This is an important volume that deserves careful consideration. It will no doubt occupy a significant position within modern discussions of the Greek verbal system, and rightly so.

—Constantine R. Campbell, associate professor of New Testament, Trinity Evangelical Divinity School

The Greek verb is the engine of the language, driving the direction in which clauses, sentences, paragraphs and whole works go. The editors of this fine book have brought together an impressive international group of scholars to assess and expand the state of our knowledge of the Greek verb in antiquity. This is no mere "academic" (read, irrelevant) enquiry: they do this in order to illuminate reading of key Greek texts, especially the New Testament and the Greek Old Testament, and achieve that aim very well with lots of examples and ideas to use. Scholars and students of the New Testament and the Greek Old Testament will find their reading of these important texts deepened, strengthened and (in places) corrected by this fine book. These scholars bring together expertise in classics, linguistics and New Testament studies in highly fruitful cross-disciplinary interaction and *together* move this conversation about the Greek verb forward much more quickly than might have happened through each working alone. I hope it receives the wide use it deserves as the conversation continues.

—Steve Walton, professorial research fellow in New Testament, St Mary's University, Twickenham (London), UK

*The Greek Verb Revisited* (ed. Runge and Fresch) is an exceptional and ground-breaking volume which opens new vistas of interpretation for our understanding of the diachronic development of ancient Greek and its interpretation.

—Michael P. Theophilos, senior lecturer, Biblical Studies and Ancient Languages, Australian Catholic University

A collection of essays from the 2015 Cambridge Verb Conference, *The Greek Verb Revisited* is the most significant book on the Koine Greek verb to be published in over a quarter century. The essays in this volume are well-informed by up-to-date research in linguistics and present a good mix of theoretical and practical treatments of the Greek verb. Comprehensive, correct, and current, this book ought to be mandatory reading for anyone serious about the grammar of the verb in the Greek New Testament, for both students and seasoned scholars alike.

—Stephen C. Carlson, postdoctoral research fellow, Institute for Religion & Critical Inquiry, A

D1563828

This interdisciplinary collection of studies will now provide a basis for any further work on the Greek verb, and it is clear that refining our understanding of Greek verbs is crucial for an accurate grasp of any Greek sentence.

—Larry Hurtado, emeritus professor of New Testament language, literature & theology, School of Divinity, University of Edinburgh

Steve Runge and Chris Fresch are to be congratulated for bringing together such important contributions to our understanding of the verb in Koine Greek. This volume reflects the cutting edge of the ongoing discussion. It should now be the starting point for students and scholars, as most previous discussions must now be considered outdated. Contributors do not agree on all the details, but we can see a clear consensus forming and these very capable scholars have left us all in their debt. This will certainly be required reading for my course on advanced Greek as I cannot recommend it highly enough!

—Roy E. Ciampa, Nida Institute for Biblical Scholarship, Gordon-Conwell Theological Seminary

*The Greek Verb Revisited: A Fresh Approach for Biblical Exegesis* offers a coherent and compelling account of the Greek verb through the combined efforts of a diverse, multidisciplinary team of linguists and scholars. Crucially, this notable volume also demonstrates the incomparable fruitfulness of long-term multidisciplinary collaborative scholarship. It is hoped that this exemplary collegial collaboration will help inspire a new wave of similar projects in biblical studies to move the discussion forward on any and all issues of consequence.

—Randall K. J. Tan, vice president, biblical research, Global Bible Initiative

This book is fascinating and hard to put down despite some of the technicality of the treatments. I particularly appreciated the multidisciplinary representation (classical, biblical, linguistic) and diachronic perspective from Homer to modern Greek. Helpful frameworks are provided to understand the Greek verb such as semantics, pragmatics, and discourse information structure. Through all of this, particular conclusions continue to reverberate in my thinking: Certainly, the augment in the indicative marks past time (allowing for pragmatic uses); most likely the Greek verb system is primarily aspectual (as opposed to tense-based); and clearly the choice of verbal aspect is exegetically significant (amplifying our need to properly understand it). I am already incorporating insights gleaned from The Greek Verb Revisited in my pedagogy and research.

—Fredrick J. Long, professor of New Testament and director of Greek instruction, Asbury Theological Seminary; international coordinator of ΓPK Greek Honor Society, GlossaHouse

# The Greek Verb Revisited

## A Fresh Approach for Biblical Exegesis

# The Greek Verb Revisited

## A Fresh Approach for Biblical Exegesis

## Steven E. Runge & Christopher J. Fresch

Editors

Proceedings of the
Linguistics and the Greek Verb Conference,
Cambridge University, 2015

LEXHAM PRESS

*The Greek Verb Revisited: A Fresh Approach for Biblical Exegesis*
Edited by Steven E. Runge and Christopher J. Fresch

Lexham Press, 1313 Commercial St., Bellingham, WA 98225
LexhamPress.com

Unless otherwise noted, Scripture quotations are the author's own translation.

Print ISBN 9781577996361
Digital ISBN 9781577996378

Lexham Editorial: James Spinti, Abigail Stocker, Joel Wilcox
Cover Design: Josh Warren
Typesetting: ProjectLuz.com

# Contents

Abbreviations     xi

Foreword     xix
ANDREAS J. KÖSTENBERGER

Introduction     1
    Bibliography     4

**Overview**

Chapter 1: Porter and Fanning on New Testament Greek Verbal
Aspect: Retrospect and Prospect     7
    BUIST FANNING
    Bibliography     11

Chapter 2: What is Aspect?: Contrasting Definitions in General
Linguistics and New Testament Studies     13
    CHRISTOPHER J. THOMSON
    1. Introduction     13
    2. Aspect in General Linguistics     18
    3. Definitions of Aspect in Recent New Testament Studies     38
    4. Verbal Aspect and Procedural Character     48
    5. Conclusion     70
    Bibliography     73

Chapter 3: Tense and Aspect in Classical Greek: Two Historical
Developments; Augment and Perfect     81
    RUTGER J. ALLAN
    1. Introduction     81
    2. The Augment: Immediacy or Distance?     83
    3. The Historical Semantic Development of the Perfect     100
    4. Conclusion     114
    Bibliography     114

Chapter 4: Aspect-Prominence, Morpho-Syntax, and a
Cognitive-Linguistic Framework for the Greek Verb     122
    NICHOLAS J. ELLIS
    1. Introduction     122
    2. Verbal Prominence: An Overview     124
    3. The Grammatical Prominence of Tense, Aspect, and Mood     127
    4. Verbal Prominence in English     130
    5. Verbal Prominence in Greek     132
    6. Why Grammatical Prominence Matters     136
    7. Perfective Aspect     138
    8. Imperfect Aspect     139
    9. Combinative Aspect     141
    10. The Greek Aspect/Tense System in Summary     143
    11. Tense, Mood, and Voice: Implications for Nonprominent
       Categories in the Greek Verbal System     154

12. Return to Matthew 2:20                                    158
13. Conclusions                                               159
Bibliography                                                  159

## Application

Chapter 5 : Verb Forms and Grounding in Narrative             163
STEPHEN H. LEVINSOHN
   1. Events Versus Nonevents                  164
   2. Tense-Aspect of Indicative Verbs         166
   3. Subordination and Tail-Head Linkage      172
   4. Specific Constructions                   176
   5. Summary and Concluding Comments          179
   Bibliography                                181

Chapter 6: Imperfects, Aorists, Historic Presents, and Perfects in
John 11: A Narrative Test Case                                184
PATRICK JAMES
   Bibliography                                217

Chapter 7: The Contribution of Verb Forms, Connectives, and
Dependency to Grounding Status in Nonnarrative Discourse      221
STEVEN E. RUNGE
   1. Introduction                             221
   2. Verb Forms and Grounding Status: Theme Line versus Support   232
   3. Connectives and Grounding                239
   4. Grammatical Dependency, Relative Salience, and
      Grounding                  253
   5. Summary                                  267
   Bibliography                                269

Chapter 8: Participles as a Pragmatic Choice: Where Semantics
Meets Pragmatics                                              273
RANDALL BUTH
   1. Introduction                             273
   2. Definition of a Participle for This Paper   274
   3. Basic Aspects of the Participles          275
   4. Participles as Simple Replacements for Finite Verbs:
      Verb Prominence and Participle Ranking   276
   5. Participles Adding Content to Lexical, Phasal Aspect:
      Continuing and Ending       279
   6. Participles Streamline a Communication But Leave the
      Semantic Relationship Unspecified   280
   7. Prominence is Helpful in following a Main Point   286
   8. Participles and the Historical Present    290
   Bibliography                                305

Chapter 9: Functions of Copula-Participle Combinations
("Periphrastics")                                             307
STEPHEN H. LEVINSOHN
   1. Introduction                             307

2. Simple and Copular Imperfectives ........................ 311
3. Simple and Copular Perfects ............................. 315
4. Fronted Participles ..................................... 321
5. Conclusions ............................................. 323
Bibliography .............................................. 324

## Linguistic Investigations

Chapter 10: The Historical Present in NT Greek: An Exercise in
Interpreting Matthew ...................................... 329
ELIZABETH ROBAR
    1. Historical Present Cross-linguistically ............. 329
    2. Koine Greek ........................................ 335
    3. New Testament > Matthew ............................ 337
    Bibliography ......................................... 351

Chapter 11: The Function of the Augment in Hellenistic Greek ... 353
PETER J. GENTRY
    1. Introduction ....................................... 353
    2. Origins and Usage (Described Diachronically) ....... 355
    3. The Personal Endings ............................... 364
    4. A Holistic Picture: Diachronic and Synchronic ..... 368
    5. Conclusion ......................................... 374
    Bibliography ......................................... 375

Chapter 12: Typology, Polysemy, and Prototypes: Situating
Nonpast Aorist Indicatives ................................ 379
CHRISTOPHER J. FRESCH
    1. The Aorist Indicative in Greek Scholarship ........ 380
    2. Verbal Systems and Linguistic Typology ............ 387
    3. Polysemy ........................................... 397
    4. Prototype Categories ............................... 404
    5. Conclusion ......................................... 410
    Bibliography ......................................... 411

Chapter 13: Perfect Greek Morphology and Pedagogy ......... 416
RANDALL BUTH
    Bibliography ......................................... 428

Chapter 14: The Semantics of the Perfect in the Greek of the
New Testament ............................................. 430
ROBERT CRELLIN
    1. Introduction ....................................... 430
    2. Event and Situation Structure ..................... 435
    3. Tense and Aspect ................................... 438
    4. Tense and Aspect in Greek .......................... 439
    5. Problem of the Perfect in Terms of Tense and Aspect . 440
    6. Proposal for the Semantics of the Greek Perfect ... 449
    7. Semantic Relationship and Merger with the Aorist .. 453
    8. Conclusion ......................................... 454
    Bibliography ......................................... 455

Chapter 15: Discourse Function of the Greek Perfect 458
STEVEN E. RUNGE
  1. Introduction 458
  2. Perfects Preceding That to Which They Are Relevant 463
  3. Perfects That Follow That to Which They Are Relevant 467
  4. Perfects on the Theme Line of the Discourse 472
  5. Apparent exceptions 480
  6. Areas for further research 482
  7. Addendum 484
  Bibliography 485

Chapter 16: Greek Prohibitions 486
MICHAEL AUBREY
  1. Introduction 486
  2. Aspect, Negation, and Predicate Types in Prohibitions 501
  3. Layers of Scope and Negation 520
  4. Conclusion: Prohibitions as Complex Constructions 534
  Bibliography 536

Chapter 17: Tense and Aspect after the New Testament 539
AMALIA MOSER
  1. Introduction 539
  2. The Greek Verb: Modern vs. Classical 540
  3. *Aktionsart* and Aspect 544
  4. A Retrospective Look at Greek Aspect 550
  5. Conclusions 559
  Bibliography 561

Chapter 18: Motivated Categories, Middle Voice, and Passive Morphology 563
RACHEL AUBREY
  1. Introduction 563
  2. Synchronic Variety and Diachronic Development 575
  3. Conceptual Prototypes and the Nature of Voice 585
  4. Semantic Map 612
  Bibliography 620

Chapter 19: Envoi 626
GEOFFREY HORROCKS
  1. Introduction 626
  2. Generalities 627
  3. Specifics 630
  4. Conclusion 635

Contributors 636

Subject/Author Index 637

Index of Ancient Sources 651

# Abbreviations

| | |
|---|---|
| 2 Clem | 2 Clement |
| acc. | accusative |
| act. | active |
| Acts Pil. | Acts of Pilate |
| *Adol. poet. aud.* | Plutarch, *Quomodo adolescens poetas audire debeat* |
| *A.J.* | Josephus, *Antiquitates judaicae* (*Jewish Antiquities*) |
| a.k.a. | also known as |
| *ALH* | *Acta Linguistica Hafniensia: International Journal of Linguistics* |
| Ammon. | Ammonius Grammaticus |
| *Ant.* | Sophocles, *Antigone* |
| aor. | aorist |
| App. | Appian |
| *Aristocr.* | Demosthenes, *Against Aristocrates* |
| Arm. | Armenian |
| ASCP | Amsterdam Studies in Classical Philology |
| AST | Amsterdam Studies in the Theory and History of Linguistic Science, Series IV: Current Issues in Linguistic Theory |
| aug. | augment(ed) |
| AV. | Atharvaveda |
| BCAW | Blackwell Companions to the Ancient World |
| BCLL | Bibliothèque des Cahiers de Linguistique de Louvain |
| BDAG | Bauer, Walter, F. W. Danker, W. F. Arndt, and F. W. Gingrich. *A Greek-English Lexicon of the New Testament and Other Early Christian Literature.* 3rd ed. Chicago: University of Chicago Press, 2000. |
| BDF | Blass, F. and A. Debrunner. *A Greek Grammar of the New Testament and Other Early Christian* |

|         |                                                                                 |
|---------|---------------------------------------------------------------------------------|
|         | *Literature*. Translated by Robert W. Funk. Revised ed. Chicago: University Of Chicago Press, 1961. |
| BHAW    | Brief Histories of the Ancient World                                            |
| BHL     | Blackwell Handbooks in Linguistics                                              |
| BICS    | *Bulletin of the Institute of Classical Studies*                                |
| Bis acc. | Lucians, *Bis accusatus*                                                        |
| B.J.    | Josephus, *Bellum judaicum* (*Jewish War*)                                       |
| BJL     | *Belgian Journal of Linguistics*                                                |
| BLG     | Biblical Languages: Greek                                                       |
| BLS     | *Proceedings of the Berkeley Linguistics Society*                               |
| BTL     | Blackwell Textbooks in Linguistics                                             |
| c.      | common                                                                          |
| CCS     | Cambridge Classical Studies                                                     |
| CCTC    | Cambridge Classical Texts and Commentaries                                      |
| CEWAL   | *The Cambridge Encyclopedia of the World's Ancient Languages*. Edited by Roger D. Woodard. Cambridge: Cambridge University Press, 2004. |
| CGLC    | Cambridge Greek and Latin Classics                                              |
| CHLL    | Cambridge Handbooks in Language and Linguistics                                 |
| CILT    | Current Issues in Linguistic Theory                                            |
| CJL     | *Canadian Journal of Linguistics*                                               |
| ClAnt   | *Classical Antiquity*                                                           |
| ClQ     | *Classical Quarterly*                                                           |
| ClR     | *Classical Review*                                                              |
| CLR     | Cognitive Linguistics Research                                                 |
| Con.    | Demosthenes, *Against Conon*                                                     |
| Cor.    | Demosthenes, *De corona*                                                         |
| CSL     | Cambridge Studies in Linguistics                                               |
| CTL     | Cambridge Textbooks in Linguistics                                             |
| CurBR   | *Currents in Biblical Research*                                                  |
| CurSL   | Current Studies in Linguistics                                                 |
| CurTL   | *Current Trends in Linguistics*                                                 |
| Cyr.    | Xenophons, *Cyropaedia*                                                          |
| dat.    | dative                                                                          |
| DBSJ    | *Detroit Baptist Seminary Journal*                                              |
| Def. orac. | Plutarch, *De defectu oraculorum* (*On the Demise of Oracles*)               |
| Dem.    | Demosthenes                                                                     |

| | |
|---|---|
| dept. | department |
| *Diff.* | Ammonius, *De adfinium vocabulorum differentia.* Edited by K. Nickau. Liepzig: Teubner, 1966. |
| Diogn. | Letter to Diognetus |
| *EAGLL* | *Encyclopedia of Ancient Greek Language and Linguistics.* Edited by Georgios K. Giannakis. 3 vols. Leiden: Brill, 2014. |
| EALT | Empirical Approaches to Language Typology |
| ed(s). | edition, editor, editors, edited by |
| EEC | Evangelical Exegetical Commentary |
| *ELL* | *English Language and Linguistics* |
| enl. | enlarged |
| esp. | especially |
| EstNT | Estudios de Nuevo Testamento |
| ex. | example |
| fem. | feminine |
| FGLG | Forschungen zur griechischen und lateinischen Grammatik |
| *FilNeot* | *Filología Neotestamentaria* |
| *FL* | *Foundations of Language* |
| *FLin* | *Folia Linguistica* |
| frag. | fragment |
| fut. | future |
| GA | genitive absolute |
| gen. | genitive |
| Gk. | Greek |
| *Glotta* | *Zeitschrift für griechische und lateinische Sprache* |
| *GTJ* | *Grace Theological Journal* |
| h. Ap. | Homeric Hymn to Apollo (Delion)/"Hymn 3 to Apollo" |
| HAW | Handbuch der altertumswissenschaft |
| Hdt. | Herodotus |
| *Hell.* | Xenophon, *Hellenica* (also known as *Historia Graeca*) |
| Herm. Sim. | Shepherd of Hermas, Similitudes |
| *Hist* | Herodotus, *Historiae* |
| Hom. | Homer, homeric |
| HP | historical present |

| | |
|---|---|
| HSK | Handbücher zur Sprach- und Kommunikationswissenschaft/Handbooks of Linguistics and Communication Science |
| ICC | International Critical Commentary |
| IE | Interface Explorations |
| IEED | Leiden Indo-European Etymological Dictionary |
| IF | *Indogermanische Forschungen* |
| Ign. *Trall.* | Ignatius, *To the Trallians* |
| IITSC | Invited Inferencing Theory of Semantic Change |
| *Il.* | Homer, *Iliad* |
| impf. | imperfect |
| impv. | imperative |
| indic. | indicative |
| inf. | infinitive |
| IPFV | imperfective |
| *IPrag* | *Intercultural Pragmatics* |
| *JBL* | *Journal of Biblical Literature* |
| *JGL* | *Journal of Greek Linguistics* |
| *JL* | *Journal of Linguistics* |
| JLSMin | Janua Linguarum, Series Minor |
| Jos. | Josephus |
| *JOTT* | *Journal of Translation and Textlingusitics* |
| *JPh* | *Journal of Philology* |
| *JSNT* | *Journal for the Study of the New Testament* |
| JSNTSup | Journal for the Study of the New Testament Supplement Series |
| JSOTSup | Journal for the Study of the Old Testament Supplement Series |
| *JT* | *Journal of Translation* |
| LA | Linguistik Aktuell/Linguistics Today |
| LANE | Languages of the Ancient Near East |
| LBS | Linguistic Biblical Studies |
| LCL | Loeb Classical Library |
| LCLib | Language and Communications Library |
| *Ling&P* | *Linguistics and Philosophy* |
| *Linguistics* | *Linguistics: An Interdisciplinary Journal of the Language Sciences* |
| *LiTy* | *Linguistic Typology* |
| LLL | Longman Linguistics Library |

| | |
|---|---|
| LLSEE | Linguistic and Literary Studies in Eastern Europe |
| LOC | Lettres Orientales et Classiques |
| LSJ | Liddel, Henry George, Robert Scott, Henry Stuart Jones. *A Greek-English Lexicon*. 9th ed. with revised supplement. Oxford: Clarendon, 1996. |
| LSAWS | Linguistic Studies in Ancient West Semitic |
| Luc. | Lucian |
| Lys. | Lysias |
| *Macr.* | Lucian, *Macrobii* |
| masc. | masculine |
| Men. | Menander |
| mid. | middle |
| *Mon.* | *Monostichoi* |
| MP | middle-passive |
| MS | Mnemosyne Supplementum |
| NA²⁷ | *Novum Testamentum Graece*, Nestle-Aland, 27th ed. |
| NA²⁸ | *Novum Testamentum Graece*, Nestle-Aland, 28th ed. |
| neut. | neuter |
| nom. | nominative |
| *NovT* | *Novum Testamentum* |
| NPC | nominative participial clause |
| NTM | New Testament Monographs |
| OCM | Oxford Classical Monographs |
| *Od.* | Homer, *Odyssey* |
| ODL | Outstanding Dissertations in Linguistics |
| OG | Old Greek |
| OrbisSup | Orbis Supplementa |
| OSSM | Oxford Survey in Syntax and Morphology |
| OTLing | Oxford Textbooks in Linguistics |
| OTM | Oxford Theological Monographs |
| OUSE | Odense University Studies in English |
| P&B NS | Pragmatics & Beyond, New Series |
| *Para.* | Plutarch, *Parallel Lives* |
| *Parm.* | Plato, *Parmenides* |
| PBA | Proceedings of the British Academy |
| per. | person |
| pers. comm. | personal communication |
| pf. | perfect |

| PFV | perfective |
| PG | Proto-Greek |
| PG Migne | Patrologia Graeca [= *Patrologiae Cursus Completus*: Series Graeca]. Edited by Jacques-Paul Migne. 162 vols. Paris, 1857–1886. |
| *Philip.* | Demosthenes, *Philippica* |
| *PhR* | *The Philosophical Review* |
| PIE | Proto-Indo-European |
| Pl. | Plato |
| pl. | plural |
| PLAL | Perspectives on Linguistics and Ancient Languages |
| Plb. | Polybius |
| plupf. | pluperfect |
| Plut. | Plutarch |
| PNTC | Pillar New Testament Commentary |
| P.Petr. | The Flinders Petrie Papyri |
| pres. | present |
| ptc. | participle |
| *Pun.* | Appian, Λιβυκή (*Punic Wars*) |
| RCG | Routledge Comprehension Grammars |
| redup. | reduplication |
| *Resp.* | Plato, *Respublica* (*Republic*) |
| rev. | revised |
| RSL | Research Surveys in Linguistics |
| RV. | Rigveda |
| S. | Sophocles |
| SAG | Stuttgarter Arbeiten zur Germanistik |
| SBG | Studies in Biblical Greek |
| SBL | Society of Biblical Literature |
| sg. | singular |
| Sib. Or. | Sibylline Oracles |
| Skt. | Sanskrit |
| SLCS | Studies in Language Companion Series |
| SLi | Sprache und Literatur |
| SLL | Synthese Language Library |
| SLP | Studies in Linguistics and Philosophy |
| *SPh* | *Studies in Philology* |
| SSLL | Studies in Semitic Languages and Linguistics |

| | |
|---|---|
| StBibLit | Studies in Biblical Literature (Lang) |
| *StudLang* | *Studies in Language: International Journal Sponsored by the Foundations of Language* |
| *SWJL* | *Southwest Journal of Linguistics* |
| *STUF* | *Sprachtypologie und Universalienforschung* |
| T.Dan | Testament of Dan |
| TDSA | Testi e documenti per lo studio dell' antichità |
| T.Gad | Testament of Gad |
| Th. | Thucydides |
| TiCSup | Trends in Classics Supplemental Volumes |
| TiEL | Topics in English Linguistics |
| TiLSM | Trends in Linguistics: Studies and Monographs |
| T.Levi | Testament of Levi |
| *TLG* | *Thesaurus Linguae Graecae* (http://stephanus.tlg.uci.edu/) |
| TLL | Topics in Language and Linguistics |
| TPostSit | Time after the Situation |
| TSit | Situation Time |
| TSL | Typological Studies in Language |
| TTop | Topic Time |
| TUtt | Utterance Time |
| *TPhS* | *Transactions of the Philological Society* |
| *TynBul* | *Tyndale Bulletin* |
| *UCLWPL* | *University College London Working Papers in Linguistics* |
| VKNWL | Verhandelingen der Koninklijke Nederlandse Akademie van Wetenschappen, afdeling Letterkunde |
| voc. | vocative |
| VP | Verb Phrase |
| vs. | versus |
| *WTJ* | *Westminster Theological Journal* |
| WUNT | Wissenschaftliche Untersuchungen zum Neuen Testament |
| Xen. | Xenophon |
| XN | Extended-Now |

**Translations cited:**

| | |
|---|---|
| ASV | American Standard Version |
| ESV | English Standard Version |
| GNB | Good News Bible |
| GWN | God's Word to the Nations |
| LEB | Lexham English Bible |
| NASB | New American Standard Bible |
| NEB | New English Bible |
| NET | New English Translation |
| NIV | New International Version |
| NLT | New Living Translation |
| NRSV | New Revised Standard Version |
| RSV | Revised Standard Version |

# Foreword

ANDREAS J. KÖSTENBERGER

## MY PERSONAL PILGRIMAGE

I was there almost from the beginning. I remember when in the early 1990s, as a Ph.D. student in D. A. Carson's Advanced Greek Grammar class at Trinity Evangelical Divinity School, I was assigned to read Stan Porter's then-recently published dissertation on Greek verbal aspect.[1] I also distinctly remember the disbelief when I was told in the Trinity bookstore what the price of his book was (close to $100 if memory serves!), but I bit the bullet and bought it anyway, and worked through it cover to cover.[2] Then, over the next few years, I participated in several Greek Linguistics sessions at the Annual Meeting of the Society of Biblical Literature which at that time were cochaired by Carson and Porter.[3] I even tried my own hand on apply-

---

1   Stanley E. Porter, *Verbal Aspect in the Greek of the New Testament: With Reference to Tense and Mood*, SBG 1 (New York: Lang, 1989). Porter subsequently produced the more accessible *Idioms of the Greek New Testament*, BLG 2 (Sheffield: Sheffield Academic Press, 1992).
2   The book is now in its third edition and (mercifully) available in paperback for about $25.
3   See the volumes edited by Stanley E. Porter and D. A. Carson, *Biblical Greek Language and Linguistics: Open Questions in Current Research*, JSNTSup 80 (Sheffield: JSOT Press, 1995); and *Discourse Analysis and Other Topics in Biblical Greek*, JSNTSup 113 (Sheffield: JSOT Press, 1995). The latter volume includes my article "Syntactical Background Studies in 1 Timothy 2.12 in the New Testament and Extrabiblical Greek Literature," 156–79. The former volume contains the following relevant articles: D. A. Carson, "An Introduction to the Porter/Fanning Debate," 18–25; Stanley E. Porter, "In Defence of Verbal Aspect," 26–45; Buist M. Fanning, "Approaches to Verbal Aspect in New Testament Greek: Issues in Definition and Method," 46–62; Daryl D. Schmidt, "Verbal Aspect in Greek: Two Approaches," 63–73; and Moisés Silva, "A Response to Fanning and Porter on Verbal Aspect," 74–82 (much of which appears in his review of Porter and Fanning, *WTJ* 54 [1992]: 179–82).

ing these ideas about verbal aspect to a particular pericope found in all four Gospels, the anointing of Jesus.[4]

## TUNING OUT (WHILE WATCHING FROM A DISTANCE)

Then, busyness set in. I finished my dissertation, graduated with my PhD, and got my first job teaching New Testament at Briercrest Bible College in Saskatchewan, Canada. I still went to the Annual Meetings of ETS and SBL every year, but for the next several years was busy keeping my head above water, developing lecture notes, translating Schlatter (a therapeutic pastime),[5] and publishing various other bits and pieces of my work. On the side, I still tried to keep one eye on the ongoing debates on aspect.

Who was right, Porter or (Buist) Fanning? I must confess my sympathies lay decidedly with Porter, not only because of my mentor, Don Carson's, influence (whether or not he realized it), but also because of my own independent assessment. I agreed with Porter's radicalism: what was needed was not merely a tweaking of the conventional way of thinking about Greek verbs; the field needed a revolution from the ground up.

It made sense to me that the study of New Testament Greek had been unduly linked to the study of classical Latin and assumptions about the latter language had been transferred to the former.

It made sense that a writer's or speaker's perception of a given action or event had a part, even a crucial part, in the way in which it was portrayed by the choice of a particular verb tense.

It made sense that mere labels had no intrinsic explanatory value: to label a given type of usage as, say, "futuristic aorist," or "historical present," didn't explain *why* there was such a thing in the first place.

---

4   Andreas Köstenberger, "A Comparison of the Pericopae of Jesus' Anointing," in *Studies in John and Gender: A Decade of Scholarship*, StBibLit 38 (New York: Lang, 2001), 49–63.

5   1,100 pages of it! Adolf Schlatter, *The History of the Christ: The Foundation for New Testament Theology*, trans. Andreas J. Köstenberger (Grand Rapids: Baker, 1997); and *The Theology of the Apostles: The Development of New Testament Theology*, trans. Andreas J. Köstenberger (Grand Rapids: Baker, 1998).

It made sense that cases where the synoptic writers, for example, depicted one and the same historical action by different verb tense-forms, required an explanation, because in such instances the distinction clearly couldn't lie on the *kind of action (Aktionsart)*—they all portrayed the exact same action which unfolded in a particular kind of way.

Language use, when it came to Koine Greek, cannot be reduced to an objective system of grammatical classification with a sophisticated taxonomy of labels; it has an inescapable subjective element that conventional grammars have failed to adequately recognize.

In other words, I'd been won over to a new way of thinking about the Greek verb. Not that there weren't residual lingering questions about the more radical claims that Porter and others were espousing.

What about the Greek augment? Was it really completely unconnected to (past) time as Porter strenuously contended? I wanted to believe that was the case in order to maintain the neatness of the theory, but couldn't quite muster enough confidence in that part of the proposal as I would have liked.

I also believed that the specific lexical meaning of a given word and a number of morphological and other factors needed more consideration when it came to analyzing specific verb usage in particular New Testament passages. Then, I lost track of the debate altogether for a few years (about a decade or so, in fact).

## TUNING BACK IN

Meanwhile, I had been able to contribute several works to the field, particularly Johannine studies, when the opportunity arose to co-author an intermediate Greek grammar, *Going Deeper with New Testament Greek*.[6] Among other things, we wanted our grammar to introduce students to verbal aspect, and so decided to devote an

---

6    Andreas J. Köstenberger, Benjamin L. Merkle, and Robert L. Plummer, *Going Deeper with New Testament Greek: An Intermediate Study of the Grammar and Syntax of the New Testament* (Nashville: B&H Academic, 2016). I was also appointed editor of the 20-volume Exegetical Guide to the Greek New Testament (EGGNT) published by B&H Academic (publication in progress) and was asked to develop a method of diagramming that could be used as standard for all volumes in the series.

entire chapter to it.[7] An initial draft was produced, and then sent to someone very familiar with verbal aspect (in fact, he had written a highly regarded book on the subject). His assessment of the chapter was candid, and he noted several areas of pointed disagreement and concern.

At the Annual Meeting of the Society of Biblical Literature, I sat down with Con Campbell over lunch, and he was kind enough to explain to me several of his views on Greek verbal aspect, particularly on the perfect tense.[8] Then, through a set of twists and turns, I made the acquaintance of Nick Ellis, who has since become a good friend.[9] In about an hour and a half, Nick brought me up to speed on some recent developments in the study of the Greek verb, and I quickly realized that events had moved on considerably since the Porter-Fanning debates of a decade or so ago. No one, it seemed, had gotten everything right, and, almost under the radar, a new paradigm was beginning to emerge.

Again, as with my first introduction to verbal aspect, I was intrigued. I asked a lot of questions, and with some gracious help from Nick and another new friend of mine, Steven Runge, I was able to reconceive the chapter on the Greek verb in our intermediate Greek book, writing large portions entirely from scratch. In addition, I was able to work my way through Steve's groundbreaking *Discourse Grammar of the Greek New Testament* and to introduce some of my doctoral students to it in my seminars.[10] In revising my work on the syntax of 1 Timothy 2:12, I was able to add a new section on the discourse analysis of 1 Timothy 2:8–15 (with input from Steve) that

---

7   Ch. 7, "Tense and Verbal Aspect," in ibid.

8   See Constantine R. Campbell, *Basics of Verbal Aspect in Biblical Greek* (Grand Rapids: Zondervan, 2008). More recently, he wrote *Advances in the Study of Greek: New Insights for Reading the New Testament* (Grand Rapids: Zondervan, 2015). For our present purposes, see esp. ch. 5, "Verbal Aspect and *Aktionsart*," 105–33. The Annual Meeting of the Society of Biblical Literature in November 2013 featured a panel session on "The Perfect Storm" featuring Campbell, Fanning, and Porter.

9   His dissertation, completed under the supervision of Markus Bockmuehl in Oxford, was published: Nicholas J. Ellis, *The Hermeneutics of Divine Testing: Cosmic Trials and Biblical Interpretation in the Epistle of James and Other Jewish Literature*, WUNT 2/396 (Tübingen: Mohr Siebeck, 2015).

10  Steven E. Runge, *Discourse Grammar of the Greek New Testament: A Practical Introduction for Teaching and Exegesis* (Peabody, MA: Hendrickson, 2010).

I believe will contribute significantly to the discussion of this important passage.[11]

## THE RISE OF A NEW PARADIGM

All in all, the development of our thinking about Greek verbal aspect over the past two and a half decades seems to provide a fascinating case study in how new paradigms vie to replace old ones in a given field of study.[12] First, there is an entrenched old paradigm. This paradigm is supported by a massive amount of literature, in the present case grammars, other literature on New Testament Greek, commentaries, etc. In this way, an entire plausibility structure is created that is mutually reinforcing and gives the appearance of a well-established, virtually insurmountable paradigm.

Then, someone, or even several individuals independently, rise up to challenge the paradigm. In fact, as it turns out, there had been small cracks in the foundation all along, but they had been too minor to be recognized at the time and can be identified only in hindsight once the challenge has been lodged. The proposal vying to become the new paradigm, however, itself faces critical scrutiny.

On the one hand, there is the predictable backlash from those who have an entire career and body of scholarship invested in the old paradigm, not to mention a lifetime of teaching. In some (if not many) cases, moreover, these individuals are past their most formative years, that is, their doctoral work at a university or seminary, where they learned the prevailing paradigm. This, of course, is no problem for the younger generation, which is quite open to new ideas, and in some cases is quick (perhaps too quick) to embrace the new paradigm.

On the other hand, there are those who provide judicious assessments of the new proposal. Those are individuals who have never embraced the old paradigm completely, or if they have, are sufficiently open to the rationale advanced by those challenging the old

---

11  "A Complex Sentence: The Syntax of 1 Timothy 2:12," in *Women in the Church: An Analysis and Application of 1 Timothy 2:9–15*, ed. Andreas J. Köstenberger and Thomas R. Schreiner, 3rd ed. (Wheaton, IL: Crossway, 2016), 119–64.

12  The classic work, of course, is Thomas S. Kuhn, *The Structure of Scientific Revolutions* (Chicago: University of Chicago Press, 1962).

paradigm to assess it on its merits. They may find some aspects of the new proposal convincing, but note problems with other parts of it. The process of moving, in Hegelian terms, from thesis to antithesis and from there to a new synthesis, is now fully underway (no, I'm not a Hegelian, though I do have German heritage).

This is an important stage in the process, because it is here that some of the legitimate aspects of the new proposal are embraced while other hard edges are smoothed out and elements that don't fit the evidence are corrected. Finally, if the process works, and actual desire for progress prevails over entrenched academic, professional, and institutional interests, a new paradigm is hammered out, and the process begins anew.

## WHERE ARE WE NOW?

When it comes to our thinking about Greek verbal aspect, where are we in this process? I would argue that we are past the old paradigm, for sure. There are too many problems with it (though this is not the place to enumerate them), and it will likely prove futile to try to keep it on life support for long.

But which paradigm will take its place? Will it be a slight modification, a mere tweaking, of the old paradigm? This will hardly be sufficient, though there may be elements of the old paradigm worth retaining in the new one. As Jesus said, we must put new wine into new wineskins; if we try to put new wine into old wineskins, they will burst and prove unable to contain the new wine.

Will it be a radical reaction to the old paradigm, a sort of antiversion that defines itself significantly in opposition to what it rejects?

Or will it be a paradigm that seeks to identify deeper plausibility structures underlying the linguistic realities that characterize the pattern of usage of New Testament Koine Greek verb tense-forms?

This is the critical juncture of the debate as it presents itself at the moment. What is more, this new paradigm needs more than one or two doctoral dissertations arguing it. It needs a broader consensus undergirding it by a critical mass of scholars who use a collaborative approach that focuses, not on personalities, but on issues, and that keeps trying to find solutions until the new paradigm has coalesced and is ready to be tested and validated by the data as they present themselves in the available Koine Greek literature, including the New Testament.

## A NEW WAY FORWARD

The book you're holding in your hands (or viewing on your screen) represents the product of years of such collaborative efforts to move past the stalemate of previous debates and to make real progress in understanding how the Greek verb works. I will not go into detail here, because I want the contributions of the authors of the various essays included in this volume to speak for themselves.

What I will do, however, is commend this volume to you as a new way forward beyond the impasse in New Testament Greek studies, particularly with regard to verbal aspect. If you're like me, and you've tuned out of the debate surrounding the use of the Greek verb for a while, or even if you've never been a part of the debate at all, now is the time to tune back in and to listen and learn from this team of scholars who, I'm convinced, have managed to arrive at a deeper level of understanding of how the Greek verb was used by first-century New Testament Greek writers, in a balanced and cogent way.

I'm personally very grateful for the friendship of several of these writers and for what they've done to get me back up to speed in this important area of New Testament study. I'm convinced that the same will happen for you as you read the following pages with an open mind and an open heart and as you strive to show yourself approved by God, handling accurately his word of truth.

Andreas J. Köstenberger, PhD, Dr. rer. soc. oec.
Wake Forest, North Carolina, Christmas 2015
Senior Research Professor of New Testament & Biblical Theology
Southeastern Baptist Theological Seminary, Wake Forest, NC
Founder, Biblical Foundations™ (www.biblicalfoundations.org)

## BIBLIOGRAPHY

Campbell, Constantine R. *Advances in the Study of Greek: New Insights for Reading the New Testament*. Grand Rapids: Zondervan, 2015.

————. *Basics of Verbal Aspect in Biblical Greek*. Grand Rapids: Zondervan, 2008.

Carson, D. A. "An Introduction to the Porter/Fanning Debate." Pages 18–25 in *Biblical Greek Language and Linguistics: Open Questions in Current Research*. Edited by Stanley E. Porter and D. A. Carson. JSNTSup 80. Sheffield: JSOT Press, 1995.

Ellis, Nicholas J. *The Hermeneutics of Divine Testing: Cosmic Trials and Biblical Interpretation in the Epistle of James and Other Jewish Literature*. WUNT 2/396. Tübingen: Mohr Siebeck, 2015.

Fanning, Buist M. "Approaches to Verbal Aspect in New Testament Greek: Issues in Definition and Method." Pages 46–62 in *Biblical Greek Language and Linguistics: Open Questions in Current Research*. Edited by Stanley E. Porter and D. A. Carson. JSNTSup 80. Sheffield: JSOT Press, 1995.

Köstenberger, Andreas J. "A Comparison of the Pericopae of Jesus' Anointing." Pages 49–63 in *Studies in John and Gender: A Decade of Scholarship*. StBibLit 38. New York: Lang, 2001.

————. "A Complex Sentence: The Syntax of 1 Timothy 2:12." Pages 119–64 in *Women in the Church: An Analysis and Application of 1 Timothy 2:9–15*. Edited by Andreas J. Köstenberger and Thomas R. Schreiner. 3rd ed. Wheaton, IL: Crossway, 2016.

————. "Syntactical Background Studies to 1 Timothy 2.12 in the New Testament and Extrabiblical Greek Literature." Pages 156–79 in *Discourse Analysis and Other Topics in Biblical Greek*. Edited by Stanley E. Porter and D. A. Carson. JSNTSup 113. Sheffield: JSOT Press, 1995.

Köstenberger, Andreas J., Benjamin L. Merkle, and Robert L. Plummer. *Going Deeper with New Testament Greek: An Intermediate Study of the Grammar and Syntax of the New Testament*. Nashville: B&H Academic, 2015.

Kuhn, Thomas S. *The Structure of Scientific Revolutions*. Chicago: University of Chicago Press, 1962.

Porter, Stanley E. *Idioms of the Greek New Testament*. BLG 2. Sheffield: Sheffield Academic Press, 1992.

————. "In Defence of Verbal Aspect." Pages 26–45 in *Biblical Greek Language and Linguistics: Open Questions in Current Research*. Edited by Stanley E. Porter and D. A. Carson. JSNTSup 80. Sheffield: JSOT Press, 1995.

————. *Verbal Aspect in the Greek of the New Testament: With Reference to Tense and Mood*. SBG 1. New York: Lang, 1989.

Porter, Stanley E., and D. A. Carson, eds. *Biblical Greek Language and Linguistics: Open Questions in Current Research.* JSNTSup 80. Sheffield: JSOT Press, 1995.

———. *Discourse Analysis and Other Topics in Biblical Greek.* JSNTSup 113. Sheffield: JSOT Press, 1995.

Runge, Steven E. *Discourse Grammar of the Greek New Testament: A Practical Introduction for Teaching and Exegesis.* Peabody, MA: Hendrickson, 2010.

Schlatter, Adolf. *The History of the Christ: The Foundation for New Testament Theology.* Translated by Andreas J. Köstenberger. Grand Rapids: Baker, 1997.

———. *The Theology of the Apostles: The Development of New Testament Theology.* Translated by Andreas J. Köstenberger. Grand Rapids: Baker, 1998.

Schmidt, Daryl D. "Verbal Aspect in Greek: Two Approaches." Pages 63–73 in *Biblical Greek Language and Linguistics: Open Questions in Current Research.* Edited by Stanley E. Porter and D. A. Carson. JSNTSup 80. Sheffield: JSOT Press, 1995.

Silva, Moisés. "A Response to Fanning and Porter on Verbal Aspect," 74–82 in *Biblical Greek Language and Linguistics: Open Questions in Current Research.* Edited by Stanley E. Porter and D. A. Carson. JSNTSup 80. Sheffield: JSOT Press, 1995.

# Introduction

In 1991 a panel was organized at the Annual Meeting of the Society of Biblical Literature in Kansas City to review the claims of two scholars who had recently published dissertations on the Greek verb, what came to be known as the Porter/Fanning debate.[1] While there was agreement about the important role of verbal aspect in the Greek verb, there was sharp disagreement about whether indicative verbs encoded temporal reference or not. New voices weighed in with contributions from Kenneth McKay, Trevor Evans, Constantine Campbell, and Rodney Decker, but little changed in regard to whether Koine Greek was tenseless or not. Over the years, distinct camps formed, each one having its own view not only on the presence of tense in the Greek verb but also of the Greek verbal system more generally. Themed sessions on the verb were held at the Annual Meetings of the Society of Biblical Literature in 2009 and 2013, but these did little more than reaffirm entrenched positions.

An informal working group of linguists and New Testament scholars began to discuss the need for an alternative view that rightly recognized the importance of aspect without dispensing with tense in the indicative mood. New research into the Greek perfect verb provided the impetus. Crellin's 2012 dissertation and paper at the International Meeting of the Society of Biblical Literature along with Runge's paper on the discourse function of the perfect served as a foil against which the "Perfect Storm" papers were evaluated at the 2013 Annual Meeting in Baltimore. The ad hoc working group recognized that Porter, Fanning, and Campbell were each highlighting important elements of the perfect. Work began that year assembling a unified description of the perfect that incorporated the valid

---

1    D. A. Carson and Stanley E. Porter, "Preface," in *Biblical Greek Language and Linguistics: Open Questions in Current Research*, ed. Stanley E. Porter and D. A. Carson, JSNTSup 80 (Sheffield: JSOT Press, 1993), 9.

observations of Porter, Fanning, and Campbell and was presented at the Annual Meetings of the Evangelical Theological Society and the Society of Biblical Literature in 2014. This work was more than the combining the best of all worlds, though. It also incorporated insights from Cognitive Linguistics and linguistic typology.

The positive response to this new approach to the perfect inspired us to develop a more comprehensive account of the verb in light of the latest research from the fields of Classics, New Testament studies, and Linguistics. Instead of a few scholars taking several years to develop a monograph, we chose to convene a special conference with invited papers. Each scholar was tasked with addressing a specific issue of the verb, where the conference would build from a general introduction to the more problematic topics. The goal was to provide a coherent account of the Greek verb that benefited from insights across disciplinary lines. Nothing like this had been attempted before in any of the disciplines, so we were pleasantly surprised by the overwhelming support from both the presenters and attendees for the results. The papers that follow are the byproduct of this conference, an affiliate conference of the Tyndale Fellowship 2015 meeting, hosted by Tyndale House, Cambridge, and sponsored by the University of Cambridge School of Arts and Humanities and the Lexham Research Institute.

The opening paper by Buist Fanning offers a glimpse of the state of affairs in New Testament studies that led Porter and Fanning to tackle the topic of aspect in the Greek verb. Chris Thomson offers an important overview of aspect, highlighting the significance of internal temporal structure to truly understand the nature of aspect. Next, Rutger Allan offers a glimpse into the historical development of the Greek verbal system, investigating specifically the ε- (*epsilon*) augment and the perfect tense. Nicholas Ellis builds upon this by offering a synchronic overview of the verbal system in Koine, correlating the morphology of the forms to the semantics of the various forms.

Following this overview, Stephen Levinsohn describes the correlation of the tense-forms to signaling foreground and background in narrative proper. Patrick James then applies Levinsohn's model to John 11 to illustrate its explanatory value. This is followed by an essay by Runge in which he investigates the contribution of tense-forms and connectives to themeline and supporting material in nonnarrative texts. Next, Randall Buth describes the pragmatic effects achieved by the use of adverbial participles to background information, followed by Levinsohn's account of periphrastic constructions as an alternative to simple finite verbs.

The balance of the volume is devoted to factors that advocates of a tenseless view cite as evidence against temporal reference in the indicative mood. Elizabeth Robar investigates pragmatic issues surrounding the function and semantics of the historical present. Peter Gentry traces the development of the ε- augment from Indo-European into Greek as a marker of past temporal reference. This is followed by Christopher Fresch's paper detailing why nonpast aorists are found in Koine and how this reconciles with a tensed view of the indicative.

The next several papers tackle the problematic topic of the Greek perfect. Randall Buth leads off by correlating the morphology of the perfect with its semantic value. This is followed by Robert Crellin's account of the perfect's internal semantic representation of an action. Steven Runge builds on these papers to describe the perfect's function within the discourse.

Next, Michael Aubrey demonstrates how the concept of predicate classes from Role and Reference Grammar can help us better understand prohibitions in Greek. Amalia Moser offers a linguist's perspective on how a diachronic understanding of tense and aspect in Greek can inform our synchronic understanding of these features in the Koine period. Rachel Aubrey then offers a unified account of the middle voice focusing on -θη- that moves beyond deponency to describe this feature on its own terms rather than with reference to English. Finally, Geoffrey Horrocks offers a retrospective and prospective reflection on the impact of this volume for future research.

The vision of this volume was much broader than simply offering an alternative view of the verb. We wanted to see what a diverse team of scholars, working within compatible linguistic frameworks, could achieve in solving a problem that none of us felt had been adequately resolved. Instead of bickering or posturing, the conference and the ensuing discussion resulted in a collegial collaboration that few of us had ever experienced.

Each contribution offered an important piece to the overall puzzle of better understanding the Koine Greek verb, demonstrating that a mixed tense/aspect view is indeed linguistically viable.

Our goal for this volume is not to end the entrenched debate, but rather to break the impasse and to see the discussion move forward. To this end we commend this volume to the reader with the hope that it will deepen and clarify your understanding of the verb as much as it has for us.

Steven E. Runge
Christopher J. Fresch
Atlanta
November 2015

## BIBLIOGRAPHY

Carson, D. A., and Stanley E. Porter. "Preface." Pages 7–11 in *Biblical Greek Language and Linguistics: Open Questions in Current Research*. Edited by Stanley E. Porter and D. A. Carson. JSNTSup 80. Sheffield: JSOT Press, 1993)

# Overview

# CHAPTER 1

# Porter and Fanning on New Testament Greek Verbal Aspect: Retrospect and Prospect

BUIST FANNING

DALLAS THEOLOGICAL SEMINARY

I hope the reader will forgive the personal flavor of these comments. Because I was living and studying at Tyndale House at the time of the conference reflected in the essays in this book, the conveners kindly encouraged me to make a brief presentation at the outset. They asked me to reflect on what Stan Porter and I were trying to address when we took up the topic of New Testament Greek verbal aspect and later published our resulting studies in 1989 and 1990. I hope that some glances back, and a few thoughts on where the broader field is going from here, will be valuable as a part of this collection of essays.

I should make several disclaimers at the start: first, my comments will address Porter and Fanning to some degree, but of course I am more familiar with one side of that tandem than the other. I will try to represent fairly what I think led Stan into this topic and where he probably thinks it should go, but my perceptions of those things may be skewed. Secondly, as the following essays themselves show, the linguistic study of *ancient* Greek verbs is broader than the study of *New Testament* Greek verbs, and the linguistic study of even New Testament Greek verbs is broader than the study of *tense-aspect* forms. So having someone write about two works on New Testament verbal aspect published twenty-five years ago is not intended to stifle discussion or progress on other fronts. I do like very much, however, the focusing effect of this book's subtitle: "A Fresh Approach for Biblical Exegesis."

I think the theme of contributing to exegetical insight is the place to begin in addressing what Stan and I were trying to do in our studies of verbal aspect. Both of us came to this linguistic topic from an interest in New Testament interpretation and theology and a conviction that sound exegesis must be based on a clear grasp of language and how it works. James Barr's book, *Semantics of Biblical Language*,[1] had a formative influence on both of us. In my own case, I read Barr's *Semantics* in the summer of 1972 and was convinced that his critique of *lexical* work in biblical studies—work that was sloppy and subject to popular misconceptions of how language should be understood—applied equally well to grammar and syntax. I was passionate about the interpretation of the New Testament and its value for Christian life and ministry, and the study of New Testament Greek to try to put that interpretation on a more sound footing seemed tremendously valuable to me both then and now. Not long after that encounter with Barr, I read Frank Stagg's article on "The Abused Aorist" in *JBL*[2] and discovered Kenneth McKay's article on Greek verbs and exegesis in the *Tyndale Bulletin*.[3] In the next year or so I read Burton's *Moods and Tenses*, Moule's *Idiom-Book*, and Blass-Debrunner-Funk's *Grammar* cover to cover.[4] I began trying to teach New Testament interpretation to seminary students in 1974 and started to find out how much I actually still had to learn about Greek language and exegesis. In the process I became convinced that linguistics in general and linguistic studies of ancient Greek in particular as well as of other languages would inform exegesis in very

---

1    James Barr, *Semantics of Biblical Language* (London: Oxford University Press, 1961).

2    Frank Stagg, "The Abused Aorist" *JBL* 91 (1972): 222–31.

3    Kenneth L. McKay, "Syntax in Exegesis," *TynBul* 23 (1972): 39–57.

4    Ernest DeWitt Burton, *Syntax of the Moods and Tenses in New Testament Greek*, 3rd ed. (Edinburgh: T&T Clark, 1973); C. F. D. Moule, *An Idiom Book of New Testament Greek* (Cambridge: Cambridge University Press, 1953); F. Blass and A. Debrunner, *A Greek Grammar of the New Testament and Other Early Christian Literature*, trans. Robert W. Funk, revised ed. (Chicago: University Of Chicago Press, 1961).

significant ways. I read Bernard Comrie's book on *Aspect*[5] and John Lyons' two volumes on *Semantics*[6] and found them really helpful for working with issues in New Testament Greek. By the time I started looking for a PhD program in New Testament in the late 1970s, I was convinced that working on verbal aspect from a linguistic perspective would be fascinating as well as valuable for New Testament exegesis, if only to help discover how to ask better questions about the Greek usage and find better answers to those questions. I am sure that Stan was motivated by similar concerns.

I want to trace at this point a couple of contrasts between our approaches. The first contrast concerns our respective stances with reference to earlier scholarship. My own instincts and background led me to think that understanding what aspect is and how it works in ancient Greek was something that had become clearer and clearer through a long tradition of study by classicists, exegetes, and linguists over a century or so of prior study. It seemed to me that the linguistic, or at least philological, insights of earlier scholars who knew Greek well and had worked extensively with its ancient texts were not so much mistaken or misguided but simplistic and in need of refinement and specification. I am thinking here of work by people like Ellicott, Lightfoot, Westcott, Burton, Moulton, Debrunner, and Zerwick to name only a few who worked with *New Testament* Greek. What could clarify their insights, I thought, was exposure to studies of how aspect worked in other languages in order to grasp the patterns of usage in Greek more adequately. What I thought was needed was not an intellectual revolution but a process of correcting and extending the work of others.

Stan on the other hand found earlier work on ancient Greek aspect to be seriously flawed and confused. What was necessary in his view was not renovation but a new foundation, a completely new paradigm, a scientific revolution à la Thomas Kuhn. That revolution exploded on the scene, according to Stan, in 1989. The old explanations of the ancient Greek verbal system that had anything to do with temporal location or with *Aktionsart* distinctions had to be cleared away and forgotten in order to make real progress.

---

5   Bernard Comrie, *Aspect: An Introduction to the Study of Verbal Aspect and Related Problems*, CTL (Cambridge: Cambridge University Press, 1976).

6   John Lyons, *Semantics*, 2 vols. (Cambridge: Cambridge University Press, 1977).

The second contrast between us concerns how to construct our own solution to the issues we discovered. In Stan's view what was needed was a rigorous linguistic approach that displayed the structure of discrete choices built into the Greek verbal network. It must be a system that tolerates as few "leaks" as possible and it must capture the choices at the larger network level, not the level of specific contextual features that may obscure the systemic structure. There are solid theoretical reasons for that approach, but I think it comes up short in accomplishing the goal of aiding interpretation of specific examples of usage. My preference instead was to avoid a grand, abstract system that seemed to me to provide little real help in understanding aspect in specific texts, and to seek explanations that took contextual features into account in a greater way. This approach is also, as I see it, the one followed by most scholars who work with aspect across a wide variety of the languages of the world regardless of the particular linguistic theories they espouse.

What I just articulated is a gross oversimplification, from my point of view, of the two approaches that Stan and I took. The reality is far more nuanced on both sides and neither is clearly right or wrong on the face of it. Both involve trade-offs with relative advantages and disadvantages. I will not try to defend my view or critique Stan's further on this occasion, since both of us have weighed in on these points before, and people are tired, I am sure, of the back and forth that seems to have no resolution. I will leave it to others to decide how to work with these issues for themselves. If you are inclined to approach Greek verbs using an abstract network of oppositions, feel free to do so, but my appeal to you is to do your best to bring it down to a level of explanation that provides help for construing the meaning of examples in specific texts.

One further thing to mention, however, is the level of consensus between Stan and me—and a number of other writers including Kenneth McKay, Rod Decker, Con Campbell, and others who could be named—on a few central points regarding New Testament Greek verbal aspect. These came to the fore to some degree in our 1993 exchange of papers (from the Society of Biblical Literature's Annual Meeting of 1991), and we revisited them more recently in an exchange of essays on the Greek perfect that will be published in late 2015 (from the Society of Biblical Literature's Annual Meeting in 2013).[7] Four of these points of consensus are: (1) verbal aspect as central to understanding ancient Greek verbal meaning; (2) aspect as a matter of viewpoint, that is, the speaker's perspective on an action or state, a category semantically different from procedural or actional characteristics often called *Aktionsarten* or kinds of action; (3) the Greek aorist as perfective aspect and the present/imperfect as imperfective aspect; (4) Greek verbal aspect as important to some kinds of discourse structuring. I believe these points of consensus are an important baseline to build on for the future. There are still debatable details within this broad outline and much of it can certainly be refined and clarified further. One of the main appeals that I want to make to all the readers of these comments is a warm and friendly invitation for them to pitch in and help with this ongoing process of correcting, improving, and extending our understanding of the ancient Greek verbal system. Please! Pick up a hammer and chisel and work away at this—with my blessings and gratitude. Feel free to confirm and correct these basic points as you think is necessary. And I do not plan to stop working with these topics anytime soon, so I likewise will feel free to push back on your ideas as I think is necessary.

One final appeal along the same line: there is a great need for help in packaging these concepts in ways that students at various levels of Greek instruction can readily understand and then use in New Testament exegesis. One of the regrettable failures of the past twenty-five years is that these points of consensus have not been more effectively communicated to a wider, less academically-inclined group of users. Any help that can be given at this more popular and utilitarian level would be most welcome.

# BIBLIOGRAPHY

Barr, James. *Semantics of Biblical Language.* London: Oxford University Press, 1961.

---

7   Stanley Porter, Buist Fanning, and Constantine Campbell, *The Perfect Volume: Critical Discussion of the Semantics of the Greek Perfect Tense under Aspect Theory*, SBG 17 (New York: Lang, forthcoming).

Blass, F. and A. Debrunner. *A Greek Grammar of the New Testament and Other Early Christian Literature*. Translated by Robert W. Funk. Revised ed. Chicago: University Of Chicago Press, 1961.

Burton, Ernest DeWitt. *Syntax of the Moods and Tenses in New Testament Greek*. 3rd ed. Edinburgh: T&T Clark, 1973.

Comrie, Bernard. *Aspect: An Introduction to the Study of Verbal Aspect and Related Problems*. CTL. Cambridge: Cambridge University Press, 1976.

Lyons, John. *Semantics*. 2 vols. Cambridge: Cambridge University Press, 1977.

McKay, Kenneth L. "Syntax in Exegesis." *TynBul* 23 (1972): 39-57.

Moule, C. F. D. *An Idiom Book of New Testament Greek*. Cambridge: Cambridge University Press, 1953.

Porter, Stanley, Buist Fanning, and Constantine Campbell. *The Perfect Volume: Critical Discussion of the Semantics of the Greek Perfect Tense under Aspect Theory*. SBG 17. New York: Lang, forthcoming.

Stagg, Frank. "The Abused Aorist." *JBL* 91 (1972): 222-31.

# CHAPTER 2

# What is Aspect?: Contrasting Definitions in General Linguistics and New Testament Studies[1]

CHRISTOPHER J. THOMSON

UNIVERSITY OF EDINBURGH

## 1. INTRODUCTION

It is common ground among scholars of New Testament Greek that in the nonindicative moods the so-called "tenses" do not encode tense in its narrower sense of location in time (past, present, future, etc.), but rather a property termed *aspect*.[2] Moreover, it is common ground that in the indicative, too, at least some tenses express

---

1  I am grateful to Constantine Campbell, Buist Fanning, and Stanley Porter for their responses to various queries, to Wally Cirafesi, Rob Crellin, James Hely Hutchinson, Mickey Mantle, Steve Runge, Stephen Shead, and Steve Walton for their helpful comments on a draft of this chapter, and to the participants in the conference "Linguistics and the Greek Verb" for their feedback on the abridged version presented there.

2  The term "tense" is used in both a broader and a narrower sense. As John Lyons notes, it has traditionally been used to cover "not only what is here classified as tense, but a range of other time-related distinctions which are nowadays subsumed, by linguists at least, under the term 'aspect.'" *Semantics* (Cambridge: Cambridge University Press, 1977), 2:687. Some scholars prefer to refer to the Greek present, aorist, and so on as "tense-forms" rather than "tenses," because they see the distinctions between them as non-temporal; e.g., Constantine R. Campbell, *Basics of Verbal Aspect in Biblical Greek* (Grand Rapids: Zondervan, 2008), 24.

aspect, whether or not they also express location in time.[3] There is no doubt, therefore, concerning the importance of aspect for understanding the Greek verb.[4]

But despite this consensus there is considerable confusion among New Testament scholars as to what is actually meant by "aspect." Although real progress in understanding the subject has been made over the last thirty years or so, not least through the application of insights from general linguistics, this chapter will argue that the understanding of aspect which has emerged reflects a misunderstanding of the linguistic literature.

Recent studies of aspect in New Testament Greek have taken as their starting point the important doctoral dissertations of Porter and Fanning, published in 1989 and 1990 respectively.[5] There are sig-

---

3  A few scholars have followed Kenneth McKay and Stanley Porter (see n. 5 below) in arguing that there is no tense (in the narrower sense) even in the indicative. As Campbell notes, this position "is still in the minority, being rejected by most grammarians." *Advances in the Study of Greek: New Insights for Reading the New Testament* (Grand Rapids: Zondervan, 2015), 111.

4  See Stanley E. Porter, *Linguistic Analysis of the Greek New Testament: Studies in Tools, Methods, and Practice* (Grand Rapids: Baker Academic, 2015), 198; Campbell, *Advances*, 109.

5  S. E. Porter, *Verbal Aspect in the Greek of the New Testament: With Reference to Tense and Mood*, SBG 1 (New York: Lang, 1989); Buist M. Fanning, *Verbal Aspect in New Testament Greek*, OTM (Oxford: Oxford University Press, 1990). The book-length treatments which have ensued are Mari Broman Olsen, *A Semantic and Pragmatic Model of Lexical and Grammatical Aspect*, ODL (New York: Garland, 1997); Rodney J. Decker, *Temporal Deixis of the Greek Verb in the Gospel of Mark with Reference to Verbal Aspect*, SBG 10 (New York: Lang, 2001); Constantine R. Campbell, *Verbal Aspect, the Indicative Mood, and Narrative: Soundings in the Greek of the New Testament*, SBG 13 (New York: Lang, 2007); Campbell, *Verbal Aspect and Non-Indicative Verbs: Further Soundings in the Greek of the New Testament*, SBG 15 (New York: Lang, 2008); Toshikazu S. Foley, *Biblical Translation in Chinese and Greek: Verbal Aspect in Theory and Practice*, LBS 1 (Leiden: Brill, 2009); David L. Matthewson, *Verbal Aspect in the Book of Revelation: The Function of Greek Verb Tenses in John's Apocalypse*, LBS 4 (Leiden: Brill, 2010); Wally V. Cirafesi, *Verbal Aspect in Synoptic Parallels: On the Method and Meaning of Divergent Tense-Form Usage in the Synoptic Passion Narrative*, LBS 7 (Leiden: Brill, 2013); Douglas S. Huffman, *Verbal Aspect Theory and the Prohibitions in the Greek New Testament*, SBG 16 (New York: Lang, 2014). Campbell has also produced a short introduction, *Basics of Verbal Aspect in Biblical Greek* (see n. 2). Important treatments prior to those of Porter and Fanning are Juan Mateos, *El aspecto verbal en el Nuevo Testamento*, EstNT 1 (Madrid: Ediciones Cristiandad, 1977), and various contributions from Kenneth L. McKay on both Classical Greek and New Testament

nificant differences between Porter's approach and Fanning's, and it is unfortunate that the phrase "verbal aspect theory" has sometimes been used to refer to distinctives of the former, such as the view that Greek tenses do not encode location in time even in the indicative.[6] But there is considerable agreement between these two scholars as to the essential nature of aspect. In particular, both see aspect as a matter of the speaker or author's choice of "viewpoint" on the situation to which the verb relates,[7] although differing as to the extent to which this choice is a subjective one.[8] Moreover, both deny that aspect is a temporal category,[9] seeing the expression of a situation's temporal structure as at most a secondary effect of the choice of aspect in combination with other elements of a clause and its context.

This level of agreement in two independent studies has been described as "nothing short of stunning,"[10] and probably accounts for the fact that subsequent New Testament scholarship on aspect has generally accepted Porter and Fanning's understanding of the

---

Greek, especially *Greek Grammar for Students: A Concise Grammar of Classical Attic with Special Reference to Aspect in the Verb* (Canberra: Dept. of Classics, Australian National University, 1974) and "On the Perfect and Other Aspects in New Testament Greek," *NovT* 23 (1981): 289–329. See now McKay, *A New Syntax of the Verb in New Testament Greek: An Aspectual Approach*, SBG 5 (New York: Lang, 1994). Trevor V. Evans discusses verbal aspect in the Septuagint in *Verbal Syntax in the Greek Pentateuch: Natural Greek Usage and Hebrew Interference* (Oxford: Oxford University Press, 2001), and makes a number of important observations in "Future Directions for Aspect Studies in Ancient Greek," in *Biblical Greek Language and Lexicography: Essays in Honor of Frederick W. Danker*, ed. Bernard A. Taylor et al. (Grand Rapids: Eerdmans, 2004), 199–206.

6   E.g., Andrew David Naselli, "A Brief Introduction to Verbal Aspect in New Testament Greek," *DBSJ* 12 (2007): 18; Stanley E. Porter, "Prominence: A Theoretical Overview," in *The Linguist As Pedagogue: Trends in the Teaching and Linguistic Analysis of the Greek New Testament*, ed. Stanley E. Porter and Matthew Brook O'Donnell, NTM 11 (Sheffield: Sheffield Phoenix, 2009), 58; Matthewson, *Verbal Aspect*, 24–25.

7   Porter, *Verbal Aspect*, 98; Fanning, *Verbal Aspect*, 84–85.

8   Porter sees "no necessary correlation between aspect form and objective action" ("Aspect Theory and Lexicography," in Taylor, *Biblical Greek Language and Lexicography*, 208). Fanning considers aspect "a rather subjective category," but notes that "fully subjective choices between aspects are not common" (*Verbal Aspect*, 85; similarly 50).

9   See §§3.2 and 3.3 below.

10  D. A. Carson, "An Introduction to the Porter/Fanning Debate," in *Biblical Greek Language and Linguistics: Open Questions in Current Research*, ed. Stanley E. Porter and D. A. Carson, JSNTSup 80 (Sheffield: JSOT Press, 1993), 22.

concept rather uncritically. Campbell has noted that while the disagreements between Porter and Fanning provoked interest and debate, the agreements offered "a relatively stable foundation for future aspectual research."[11] He lists aspect as one of the "significant issues within Greek verbal aspect studies" concerning which "there is a great deal of agreement,"[12] and others have made similar comments in recent publications.[13]

It is hoped that the present chapter will prompt scholars to reexamine this foundational question. It will be noted below that despite considerable debate within general linguistics as to precisely how aspect should be defined,[14] there is a consensus that it is a temporal concept, having to do with the way in which a situation is presented not in some abstract or spatial sense but specifically *in relation to time*. For this reason the actual temporal structure of the situation often constrains the speaker or author's choice of aspect, so that the choice is a subjective one only in certain circumstances. Fanning, indeed, recognizes this latter point, but is nevertheless reluctant to define aspect in relation to time, and most of the recent work on aspect within New Testament studies has followed Porter's more subjective approach.

In order to avoid any possible misunderstanding it is worth stressing that the concern of the present chapter is whether *aspect* is or is not a temporal concept. It is not whether the Greek "tenses" ever encode tense (in the narrower sense of location in time) alongside aspect. Because the second question is one of the major areas of disagreement between Porter and Fanning, it is sometimes supposed

---

11  Campbell, *Advances*, 46–47 (quoted text from p. 47).

12  Ibid., 130.

13  Cirafesi notes that "a somewhat unified definition of verbal aspect has emerged" (*Verbal Aspect*, 22), and Porter describes the definition of verbal aspect as a "point of agreement" between himself, Fanning, and Campbell (*Linguistic Analysis*, 199). Of the scholars cited in n. 5, above, only Olsen and Evans refer to time in their definitions of aspect. Olsen, whose field is general linguistics, follows Comrie's temporal definition (on which see §2.2 below), as does Evans in his study of the Greek Pentateuch (Olsen, *Semantic and Pragmatic Model*, 6–7; Evans, *Verbal Syntax*, 18–19).

14  Carl Bache noted some time ago that "aspect is probably one of the most controversial areas not only in language-specific grammars but also in general linguistics," so that "it is impossible to refer to any single generally accepted definition." *Verbal Aspect: A General Theory and Its Application to Present-Day English*, OUSE 8 (Odense: Odense University Press, 1985), 5.

that the "verbal aspect debate" is really a debate about tense, or that aspect and tense are somehow in competition. As Campbell rightly points out, this is not the case.[15] Nevertheless, the questions are related,[16] and some of the same methodological issues arise in relation to both. For example, arguments presented in support of the "no tense" view often depend on the assumption that grammatical categories have invariable and "uncancelable" semantic meanings, so that the existence of non-past-referring imperfects (for example) is evidence that the imperfect is not a past tense.[17] In fact there is much to be said for the view that grammatical categories can be polysemous, so that there need not be a single core of meaning found in every context.[18] It will be argued here that a temporal view of aspect is the norm among linguists, and has considerable power to explain aspectual usage in the Greek New Testament. But this should not be interpreted as a claim that there are no idiomatic examples or special cases.

Section 2 below offers an overview of representative approaches to aspect in general linguistics, pointing out that although these

---

15  Campbell, *Advances*, 109. Both Porter and Decker appear to confuse the two questions when they accuse Fanning of inconsistency for defining aspect without reference to time but seeing the tenses as expressing time in the indicative (Stanley E. Porter, "In Defence of Verbal Aspect," in Porter, *Biblical Greek Language and Linguistics*, 37; Decker, *Temporal Deixis*, 20).

16  See the comments in the conclusion to this chapter.

17  See, e.g., Porter, *Verbal Aspect*, 104, 184; Decker, *Temporal Deixis*, 44–48; Campbell, *Indicative Mood*, 24–27. The notion of semantic meaning as "uncancelable" meaning has been borrowed from the field of pragmatics, where it is used very differently. Broadly, pragmatic meaning is meaning that is implied by the use of a sentence in a particular extralinguistic context. See generally Stephen C. Levinson, *Pragmatics*, CTL (Cambridge: Cambridge University Press, 1983); Mira Ariel, *Defining Pragmatics*, RSL (Cambridge: Cambridge University Press, 2010).

18  See, e.g., Bernard Comrie, *Tense*, CTL (Cambridge: Cambridge University Press, 1985), 18–23; Moisés Silva, "A Response to Fanning and Porter on Verbal Aspect," in Porter, *Biblical Greek Language and Linguistics*, 79; John R. Taylor, *Linguistic Categorization*, 3rd ed., OTLing (Oxford: Oxford University Press, 2003), 176–81; Lotte Hogeweg, "What's So Unreal About the Past: Past Tense and Counterfactuals," in *Studies on English Modality in Honour of Frank R. Palmer*, ed. Anastasios Tsangalidis and Roberta Facchinetti, Linguistic Insights 111 (Bern: Lang, 2009), 181–208; William Croft, *Verbs: Aspect and Causal Structure* (Oxford: Oxford University Press, 2012), 127; Klaas Bentein, "Tense and Aspect from Hellenistic to Early Byzantine Greek," *EAGLL* 3:380. See also Christopher J. Fresch's contribution in ch. 12 of the present volume.

differ in their descriptions they are in agreement that aspect is a temporal concept. It will be suggested, however, that in some cases this is obscured by linguists' use of visual and spatial metaphors to describe aspect, which may be a contributing factor in the current confusion within New Testament scholarship. It will be suggested that for this reason a "time-relational" analysis (to use Klein's term) is preferable. Moreover, such an approach clarifies the different ways in which aspect and *Aktionsart* relate to time. Section 3 surveys the definitions of aspect by four New Testament scholars, namely Mateos, Porter, Fanning, and Campbell, showing how the latter three downplay or deny the temporal nature of aspect, in contrast to the linguists discussed in section 2. Section 4 then demonstrates how a temporal understanding of aspect explains the various effects of aspectual choice in combination with different types of verb, and section 5 offers concluding reflections and suggests some desiderata for further work in this area.

For the sake of simplicity this chapter focuses primarily on perfective and imperfective aspects, concerning which there is the most consensus among New Testament scholars, and on the indicative mood. However, it will be suggested that a time-relational approach also offers potential for explaining the aspect of the perfect and pluperfect tenses,[19] and that of the future tense in the nonindicative moods.[20]


## 2. ASPECT IN GENERAL LINGUISTICS

A comprehensive survey of approaches to aspect in general linguistics would be well beyond the possibilities of this chapter.[21] Instead

---

19  The aspectual value of these tenses is complex and disputed. Porter describes it as "stative," grammaticalizing "the speaker's conception of the verbal process as a state or condition" (*Verbal Aspect*, 257). Fanning sees the perfect as "a complex verbal category denoting, in its basic sense, a state which results from a prior occurrence," combining "the *Aktionsart*-feature of stative situation, the tense-feature of anteriority, and the aspect of summary viewpoint concerning the occurrence" (*Verbal Aspect*, 119). Campbell sees it as imperfective (*Indicative Mood*, 186).

20  See §2.4 below.

21  The literature is vast. As of 2006, Robert Binnick's "Project on Annotated Bibliography of Contemporary Research in Tense, Grammatical Aspect, *Aktionsart*, and Related Areas" had reached around 9,000 items (http://www.

the range of opinion will be illustrated with reference to a few of the works that have proved most influential, both on aspect studies in general and on New Testament scholarship in particular.

Perhaps the biggest difference among linguists when it comes to defining aspect is precisely which of a number of related phenomena should be included under that umbrella, the difficulty being that languages behave rather differently with respect to the phenomena in question. One approach starts with a particular language and uses the term "aspect" to refer to particular grammaticalized distinctions found in that language, while another seeks a broader definition that can be applied cross-linguistically.[22] Studies of aspect in New Testament Greek have drawn on both approaches. As an example of the former we will begin by considering aspect in Russian, and in particular Isačenko's "parade" illustration, a modified version of which has made its way, via Porter, into discussion of New Testament Greek. The remainder of the section will examine various attempts to define aspect as a cross-linguistic category, beginning with the idea of aspect as a view of the "internal temporal constituency" of a situation, of which Comrie is perhaps the most frequently-cited exponent.[23] After explaining Comrie's view, we will consider Bache's critique of Comrie, and Bache's explanation of the distinction between aspect and *Aktionsart*. It will be noted that he and others who make such a distinction nevertheless define both concepts in relation to time. It will be suggested, however, that their temporal understanding of aspect is in some cases obscured by the use of visual and spatial metaphors, and that a time-relational definition, such as those of Johnson and Klein, is to be preferred.

---

utsc.utoronto.ca/~binnick/TENSE/Bibliography.html). A useful short introduction to the subject is Hans-Jürgen Sasse, "Aspect and Aktionsart," in *Encyclopedia of Language & Linguistics*, ed. Keith Brown, 2nd ed. (London: Elsevier, 2006), 1:535–38, and an up-to-date overview of the field is offered by Robert I. Binnick, ed., *The Oxford Handbook of Tense and Aspect* (New York: Oxford University Press, 2012). See also Hans-Jürgen Sasse, "Recent Activity in the Theory of Aspect: Accomplishments, Achievements, or Just Non-Progressive State?" *LiTy* 6 (2002): 199–271.

22  See Bernard Comrie, *Aspect: An Introduction to the Study of Verbal Aspect and Related Problems*, CTL (Cambridge: Cambridge University Press, 1976), 6–7.

23  Ibid., 3.

## 2.1 Aspect in Russian and Isačenko's "Parade" Analogy

The narrower approach to aspect usually takes as its starting point the distinction between *perfective* and *imperfective* verbs in Slavonic languages such as Russian, which has been called "the aspect language *par excellence*."[24] Indeed, the use of "aspect" as a grammatical term originated in the nineteenth century as a calque or loan translation of the Russian term вид (*vid*). The latter can mean both "form" and "view," and was originally adopted by grammarians as an equivalent to the Greek term εἶδος, referring to a morphological form or type. Smotrickij used the term in the early seventeenth century to distinguish "primary" nouns and verbs from "derived" ones, and Greč in his 1827 grammar used it to distinguish various semantic classes of verb. It was only later that the term came to be reinterpreted in its alternative sense of "view" and used to refer to the distinction between perfective and imperfective verbs.[25] Reiff's use of the calque "aspect" in his 1828 French translation of Greč's grammar was no doubt partly responsible for the first of these developments,[26] even if, contrary to what is usually supposed,[27] he may not have been the first to use "aspect" as an equivalent for вид.[28]

---

24  Bache, *Verbal Aspect*, 1. Östen Dahl observes, however, that the Slavonic languages are in fact "rather idiosyncratic in many ways" when it comes to aspect. "Perfectivity in Slavonic and Other Languages," in *Aspect Bound: A Voyage into the Realm of Germanic, Slavonic and Finno-Ugrian Aspectology*, ed. Casper de Groot and Hannu Tommola (Dordrecht: Foris, 1984), 4.

25  See Lawrence W. Newman, "The Notion of Verbal Aspect in Eighteenth Century Russia," *Russian Linguistics* 3 (1976): 38; C. J. Ruijgh, review of *Kontext und Aspekt in der altgriechischen Prosa Herodots*, by Heinrich Hettrich, *Gnomon* 51 (1979): 222–23; Robert I. Binnick, *Time and the Verb: A Guide to Tense and Aspect* (New York: Oxford University Press, 1991), 139–40.

26  Nikolaj Ivanovič Greč, *Grammaire raisonnée de la langue russe*, trans. Charles Philippe Reiff (St. Petersburg: Gretsch,1828–29). Reiff's own grammar of 1821 uses "branche" rather than "aspect" as an equivalent to вид, contrary to what is stated in H. M. Sørensen, "Om definitionerne af verbets aspekter," in *In memoriam Kr. Sandfeld udgivet paa 70-aarsdagen for hans fødsel*, ed. Rosally Brøndal et al. (Copenhagen: Gyldendal, 1943), 221. See Charles Philippe Reiff, *Grammaire russe précédée d'une introduction sur la langue slavonne* (Paris: Barrois, 1851), 110 (as p. xv indicates, the 1851 Paris edition is simply a reissue of the 1821 St. Petersburg edition, which I was unable to consult).

27  For this view see, e.g., Newman, "Notion of Verbal Aspect," 38; Ruijgh, review of *Kontext und Aspekt* (by Hettrich), 222; Binnick, *Time and the Verb*, 140.

28  Auroux notes that de Neuville seems to have used "aspect" in the sense of вид in a short article published in 1818; Sylvain Auroux, "Innovation et sys-

The precise distinction between perfective and imperfective aspect in Russian has been much debated. Some earlier scholars saw the distinction as one between completed action and continuous action, or between actions of shorter and longer duration.[29] But Forsyth represents what is probably the standard view today when he defines a perfective verb as one that *"expresses the action as a total event summed up with reference to a single specific juncture,"*[30] and an imperfective verb as one that is neutral with respect to perfectivity.[31] Isačenko, who understood the distinction similarly, illustrated it using the analogy of a parade, which is often cited in studies of aspect in New Testament Greek.[32] However, the version of the analogy familiar to New Testament scholars is Porter's adaptation, and differs strikingly from Isačenko's own version.

Isačenko suggested that when one uses a perfective verb such as он переписал (*on perepisal*, he rewrote) or он прочитал (*on pročital*, he read), one's perspective can be compared to that of a person watching a parade from the stand. Such a person stands outside the event and experiences the whole thing from beginning to end.

---

tème scientifique: Le temps verbal dans la Grammaire génerale," in *Hommage à Jean-Toussaint Desanti*, ed. Sylvain Auroux et al. (Mauvezin: Trans-Europ-Repress, 1991), 80, citing Michel de Neuville, "Système des formes du verbe français," *Annales de grammaire* 1 (1818): 543. Archaimbault argues that Maudru also did so in his 1802 grammar, but this seems less clear; Sylvie Archaimbault, "L'aspect: Fortune d'un terme, avatars d'un concept," in *Métalangage et terminologie linguistique: Actes du colloque international de Grenoble (Université Stendhal-Grenoble III, 14-16 mai 1998)*, ed. Bernard Colombat and Marie Savelli, OrbisSup 17 (Leuven: Peeters, 2001), 86, citing Jean-Baptiste Maudru, *Éléments raisonnés de la langue russe ou principes généraux de la grammaire appliqués à la langue russe* (Paris: Maudru, 1802), 222.

29 A survey of major views is presented in A. V. Isačenko, *Grammatičeskij stroj russkogo jazyka v sopostavlenii c slovackim: Morfologija*, part 2 (Bratislava: Slovak Academy of Sciences, 1960), 133-36, and more briefly in Isačenko, *Formenlehre*, pt. 1 of *Die russische Sprache der Gegenwart* (Halle: Niemeyer, 1962), 349.

30 James Forsyth, *A Grammar of Aspect: Usage and Meaning in the Russian Verb*, Studies in the Modern Russian Language Extra Volume (Cambridge: Cambridge University Press, 1970), 8 (emphasis original).

31 Ibid., 14.

32 See, e.g., Porter, *Verbal Aspect*, 91; Porter, *Idioms of the Greek New Testament*, 2nd ed. BLG 2 (Sheffield: Sheffield Academic, 1994), 24; Daniel B. Wallace, *Greek Grammar Beyond the Basics: An Exegetical Syntax of the New Testament* (Grand Rapids: Zondervan, 1996), 500; Campbell, *Indicative Mood*, 50; Campbell, *Basics*, 19-20.

By contrast, the perspective expressed by the imperfective equivalents он переписывал (*on perepisyval*; "he was rewriting") and он читал (*on čital*; "he was reading") can be compared to that of a participant marching in the parade, who does not experience the complete event because he or she cannot see its beginning or end.[33] Isačenko represented the distinction graphically as follows:[34]

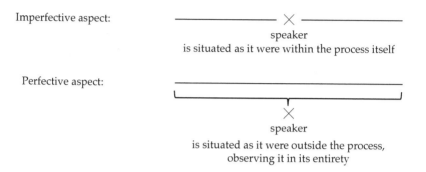

Imperfective aspect:

speaker
is situated as it were within the process itself

Perfective aspect:

speaker
is situated as it were outside the process,
observing it in its entirety

Figure 1: Isačenko's Parade Analogy

A weakness which has been noted in Isačenko's analogy, so far as Russian is concerned, is that the comparison of the imperfective to the view from within the parade, not taking in its beginning and end, contradicts Isačenko's own understanding of the imperfective as a neutral form.[35] In other words, the so-called imperfective aspect in Russian *can* be used when speaking of an entire situation from beginning to end, although unlike the perfective aspect it *need* not.[36] Forsyth notes, for example, that the question "Have you read *War and Peace*?" can be phrased using an imperfective verb: Вы <u>читали</u>

---

33  The examples using переписать/переписывать (rewrite) and прочитать/читать (read) appear in Isačenko, *Grammatičeskij stroj*, 132–33 and Isačenko, *Russische Sprache*, 348, respectively.

34  Isačenko, *Grammatičeskij stroj*, 133 (my translation); cf. Isačenko, *Russische Sprache*, 348.

35  Forsyth, *Grammar of Aspect*, 349. For Isačenko's view of imperfective aspect see his *Grammatičeskij stroj*, 132.

36  Forsyth argues that this is true even in the case of those verbs where the imperfective is a secondary formation from a perfective verb (*Grammar of Aspect*, 29).

"Войну и мир"? (*Vy čitali "Vojnu i mir"?*).[37] But although Isačenko's illustration of imperfective aspect does not completely fit his understanding of Russian, it does fit the usual understanding of imperfective aspect when considered as a cross-linguistic typological category. That is, some languages differ from Russian in having a form that is used only when the temporal boundaries of a situation are positively excluded,[38] and within general linguistics the term "imperfective" is normally used to refer to such a form.[39]

It is important to stress (as, indeed, Isačenko himself stressed) that his parade analogy is merely an analogy, and can be accepted only with certain reservations.[40] The analogy can be understood correctly only in the light of Isačenko's accompanying explanation and examples, which suggest that he sees the totality expressed by perfective aspect as primarily *temporal* rather than spatial. The analogy works because a parade moves through time and space simultaneously; those observing from the stand see the whole length of the parade not at once but over time as it passes by. But Isačenko's examples involve verbs for "reading" and "rewriting," which normally take place in a single location. The difference between referring to the action "to read a book" using the perfective прочитать книгу (*pročitat' knigu*) and the imperfective читать книгу (*čitat' knigu*) is not that the first takes in all of the *space* occupied by the action while the second views it in close-up, with only part of the scene visible. Rather, the difference is that the perfective includes the whole *time-span* of the event from beginning to end, while the imperfective does not (or does not *necessarily*, being aspectually neutral). It is true that Isačenko avoids defining aspect in explicitly temporal terms, and

---

37  Likewise, the answer "Yes, I've read it" can be expressed using the imperfective verb Читал (*Čital*) (ibid., 83). The speaker in such cases "is merely interested in the fact that the type of action named did occur" (ibid., 82).

38  Recent works have taken the view that the opposition between perfective and imperfective aspects in New Testament Greek is equipollent, i.e., that neither is aspectually neutral or unmarked (Fanning, *Verbal Aspect*, 124–25; Porter, *Verbal Aspect*, 90; Campbell, *Indicative Mood*, 20–21). If this is correct, then the imperfective aspect can fairly be compared to the "internal" view of the participant in Isačenko's parade. But the question of markedness deserves further attention, given the complexities noted by Comrie (*Aspect*, 111–22) and Fanning (*Verbal Aspect*, 55–72).

39  E.g., Pier Marco Bertinetto, "Perfectives, Imperfectives, and Progressives," in Brown, *Encyclopedia of Language & Linguistics*, 9:266.

40  Isačenko, *Grammatičeskij stroj*, 133.

even states that aspect lies "außerhalb der temporalen Kategorien" (outside temporal categories).[41] But this needs to be understood in the context of his rejection of alternative definitions of aspect that identified it with temporal features of the situation itself such as duration or completion. It should also be noted that while Isačenko approved Dostal's description of aspect as expressing the speaker's attitude to a situation, he stressed that this was not a *subjective* attitude, for in most cases the "choice" of aspect is dictated by the semantic task of the utterance.[42]

In Porter's version of the parade analogy the perspective of the person watching from the stand represents not perfective aspect, as it does for Isačenko, but *imperfective* aspect, while perfective aspect is represented by the view from a helicopter, taking in the whole parade at once. This perhaps reflects Porter's move away from a temporal understanding of aspect, since the aspects are now represented by what can be seen of the parade at a particular moment, not what is seen over the course of time.[43] The fact that the view from the stand has been used to illustrate both perfective aspect (by Isačenko) and imperfective aspect (by Porter) is perhaps an indication that the analogy is rather less helpful than it appears at first sight.

## 2.2 Comrie and Aspects as Views of Internal Temporal Constituency

Although some linguists have insisted that the term "aspect" should be reserved only for the perfective/imperfective distinction found in Slavonic languages, Bache notes that "the aim of general linguistics is to provide a technical terminology and a linguistic model which may serve as a useful framework for the analysis of any specific language."[44] Not all languages have a straightforward perfective/imperfective contrast. English, for example, can express actions as "simple" (e.g., I walk, I walked), "progressive" (I am walking, I was

41  Isačenko, *Russische Sprache*, 348.
42  Isačenko, *Grammatičeskij stroj*, 132.
43  On Porter's view of aspect see §3.2 below.
44  Carl Bache, "Aspect and Aktionsart: Towards a Semantic Distinction," *JL* 18 (1982): 57.

walking), "perfect" (I have walked, I had walked),[45] or perfect progressive (I have been walking, I had been walking).[46] None of these categories corresponds precisely to what one finds in Russian, but it seems too narrow to consider them nonaspectual.[47] Accordingly linguists have sought a broader definition of aspect that can be applied cross-linguistically.

A common understanding of aspect within general linguistics is that the term refers to an expression or "view" of the internal temporal structure of a situation, where the word "situation" serves as a catchall for actions, events, activities, and states.[48] Thus Klein notes that aspect, according to the conventional view, "concerns the different perspectives which a speaker can take and express with regard to the temporal course of some event, action, process, etc.: the speaker may view it as completed, as on-going, as imminent, and possibly in other ways."[49] Perhaps the most influential and frequently-cited representative of this approach is Comrie, who defines aspects as "different ways of viewing the internal temporal constituency of a situation."[50] The phrase "internal temporal constituency" refers to the way in which the situation unfolds through different temporal phases, especially its beginning, middle, and end.[51] Comrie defines perfective aspect as indicating "the view of a situation as a single whole, without distinction of the various separate phases that make up that situation," while imperfective aspect

---

45  Perfect aspect is not to be confused with perfective aspect. On the distinction see §2.4 below.

46  The simple aspect is usually considered neutral, like the so-called "imperfective" in Russian. See, e.g., Binnick, *Time and the Verb*, 296; Olsen, *Semantic and Pragmatic Model*, 182–89; Henriëtte de Swart, "Verbal Aspect," in Binnick, *Oxford Handbook*, 761. However, Carlota Smith argues for its perfectivity. *The Parameter of Aspect*, 2nd ed., SLP 43 (Dordrecht: Kluwer, 1997), 106–7.

47  Bache, "Aspect and Aktionsart," 57.

48  Among those who use "situation" in this way are Comrie, Lyons, Bache, and Smith. See Comrie, *Aspect*, 13; Lyons, *Semantics*, 2:483; Carl Bache, *The Study of Aspect, Tense and Action: Towards a Theory of the Semantics of Grammatical Categories*, 2nd ed. (Frankfurt am Main: Lang, 1997), 119; Smith, *Parameter*, xiii–xiv. Others use the term "eventuality;" see, e.g., Emmon Bach, "The Algebra of Events," *Ling&P* 9 (1986): 6.

49  Wolfgang Klein, *Time in Language*, Germanic Linguistics (London: Routledge, 1994), 16. Klein himself adopts a time-relational approach similar to Johnson's, on which see §2.4 below.

50  Comrie, *Aspect*, 3.

51  Ibid., 3–4.

"pays essential attention to the internal structure of the situation."[52] This definition enables Comrie to include within "imperfective aspect" a variety of more specific aspects such as habitual and progressive aspects.

Comrie's definition of aspect is a semantic rather than a formal one. That is, it is not restricted to distinctions that are grammaticalized in a particular way, or indeed at all, but encompasses the diversity of ways in which the world's languages express internal temporal constituency. For example, Comrie notes that in Finnish the distinction between "He read the book" and "He was reading the book" is expressed not by using different forms of the verb but by placing the object of the sentence (book, *kirja*) in different cases, namely the accusative (*hän luki kirjan*) and partitive (*hän luki kirjaa*) respectively. This distinction can nevertheless be considered an aspectual one within Comrie's definition,[53] as can information about temporal constituency expressed lexically, through one's choice of vocabulary.[54]

It is important to note that Comrie does not identify aspect with internal temporal constituency, but with a *view* of internal temporal constituency. Aspect, in other words, is a linguistic feature, a feature of utterances about situations rather than of the situations themselves. But there is a connection between the two; the objective nature of a situation constrains the utterances one may fittingly make about it. Someone who regularly played in their school football team could refer to that situation using either of the sentences "I played football for my school" or "I used to play football for my school." The two differ not in the internal temporal constituency of the situation they describe, but in the way they *view* that internal temporal constituency. The first simply views the situation as a whole, while the second looks "inside" the situation and expresses something of its temporal constituency as a regular occurrence. On the other hand, someone who had played only one match could truthfully say "I played football for my school" but not "I used to play football for my school." Similarly, the sentence "The light flashed" could refer to either a single flash or a sequence of flashes, but the

---

52  Ibid., 16.
53  Ibid., 8.
54  On the latter see §4 below.

sentence "The light was flashing" would normally suit only the second scenario. The reason is that a single flash is usually conceived of as a momentary or *punctual* event, which therefore lacks internal temporal constituency, having no middle phase.[55]

The idea of aspect as a "view" or "perspective" is similar to that reflected in Isačenko's parade illustration, and goes back to the nineteenth-century reinterpretation of the term вид noted above. Whether this metaphor is in fact a helpful one will be questioned below, but it is important to stress that when Comrie and others explain aspect as a "view" they are speaking of a view of the *temporal* structure of a situation. Like Isačenko, Comrie describes perfective and imperfective aspect using the language of "exterior" and "interior" viewpoint, respectively. But these terms refer to positions relative to the *temporal* course of the situation from beginning to end.[56] The imperfective aspect pays attention to the internal temporal structure of the situation, whereas the perfective does not, as it were, "look inside" that temporal structure.[57] So aspect, like tense, has to do with time.[58] But it has to do with "*how* the situation relates to time, rather than *when*"[59] or, to put it another way, with "situation-internal time" rather than "situation-external time."[60]

Comrie defines tense as "grammaticalised expression of location in time."[61] It is said to be *deictic* in that it relates the time of the situation to a particular reference point or *deictic center*. In the case of temporal deixis this is a point in time, a "now,"[62] which is normally (but not necessarily) the time of the utterance.[63] As Lyons puts it, tense "grammaticalizes the relationship which holds between

---

55  Comrie, *Aspect*, 26, 42. Comrie notes, however, that it is possible to imagine situations where a seemingly momentary event is represented as having duration (42–43). As Bache points out, what matters is whether the event is *conceived of* as momentary or durative ("Aspect and Aktionsart," 65).

56  Comrie, *Aspect*, 4.

57  Ibid.

58  See ibid., 5.

59  M. Lynne Murphy, *Lexical Meaning*, CTL (Cambridge: Cambridge University Press, 2010), 200 (emphasis original).

60  Comrie, *Aspect*, 5.

61  Comrie, *Tense*, 9.

62  On deixis see ibid., 13–18; Lyons, *Semantics*, 2:677–90.

63  In narrative the deictic center can be a point within the narrative, which explains at least some instances of the historic present (see Binnick, *Time and the Verb*, 128).

the time of the situation that is being described and the temporal zero-point of the deictic context."[64] An example of a difference in tense is the contrast between the sentences "I am playing football" and "I was playing football." The first communicates the idea that I am playing at the present moment, the second that I was playing at a reference point in the past. Aspect, on the other hand, is usually said to be *nondeictic*, meaning that it does not indicate *when* the situation occurred in relation to a particular deictic center.[65] But to say that aspect is non*deictic* is not to say that it is non*temporal*, as can be seen from the examples discussed above.

## 2.3 Bache and the Aspect / *Aktionsart* Distinction

Bache argues that Comrie's definition of aspect is too broad, in that he fails to distinguish it from *Aktionsart*, a German term that literally means "kind of action."[66] It is important to understand precisely what Bache means by this distinction, because the word *"Aktionsart"* has been used in a variety of ways, both in general linguistics and in New Testament studies. At least six different senses can be discerned in recent literature, and it will be useful to list these before turning to Bache's argument, for confusion arises if they are not carefully distinguished.

First, some scholars have used *"Aktionsart"* to refer to what Comrie calls "internal temporal constituency"—that is, to the way in which a situation actually takes place in time. According to this understanding *Aktionsart* is something objective, pertaining to the situation itself, not to the way in which it is conceptualized or described.[67]

---

64  Lyons, *Semantics*, 2:678.

65  However, Lyons notes that "the distinction between tense and aspect is hard to draw with respect to what is sometimes described as relative, or secondary, tense" (ibid., 2:705).

66  Bache, "Aspect and Aktionsart." The term *actionality* is sometimes used as an English equivalent; e.g., Sergej Tatevosov, "The Parameter of Actionality," *LiTy* 6 (2003): 317–401. Bache also critiques Lyons, whose approach is broadly similar to Comrie's and is not discussed here (see Lyons, *Semantics*, 2:703–18).

67  Amalia Moser, "From Aktionsart to Aspect: Grammaticalization and Subjectification in Greek," *ALH* 46 (2014): 67.

A second way that some, including Bache, have used the term is with reference to one's psychological conception of a situation. Borrowing an example from Dowty,[68] Bache notes that one may conceptualize the activity of reading a book for an hour as a continuous one, even if in actual fact it was interrupted by a visit to the bathroom, periods looking out of the window, blinking, and so on.[69] Since *Aktionsart* is a matter of one's conception of a situation, Bache describes it not as objective but as "quasi-objective."[70]

A third approach understands *Aktionsart* as a property not of situations themselves, nor of conceptions of situations, but of sentences (or more precisely, clauses) about them. In this case the term refers to what is *expressed* of the situation's internal temporal constituency through the various components of the clause, including the choice of verbal aspect and the semantics of the verbal lexeme. Thus Wallace explains *Aktionsart* as "aspect in combination with lexical, grammatical, or contextual features."[71] This understanding of *Aktionsart* is close to Comrie's understanding of *aspect*.

A fourth understanding sees *Aktionsart* as a property not of complete clauses but of the verbal lexeme together with its arguments,[72] arguments being those elements of a clause such as its subject(s) and object(s) "which have a close semantic relationship to their predicate," and "which must be involved because of the very nature of the relation or activity named by the predicate."[73] According to this approach, it is the interaction of *Aktionsart* with the grammatical aspect of the verb (perfective, imperfective, etc.) and with other elements of the clause that expresses the internal temporal structure of a situation. The significance of including arguments is that they can make a difference to the relevant temporal characteristics of the situation described, as explained in more detail in section 4

---

68  David R. Dowty, "Studies in the Logic of Verb Aspect and Time Reference in English" (PhD diss., University of Texas at Austin, 1972), 55.

69  Bache, "Aspect and Aktionsart," 65–66.

70  Ibid., 71.

71  Wallace, *Greek Grammar*, 499. This also seems to be Campbell's approach (see, e.g., *Basics*, 55), despite statements such as "*Aktionsart* refers to what actually happened" (ibid., 22)

72  Smith refers to the combination of the verb with its arguments as the *verb constellation* (*Parameter*, 17). This terminology will be employed in §4 below.

73  Paul R. Kroeger, *Analyzing Grammar: An Introduction* (Cambridge: Cambridge University Press, 2005), 58.

below.[74] For example, "Bloggs ran" and "Bloggs ran a mile" behave differently because the latter includes the idea of reaching an endpoint. Similarly "Bloggs scored a goal" speaks of a single event, whereas "Bloggs scored goals" speaks of a series of events spread over a period of time. A wide range of other terms have been used to refer to *Aktionsart* in this sense, including aspectual character,[75] aspectual class,[76] procedural character,[77] situation type,[78] and inherent meaning.[79]

A fifth approach is to see *Aktionsart* as a property of the verb alone, so that the verb "run" has the same *Aktionsart* in the sentences "Bloggs ran" and "Bloggs ran a mile."[80] Robert Crellin, who classifies "run" as an "activity" verb, notes that, "while not finally determining the structure of an event expressed at the sentence level, verbs determine the 'kind of event' that a sentence describes."[81] *Aktionsart* in this sense is sometimes referred to as "lexical aspect."[82] Although the latter term is also used for *Aktionsart* in the fourth sense, Filip argues that it is strictly appropriate only "when just verbs, taken as lexical items, are at stake."[83]

Sixth, within Slavonic linguistics the term has been used to refer to the temporal characteristics of a particular class of verbs also known as "procedurals." These are verbs derived from other verbs through the addition of prefixes or suffixes, and indicate how the action "develops or proceeds in particular circumstances."[84]

---

74  See also Hana Filip, "Lexical Aspect," in Binnick, *Oxford Handbook*, 725; de Swart, "Verbal Aspect," 754.
75  Lyons, *Semantics*, 2:706.
76  Filip, "Lexical Aspect," 725.
77  Fanning, *Verbal Aspect*, 41.
78  Smith, *Parameter*, 17–37.
79  Comrie, *Aspect*, 41–51.
80  Geoffrey Horrocks and Melita Stavrou, "Grammaticalized Aspect and Spatio-Temporal Culmination," *Lingua* 117 (2007): 637.
81  Robert Crellin, "The Greek Perfect Active System: 200 BC–AD 150" (PhD diss., University of Cambridge, 2012), 47. Crellin understands "event aspect" as synonymous with *Aktionsart* (40). See also Susan D. Rothstein, "Introduction," in *Theoretical and Crosslinguistic Approaches to the Semantics of Aspect*, ed. Susan D. Rothstein, Linguistik Aktuell 110 (Amsterdam: Benjamins, 2008), 2–3.
82  Filip, "Lexical Aspect," 725.
83  Ibid.
84  Forsyth, *Grammar of Aspect*, 19. See generally ibid., 19–31.

In Russian, for example, the prefix за- (*za-*) can be added to certain imperfective verbs to generate a perfective verb referring to the beginning of the relevant action. Thus плакать (*plakat'*) means "cry" but the procedural заплакать (*zaplakat'*) means "burst into tears."[85]

As noted above, Bache understands *Aktionsart* in the second of these senses, as one's conception of the temporal course of a situation. In contrast to *Aktionsart*, he sees aspect as reflecting a speaker's or writer's choice of "situational focus" in representing the situation,[86] whether as "a unit, or 'total event' ... or as something unfolding, with specific attention to the internal structure of the situation."[87] It is important to note that his objection to Comrie is not related to Comrie's understanding of aspect as a temporal concept. Indeed, he has referred to Comrie's formulation of the distinction between perfective and imperfective aspect as "one of the very best," though critiquing it on the grounds that strictly speaking it is the "locutionary agent" and not the aspects themselves that "look at" the situation from the outside or inside.[88] For Bache, similarly to Comrie, "looking at a situation from outside, i.e. with an external situational focus, means to look at it in its entirety, with all its constituent phases viewed as a whole," whereas "looking at a situation from inside, i.e. with an internal situational focus, means to look at it as it unfolds, with special attention paid to the middle part."[89] Thus perfective aspect presents a situation "as a whole," while imperfective aspect presents the situation "as unfolding or continuing over an explicit or implicit stretch of time."[90] The reference in these descriptions to constituent phases and to unfolding or continuing over time should leave no doubt that Bache, like Comrie, relates aspect to time.

Bache also recognizes that "there is telling evidence, both syntactic and semantic, against the optional nature of aspectual choice." For example, "the logical incompatibility of the perfective aspect with reference to a process or activity in progress at the time of speaking is usually considered a central theorem in discussions on

---

85  Ibid., 20.
86  Bache, "Aspect and Aktionsart," 70.
87  Ibid., 65.
88  Bache, *Study*, 258.
89  Ibid., 259–60. See also Bache, *Verbal Aspect*, 6–7.
90  Bache, *Verbal Aspect*, 126.

aspect."[91] The situations in which there is a genuinely free choice are those which are "DISTANT from the concrete present either temporally or modally,"[92] and which are "conceived of as objectively (a) durative, (b) atelic … and (c) non-stative."[93] These latter three terms will be explained in more detail in section 4, but essentially the situation must be conceptualized as lasting longer than a moment, not having an inherent terminal point, and involving change. The requirement for distance from the "concrete present" means that the situation must "be placed in the past, in the future or be conceived of as hypothetical, necessary etc."[94] Where these conditions are satisfied, there is what Bache calls a "pure aspectual opposition" between perfective and imperfective aspect, and the speaker or writer has a subjective choice whether to present the situation "as a unit" or "as something unfolding."[95]

In all other cases, however, the choice of aspect is constrained by the *Aktionsart* of the situation. For example, "punctual situations cannot be referred to by a construction marked as truly imperfective."[96] Punctual *verbs* can be combined with imperfectivity, but "such constructions invariably express repetition or refer to the period leading up to the act or event concerned."[97] As discussed in section 4.4 below, whether what is expressed in such a case is repetition or a run-up will depend on the semantics of the verb in question. The sentence "The light was flashing" is of the first type, while an example of the second is "Bloggs was finding his coat," which in fact relates to the period when Bloggs was *looking for* his coat and had not yet found it. The choice of aspect is likewise not a subjective one in the case of durative but telic situations, which Bache defines as those "which move towards a logical conclusion."[98] In such cases imperfective aspect is used to refer "to the process tending towards, but not necessarily reaching, its goal, whereas a perfective

---

91  Bache, "Aspect and Aktionsart," 66.
92  Ibid., 67.
93  Ibid., 68.
94  Ibid., 67.
95  Ibid., 65.
96  Ibid., 68.
97  Ibid., 68; cf. 70.
98  Ibid., 60.

construction makes explicit reference to the goal."[99] Thus the Russian imperfective sentence он умирал (*on umiral*, he was dying) speaks of the period before death, whereas the perfective он умер (*on umer*, he died) refers to death itself.[100]

Since the choice between imperfective and perfective in such cases is not a subjective one, Bache considers it not to be "purely aspectual." Rather, it "involves *Aktionsart*,"[101] and Bache uses the term "aspectual functions" to refer to the uses of the imperfective and perfective in such cases.[102] Yet for Bache the true nature of aspect is displayed in cases where there is a subjective choice between perfective and imperfective, and for this reason he describes aspect as "quasi-subjective." Nevertheless, it is only *quasi*-subjective, because in many cases there is no such subjective choice.[103] Bache is surely right to note that there is a distinction between cases where aspectual choice is constrained by objective (or quasi-objective) factors and those where the choice is more subjective. Yet it may be observed that his argument that only the latter display "pure" aspect is circular, since it is based on the *a priori* assumption that aspect is a subjective category.[104]

Smith makes a distinction between "viewpoint aspect" and "situation aspect" that is similar to Bache's distinction between aspect and *Aktionsart*. As with Comrie and Bache, when she speaks of "viewpoint" she is referring to a "*temporal* perspective."[105] "The main semantic difference among aspectual viewpoints is in how much of a situation they make visible. Perfective viewpoints focus a situation in its entirety, including endpoints; imperfective viewpoints focus an interval that excludes endpoints."[106] Comrie, Bache, and Smith, are not atypical in defining aspect in terms of temporal phases or

---

99   Ibid., 69.
100  Ibid., 68–69, citing Forsyth, *Grammar of Aspect*, 49.
101  Bache, "Aspect and Aktionsart," 69.
102  Ibid., 67–68.
103  Ibid., 70.
104  See ibid., 67.
105  Carlota S. Smith, "A Theory of Aspectual Choice," *Language* 59 (1983): 479; Smith, *Parameter*, xiv, 2 (emphasis added).
106  Smith, *Parameter*, 62.

intervals; there is widespread agreement on this in the linguistic literature.[107]

## 2.4 Marion Johnson and Time-Relational Approaches

Within general linguistics, therefore, definitions of perfective and imperfective aspect in terms of external and internal "viewpoint" are metaphorical, expressing a distinction in the relationship of the verb to time. But although such definitions are common, even commonplace, they are not unproblematic. As Klein notes, "situations, that is, events, actions, processes, states, do not have an inside or an outside, like a house or a tomato."[108] Since "the characterization is purely metaphorical," it is "far from being clear. Characteristically, it is accompanied by spatial and other circumlocutions, such as 'der Prozeß ... liegt geschlossen im Blickfeld des Sprechers [the process as a whole ... is in the speaker's field of vision]' (Ružička 1952:4), as if the process were a matchbox or the Eiffel tower."[109] Here Klein notes Isačenko's parade illustration as "a particularly vivid formulation."[110]

If one must use the language of "view" then aspect is in fact more to do with what is *in* view—whether the entire course of a situation (perfective aspect) or a phase excluding endpoints (imperfective aspect)—than the position or viewpoint one views it from. But the language of "viewing" is itself problematic, because a speaker or writer does not use language to view situations, but rather to *speak about* them. To be sure, language sometimes creates a mental picture. But that is a pragmatic effect arising from the way it is used in context, and aspectual forms can be used in abstract prose that does not create any mental picture whatsoever. As noted above, the idea of aspect as "view" or "viewpoint" seems to have arisen from an

107  Sasse notes a "general consensus that 'aspectuality' is a matter of 'boundaries,'" in the sense of "initial and final endpoints" (i.e., *temporal* boundaries). "Situations may be conceived of as including their starting points or endpoints or both, or may be conceived of as persistent situations with no boundaries implied" ("Recent Activity," 201).
108  Klein, *Time in Language*, 29.
109  Klein, "A Time-Relational Analysis of Russian Aspect," *Language* 71 (1995): 674, citing Rudolf Ružička, "Der russische Verbalaspekt," *Der Russischunterricht* 5 (1952): 161–69 (page numbers cited by Klein *sic*).
110  Klein, "Time-Relational Analysis," 674.

infelicitous translation of the word вид.[111] It would be preferable to define aspect more literally, as the temporal phase or phases about which the speaker or writer is speaking, rather than the phases they have "in view."

Johnson takes just such an approach, building on Reichenbach's work on tenses and that of Bennett and Partee on aspect and truth conditions.[112] She distinguishes "three categories of time which are significant in relation to an act of speaking." The "speech time" (S) is "the time at which the act of speaking itself takes place," the "event time" (E) is the time at which an event takes place, and the "reference time" (R) is the time the speaker "is principally referring to."[113] Whereas tense concerns the relationship between reference time (R) and speech time (S),[114] aspect is concerned with the relationship between reference time (R) and event time (E).[115] Although Johnson uses the word "event," her analysis also holds for other forms of situation such as activities and states.

Johnson defines perfective aspect (which she terms "completive aspect") using the formula "R = E" and imperfective aspect as "For some $t$ in E, R $(<)$ $\{t\}$."[116] In other words, perfective/completive aspect is used when speaking of the whole of the situation expressed

111  Lyons describes "aspect" as a "rather unsatisfactory ... translational equivalent" (*Semantics*, 2:705). Similarly C. J. Ruijgh, "Les valeurs temporelles des formes verbales en grec ancien," in *The Function of Tense in Texts*, ed. Jadranka Gvozdanović and Theo A. J. M. Janssen, VKNWL NS 144 (Amsterdam: Royal Netherlands Academy of Arts and Sciences, 1991), 222–23; Sarah de Voguë et al., "Aspect," in *Dictionary of Untranslatables: A Philosophical Lexicon*, ed. Barbara Cassin, trans. Steven Rendall et al. (Princeton: Princeton University Press, 2014), 50.

112  Hans Reichenbach, *Elements of Symbolic Logic* (New York: Macmillan, 1947), 287–98; Michael Bennett and Barbara H. Partee, *Toward the Logic of Tense and Aspect in English* (Santa Monica, Calif.: System Development Corporation, 1972; repr., Bloomington, IN: University Linguistics Club, 1978). The latter paper is now available in Barbara H. Partee, *Compositionality in Formal Semantics: Selected Papers by Barbara H. Partee*, Explorations in Semantics 1 (Oxford: Blackwell, 2004), 59–109.

113  Marion R. Johnson, "A Unified Temporal Theory of Tense and Aspect," in *Tense and Aspect*, ed. Philip J. Tedeschi and Annie Zaenen, vol. 14 of *Syntax and Semantics* (New York: Academic Press, 1981), 148.

114  This definition perhaps requires slight modification to reflect the fact, noted above, that S is not the only possible deictic center.

115  Johnson, "Unified Temporal Theory," 148.

116  Ibid., 154. For further explanation of her notation see ibid., 150–51.

by the verb, whereas imperfective aspect is used when there is some part of the event time that is after the reference time, i.e., when the endpoint is excluded from the reference time.[117] Although Johnson's understanding of the distinction is similar to those discussed above,[118] her approach has the advantage that it avoids defining aspect in metaphorical terms, and instead offers a precise definition which clarifies both the temporal nature of aspect and its distinction from tense on the one hand and *Aktionsart* (however defined) on the other.

A further attraction of Johnson's approach over Comrie's is that whereas Comrie's definition refers only to *internal* temporal structure, Johnson's allows for reference to times before and after the situation itself.[119] This enables her to offer a straightforward explanation of perfect aspect, which is not easily accommodated within Comrie's system.[120] Perfect aspect, also known as anterior or retrospective aspect (and not to be confused with perfective aspect), is used when "E (<) R"—that is, when the whole of the event time precedes the reference time. Johnson illustrates the various aspects

---

117 Note that if the clause in question contains a temporal adverb, the adverb does not necessarily designate R itself, but may designate a period of time containing R. E.g., "Bloggs was running yesterday" does not mean that Bloggs was running all day, only that at some time (R) during the day he was doing so. See also Binnick, *Time and the Verb*, 210.

118 Binnick notes that Johnson's understanding at first appears incompatible with the "viewpoint" approach (Binnick, *Time and the Verb*, 211), but that there "need be no profound contradiction" between the two (212).

119 Johnson, "Unified Temporal Theory," 152.

120 Bernd Kortmann, e.g., argues that the perfect is not an aspect because it is concerned with "situation-external" rather than "situation-internal" time. "The Triad 'Tense-Aspect-Aktionsart': Problems and Possible Solutions," in *Perspectives on Aspect and Aktionsart*, BJL 6 (Amsterdam: Benjamins, 1991), 18. Comrie himself notes that many linguists "doubt whether the perfect should be considered an aspect," but because it has traditionally been regarded as such he considers it convenient to deal with it in his book, "while bearing in mind continually that it is an aspect in a rather different sense from the other aspects treated so far" (*Aspect*, 52).

diagrammatically as follows, with the brackets indicating the event time (E):

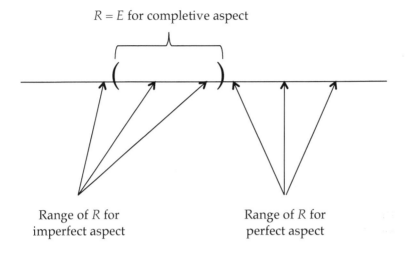

$R = E$ for completive aspect

Range of $R$ for imperfect aspect

Range of $R$ for perfect aspect

Figure 2: Aspect in Johnson's Unified Temporal Theory

The application of this sort of approach has promise for the analysis of New Testament Greek, and may help to resolve some of the outstanding problems. Klein terms such approaches "time-relational."[121] His own approach is similar to Johnson's,[122] and has been fruitfully applied by Crellin in his analysis of the perfect in Koine Greek.[123]

Although Johnson distinguishes only three aspects, it would clearly also be possible to define posterior or prospective aspect in a similar way, namely as "R (<) E"—that is, the reference time precedes the event time. This offers a satisfying explanation of

121 Klein, *Time in Language*, 29; Klein, "Time-Relational Analysis," 674.
122 Klein, *Time in Language*, 99–119; Klein, "Time-Relational Analysis." Similarly Sandra Chung and Alan Timberlake, "Tense, Aspect, and Mood," in *Grammatical Categories and the Lexicon*, ed. Timothy Shopen, vol. 3 of *Language Typology and Syntactic Description* (Cambridge: Cambridge University Press, 1985), 213; Binnick, *Time and the Verb*, 213.
123 Crellin, "Greek Perfect Active System." See also his contribution in ch. 14 of the present volume.

the aspect of the future tense in the nonindicative moods of New Testament Greek.[124] For example:

> ἰδόντες δὲ οἱ περὶ αὐτὸν <u>τὸ ἐσόμενον</u> εἶπαν· κύριε, εἰ πατάξομεν ἐν μαχαίρῃ; (Luke 22:49)
> When Jesus' followers saw <u>what was going to happen</u>, they said, "Lord, should we strike with our swords?" (NIV)

> ἀλλ' εἰσὶν ἐξ ὑμῶν τινες οἳ οὐ πιστεύουσιν. ᾔδει γὰρ ἐξ ἀρχῆς ὁ Ἰησοῦς τίνες εἰσὶν οἱ μὴ πιστεύοντες καὶ τίς ἐστιν <u>ὁ παραδώσων</u> αὐτόν. (John 6:64)
> "But there are some of you who do not believe." (For Jesus knew from the beginning who those were who did not believe, and who it was <u>who would betray</u> him.) (ESV)

## 3. DEFINITIONS OF ASPECT IN RECENT NEW TESTAMENT STUDIES

New Testament scholarship since Porter and Fanning has generally adopted a viewpoint approach to aspect but, in contrast to the linguists mentioned above, has tended to downplay or deny the temporal nature of aspect. This section will briefly survey the definitions of aspect, perfectivity, and imperfectivity offered by four New Testament scholars, namely Mateos, Porter, Fanning, and Campbell. Mateos's 1977 monograph *El aspecto verbal en el Nuevo Testamento* was the first book-length treatment of aspect in New Testament Greek, predating those of Porter and Fanning, and adopts a more clearly time-based approach than subsequent treatments. Most works subsequent to Porter and Fanning largely follow their definitions (and particularly Porter's), and will not be considered separately here.[125]

---

124  In the New Testament the future is relatively rare outside the indicative, with just 13 instances of the future participle and 5 of the future infinitive according to a search using Accordance software. These forms are more common in the Septuagint, which also contains a few instances of the future optative.

125  Decker, *Temporal Deixis*; Foley, *Biblical Translation*; Matthewson, *Verbal Aspect*; Cirafesi, *Verbal Aspect*; Huffman, *Verbal Aspect Theory*.

However, Campbell's view merits attention because he departs from Porter and Fanning on a number of points, and because in addition to two monographs he has written a short introduction to aspect, which will provide many students' first orientation to the subject.

## 3.1 Mateos

Mateos assumes a broad definition of aspect similar to that used by Comrie, and sees the aspect expressed by a verbal form in context as depending on three factors, which he terms "lexematic," "morphematic," and "syntagmatic" aspect. "Lexematic aspect" essentially refers to *Aktionsart* in the fifth sense mentioned in section 2.3, "morphematic aspect" refers to the aspect of the verbal form (perfective, imperfective, etc.), and "syntagmatic aspect" refers to the aspectual information conveyed by the various syntagmatic relationships in which the verb occurs, such as auxiliaries ("try," "begin," "stop," etc.), arguments (e.g., "throw a stone" vs. "throw stones") and adverbs like "frequently."[126]

Mateos sees the aorist as having *punctual* aspect, not meaning that it represents a situation as momentary, but that it presents the situation as a single whole, without regard to its duration. This is essentially the widely accepted "totality" understanding of perfective aspect discussed above. He sees the present stem as ordinarily (except in the present and future indicative) expressing durative aspect, whether iterative or habitual.[127] But although durativity is necessarily *implied* by imperfective aspect, as noted above, scholars now tend to see the defining feature of imperfective aspect as the lack of reference to endpoints, rather than durativity per se. Mateos's analysis of the relationship between lexematic and morphematic aspect (i.e., procedural character and verbal aspect) reflects the sort of interactive approach discussed in section 4.4 below. Accordingly, he first divides lexemes into different classes and then examines the effect of the various verb forms on them.[128] Although Mateos's work is now somewhat dated and lacking in detailed analysis, Porter and Pitts assess his contribution to the study of aspect in

---

126 Mateos, *Aspecto verbal*, 20–22.
127 Ibid., 31.
128 Ibid., 41–133.

New Testament Greek somewhat unfairly when they describe it as only a "significant forerunner" and "a form of *Aktionsart* theory that goes back to the nineteenth century."[129]

## 3.2 Porter

Porter defines aspect as "a synthetic semantic category (realized in the forms of verbs) used of meaningful oppositions in a network of tense systems to grammaticalize the author's reasoned subjective choice of conception of a process."[130] Perfective aspect expresses the conception of an action as "*a complete and undifferentiated process*," and imperfective aspect a conception of the action "*as being in progress. In other words, its internal structure is seen as unfolding*."[131]

The words "process," "progress," and "unfolding" in these definitions might seem at first to point toward an understanding of at least imperfective aspect as having to do with *temporal* structure. But it is striking that the word "temporal" does not appear in these definitions. Instead of Comrie's phrase "internal temporal structure" Porter refers simply to "internal structure," and likewise Porter speaks of "constituency" rather than "temporal constituency." This appears deliberate, for Porter states that, "aspect is not properly speaking a temporal category," although like tense and attitude it is "concerned with processes which occur in time."[132] Moreover, in denying that aspect is temporal he appears not merely to exclude *external* or *deictic* time (i.e., tense), for he critiques Hockett, Comrie, and Moorhouse for defining aspect in terms of temporal distribution or constituency,[133] claiming that Comrie's "attempt to correlate aspect with 'situation-internal time' and tense with 'situation-external time' … runs contrary to his view of aspect as non-deictic" and shifts "to a view of aspect as *Aktionsart*."[134]

---

129  Stanley E. Porter and Andrew W. Pitts, "New Testament Greek Language and Linguistics in Recent Research," *CurBR* 6 (2008): 216; similarly Porter, *Verbal Aspect*, 61.
130  Porter, *Verbal Aspect*, 88.
131  Porter, *Idioms*, 21 (emphasis original).
132  Porter, *Verbal Aspect*, 98; see also 46, 50, 99, 105; Porter, "Aspect Theory and Lexicography," 208.
133  Porter, *Verbal Aspect*, 84, 105, 181.
134  Ibid., 105; cf. 46.

Porter's rejection of a temporal understanding of aspect is also reflected in the reconfiguration of Isačenko's parade illustration noted above.[135] Whereas Isačenko's perfective aspect takes in the whole event over the course of time, Porter's perfective aspect views it all at once "in its immediacy."[136] And whereas Isačenko's imperfective aspect never views the beginning or end of the parade, Porter's imperfective aspect simply does not see it at a particular moment in time. Porter's understanding of viewpoint thus leaves out the idea of temporal development, which, it was argued, is implicit in Isačenko's approach.

Porter also rejects the idea that the choice of aspect is affected by the lexical semantics of the verb or by the objective temporal constituency of a situation,[137] an issue to which we will return in section 4. Whereas Isačenko, Forsyth, Comrie, Bache, and others agree that the choice of aspect is not always a *subjective* choice, the element of subjectivity is intrinsic to Porter's definition, and he considers that "there is no necessary correlation between aspect form and objective action."[138]

## 3.3 Fanning

Fanning defines aspect as "that category in the grammar of the verb which reflects the focus or viewpoint of the speaker in regard to the action or condition which the verb describes. It shows the perspective from which the occurrence is regarded or the portrayal of the occurrence itself apart from the actual or perceived nature of the situation itself."[139] The aorist (i.e., perfective) aspect "presents an occurrence *in summary, viewed as a whole from the outside, without regard for the internal make-up of the occurrence*,"[140] while the present (imperfective) aspect "reflects an *internal* viewpoint concerning the occurrence which *focuses on its development or progress* and sees the

135  See §2.1.
136  Porter, *Verbal Aspect*, 91
137  Ibid., 29–35, 87; Porter, "Aspect Theory and Lexicography."
138  Porter, *Verbal Aspect*, 208.
139  Fanning, *Verbal Aspect*, 84–85.
140  Ibid., 97 (emphasis original). See also 27.

occurrence *in regard to its internal make-up, without beginning or end in view.*"[141]

The phrase "apart from the actual or perceived nature of the situation itself" gives the impression that Fanning, like Porter, regards aspect as essentially subjective, although he admits that "fully subjective choices are not common."[142] Like Porter, Fanning describes aspect using the language of "viewpoint" and "perspective," and is reluctant to describe aspect in temporal terms, although he seems more ambivalent than Porter on this point. Like Porter, he describes the imperfective using apparently temporal categories, namely "development," "progress," "beginning," and "end." Moreover, in the very first sentence of Fanning's introduction he appears to approve Hockett's definition of verbal aspect as concerned with an event's "temporal distribution or contour"[143] (a definition which Porter expressly rejects).[144] Yet Fanning's own definition does not use the word "temporal." Similarly to Porter, he refers to "internal make-up" rather than Comrie's "internal *temporal* constituency" And although Fanning recognizes that temporal meanings such as duration, progression, and completion can be produced as "a *secondary* function of aspect when combined with other elements like the verb's inherent meaning, adverbs, and so forth,"[145] he does not allow that this is a consequence of aspect itself being a temporal concept.[146]

---

141  Ibid., 103 (emphasis original). Similarly 27, 124.
142  Ibid., 421.
143  Ibid., 1, citing Charles F. Hockett, *A Course in Modern Linguistics* (New York: Macmillan, 1958), 237.
144  Porter, *Verbal Aspect*, 84.
145  Fanning, *Verbal Aspect*, 26 (emphasis original).
146  Fanning mistakenly cites Comrie in support of the idea that these temporal ideas are "secondary effects of the aspects, rather than a reflection of the essential nature of the aspects as temporal" (ibid., citing Comrie, *Aspect*, 5). As noted above, Comrie *does* consider aspect to be a temporal concept, which is why it combines with other elements of a clause to produce the sorts of temporal meanings Fanning notes. For Comrie, the distinction between tense and aspect is one not between temporal and nontemporal meaning, but between deictic and nondeictic temporal meaning. What Comrie describes as a secondary effect in the passage to which Fanning refers is the *deictic* function of aspectual forms in context, i.e., the function of relating the time of a situation to another point in time. E.g., "a sequence of forms with perfective meaning will normally be taken to indicate a sequence of events" (Comrie, *Aspect*, 5). As de Swart notes, the sentence "When Bill came into the office, Sara left through the back door" im-

Like Porter, it seems that Fanning wants to say more than simply that aspect is nondeictic. For example, he criticizes Johnson's view, discussed above, for giving "too much emphasis to the *temporal* relation of the event to the reference-point."[147] According to Fanning, the "relationship between the action and the reference-point from which it is viewed is not primarily a *chronological* one, even though it can produce that effect. If the relationship must be pictured in any dimension, a *spatial* one fits better, since the distinction is one of proximity vs. distance."[148]

It is not obvious what Fanning means by picturing the relationship in a spatial dimension. He states that "in order to view the action from within and ignore the initial and final limits, the vantage-point must be *near*, an internal perspective; on the other hand, viewing the whole action from beginning to end without focus on the internal make-up of the action most naturally fits a *remote* or distanced perspective."[149] Fanning cites Bache in support of the view that perfective aspect requires distance, whether temporal or modal.[150] However, Bache does not argue that imperfective aspect requires proximity. His point is rather that it is only where there is distance that there can be a subjective choice between perfective and imperfective aspects.[151] Fanning is certainly correct that aspect is not primarily concerned with the *sequence* of events (although this is less true of the perfect and prospective aspects than of the perfective and imperfective). However, he is mistaken in supposing that it must therefore be to do with *space*, whether literal or metaphorical. The question is which phase or phases of the situation the speaker or writer is speaking about, not from how far away the situation is being presented.

In a footnote Fanning cites several linguists who, he claims, advocate or at least entertain a "spatial" approach.[152] However, in each

---

plies that Sara's leaving followed Bill's entering, whereas "When Bill came into the office, Sara was leaving through the back door" implies that she had started to leave before Bill entered ("Verbal Aspect," 753).

147 Fanning, *Verbal Aspect*, 27 n. 65 (emphasis original).
148 Ibid., 27 (emphasis original).
149 Ibid., 27–28 (emphasis original).
150 Ibid., 28 n. 69, citing Bache, "Aspect and Aktionsart," 67.
151 Bache, "Aspect and Aktionsart," 67. See §2.3 above.
152 Fanning, *Verbal Aspect*, 27–28 n. 68.

case this appears to reflect a misunderstanding of their position. Windfuhr understands aspect temporally,[153] but adopts a spatial *model* as a means of *plotting* distinctions in tense, aspect, and mood, given that a third of Persian forms "participate in two different categories each, either in two tenses, and/or two moods, and/or two pasts."[154] Anderson also clearly sees aspect as temporal, being "concerned with the relation of an event or state to a particular reference point: it is located before (retrospective), after (prospective), around (progressive) or simply at (AORIST) a particular point *in time*,"[155] these temporal relationships being expressed in spatial *language*.[156] Similarly, Harweg does not consider that aspect could be concerned with spatial rather than temporal relationships, only that applying a notion of perspective to aspect involves picturing time in terms of space.[157]

## 3.4 Campbell

Similarly to Porter and Fanning, Campbell sees aspect as a matter of "viewpoint,"[158] defining it as "the manner in which verbs are used to view an action or state. An author/speaker will portray an event either from the inside, as though it is seen as unfolding, or from the outside, as though it is seen as a whole."[159] Campbell approves Porter's understanding of imperfective aspect as conceiving of an action as "being in progress" and its internal structure as "unfolding,"[160] as well as Fanning's understanding of imperfective aspect as focusing on an occurrence's "development or progress ... without beginning or end in view."[161] As noted above, the words "prog-

153  Gernot L. Windfuhr, "A Spatial Model for Tense, Aspect, and Mood," *FLin* 19 (1985): 428–31.
154  Ibid., 416.
155  John Anderson, *An Essay Concerning Aspect: Some Considerations of a General Character Arising from the Abbé Darrigol's Analysis of the Basque Verb*, JLSMin 167 (The Hague: Mouton, 1973), 39–40 (emphasis added).
156  On localist approaches such as Anderson's see Lyons, *Semantics*, 2:718–24; Comrie, *Aspect*, 129–30.
157  Roland Harweg, "Aspekte als Zeitstufen und Zeitstufen als Aspekte," *Linguistics* 181 (1976): 6.
158  Campbell, *Indicative Mood*, 8.
159  Ibid., 1; similarly 8.
160  Ibid., 35–36, citing Porter, *Idioms*, 21; Campbell, *Verbal Aspect*, 91.
161  Ibid., 36, citing Fanning, *Verbal Aspect*, 103.

ress," "unfolding," "development," "beginning," and "end" suggest temporality.[162] Yet Campbell is even more emphatic than Porter and Fanning that aspect is not a temporal concept, whether deictic or nondeictic. He comments, "It is unfortunate that aspect is occasionally defined in terms of temporal relations rather than simply viewpoint,"[163] and even critiques the idea that imperfective aspect views action as being "in progress," stating that "imperfective aspect views an action internally, but that action need not necessarily be in progress." According to Campbell, such a notion has to do with how the action occurs objectively, "and thus belongs to the realm of *Aktionsart.*"[164]

Elsewhere Campbell comments: "While there is a tendency in some quarters to describe this internal viewpoint in terms of internal temporal relations, imperfective aspect is here understood apart from reference to temporal considerations. ... Comrie's now standard definition of imperfective aspect as 'the internal temporal structure of a situation' is *not* adopted here, as the reference to temporality is potentially misleading, especially as we distinguish aspect from tense."[165] Campbell's reference to "some quarters" rather misleadingly implies that a temporal view of aspect is a minority view rather than the norm among linguists.[166] He concedes that "Comrie's approach has its own logic," but states that "it is more useful to avoid temporal descriptions of aspect altogether. Rather, aspect is here regarded as a spatial phenomenon."[167] Campbell cites Fanning in support of this view,[168] but goes far beyond Fanning in the emphasis he places on aspect being spatial. As with Fanning, it is not clear quite what Campbell means by describing aspect as

---

162  Even when not citing other scholars, Campbell describes the internal viewpoint as one in which "the beginning and endpoint of an action are not taken into account" (*Indicative Mood*, 116).

163  Ibid., 9n8.

164  Ibid., 11.

165  Ibid., 36 (emphasis original), citing Comrie, *Aspect*, 24. Campbell also criticizes Olsen for her dependence on "temporal categories" (Campbell, *Indicative Mood*, 104).

166  Campbell cites Evans, *Verbal Syntax*, 18 and Bache, "Aspect and Aktionsart," 64 in support of his understanding of aspect as viewpoint, without noting that both of these scholars clearly understand it in temporal terms (Campbell, *Indicative Mood*, 8n18).

167  Campbell, *Indicative Mood*, 36.

168  Ibid., citing Fanning, *Verbal Aspect*, 27.

"spatial."[169] But following Porter's adaptation of Isačenko's parade analogy,[170] he sees perfective aspect as offering a "helicopter view" of an action,[171] so that "exactly how the parade is unfolding is not seen."[172] Surprisingly, he takes this to mean that the aorist is not normally used for presenting the details of a narrative,[173] presumably because he rejects the idea that it is internal temporal constituency that is "not seen" by the perfective.

## 3.5 Observations

A full examination of the aspectual theories of these New Testament scholars cannot be undertaken here. However, this brief summary of their definitions is sufficient to highlight the fact that Porter, Fanning, and Campbell each depart, though to varying degrees, from the consensus in general linguistics that aspect is at its root a temporal concept. This appears to be not so much a deliberate rejection of the consensus as a misunderstanding of it, for each of the three criticizes the temporal definitions of certain linguists without acknowledging that a temporal understanding is the norm. Moreover, Porter, Fanning, and Campbell each cite linguists such as Isačenko, Comrie, Bache, and Smith in support of a "viewpoint" definition, but without attention to the way these linguists actually use the metaphor. The problems with the metaphor itself noted in section 2.4 seem partly to blame for the misunderstanding. Another indication that it is indeed a misunderstanding rather than a deliberate departure from the consensus is that Porter, Fanning, and Campbell offer very little by way of argument against the temporal

---

169 Campbell also replaces the traditional tense distinctions between the present and imperfect indicative and between the perfect and pluperfect indicative with distinctions of spatial remoteness and proximity. In a "Concluding Postscript" in his *Basics of Verbal Aspect in Biblical Greek* he expands on what he means by "spatial" in that context, noting that he uses the terms of "remoteness" and "proximity" as "metaphors" (*Basics*, 129). Although Campbell does not directly address aspect in this postscript, he appears to see aspect as likewise spatial only in a metaphorical sense.

170 Campbell, *Indicative Mood*, 50; Campbell, *Basics*, 19-20.

171 Campbell, *Basics*, 38.

172 Ibid., 34.

173 Ibid., 34-35. Similarly Buist M. Fanning, "Approaches to Verbal Aspect in New Testament Greek: Issues in Definition and Method," in Porter, *Biblical Greek Language and Linguistics*, 49.

view, besides the observation that aspect is distinct from both tense and *Aktionsart*. Yet the discussion in section 2 shows that it is possible to keep these three concepts distinct while recognizing that they all have to do with time in different ways. The distinction is clearest when a time-relational definition of aspect is adopted.

The remainder of this chapter will attempt to demonstrate how clarity concerning the temporal nature of aspect illuminates the various ways in which aspect interacts with the semantic properties of particular types of verbs.[174] Fanning in particular offers an excellent treatment of such interactions, but his rejection of a temporal definition of aspect leaves him unable to explain quite *why* they occur. Such an explanation will be offered below by combining Johnson's time-relational definition of aspect with Croft's two-dimensional geometric approach to representing aspectual structure.

The account offered below is merely a sketch of the sort of lines along which a fuller investigation of these matters might proceed. As Evans has noted, much more work in this area is needed.[175] The fact that it has received so little attention in the last twenty-five years is no doubt partly a result of Porter's dismissal of such analysis as concerned not with aspect but with *Aktionsart*, and consequently outmoded.[176] But as Fanning himself has noted, "many other writers on aspect in general linguistics and semantics have given attention to such matters and have included them as a central part of their discussion of aspect. A full treatment of aspect in New Testament Greek which professes to be rooted in linguistic theory should hardly ignore or bypass such discussions."[177] This continues to be the case. We shall return to this in the conclusion, but it is worth noting here that Fanning's treatment of aspect has much more in common with

---

174 As noted below (see n. 184), analysis is possible both at the level of the verb itself and at the level of the verb with its arguments.

175 Evans, "Future Directions," 205; similarly Evans, *Verbal Syntax*, 20.

176 Porter considers that the works of Comrie and Fanning are really treatments of *Aktionsart* rather than aspect. Porter, *Verbal Aspect*, 46; Porter, review of *Verbal Aspect in New Testament Greek*, by Buist M. Fanning, *JSNT* 43 (1991): 127. As noted above, he and Pitts judge that Mateos's similar approach "goes back to the nineteenth century" (Porter and Pitts, "New Testament Greek Language and Linguistics," 216).

177 Fanning, "Introduction," 61.

the sort of approach found within aspect studies in general linguistics than do those of Porter and Campbell.[178]

# 4. VERBAL ASPECT AND PROCEDURAL CHARACTER

It was noted in section 2 that with certain types of verbs the choice of perfective or imperfective aspect is constrained by the objective (or quasi-objective) temporal constituency of the situation concerned. With such verbs perfective and imperfective aspects express different situations (e.g., "he died" versus "he was dying"),[179] not merely different views of the same situation. This is a point of widespread consensus in aspect studies,[180] although Porter dissents.[181] Fanning in particular has helpfully discussed these interactions between verbal aspect and lexical semantics in relation to New Testament Greek,[182] and this section will show how a time-relational view of aspect offers a straightforward explanation for them.

To be precise, it is the verbal lexeme together with its arguments that interacts with aspect in this way.[183] Following Smith this combination will be called the *verb constellation*, and verb constellations will be expressed using square brackets.[184] For example, the sentence "Bloggs ran a mile" contains the constellation [Bloggs run a mile], which behaves differently from [Bloggs run], as discussed

---

178  Fanning is influenced especially by Bache and Smith (Fanning, *Verbal Aspect*, v, 41), which perhaps explains why his analysis seems to reflect their temporal understanding of aspect, despite his assertions to the contrary.

179  As noted above, the distinction between the simple and progressive past tenses in English is not identical to the perfective/imperfective distinction, but the effect in this case is similar.

180  The consensus is noted by Lyons (*Semantics*, 2:706) and Sasse ("Recent Activity," 230).

181  See §3.2 above.

182  Fanning, *Verbal Aspect*, 126–96.

183  Telicity in particular is not determined by the verb alone (see Crellin, "Greek Perfect Active System," 44). However, Crellin points out that the verb "determines certain parameters according to which the property of telicity is set" (47), so that analysis at the level of the verb itself is also possible. See also Susan D. Rothstein, *Structuring Events: A Study in the Semantics of Lexical Aspect*, Explorations in Semantics 2 (Oxford: Blackwell, 2004), 29–34.

184  Smith, *Parameter*, 2, 7.

below.[185] Verb constellations can be divided into a number of classes, differing in their temporal characteristics. The standard taxonomy is that of Vendler, who distinguished four classes, namely *states, activities, accomplishments,* and *achievements*.[186] These differ with respect to the properties of *stativity, durativity,* and *telicity* (or *boundedness*), a telic situation being one with an inherent terminal point. As noted above, a wide range of different umbrella terms have been used to refer to these classes and their semantic characteristics, but the terms "procedural class" and "procedural character" are adopted here. Table 1 indicates the characteristics of each class together with English examples (omitting subjects, since Vendler did not include these in his analysis):

Table 1

| Class | Stativity | Durativity | Telicity | Examples |
|---|---|---|---|---|
| State | + | + | - | love somebody, believe something |
| Activity | - | + | - | run, push a cart |
| Accomplishment | - | + | + | run a mile, draw a circle |
| Achievement | - | - | + | find an object, win a race |

Before turning to a discussion of these classes and their interaction with verbal aspect, three caveats should be noted.

First, these classes are *Aktionsarten* in the fourth of the six senses distinguished in section 2.3 above. Thus they do not classify states of affairs objectively existing in the real world, or conceptions of states of affairs, but sets of temporal characteristics communicated by the verb constellation. In Smith's words, they are "semantic categories of language, classes of idealized situations with distinctive temporal features."[187] Someone who is drawing a circle (an accom-

---

185 See §4.2; Filip, "Lexical Aspect," 725; de Swart, "Verbal Aspect," 754.
186 Zeno Vendler, "Verbs and Times," *PhR* 66 (1957): 143–60.
187 Smith, *Parameter*, 17. Fanning, similarly, notes that "this taxonomy does not classify the characteristics of actual situations, but the *linguistic portrayals* of situations" (*Verbal Aspect*, 127 n. 2; emphasis original).

plishment) is also drawing (an activity), so the sentences "Bloggs is drawing" and "Bloggs is drawing a circle" could be used to speak of the same real-world event. But the latter expresses the idea of an inherent endpoint whereas the former does not. Nevertheless, there is clearly a *correspondence* between these verb constellations and the situations they express.[188]

A second caveat is that although the four classes noted above are the ones most commonly identified, further distinctions and subdivisions are possible, some of which are noted below. The distinction between "prefaced" and "nonprefaced" achievements is particularly significant, as discussed in section 4.3. Croft offers a useful method of representing the various possibilities in a two-dimensional graphical format, and his diagrams have been adopted here with slight modifications.[189] In section 4.4 this graphical approach will be used to illustrate the predictable interactions of procedural character with verbal aspect.

Third, much more work is needed on the relevant semantic properties of Greek verbs. As Evans notes, applications of Vendler's categories to Greek so far "seem to be somewhat arbitrary, and to depend ultimately on the sadly dated English glosses of LSJ. More work on these issues is vitally needed before the relationship between inherent lexical meaning and aspectual choice can be fully explored."[190] The problem is illustrated by the fact that Fanning and Mateos differ in their classifications of certain verbs. For example, Shain notes that "Fanning lists *erchomai* as an activity verb and *eiserchomai* as an accomplishment," while "Mateos lists *erchomai*

---

188  For this reason it is not "disingenuous" of Fanning to maintain that these are *linguistic* portrayals (see n. 188 above) and at the same time to discuss the way in which they represent actual situations; *pace* Porter, "Introduction," 37 n. 3.

189  See Croft, *Verbs*, 53. One difference is the labeling of the axes, which Croft marks simply as "t" (for "time") and "q" (for "qualitative state"). Another is that the diagrams are used here to represent construals of verb constellations rather than complete sentences, similarly to Elena Paducheva, who adopts a similar but simpler two-dimensional representation. "Taxonomic Categories and Semantics of Aspectual Opposition," in *Temporal Reference, Aspect and Actionality*, ed. Pier Marco Bertinetto et al., vol. 1 of *Semantic and Syntactic Perspectives* (Turin: Rosenberg & Sellier, 1995), 80. Croft uses a third dimension to represent the distinct subevents involved in a situation with multiple participants, but this need not be discussed here.

190  Evans, "Future Directions," 205; similarly Evans, *Verbal Syntax*, 20.

as an accomplishment and *eiserchomai* as an achievement."[191] Shain herself offers a step in the right direction by describing objective tests for procedural class, which she then applies to these verbs.[192] This type of analysis has not been carried out for the verbs used in the examples below, so their classification here is tentative and provisional. However, verbs have been chosen that Fanning and Mateos assign to the same class, in order to increase the likelihood of a correct classification. English examples will also be offered, and for present purposes it may be assumed that the contrast between simple and progressive aspect in English, at least in the past tense with dynamic verbs, roughly corresponds to the perfective/imperfective contrast discussed above.

## 4.1 States

As the name suggests, state verb constellations differ from those belonging to other classes in being stative. That is, they do not indicate change over time. They are also generally durative, representing a situation lasting longer than a moment.[193] Moreover, they are unbounded or *atelic*, meaning that the verb constellation itself does not express a natural endpoint to the situation. As Croft notes, it is possible to subdivide the class of states into a number of subclasses, depending on whether the state is transitory or permanent, and in the latter case whether it is acquired or inherent. These types of state are illustrated by the sentences "The door is open," "The window is shattered," and "She is French," respectively.[194] To take just one of these types by way of example, the state expressed by the verb constellation [the door be open] can be represented as in figure 3,[195] with time along the x-axis, and state on the y-axis:

---

191 Rachel Shain, "Exploring Aktionsart in Corpora: A Case Study of Koine Greek *Erchomai* and *Eiserchomai*," *JGL* 11 (2011): 230, citing Fanning, *Verbal Aspect*, 144, 151 and Mateos, *Aspecto verbal*, 85, 97.

192 Shain, "Exploring Aktionsart," 232–47. See below, §5.3.

193 Croft, following Mittwoch, recognizes a category of nondurative "point states," e.g., "the sun is at its zenith" (Croft, *Verbs*, 43, 58). See Anita Mittwoch, "Aspects of English Aspect: On the Interaction of Perfect, Progressive and Durational Phrases," *Ling&P* 11 (1988): 234. However, these are not typical and may be overlooked for present purposes.

194 Croft adds a further category of "point states," on which see n193 above.

195 Croft, *Verbs*, 58

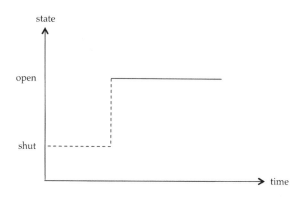

Figure 3

In this diagram the horizontal dashed line represents the situation preceding entry into the state, i.e., while the door is shut. The vertical dashed line represents entry into the state, i.e., the opening of the door, and the solid line represents the situation after the door has been opened, i.e., the state of openness. In cognitive-linguistic terms, it is this latter state which is "profiled" by "be open" in the verb constellation [the door be open],[196] while the phases represented by the dashed lines are part of the presupposed semantic frame of conceptual knowledge associated with open doors.[197] The solid line is horizontal to represent the fact that there is no change of state during the profiled phase.

The verb constellation [ἡμεῖς (οἱ μαθηταί) πιστεύειν ὅτι κτλ.] ([we (the disciples) believe that etc.]) seems to be used in a stative sense in the following sentence,[198] which can be represented diagrammatically as in figure 4.[199]

---

196  Croft describes the profiled phase as "the phase asserted to hold in the world at ... the time reference denoted by the tense of the construction" (ibid., 55). But the approach followed here differs from Croft's in that it sees what Johnson calls the "event time" as a profiled phase of the verb constellation, and aspect as relating that event time to the reference time.

197  See ibid., 11–13, 53–57.

198  In Greek examples the present infinitive is used here for the purposes of representing the uninflected verb within the verbal constellation.

199  The verb πιστεύειν is classified as a state by Fanning (*Verbal Aspect*, 136) and Mateos (*Aspecto verbal*, 43).

ἐν τούτῳ <u>πιστεύομεν</u> ὅτι ἀπὸ θεοῦ ἐξῆλθες. (John 16:30)
"By this <u>we believe</u> that you came from God." (RSV)

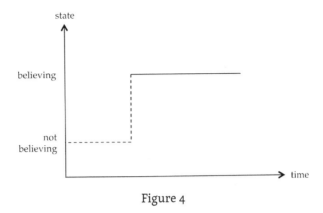

Figure 4

This sentence presupposes a time when the disciples did not believe, and a point at which they came to believe. However, what the verb πιστεύομεν itself expresses is the state of believing that follows that point.

## 4.2 Activities and Accomplishments

Activities such as [Bloggs run] are nonstative, but share with states the properties of being durative and atelic. One cannot run for just a moment, and the verb constellation [Bloggs run] does not express an inherent endpoint. By contrast [Bloggs run a mile] is an accomplishment because it is telic; to run a mile is to run until a particular point is reached. It follows that if Bloggs were to stop before that point, Bloggs would not have run a mile.[200] This is not the case with [Bloggs run], for if Bloggs runs for any length of time then Bloggs has run. Figures 5 and 6 represent the verb constellations [Bloggs run] and [Bloggs run a mile] respectively.[201] As in figures 3 and 4, the solid lines in the diagrams represent the situations profiled by the relevant verb constellations. In figures 5 and 6 these lines slope because both situations involve a change of state; running is a

---

200 See Vendler, "Verbs and Times," 146.
201 See Croft, *Verbs*, 61–62, where different examples are given and further distinctions are made.

dynamic activity. But in figure 5 ([Bloggs run]) the change does not involve progress towards a goal, only a repeated pattern of movements, represented by a zigzag line, whereas in figure 6 ([Bloggs run a mile]) there is progress towards a goal, represented by a line sloping steadily upward toward the finish state.

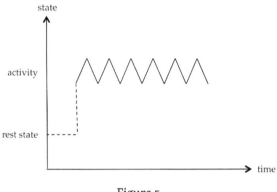

Figure 5

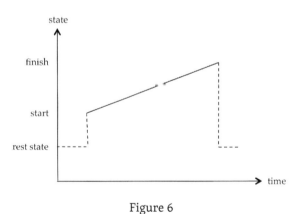

Figure 6

An example of an activity in New Testament Greek might be [γυναῖκες διακονεῖν αὐτῷ] ([women serve him]) in the sentence καὶ διηκόνουν αὐτῷ (and they were serving him, Mark 15:41).[202] This can therefore be represented by figure 5. A likely example of an

---

202 Mateos and Fanning both classify διακονεῖν as an activity (Mateos, *Aspecto verbal*, 65; Fanning, *Verbal Aspect*, 144).

accomplishment (figure 6) is [Νῶε κατασκευάζειν κιβωτόν] ([Noah construct an ark]) in the following sentence:[203]

Πίστει ... Νῶε ... <u>κατεσκεύασεν</u> κιβωτόν. (Heb 11:7)
By faith ... Noah ... <u>constructed</u> an ark. (ESV)

## 4.3 Achievements

Achievements such as [the door open] or [the light flash] share with accomplishments the property of telicity, but unlike accomplishments they are momentary rather than durative. In other words, they express a situation conceptualized as occupying a single point in time. Some achievements, for example [the door open], involve the subject ending up in a new resulting state. Others, such as [the light flash] do not. These two types of achievements can be represented by figures 7 and 8, respectively.

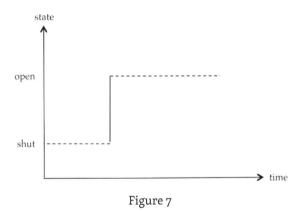

Figure 7

---

203 Fanning classifies κατασκευάζειν as an accomplishment (*Verbal Aspect*, 151), as does Mateos, who calls accomplishments "lexemas dinámicos de acción resultativa" (dynamic lexemes of resultative action) (*Aspecto verbal*, 97).

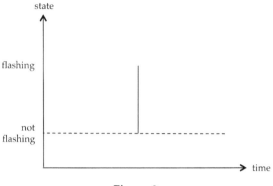

Figure 8

Figure 7 is similar to figure 3, which represented the state [the door be open], but now the solid line indicating the profiled phase marks the transition between states, rather than the resulting state. Figure 8 [the light flash] is similar, except that there is no resulting state, and the light returns to its original state after flashing. An apparent Greek example of this latter kind is the verb constellation [ἄνθρωπος βάλλειν κόκκον σινάπεως] ([a man throw a mustard seed]) in the following sentence:[204]

> ὁμοία ἐστὶν κόκκῳ σινάπεως, ὃν λαβὼν ἄνθρωπος ἔβαλεν εἰς κῆπον ἑαυτοῦ. (Luke 13:19)
> "It is like a mustard seed, which a man took and threw into his own garden." (NASB)

A possible example of the first type is the verb constellation [ὁ πύργος πίπτειν] ([the tower fall]) in the following:[205]

> ἢ ἐκεῖνοι οἱ δεκαοκτὼ ἐφ᾽ οὓς ἔπεσεν ὁ πύργος ἐν τῷ Σιλωὰμ καὶ ἀπέκτεινεν αὐτούς, δοκεῖτε ὅτι αὐτοὶ ὀφειλέται ἐγένοντο παρὰ πάντας τοὺς ἀνθρώπους τοὺς κατοικοῦντας Ἰερουσαλήμ; (Luke 13:4)
> Or those eighteen on whom the tower in Siloam

---

204  The *seed*, of course, changes state (location) as a result of the throwing. But our present concern is with the *subject's* change of state or otherwise.

205  Fanning classes both βάλλειν and πίπτειν as punctual achievements (*Verbal Aspect*, 157), while Mateos calls them "lexemas dinámicos de acción instantánea" (dynamic lexemes of instantaneous action) (*Aspecto verbal*, 85).

<u>fell</u> and killed them: do you think that they were
worse offenders than all the others who lived in
Jerusalem? (ESV)

It was noted above that the Greek verb πιστεύειν can be used in a
stative sense, as in John 16:30. However, it seems that it can also be
used in an achievement sense, expressing the transition between
states. For example, the verb constellation [ὁ ἀνθύπατος πιστεύειν]
([the proconsul believe]) seems to be an achievement in the following sentence:

τότε ἰδὼν ὁ ἀνθύπατος τὸ γεγονὸς <u>ἐπίστευσεν</u>. (Acts 13:12)
When the proconsul saw what had happened, <u>he
believed</u>. (NIV)

This can be represented as in figure 9:

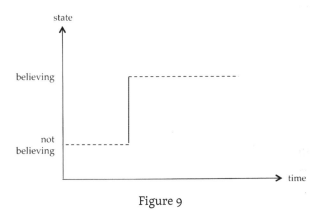

Figure 9

Many state verbs can similarly be used in an achievement sense,
illustrating the important point that verbs and verbal constellations
are often polysemous with respect to procedural class, or can be
construed in different ways depending on context.[206] Croft relates
the availability of these different construals to our rich experience
of the way in which different types of situations typically unfold.[207]

---

206 See Croft, *Verbs*, 83–92. For further examples see Smith, *Parameter*, 18.
207 "The particular words and constructions used to verbalize a particular
   scene highlight or draw out certain details over others in the rich understanding we have of those particular scenes" (Croft, *Verbs*, 16). E.g., "reach

Fanning, following Østergaard, has noted that some achievements are "prefaced," meaning that they occur in a moment but as "the culmination of a separate process which is its preface: e.g., 'he arrived just in time,' 'she found her coat.' These imply a separate approach-phase which affects their aspectual function."[208] Fanning terms such achievements "climaxes," while those without an approach phase (as in figures 7 and 8) he terms "punctuals."[209] Figure 10 represents the climax [Bloggs find his coat]:

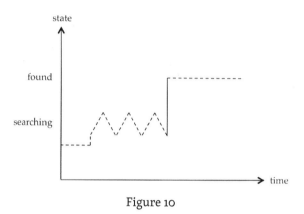

Figure 10

In this diagram the achievement itself (the finding) is represented by the solid vertical line marking entry into the new state in which the coat is found. The dashed lines preceding it represent the preface, i.e., the activity of searching.[210] A possible example of a cli-

---

the summit" can be construed either as momentary ("They reached the summit") or durative ("It took them two hours to reach the summit") (ibid., 37). Croft argues that "state and achievement are not inherent aspectual types of predicates but aspectual types or construals that different predicates have the potential to possess," and calls "the class of predicates that have the aspectual potential of states or achievements that result in the state INCEPTIVE STATES" (ibid., 38).

208 Fanning, Verbal Aspect, 155.

209 In the case of punctuals, "the event is not linked with another action as its preface" (ibid., 156). Punctuals are sometimes called "semelfactives" (semel means "once" in Latin), but the latter term is not entirely felicitous, for a punctual verb constellation can be used to express a repeated occurrence (e.g., "he was coughing") (see Comrie, Aspect, 42).

210 [Bloggs find his coat] can also be construed as a punctual, i.e., as an achievement without a preface, if the sense is that Bloggs stumbled on his coat without looking for it.

max in Greek is [ἡ παῖς ἀποθνῄσκειν] ([the girl die]) in the following sentence:[211]

> καὶ κατεγέλων αὐτοῦ εἰδότες ὅτι <u>ἀπέθανεν</u>. (Luke 8:53)
> And they began laughing at Him, knowing that <u>she had died</u>. (NASB)

This can be represented as in figure 11.[212]

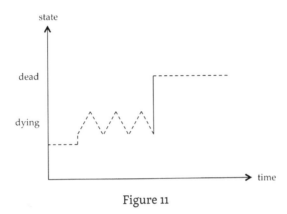

Figure 11

## 4.4 The Interaction of Verbal Aspect and Procedural Character

As mentioned above, it is widely recognized that aspect interacts with the procedural character of a verb constellation. These interactions are predictable,[213] and can be easily explained if the temporal nature of aspect is kept in mind. For example, one consequence of accomplishments having an inherent endpoint is that perfective aspect communicates the idea of reaching that endpoint, since it speaks of a complete situation from beginning to end. In figure 12,

---

211 Fanning lists ἀποθνῄσκειν as a climax (*Verbal Aspect*, 157). Mateos, who does not distinguish punctuals and climaxes, classes it as a "lexema dinámico de acción instantanea" (dynamic lexeme of instantaneous action) (*Aspecto verbal*, 85).

212 Other construals of ἀποθνῄσκειν are possible, depending on what is understood about the event from the context. E.g., if death were sudden and unexpected then it could be construed as a punctual rather than a climax.

213 Fanning, *Verbal Aspect*, 41, 43.

the shaded area highlights the period of time Johnson calls the "reference time" (the time being spoken about) when perfective aspect is used with an accomplishment verb. In the case of perfective aspect the reference time is identical with the event time, and it can be seen that in such a case the reference time includes the endpoint of the situation.

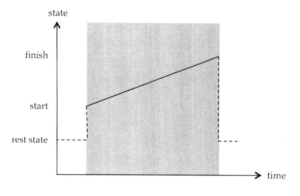

Figure 12

Assuming that the Greek aorist is perfective rather than aspectually neutral,[214] figure 12 could represent a sentence such as Νῶε κατεσκεύασεν κιβωτόν (Noah constructed an ark). This sentence would simply be untrue if Noah gave up construction at the halfway point and did not complete the project. This is probably why some earlier linguists understood the essence of perfective aspect to be completion. But the better analysis seems to be that the decisive feature is completeness rather than completion. The idea of completion comes from the combination of perfective aspect with a telic verb constellation.

But although one cannot be said to have constructed an ark or to have run a mile if one stops before the end, one can truthfully be said to have been constructing an ark or running a mile. This so-called "imperfective paradox" is partly explained by the fact that imperfective aspect and progressive aspect in English, speak of a phase of the situation not including its terminal point, i.e., a point

---

214  On this point Mateos, Porter, Fanning, and Campbell are in agreement. See Mateos, *Aspecto verbal*, 31; Porter, *Idioms*, 21; Fanning, *Verbal Aspect*, 71, 97; Campbell, *Indicative Mood*, 21, 125.

in time or a period of time before the endpoint has been reached.[215]
This is illustrated by the shaded portion of the timeline in figure 13.

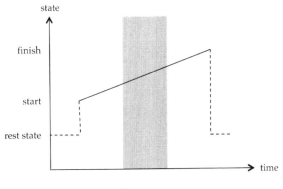

Figure 13

If the Greek imperfect tense is indeed imperfective, as is widely believed,[216] then the shaded portion of the timeline in figure 13
can serve to represent the reference time of the sentence Νῶε
κατεσκεύαζεν κιβωτόν (Noah was constructing an ark). This sentence
would remain true if Noah began construction but did not finish;
what actually happens in the time subsequent to the reference time
is not material.

The question remains how a verbal constellation can be conceptualized as having an endpoint when the endpoint is not in fact
reached, or even known not to have been reached. One answer that
suggests itself is that the constellation is telic because of an *intention* at the reference time that the endpoint would be reached. This
would account for the so-called *conative* use of the imperfective,
speaking of *attempted* accomplishments. For example:

ἐδίωκον τὴν ἐκκλησίαν τοῦ θεοῦ καὶ ἐπόρθουν αὐτήν.
(Gal 1:13)

---

215  For the term "imperfective paradox" see David R. Dowty, "Toward a Se-
     mantic Analysis of Verb Aspect and the English 'Imperfective' Progressive,"
     *Ling&P* 1 (1977): 45–77.
216  See Porter, *Idioms*, 21; Fanning, *Verbal Aspect*, 240; Campbell, *Indicative
     Mood*, 101. Mateos speaks of durativity rather than imperfectivity (*Aspecto
     verbal*, 31; see §3.1 above).

> I persecuted the church of God violently and tried to
> destroy it. (ESV)

Assuming that πορθεῖν here is a telic verb, Paul "was destroying" (ἐπόρθουν) the church in the sense that at the past reference time (indicated by ποτέ earlier in the verse) he was pursuing a project which, if carried on to completion as he intended, would culminate in the extinction of the church. Yet Dowty notes that not all cases of the imperfective paradox can be solved this way, for example those where the accomplishment has no sentient agent.[217] The problem is a complex one which cannot be discussed in detail here.

In contrast to the situation with telic verb constellations, perfective forms in conjunction with atelic verb constellations do not imply completion, because the situation has no natural endpoint. This can be seen from figure 14, which illustrates the combination of perfective aspect with the activity [(Ὀνησίφορος) διηκόνειν] ([he (Onesiphorus) serve] in the following sentence:

> καὶ ὅσα ἐν Ἐφέσῳ <u>διηκόνησεν</u>, βέλτιον σὺ γινώσκεις.
> (2 Tim 1:18)
> And you well know all the <u>service he rendered</u> at
> Ephesus. (ESV)

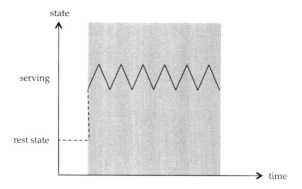

Figure 14

---

217 Dowty, "Toward a Semantic Analysis," 46. Among the examples Dowty gives is the sentence "The river was cutting a new channel to the sea, but the men with the sandbags stopped it from doing so" (ibid.).

The aorist tense, being perfective, expresses the totality of the situation of Onesiphorus's serving expressed by the verb constellation, but since this situation does not include an inherent endpoint, the use of the aorist does not imply that such an endpoint is reached. This is a case where the imperfect ὅσα ἐν Ἐφέσῳ διηκόνει could perhaps have been used instead. If so, this would be an example of what Bache calls "pure aspectual opposition." A New Testament example using the imperfect is Mark 15:41, mentioned already in section 4.2:

αἳ ὅτε ἦν ἐν τῇ Γαλιλαίᾳ ἠκολούθουν αὐτῷ καὶ <u>διηκόνουν</u> αὐτῷ. (Mark 15:41)
When he was in Galilee, they followed him and <u>ministered</u> to him. (ESV)

The sort of analysis offered here explains why "Bloggs was swimming" implies "Bloggs swam" (swimming being an atelic activity), whereas "Bloggs was drowning" doesn't necessarily imply "Bloggs drowned." There is nothing contradictory about the sentence "Bloggs was drowning, but the lifeguard rescued him." On the other hand, it would be contradictory to say "Bloggs drowned, but the lifeguard rescued him." Indeed, it is hard to imagine a context in which "Bloggs drowned" does not express Bloggs's death, indicating that this is a semantic feature, not a pragmatic one.[218] Whether drowning is considered to be a climax (i.e., an achievement with a preface) or an accomplishment is a moot point, and arguably either construal is possible. However, it is certainly telic; there is a definite point at which one dies. Perfective aspect is used to speak of the whole situation including that endpoint, while imperfective aspect is used to speak of a period before the endpoint has been reached.

Similar considerations explain why in the case of punctual verbs imperfective or progressive aspect conveys an iterative sense, and cannot be used with reference to a single instance.[219] The English

218  See Smith, *Parameter*, 106–7. On pragmatics see n. 17 above. It has become common in New Testament studies of aspect to state that *Aktionsart* is a pragmatic rather than a semantic category (e.g., Decker, *Temporal Deixis*, 26; Campbell, *Basics*, 23), but this reflects a use of the terminology which is misleading and unconventional.

219  Comrie, *Aspect*, 26; Bache, "Aspect and Aktionsart," 58. It is in fact possible to contrive counterexamples, but these involve construing the situation as nonpunctual (see Comrie, *Aspect*, 42–43).

verb constellation [the light flash] can be construed as referring either to a single flash (figure 15) or a series of flashes (figure 16).[220]

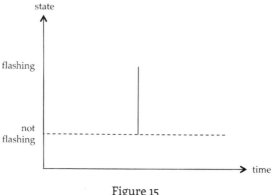

Figure 15

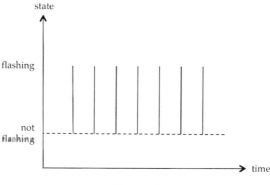

Figure 16

But imperfective aspect, or the progressive aspect in a sentence such as "the light was flashing," cannot normally be used to speak of a single momentary event, since there is no possible reference time, however small, that does not include the situation's endpoint (see figure 17). A single flash does not have what Comrie calls "internal temporal structure."[221] Accordingly, the use of the imperfective aspect requires an interpretation such as that shown in figure 18.

---

220  See Croft, Verbs, 94.
221  See n. 56 above.

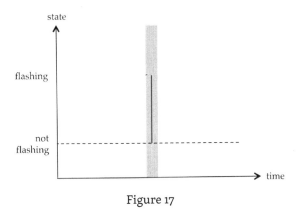

Figure 17

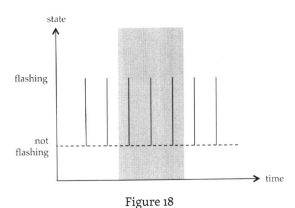

Figure 18

If βάλλειν (throw, put) is rightly classified as a punctual verb, then the following sentence using the imperfect must refer to a *series* of deposits, rather than a single simultaneous deposit:

καὶ πολλοὶ πλούσιοι <u>ἔβαλλον</u> πολλά· (Mark 12:41)
And many rich people <u>were putting in</u> large
sums. (NIV)

As noted above, therefore, imperfective aspect can be used with punctual *verbs*, but not to speak about punctual *situations*. With punctual verbs the imperfective indicates repetition.

In the case of climaxes, imperfective aspect is normally construed as speaking of the preface rather than the moment of the achievement itself. The imperfective effectively forces the climax to be construed as an accomplishment, i.e., as having duration, so that its endpoint can be excluded from the reference time. Thus the imperfective sentence αὐτὴ ἀπέθνῃσκεν (Luke 8:42) means "she was dying" (and had not yet died),[222] whereas the perfective ἀπέθανεν (Luke 8:53) means "she died" (and subsequently was no longer alive). These two sentences are represented in figures 19 and 20, respectively.

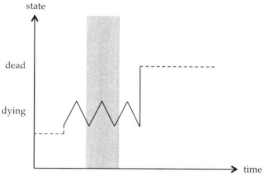

Figure 19

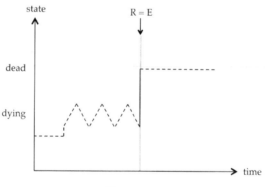

Figure 20

It is perhaps because of effects such as these that the essence of imperfective aspect has sometimes been thought to be durativity. Since the imperfective can only be used with reference to a situation having duration, its use necessarily *implies* duration. But durativity is not generally considered to be the *defining* characteristic of the

---

222  See Fanning, *Verbal Aspect*, 158.

imperfective, since it cannot be used to speak of a durative situation including its endpoints.[223] Thus Fanning notes that "with verbs of a 'bounded' sort" the present aspect (Fanning's term for the imperfective aspect in Greek) "usually denotes the action as 'in progress but not carried to completion.'"[224] For example:

ὁ δὲ Ἰωάννης <u>διεκώλυεν</u> αὐτόν. (Matt 3:14)
But John <u>tried to deter</u> him. (NIV)

Fanning comments: "This is difficult to account for on the basis of the durative view of the present, since there is nothing in the concept of *duration* which is inimical to completion."[225]

The type of analysis and graphical representation outlined in the preceding paragraphs explains why there is only in certain circumstances a subjective choice between perfective and imperfective aspect. It also has the potential to explain the various nuances of the perfect or retrospective aspect, and although space prevents a detailed discussion of this here a few brief comments are worthwhile. As noted above, perfect aspect normally has as its reference time a time after the situation expressed by the verb constellation. This explains why, when the perfect is used with verb constellations that involve the subject transitioning into a resulting state, the perfect expresses the idea of the subject being in that state.[226] For example, figure 21 represents the following sentence:

<u>τέθνηκεν</u> ἡ θυγάτηρ σου. (Luke 8:49)
Your daughter <u>has died</u>. (NASB)

---

223 As noted above, the Russian "imperfective" can be used in this way, but only because it is aspectually neutral and not marked for imperfectivity.
224 Fanning, *Verbal Aspect*, 99.
225 Ibid., (emphasis original). A possible weakness in this argument is that Fanning does not demonstrate that the lack completion is conveyed by the semantics of the verb form διεκώλυεν, rather than by the context.
226 See Crellin, "Greek Perfect Active System," 281–82.

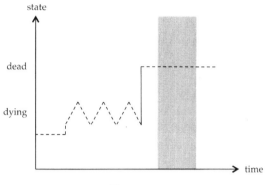

Figure 21

In the case of a lexeme such as "believe" which can denote either a continuing state or entry into that state, the use of perfect aspect normally requires the latter interpretation, because the state itself cannot usually be construed as prior to the reference time. For example, ἡμεῖς πεπιστεύκαμεν in the following sentence can be represented as in figure 22, which explains why it has a stative sense close to that of the present πιστεύομεν (compare figure 4).

> ἡμεῖς πεπιστεύκαμεν καὶ ἐγνώκαμεν ὅτι σὺ εἶ ὁ ἅγιος τοῦ
> θεοῦ. (John 6:69)
> We have come to believe and to know that you are the
> Holy One of God. (NIV)

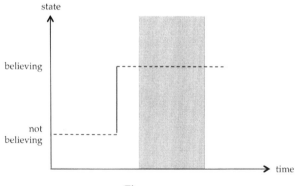

Figure 22

Contrary to what is supposed by Porter, however, stativity does not appear to be the *essence* of perfect aspect,[227] any more than durativity is the essence of imperfective aspect or completion the essence of perfective aspect. Rather, the stative effect depends on the procedural character of the verb in question. Crellin has argued that in the case of verbs that do not involve the subject participating in a state, the perfect has an anterior rather than a stative sense.[228]

The purpose of going into these interactions between procedural character and verbal aspect in some detail is to make the point that they are readily intelligible—indeed predictable[229]—precisely because aspect is related to time, and in particular to temporal phases and boundaries. Mateos and especially Fanning have offered useful accounts of these relationships in New Testament Greek, although Fanning's ambivalence concerning the temporal nature of aspect leaves him unable to explain quite *why* these predictable effects occur. The same is true of Campbell's brief account in *Basics of Verbal Aspect in Biblical Greek*, which is rather less successful than Fanning's because his account of the relevant lexical-semantic characteristics is idiosyncratic, treating punctuality as a subset of transitivity and ignoring telicity, which is arguably the most important factor alongside durativity.[230] Porter, on the other hand, seems to deny the existence of this kind of interaction between aspect and lexical semantics altogether, seeing the two as independent. His reasoning suffers from the flaw that it is based on the statistical co-occurrence of aspects with particular lexemes,[231] without regard to the constraints on the types of *situations* (or more precisely, *conceptualizations* of situations) that can be expressed by those combinations.

It is because of these interactions between aspectual distinctions such as perfectivity or imperfectivity on the one hand and procedural character on the other that some linguists consider the latter to be itself an aspectual phenomenon, using the term "lexical aspect" to distinguish it from verbal or grammatical aspect. The appeal of treating lexical and grammatical aspect as subcategories

---

227  See Porter, *Verbal Aspect*, 251–59.
228  Crellin, "Greek Perfect Active System," 279, 283, 297. See also Crellin's contribution in ch. 14 of the present volume.
229  See Fanning, *Verbal Aspect*, 41.
230  Campbell, *Basics*, esp. 55–59.
231  See Porter, "Aspect Theory and Lexicography."

of the same overarching category is that the two interact because they both have to do with the expression of the temporal constituency of a situation, and in particular with its temporal boundaries.[232] But doing so obscures the fact that they interact precisely because they perform different functions within the temporal domain. The procedural character of the verbal constellation conveys information (or activates background knowledge) about the phases and boundaries of the situation in question, and the choice of verbal aspect then selects one or more of those phases as the reference time.[233] Thus what Sasse terms "unidimensional" and "bidimensional" approaches both contain an element of truth,[234] at least in relation to a language such as Greek with clear grammaticalized aspectual distinctions.

## 5. CONCLUSION

This chapter has argued that the denial by Porter, Fanning, and Campbell that aspect is a temporal concept is at odds with the prevailing understanding within general linguistics. I have suggested that the precise sense in which aspect relates to time, and the various ways in which it interacts with procedural character, are clarified when one abandons visual and spatial metaphors and adopts a more literal time-referential definition. Fanning's account of the interactions between aspect and procedural character is extremely helpful and insightful, but would be strengthened by a recognition that these interactions occur because of the temporal nature of aspect.

---

232  See, e.g., Smith, *Parameter*, xiv.
233  Another way of putting this is to say that aspect and procedural character have to do with different kinds of boundaries. As Croft puts it, "the property of boundedness that is considered to be a part of the root of the verbal meaning, i.e. the existence of a natural endpoint or telos for the event, is represented by the states defined on the q dimension, while boundedness of a particular event in a particular occurrence is defined by the existence of profiled beginning and ending phases on the t dimension" (Croft, *Verbs*, 81). See also Sasse, "Recent Activity," 205-6.
234  See Sasse, "Recent Activity," 202.

I will conclude by suggesting some desiderata for future work on aspect in New Testament Greek that emerge from the present examination.

## 5.1 Recognition of the Temporal Nature of Aspect

First, it follows from the preceding discussion that future studies would do well to revisit the definition of aspect and the question of aspect's relationship to time.

## 5.2 Engagement with Literature on Aspect within General Linguistics

Second, future work on aspect in New Testament Greek will benefit from engaging widely and carefully with the work that has been done and continues to be done on the subject within the field of general linguistics. Whether or not one accepts Porter's argument that the adoption of a specific linguistic theory is a prerequisite for identifying and interpreting linguistic evidence,[235] the adoption of a particular theory should not lead one to overlook the insights of those working within a different framework.

## 5.3 Analysis of Procedural Character

Third, as Evans has noted, much more analysis is needed of the procedural character of Greek verbs and verb constellations.[236] Shain makes an important step forward by investigating procedural character using tests of the sort typically utilized by linguists. For example, "An appropriate test for dynamicity ... is whether a predicate can have a habitual interpretation in an imperfective aspect: if it can, then it is not stative."[237] In addition to the tests she employs, she notes that many others could be developed. For example, "adverbial phrases, particularly time phrases" can be used to diagnose

235 Porter adopts a particular theoretical framework, namely Systemic Functional Linguistics, and argues that "without a linguistic theory as the basis of examination of the language, it is very difficult to determine what counts as evidence and how any such evidence should be interpreted" (*Linguistic Analysis*, 200).
236 Evans, "Future Directions," 205; similarly Evans, *Verbal Syntax*, 20.
237 Shain, "Exploring Aktionsart," 227.

procedural character. Typically "atelic predicates take duration adverbials, and telic predicates take time-frame adverbials."[238] This is
a promising avenue, despite some weaknesses in Shain's analysis
that illustrate the complications inherent in such an approach.[239]

Attention to procedural character is relevant not only for understanding aspectual usage in the Greek New Testament, but also
for the ongoing debate over whether Greek verbs express tense (location in time) alongside aspect. For example, Campbell cites the
clause ἐν σοὶ εὐδόκησα in Mark 1:11 as an example of a non-past-referring aorist, on the basis of the translation "with you I am well
pleased." He comments "Suffice to say that *no one* translates the last
clause of this verse, '*in you I was well pleased.*'"[240] But this does not
suffice. What is needed is a principled consideration of the procedural character of εὐδοκέω along the lines suggested above. Campbell
appears to assume, on the basis of its English translation equivalent,
that it is a stative verb meaning "be pleased." But if a possible construal of εὐδοκέω is as an achievement expressing *entry into* a state
(i.e., if it is what Croft calls an inceptive state),[241] then the event time
is indeed prior to the speech time.[242]

---

238  Ibid., 246.
239  Some of Shain's tests seem difficult to apply without circularity. E.g., she
states that "the discovery of an instance in a text in which an event is ultimately unrealized and the predicate denoting it is in an imperfective aspect constitutes conclusive evidence of the telicity of that utterance" (ibid.,
227). But the question whether an event is unrealized or not involves a
judgment concerning its telicity. Thus her conclusion that ἀναγκάζειν in Gal
6:12 refers to an unrealized event depends on the assumption that it has the
telic sense "compel." If it had an atelic sense such as "urge," then the event
would have been realized and the test would fail. Similarly, Shain assumes
that the existence of a goal or destination indicates telicity (228). However,
this is only true if the use of perfective aspect implies that the goal has
been reached. Thus [Bloggs move to the door] is telic but [Bloggs move toward the door] is atelic. Telicity is determined here by the difference between "move to" and "move toward," not by the presence of "the door."
240  Campbell, *Basics*, 36 (all emphasis original).
241  Compare ἐπιστεύσαμεν in Gal 2:16, which clearly does not indicate that Paul
has stopped believing.
242  Campbell's argument is all the more surprising given that the English construction "I am pleased" is a resultative, and resultatives typically "signal
that a state exists as a result of a past action." Joan Bybee, Revere Perkins,
and William Pagliuca, *The Evolution of Grammar: Tense, Aspect, and Modality in the Languages of the World* (Chicago: University of Chicago Press,
1994), 54.

## 5.4 Scrutiny of Linguistic Assumptions

A final desideratum for future work on aspect in New Testament Greek is that the linguistic assumptions on which it and earlier studies are based be identified and scrutinized. A case in point is the assumption, noted in section 1, that each tense (present, aorist, etc.) has one and only one meaning, regardless of the mood, lexeme, or construction in which it occurs. This is a bold claim and one that is hardly self-evident, since many linguists take the opposite position.[243] It cannot be assumed without argument, for example, that the tenses have the same aspectual value in every mood, or that a particular aspect always has the same markedness.[244] Thus the fact that the present appears to be imperfective in the nonindicative moods does not exclude the possibility that it is aspectually neutral in the indicative.[245] A methodologically sound investigation will so far as possible investigate aspectual contrasts by means of minimal pairs, where other elements of the sentence (mood, lexeme, etc.) remain constant and only the tense changes.

In short, much work remains to be done, and despite the criticisms articulated here, Porter, Fanning, and Campbell are to be thanked for stimulating interest in this important area of New Testament Greek research.

## BIBLIOGRAPHY

Anderson, John. *An Essay Concerning Aspect: Some Considerations of a General Character Arising from the Abbé Darrigol's Analysis of the Basque Verb.* JLSMin 167. The Hague: Mouton, 1973.

---

243 See, e.g., those cited at n. 18 above. Some scholars have sought to justify this position by suggesting that any variation in meaning is *by definition* "pragmatic." But this is based on a misunderstanding of what linguists mean when they distinguish semantics and pragmatics (see n. 17 above).

244 Comrie notes that "in combination with past tense there is generally in languages a tendency for the perfective aspect to be unmarked, while with present tense the tendency is for imperfective aspect to be unmarked" (Comrie, *Aspect*, 121).

245 For the view that the present indicative is aspectually neutral see, e.g., Mateos, *Aspecto verbal*, 31; Yves Duhoux, *Le verbe grec ancien: Éléments de morphologie et de syntaxe historiques*, 2nd ed., BCLL 104 (Leuven: Peeters, 2000), 143; Comrie, *Aspect*, 71.

Archaimbault, Sylvie. "L'aspect: Fortune d'un terme, avatars d'un concept." Pages 83–89 in *Métalangage et terminologie linguistique: Actes du colloque international de Grenoble (Université Stendhal-Grenoble III, 14-16 mai 1998)*. Edited by Bernard Colombat and Marie Savelli. OrbisSup 17. Leuven: Peeters, 2001.

Ariel, Mira. *Defining Pragmatics*. RSL. Cambridge: Cambridge University Press, 2010.

Auroux, Sylvain. "Innovation et système scientifique: Le temps verbal dans la grammaire générale." Pages 55–86 in *Hommage à Jean-Toussaint Desanti*. Edited by Sylvain Auroux, Bernard Besnier, Maurice Caveing, and Simone Debout. Mauvezin: Trans-Europ-Repress, 1991.

Bach, Emmon. "The Algebra of Events." *Ling&P* 9 (1986): 5–16.

Bache, Carl. "Aspect and Aktionsart: Towards a Semantic Distinction." *JL* 18 (1982): 57–72.

———. *Verbal Aspect: A General Theory and Its Application to Present-Day English*. OUSE 8. Odense: Odense University Press, 1985.

———. *The Study of Aspect, Tense and Action: Towards a Theory of the Semantics of Grammatical Categories*. 2nd ed. Frankfurt am Main: Lang, 1997.

Bennett, Michael and Barbara H. Partee. *Toward the Logic of Tense and Aspect in English*. Santa Monica, CA: System Development Corporation, 1972. Repr., Bloomington, IN: University Linguistics Club, 1978.

Bentein, Klaas. "Tense and Aspect from Hellenistic to Early Byzantine Greek." *EAGLL* 3:379–82.

Bertinetto, Pier Marco "Perfectives, Imperfectives, and Progressives." Pages 266–70 in vol. 9 of *Encyclopedia of Language & Linguistics*. Edited by Keith Brown. 2nd ed. 14 vols. Oxford: Elsevier, 2006.

Binnick, Robert I. *Time and the Verb: A Guide to Tense and Aspect*. New York: Oxford University Press, 1991.

———, ed. *The Oxford Handbook of Tense and Aspect*. New York: Oxford University Press, 2012.

Bybee, Joan, Revere Perkins, and William Pagliuca. *The Evolution of Grammar: Tense, Aspect, and Modality in the Languages of the World*. Chicago: University of Chicago Press, 1994.

Campbell, Constantine R. *Advances in the Study of Greek: New Insights for Reading the New Testament*. Grand Rapids: Zondervan, 2015.

———. *Basics of Verbal Aspect in Biblical Greek*. Grand Rapids: Zondervan, 2008.

———. *Verbal Aspect and Non-Indicative Verbs: Further Soundings in the Greek of the New Testament.* SBG 15. New York: Lang, 2008.

———. *Verbal Aspect, the Indicative Mood, and Narrative: Soundings in the Greek of the New Testament.* SBG 13. New York: Lang, 2007.

Carson, D. A. "An Introduction to the Porter/Fanning Debate." Pages 18–25 in *Biblical Greek Language and Linguistics: Open Questions in Current Research.* Edited by Stanley E. Porter and D. A. Carson. JSNTSup 80. Sheffield: JSOT Press, 1993.

Chung, Sandra and Alan Timberlake. "Tense, Aspect, and Mood." Pages 202–58 in *Grammatical Categories and the Lexicon.* Edited by Timothy Shopen. Vol. 3 of *Language Typology and Syntactic Description.* Cambridge: Cambridge University Press, 1985.

Cirafesi, Wally V. *Verbal Aspect in Synoptic Parallels: On the Method and Meaning of Divergent Tense-Form Usage in the Synoptic Passion Narratives.* LBS 7. Leiden: Brill, 2013.

Comrie, Bernard. *Aspect: An Introduction to the Study of Verbal Aspect and Related Problems.* CTL. Cambridge: Cambridge University Press, 1976.

———. *Tense.* CTL. Cambridge: Cambridge University Press, 1985.

Crellin, Robert. "The Greek Perfect Active System: 200 BC–AD 150." PhD diss., University of Cambridge, 2012.

Croft, William. *Verbs: Aspect and Causal Structure.* Oxford: Oxford University Press, 2012.

Dahl, Östen. "Perfectivity in Slavonic and Other Languages." Pages 3–22 in *Aspect Bound: A Voyage into the Realm of Germanic, Slavonic and Finno-Ugrian Aspectology.* Edited by Casper de Groot and Hannu Tommola. Dordrecht: Foris, 1984.

Decker, Rodney J. *Temporal Deixis of the Greek Verb in the Gospel of Mark with Reference to Verbal Aspect.* SBG 10. New York: Lang, 2001.

Dowty, David R. "Studies in the Logic of Verb Aspect and Time Reference in English." PhD diss., University of Texas at Austin, 1972.

———. "Toward a Semantic Analysis of Verb Aspect and the English 'Imperfective' Progressive." *Ling&P* 1 (1977): 45–77.

Duhoux, Yves. *Le verbe grec ancien: Éléments de morphologie et de syntaxe historiques.* 2nd ed. BCLL 104. Leuven: Peeters, 2000.

Evans, Trevor V. "Future Directions for Aspect Studies in Ancient Greek." Pages 199–206 in *Biblical Greek Language and Lexicography: Essays in Honor of Frederick W. Danker.* Edited by Bernard A. Taylor, John A. L. Lee, Peter R. Burton, and Richard E. Whitaker. Grand Rapids: Eerdmans, 2004.

———. *Verbal Syntax in the Greek Pentateuch: Natural Greek Usage and Hebrew Interference.* Oxford: Oxford University Press, 2001.

Fanning, Buist M. "Approaches to Verbal Aspect in New Testament Greek: Issues in Definition and Method." Pages 46–62 in *Biblical Greek Language and Linguistics: Open Questions in Current Research.* Edited by Stanley E. Porter and D. A. Carson. JSNTSup 80. Sheffield: JSOT Press, 1993.

———. *Verbal Aspect in New Testament Greek.* OTM. Oxford: Oxford University Press, 1990.

Filip, Hana. "Lexical Aspect." Pages 721–51 in *The Oxford Handbook of Tense and Aspect.* Edited by Robert I. Binnick. New York: Oxford University Press, 2012.

Foley, Toshikazu S. *Biblical Translation in Chinese and Greek: Verbal Aspect in Theory and Practice.* LBS 1. Leiden: Brill, 2009.

Forsyth, James. *A Grammar of Aspect: Usage and Meaning in the Russian Verb.* Studies in the Modern Russian Language Extra Volume. Cambridge: Cambridge University Press, 1970.

Greč, Nikolaj Ivanovič. *Grammaire raisonnée de la langue russe.* Translated by Charles Philippe Reiff. 2 vols. St Petersburg: Gretsch, 1828–29.

Harweg, Roland. "Aspekte als Zeitstufen und Zeitstufen als Aspekte." *Linguistics* 181 (1976): 5–28.

Hockett, Charles F. *A Course in Modern Linguistics.* New York: Macmillan, 1958.

Hogeweg, Lotte. "What's So Unreal About the Past: Past Tense and Counterfactuals." Pages 181–208 in *Studies on English Modality in Honour of Frank R. Palmer.* Edited by Anastasios Tsangalidis and Roberta Facchinetti. Linguistic Insights 111. Bern: Lang, 2009.

Horrocks, Geoffrey and Melita Stavrou. "Grammaticalized Aspect and Spatio-Temporal Culmination." *Lingua* 117 (2007): 605–44.

Huffman, Douglas S. *Verbal Aspect Theory and the Prohibitions in the Greek New Testament.* SBG 16. New York: Lang, 2014.

Isačenko, A. V. *Grammatičeskij stroj russkogo jazyka v sopostavlenii c slovackim: Morfologija.* Part 2. Bratislava: Slovak Academy of Sciences, 1960.

———. *Formenlehre.* Part 1 of *Die russische Sprache der Gegenwart.* Halle: Niemeyer, 1962.

Johnson, Marion R. "A Unified Temporal Theory of Tense and Aspect." Pages 145–75 in *Tense and Aspect.* Edited by Philip J. Tedeschi and Annie Zaenen. Vol. 14 of *Syntax and Semantics.* New York: Academic Press, 1981.

Klein, Wolfgang. *Time in Language*. Germanic Linguistics. London: Routledge, 1994.

———. "A Time-Relational Analysis of Russian Aspect." *Language* 71 (1995): 669–95.

Kortmann, Bernd. "The Triad 'Tense-Aspect-Aktionsart': Problems and Possible Solutions." Pages 9–30 in *Perspectives on Aspect and Aktionsart*. Edited by Carl Vetters and Willy Vandeweghe. *BJL* 6. Amsterdam: Benjamins, 1991.

Kroeger, Paul R. *Analyzing Grammar: An Introduction*. Cambridge: Cambridge University Press, 2005.

Levinson, Stephen C. *Pragmatics*. CTL. Cambridge: Cambridge University Press, 1983.

Lyons, John. *Semantics*. 2 vols. Cambridge: Cambridge University Press, 1977.

Mateos, Juan. *El aspecto verbal en el Nuevo Testamento*. EstNT 1. Madrid: Ediciones Cristiandad, 1977.

Matthewson, David L. *Verbal Aspect in the Book of Revelation: The Function of Greek Verb Tenses in John's Apocalypse*. LBS 4. Leiden: Brill, 2010.

Maudru, Jean-Baptiste. *Élémens raisonnés de la langue russe ou principes généraux de la grammaire appliqués à la langue russe*. Paris: Maudru, 1802.

McKay, Kenneth L. *Greek Grammar for Students: A Concise Grammar of Classical Attic with Special Reference to Aspect in the Verb*. Canberra: Dept. of Classics, Australian National University, 1974.

———. *A New Syntax of the Verb in New Testament Greek: An Aspectual Approach*. SBG 5. New York: Lang, 1994.

———. "On the Perfect and Other Aspects in New Testament Greek." *NovT* 23 (1981): 289–329.

Mittwoch, Anita. "Aspects of English Aspect: On the Interaction of Perfect, Progressive and Durational Phrases." *Ling&P* 11 (1988): 203–54.

Moser, Amalia. "From Aktionsart to Aspect: Grammaticalization and Subjectification in Greek." *ALH* 46 (2014): 64–84.

Murphy, M. Lynne. *Lexical Meaning*. CTL. Cambridge: Cambridge University Press, 2010.

Naselli, Andrew David. "A Brief Introduction to Verbal Aspect in New Testament Greek." *DBSJ* 12 (2007): 17–28.

Neuville, Michel de. "Système des formes du verbe français." *Annales de grammaire* 1 (1818): 543–51.

Newman, Lawrence W. "The Notion of Verbal Aspect in Eighteenth Century Russia." *Russian Linguistics* 3 (1976): 35–53.

Olsen, Mari Broman. *A Semantic and Pragmatic Model of Lexical and Grammatical Aspect.* ODL. New York: Garland, 1997.

Paducheva, Elena. "Taxonomic Categories and Semantics of Aspectual Opposition." Pages 71–90 in *Semantic and Syntactic Perspectives.* Edited by Pier Marco Bertinetto, Valentina Bianchi, Östen Dahl, James Higginbotham, and Mario Squartini. Vol. 1 of *Temporal Reference, Aspect and Actionality.* Turin: Rosenberg & Sellier, 1995.

Partee, Barbara H. *Compositionality in Formal Semantics: Selected Papers by Barbara H. Partee.* Explorations in Semantics 1. Oxford: Blackwell, 2004.

Porter, Stanley E. "Aspect Theory and Lexicography." Pages 207–22 in *Biblical Greek Language and Lexicography: Essays in Honor of Frederick W. Danker.* Edited by Bernard A. Taylor, John A. L. Lee, Peter R. Burton, and Richard E. Whitaker. Grand Rapids: Eerdmans, 2004.

———. *Idioms of the Greek New Testament.* 2nd ed. BLG 2. Sheffield: Sheffield Academic, 1994.

———. "In Defence of Verbal Aspect." Pages 26–45 in *Biblical Greek Language and Linguistics: Open Questions in Current Research.* Edited by Stanley E. Porter and D. A. Carson. JSNTSup 80. Sheffield: JSOT Press, 1993.

———. *Linguistic Analysis of the Greek New Testament: Studies in Tools, Methods, and Practice.* Grand Rapids: Baker Academic, 2015.

———. "Prominence: A Theoretical Overview." Pages 45–74 in *The Linguist As Pedagogue: Trends in the Teaching and Linguistic Analysis of the Greek New Testament.* Edited by Stanley E. Porter and Matthew Brook O'Donnell. NTM 11. Sheffield: Sheffield Phoenix, 2009.

———. Review of *Verbal Aspect in New Testament Greek,* by Buist M. Fanning. *JSNT* 43 (1991): 127–28.

———. *Verbal Aspect in the Greek of the New Testament: With Reference to Tense and Mood.* SBG 1. New York: Lang, 1989.

Porter, Stanley E. and Andrew W. Pitts. "New Testament Greek Language and Linguistics in Recent Research." *CurBR* 6 (2008): 214–55.

Reichenbach, Hans. *Elements of Symbolic Logic.* New York: Macmillan, 1947.

Reiff, Charles Philippe. *Grammaire russe précédée d'une introduction sur la langue slavonne.* Paris: Barrois, 1851.

Rothstein, Susan D. "Introduction." Pages 1–10 in *Theoretical and Crosslinguistic Approaches to the Semantics of Aspect*. Edited by Susan D. Rothstein. Linguistik Aktuell 110. Amsterdam: Benjamins, 2008.

———. *Structuring Events: A Study in the Semantics of Lexical Aspect*. Explorations in Semantics 2. Oxford: Blackwell, 2004.

Ruijgh, C. J. "Les valeurs temporelles des formes verbales en grec ancien." Pages 197–217 in *The Function of Tense in Texts*. Edited by Jadranka Gvozdanović and Theo A. J. M. Janssen. VKNWL NS 144. Amsterdam: Royal Netherlands Academy of Arts and Sciences, 1991.

———. Review of *Kontext und Aspekt in der altgriechischen Prosa Herodots*, by Heinrich Hettrich. *Gnomon* 51 (1979): 217–27.

Růžička, Rudolf. "Der russische Verbalaspekt." *Der Russischunterricht* 5 (1952): 161–69.

Sasse, Hans-Jürgen. "Aspect and Aktionsart." Pages 535–38 in vol. 1 of *Encyclopedia of Language & Linguistics*. Edited by Keith Brown. 2nd ed. 14 vols. Oxford: Elsevier, 2006.

———. "Recent Activity in the Theory of Aspect: Accomplishments, Achievements, or Just Non-Progressive State?" *LiTy* 6 (2002): 199–271.

Shain, Rachel. "Exploring Aktionsart in Corpora: A Case Study of Koine Greek *Erchomai* and *Eiserchomai*." *JGL* 11 (2011): 221–48.

Silva, Moisés. "A Response to Fanning and Porter on Verbal Aspect." Pages 74–82 in *Biblical Greek Language and Linguistics: Open Questions in Current Research*. Edited by Stanley E. Porter and D. A. Carson. JSNTSup 80. Sheffield: JSOT Press, 1993.

Smith, Carlota S. "A Theory of Aspectual Choice." *Language* 59 (1983): 479–501.

———. *The Parameter of Aspect*. 2nd ed. SLP 43. Dordrecht: Kluwer, 1997.

Sørensen, H. M. "Om definitionerne af verbets aspekter." Pages 221–33 in *In memoriam Kr. Sandfeld udgivet paa 70-aarsdagen for hans fødsel*. Edited by Rosally Brøndal, Viggo Brøndal, Christen Møller, and Hedvig Olsen. Copenhagen: Gyldendal, 1943.

Swart, Henriëtte de. "Verbal Aspect." Pages 752–80 in *The Oxford Handbook of Tense and Aspect*. Edited by Robert I. Binnick. New York: Oxford University Press, 2012.

Tatevosov, Sergej. "The Parameter of Actionality." *LiTy* 6 (2003): 317–401.

Taylor, John R. *Linguistic Categorization*. 3rd ed. OTLing. Oxford: Oxford University Press, 2003.

Vendler, Zeno. "Verbs and Times." *PhR* 66 (1957): 143–60.

Voguë, Sarah de, Rémi Camus, Ilse Depraetere, Sylvie Mellet, Albert
    Rijksbaron, and Maria Tzevelekou. "Aspect." Pages 48–64 in
    *Dictionary of Untranslatables: A Philosophical Lexicon.* Edited
    by Barbara Cassin. Translated by Steven Rendall, Christian
    Hubert, Jeffrey Mehlman, Nathanael Stein, and Michael
    Syrotinski. Princeton: Princeton University Press, 2014.
Wallace, Daniel B. *Greek Grammar Beyond the Basics: An Exegetical
    Syntax of the New Testament; With Scripture, Subject, and Greek
    Word Indexes.* Grand Rapids: Zondervan, 1996.
Windfuhr, Gernot L. "A Spatial Model for Tense, Aspect, and Mood."
    *FLin* 19 (1985): 415–61.

CHAPTER 3

# Tense and Aspect in Classical Greek: Two Historical Developments; Augment and Perfect

RUTGER J. ALLAN

FREE UNIVERSITY AMSTERDAM

## 1. INTRODUCTION

The historical development of the aspect system in Classical Greek has received relatively little attention in the intense scholarly debate on Greek aspect.[1] There appears to be a wide consensus that the

---

1  There have been a number of approaches to the pres. vs. aor. distinction in Classical Greek, e.g., aspectual, structuralist: Martín S. Ruipérez, *Estructura del sistema de aspectos y tiempos del verbo greco antiguo: Análisis funcional sincrónico* (Salamanca: Consejo Superior de Investigaciones Científicas, 1954). Relative tense: Cornelis J. Ruijgh, *Autour de "τε épique": études sur la syntaxe grecque* (Amsterdam: Hakkert, 1971); idem, "L'emploi 'inceptif' du thème du présent du verbe grec: Esquisse d'une théorie de valeurs temporelles des thèmes temporels," *Mnemosyne* 38 (1985): 1–61; idem, "Les valeurs temporelles des formes verbales en grec ancien," in *The Function of Tense in Texts*, ed. Jadranka Gvozdanović and Theo A. J. M. Janssen (Amsterdam: North-Holland, 1991), 197–217; Heinrich Hettrich, *Kontext und Aspekt in der altgriechischen Prosa Herodots* (Göttingen: Vandenhoeck & Ruprecht, 1976). Relative tense/aspectual: Albert Rijksbaron, *The Syntax and Semantics of the Verb in Classical Greek: An Introduction*, 3rd ed. (Chicago: The University of Chicago Press, 2006). Pragmatic: Christiaan M.J. Sicking and Peter Stork. *Two Studies in the Semantics of the Verb in Classical Greek*, MS 160 (Leiden: Brill, 1996), Christiaan M.J. Sicking, "The Distribution of Aorist and Present Tense Stem Forms in Greek, Especially in the Imperative," *Glotta* 69 (1991):

aspectual system as we find it in Homer and the system of Classical Greek are essentially the same. In our most authoritative grammars, Kühner-Gerth and Schwyzer-Debrunner, we find definitions of the core meanings of the present and aorist stems that are meant to cover both Homeric and Classical Greek. The descriptions of the specific usages of the aspects stems, such as the iterative use of the imperfect or the ingressive use of the aorist, are illustrated by examples taken from Homer and from Classical Greek with the implication that there is essentially a historical continuity between the Homeric and the Classical use of verbal aspect.[2]

Even though there seem to be no spectacular developments in the present vs. aorist opposition from Homer to Classical Greek, there are some elements of the tense-aspect system that do show a clear development over time. Two of these elements will be the topic of this paper: (1) the *augment* and (2) the semantic development of the *perfect* stem.[3]

---

14–43, 154–70. Aspectual, Guillaume-inspired: John Hewson and Vit Bubenik, *Tense and Aspect in Indo-European Languages. Theory, Typology, Diachrony*, AST 135 (Amsterdam: Benjamins, 1997). Aspectual: Maria Napoli, *Aspect and Actionality in Homeric Greek: A Contrastive Analysis*, Materiali linguistici 54 (Milan: FrancoAngeli, 2006). Aspectual, Discourse Representation Theory: Corien L. A. Bary, "Aspect in Ancient Greek: A Semantic Analysis of the Aorist and Imperfective" (PhD diss., Radboud University Nijmegen, 2009. Aspectual, Cognitive Linguistics: Rutger.J. Allan, "The Imperfect Unbound: A Cognitive Linguistic Approach to Greek Aspect," in *Language Variation and Change. Tense, Aspect and Modality in Ancient Greek*, ed. Klaas Bentein, Mark Janse, and Jorie Soltic (Leiden: Brill, forthcoming).

2    E.g., Raphael Kühner and Bernhard Gerth, *Ausführliche Grammatik der griechischen Sprache. 2. Teil: Satzlehre* (Hanover: Hahnsche Buchhandlung, 1898), 129–69; Eduard Schwyzer and Albert Debrunner, *Griechische Grammatik Grammatik: Auf der Grundlage von Karl Brugmanns Griechischer Grammatik*, Zweiter Band; Syntax und Syntaktische Stilistik, HAW 2 (Munich: Beck, 1950), 246–86. For a different view, see Amalia Moser, "The Changing Relationship of Tense and Aspect in the History of Greek," *STUF* 61 (2008): 5–18 and Moser (ch. 17 in this volume), who argues that the Greek verb system initially was based on *Aktionsart* while Classical Greek was aspect-oriented.

3    Also the fut. tense form and the fut. auxiliary μέλλω show a significant diachronical semantic change from PIE via Homeric Greek to Classical Greek; see Rutger J. Allan, "The History of the Future: Subjectification and Semantic Change in Ancient Greek Future Expressions," in *The Greek Future and its History*, ed. Rutger J. Allan, Frédéric Lambert, and Theodore Markopoulos (Leuven: Peeters, forthcoming).

In section 2, I will address the intriguing distribution of the augment in Homer. I will defend the traditional view that the augment expresses past time against the more recently forwarded view that the augment is a marker of immediacy. I will also argue that the gnomic aorist has evolved from a past time referring expression. In connection with the gnomic aorist, the more general issue will be addressed whether genericity and iterativity are, as is often assumed, inherent to the semantics of the present (i.e., imperfective) aspect or should, rather, be regarded as semantic classes that function independently from grammatical aspect marking. In section 3, I will give a broad overview of the most important semantic changes of the perfect from PIE to Classical Greek. I will argue that the best approach to the analysis of the semantics of the perfect is to view the perfect as a polysemous chain of semantic extensions. Section 4 contains the conclusion.

## 2. THE AUGMENT: IMMEDIACY OR DISTANCE?

In Classical Greek the augment is an obligatory morpheme in the secondary indicative forms. The augmented form typically expresses past states of affairs, but it can also refer to counterfactual states of affairs.

In Homeric Greek, the augment is not yet obligatory in the formation of the secondary indicative. Sometimes the augment appears, sometimes it is omitted. However, the distribution of the augment is not arbitrary neither is it completely dependent on metrical factors. A number of intriguing rules and tendencies seem to govern the use of the augment. The following list of distributional factors is derived from recent work on the Homeric augment by Egbert Bakker:[4]

---

4   See Egbert J. Bakker, "Pointing to the Past: Verbal Agreement and Temporal Deixis in Homer," in *Euphrosyne: Studies in Ancient Epic and Its Legacy in Honor of Dimitris N. Maronitis*, ed. John N. Kazazis and Antonios Rengakos (Stuttgart: Steiner, 1999), 50–65; idem, "Similes, Augment, and the Language of Immediacy," in *Speaking Volumes: Orality and Literacy in the Greek and Roman World*, ed. Janet Watson, MS 218 (Leiden: Brill, 2001), 1–23; idem, *Pointing at the Past: From Formula to Performance in Homeric Poetics*, Hellenic Studies 12 (Washington, DC: Center for Hellenic Studies, 2005). Important earlier work on the textual distribution of the augment has been done by Arthur

- Metrical form may require presence or absence of augment
- Augment more frequent in direct discourse than in narrative
- Augment obligatory in gnomic aorist
- No augment on imperfects in -σκ-
- Augment less frequent in discourse with negated aorists
- Augment more frequent in speech introductions
- Augment less frequent in ἐπεί-clauses in narrative and in discourse

The question arises as to how the distribution of the augment can be accounted for if we factor out those cases that are determined by metrical necessity. What can we say about the meaning of the augment on the basis of these distributional patterns in Homeric discourse? In order to explain the augment's distribution, Bakker proposes the following characterization of the semantics of the augment:

> [T]he augment expressed the actual occurrence of an event in a specific time and place. ... verbal augment originally was a deictic suffix marking an event as "near" with respect to the speaker's present and immediate situation. The augment marks not so much present tense as presence: closeness, positive, observable occurrence.[5]

Bakker sees the augment as a marker of *immediacy/presence*.[6] This semantic feature, according to Bakker, explains its occurrence

---

Platt, "The Homeric Augment." *JPh* 19 (1891): 211–37 and J. A. J. Drewitt, "The Augment in Homer," *ClQ* 6 (1912): 44–59, 104–20. For an overview of the historical development of the augment from PIE to Koine Greek, see Gentry (ch. 11 in this volume).

5    Bakker, *Pointing at the Past*, 127.

6    Note that Drewitt had already analyzed the augment's original function as "an interjection or particle which would mark some connexion with or reference to the present" (Drewitt, "Augment in Homer," 44). Bakker's analysis of semantics of the augment has been the starting point of the studies of Frederick J. Pagniello, "The Homeric Augment: A Deictic Particle" (PhD diss., University of Georgia, 2002) and Peter-Arnold Mumm, "Zur Funktion des homerischen Augments," in *Analecta homini universali dicata: Arbeiten zur Indogermanistik, Linguistik, Philologie, Politik, Musik und Dichtung; Festschrift*

in direct discourse, similes, general statements, and speech introductions. Bakker's account is appealing but it also raises a number
of problems.

The first problem is: If indeed the augment has to do with immediacy, presence, and observability, how can we explain the fact
that present tense forms *never* have the augment—even though they
refer to immediate, present, positive, and observable events most of
the time? (If the answer is that the present tense is already a marker
of immediacy, what is the difference between the two formations?)
And why, as Wakker observes, is the augment also used in counterfactual (irrealis) events even though these are clearly distant from
actual observable reality?[7]

This issue brings us to a second problem attached to Bakker's
thesis, one of diachronical nature. In Classical Greek, we see that
the augment has become obligatory in secondary indicative forms.
Secondary indicative forms are typically used to express past time,
but they are also used to express counterfactual (irrealis) states of
affairs, for example, in conditional clauses or in wishes. It is therefore justified to analyze the augment in Classical Greek as a marker
of *distance* from the speaker's present reality, either of a temporal
nature (when used as a marker of past time) or of a modal-epistem-
ic nature (when used as a marker of counterfactuality).[8] Now, if the
augment in Classical Greek denotes temporal-epistemic distance it
is not easy to explain how a marker of *distance* could have evolved
from a marker that expressed *immediacy* in Homer.

*Oswald Panagl zum 65. Geburtstag, Band 1*, ed. Thomas Krisch, Thomas Lindner, and Ulrich Müller, SAG 421 (Stuttgart: Heinz, 2004), 148–58.

7   Gerry C. Wakker, "The Gnomic Aorist in Hesiod," in *Language Variation and
Change: Tense, Aspect and Modality in Ancient Greek*, ed. Klaas Bentein, Mark
Janse, and Jorie Soltic (Leiden: Brill, forthcoming).

8   See also Kenneth L. McKay, "The Use of the Perfect down to the Second Century A.D." *BICS* (1965): 1–21. For the link between past tense and counterfactuality and its analysis as distance from present reality, see e.g., Deborah
James, "Past Tense and the Hypothetical: A Cross-linguistic Study," *StudLang*
6 (1982): 375–403; Suzanne Fleischman, "Imperfective and Irrealis," in *Modality in Grammar and Discourse*, ed. Joan L. Bybee and Suzanne Fleischman,
TSL 32 (Amsterdam: Benjamins, 1995), 519–51; Ronald W. Langacker, *Foundations of Cognitive Grammar, Vol. II: Descriptive Application* (Stanford: Stanford
University Press, 1991); Eve Sweetser and Barbara Dancygier, *Mental Spaces
in Grammar: Conditional Constructions*, CSL (Cambridge: Cambridge University Press, 2005).

A third objection pertains to the gnomic aorist. An important argument for Bakker is the (almost) universal use of the augment in similes, and similes obviously tend to have a strong visual quality and convey a feeling of "presence" to the hearer. However, the use of the gnomic aorist in similes is merely a *subtype* of the gnomic aorist. It only occurs so frequently in Homeric epic because the narrator is particularly fond of similes. However, there is no reason to assume that the gnomic aorist in typical gnomic utterances such as ῥεχθὲν δέ τε νήπιος ἔγνω (Hom. *Il.* 17.32) ("Once a thing has been done, a fool understands it")[9] has a special visualizing or otherwise immediate quality.

A final problem with Bakker's account of the augment is that it seems to be in tension with his general view on the character of Homeric epic poetry. According to Bakker, "epic narrative is typically presented as, in narratological terms, the *description of things seen,* with the narrator (performer) posing as eye-witness."[10] The "descriptive quality of epic," Bakker states, is "a matter of speech in performance in which the narrator/performer is not so much concerned with the transmission of narrative information as with the *reenactment* of events from the past, with the *recreation* in the present of a past on which (importantly) both the poet and the audience agree."[11] This general characterization of epic narrative seems not so easy to reconcile with Bakker's explanation of the augment. If the augment would really mark the presence, closeness, and observability of an event, we would expect that it would be highly frequent in epic narrative. However, in Homeric narrative the augment is relatively infrequent.

We have to conclude that viewing the augment as a marker of immediacy raises a number of issues that still have to be accounted for. In my view, therefore, the traditional conception of the augment as a marker of past tense is still the most attractive starting point.[12]

---

9   All translations are by the author unless otherwise indicated.
10  Egbert J. Bakker, "Discourse and Performance. Involvement, Visualization, and 'Presence' in Homeric Poetry," *ClAnt* 12 (1993), 15 (emphasis original).
11  Ibid. (emphasis original). Similar views are expressed by idem in *Poetry in Speech: Orality and Homeric Discourse* (Ithaca: Cornell University Press, 1997) and in Bakker, *Pointing at the Past.*
12  The traditional view of the augment as a past tense marker is also more plausible from a historical point of view. An attractive etymology of the

To explain the peculiar distribution of the augment in Homer, we have to realize that the augment, even though it is strictly speaking redundant, is nonetheless a useful morphological element: it facilitates the interpretation of the form as a past tense.[13] Because forms without the augment do not contain a specialized past tense morpheme, past time reference is indicated only indirectly: in order to identify an unaugmented form as a past tense form, a hearer has to combine two different morphological signals. First, the hearer has to note that the form does *not* contain a special mood-marking morpheme (such as imperative endings, an optative marker -ι- or a subjunctive marker -ω-/-η-) and therefore has to be indicative. Second, on the basis of its *secondary endings*, the hearer will interpret the form as referring to the past.[14] In other words, the past tense meaning is not coded in a direct way but only by the *combination* of (1) the unmarked (indic.) mood and (2) secondary endings. The augment as a specialized past-marking morpheme helps the hearer to identify the form as a past tense in a straightforward way. The Homeric augment can thus be characterized as an optional deictic element with the function of *highlighting* for the hearer that the state of affairs is located in the past.[15]

---

augment is that it goes back to a PIE distal deictic (first spatial and then temporal?) adverb or proclitic particles *$h_1e$(-) "there, then," of which relics can be also found in ἐ-κεῖνος and ἐ-χθές (Eva Tichy, *Indogermanistisches Grundwissen: Grundwissen für Studierende sprachwissenschaftlicher Disziplinen*, 3rd ed. (Bremen: Hempen, 2009), 126; Robert S. P. Beekes and Lucien van Beek, *Etymological Dictionary of Greek*, IEED 10 (Leiden: Brill, 2010), 397, 1632. An alternative view is given by Andreas Willi, "Of Aspects, Augments, Aorists–Or How to Say to Have Killed a Dragon," in *Greek and Latin from an Indo-European Perspective*, ed. Coulter H. George (Cambridge: Cambridge Philological Society, 2007), 34–48, who explains the augment on the basis of a reduplication *$h_1e$-$h_1$- of roots with initial *$h_1$-.

13  Note that there are also forms (such as the 1st and 2nd pl. indic.) that are simply ambiguous without the augment.

14  Note that the secondary endings alone are not enough to identify a form as a past tense since secondary endings also occur in the optative mood.

15  Cf. Chantraine's characterization of the augment: "L'augment était, du point de vue indo-européen, un mot accessoire que l'on préposait à un indicatif à désinences secondaires *pour marquer plus nettement le sens passé*." ["The augment was, from an Indo-European point of view, an accessory word that one placed before an indicative with secondary endings *to mark the past meaning more clearly*."] (*Grammaire Homérique, I: Phonétique et morphologie* [Paris: Klincksieck, 1958³], 479 [emphasis mine].) It should be noted that the

The need to emphatically mark out past time reference is dependent on the discourse context. In contexts in which there is a shift toward past time, the augment will tend to be used in order to help the hearer in keeping track of the shift in temporal reference. In contexts in which past time reference is already contextually given by other means, the augment can be omitted.

In direct discourse, speakers tend to refer to the *present* world surrounding the interlocutors, or to the *future*, predicting what will happen or indicating what should happen.[16] When the speaker wishes to refer to a past state of affairs relevant to the current speech situation, this temporal shift tends to be signaled explicitly by using an augmented verb. In narrative, on the other hand, the

---

augment already had lost much of its original function by Homer's time: the fuzziness of the distributional rules shows that the occurrence of the augment is also determined by metrical factors. The distributional tendencies can therefore only be regarded as *traces* of the augment's older distribution. The semantic change from Homeric to Classical Greek can be seen as a form of generalization and bleaching. The augment becomes obligatory on all secondary indicative forms and it develops semantically from a marker *highlighting* past time reference to a *neutral* past tense marker. The introduction of the augment brings Ancient Greek into alignment with the typological tendency for past tenses to be the morphologically marked category with respect to the (often morphologically unmarked) present tense (see, e.g., Östen Dahl, *Tense and Aspect Systems* [Oxford: Blackwell, 1985], 117).

16    For example, if you look at the first 100 finite verbs in direct speech in the *Iliad*, only 14 refer to *past* states of affairs (13 aor. indic. and 1 impf.), while 31 forms (pres., pfs.) refer to *present* states of affairs and 55 refer to (possible) *future* states of affairs (futs., impvs., subjunctives, cupitive optatives). This is a ratio very typical of what Émile Benveniste (*Problèmes de linguistique générale*, vol. 1. [Paris: Gallimard, 1966], 238–43) calls *discours* (vs. *histoire*). The relevance of Benveniste's distinction between *discours* and *histoire* to the function of the augment is also noted by Louis Basset ("L'augment et la distinction discours/récit dans l'*Iliade* et l'*Odyssée*," in *Études homériques: Séminaire de recherche*, ed. Michel Casevitz [Lyon: Maison de l'Orient méditerranéen, 1989], 9–16). In my typology of the modes of discourse (see Rutger J. Allan, "Towards a Typology of the Narrative Modes in Ancient Greek: Text Types and Narrative Structure in Euripidean Messenger Speeches," in *Discourse Cohesion in Ancient Greek*, ed. Stéphanie J. Bakker and Gerry C. Wakker, ASCP 16 [Leiden: Brill, 2009], 171–203 and idem, "History as Presence: Time, Tense and Narrative Modes in Thucydides," in *Thucydides between History and Literature*, ed. Antonis Tsakmakis and Melina Tamiolaki, TiCSup 17 [Berlin: de Gruyter, 2013], 371– 89) direct discourse is classified as Discursive Mode (distinct from the Immediate/Displaced Diegetic Mode and the Descriptive Mode).

need to signal past time reference is less strong: once the narrator has entered into the past story world, it is unnecessary to continually mark every event as being anterior to speech time. The tendency to omit the augment in narrative is in accordance with the cross-linguistic tendency that narrative forms are morphologically unmarked.[17]

The absence of the augment with imperfects in -σκ- can be explained in a similar way. Habitual-iterative imperfects typically serve as a background to main (narrative) events. This means that there is no need to separately mark their anteriority to speech time since they are already temporally linked to a foreground event.[18] In the same way, ἐπεί-clauses are temporally anchored to the main clause and do not need a separate tense marking.

The tendency for the augment to be absent with negated aorists can be explained by the fact that negated aorists (often combined with πω) often do not locate an event at a specific moment in the past. They typically express that an event did not take place at any time anterior to speech time. The deictic relation between the speaker's deictic center and the temporal location of the state of affairs is therefore rather diffuse.[19]

The occurrence of the augment in speech introductions can be accounted for by the need to indicate the location in time especially at those moments in which the narrator switches from the narrative

---

17  Cf. Dahl's observation: "More common than marking narrative context, however, is not marking them—quite a considerable number of languages use unmarked verb forms in narrative contexts" (Dahl, *Tense and Aspect Systems*, 113). According to Dahl, there are languages that only mark past tense in nonnarrative contexts (ibid., 119).

18  See also Frederick J. Pagniello, "The Past-Iterative and the Augment in Homer," *IF* 112 (2007): 105–23. By the same token, the less frequent occurrence of the augment in impfs. (as compared to aors.) observed by Chantraine, can be explained by the fact that impf. verbs typically express background events temporally linked (i.e., simultaneous) to a main narrative event. Another factor that might be relevant is the fact that habitual-iteratives do not refer to one specific moment in time: the deictic relation between the deictic center (speech time) and the reference time is more diffuse.

19  An example of a negated aor. not referring to a specific moment in the past is: οὐ γάρ πω τοίους ἴδον ἀνέρας οὐδὲ ἴδωμαι (Hom. *Il.* 1.262) ("For I have not seen such men since, nor will I ever see.").

world to the embedded world referred to by the speech of the character and vice versa.[20]

The fact that gnomic aorists show a strong tendency to have the augment is more difficult to explain. A classic example of the gnomic aorist is:

(2) ῥεχθὲν δέ τε νήπιος ἔγνω (Hom. *Il.* 17.32)
Once a thing has been done, a fool understands it.

The gnomic aorist derives its name from its use in γνῶμαι such as these, but it occurs in various types of generic statements such as Homeric similes and descriptions of procedures.[21] The status of the gnomic aorist in the Ancient Greek verbal system has been (and still is) a hard nut to crack. The issue of the gnomic aorist

---

20 I should note here that I have some doubts about the significance of the statistics concerning the occurrence of the augment in speech introductions and conclusions. Speech introductions are generally highly formulaic lines. The occurrence of the augment is bound to be strongly determined by metrical convenience. The significance of the numbers of instances is distorted by the fact that the *token* frequency is so much higher than the *type* frequency. E.g., ἠμείβετο occurs 78 times but only in three different formulas, ἀμείβετο occurs 19 times but in six different formulas and twice in a nonformulaic line. On the basis of the *type* frequency we may even conclude that the unaugmented form is more frequent and less determined by formulaic considerations. Another reason to have suspicions about the use of the augment in speech introductions is the complete absence of an unaugmented variant in highly frequent compound verbs such as προσέειπε (171x) and προσέφη (214x). The simple verbs, however, do show formal variation (ἔειπε: εἶπε; ἔφη: φῆ) without any significant correlation between augments and speech introductions. The suspicious absence of unaugmented variants to προσέειπε and προσέφη could be accounted for by assuming that the poets replaced the older *unaugmented* forms *π(ρ)οτίϝειπε, and *π(ρ)οτιφᾶ in formulas by the augmented metrical equivalents προσέειπε and προσέφη.

21 For descriptions of the gnomic aor., see Kühner and Gerth, *Ausführliche Grammatik,* 158–63; Schwyzer and Debrunner, *Griechische Grammatik,* 283–86; Chantraine, *Grammaire Homérique,* 185–87; Ruijgh, "τε épique," 255–65; Kenneth L. McKay, "Aspectual Usage in Timeless Contexts in Ancient Greek," in *In the Footsteps of Raphael Kühner: Proceedings of the International Colloquium in Commemoration of the 150th Anniversary of the Publication of Raphael Kühner's Ausführliche Grammatik der griechischen Sprache, II. Theil: Syntaxe, Amsterdam, 1986,* ed. Albert Rijksbaron, Hotze A. Mulder, and Gerry C. Wakker (Amsterdam: Gieben, 1988), 193–208; Rijksbaron, *Syntax and Semantics,* 31–33; Bakker, "Pointing to the Past," "Similes," and *Pointing at the Past.*

revolves around two questions that should be kept separate as much as possible:

> (1) Why is a *perfective* form (aorist) used to express a generic state of affairs?
>
> (2) Why is a *past tense* form used to express a generic state of affairs?

(1) That a generic meaning is expressed by a perfective form is a relatively rare phenomenon from a cross-linguistic point of view. However, in his typological survey of generic expressions, Dahl did find some exceptions to the typical link between generics and imperfective aspect. Dahl points to generic perfectives in a number of Slavic languages used in opposition to imperfective generics, and he observes that the same aspectual distinction is upheld in generics as in the rest of the aspectual system.[22]

A similar phenomenon seems to play a role in Ancient Greek: the gnomic aorist shows the same usage types as the aorist elsewhere. It can be used, for example, to express a completed, ingressive or complexive meaning.[23] Consider example (3):

> (3) ἄλλῳ μὲν γὰρ ἔδωκε θεὸς πολεμήϊα ἔργα,
> ἄλλῳ δ' ὀρχηστύν, ἑτέρῳ κίθαριν καὶ ἀοιδήν,
> ἄλλῳ δ' ἐν στήθεσσι τιθεῖ νόον εὐρύοπα Ζεὺς
> ἐσθλόν, τοῦ δέ τε πολλοὶ ἐπαυρίσκοντ' ἄνθρωποι,
> καί τε πολέας ἐσάωσε, μάλιστα δὲ καὐτὸς ἀνέγνω. (Hom. *Il.*
> 13.730–34)
> God gives one man skill in battle, and to another he
> gives dancing, and to a third the playing of the lyre
> and song: and in another man's breast wide-seeing

---

22  Östen Dahl, "The Marking of the Episodic/Generic Distinction in Tense-Aspect Systems," in *The Generic Book*, ed. Gregory N. Carlson and Francis Jeffry Pelletier (Chicago: University of Chicago Press 1995), 420.

23  See, e.g., Kühner and Gerth, *Ausführliche Grammatik*, 161; McKay, "Aspectual Usage in Timeless Contexts,"193–208; Rijksbaron, *Syntax and Semantics*, 31–33; Bary, "Aspect in Ancient Greek," 20–21, 131–32, 175; Wakker, "Gnomic Aorist."

> Zeus puts wisdom, which brings benefit to many men
> and is the saving of many too, as he knows best of all.[24]

McKay explains the aorist ἔδωκε in l. 730 as expressing a completed action; the present τιθεῖ he explains as distributive and general; the other present and aorist forms (ἐπαυρίσκοντ᾿, ἐσάωσε, ἀνέγνω) should, according to McKay, also be accounted for in terms of *process vs. completeness*.[25]

In the terminology of Cognitive Grammar, the choice between perfective or imperfective aspect in generic expressions can be seen as a choice between two *construals*. Construal is a central notion in Cognitive Grammar that refers to our ability as speakers to portray the same situation in alternative ways. A linguistic expression does not only evoke a particular conceptual content, it always also involves a specific way of *construing* the conceptual content: the level of *specificity* at which a situation is described, the element in the situation which is *focused* on, which elements are presented as more prominent (foregrounded), and which elements are viewed as less salient (backgrounded).[26]

Aspectual differences can be described as differences in construal: the aspects differ in the way in which a situation is viewed. More specifically, the aspects differ in the particular portion of the event that is focused ("zoomed in") on. The aorist (perfective) aspect imposes a scope of view on the event such that it includes one or both boundaries of the event, while the present (imperfective) aspect imposes a temporal scope that *excludes* the boundaries of the event.[27]

The contrast between a gnomic aorist and a generic present can also be described in terms of construal. The gnomic aorist focuses the attention on the fact that each individual instance (subevent) out of all potential iterations is *bounded*. For example, in ἄλλῳ μὲν γὰρ ἔδωκε θεὸς πολεμήϊα ἔργα (l. 730) (lit.: "to another the god gave battle skills"), the aorist signals that each individual *instance* of the act of giving is viewed as bounded.

---

24  The translation is taken from Homer, *The Iliad*, trans. Martin Hammond (Harmondsworth: Penguin, 1987).

25  McKay, "Aspectual Usage in Timeless Contexts," 198.

26  For a general discussion of construal, see Ronald W. Langacker, *Cognitive Grammar: A Basic Introduction* (Oxford: Oxford University Press, 2008), 3–89.

27  For construal and aspect in Ancient Greek, see also Allan, "Imperfect Unbound."

In the second way of construal—involving a generic present (i.e., imperfective aspect)—, the speaker defocuses ("zooms out") from the individual subevents and conceptualizes the series of subevents as a higher-order macroevent. The speaker does not wish to be specific about the internal structure of the subevents but construes the chain of subevents as a macroevent without initial or final boundaries: the open-ended chain of iterations is regarded as holding for an unbounded span of time.[28] In ἄλλῳ δ' ἐν στήθεσσι τιθεῖ νόον εὐρύοπα Ζεὺς / ἐσθλόν (l. 732-33) ("and in another man's breast wide-seeing Zeus puts wisdom"), for example, the present (imperfective) aspect conveys that the series of iterations extends indefinitely into the past and into the future.

Even though the imperfective aspect seems the natural option to express a generic state of affairs, it is important to realize that aspect marking is unnecessary to mark the utterance as generic. The semantic feature of genericity is always also inherent in the generic subject (or other argument) of the clause "humankind," "a fool," "horses," etc. In Homer, furthermore, genericity is often explicitly marked by the presence of the particle τε ("epic τε"). In other words, because the generic meaning is also conveyed by other elements of the clause, aspect morphology can be employed freely to express subtle aspectual distinctions.

In fact, the gnomic aorist is not the only generic expression in Greek where we find aspectual variation. There are several other generic and iterative expressions in which the aorist stem readily occurs, e.g., (1) the generic-iterative subjunctive (with ἄν), (2) the iterative optative, and (3) the iterative use of the secondary indicative with ἄν (ἄν iterativum, e.g., ἤτησ' ἄν "he asked repeatedly"). In these constructions, the perfective (aorist) aspect is used to signal that each of the individual subevents is viewed as bounded. In other words, these expressions refer to iterations of *bounded* subevents.

Also interesting in this respect are Homeric forms with the suffix -σκ-ε/ο- built on aorist stems, e.g., δόσκεν "he would give" and

---

28  Even though there seems to be a considerable freedom to choose between a gnomic aor. and a generic pres., an important factor influencing the speaker's choice seems to be the inherent *Aktionsart* of the verb: the gnomic aor. occurs with verbs that are inherently telic, while generic statements with atelic verbs tend to be expressed with a (generic) pres.

στρέψασκον "they would turn" (both in *Il.* 18.546).[29] These formations show a complex hierarchical scope relation between aspectual marking and iterative marking. In these hybrid formations, the
aorist stem (δο-/στρέψα-) signals that each individual subevent is
bounded (completed), the suffix -σκ- indicates that the subevent is
iterated, and the imperfective endings express that the subevents
constitute a chain (macroevent) that is construed as *unbounded*.
In the typical case, the chain of iterated state of affairs is construed
as unbounded in order to present it as a temporal framework in
which another state of affairs occurs.

These various constructions make it clear that genericity and
iterativity should not be seen as an inherent meaning of the present stem. The usual association between genericity/iterativity and
imperfective (present) aspect in Greek should instead be explained
by the speaker's choice to *construe* a chain of iterated events (macroevent) as an *unbounded* (ongoing) macroevent. However, a speaker
also has the alternative option to construe a chain of iterated events
as *bounded* by marking it with an aorist.[30] For example,

(4) [Men should not even punish slaves in anger.]
πολλάκις γὰρ καὶ δεσπόται ὀργιζόμενοι μείζω κακὰ <u>ἔπαθον</u> ἢ
<u>ἐποίησαν</u>. (Xen. *Hell.* 5.3.7)
For also masters in anger <u>have</u> often <u>suffered</u> greater
harm than they <u>have inflicted</u>.

This use of the aorist is sometimes called the empiric aorist.
The reason to construe this iterative state of affairs as bounded is to
view it holistically as a fact based on past experience in order to use
it as an argument to make a claim about the present.[31] The iterated
state of affairs, furthermore, does *not* function as a temporal framework to another past state of affairs.

These deviations from the pattern *iterative/generic meaning-
imperfective aspect* demonstrates that aspect marking is in fact independent from iterative or generic semantics. Instead, it can be

---

29 See Chantraine, *Grammaire Homérique*, 324–25.
30 See also Ronald W. Langacker, *Grammar and Conceptualization*, CLR 14 (Berlin: Mouton de Gruyter, 2000), 247–49, who calls this type of construal a
*higher-order perfective*.
31 Cf. Rijksbaron, *Syntax and Semantics*, 33 on the empiric aor.: "it is used in
utterances based on experience." I will return to the empiric aor. below.

employed freely by the speaker to conceptualize the state of affairs in a particular way.

(2) The second problem attached to the gnomic aorist concerns its apparent past tense morphology. This is the most thorny aspect of the gnomic aorist. How can a form normally used for past time reference be employed to refer to a generic state of affairs? In my view, to conclude that the aorist indicative *in general* is not a real past tense, as has been claimed by, for example, Rijksbaron and Bakker, is too radical.[32] If we follow this line of reasoning, we would also have to conclude that the *imperfect* is not a past tense either, since the imperfect frequently shows a nontemporal *modal* meaning, for example in counterfactual (irrealis) conditional sentences, in unrealizable wishes, and in the modal use of imperfects (without ἄν) such as ἐβουλόμην "I would like'" and ἔδει "it would be necessary." However, that the imperfect is not a past tense is never claimed, at least, not in the debate on Classical Greek aspect.[33]

How should we explain the presence of apparent past tense markers (augment plus secondary endings) in the gnomic aorist? This question can be approached from a synchronical and a historical point of view. The first thing to note is that, from a synchronical point of view, there is no doubt that the gnomic aorist is to be regarded as referring to the *present* time. This is shown by the fact that it always combines with subordinate clauses featuring the

32  See Albert Rijksbaron, "The Discourse Function of the Imperfect," in Rijksbaron, *In the Footsteps of Raphael Kühner*, 237–54; Egbert J. Bakker, "Verbal Aspect and Mimetic Description in Thucydides," in *Grammar as Interpretation: Greek Literature in its Linguistic Contexts*, ed. Egbert J. Bakker, MS 171 (Leiden: Brill, 1997), 7–54. A similar debate is going on with regard to Koine Greek: see Fresch (ch. 12 in this volume). I agree with Fresch's polysemy account: past time reference should be seen as the prototypical meaning of the aor. indic. while the gnomic aor. is a peripheral extension of the prototype (see also Rutger J. Allan, "The Historical Present in Thucydides. Capturing the Case of αἱρεῖ and λαμβάνει," in *The Historical Present in Thucydides: Semantics and Narrative Function*, ed. J. Lallot et al., ASCP 18 [Leiden/Boston: Brill, 2011], 38).

33  On the contrary, the impf. is often considered the only "true" past tense form. For example, Rijksbaron states that the impf. "unequivocally brings us to the past" (Rijksbaron, "Discourse Function of the Imperfect," 247) and Bakker: "Unlike the imperfect, then, the aorist does not by itself effect a displacement from the present to the past" (Bakker, "Verbal Aspect," 21).

(generic-iterative) *subjunctive*, never the optative.[34] Apparently, the possible tension between the presence of the augment and present time reference is overruled by the need to express aspectual distinctions.

For a synchronical approach, the theory of Cognitive Grammar and especially its treatment of grammatical categories may be helpful. In the framework of Cognitive Grammar, linguistic categories are seen as polysemous networks consisting of a *prototypical* (most central) meaning and its *extensions* (peripheral meanings). Cognitive grammar is a *usage-based* model: a speaker may—but need not— mentally extract an abstract core meaning (*abstract schema*) shared by the prototype and the extensions. In Langacker's usage-based approach, the extraction of an abstract schema is based on the perception of commonalities between repeated instances of language use. If there is no abstract schema, the category can be characterized as a network of family resemblances (cf. Wittgenstein's "Netz von Familieähnlichkeiten" ["network of family resemblances"]).[35]

In Cognitive Grammar terms, the past tense meaning is the prototypical meaning of the secondary aorist form, while the gnomic aorist is an extension from the prototype.[36] In a similar way, the counterfactual (irrealis) meaning of the past tense form can be analyzed as a semantic extension from its prototypical temporal meaning.[37] Such an approach to the issue has the advantage that it

---

34  See Kühner and Gerth, *Ausführliche Grammatik*, 160–61 and Wakker, "Gnomic Aorist in Hesiod." The iterative optative is used in subordinate clauses (instead of a generic-iterative subjunctive + ἄν), if the main clause refers to a habitual state of affairs in the *past* (see, e.g., Rijksbaron, *Syntax and Semantics*, 83).

35  For an introduction to the Cognitive Grammar approach to linguistic categorization, see Ronald W. Langacker, *Foundations of Cognitive Grammar, Vol. I: Theoretical Prerequisites* (Stanford: Stanford University Press, 1987), 369–408; John R. Taylor, *Linguistic Categorization*, OTLing (Oxford: Oxford University Press, 2003). In Rutger J. Allan, *The Middle Voice in Ancient Greek: A Study in Polysemy*, ASCP 11 (Amsterdam: Gieben, 2003), I analyzed the middle voice as a polysemous network category.

36  See also Wakker, "Gnomic Aorist" and Fresch, ch. 12 in this volume.

37  In Allan ("Historical Present," 38), I proposed (following Langacker's analysis of the English past tense; see *Foundations of Cognitive Grammar, Vol. II*, 242–46) to describe the abstract meaning of the secondary indicative form (i.e., subsuming its past time and counterfactual [irrealis] uses) as expressing deictic *distance* from the vantage point of the conceptualizer (speaker/ hearer): the event referred to by a secondary indicative is construed as *not*

acknowledges that not all the actual uses of the secondary indicative can be interpreted as referring to past time, while it does not
ignore the important observation that past time reference is by far
the most frequent use of the secondary indicative. In other words, a
Cognitive Grammar approach enables a synthesis of a temporal and
a nontemporal view of the Greek verbal tenses.

Cross-linguistically, genericity is typically expressed by the
present tense. However, genericity should not be seen as an inherent meaning of the present tense. The relationship between genericity and present tense can be explained in a different way. In a
typological study on generic expressions, Dahl concludes that, "the
most general statement that can be made about generics is indeed
that they are not overtly marked for tense and aspect, or alternatively, that they employ the least marked tense-aspect choice in the
language."[38]

Dahl calls this principle the Minimal Marking Tendency. In other words, that generics are expressed by the present tense in most
languages can be explained by the fact that in most language the
present tense is morphologically the least marked tense.

If we apply Dahl's Minimal Marking Tendency to (Homeric)
Greek, it turns out that the present indicative is not unequivocally
the least marked form. With many verbs, the aorist indicative is in
fact the least marked form; for example, aorist third singular ἔ-γνω
(two morphemes) vs. present γι-γνώ-σκ-ε-ι (five morphemes[39]); aorist ἥμαρτ-ε (three morphemes, including *augmentum temporale*) vs.
ἁμαρτ-άν-ε-ι (four morphemes). Conversely, other verbs have present indicative forms that are less marked than the aorist indicative,
e.g., στρέφ-ε-ι (three morphemes) vs. ἔ-στρεπ-σ-ε (four morphemes).
In other words, that both present indicative and the aorist indicative

---

*directly accessible* to the experience of the speaker and hearer. In the prototypical case, distance is interpreted in terms of *temporal* distance. In its
counterfactual use, on the other hand, the past tense form signals that the
event is located in a virtual world that is *epistemically* at a distance from the
actual reality surrounding the interlocutors. Similar to past and counterfactual events, the gnomic aor. does not refer to an actual, directly perceiv-
able, event but to a virtual event epistemically at a distance from reality.

38 Dahl, "Marking of the Episodic/Generic Distinction," 415.
39 I.e., [reduplication] - [root] - [σκ-suffix] - [thematic vowel] - [proximal deictic marker -ι-].

can be used to express generic states of affairs seems to be in accordance with the Minimal Marking Tendency.

There are, however, also *conceptual* aspects to genericity that explain that there is no exclusive link between genericity and the present tense. Genericity is a relatively complex conceptual domain, comprising a number of dimensions.[40] What is important in understanding the nature of generics is the idea that part of our knowledge of the world consists of generalizations about how we think the world is structured. These generalizations can be of a physical nature (laws of nature) or they may be based on established social practice.

A structural generalization is of a *virtual* character: it involves a *mental* construction of a generic event type. A generalization, however, also indirectly invokes *actual* instantiations (tokens) experienced in the *past*. The generalization is, after all, based on the observation of structural similarities between the actually experienced events. A structural generalization also has a *future* dimension: a generalization can be employed to project the occurrence of similar events in the future.

The complex temporal structure of genericity is reflected in the way it is coded in language. To highlight that the generic event type is part of the world's *present* structure and therefore currently relevant to the speaker, the present tense is used. In Greek as well as in many other languages, this is the most typical option. However, in order to emphasize the fact that the generalization was relevant from the point of view of a story character at a moment in the past, an imperfect can also be used even though its validity is not restricted to the past.[41]

> (5) ἐκεῖθεν δ' εὐθὺς ἐπισιτισάμενοι ἔπλευσαν εἰς Αἰγὸς ποταμοὺς ἀντίον τῆς Λαμψάκου· <u>διεῖχε</u> δ' ὁ Ἑλλήσποντος ταύτῃ σταδίους ὡς πεντεκαίδεκα. (Xen. *Hell.* 2.1.21)
> From there, as soon as they had provisioned, they sailed to Aegospotami, which is opposite Lampsacus,

---

40  My account of the conceptual structure of genericity is based on Ronald W. Langacker's analysis in "The English Present Tense," *ELL* 5 (2001): 251 and idem, *Investigations in Cognitive Grammar*, CLR 42 (Berlin: Mouton de Gruyter, 2009), 197–98.

41  More examples in Kühner and Gerth, *Ausführliche Grammatik*, 145–46.

the Hellespont at this point being about fifteen stadia
wide. (Brownson, LCL)

A speaker may also wish to highlight the predictive power of a
generalization, in which case a future tense or (in subordinate clauses) a general subjunctive (+ ἄν) can be used in Greek.[42] For example,

> (6) φαμὲν δὲ δὴ ὅτι ὁ ἐπιεικὴς ἀνὴρ τῷ ἐπιεικεῖ, οὗπερ καὶ
> ἑταῖρός ἐστιν, τὸ τεθνάναι οὐ δεινὸν ἡγήσεται. (Pl. *Resp.*
> 387d)
> We say that a decent man will not think that death is a
> terrible thing for another decent man whose friend he
> is.

The variety in tense-aspect marking of generic states of affairs
in Greek shows that genericity is not married to the present tense.
This observation also makes the occurrence of past tense morphology in the gnomic aorist less remarkable. The traditional explanation
of the past tense marking is, in my view, still the most satisfactory.
Traditionally, the past tense of the gnomic aorist is explained by the
idea that the gnomic utterance has evolved from a past time referring expression. This expression referred to a past state of affairs
with a strong implication that the individual past state of affairs
stands for a general pattern in the world.[43] Over time, the pragmatic
implicature of generality became stronger (while the feature of past
time reference became weaker) until eventually genericity became
part of the coded meaning (semanticized).

The so-called *empiric aorist* may possibly be the historical missing link between the past time and the generic meaning. The empiric aorist (also referred to as *aorist of experience*) is used to refer to
facts that are based on experience.[44] Consider the following examples from Smyth:[45]

---

42  More examples in Kühner and Gerth, *Ausführliche Grammatik*, 171–72. Cf.
    English "Water will boil at 100° Celsius."
43  See also Wakker, "Gnomic Aorist."
44  For the empiric aor., see Herbert W. Smyth, *Greek Grammar*, rev. Gordon M.
    Messing. (Harvard: Harvard University Press, 1956), §1930; Rijksbaron, *Syn-
    tax and Semantics*, 33.
45  Smyth, *Greek Grammar*, §1930.

(7) a. πολλοὶ πολλάκις μειζόνων ἐπιθυμοῦντες τὰ παρόντ'
ἀπώλεσαν. (Dem. Aristocr. 113)
people often <u>lose</u> what they have because they desire
for more

b. ἀλλὰ γὰρ ἀθυμοῦντες ἄνδρες οὔπω τρόπαιον <u>ἔστησαν</u> (Pl.
Critias 108c)
But the faint-hearted <u>have</u> never yet <u>set up</u> a victory
monument.[46]

c. Ἡ γλῶσσα πολλοὺς εἰς ὄλεθρον <u>ἤγαγεν</u>. (Men. Mon. 205)
The tongue <u>has brought</u> many men to ruin.

The aorists refer to states of affairs in the past. However, it is
strongly implied by the speaker that the experience based on these
past states of affairs is equally valid for the present and future.

Even if one does not accept the idea that the empirical aorist is in
some way historically related to the gnomic aorist, what the empiric
aorist *does* show is that a speaker may convey a generic message by
referring to a past state of affairs.[47]

## 3. THE HISTORICAL SEMANTIC DEVELOPMENT OF THE PERFECT

I turn to the second topic of this paper: the historical semantic development of the Greek perfect. Compared to the vast literature on
the *present : aorist* opposition, the Classical Greek perfect and its
diachronical development have received relatively little attention.[48]

---

46   The translation is taken from Plato, *Complete Works*, ed. John M. Cooper and
     D. S. Hutchinson (Indianapolis: Hackett, 1997).
47   Kühner and Gerth regard the terms "gnomisch" and "empirisch" simply as
     synonymous terminological alternatives (Kühner and Gerth, *Ausführliche
     Grammatik*, 159). For the difficulties of distinguishing the empiric from the
     gnomic aor. in some contexts, see Wakker, "Gnomic Aorist."
48   E.g., Jacob Wackernagel, "Studien zum griechischen Perfectum," *Programm
     zur akademischen Preisverteilung* (Göttingen, 1904), 3–24; Pierre Chantraine,
     *Histoire du parfait grec* (Paris: Champion, 1927); Martin Haspelmath, "From
     Resultative to Perfect in Ancient Greek," in *Nuevos estudios sobre construc-
     ciones resultativas*, ed. José Luis Iturrioz Leza, Función 11–12 (Guadalajara:
     Universidad de Guadalajara, 1992), 187–224; Christiaan M. J. Sicking and
     Peter Stork, *Two Studies in the Semantics of the Verb*; Yves Duhoux, *Le verbe
     grec ancien: Éléments de morphologie et de syntaxe historique*, BCLL 61 (Leuven:
     Peeters, 2000), 396–440; André Sauge, *Les degrés du verbe: Sense et formation*

The aim of this section is to provide a broad outline of the main diachronic semantic developments of the Greek perfect.

In the history of the Greek perfect, roughly three stages can be distinguished.[49]

---

*du parfait en grec ancien* (Bern: Lang, 2000); Eva-Carin Gerö and Arnim von Stechow, "Tense in Time: The Greek Perfect," in *Words in Time: Diachronic Semantics from Different Points of View*, ed. Regine Eckardt, Klaus von Heusinger, and Christoph Schwarze, TiLSM 143 (Berlin: Mouton de Gruyter, 2003), 251–94; Dag Haug, "From Resultatives to Anteriors in Ancient Greek: On the Role of Paradigmaticity in Semantic Change," in *Grammatical Change and Linguistic Theory: The Rosendal Papers*, ed. Thórhallur Eythórsson, LA 113 (Amsterdam: Benjamins, 2008), 285–305; Sander Orriens, "Involving the Past in the Present: The Classical Greek Perfect as a Situating Cohesion Device," in *Discourse Cohesion in Ancient Greek*, ed. Stéphanie Bakker and Gerry Wakker, ASCP 16 (Leiden: Brill, 2009), 221–39; Klaas Bentein, "Verbal Periphrasis in Ancient Greek. Cognitive and Diachronic Studies" (PhD diss., Universiteit Gent, 2012); Robert Crellin, "The Greek Perfect Active System: 200 BC–AD 150" (PhD diss., University of Cambridge, 2012); Arjan A. Nijk, "The Rhetorical Function of the Perfect in Classical Greek," *Phil* 157 (2013): 237–62; see also Crellin, ch. 14 in this volume. Sander Orriens (University of Groningen) is preparing a doctoral dissertation that aims to provide a detailed description of the diachronic development of the Greek pf. informed by grammaticalization theory.

49  Similar stages are distinguished by Bentein, *Verbal Periphrasis*, and Bentein, "Perfect," *EAGLL* 3:46–49. These three stages are in accordance with recent typological research on semantic shifts of perfect-like verbal categories. A groundbreaking typological study (not only with respect to the pf. but also more generally on the methodology of semantic spaces) is Lloyd B. Anderson, "The 'Perfect' as a Universal and Language-Specific Category," in *Tense-Aspect: Between Semantics and Pragmatics; Containing the Contributions to a Symposium on Tense and Aspect, held at UCLA, May 1979*, ed. Paul J. Hopper, TSL 1 (Amsterdam: Benjamins, 1982), 227–64. He observed a cross-linguistic diachronical path *result-state intransitive > current relevance intransitive > current relevance transitive > anterior perfective > past perfective*. Compare also Joan L. Bybee, Revere Perkins, and William Pagliuca, *The Evolution of Grammar: Tense, Aspect and Modality in the Languages of the World* (Chicago: The University of Chicago Press, 1994), 68–87, who propose a path *resultative > anterior > perfective/simple past*. The term *anterior* is used as an equivalent to *current relevance* perfect.

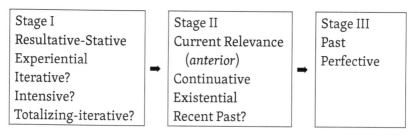

Figure 1. Semantic developments of the Greek Perfect

## 3.1 Stage I

The first stage is represented by the PIE and the Homeric perfect. Both in PIE and in Homeric Greek, the prototypical meaning of the perfect was to express a resulting state: the perfect designated that the subject was in a physical or mental state resulting from a prior event.[50] For example,

(8) Ἥρη τίπτε βέβηκας; (Hom. *Il.* 15.90)
Hera, why have you come?

It should be noted that the two semantic elements of the perfect are not on a par. The focus of the perfect is on the *present state*; the past event is only evoked *in the background* of the conceptualization.[51] The perfect *denotes* a present state, while it *presupposes* a past

---

50  According to Chantraine, (*Grammaire homérique*, 197), the Homeric pf. expressed an "état acquis" (an acquired state). The idea of an *acquired state* is roughly equivalent to the more recent notion of *resultative state*. Chantraine does use the term "parfait résultatif" but in a different sense, namely to refer to the pf. "qui exprime non l'état du sujet, mais le résultat qui porte sur l'objet et qui finira, au course de l'histoire du grec, à équivaloir à peu près à un aoriste emphatique" ["that expresses not the state of the subject but the result that bears on the object and that will eventually, in the course of the history of Greek, become more or less equivalent to an emphatic aorist."] (Chantraine, ibid., 199).

51  In Cognitive Grammar terminology, the present state is *profiled*, whereas the preceding event is part of the *conceptual base* (see Allan, "Imperfect Unbound"). An example from a different semantic domain illustrating the difference between profile and conceptual base is the word "uncle." This word not only evokes the conception of the person designated by uncle but it also encompasses as a conceptual base a network of kinship relations including the ego (a niece or nephew) and his or her parents (Langacker, *Foundations I*, 184–87).

event.[52] The anterior event, in other words, is seen as less relevant or even as completely irrelevant as compared to the present state of the subject.

It is sometimes claimed that the resultative meaning of the perfect only emerged after PIE and that the PIE perfect was still a purely stative formation.[53] There are several reasons to reject this view. Clackson points out that in most Indo-European languages the perfect has been reinterpreted as a tense with past reference and he rightly observes that "this shift to past reference offers support for the notion that the perfect originally referred to the state *following an action in the past*, and was not just a stative."[54]

A very old perfect like οἶδα (< *u̯oid -, cf. Skt. *véda*, Goth. *wait*) shows that the resultative meaning must go back to an early stage of PIE since already within PIE the resultative meaning *u̯oid-h₂e* "I have seen" (root *u̯eid-* "see") had developed into "know."

The resultative character of the PIE perfect can also be inferred from the fact that the perfect forms that can be reconstructed for PIE were built next to an unmarked (root) aorist.[55] Root aorists are morphologically unmarked in that they do not have an additional morpheme expressing aorist aspect. These morphologically *unmarked* aorist forms expressed a *change* of state (i.e., they had a telic lexical *Aktionsart*). Since the change of state meaning cannot be ascribed to a specific aorist morpheme, it means that the lexical semantics of the verbal root itself designated a change of state.[56] On the other

---

52  Cf. Sicking and Stork, *Two Studies in the Semantics of the Verb*, 160 and elsewhere.

53  See e.g., Stanley E. Porter, *Verbal Aspect in the Greek of the New Testament: With Reference to Tense and Mood*, SBG 1 (New York: Lang, 1989), 252; Andrew L. Sihler, *New Comparative Grammar of Greek and Latin* (Oxford: Oxford University Press, 1995), 564; Benjamin W. Fortson, *Indo-European Language and Culture: An Introduction*, BTL 19 (Oxford: Wiley-Blackwell, 2004), 95. For the PIE pf. as a resultative state, see Helmut Rix et al., *Lexikon der Indogermanischen Verben* (Wiesbaden: Reichert, 1998), 21; James Clackson, *Indo-European Linguistics: An Introduction*, CTL (Cambridge: Cambridge University Press, 2007), 121; Tichy, *Indogermanistisches Grundwissen*, 93; Michael Meier-Brügger, *Indogermanische Sprachwissenschaft*, 9th ed. (Berlin: de Gruyter, 2010), 391.

54  Clackson, *Indo-European Linguistics*, 121 (emphasis original).

55  This observation is based on the inventory of reconstructed pf. forms in Rix, *Lexikon der Indogermanischen Verben*, 21.

56  Cf. Clackson, ibid., 133–34.

hand, the perfect forms built from these roots *are* morphological-ly marked (reduplicated). The marked perfect expressed the state resulting from the change of state designated by the root. In other words, perfect morphology is used to turn the change of state mean-ing of the root into a resultative state. For example,

(9) PIE: Aorist change of state → Perfect resulting state

Aorist *$(h_1e\text{-})g^weh_2\text{-}t$ → Perfect *$g^we\text{-}g^woh_2\text{-}e$ "has "made a step, went"[57]     gone"[61]

Aorist *$(h_1e\text{-})g^wreh_3\text{-}t$ → Perfect *$g^we\text{-}g^worh_3\text{-}e$ "has "swallowed"[58]     swallowed"[62]

Aorist *$(h_1e\text{-})mn\text{-}to$ → Perfect *$me\text{-}mon\text{-}e$ "has in "brought into mind"[59]     mind"[63]

Aorist *$(h_1e\text{-})steh_2\text{-}t$ "stood → Perfect *$se\text{-}stoh_2\text{-}e$ up"[60]     "stands"[64]

Another indication that the PIE perfect was primarily *resulta-tive*-stative rather than just stative is the fact that there was also a

---

57  Cf. ἔβη, Skt. *ágāt.*

58  Cf. ἔβρως (h. Ap. 127); Skt. Vedic subj. *garan* "sollen verschlingen" (Rix et al., ibid., 189).

59  Cf. Skt. *ámata* (RV. 10,68,7) "hat an etw. gedacht" (Rix, *Lexikon der Indoger-manischen Verben*, 391). The gloss given by Rix is ambiguous as to a state or a change of state reading. However, the context of RV. 10,68,7 clearly points to a change of state meaning: "brought to mind," "remembered," "discovered."

60  Cf. ἔστη; Skt. *ásthāt.*

61  Cf. Hom. βεβάασι; Skt. opt. *jagāyāt* (RV. 10,28,1) "wäre gegangen" (Rix, *Lex-ikon der Indogermanischen Verben*, 183).

62  Cf. Hom. βεβρωκώς; Skt. *jagāra* "hat verschlungen" (Rix, *Lexikon der Indoger-manischen Verben*, 189).

63  Cf. μέμονα; Lat. *meminī.*

64  Cf. ἔσταμεν; Skt. *tastháu* "steht, hat sich gestellt" (Rix, *Lexikon der Indog-ermanischen Verben*, 536). Also pfs. such as δέδορκα "fix one's gaze", δείδω (δέδοικα) "be afraid", τέθηλα "be in bloom", εἴωθα "be wont" originally had an unmarked (root) aor. form (or a thematic aor. derived from a root aor.) that denoted a change of state (see Beekes, *Etymological Dictionary of Greek,* and Rix, *Lexikon der Indogermanischen Verben,* 536). This means that even though from a synchronical point of view these pfs. may seem to be purely stative, they are originally *resultative*-stative. A special case is εἴωθα as it possibly goes back to a compound *$sue\ d^heh_1\text{-}$ "put/make self'" (see Beekes, *Etymologi-cal Dictionary of Greek,* 395)

distinct stative category in PIE, with an e-vocalism in the root and a different set of endings.[65] Examples are:

(10) The Stative in PIE:
*$h_1éh_1s$-oi "he is seated" (cf. ἧσται, Hitt. ešar(ri)),
*$ḱéi$-oi "he lies"(cf. κεῖται, Skt. śáye),
*$u̯és$-toi "he is wearing" (cf. ἔστο, Skt. váste).

These stative verbs do not evoke a preceding event.

It is probable that the PIE resultative perfect had already developed an *experiential* meaning. The experiential perfect is used to express that a past event has had a persistent effect on the present in the form of the subject's knowledge or experience.[66] Evidence for the experiential perfect in PIE is the verb *$u̯oid$-$h_2e$ "I have seen" > "I know" which shows that the perfect has been interpreted as signaling that the subject acquired a lasting knowledge through previous perception. There are also cases of the experiential perfect in Homer. Ruijgh mentions the following example:[67]

(11) ἐγὼ δέ μιν αὐτὸς ὄπωπα,
καὶ γὰρ μνήμων εἰμί, πάϊς δ᾽ ἔτι νήπιος ἦα. (Hom. Od. 21.94)

---

65  See Tichy, *Indogermanistisches Grundwissen*, 96–97; Meier-Brügger, *Indogermanische Sprachwissenschaft*, 314, and Rutger J. Allan, "Stative (and Medium Middle) Verbs," *EAGLL* 3:316–18.

66  In the literature, the term experiential pf. is used in two different ways: (1) as expressing the subject's resulting experience/knowledge, and (2) as expressing "that a given situation has held at least once during some time in the past leading up to the present" (Bernard Comrie, *Aspect: An Introduction to the Study of Verbal Aspect and Related Problems*, CTL [Cambridge: Cambridge University Press, 1976], 58). These two types should be carefully distinguished from one another. The first type refers to the subject's mental state typically resulting from having perceived/experienced something (e.g., ὄπωπα "I have seen [and therefore know]") and it is therefore semantically related to the resultative pfs. of mental verbs (e.g., ἔγνωκα "I have understood, realized"). The other type does not necessarily involve the subject's mental state, e.g., "The Olympics have been in London twice before." The pf. does not pertain to the subject's resulting mental state in the present but should, in my view, by analyzed as a subtype of the current relevance pf.: It expresses that the occurrence(s) of a particular event in the past is somehow relevant to the speaker's present. I would assume that the latter type of experiential (or better: *existential*) pf. is a later development in the path of grammaticalization, connected to the emergence of the current relevance pf. I will return to the existential pf. later.

67  Ruijgh, "Valeurs temporelles", 208.

I <u>have seen</u> him myself and I remember him, though I was still a child.

Besides the resultative perfect and the related experiential meaning, there seem to be traces of other perfect meanings.[68] It is attractive to assume that the source meaning of the perfect form was to express iterativity. Cross-linguistically, reduplicated forms overwhelmingly expressed iterativity (no doubt a case of form-function iconicity), or otherwise their history can be traced back to an older stage of iterativity.[69] In Homeric Greek, there are still perfects with iterative meaning, which may be explained as relics of an older iterative meaning of the perfect. Many of these perfects express a repetitive sound, e.g., βέβρυχε "roar," κεκληγώς "scream, bark," μεμυκώς "bellow," πεπληγώς "strike, hit."[70]

Ruijgh also distinguishes a *totalizing-iterative* perfect ("*up-to-now perfect*") in Homer, e.g.,

---

68  I also regard as resultative examples such as μέσσῳ δ' ἐν σκοπέλῳ ἐστὶ σπέος ἠεροειδές,/ πρὸς ζόφον εἰς Ἔρεβος τετραμμένον ("Halfway up the cliff is a dark cave, turned west towards Erebos", Hom. *Od.* 12.81–82) where there is obviously no real event that has led to the existent state. This use of the resultative pf. can be seen as involving what is called "fictive motion." As Langacker puts it, in fictive motion, "cognitive operations inherent in the conception of spatial motion are applied to static scenes as a way of mentally accessing them" (Langacker, *Cognitive Grammar*, 529). An English example given by Langacker is: "An ugly scar runs from his elbow to his wrist." He also gives examples of the English pf. used in this way: "scattered villages" and "a detached garage." The villages have obviously never been clustered together and the garage has never been attached (ibid., 530). For the Greek pf. used to refer to fictive motion, see José Miguel Jiménez Delgado, José Miguel, and Rafael Martínez Vázquez, "Verbos de movimiento virtual en griego antiguo," *Emerita* 69 (2011): 277–300.

69  Bybee, Perkins, and Pagliuca, *Evolution of Grammar* (172), find cross-linguistic evidence that reduplicated formations start off as iteratives and eventually develop an intransitive-stative meaning. See also Bridget Drinka, "The Development of the Perfect in Indo-European: Stratigraphic Evidence of Prehistoric Areal Influence," in *Language Contacts in Prehistory: Studies in Stratigraphy*, ed. Hennning Andersen (Amsterdam: Benjamins, 2003), 77–105.

70  See Ruijgh, "Valeurs temporelles." I would also tentatively explain the following nonresultative/nonstative pfs. as going back to an old iterative meaning: ὄρωρει "arose (repeatedly)" (typically of sounds), πέποτηται "fly hither and thither" (the pf. intensifies the iterative meaning of ποτάομαι?), πέπορδα "fart" (repetitive sound).

(12) ὢ πόποι, ἦ δὴ μυρί᾽ Ὀδυσσεὺς ἐσθλὰ ἔοργε ... νῦν δὲ
τόδε μέγ᾽ ἄριστον ἐν Ἀργείοισιν ἔρεξεν. (Hom. Il. 2.272–74)
Oh yes, Odysseus <u>has done</u> thousands of fine things
before now.... But this now is far the best thing he <u>has
done</u> among the Argives. (Hammond, LCL)

According to Ruijgh, the perfect ἔοργε in l. 272 refers to the totality of the series of iterative actions, while the aorist ἔρεξεν refers to
the most recent single action.

Another function that is cross-linguistically strongly associated with reduplication is *intensification*.[71] In Homer (as well as in
Classical Greek), we find perfects that traditionally have been interpreted as intensive perfects. The intensive perfect is used with
verbs of which the lexical semantics is already stative. The intensive
perfect denotes "the highest degree of that state."[72] Synchronically,
the intensive meaning can be explained by assuming that the stative
meaning of the perfect doubles and therefore reinforces the stative
semantics of the verb. Homeric examples are: βέβριθα "be heavy,"
ἔολπα "hope," μέμηλε "concern, trouble," ὄδωδα "smell," τέθηλα "be
in full bloom." Classical example are: ἥγημαι "be firmly convinced,"
πεφόβημαι "be terrified," σεσιώπηκα "maintain complete silence,"
τεθαύμακα "be surprised."[73] It is tempting to see the intensive perfect as a relic of an older stage in which the perfect expressed
intensification.[74]

---

71 See Terry Regier, *A Preliminary Study of the Semantics of Reduplication*, Technical Report TR-94-019 (Berkeley, CA: International Computer Science Institute, 1994) and Sharon Inkelas, "Non-concatenative Derivation: Reduplication," in *The Oxford Handbook of Derivational Morphology*, ed. Rochelle
   Lieber and Pavol Štekauer (Oxford: Oxford Univeristy Press, 2014), 169–89.
   Regier hypothesizes that intensification may have been the missing link between iterativity and the *completion* meaning of the Indo-European pf.
72 Rijksbaron, *Syntax and Semantics*, 38.
73 For the intensive pf., see Kühner-Gerth, *Ausführliche Grammatik*, 148–49;
   McKay, "Use of the Perfect", 6; Ruijgh, "τε épique", 249 and "Valeurs temporelles", 211; Duhoux, *Verbe grec ancien*, 414–16; Sauge, *Degrés du verbe*;
   Rijksbaron, *Syntax and Semantics*, 38. Chantraine (*Histoire*, 17) denies the
   existence of a distinct intensive pf. Sicking and Stork (*Two Studies in the Semantics of the Verb*, 169) analyze these pfs. as referring to an *inalterable* state.
74 For the historical connection between iterativity/intensification and the pf.,
   see also Drinka, "Development of the Perfect."

## 3.2 Stage II

The second stage starts roughly after Homer. The most important change is the emergence of the *current relevance perfect* or *anterior*.[75] Bybee, Perkins, and Pagliuca define anteriors as: "An anterior signals that the situation occurs prior to reference time and is relevant at reference time."[76]

Crucial to this semantic change is the creation of *transitive* perfects, which fill up a gap in the verbal system. Already in the seventh and the beginning of the sixth century forms like δέδωκε "has given" (Tyrtaeus) and τετίμακ(ε) "has honored" (Sappho) make their appearance. But in the second half of the fifth century and especially in the fourth century the frequency of these transitive perfects (often built with -κ-) rapidly increases.[77] The newly built transitive perfects are still *subject-oriented*.[78]

The semantic shift connected to these new perfects can be explained well in terms of *the Invited Inferencing Theory of Semantic Change* (IITSC).[79] The role of pragmatic inferencing in the diachronical process of subjectification is demonstrated by Traugott in many of her studies on grammaticalization. According to Traugott's IITSC, semantic change occurs when pragmatic implicatures that arise

---

75  Haspelmath, "From Resultative to Perfect"; Simon R. Slings, "Geschiedenis van het perfectum in het oud-Grieks," in *Nauwe betrekkingen: Voor Theo Janssen bij zijn vijftigste verjaardag*, ed. Ronny Boogaart and Jan Noordegraaf (Amsterdam: Stichting Neerlandistiek VU, 1994), 239–47; Haug, "From Resultatives to Anteriors."

76  Bybee, Perkins, and Pagliuca, *Evolution of Grammar*, 54.

77  See Cornelis J. Ruijgh, "Over de gebruikswijzen van het Griekse perfectum: Met speciale aandacht voor Plato's *Politeia*," *Lampas* 37 (2004): 24–45.

78  Wackernagel, "Studien zum griechischen Perfectum," and Chantraine, *Histoire du parfait grec*, have argued that transitive pfs. in Classical Greek came to express the resulting state of the grammatical *object* (object-resultative): "Le parfait exprime bien encore un état; mais ce n'est plus l'état du sujet, c'est celui de l'objet" ["The perfect does still express a state; but it is not the state of the subject: it is the state of the object."] (Chantraine, ibid., 122). However, McKay ("Use of the Perfect" and "On the Perfect and Other Aspects in the Greek Non-literary Papyri," *BICS* 27 [1980]: 23–49) has demonstrated convincingly that this view is untenable and that the pf. continued to be subject-oriented throughout Classical and Hellenistic Greek (see also Porter, *Verbal Aspect*, 273–81).

79  Elizabeth Closs Traugott and Richard B. Dasher, *Regularity in Semantic Change*, CSL 97 (Cambridge: Cambridge University Press, 2002).

in specific contexts become conventionalized as part of the coded meaning.[80]

The process of semantic change starts off when an individual speaker uses a word or grammatical form ad hoc in a new context of use. In the case of the perfect, a speaker experiments by creating a new perfect form of an agentive transitive verb.[81] By using the perfect in a new context, i.e., with an agentive transitive verb, the perfect cannot be interpreted by the hearer in the usual way, that is, as a signal that the subject is in a certain psychological or physical state as a result of a prior event. The speaker invites the hearer to interpret the subject's prior action as otherwise relevant to the current speech situation. By repeated use of this implicature by other speakers and with other verbs it eventually became a new conventional meaning of the perfect form: the *current relevance perfect*. The older resultative-stative meaning, however, did not disappear.[82]

A typical interpretation of these new transitive perfects is that the subject is construed as somehow still responsible (accountable) for his or her past action.[83] Examples (13) and (14), taken from Rijksbaron,[84] illustrate this meaning:

(13) a. Κρ. φής, ἦ καταρνῇ μὴ <u>δεδρακέναι</u> τάδε;
Αν. καὶ φημὶ <u>δρᾶσαι</u> κοὐκ ἀπαρνοῦμαι τὸ μή. (S. *Ant.* 442–43)
Kreon: "Do you admit or deny that you <u>are guilty</u> of these actions?"
Antigone: "I admit that I <u>did</u> them and I do not deny it."
b. <u>Γέγραφε</u> δὲ καὶ ταῦτα ὁ αὐτὸς Θουκυδίδης Ἀθηναῖος (Th. 5.26.1)

---

80  See ibid., 34–40; Paul J. Hopper and Elizabeth Closs Traugott, *Grammaticalization*, 2nd ed., CTL (Cambridge: Cambridge University Press 2003), 71–98.

81  The new form δέδωκε might have been created after the proportional analogy πέποται : πέπωκε = δέδοται : X (>> δέδωκε) (see Ruijgh, "Over de gebruikswijzen," 32.

82  When new meanings emerge, older meanings often continue to exist. The coexistence of older and newer meanings is called layering (Hopper and Traugott, *Grammaticalization*,126–27).

83  See McKay, "Use of the Perfect"; Duhoux, *Verbe grec ancien*, 416–17; Rijksbaron, *Syntax and Semantics*, 36–37.

84  Ibid.

Of this too the same Thucydides of Athens is the author.

(14)

| | |
|---|---|
| ὤμοσα "I swore an oath" | vs. ὀμώμοκα "I am under oath" |
| ἀπέκτεινα "I killed" | vs. ἀπέκτονα "I am (someone's) murderer" |
| ἠδίκησα "I committed a crime" | vs. ἠδίκηκα "I am guilty of a (number of) crime(s)" |

In (13a.), Kreon uses a perfect because what he wants to hear is that Antigone admits she is *guilty* of having buried her brother. Antigone, however, replies with an aorist. She does admit that she performed the actions but she denies that she can be presently held guilty of them. In (13b.), Thucydides emphasizes his role as the author and his responsibility for his activity as historian.[85]

The emergence of the current relevance meaning of the perfect can be described as a form of *subjectification*: the *objective* (event-oriented) mental or physical property of the subject has bleached away and is replaced by the *subjective* (speaker-oriented) feature of current relevance.[86]

A use of the perfect that can be regarded as a subtype of the current relevance perfect is the *existential* perfect, characterized by Comrie as expressing "that a given situation has held at least once

---

85  More examples can be found in McKay, "Use of the Perfect."

86  Subjectification is a notion from cognitive linguistics referring to a frequent type of diachronical semantic change. Subjectification is described by Langacker as "a gradual process of progressive attenuation," in which "an objective relationship fades away, leaving behind a subjective relationship that was originally immanent in it" (Ronald W. Langacker, "On Subjectification and Grammaticalization," in *Discourse and Cognition: Bridging the Gap*, ed. Jean-Pierre Koenig [Stanford: CSLI, 1998], 75). The objective physical or mental property of the grammatical subject fades away and the subjectively construed (i.e., completely dependent on the speaker's judgment) element of current relevance remains. For subjectification, see also Traugott and Dasher, *Regularity in Semantic Change*. The role of subjectification in the history of the English pf. is addressed by Kathleen Carey, "Subjectification and the Development of the English Perfect," in *Subjectivity and Subjectivisation*, ed. Dieter Stein and Susan Wright (Cambridge: Cambridge University Press, 1995), 83–102. In Allan, "History of the Future," the semantic development of the Greek fut. is described as a form of subjectification.

during some time in the past leading up to the present."[87] An example of the existential perfect given by Gerö and von Stechow is:[88]

(15) σκέψασθε δὲ ... ζητοῦντες εἴ τις ἐμοὶ καὶ Ἐρατοσθένει
ἔχθρα πώποτε γεγένηται πλὴν ταύτης. (Lys. 1.43)
Consider ... asking yourselves whether any enmity <u>has</u>
ever <u>arisen</u> before this between me and Eratosthenes.

Whether any enmity has arisen in the past between the speaker and his victim Eratosthenes is highly relevant for the speaker's current situation. He is charged for the murder of Eratosthenes and tries to convince the judges that there had not been any hostility between him and his victim until his victim seduced his wife.

In Classical Greek, we also find cases of the *continuative perfect* (or *perfect of persistent situation*). An example is:

(16) τό τε σιδηροφορεῖσθαι τούτοις τοῖς ἠπειρώταις ἀπὸ τῆς
παλαιᾶς λῃστείας <u>ἐμμεμένηκεν</u>· (Th. 1.5.3)
[A]nd the custom of carrying arms <u>is still kept up</u>
among these continentals, from the old piratical
habits.[89]

The perfect expresses that the event started in the past and continued into the present.[90]

With Ruijgh, I do not assume a distinct *perfect of recent past* in Classical Greek (*pace* Slings and Bentein).[91] Perfects combined with adverbs such as ἄρτι and νεωστί can be explained otherwise, either as (1) *resultative* or *experiential* perfects: the subject has entered a

87  Comrie, *Aspect*, 58.
88  Gerö and von Stechow, "Tense in Time," 237.
89  The translation is from Crawley, revised by Strassler in *The Landmark Thucydides: A Comprehensive Guide to the Peloponnesian War* (New York: Simon & Schuster, 1998).
90  See also Ruijgh, "Valeurs temporelles", 209-10 (who calls it the totalizing-continuative use of the pf.). The example is also discussed by McKay, "Use of the Perfect," 12. This continuative pf. can also be negated, expressing that something has not occurred up until the present, e.g., Demosthenes, *Philip.* 1.9: κατεστήσαμεν τηλικοῦτον ἡλίκος οὐδείς πω βασιλεὺς γέγονε Μακεδονίας ("We made him greater than any king of Macedonia has ever been"). The "perfect of persistent situation" is also discussed by Sicking and Stork, *Two Studies in the Semantics of the Verb*, 158.
91  See Ruijgh, "Over de gebruikswijzen," 36; Slings, "Geschiedenis van het perfectum"; Bentein, "Verbal Periphrasis."

certain (mental) state as a result of a recent event, or as (2) *current relevance* perfects: recent events are more likely to be currently relevant than events that occurred in the more distant past. As Ruijgh points out, the ancient Stoic grammarians paraphrased the value of the perfect πεποίηκα ("I have done") with ἐποίησα$_{AOR}$ ἄρτι ("I have just done").[92] The grammarians' native intuition may be based on the high frequency of this particular use of the perfect in everyday conversation.

## 3.3 Stage III

In the final stage, a new meaning of the perfect emerges in which there is no reference to the present time: the perfect came to be used as a past perfective tense very similar to the aorist indicative.[93] There is much debate about the period in which this development took place. Chantraine points to a number of Classical instances in which, according to him, the perfect had already approximated the aorist and came to be used for "affective" purposes.[94] Chantraine's view, however, has not gained much support. McKay and Porter have argued that the change did not occur until the fourth or fifth centuries AD.[95] Duhoux gives an example of the perfect used as a past tense in John (17:7-8) and he argues that the evolution of the perfect into a past tense had been completed in the second century AD.[96] Crellin (ch. 14 in this volume) gives examples from Revelation and Matthew. In his handbook on the history of Greek, Horrocks sees signs of a functional merger of the perfect and aorist already

---

92  Ruijgh, "Valeurs temporelles," 208.

93  This type of semantic change is cross-linguistically very frequent (Haspelmath, "From Resultative to Perfect"; Bybee, Perkins, and Pagliuca, *Evolution of Grammar*, 81–87). It can be seen as a process of semantic bleaching and subjectification: The semantic feature of a *state/current relevance* at speech time fades away. Speech time now only functions as a temporal vantage point to view the past event. The pf. gradually shifts from denoting a present state towards denoting a past event. Note that the older meanings from Stage I and II did not immediately disappear but remained in existence alongside the novel past perfective meaning.

94  Chantraine, *Histoire du parfait grec*, 184–89.

95  McKay, "Use of the Perfect" and "On the Perfect", 23; Porter, *Verbal Aspect*, 273.

96  Duhoux, *Verbe grec ancien*, 430–31.

in the language of Menander, but unfortunately he does not give an example of this functional merger.[97]

If we consider the various semantic extensions throughout the history of the Greek perfect, the question arises as to whether it is possible to assign an abstract core meaning (abstract schema) to the perfect form, a semantic feature that is present in all different varieties of the perfect category. An obvious candidate to serve as a core meaning is *stativity*. Stativity indeed appears to be present in many semantic varieties of the perfect. However, it is questionable whether the current relevance meaning can still be described as being stative. Take an example like (15b): To what extent is Thucydides in a particular mental or physical state as a result of his having written the *Histories*? Isn't it somewhat stretching the concept of stativity too much to call cases such as these also stative? Whatever your answer to this question may be, stativity cannot be taken as the core meaning of the perfect for another reason as well: from the aorist-like past tense meaning that finally emerged, the feature of stativity is clearly absent.

Perhaps the most attractive alternative is to take *current relevance* as the feature that subsumes most of the semantic variants of the perfect. One could maintain that the current relevance meaning is already present as a side effect in the older resultative-stative meaning. After all, when a subject is currently in a mental or physical state resulting from a prior event, this present state can be said to be (by definition) also currently relevant. But again, taking current relevance as the abstract core meaning of the perfect shatters if we also want to include into its abstract definition its final development into a past tense form.

Now, what happens if we would accept that the Greek perfect does not have a core meaning? In that case, we would have to conclude that the perfect is best analyzed as a chain of related meanings, a polysemous network of family resemblances, a complex layering of variant meanings that resulted from a long historical process of semantic extensions.

---

97 Geoffrey Horrocks, *Greek: A History of the Language and Its Speakers*, 2nd ed. (Chichester: Wiley-Blackwell, 2010), 131–32, 154, 176–78.

## 4. CONCLUSION

In this paper, two grammatical topics were addressed that show a considerable change throughout the history of Ancient Greek: the augment and the perfect. I argued that the puzzling distribution of the augment in Homer can best be approached by analyzing the augment as a means to highlight that the state of affairs is located in the past. The need to highlight past reference is dependent on the discourse context. I also argued that the semantic development of the perfect can be described as a polysemous chain of semantic extensions. Whether or not there is an abstract core meaning shared by all semantic extensions is a difficult question that still lacks a definitive answer.

In the last decades, the Greek aspect system and, more specifically, the augment and the perfect, have been the objects of intense scholarly debate. The coming years will undoubtedly also see the birth of a host of publications on these subjects. One of the developments that has, in my view, considerably contributed to a better understanding of the peculiarities of the Ancient Greek system is our increased knowledge of tense-aspect systems across the languages of the world. However, there is also an area of the study of Classical Greek tense and aspect where unfortunately relatively little progress has been made: the performance of large-scale corpus studies of particular grammatical phenomena such as the augment or the perfect. Analyses are still too often based on a limited set of standard examples that are used and reused by one scholar after another. Large corpus studies are dearly needed to give a new impulse to long-lasting debates.

## BIBLIOGRAPHY

Allan, Rutger J. "The Historical Present in Thucydides: Capturing the Case of αἱρεῖ and λαμβάνει." Pages 37–67 In *The Historical Present in Thucydides: Semantics and Narrative Function*. Edited by J. Lallot, Albert Rijksbaron, Bernard Jacquinod, and Michel Buijs. ASCP 18. Leiden: Brill, 2011.

———. "History as Presence: Time, Tense and Narrative Modes in Thucydides." Pages 371–89 in *Thucydides between History and Literature*. Edited by Antonis Tsakmakis and Melina Tamiolaki. TiCSup 17. Berlin: de Gruyter, 2013.

————. "The History of the Future: Subjectification and Semantic Change in Ancient Greek Future Expressions." In *The Greek Future and its History*. Edited by Rutger J. Allan, Frédéric Lambert, and Theodore Markopoulos. Leuven: Peeters, forthcoming.

————. "The Imperfect Unbound: A Cognitive Linguistic Approach to Greek Aspect." In *Language Variation and Change: Tense, Aspect and Modality in Ancient Greek*. Edited by Klaas Bentein, Mark Janse, and Jorie Soltic. Leiden: Brill, forthcoming.

————. *The Middle Voice in Ancient Greek: A Study in Polysemy*. ASCP 11. Amsterdam: Gieben, 2003.

————. "Stative (and Medium Middle) Verbs." *EAGLL* 3:316–18.

————. "Towards a Typology of the Narrative Modes in Ancient Greek: Text Types and Narrative Structure in Euripidean Messenger Speeches." Pages 171–204 In *Discourse Cohesion in Ancient Greek*. Edited by Stéphanie J. Bakker and Gerry C. Wakker. ASCP 16. Leiden: Brill, 2009.

Anderson, Lloyd B. "The 'Perfect' as a Universal and Language-Specific Category." Pages 227–64 in *Tense-Aspect: Between Semantics and Pragmatics; Containing the Contributions to a Symposium on Tense and Aspect, held at UCLA, May 1979*. Edited by Paul J. Hopper. TSL 1. Amsterdam: Benjamins, 1982.

Bakker, Egbert J. "Discourse and Performance: Involvement, Visualization, and 'Presence' in Homeric Poetry." *ClAnt* 12 (1993): 1–29.

————. *Poetry in Speech: Orality and Homeric Discourse*. Myth and Poetics. Ithaca: Cornell University Press, 1997.

————. *Pointing at the Past: From Formula to Performance in Homeric Poetics*. Hellenic Studies 12. Washington, DC: Center for Hellenic Studies, 2005.

————. "Pointing to the Past: Verbal Agreement and Temporal Deixis in Homer." Pages 50–65 in *Euphrosyne: Studies in Ancient Epic and Its Legacy in Honor of Dimitris N. Maronitis*. Edited by John N. Kazazis and Antonios Rengakos. Stuttgart: Steiner, 1999.

————. "Similes, Augment, and the Language of Immediacy." Pages 1–23 in *Speaking Volumes: Orality and Literacy in the Greek and Roman World*. Edited by Janet Watson. MS 218. Leiden: Brill, 2001.

————. "Verbal Aspect and Mimetic Description in Thucydides." Pages 7–54 in *Grammar as Interpretation: Greek Literature in its Linguistic Contexts*. Edited by Egbert J. Bakker. MS 171. Leiden: Brill, 1997.

Bary, Corien L.A. "Aspect in Ancient Greek: A Semantic Analysis of the Aorist and Imperfective." PhD diss., Nijmegen: Radboud University, 2009.

Basset, Louis. "L'augment et la distinction discours/récit dans l'Iliade et l'Odyssée." Pages 9–16 in *Études homériques: Séminaire de recherche*. Edited by Michel Casevitz. Lyon: Maison de l'Orient méditerranéen, 1989.

Beekes, Robert S. P., and Lucien van Beek. *Etymological Dictionary of Greek*. IEED 10. Leiden: Brill, 2010.

Bentein, Klaas. "Perfect." *EAGLL* 3:46–49

———. . "Verbal Periphrasis in Ancient Greek: Cognitive and Diachronic Studies." PhD diss., Universiteit Gent, 2012.

Benveniste, Émile. *Problèmes de linguistique générale*. Vol. 1. Paris: Gallimard, 1966.

Bybee, Joan L., Revere Perkins, and William Pagliuca. *The Evolution of Grammar: Tense, Aspect and Modality in the Languages of the World*. Chicago: The University of Chicago Press, 1994.

Carey, Kathleen. "Subjectification and the Development of the English Perfect." Pages 83–102 in *Subjectivity and Subjectivisation: Linguistic Perspectives*. Edited by Dieter Stein and Susan Wright. Cambridge: Cambridge University Press, 1995.

Chantraine, Pierre. *Grammaire Homérique, II: Syntaxe*. Paris: Klincksieck, 1953.

———. *Histoire du parfait grec*. Paris: Champion, 1927.

Clackson, James. *Indo-European Linguistics: An Introduction*. CTL. Cambridge: Cambridge University Press, 2007.

Comrie, Bernard. *Aspect: An Introduction to the Study of Verbal Aspect and Related Problems*. CTL. Cambridge: Cambridge University Press, 1976.

Crellin, Robert. "The Greek Perfect Active System: 200 BC–AD 150." PhD diss., University of Cambridge, 2012.

Dahl, Östen. "The Marking of the Episodic/Generic Distinction in Tense-Aspect Systems." Pages 412–25 in *The Generic Book*. Edited by Gregory N. Carlson and Francis Jeffry Pelletier. Chicago: University of Chicago Press, 1995.

———. *Tense and Aspect Systems*. Oxford: Blackwell, 1985.

Drewitt, J. A. J. "The Augment in Homer." *ClQ* 6 (1912): 44–59, 104–20.

Drinka, Bridget. "The Development of the Perfect in Indo-European: Stratigraphic Evidence of Prehistoric Areal Influence." Pages 77–105 in *Language Contacts in Prehistory: Studies in Stratigraphy*. Edited by Hennning Andersen. Amsterdam: Benjamins, 2003.

Duhoux, Yves. *Le verbe grec ancien: Éléments de morphologie et de syntaxe historiques*. BCLL 61. Leuven: Peeters, 1992

Fleischman, Suzanne. "Imperfective and Irrealis." Pages 519–51 in *Modality in Grammar and Discourse*. Edited by Joan L. Bybee and Suzanne Fleischman. TSL 32. Amsterdam: Benjamins, 1995.

Fortson, Benjamin W. *Indo-European Language and Culture: An Introduction*. BTL 19. Oxford: Wiley-Blackwell, 2004.

Gerö, Eva-Carin and Arnim von Stechow. "Tense in time: The Greek Perfect." Pages 251–94 in *Words in Time: Diachronic Semantics from Different Points of View*. Edited by Regine Eckardt, Klaus von Heusinger, and Christoph Schwarze. TiLSM 143. Berlin: Mouton de Gruyter, 2003.

Haspelmath, Martin. "From Resultative to Perfect in Ancient Greek." Pages 187–224 in *Nuevos estudios sobre construcciones resultativas*. Edited by José Luis Iturrioz Leza. Función 11–12. Guadalajara: Universidad de Guadalajara, 1992.

Haug, Dag. "From Resultatives to Anteriors in Ancient Greek: On the Role of Paradigmaticity in Semantic Change." Pages 285–305 in *Grammatical Change and Linguistic Theory: The Rosendal Papers*. Edited by Thórhallur Eythórsson. LA 113. Amsterdam: Benjamins, 2008.

Hettrich, Heinrich. *Kontext und Aspekt in der altgriechischen Prosa Herodots*. Göttingen: Vandenhoeck & Ruprecht, 1976.

Hewson, John and Vit Bubenik. *Tense and Aspect in Indo-European Languages: Theory, Typology, Diachrony*. AST 135. Amsterdam: Benjamins, 1997.

Homer. *The Iliad*. Translated by Martin Hammond. Harmondsworth: Penguin, 1987.

Hopper, Paul J., and Elizabeth Closs Traugott. *Grammaticalization*. 2nd ed. CTL. Cambridge: Cambridge University Press, 2003.

Horrocks, Geoffrey. *Greek: A History of the Language and Its Speakers*. 2nd ed. Chichester: Blackwell, 2010.

Inkelas, Sharon. "Non-concatenative Derivation: Reduplication." Pages 169–189 in *The Oxford Handbook of Derivational Morphology*. Edited by Rochelle Lieber and Pavol Štekauer. Oxford: Oxford University Press, 2014.

James, Deborah. "Past Tense and the Hypothetical: A Cross-linguistic Study." *StudLang* 6 (1982): 375–403.

Jiménez Delgado, José Miguel, and Rafael Martínez Vázquez. "Verbos de movimiento virtual en griego antiguo." *Emerita* 69 (2011): 277–300.

Kühner, Raphael and Bernhard Gerth. *Ausführliche Grammatik der griechischen Sprache: 2. Teil; Satzlehre*. 2 vols. Hanover: Hahnsche Buchhandlung, 1898-1904.

Langacker, Ronald W. *Cognitive Grammar: A Basic Introduction*. Oxford: Oxford University Press, 2008.

———. "The English Present Tense." *ELL* 5 (2001): 251-72.

———. *Foundations of Cognitive Grammar*. Vol. I: *Theoretical Prerequisites*. Stanford: Stanford University Press, 1987.

———. *Foundations of Cognitive Grammar*. Vol. II: *Descriptive Application*. Stanford: Stanford University Press, 1991.

———. *Grammar and Conceptualization*. CLR 14. Berlin: Mouton de Gruyter, 2000.

———. *Investigations in Cognitive Grammar*. CLR 42. Berlin: Mouton de Gruyter, 2009.

———. "On Subjectification and Grammaticalization." Pages 71-89 in *Discourse and Cognition: Bridging the Gap*. Edited by Jean-Pierre Koenig. Stanford: CSLI, 1998.

McKay, Kenneth L. "Aspectual Usage in Timeless Contexts in Ancient Greek." Pages 193-208 in *In the Footsteps of Raphael Kühner: Proceedings of the International Colloquium in Commemoration of the 150th Anniversary of the Publication of Raphael Kühner's Ausführliche Grammatik der griechischen Sprache, II. Theil: Syntaxe, Amsterdam, 1986*. Edited by Albert Rijksbaron, Hotze A. Mulder, and Gerry C. Wakker. Amsterdam: Gieben, 1988.

. "On the Perfect and Other Aspects in the Greek Non literary Papyri." *BICS* 27 (1980): 23-49.

———. "The Use of the Perfect down to the Second Century A.D." *BICS* (1965): 1-21.

Meier-Brügger, Michael. *Indogermanische Sprachwissenschaft*. 9th ed. Berlin: de Gruyter, 2010.

Moser, Amalia. "The Changing Relationship of Tense and Aspect in the History of Greek." *STUF* 61 (2008): 5-18.

Mumm, Peter-Arnold. "Zur Funktion des homerischen Augments." Pages 148-58 in *Analecta homini universali dicata: Arbeiten zur Indogermanistik, Linguistik, Philologie, Politik, Musik und Dichtung; Festschrift für Oswald Panagl zum 65. Geburtstag*. Edited by Thomas Krisch, Thomas Lindner, and Ulrich Müller. SAG 421. Stuttgart: Heinz, 2004.

Napoli, Maria. *Aspect and Actionality in Homeric Greek: A Contrastive Analysis*. Materiali linguistici 54. Milan: FrancoAngeli, 2006.

Nijk, Arjan A. "The Rhetorical Function of the Perfect in Classical Greek." *Phil* 157 (2013): 237-62.

Orriens, Sander. "Involving the Past in the Present: The Classical
    Greek Perfect as a Situating Cohesion Device." Pages 221–39
    in *Discourse Cohesion in Ancient Greek*. Edited by Stéphanie
    Bakker and Gerry Wakker. ASCP 16. Leiden: Brill, 2009.
Pagniello, Frederick J. "The Homeric Augment: A Deictic Particle." PhD
    diss., University of Georgia, 2002.
———. "The Past-Iterative and the Augment in Homer." *IF* 112
    (2007): 105–23.
Plato. *Complete Works*. Edited by John M. Cooper and D. S. Hutchinson.
    Indianapolis: Hackett, 1997.
Platt, Arthur. "The Homeric Augment." *JPh* 19 (1891): 211–37.
Porter, Stanley E. *Verbal Aspect in the Greek of the New Testament: With
    Reference to Tense and Mood*. SBG 1. New York: Lang, 1989.
Regier, Terry. *A Preliminary Study of the Semantics of Reduplication*.
    Technical Report TR-94-019. Berkeley, CA: International
    Computer Science Institute, 1994.
Rijksbaron, Albert. "The Discourse Function of the Imperfect." Pages
    237–54 in *In the Footsteps of Raphael Kühner: Proceedings of
    the International Colloquium in Commemoration of the 150th
    Anniversary of the Publication of Raphael Kühner's Ausführliche
    Grammatik der griechischen Sprache, II. Theil: Syntaxe,
    Amsterdam, 1986*. Edited by Albert Rijksbaron, Hotze A.
    Mulder, and Gerry C. Wakker. Amsterdam: Gieben, 1988.
———. *The Syntax and Semantics of the Verb in Classical Greek: An
    Introduction*. 3rd ed. Chicago: The University of Chicago
    Press, 2006.
Rix, Helmut, Martin Kümmel, Thomas Zehnder, Reiner Lipp, and
    Brigitte Schirmer. *Lexikon der Indogermanischen Verben*.
    Wiesbaden: Reichert, 1998.
Ruijgh, Cornelis J. *Autour de "τε épique": études sur la syntaxe grecque*.
    Amsterdam: Hakkert, 1971.
———. "L'emploi 'inceptif' du thème du présent du verbe grec:
    Esquisse d'une théorie de valeurs temporelles des thèmes
    temporels." *Mnemosyne* 38 (1985): 1–61.
———. "Les valeurs temporelles des formes verbales en grec ancien."
    Pages 197–217 in *The Function of Tense in Texts*. Edited by
    Jadranka Gvozdanović and Theo A. J. M. Janssen. Amsterdam:
    North-Holland, 1991
———. "Over de gebruikswijzen van het Griekse perfectum:
    Met speciale aandacht voor Plato's *Politeia*." *Lampas* 37
    (2004): 24–45.

Ruipérez, Martín S. *Estructura del sistema de aspectos y tiempos del verbo griego antiguo: Análisis funcional sincrónico.* Salamanca: Consejo Superior de Investigaciones Científicas, 1954.

Sauge, André. *Les degrés du verbe: sens et formation du parfait en grec ancien.* Bern: Lang, 2000.

Schwyzer, Eduard and Albert Debrunner. *Griechische Grammatik: Auf der Grundlage von Karl Brugmanns* Griechischer Grammatik, Zweiter Band; Syntax und Syntaktische Stilistik. *HAW 2. Munich: Beck, 1950.*

Sicking, Christiaan M.J. "The Distribution of Aorist and Present Tense Stem Forms in Greek, Especially in the Imperative." *Glotta* 69 (1991): 14–43, 154–70.

Sicking, Christiaan M.J and Peter Stork. *Two Studies in the Semantics of the Verb in Classical Greek.* MS 160. Leiden: Brill, 1996.

Sihler, Andrew L. *New Comparative Grammar of Greek and Latin.* Oxford: Oxford University Press, 1995.

Slings, Simon R. "Geschiedenis van het perfectum in het oud-Grieks." Pages 239–47 in *Nauwe betrekkingen: Voor Theo Janssen bij zijn vijftigste verjaardag.* Edited by Ronny Boogaart and Jan Noordegraaf. Amsterdam: Stichting Neerlandistiek VU, 1994.

Smyth, Herbert W. *Greek Grammar.* Revised by Gordon M. Messing. Harvard: Harvard University Press, 1956.

Strassler, Robert B. *The Landmark Thucydides: A Comprehensive Guide to the Peloponnesian War.* New York: Simon & Schuster, 1998.

Sweetser, Eve and Barbara Dancygier, *Mental Spaces in Grammar: Conditional Constructions.* CSL. Cambridge: Cambridge University Press, 2005.

Taylor, John R. *Linguistic Categorization.* OTLing. Oxford: Oxford University Press, 2003.

Tichy, Eva. *Indogermanistisches Grundwissen für Studierende sprachwissenschaftlicher Disziplinen.* 3rd ed. Bremen: Hempen, 2009.

Traugott, Elizabeth Closs and Richard B. Dasher. *Regularity in Semantic Change.* CSL 97. Cambridge: Cambridge University Press, 2002.

Wackernagel, Jacob. "Studien zum griechischen Perfectum." *Programm zur akademischen Preisverteilung.* Göttingen, 1904.

Wakker, Gerry C. "The Gnomic Aorist in Hesiod." In *Language Variation and Change: Tense, Aspect and Modality in Ancient Greek.* Edited by Klaas Bentein, Mark Janse, and Jorie Soltic. Leiden: Brill, forthcoming.

Willi, Andreas. "Of Aspects, Augments, Aorists-Or How to Say to Have Killed a Dragon." Pages 34–48 in *Greek and Latin from an Indo-*

*European Perspective*. Edited by Coulter H. George. Cambridge: Cambridge Philological Society, 2007.

Xenophon. *Hellenica*. Translated by Carleton L. Brownson. 2 vols. LCL. Cambridge: Harvard University Press, 1918–1921.

CHAPTER 4

# Aspect-Prominence, Morpho-Syntax, and a Cognitive-Linguistic Framework for the Greek Verb

NICHOLAS J. ELLIS

BIBLEMESH

## 1. INTRODUCTION

I am privileged to contribute this chapter on the basic linguistic framework for the Greek verb.[1] My task will be to set out clearly the aspect-prominence of the Greek language, propose a morpho-syntactical system that is coherent with this aspect prominence, and examine the cognitive-linguistic implications of this system.

## 1.1 Opening Illustration: Matthew 2:20

First, let us consider a question that arises from the Greek text of Matthew 2:20:

---

1   While I was privileged to present this paper at the 2015 Cambridge Verb Conference, I can hardly claim this chapter as exclusively my own research. Fundamental to the argument has been the work performed by myself, Mark Dubis and Michael Aubrey under the auspice of the BibleMesh Greek Readings project (www.biblemesh.com/biblemesh-biblical-languages). Our work in turn has been seminally influenced by the thought of Stephen Levinsohn and Randall Buth, with significant contributions by way of conversations with Christopher Fresch and Steve Runge. Many other contributors to this book have influenced our thinking in one way or another. We are therefore indebted to the ongoing conversation stimulated by this growing community of linguists, philologists, and biblical scholars.

ἐγερθεὶς παράλαβε τὸ παιδίον καὶ τὴν μητέρα αὐτοῦ καὶ
πορεύου εἰς γῆν Ἰσραήλ· <u>τεθνήκασιν γὰρ οἱ ζητοῦντες</u> τὴν
ψυχὴν τοῦ παιδίου.

"Arise and take the child and His mother, and go into
the land of Israel; for <u>those who were seeking the
child's life have died</u>."[2]

In the phrase τεθνήκασιν γὰρ οἱ ζητοῦντες τὴν ψυχὴν τοῦ παιδίου, we
find the substantival participle οἱ ζητοῦντες. Traditionally, ζητοῦντες
would be labeled a "present participle." But is there anything in the
semantics of this term that justify this nomenclature? As we can see
quite plainly, there can be no "present time," for logically those who
"have died" (τεθνήκασιν) can not now be "searching" (ζητοῦντες) for
the child at the time of the speech act. Indeed, the seekers are dead!
Moreover, neither can there be "contemporaneous time," as would
typically be taught, given that the searching necessarily occurred
prior to dying. Rather, something else fundamentally seems to be
in view here, guiding the choice of the verb. In what follows, we
will examine how the Greek verbal system matches structure with
function, and suggest a nomenclature that matches this structural
framework better than the traditional nomenclature.

## 1.2 The Traditional Approach

As any beginning Greek student will know, the standard approach
to describing the morphological possibilities of the Greek verb are
the six principle parts: present (I), future (II), aorist (III), perfect
(IV), perfect middle (V) and aorist passive (VI). The fundamental
observation about this system is that it provides a descriptive, organizational, and therefore cognitive framework for the Greek system
that is based on tense-prominence, prioritizing the present tense
within the indicative mood.

I will argue in what follows that this framework is fundamentally flawed. It fails to reflect the essential organizational principles behind Greek morpho-syntax and semantic prominence. I will
argue that Greek, as an aspect-prominent language, is primarily
oriented along a three-part aspect morphology rather than tense

---

2    All translations are the author's own.

morphology. Recognizing this simple prototypical structure and reflecting it in our descriptive language has significant implications for both exegesis and pedagogy.

## 2. VERBAL PROMINENCE: AN OVERVIEW

First of all, let us consider what we mean by "verbal prominence." Languages tend to emphasize one of three verbal parameters: tense, aspect, or mood.[3] Thus, some languages are tense prominent, other languages are aspect prominent, and still others are mood prominent.[4] In the section that follows, let us examine a brief definition of these categories.

### 2.1 Introduction to Tense

Tense includes a number of nuanced variables across languages, but generally speaking tense provides a temporal frame for an event. *Tense* is concerned with a situation's *relative location in time*, usually in terms of being in the *past, present,* or *future*. Consider, in English, how tense is portrayed in example 1 below:

> a. "Your mother was reading a book." (past time)
> b. "Your mother is reading a book." (present time)
> c. "Your mother will be reading a book." (future time)

In the three sentences of example 1, the speaker adopts the moment of speaking as his reference point (as is typically the case). Taking that moment as his reference point, we see three tense choices that the speaker might make as he expresses the relative time of the verbal event of the mother reading a book. The speaker's choice of a tense (past, present, or future) is, indeed, a choice. It should be noted that, while the above three sentences represent a default

---

3   There are, of course, a number of other grammatical categories related to the verb, including voice, subject agreement, and in some languages, gender, transitivity, causativity, and even object agreement. The typology we present here is oriented around tense, aspect, and mood. Linguists have recognized that these three categories are closely related (so much so that they are often simply referred to with the abbreviation TAM).

4   This typology is based on D. N. S. Bhat, *The Prominence of Tense, Aspect, and Mood* (Amsterdam: Benjamins, 1999). Bhat's work has been found to be an effective typology for a large variety of languages.

description of time, the speaker might for some practical reason choose to use a different tense and create a mismatch between the historical event and his description of the event. For example, the speaker could have framed a past event with a present tense verb-form for heightened effect: "so yesterday, your mother is reading a book, and she sees this huge spider..." In this case, the speaker's reference point is not the speaker's own time of speaking but instead the past time in which the mother has her experience. Even though the speaker is describing a *past* event, the speaker uses *present* tense verbs. This is an example of what we mean when we say that tense is a "choice." Although the speaker could have used the past-tense verbs "read" and "saw," instead the speaker uses "is reading" and "sees." Greek speakers can make similar tense choices.[5]

## 2.2 Introduction to Aspect

If we have a clear mental picture of tense (which, as English speakers, we likely do), then what about aspect? Chris Thomson has provided in this volume a very good summary on the history of the aspectual discussion, so I will keep these comments brief.[6] Broadly speaking *aspect* is concerned with a situation's *internal structure*, usually in terms of being *bounded (self-contained)* or *unbounded (uncontained)*. Rather than denoting a situation's location in time, aspect is concerned with an event's internal temporal structure, or to put it another way, the manner and extent to which time unfolds within a situation.

English utilizes two aspects: these have been described using the terms *perfective aspect* and *imperfective* (or "*progressive*") *aspect*. Take example 2, below:

a. Jane ate an entire box of chocolates.
b. Jane was eating an entire box of chocolates.

---

5    Note the pragmatic use of the so-called "historical present", as described by Elizabeth Robar, "Historical Present" (ch. 10 in this volume); cf. Steven E. Runge, "The Verbal Aspect of the Historical Present Indicative in Narrative," in *Discourse Studies and Biblical Interpretation: A Festschrift in Honor of Stephen H. Levinsohn*. ed. Steven E. Runge (Bellingham, WA: Logos Bible Software, 2011), 191–224.

6    Christopher J. Thomson, "What is Aspect?: Contrasting Definitions in General Linguistics and New Testament Studies," ch. 2 in the present volume.

If the term *aspect* was foreign to you before, perhaps you can intuit its meaning from the above example. The clause in example (2a) is in the so-called *perfective aspect*. The perfective aspect presents an event as self-contained. The entire event, with its initiation and conclusion, are presented as a single whole with no reference to anything that happened between the initiation and the conclusion of the event. The "historical Jane" might have paused from eating the chocolates, called her mother, and then resumed eating the chocolates, but as far as the presentation of the event's aspect in (2a) is concerned, this is irrelevant. When a speaker chooses to present an event using perfective aspect, all that matters is the claim "This happened."

On the other hand, in example (2b) the so-called *imperfective aspect* conveyed by "was eating" communicates a different choice in portraying the event. The English past progressive form assumes that an event has begun but makes no reference to its conclusion. In the case of Jane and her box of chocolates, Jane might still be eating them now, or she might have never finished eating the box of chocolates. The English progressive does not say anything about a conclusion. It leaves the event entirely open-ended. It simply describes the action as in progress. In the linguistic literature, the terms, *"self-contained"* and *"open-ended,"* used to describe *perfective* and *imperfective* aspect, are often referred to as *bounded* and *unbounded*, respectively.[7]

Similarly, the Greek verb can utilize perfective and imperfective aspect to describe the inner workings of an event or action, or a third aspect to convey a past event that displays ongoing relevance. We will examine these categories in greater depth in what follows.

## 2.3 Introduction to Mood

The category of mood is a little more complicated than tense and aspect. As our concern here is primarily on the distinction between tense/aspect, note a few illustrative examples. In English, mood is expressed through auxiliary or helping verbs.[8] Consider example 3:

---

7    Bernard Comrie, *Aspect: An Introduction to the Study of Verbal Aspect and Related Problems*, (Cambridge: Cambridge University Press, 1976), 3–4.

8    These are often called *helping verbs* in primary and secondary English grammar texts but reference grammars prefer the term *auxiliary*. For a stu-

a. Actuality:     He landed at Heathrow rather late.

b. Probability:   She *might* arrive home by dinner if traffic is good.

c. Permission:    You *may* substitute asparagus for the baked potato.

d. Ability:       He *can* type 50 words per minute.

English modal auxiliary verbs can also express functions such as possibility, necessity, and obligation. For our current purposes, note that mood functions in a language to express a range of expressions, from describing a factual event (so-called *realis*), to describing something that is extrafactual (so-called *irrealis*). This *irrealis* category can express a possibility (e.g., "might," "could") or obligation (e.g., "should," "must"). Greek has four moods: indicative (a *realis* mood used for statements/questions), the *irrealis* imperative (used for commands), subjunctive, and optative moods (expressing probability and possibility, respectively).

# 3. THE GRAMMATICAL PROMINENCE OF TENSE, ASPECT, AND MOOD

As already noted, languages have a tendency to give greater prominence to one of the three: tense, aspect, or mood. This is critical to understand since Greek and English operate differently in this respect. In what follows, we will argue that English is tense prominent, and Greek is aspect prominent.

Before we examine what "grammatical prominence" means, it is important to emphasize what it does *not* mean. It does *not* mean that the prominent category (whether tense, aspect, or mood) is dominant to the exclusion of the other two categories. It also does not mean that one category is more important than the other two, or that the other two become irrelevant. That is not how grammatical prominence works. Rather, grammatical prominence involves the extent to which one of these categories provides the primary or central concept for

---

dent-oriented discussion of mood in English, see Rodney Huddleston and Geoffrey K. Pullum, *A Student's Introduction to English Grammar* (Cambridge: Cambridge University Press, 2005), 53–56.

how a particular verbal system is arranged. The prominent category functions as a sort of organizing principle for the other two categories. For example, there is a close relationship between tense and mood: because mood deals closely with the certainty of an event, it should not be surprising that there are correlations between a clause referring to the past (tense) and that clause also being more certain in its existence (mood). In other words, if something has already happened, it is pretty certain! The same can be said of a future event (tense) being *less* certain (mood) since a future event has not yet happened. Similarly, a completed (and thus "bounded") event (aspect) is more real (mood) than an incomplete event. Bhat shows how these three categories provide an interconnected system for organizing language and for assigning verbal prominence to one of these categories.[9] Visually, we could represent this typology of possible verbal prominence in languages as a triangle, with tense, aspect, and mood each representing a corner.

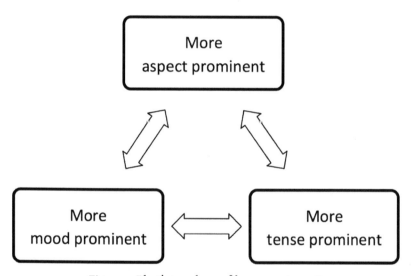

Figure 1. Bhat's typology of language types[10]

So what criteria do linguists use when classifying a language as tense prominent, aspect prominent, or mood prominent? Most

9   Bhat, *Prominence*, 93–94.
10   Adapted from Michael Aubrey, "The Greek Perfect and the Categorization of Tense and Aspect" (MA thesis, Trinity Western University, 2014), 137.

of these criteria involve the structure and grammatical forms of the language.

## 3.1 Grammaticalization within the Language

The first criterion is the degree to which the category is grammaticalized within a language. This refers to the difference between *grammatical meaning* and *lexical meaning*. In the English clause "I wanted a new hat," the verb "wanted" denotes the *lexical* meaning of "desire," but the suffix attached to the end of "wanted" denotes past tense. Thus the -ed suffix encodes *grammatical* meaning. One can assess whether a language gives greater prominence to tense, aspect, or mood by observing which of these has a higher level of grammatical encoding within the language.

## 3.2 The Formation of a Complete Paradigm

The second criterion is the degree to which tense, aspect, or mood forms a complete paradigm. In English, we use suffixes such as -s or -ed to grammaticalize tense (thus *jumps* is present but *jumped* is past). This will be more fully illustrated in what follows.

## 3.3 Pervasive and Obligatory

Finally, a third and fourth criteria for verbal prominence includes whether the category is pervasive and obligatory across the various forms within the verbal system. We will see below how aspect is the category most pervasive in Greek across all six major verb types: tense occurs in the indicative mood; mood is central to the indicative, subjunctive, imperative, and optative verb-types; aspect, however, is central to all verbal categories of participles and infinitives.

## 3.4 Correlative Implications of Verbal Prominence

When a language structurally aligns itself with tense, aspect, or mood against the other two, there are a number of correlative implications.[11] Three of the most important can be summarized as follows:

---

11   See a full examination in Bhat, *Prominence*, 101–2.

- The prominent category becomes especially apparent outside the indicative mood, as the other two categories tend to recede outside the indicative. In a sense, the nonindicative verb forms provide a litmus test for verbal prominence.
- Less-prominent grammatical categories become associated with the prominent category, with many languages tending to use the prominent category to help form the less prominent categories.[12]
- The prominent category will tend to be encoded through morphological inflection, while the less-prominent categories will tend to be encoded by less direct means (e.g., through the use of auxiliary verbs).

With the above descriptors of verbal prominence in mind, let us examine both English and Greek with an eye towards their respective prominent verbal categories.

## 4. VERBAL PROMINENCE IN ENGLISH

English is widely considered to be a tense-prominent language. Let us see what features of the language implicate this designation.

In English, past tense is grammaticalized on many verbal forms using the suffix -ed. Indeed, tense is the primary category grammaticalized in English verbs, and accordingly linguists widely describe English as a tense prominent language.[13] The English verb, unlike Greek, inherently involves very little explicit verbal morphology. In other words, English verbs tend to be fairly static in their forms, with only the addition of simple changes such as an "s" or an "ing" to distinguish forms. However, when English does utilize morphological changes, these changes tend to encode tense.

---

12  In Greek, this is particularly the case for how future time reference and habituality become interrelated with aspect.

13  E.g., Adeline Patard and Frank Brisard, eds., *Cognitive Approaches to Tense, Aspect, and Epistemic Modality* (Amsterdam: Benjamins, 2011), esp. pp. 217–48; cf. Bhat, *Prominence*, 120. The same could be said for German and other Austro-Asiatic languages.

| Type of Grammatical Form | Give | Walk | Sing |
|---|---|---|---|
| 1st & 2nd Present Form | give | walk | sing |
| 3rd Singular Present Form | gives | walks | sings |
| Past Tense Form | gave | walked | sang |
| Past Participle Form | given | walked | sung |
| Present Participle Form | giving | walking | singing |

In terms of our three categories (tense, aspect, and mood) it becomes clear quite quickly that English only explicitly grammaticalizes the tense category on its verbs. The other two categories, aspect and mood, are expressed with the use of helping words (for example, where mood may use "should give", "could walk", "might sing", etc.) or are communicated through a tense form (for example, English tends to communicate aspect using a tense formative rather than a uniquely aspectual formation; see the following example):

*Example 4*

    a. Progressive aspect:    John was giving Sally an apple.
    b. Perfective aspect:    John gave Sally an apple.

Note how tense formatives are the primary grammaticalized features within these verbal forms. The progressive aspect in clause (a) is formed by using a helping verb, while the perfective aspect in clause (b) is expressed by the past tense form "gave." In both instances, English aspect is communicated using English *tense* morphology, although with progressive aspect a helping word is also used. As Bhat predicts, we can see that English's tense-prominent features as well as helping words are used to convey the less-prominent aspectual distinction. We could make similar observations about English's mood category, where the various moods are expressed by means of helping words like *can* and *could*, *shall* and *should*, *will* and *would*, *may* and *might*. Similar to aspect, mood is not grammaticalized on the English verb itself.

Now, since the subject of this investigation is the Greek verb, let us ask the obvious operative question: is Greek like English: a tense-prominent language? To this question, I will answer a simple and yet hearty, "No, it is not a tense-prominent language, either in semantics or in structure!" Let us examine the reasons for this argument in what follows.

## 5. VERBAL PROMINENCE IN GREEK

Unlike English, with its tense-prominence, other languages will primarily grammaticalize mood (e.g., the Papuan language Amele and the Tibeto-Burman languages of Nepal). Still other languages will primarily grammaticalize aspect (e.g., Greek and other Indo-Aryan languages). In what follows, we will examine how Greek is strongly aspect prominent in its morphological meaning and structure, and argue that this prominence should be reflected in its structural labels, cognitive framework, and pedagogy.

### 5.1 Greek as a Three-Aspect Prominent System

The aspect-prominent nature of Greek is encoded within its morphology (as we will see below), and this reveals a three-part aspectual system: perfective aspect, imperfective aspect, and a third aspect, alternately called perfect, stative, or my preference "combinative" aspect, due to its combination of semantic categories of the other two aspects.

How then are these aspectual categories communicated in the Greek verbal system? As noted above, one criterion of verbal prominence is the degree to which tense, aspect, or mood form a complete paradigm. Let us now turn to how tense, aspect, and mood are grammaticalized in the Greek morphological system.

### 5.2 Greek Aspect-Prominence: Morphological Considerations

In parsing the structure of the Greek verb, we build the Greek paradigm from the inside out. We begin with the lexical core of the verb. This is the most basic element of any verb. It is what makes that verb distinct in the lexicon from other verbs.[14] Some examples of lexical cores are presented below.

---

14  In linguistics this would be called the verbal root. However, the term 'root' in discussion of Ancient Greek usually refers to historical reconstructions

- λυ- "loosen, destroy, release"
- καλε- "to call"
- ἀγαπα- "love"
- φανερο- "reveal, make known"

None of these lexical cores will ever appear in the text by themselves. They need some inflectional morphology before they can be used in a sentence.

First of all, the lexical core requires some kind of morphological marker for aspect, its most prominent grammatical feature. Aspect morphology forms the verb's structural backbone. In table 1 below, note how aspect morphology attaches directly to the lexical core. The combination of the lexical core and the aspect markers forms the aspect stem. The aspect stem of any Greek verb comprises its most basic grammaticalized feature.

Table 1: Formation of aspect stems

| Tense indicator (indicative mood only) | Aspect stem | | | Personal endings |
|---|---|---|---|---|
| | Imperfective aspect marker | Lexical core | Perfective aspect marker | |

Cross-linguistically, verbal prominence tends to move from the inside out, with the more-prominent, more foundational, and generally less static elements located closer to the lexical core, and the less-prominent and more variable elements located on the periphery of the verbal form. This feature of verbal prominence correlates to the placement of aspect indicators, modal indicators, the temporal indicator, and personal endings, as we will discuss below.[15]

Greek verbs are therefore comprised of three basic aspect stems: the perfective, imperfective, and combinative aspects. You should

---

of the proto-language. In order to avoid confusion on that point, we use the term "lexical core."

15  See here Joan L. Bybee, *Morphology: A Study of the Relation between Meaning and Form* (Amsterdam: Benjamins, 1985), e.g., p. 22; also Bhat, *Prominence*, 155.

note that any given lexeme can utilize these three aspect stems in its inflectional morphology.

Table 2 shows an analysis of the tense, aspect, and mood markers for three different forms of the Greek verb with the root δω: δίδωμι ("I am giving") ἔδωκα ("I gave"), and δέδωκα ("I have given").

Table 2: Tense and aspect morphology in first singular forms of δίδωμι

| | Tense indicator | Aspect prefix | Lexical core | Aspect suffix | Voice, mood, person, number |
|---|---|---|---|---|---|
| Imperfective aspect/ nonpast tense | ∅ | δι | δω | ∅ | μι |
| Perfective aspect/ past tense | ε | ∅ | δω | κ | α |
| Combinative aspect/ nonpast tense | ∅ | δε | δω | κ | α |

In the above chart, we can observe how Greek grammaticalizes tense, aspect, and lexeme, as well as a number of other features. Take the form δίδωμι: morphologically, this indicative form lacks the past-tense marker; it is therefore nonpast (specifically, the present tense). It is unbounded/imperfective in aspect ("am giving"), utilizing an imperfective aspect marker preceding its lexical core. In contrast, the form ἔδωκα is past tense (so-marked via the ε augment). It is also bounded/perfective in aspect ("gave"), so-marked via a perfective aspect marker (σ) following its lexical core. Finally, the form δέδωκα is also nonpast (i.e., marking the present relevance of the event), though it marks a more complex aspectual relationship: both imperfective and perfective aspect markers precede and follow the lexical core, respectively. We can observe here that Greek has a well-developed paradigm for the category of aspect, indicating possible aspect prominence within the language.[16]

The grammaticalization of aspect within Greek forms becomes even clearer with the third and fourth criteria, that is, the prominent verbal category will be pervasive and obligatory. When we move into the Greek subjunctive, imperative, and optative moods, as well as the Greek infinitive and participle forms, we find that aspect is pervasively grammaticalized across the forms. In other words, aspect appears in all Greek verbs. Tense, on the other hand, only appears in the indicative mood.[17] Table 3 below provides representative examples from the nonindicative moods as well as from infinitives and participles. Note how the perfective aspect stem is communicated through the use of the lexical core+σ; the imperfective aspect stem is typically communicated through the lexical core alone (though note the μι-verb paradigm above for imperfective reduplication); and the combinative aspect stem is communicated through the use of a reduplicated consonant prefix and typically a κ-suffix, added to the end of the lexical core.

---

16  The mood paradigm is equally well developed since there are three moods in Greek, and indeed we cannot draw a conclusion for prominence solely on the presence of a grammaticalized category found across the verbal paradigm.

17  Mood in Greek, like tense, is also represented in a more limited fashion than aspect.

Table 3: Aspect as pervasive and obligatory in Greek

| | Active voice | | | | | |
|---|---|---|---|---|---|---|
| | **Perfective** | | **Imperfective** | | **Combinative** | |
| Infinitive | λῦσαι | | λύειν | | λελυκέναι | |
| Participle | λύσαντος | | λύοντος | | λελυκότος | |
| Imperative | λῦσον | | λῦε | | λέλυκε | |
| Subjunctive | λύσωμεν | | λύωμεν | | λελυῶμεν | |
| Optative | λύσαιμεν | | λύοιμεν | | λελύοιμεν | |
| Indicative | Past (aorist) | Nonpast (future) | Past (imperfect) | Nonpast (present) | Past (pluperfect) | Nonpast (perfect) |
| | ἐλύσαμεν | λύσομεν | ἐλύομεν | λύομεν | ἐλελύκειμεν | λελύκαμεν |

Aspect is pervasive across the entire Greek verbal system and it is also the only grammatical category of the three that is always completely obligatory. In comparison, mood is not expressed at all with infinitives and participles, and the past/nonpast distinction expressed by the Greek augment prefix disappears entirely outside of the indicative mood.

In all of this, Greek's aspect-prominent features stand in contrast to English's tense-prominent features. Aspect is more grammaticalized, more paradigmatic, more obligatory, and more pervasive than tense or mood. Understanding this linguistic framework for Greek verbal prominence, and how it differs from our own English linguistic framework, will be critical as we move forward to examine the formal morphology and semantic meaning of the Greek verb.

# 6. WHY GRAMMATICAL PROMINENCE MATTERS

This fundamental linguistic principal of verbal prominence changes the basic question we ask when examining a Greek verb-form. It is therefore worthwhile to pause and consider for a moment why a student of the New Testament should care about the question of grammatical prominence. The answer is simple. The majority of grammars of New Testament Greek over the past two centuries have all been written by speakers of tense-prominent languages, written in comparison to their native tense-prominent systems. This has invariably affected how the Greek verbal system has been portrayed so that grammarians have unintentionally placed an undue emphasis on tense over against aspect. As Bhat puts it, "It is something like trying to understand the colour of various objects around us while looking at them through a red-coloured glass."[18] Being aware of our own native linguistic bias from the beginning will help us to avoid misreading Greek.

When we utilize an aspect-prominent organizational and terminological system in our analysis of the Greek verb, suddenly our descriptions of the language become much simpler and more coherent. In what follows, note how the three aspect stems form the morphological options for any given lexeme. Let us take the standard λυ- paradigm, and observe how it is formed across the various aspect stems.

---

18  Bhat, *Prominence*, 99.

## 7. PERFECTIVE ASPECT

Table 4: Formation of perfective aspect stems

| | Tense indicator (indicative mood) | Perfective aspect stem | | | Personal endings |
|---|---|---|---|---|---|
| | | Imperfective aspect marker (reduplication) | Lexical core | Perfective aspect marker ($x$ or $\sigma$) | Personal endings |
| Past perfective (aorist) | ε | ∅ | λυ | σ | αμεν |
| Nonpast perfective (future) | ∅ | ∅ | λυ | σ | ομεν |

With perfective aspect verbs, note the use of a postlexical core aspect marker, σ, to mark this verb-form as perfective in aspect. Within the indicative mood, then, we have the choice of a past ("aorist") or nonpast ("future") binary, marked through the use of the augment. Note how this aspect prominence and indicative tense binary manifests across the verbal paradigm:

Table 5: Perfective aspect across the verbal paradigms

| Active voice | | |
|---|---|---|
| | **Perfective** | |
| Infinitive | λῦσαι | |
| Participle | λύσαντος | |
| Imperative | λῦσον | |
| Subjunctive | λύσωμεν | |
| Optative | λύσαιμεν | |
| Indicative | Past (aorist) | Nonpast (future) |
| | ἐλύσαμεν | λύσομεν |

Note how perfective verb forms morphologize their aspect stems through the use of a perfective aspect suffix, either a κ or σ, following the lexical core. To this aspect stem will be attached modal and personal endings. There are also verb-types, such as the irregular or second aorist perfectives, in which the perfective aspect stem is marked through the use of a uniquely perfective stem, rather than through a prefix or suffix.[19]

## 8. IMPERFECTIVE ASPECT

A similar framework is visible for the imperfective aspect stems. We have already seen how a complete paradigm is displayed by the older μι-type verbs. Note how a similar structure is available for the standard ω-type verbs:

---

19  On the somewhat anomalous nonpast (future) perfectives outside the indicative mood, see below.

Table 6: Formation of imperfective aspect stems

| | Tense indicator (indicative mood) | Imperfective aspect stem | | | Personal endings |
|---|---|---|---|---|---|
| | | Imperfective aspect marker (reduplication) | Lexical core | Perfective aspect marker (κ or σ) | |
| Past imperfective | ε | ∅ | λυ | ∅ | ον |
| Nonpast imperfective ω-verb | ∅ | ∅ | λυ | ∅ | ω |
| Nonpast imperfective μι-verb | ∅ | δι | δω | ∅ | μι |

Note how imperfective verb forms may morphologize their aspect stems in one of two ways: some verbs will mark imperfectivity through prefixing a reduplicated consonant to their lexical core (as is the case with δίδωμι); other verbs lack aspect markers altogether, and therefore the lexical core alone serves as the imperfective aspect stem. To this aspect stem will be attached modal and personal endings, and, in the indicative mood, a potential past-time augment (e.g., ἔλυον). As with the perfective verbs, this framework is consistent across indicative and nonindicative moods:

Table 7: Imperfective aspect across the verbal paradigms

| Active voice | |
|---|---|
| | Imperfective |
| Infinitive | λύειν |
| Participle | λύοντος |
| Imperative | λῦε |

| Subjunctive | λύωμεν | |
|---|---|---|
| Optative | λύοιμεν | |
| Indicative | Past (imperfect) | Nonpast (present) |
| | ἐλύομεν | λύομεν |

## 9. COMBINATIVE ASPECT

Note how combinative aspect forms morphologize their aspect stems through the use of an imperfective aspect prefix (reduplication), as well as a perfective aspect suffix (κ) affixed to the lexical core. To this aspect stem will be attached modal and personal endings, and, in the indicative mood, a potential past-time augment.

Table 8: Formation of combinative aspect stems

| | Tense indicator (indicative mood) | Combinative aspect stem | | | Personal endings |
|---|---|---|---|---|---|
| | | Imperfective aspect marker (reduplication) | Lexical core | Perfective aspect marker (κ or σ) | |
| Past combinative | ε | λε | λυ | κ | ειμεν |
| Nonpast combinative | ∅ | λε | λυ | κ | αμεν |

Observe how this system is consistent across the indicative and nonindicative moods and other verb-forms.

Table 9: Continuative aspect across the verbal paradigms

| Active voice | | |
|---|---|---|
| | **Combinative aspect** | |
| Infinitive | λελυκέναι | |
| Participle | λελυκότος | |
| Imperative | λελύκε | |
| Subjunctive | λελυῶμεν | |
| Optative | λελύοιμεν | |
| Indicative | Past (pluperfect) | Nonpast (perfect) |
| | ἐλελύκειμεν | λελύκαμεν |

What we have called "combinative aspect" has received various labels by scholars. Stan Porter and those who follow him have called this "stative aspect," per Porter's theory that only a resultant "state" rather than a perfective event is in view.[20] Most scholars, including Buist Fanning, have labeled this aspect as "perfect aspect."[21] Constantine Campbell has argued that this aspect is essentially imperfective in aspect, a sort of "intensive present."[22] Here, we should pause and comment on the terminological problem inherent to discussion of the perfect. In English, the term perfect is used to denote a tense category (note the tense-binary of the English perfect vs. pluperfect tenses). Thus, the traditional practice of using the term "perfect tense" to denote the nonpast combinative aspect in the indicative mood is not problematic. However, the problem arises when this temporal label is extended to the entire aspectual system. When we extend this tense-based category to describe the

---

20 E.g., Stanley E. Porter, *Idioms of the Greek New Testament*, 2nd ed., BLG 2 (Sheffield: Sheffield Academic, 1994), 21–22.

21 Cf. Buist M. Fanning, *Verbal Aspect in New Testament Greek*, OTM (Oxford: Clarendon, 1994), 112–20.

22 These three distinctions were on display at the Society of Biblical Literature session "The Perfect Storm," featuring Porter, Fanning, and Campbell; cf. the resulting volume, *The Perfect Volume: Critical Discussion of the Semantics of the Greek Perfect Tense under Aspect Theory*, SBG 17 (New York: Lang, forthcoming). On the limited value of this session for moving the conversation forward, see the response to this session by Randall Buth at http://www.biblicallanguagecenter.com/handles-greek-perfect/.

underlying aspectual system, this conflicts with the temporal no-menclature. I would be comfortable with the use of "perfect aspect", but would then describe the binary indicative tense categories as "past perfect" and "present perfect". However, given the entrenched use of pluperfect and perfect terminology for the tense category, and given the inherent temporal nature of "perfect" within English, I would argue instead for the purely aspectual category to be la-beled "combinative" (reflecting the perfective nature of the verbal event and the imperfective nature of its ongoing relevance), which allows us to retain the terms pluperfect and perfect for the indica-tive tense-forms.[23] Given the event/relevance semantics I have just described, it is clear that I would reject the term "stative" as both overly limiting and inherently misleading.[24]

## 10. THE GREEK ASPECT/TENSE SYSTEM IN SUMMARY

It is important to note that the aspect stems are the most basic fea-ture of the Greek verbal system, structuring verbal morphology across the range of moods and verb forms. Examine again how this is the case for the three aspects in the following table.

---

23  Cf. Bhat, *Prominence*, 171–75.
24  On the close relationship between morphology and semantics within the combinative aspect, note especially Randal Buth, "Perfect Greek Morpholo-gy and Pedagogy" (ch. 13 in this volume) and Robert Crellin, "The Semantics of the Perfect in the Greek of the New Testament" (ch. 14 in this volume).

Table 10: Formation of aspect stems

| Active voice | | | | | | |
|---|---|---|---|---|---|---|
| | Perfective | | Imperfective | | Combinative | |
| Infini-tive | λῦσαι | | λύειν | | λελυκέναι | |
| Partici-ple | λύσαντος | | λύοντος | | λελυκότος | |
| Impera-tive | λῦσον | | λῦε | | λέλυκε | |
| Sub-junctive | λύσωμεν | | λύωμεν | | λελυκῶμεν | |
| Optative | λύσαιμεν | | λύοιμεν | | λελύοιμεν | |
| Indica-tive | Past (aorist) | Nonpast (future) | Past (imper-fect) | Nonpast (pres-ent) | Past (pluper-fect) | Nonpast (perfect) |
| | ἐλύσαμεν | λύσομεν | ἐλύομεν | λύομεν | ἐλελύκειμεν | λελύκαμεν |

Note how all verbal forms for the verb λῦσαι, λύειν, λελυκέναι (to loosen, destroy, release), across the range of moods, can be broken down into three aspect stems: λυσ, λυ, λελυκ. In the indicative mood, these aspect stems may further be broken into a past/nonpast binary, as indicated by the use of the ἐ- augment. The above table helps clarify that the nonindicative verbs have not "lost" their tense markedness, but rather that only in the indicative mood do the verb-forms gain tense. This stands in contrast to the standard cognitive experience of most traditional Greek students, who typically orient the indicative, with its tense binaries, as the most basic verbal form, with the nonindicatives then somehow losing their tense markers. Rather, the most prominent feature (aspect) is in view across the majority of the verb forms, with the addition of tense added in the indicative mood. Keeping Greek's aspect prominence in view helps us maintain a proper orientation to the language's structure.

## 10.1 Aspect Prominence in Various Paradigm Types

In what follows, the general morphological principles in the preceding charts will be fleshed out in further detail.

## Regular -Ω Verb Paradigm

There are three basic paradigms for the Greek verb, which we discuss in order of their productivity.[25] The first and most productive consists of the regular Ω paradigm. We call it the Ω paradigm because of the form of the nonpast first-person singular ending: -ω. The formation of tense and aspect for these verbs is provided in table 11 below.

---

25  In linguistics, the term "productivity" refers to the extent to which a grammatical form and construction is pervasive in the language. The more common it is, the more productive it is. In this case, imperfective-stem verbs are the most productive kind of verb, followed by perfective-stem verbs, and lastly -μι verbs are the least productive.

Table 11: Tense and aspect for regular Ω paradigm verbs (i.e., thematic)

**Nonpast tense (i.e., primary endings)**

| | Past/ aug | Aspect redup. | Lexical core | Aspect | Act. 1st sg. | Verbal form |
|---|---|---|---|---|---|---|
| Non-past imper-fective | ∅ | ∅ | λυ | ∅ | -ω | λύω |
| Non-past perfec-tive | ∅ | ∅ | λυ | -σ | -ω | λύσω |
| Non-past combi-native | ∅ | λε- | λυ | -κ | -α | λελύκα |

**Past tense (i.e., secondary endings)**

| | Past/ aug | Aspect redup. | Lexical core | Aspect | Act. 1st sg. | Verbal form |
|---|---|---|---|---|---|---|
| Past imper-fective | ε- | ∅ | λυ | ∅ | -ον | ἐλύον |
| Past perfec-tive | ε- | ∅ | λυ | -σ | -α | ἐλύσα |
| Past combi-native | (ε-) | (λε-) | λυ | -κ | -ειν | ἐλελύκειν |

In this table, we have combined the imperfective, perfective, and combinative forms, distinguishing between the past and non-past forms. This table contains the most basic components of the verbal paradigm, and shows the three basic aspectual choices for grammaticalizing the lexical core: imperfective, perfective, and combinative. With imperfective-stem verbs of the Ω-type verbs, the imperfective aspect stem is the default aspectual interpretation of the bare root. It has no overt inflectional markers and is instead basic to the verb lexeme. Each of the aspectual formatives becomes increasingly complex in its formation as we move away from the default imperfective morphology. The perfective aspect is realized with a -σ suffix. Combinative aspect, the most complex, is realized through syllabic reduplication of the lexical core's first consonant + the vowel ε, in conjunction with the perfective -κ following the lexical core. Thus, in the case of the verb λύω, the nonpast combinative aspect takes the form: λελύκα.[26] A tense formative is then available as a prefix, and verbal agreement (person, number, etc.) is realized in the final suffix position.

Note especially how gramaticalization of tense is done outside the aspect stem. The distinction between past tense and nonpast tense is marked by the appearance of a prefix augment (typically ἐ) for past tense, in conjunction with the secondary subject agreement endings.

You should note two qualifications to the typological approach portrayed above:

1. Reduplication for the combinative aspect and also the past tense augment prefix are optional in the past tense. One possible explanation for this is that the bulkiness of the past combinative forms created an unreasonable load on the user, especially when the -κ suffix and the past combinative agreement endings (the -ειν ending above) were already the most distinctive within the rest of the verbal paradigm. Whatever the cause, what is important in recognizing combinative aspect verbs in the past tense is to pay close attention to the final agreement ending.

2. Regarding the future indicative, the exact nature of this form, especially within the complex development of Greek, must be left to more complete treatments than this chapter allows. However, a brief comment on the state of affairs is in order. For these Greek nonpast perfective forms, the

---

26 When the lexical core begins with a vowel, there is no consonant to reduplicate. Therefore, the initial consonantal reduplication goes unrealized and the epsilon merges with the initial vowel of the lexical core.

temporal location of the state-of-affairs is almost exclusively subsequent to the reference point, and for this reason the forms clearly fit within the realm of tense.[27] At the same time, Bhat notes that the notion and indeed the form of the future verb is typically attached to the prominent verbal category within a given language, whether tense, aspect, or mood.[28] Thus, in an aspect-prominent language, the future tense will likely involve forms that are organized within the aspectual system.

Without doubt, the future form in Greek has been subject to intense debate. Many linguists have observed that the concept of future often derives historically from modal forms, expressing desire, obligation, and ability.[29] Some hold that the future form is derived from the Proto-Indo-European desiderative suffix *-s.[30] Under this analysis, the future would be viewed as essentially modal in nature, coding an inherent sense of *irrealis*. Others, however, have argued that the Greek future should be viewed as derived from the perfective aspect suffix, which also takes the form -s.[31] Similarly, it appears from ancient grammatical descriptions (e.g., Dionysius Thrax) that, regardless of the origins of the -s future form, native speakers of Koine Greek reanalyzed it as aspectual: a nonpast version of the perfective aspect (the so-called "aorist of the future").[32]

---

27  For what follows on the future tense, see especially Aubrey, "Greek Perfect."
28  Bhat, *Prominence*, 176–77.
29  See here Joan Bybee, Revere Perkins, and William Pagliuca, *The Evolution of Grammar: Tense, Aspect, and Modality in the Languages of the World* (Chicago: University of Chicago Press, 1994); also Östen Dahl, ed., *Tense and Aspect in the Languages of Europe* (Berlin: de Gruyter, 2000).
30  E.g., Andrew Sihler, *New Comparative Grammar of Greek and Latin* (Oxford: Oxford University Press, 1995).
31  So Jo Willmott, *The Moods of Homeric Greek*, Cambridge Classical Studies (Cambridge: Cambridge University Press, 2008), 79, who goes as far as to suggest that both the future tense and the perfective subjunctive arose from perfective nonpast, each splitting then taking on different meanings.
32  Indeed, there is no real consensus on which view of the Greek future is the correct one. Both Willmott, *Moods of Homeric Greek* and David Lightfoot, *Natural Logic and the Greek Moods: The Nature of the Subjunctive and Optative in Classical Greek* (The Hague: Mouton, 1975) conclude on the issue that the evidence is simply too ambiguous to decide in either direction.

*Older Mι-Verb Paradigm*

Beyond the ω-type verbs, there is an older paradigm for verbs as well. This paradigm is not very productive in that there are far fewer verbs in this paradigm during the koine period than in the regular ω-verb paradigm.[33] However, the μι-verb paradigm is important because of the number of high frequency verbs represented within this paradigm. The most common of these is Greek's 'to be' verb: εἰμί. Similarly, verbs denoting common concepts like *to put* (τίθημι), *to make stand* (ἵστημι), and *to give* (δίδωμι) are all expressed by verbs in the μι-verb paradigm. The morphological structure of these verbs differs in a number of ways form the ω-verb paradigm.

Table 12: Tense and aspect for regular Ω paradigm verbs (i.e., thematic)

| Nonpast tense (i.e., primary endings) | | | | | |
|---|---|---|---|---|---|
| **Past/ aug** | **Aspect redup.** | **Lexical core** | **Aspect** | **Active 1st sg.** | **Verbal form** |
| ∅ | δι- | δω | ∅ | -μι | δίδωμι |
| ∅ | ∅ | δω | -σ | -ω | δώσω |
| ∅ | δε- | δω | -κ | -α | δέδωκα |
| **Past tense (i.e., secondary endings)** | | | | | |
| **Past/ aug** | **Aspect redup.** | **Lexical core** | **Aspect** | **Active 1st sg.** | **Verbal form** |
| ε- | δι- | δο | ∅ | -ον | ἐδίδουν |
| ε- | ∅ | δω | -κ | -α | ἔδωκα |
| (ε-) | (δε-) | δω | -κ | -ειν | ἐδεδώκειν |

First of all, imperfective aspect is no longer the default morphological form. It now has its own overt inflectional marker, the aspectual reduplication described on the proceeding pages. Second, we can see that the inflectional markers for the other aspects are rather

---

33  BDAG has roughly 130 lexical entries for -μι verbs. This contrasts with 2133 lexical entries for verbs that are a part of the -ω paradigm. At one point in the language's history, this paradigm was as productive as our first paradigm. It slowly fell out of use and eventually disappeared in the Byzantine Era; so Geoffrey Horrocks, *Greek: A History of the Language and its Speakers*, 2nd ed. (Oxford: Wiley-Blackwell, 2010).

different as well. And of course, the nonpast first-person singular ending takes the form of -μι rather than -ω.

Despite these formal differences, the basic morphological structure is essentially the same. There are still three aspects: imperfective, perfective, and combinative. Tense is still morphologically marked within a past/nonpast binary system (a morphology that includes past, present, and future reference time). Nevertheless, the inflectional markers, at least for aspect, have changed somewhat substantially. The biggest changes are in the imperfective aspect stem. It now has its own inflectional marker: the prefix reduplication δι-. This reduplication is formed in a manner similar to the combinative aspect prefix, except with the vowel *iota* rather than *epsilon*.

### Irregular Aspect Stems

Verbs with irregular aspect stems are fairly common. In general their structure is fairly simple: an aspect-specific stem (unique to each aspect) indicates the choice of aspect. As with regular aspect stems, these irregular stems also attach the augment to the front of the aspect stem, indicating past- or nonpast tense in the indicative mood. These irregular aspect stems also demonstrate more regular subject agreement endings—the subject agreement endings for the perfective aspect are exactly the same as those of the imperfective aspect in marking the past and nonpast tenses.

Nevertheless, there is a fundamental difference in the manner that these irregular aspect stems realize the category of aspect and, unfortunately, it often means basic memorization. An example of this kind of irregular aspect stem is shown below in table 13.

Table 13: Tense and aspect morphology for irregular aspect stems (i.e., 2nd aorists)

| | Nonpast tense (i.e., primary endings) | | | | |
|---|---|---|---|---|---|
| | Past/ aug | Aspect redup. | Lexical core | Aspect | Active 1st sg. |
| Nonpast imperfective | ∅ | ∅ | βαλλ | ∅ | -ω |
| Nonpast perfective | ∅ | ∅ | βαλ | ∅ | -ω |
| Nonpast combinative | ∅ | βε- | βλη | -κ | -α |
| | Past tense (i.e., secondary endings) | | | | |
| | Past/ aug | Aspect redup. | Lexical core | Aspect | Active 1st sg. |
| Past imperfective | ε- | ∅ | βαλλ | ∅ | -ον |
| Past perfective | ε- | ∅ | βαλ | ∅ | -ον |
| Past combinative | (ε-) | (βε-) | βλη | -κ | -ειν |

The difference between each of the aspects in this case is not merely in the inflectional marking, but in the modification of the lexical core itself. This modification is traditionally called "ablaut." With the perfective aspect, the modification to the lexical core itself indicates the perfective aspect stem.

The combinative aspect is unique here in that the change in the lexical core takes place in conjunction with the normal affixation pattern: reduplication and the -κ suffix. Once an aspect is selected, the rest of the agreement markers attach in the same manner as above. Still, it is important to keep in mind with these verbs that the agreement endings in the perfective and imperfective aspects only change with respect to tense (past vs. nonpast verbal endings).

Some verbs of the so-called irregular stem type might exhibit this change only partially. A good example of a verb like this is καλέω, which only has an irregular lexical core in the combinative active voice in table 11 and the perfective middle/passive voice in table 14.

Table 14: Irregular aspect stems and the combinative aspect

| | Nonpast tense (i.e., primary endings) | | | | |
|---|---|---|---|---|---|
| | Past/ aug | Aspect redup. | Lexical core | Aspect | Active 1st sg. |
| Nonpast imperfective | ∅ | ∅ | καλέ | ∅ | -ω |
| Nonpast perfective | ∅ | ∅ | καλέ | -σ | -ω |
| Nonpast combinative | ∅ | κε- | κλη | -κ | -α |
| | Past tense (i.e., secondary endings) | | | | |
| | Past/ aug | Aspect redup. | Lexical core | Aspect | Active 1st sg. |
| Past imperfective | ε- | ∅ | καλέ | ∅ | -ον |
| Past perfective | ε- | ∅ | καλέ | -σ | -α |
| Past combinative | (ε-) | (κε-) | κλη | -κ | -ειν |

Observe that the perfective middle-passive takes the same κλη lexical core as the combinative aspect.

Table 15: Irregular aspect stems in the middle-passive voice

| | Nonpast tense (i.e., primary endings) | | | | |
|---|---|---|---|---|---|
| | Past/ aug | Aspect redup. | Lexical core | Aspect | MP 1st sg. |
| Nonpast imperfective | ∅ | ∅ | καλέ | ∅ | -ομαι |
| Nonpast perfective | ∅ | ∅ | κλη | -θησ | -ομαι |
| Nonpast combinative | ∅ | κε- | κλη | ∅ | -α |
| | Past tense (i.e., secondary endings) | | | | |
| | Past/ aug | Aspect redup. | Lexical core | Aspect | MP 1st sg. |
| Past imperfective | ε- | ∅ | καλέ | ∅ | -ον |
| Past perfective | ε- | ∅ | κλη | -θη | -ν |
| Past combinative | (ε-) | (κε-) | κλη | ∅ | -μαι |

This pattern where the perfective middle-passive shares the same lexical core with the combinative aspect is fairly common for verbs with irregular aspect stems.[34]

Finally, while irregular aspect stems are most prevalent with the -ω paradigm, this is only because the -ω paradigm is the most common. Irregular aspect stems also appear with verbs of the -μι paradigm.

In sum, observe how the ω-type, μι-type, and irregular type verb forms conform to the standard tripartite aspectually prominent framework across the Greek verbal system.

---

34 Note additionally how the θη aspect marker tracks across the middle/passive in both the past and nonpast perfective forms (i.e., aorist and future middle-passive). This close morphological relationship within the middle-passive forms further suggests a close aspectual link between the aorist and future tense-forms.

Table 16: Aspect stem paradigms summary

| Aspect stem | Ω paradigm | Μι paradigm | Irregular aspect stems |
|---|---|---|---|
| **Imperfective** | No overt marker | Reduplication | Usually unique aspect stem |
| **Perfective** | σ suffix | σ or κ suffix | Unique aspect stem + agreement endings marked only for tense |
| **Combinative** | Reduplication + κ suffix | Reduplication + κ suffix | Reduplication + unique aspect stem + κ suffix |

# 11. TENSE, MOOD, AND VOICE: IMPLICATIONS FOR NONPROMINENT CATEGORIES IN THE GREEK VERBAL SYSTEM

Having examined in detail the nature of aspect-prominence in the Greek verbal system, what can we say regarding the essential role of tense and mood?

The basic tense distinction in Koine Greek is that of morphological past/nonpast binary, in which past, present, and future reference time may be communicated. Recall that past tense is marked inflectionally on the verb with a prefix augment. This past tense prefix can appear in conjunction with all three aspects: perfective, imperfective, and combinative in addition to the past tense subject agreement endings. Tense is only marked morphologically in the indicative mood, which follows Bhat's suggestion that within the indicative mood nonprominent features are elevated.

## 11.1 Tense and Imperfective Aspect

We can see this contrast between past and nonpast in imperfective verbs in the example below:

a. ἃ δὲ γράφω ὑμῖν, ἰδοὺ ἐνώπιον τοῦ θεοῦ ὅτι οὐ ψεύδομαι.

a) Now what I am writing to you, look, before God, that
I am not lying! (Galatians 1:20)

b. Ἀπὸ στόματος αὐτοῦ ἀνήγγειλέν μοι Ἰερεμίας πάντας τοὺς
λόγους τούτους, καὶ ἔγραφον ἐν βιβλίῳ.

b) Jeremiah declared to me all these words, and I was
transcribing them in a scroll (Jeremiah 43:18 LXX).

These two clauses, one from the New Testament and the other
from the Septuagint, demonstrate the contrast between past and
nonpast in the imperfective aspect. In Galatians 1:20, Paul highlights
the importance of the statement that follows. Since his note on his
writing is taking place as he writes it, he uses the imperfective aspect
and nonpast reference tense. As such, there is no prefix augment on
the verb and the agreement ending takes its nonpast form: γράφω
(I am writing). In contrast, the verse from the Septuagint consists
of Jeremiah's scribe, Baruch, stating that he wrote down the words
of prophecy that Jeremiah spoke. Baruch is describing an event that
took place prior to the moment of speech and thus the verb appears
in the past tense and has the past tense prefix augment and the past
tense agreement ending: ἔγραφον (I was writing, i.e., transcribing).
Thus, a basic binary exists within the imperfective indicative, between past and nonpast.

## Tense and the Perfective Aspect

The situation between past and nonpast tenses with perfective aspect is slightly more complicated. In English, the simple present is
used to express habitual situations, as in I eat broccoli regularly; in
Greek, the nonpast imperfective (i.e., present tense-form) fills this
role. In English, however, the present tense can also be used to communicate perfective aspect (e.g., "I eat"), much like the Greek past
perfective ("aorist") but with present reference time. In contrast,
however, Greek does not utilize a specific form that is marked for
nonpast reference time and perfective aspect. Rather, the Greek
perfective nonpast form is exclusively used to indicate future reference time. For those rare times when a perfective event needs to
be communicated with perfective aspect, the "aorist" form is chosen. In short, the binary choice available to perfective indicatives is

prototypically that of past reference time (the "aorist" tense-form), and future reference time, as in the following examples:

a. γράψω ἐπ᾽ αὐτὸν τὸ ὄνομα τοῦ θεοῦ μου καὶ τὸ ὄνομα τῆς πόλεως τοῦ θεοῦ μου, τῆς καινῆς Ἰερουσαλήμ, ἡ καταβαίνουσα ἐκ τοῦ οὐρανοῦ ἀπὸ τοῦ θεοῦ μου, καὶ τὸ ὄνομά μου τὸ καινόν.
I will write on him the name of my God and the name of the city of my God, the new Jerusalem, which comes down from heaven from my God, and my own new name (Revelation 3:12).

b. Διὰ Σιλουανοῦ ὑμῖν τοῦ πιστοῦ ἀδελφοῦ, ὡς λογίζομαι, δι᾽ ὀλίγων ἔγραψα, παρακαλῶν καὶ ἐπιμαρτυρῶν ταύτην εἶναι ἀληθῆ χάριν τοῦ θεοῦ
Through Silvanus to you as I consider him a faithful brother, by a few words I wrote this short letter to encourage you and to attest that this is the true grace of God (1 Peter 5:12).

In order to illustrate the contrast in tense between past and non-past reference time available within the perfective aspect, we again use the verb γράφω. In the nonpast perfective, Jesus, in a letter to the church at Philadelphia, makes a future statement about writing his name on the person who is victorious. The perfective aspect in conjunction with the nonpast tense agreement ending -ω function to convey future time reference. Again, in contrast, the perfective aspect with the past tense in 1 Peter 5:12 has both the prefix augment (ἐ-) and the past tense agreement ending (-α). In this verse, Peter is drawing his letter to a conclusion and speaks of what he wrote already in earlier portions of the letter.

## Tense and the Combinative Aspect

For English speakers, the combinative aspect often feels like it is already a past tense. That's because the idea of a verb referring to an event that is now a completed state sounds suspiciously like a past tense. But that is primarily because we conceive of Greek aspect in terms of tense-prominent English. Completion, however, is a property of aspect, not tense. Semantically speaking, the nonpast combinative ("perfect") forms refer to an event that is completed at the time of speaking, though it has present relevance. The "pluper-fect" indicative, however, refers to an event that is completed at the time of speaking, but the relevance was similarly in the past time. See the following examples:

a. <u>ἀναδέδειχα</u> τὸν υἱὸν Ἀντίοχον βασιλέα, ὃν πολλάκις ἀνατρέχων εἰς τὰς ἐπάνω σατραπείας τοῖς πλείστοις ὑμῶν παρεκατετιθέμην καὶ συνίστων· <u>γέγραφα</u> δὲ πρὸς αὐτὸν τὰ ὑπογεγραμμένα.
a) <u>I have appointed</u> my son Antiochus as king, whom, during the many times I hurried to the upper provinces, I entrusted and introduced to many of you. And <u>I have written</u> to him what is written [here] (2 Maccabees 9:25).

b. Ἰησοῦς κατὰ τὸν καιρὸν τοῦτον <u>ἐγεγράφει</u> πρὸς αὐτοὺς πείσειν ἐπαγγελλόμενος τὸ πλῆθος ἐλθόντας ὑποδέχεσθαι καὶ αὐτοῖς ἑλέσθαι προστεθῆναι.
b) Joseph, about this time, <u>had written</u> to them announcing that he would persuade the crowd to welcome them when they came and decide to join with them (Josephus, *Life* 271).

Thus in clause (a) above, the verb γέγραφα (I have written) re-fers to an act of writing that the speaker had finished at the time of speaking. Note that there is the combinative aspect's reduplication (γε-) and also the combinative aspect's nonpast agreement ending (-α). There is no past tense prefix augment, however. Note the bi-nary between a nonpast combinative form and a past combinative form in the above two examples.

Sentence (b) from Josephus's biography stands in contrast to the typical nonpast combinative. Here Josephus is reporting that a man named Joseph had completed a piece of writing and that piece of writing was already completed in the past before Josephus' time of writing. Once again, the past tense version of the combinative as-pect has the past tense prefix augment (ἐ-) as well as the combina-tive aspect's past tense subject agreement ending.

## 12. RETURN TO MATTHEW 2:20

In light of the above discussion, let us return briefly to Matthew 2:20, introduced at the start of this paper:

λέγων· ἐγερθεὶς παράλαβε τὸ παιδίον καὶ τὴν μητέρα αὐτοῦ καὶ πορεύου εἰς γῆν Ἰσραήλ· τεθνήκασιν γὰρ οἱ ζητοῦντες τὴν ψυχὴν τοῦ παιδίου.

We asked previously whether the participle ζητοῦντες is better described by a tense-prominent system, with tense-prominent labels, or by an aspect-prominent system, with aspect-prominent labels. The adoption of a tense-prominent approach, whether framed linguistically or simply by the nature of an implicit tense-prominent cognitive framework, creates problems. In calling this verb a "present participle," one is immediately led to the nature of the verb's tense. However, by adopting an aspect-prominent approach, and calling this verb an imperfective participle rather than a present participle, we may simply and accurately describe the nature of this verb. We are now equipped to see the event in view (the act of "seeking") as primarily an imperfective event, rather than an event with grammaticalized time. In fact, this imperfective substantival participle could stand in place of either a past or nonpast imperfective event. However, the temporal frame must be established contextually, and indeed, given the accompanying perfect tense verb, we see that the relative time of the event "to seek" is understood to be in the past, preceding the death of the seekers. Had this event been framed in the indicative mood, an "imperfect" (i.e., past-imperfective) form would have been used, and not a present-tense indicative form, as the temporal frame of "searching" *logically* precedes the primary verb "they have died." However, given the nonindicative form, the tense of the verb is simply left to context, and not to the morpho-syntactical nature of the imperfective participle.[35]

---

35  Here, we should not view the participle to have "lost" its past tense. Rather, the most prominent feature (aspect) is in view, without the addition of the tense marking found within the indicative. Once again, keeping Greek's aspect prominence in view helps us maintain a proper orientation to what the language is communicating.

## 13. CONCLUSIONS

In closing, we have made a number of claims regarding aspect-prominence that have wide-sweeping implications for the Greek language.

- We have argued that aspect prominence provides a pervasive, morpho-syntactical framework for the Greek verbal system. While both mood and tense are also found in Greek, and indeed are central to the language, aspect is more grammaticalized, more paradigmatic, more obligatory, and more pervasive than either tense or mood. Aspect in Greek manifests in three distinct forms, each of which are grammaticalized at the heart of the verbal morphology: perfective, imperfective, and combinative aspect.
- The prominence of aspect has provided a coherent, cognitive orientation for the language, which replaces the standard, tense prominent, indicative prominent orientation for mentally categorizing the Greek verbal framework.
- It should be emphasized that the fundamental morpho-syntactical features that our students should be orientating themselves toward is that of the aspectual prominence of the language. This seems to be the fundamental choice available to the author when framing a verbal concept, and it has significant implications for the pragmatic structure of the language.
- Regarding pedagogical implications: teaching students within a tripartite verbal system that remains consistent across the variables of mood and tense offers a way forward for students seeking to penetrate the dense cloud that often descends upon the first, second, and third years of traditional grammatical instruction.

## BIBLIOGRAPHY

Aubrey, Michael. "The Greek Perfect and the Categorization of Tense and Aspect." MA thesis, Trinity Western University, 2014.

Bhat, D. N. S.. *The Prominence of Tense, Aspect, and Mood*. Amsterdam: Benjamins, 1999.

Bybee, Joan L. *Morphology: A Study of the Relation between Meaning and Form*. Amsterdam: Benjamins, 1985.

Bybee, Joan, Revere Perkins, and William Pagliuca. *The Evolution of Grammar: Tense, Aspect, and Modality in the Languages of the World*. Chicago: University of Chicago Press, 1994.

Carson, D. A., ed. *The Perfect Volume: Critical Discussion of the Semantics of the Greek Perfect Tense under Aspect Theory*. SBG 17. New York: Lang, forthcoming.

Comrie, Bernard. *Aspect: An Introduction to the Study of Verbal Aspect and Related Problems*. Cambridge: Cambridge University Press, 1976.

Dahl, Östen, ed. *Tense and Aspect in the Languages of Europe*. Berlin: de Gruyter, 2000.

Fanning, Buist M. *Verbal Aspect in New Testament Greek*. OTM. Oxford: Clarendon, 1990.

Horrocks, Geoffrey. *Greek: A History of the Language and its Speakers*. 2nd ed. Oxford: Wiley-Blackwell, 2010.

Huddleston, Rodney D., and Geoffrey K. Pullum. *A Student's Introduction to English Grammar*. Cambridge: Cambridge University Press, 2005.

Lightfoot, David. *Natural Logic and the Greek Moods: The Nature of the Subjunctive and Optative in Classical Greek*. The Hague: Mouton, 1975.

Patard, Adeline, and Frank Brisard, eds. *Cognitive Approaches to Tense, Aspect, and Epistemic Modality*. Amsterdam: Benjamins, 2011.

Porter, Stanley E. *Idioms of the Greek New Testament*. 2nd ed. BLG 2. Sheffield: Sheffield Academic, 1994.

Runge, Steven E. "The Verbal Aspect of the Historical Present Indicative in Narrative." Pages 191–224 in *Discourse Studies and Biblical Interpretation: A Festschrift in Honor of Stephen H. Levinsohn*. Edited by Steven E. Runge. Bellingham, WA: Logos Bible Software, 2011.

Sihler, Andrew L. *New Comparative Grammar of Greek and Latin*. Oxford: Oxford University Press, 1995.

Willmott, Jo. *The Moods of Homeric Greek*. Cambridge Classical Studies. Cambridge: Cambridge University Press, 2007.

# Application

CHAPTER 5

# Verb Forms and Grounding in Narrative

STEPHEN H. LEVINSOHN

SIL INTERNATIONAL

The topic of grounding is a very contentious one, with opposing groups insisting in absolute terms, "This verb form is background," "No, it is foreground,"[1] and others of us crying out after them, "Hold on! Languages don't work that way!"

I begin this paper by defining some key terms, particularly as they apply to narrative texts.

Kathleen Callow relates foreground in a discourse to *thematic* information: "this is what I'm talking about." Thematic material "carries the discourse forward, contributes to the progression of the narrative or argument ... develops the theme of the discourse." In contrast, nonthematic or background material "serves as a commentary on the theme, but does not itself contribute directly to the

---

1   Compare, for instance, Stanley E. Porter, "Prominence: An Overview," in *The Linguist as Pedagogue: Trends in the Teaching and Linguistic Analysis of the Greek New Testament*, ed. Stanley E. Porter and Matthew Brook O'Donnell, NTM 11 (Sheffield: Sheffield Phoenix, 2009), 60–61; and Robert E. Longacre, "Mark 5.1–43: Generating the Complexity of a Narrative from Its Most Basic Elements," in *Discourse Analysis and the New Testament: Approaches and Results*, ed. Stanley E. Porter and Jeffrey T. Reed, JSNTSup 170 (Sheffield: Sheffield Academic, 1999), 177. See also the Mark 2:1–5 lesson of BibleMesh's forthcoming Level 4 Greek Reading course entitled, "Introduction to Background and Foreground" (http://biblemesh.com/biblemesh-biblical-languages).

progression of the theme ... [it] fills out the theme but does not develop it."[2]

Narrative is defined over against other discourse genres as agent oriented with its events organized chronologically.[3] Consequently, the theme line for narrative is made up of events that are performed in chronological sequence by agents.

## 1. EVENTS VERSUS NONEVENTS

Because narratives are made up of events, a sentence that describes an event is assumed to be communicating foreground (thematic) information unless it is marked in some way.[4] In other words, when a narrative sentence describes an event, the default interpretation is that it is foreground. For it *not* to be interpreted as foreground, a backgrounding device must be used.

In contrast, nonevents are automatically viewed as background information when appearing in a narrative, because of the nature of narratives.[5] This does not mean that the information they convey is unimportant for the narrative; indeed, it may be highlighted. Rather, their background status is simply a consequence of the fact that the sentence describes a nonevent.

Background information in narrative thus consists of the nonevents, together with those events that are marked as being of secondary importance (nonthematic).

Note that the verbs in reported speeches are not considered in this paper, as they are on a different "level" from that of the narrative superstructure.[6] So, "they said, 'X'" is a narrative event, but

---

2   Kathleen Callow, *Discourse Considerations in Translating the Word of God* (Grand Rapids: Zondervan, 1974), 52–53.

3   Robert E. Longacre (*The Grammar of Discourse*, 2nd ed. [New York: Plenum, 1996], 9) characterizes narrative as "+Agent oriented, +Contingent temporal succession."

4   "Events are viewed as foreground (theme-line) **unless** they are background-ED" (Stephen H. Levinsohn, *Self-Instruction Materials on Narrative Discourse Analysis* [http://www-01.sil.org/~levinsohns/narr.pdf, 2012], §5.2.2) (emphasis original).

5   Ibid., §5.2.1.

6   See Florencio Dormeyer and Florencio Galindo, *Comentario a los Hechos de los Apóstoles: Modelo de Nueva Evangelización* (Estella, Navarra, Spain: Verbo Divino, 2007), 8. The authors distinguish at least three levels within a

what they said (e.g., in an interaction between Jesus and the other participants in a pericope) is part of a different dimension, which is to be analyzed in its own right. Luke 4:33–35 (below) illustrates this.

## Narrative superstructure

| | | |
|---|---|---|
| 33a | background: nonevent: | καὶ ἐν τῇ συναγωγῇ ἦν ἄνθρωπος ἔχων πνεῦμα δαιμονίου ἀκαθάρτου |
| | | In the synagogue there was a man who had the spirit of an unclean demon[7] |
| 33b–34 | foreground: event: | καὶ ἀνέκραξεν φωνῇ μεγάλῃ, "X" |
| | | and he cried out with a loud voice, "X" |
| 35 | foreground: event: | καὶ ἐπετίμησεν αὐτῷ ὁ Ἰησοῦς λέγων, "Y" |
| | | But Jesus rebuked him, saying, "Y" |

## Embedded conversation between the participants

34 (X)  Ἔα, τί ἡμῖν καὶ σοί, Ἰησοῦ Ναζαρηνέ; ἦλθες ἀπολέσαι ἡμᾶς; οἶδά σε τίς εἶ, ὁ ἅγιος τοῦ θεοῦ.

"Let us alone! What have you to do with us, Jesus of Nazareth? Have you come to destroy us? I know who you are, the Holy One of God."

35 (Y)  Φιμώθητι καὶ ἔξελθε ἀπ' αὐτοῦ.

"Be silent, and come out of him!"

The rest of this paper is divided into three parts: first, consideration of tense-aspect and grounding in indicative verbs (§2); second, subordination and tail-head linkage (§3); and third, two

narrative: (1) the direct communication between author and reader; (2) the narrative itself where the events unfold and the characters interact with each other; (3) the communication between the characters reported in the speeches.

7   Free translations are based on the NRSV, but have been made more literal on occasion in order to bring out the point being illustrated.

constructions that affect the grounding of the events associated with them (§4).

## 2. TENSE-ASPECT OF INDICATIVE VERBS[8]

Most narratives in the Gospels employ more than one "tense-form."[9] The majority of narrative events are presented with the aorist, but others may be encoded with the imperfect, the historical present (HP) and/or, occasionally, the perfect and/or pluperfect. Stanley E. Porter and Robert E. Longacre have both made proposals about the effect of using these different tense-forms.[10] They agree that "the aorist tense-form characterizes the mainline or storyline of narrative discourse."[11] When it comes to the "prominence" or "dynamicity"[12] of the tense-forms, however, they hold very different positions, as the following table shows.[13]

---

8    The following paragraphs are based on Stephen H. Levinsohn, "Aspect and Prominence in the Synoptic Accounts of Jesus' Entry into Jerusalem," *FilNeot* 23 (2010) 161–62, 167–69.

9    Constantine R. Campbell, *Basics of Verbal Aspect in Biblical Greek* (Grand Rapids: Zondervan, 2008), 24.

10   For a useful introduction to and critique of Porter's approach to the tense-forms of Biblical Greek, see Jody A. Barnard, "Is Verbal Aspect a Prominence Indicator? An Evaluation of Stanley E. Porter's Proposal with Special Reference to the Gospel of Luke," *FilNeot* 19 (2006), 3–29. For a summary and critique of Longacre's "storyline scheme" with its verb ranking system in terms of "bands," see Jean-Marc Heimerdinger, *Topic, Focus and Foreground in Ancient Hebrew Narratives*, JSOTSup 295 (Sheffield: Sheffield Academic, 1999), 57–58.

11   Porter, "Prominence," 57. Longacre ("Mark 5," 177) writes in similar vein: "For the most part, then, the storyline of Koine Greek narrative is carried by clauses with verbs in the aorist."

12   Longacre, "Mark 5," 179.

13   Buist Fanning ("Greek Presents, Imperfects, and Aorists in the Synoptic Gospels: Their Contribution to Narrative Structuring" [paper presented at the Annual Meeting of the SBL, New Orleans, 2009], 11–13) makes a similar point.

| | aorist | imperfect | historical present | perfect |
|---|---|---|---|---|
| Porter | unmarked ("background") | foreground, remote in staging | foreground | foreground |
| Longacre | foreground | background | secondary storyline | (low dynamicity)[14] |

Although Porter refers to the aorist as "the background tense,"[15] it is clear from other comments that he uses "background" in the sense of "unmarked for prominence."[16] Longacre's use of the term "background" is different and corresponds more closely to the dictionary definition: "explanatory or contributory information or circumstances."[17] Even with this clarification, though, it is clear that the two men hold opposing views, particularly on the prominence of the *imperfect*, which is the theme of the next paragraphs.

A key feature of the approach of both Porter and Longacre to the prominence of different tense-forms is that they *equate* a particular degree of prominence with individual tense-forms such as the imperfect. This approach is at variance with the position of linguists such as Hopper,[18] Foley and van Valin[19] and others[20] who rather perceive "an inherent *correlation* between perfective versus imperfective aspect and foreground versus background."[21]

---

14  The dynamicity of the pf. is not discussed in Longacre, "Mark 5," but does feature in other articles written by him.

15  Porter, "Prominence," 60.

16  Cynthia Long Westfall ("A Method for the Analysis of Prominence in Hellenistic Greek," in Porter, *The Linguist as Pedagogue*, 79) calls the aor. the "unmarked" aspect.

17  *Oxford English Dictionary*.

18  Paul J. Hopper, "Aspect and Foregrounding in Discourse," in *Discourse and Syntax*, ed. Talmy Givón, Syntax and Semantics 12 (New York: Academic Press, 1979), 215–16.

19  William A. Foley and Robert D. Van Valin, *Functional Syntax and Universal Grammar* (Cambridge: Cambridge University Press, 1984) 373, 397.

20  See Fanning, *Contribution*, 11 n. 50.

21  Stephen H. Levinsohn, *Discourse Features of New Testament Greek: A Coursebook on the Information Structure of New Testament Greek*, 2nd ed. (Dallas: SIL International, 2000), §10.2.2 (emphasis added).

Treating the relation between aspect and grounding as a correlation, rather than an equation, allows us to concur with Longacre and other linguists that, cross-linguistically, imperfectives in narratives typically encode information of a background nature, without requiring that every event described with the imperfect in a Greek narrative be viewed as background.[22] Equally, such a position allows us to concur with Porter that a number of imperfects in Mark's Gospel give prominence to the event concerned, without requiring that every event described with the imperfect in Mark be prominent.

If the relation between a specific tense-form and a particular degree of prominence is not a one-to-one equation but a correlation, how are we to know when the imperfect does convey prominence and when it does not? In his article on the English progressive ("be + V-ing"), Zegarač argues for the need to distinguish between the "meaning" of the construction and the different "overtones" that arise when it is used in certain contexts, such as "mild reproof," "insincerity" or "temporariness."[23] Applying this distinction to Greek, the "meaning" of the imperfect is the portrayal of a past event as ongoing at the point of reference. The "overtones" that arise vary with the context, and may include both backgrounding and foregrounding.

Zegarač also deals with the issue of "markedness" and distinguishes between contexts in which a particular tense-form is the default or "more relevant" way of portraying an event[24] and those in which it is not ("marked" usages). Applying this distinction to Greek, on many occasions the imperfect is the most relevant way of portraying an event simply because the desire of the author is to indicate that the event is ongoing. So in Mark 10:52c (καὶ ἠκολούθει αὐτῷ ἐν τῇ ὁδῷ "and was following him on the way"), the imperfect is the most relevant way of indicating that Bartimaeus not only began

---

22 For discussion of this point, see Stephen Levinsohn, *Self-Instruction Materials on Narrative Discourse Analysis* (http://www-01.sil.org/~levinsohns/narr. pdf, 2012), §§5.3.1–2. See Fanning, *Contribution*, 15 on the need to recognize both a backgrounding role for the impf. and a "frontgrounding" one.

23 Vladimir Zegarač, "Relevance Theory and the Meaning of the English Progressive," *UCLWPL* 1 (1989) 20, 22.

24 Ibid., 29. In the rest of this article, I replace "more relevant" with "most relevant."

to follow Jesus, but was continuing to do so. Similarly, in Luke 2:41 (Καὶ ἐπορεύοντο οἱ γονεῖς αὐτοῦ κατ' ἔτος εἰς Ἰερουσαλὴμ τῇ ἑορτῇ τοῦ πάσχα "Now every year his parents used to go to Jerusalem for the festival of the Passover"), the imperfect is the most relevant way of portraying Jesus' parents' custom of going to Jerusalem each year for the Passover if the author wishes to indicate that this custom was ongoing when Jesus became 12 years old.

In contrast, if the aorist is the most relevant way of portraying an event, yet the Gospel author chooses to use the imperfect instead, then he "must have intended to convey special contextual effects."[25] By choosing a more marked form, "the communicator makes the utterance more costly to process ... [and] this would entail that [he] intended to convey additional implicatures to compensate for the increase in processing effort."[26]

In Mark 15:14a (ὁ δὲ Πιλᾶτος ἔλεγεν αὐτοῖς, Τί γὰρ ἐποίησεν κακόν; "Pilate was asking them, 'Why, what evil has he done?'"), for instance, the imperfect does not appear to be the most relevant way of portraying the act of speaking, as it does not seem to be ongoing at the point of reference (it is sandwiched between two speeches by the chief priests that are introduced with aorist ἔκραξαν "they cried out"). Consequently, the reader looks for "additional implicatures to compensate for the increase in processing effort"[27]—implicatures that vary with the context. Because the chief priests, rather than Pilate, determine the outcome of the conversation, the implicature associated with the use of the imperfect is likely to be that of backgrounding.

Now consider John 8:31-32: Ἔλεγεν οὖν ὁ Ἰησοῦς πρὸς τοὺς πεπιστευκότας αὐτῷ Ἰουδαίους, Ἐὰν ὑμεῖς μείνητε ἐν τῷ λόγῳ τῷ ἐμῷ, ἀληθῶς μαθηταί μού ἐστε καὶ γνώσεσθε τὴν ἀλήθειαν ... "Then Jesus was saying to the Jews who had believed in him, 'If you continue in my word, you are truly my disciples; and you will know the truth.'" Again, the speech is not readily perceived as ongoing at the point of reference. This time, though, the effect of using the imperfect is

---

25  Ernst-August Gutt, *Translation and Relevance: Cognition and Context* (Oxford: Blackwell, 1991), 103.

26  Ibid., 41. See also Deirdre Wilson and Dan Sperber, *Meaning and Relevance* (Cambridge: Cambridge University Press, 2012), 88.

27  Gutt, *Translation and Relevance*, 41.

likely to be that of foregrounding, because it "incites or provokes the conversational exchange of the rest of the chapter."[28]

The *perfect* is only used six times in narrative contexts (Matt 1:22, 21:4; John 19:35 *bis*, 20:31, 21:24). Bhat states that, in aspect-prominent languages, it typically portrays the event concerned as completed with a resultant imperfective state.[29] Because of its stative nature, such examples always present background information in narrative.

My paper on *"periphrastic"* combinations of a copula and a participial clause[30] such as καὶ ἦν διδάσκων αὐτοὺς ἐν τοῖς σάββασιν "and was teaching them on the sabbath" (Luke 4:31) argues that such constructions are also stative[31] and, therefore, of a background nature in narrative. Even when they are judged to be describing an event in progress, Nicholas Bailey labels them as "background-progressive."[32]

Many events presented in the *pluperfect* in narrative are backgroundED "because the event concerned takes place prior to the time of the theme-line events."[33] See, for example, Mark 14:44 (δεδώκει δὲ ὁ παραδιδοὺς αὐτὸν σύσσημον αὐτοῖς "Now the betrayer had given them a sign"). However, I have argued elsewhere that οἶδα and ἵστημι function as "stative imperfectives,"[34] as in Matt 13:2 (καὶ πᾶς ὁ ὄχλος ἐπὶ τὸν αἰγιαλὸν εἰστήκει "and the whole crowd was standing on the beach"), so present background information in narrative because of their stative nature.

The *historical present* (HP) is not the default way of portraying an event in narrative, so must have "added implicatures." The consensus

---

28 Levinsohn, *Narrative*, §5.3.3. The use of the impf. to introduce an initial question in Mark 10:17 (ἐπηρώτα) is similar.

29 D. N. S. Bhat, *The Prominence of Tense, Aspect and Mood* (Amsterdam: Benjamins, 1999), 168–74.

30 See ch. 9 in the present volume.

31 See also Stephen H. Levinsohn, "Constituent Order in and Usages of εἰμί - Participle Combinations in the Synoptics and Acts," (paper presented at the International meeting of the SBL, St. Andrews, Scotland, July 2013, and at the Congress of the International Syriac Language Project, Munich, Germany, August 2013).

32 Nicholas A. Bailey, "Thetic Constructions in Koine Greek" (PhD diss., Vrije Universiteit Amsterdam, 2009), 195.

33 Levinsohn, *Narrative*, §5.2.3, #1.

34 Stephen H. Levinsohn, "Gnomic Aorists: No Problem! The Greek Indicative Verb System as Four Ordered Pairs" (paper presented at Tyndale House, Cambridge, England, October 2014), §4.

is that the HP is associated in some way with prominence. Although Porter affirms, "the present form draws added attention to the action to which it refers,"[35] John Callow insists that, particularly in Mark and John, the HP "does *not* draw attention to the event which the HP verb itself refers to, as those events, in themselves, are not particularly important—*to go, to say, to gather together, to see, etc.* ... [I]t has a *cataphoric* function; that is, it points on beyond itself into the narrative, it draws attention to what is following."[36] So, in Mark 1:21 (Καὶ εἰσπορεύονται εἰς Καφαρναούμ "They come to Capernaum"), "it is not the action of entering Capernaum itself that is particularly important. Rather, the presence of the HP points on beyond itself and draws attention to the subsequent events that take place in Capernaum."[37] In other words, εἰσπορεύονται gives prominence not so much to the act of entering Capernaum as to Jesus teaching in the synagogue there and the amazement of the crowd (ἐδίδασκεν, ἐξεπλήσσοντο) at his teaching (1:21b-22).

This section would not be complete without a comment about sentences introduced with γάρ. This particle "constrains sentences it introduces to be interpreted as strengthening material in the immediate context."[38] This means that, in narrative, sentences introduced with γάρ never present foreground events, even when the aorist is used. See, for example, Matt 14:3: Ὁ γὰρ Ἡρῴδης κρατήσας τὸν Ἰωάννην ἔδησεν [αὐτὸν] καὶ ἐν φυλακῇ ἀπέθετο διὰ Ἡρῳδιάδα τὴν γυναῖκα Φιλίππου τοῦ ἀδελφοῦ αὐτοῦ "For Herod had arrested John, bound him, and put him in prison on account of Herodias, his brother Philip's wife." Even though the indicative verbs are in the aorist, the events concerned are understood to have occurred prior to the foreground events of 14:1-2 (Ἐν ἐκείνῳ τῷ καιρῷ ἤκουσεν Ἡρῴδης ὁ τετραάρχης τὴν ἀκοὴν Ἰησοῦ, καὶ εἶπεν τοῖς παισὶν αὐτοῦ, Οὗτός ἐστιν Ἰωάννης ὁ βαπτιστής

---

35  Stanley E. Porter, *Idioms of the Greek New Testament*, BLG 2 (Sheffield: Sheffield Academic, 1992), 31.

36  John C. Callow, "The Historic Present in Mark" (paper presented at a seminar at SIL, Horsleys Green, UK, 1996), 2. For further discussion of this point, see Levinsohn, *Discourse Features*, §12.2 and Fanning, *Contribution*, 17-19. Westfall ("Analysis of prominence," 77) also allows for the "*domain of prominence*" to be "at the level of couplet, paragraph, section or discourse" (emphasis original).

37  Levinsohn, *Discourse Features*, §12.2.

38  Ibid., Part IV.

... "At that time Herod the ruler heard reports about Jesus; and he said to his servants, 'This is John the Baptist ...' ").

In summary, then, the indicative verb forms we have considered in this section relate to grounding in narrative in the following ways:

- aorist (default way of portraying an event as a whole): default foreground (unless introduced with γάρ).
- imperfect (default way of portraying an event as ongoing): usually background, but may be foreground; when not the natural way of portraying an event, has added implicatures and may be backgrounded or highlighted.
- perfect, pluperfect and "periphrastic" combinations of a copula and a participial clause: background because of their stative nature.
- historical present: usually cataphoric, pointing forward to and giving prominence to what follows.

## 3. SUBORDINATION AND TAIL-HEAD LINKAGE

Up to this point, our concern has mostly been with "devices used to background sentences."[39] When we consider subordination, we shift our attention to "backgrounding *within* a sentence."[40]

Although it is sometimes claimed that events presented in subordinate clauses are always background,[41] many postnuclear subordinate clauses in fact present foreground information. The postnuclear genitive absolute (GA) of Acts 28:25 (ἀσύμφωνοι δὲ ὄντες πρὸς ἀλλήλους ἀπελύοντο εἰπόντος τοῦ Παύλου ῥῆμα ἕν, ὅτι Καλῶς τὸ πνεῦμα τὸ ἅγιον ἐλάλησεν διὰ Ἡσαΐου τοῦ προφήτου πρὸς τοὺς πατέρας ὑμῶν "They disagreed among themselves and began to leave after Paul had made this final statement: 'The Holy Spirit spoke the truth to your forefathers when he said through Isaiah the prophet ...'" [NIV]) is

---

39 Levinsohn, *Narrative*, §5.2.3.
40 Ibid., §5.2.4 (emphasis original).
41 See, for example, Russell S. Tomlin, "Foreground-Background Information and the Syntax of Subordination," *Text* 5 (1–2) (1985), 85, who claims that the hypothesis that "dependent clauses code background information" is correct.

particularly noteworthy, as the event described in the GA took place prior to that of the main verb, yet must be of a foreground nature.[42]

*Prenuclear* subordinate clauses that describe events in narrative, in contrast, always background those events *in relation to* that of the main clause.[43] Such backgrounding does not necessarily place them on a par with nonevents, however, as the latter are inherently background in narrative. Rather, they are simply marked as *less important* than the main clause event.

This is illustrated in Mark 5:25–27 (below). "The effect of using the series of participial clauses is to signal that all the information prior to v. 27c is of secondary importance in relation to the foreground event described in v. 27c."[44] So, for instance, 'came up behind him in the crowd' is less important than 'touched his cloak' (27b–c), though it is still higher on Longacre's "cline of dynamicity"[45] than the stative clause of verse 25.[46]

25  καὶ γυνὴ οὖσα ἐν ῥύσει αἵματος δώδεκα ἔτη
Now there was a woman who had been suffering from hemorrhages for twelve years

---

42  "It is very remarkable, that the same prophetic quotation with which our Lord opened his teaching by parables [Matt. xiii. 14, 15], should form the solemn close of the historic Scriptures" (Henry Alford, *The Greek Testament* [London: Rivingtons, 1881], II.309). See also Mark 16:20 (ἐκεῖνοι δὲ ἐξελθόντες ἐκήρυξαν πανταχοῦ, τοῦ κυρίου συνεργοῦντος καὶ τὸν λόγον βεβαιοῦντος διὰ τῶν ἐπακολουθούντων σημείων "And they went out and proclaimed the good news everywhere, while the Lord worked with them and confirmed the message by the signs that accompanied it").

43  "Preposed participles (whether nominative or genitive absolute) which are dependent on a clause with an aorist supply the immediate backup to the storyline by adding preliminary detail" (Longacre, "Mark 5," 177). For nonnarrative exceptions involving narrow focus see Stephen H. Levinsohn, "Adverbial Participial Clauses in Koiné Greek: Grounding and Information Structure" (paper presented at the International Conference on Discourse and Grammar [DG2008]; "Illocutionary Force, Information Structure, and Subordination between Discourse and Grammar," Universeit Ghent, Belgium, 2008; http://www-01.sil.org/~levinsohns/GkParticipialClauses.pdf), §2; e.g., Οὐκ ἐντρέπων ὑμᾶς γράφω ταῦτα (1 Cor 4:14).

44  Levinsohn, *Discourse Features*, §II.1.2.

45  Longacre, "Mark 5," 179.

46  NRSV is typical of modern English versions that translate the participial clauses of 5:27b–c as main events. In contrast, "She had heard about Jesus" (5:27a) is inherently background because of the plupf. (see §2).

26a  καὶ πολλὰ παθοῦσα ὑπὸ πολλῶν ἰατρῶν
and having endured much under many physicians

26b  καὶ δαπανήσασα τὰ παρ' αὐτῆς πάντα
and having spent all that she had

26c  καὶ μηδὲν ὠφεληθεῖσα
and being no better

26d  ἀλλὰ μᾶλλον εἰς τὸ χεῖρον ἐλθοῦσα,
but rather growing worse

27a  ἀκούσασα περὶ τοῦ Ἰησοῦ,
having heard about Jesus,

27b  ἐλθοῦσα ἐν τῷ ὄχλῳ ὄπισθεν
having come up behind him in the crowd

27c  ἥψατο τοῦ ἱματίου αὐτοῦ·
she touched his cloak

Mark 1:14 (Μετὰ δὲ τὸ παραδοθῆναι τὸν Ἰωάννην ἦλθεν ὁ Ἰησοῦς εἰς τὴν Γαλιλαίαν κηρύσσων τὸ εὐαγγέλιον τοῦ θεοῦ "Now after John was arrested, Jesus came to Galilee, proclaiming the good news of God") is similar in that the sentence begins with a prenuclear adverbial clause Μετὰ ... τὸ παραδοθῆναι τὸν Ἰωάννην which is backgrounded in relation to the next events.[47]

The status of *postnuclear* subordinate clauses is "to be deduced from the context".[48] Longacre stated that the "postposed participle is of the same semantic rank as the verb that it follows".[49] This observation appears to be true for all postnuclear present nominative participial clauses (NPCs) with event verbs, as well as for many aorist NPCs. For instance, I understand the postnuclear present participles of Mark 1:14–15 (... ἦλθεν ὁ Ἰησοῦς εἰς τὴν Γαλιλαίαν κηρύσσων τὸ εὐαγγέλιον τοῦ θεοῦ καὶ λέγων ὅτι Πεπλήρωται ὁ καιρὸς ... "Jesus came to Galilee, proclaiming the good news of God, and saying, 'The time is

---

47  See Levinsohn, *Discourse Features*, §11.1.3 for discussion of the significance of beginning a sentence with an adverbial clause of time rather than a ptc.

48  Ibid., §11.1.2.

49  Longacre, "Mark 5," 177. In Matt 28:19–20, for instance, "the two postposed participles continue the action of the main verb and are semantically coordinate with it, issuing in a threefold command 'Make disciples ... baptize ... teach'" (Ibid., 178).

fulfilled ...'") to be describing foreground events. Similarly, the post-nuclear aorist participle of Luke 2:16 (καὶ ἦλθαν σπεύσαντες) would appear to be an integral part of the foreground event; hence, the NRSV translation "So they went with haste." As for Acts 7:27 (ὁ δὲ ἀδικῶν τὸν πλησίον ἀπώσατο αὐτὸν εἰπών, Τίς σε κατέστησεν ἄρχοντα καὶ δικαστὴν ἐφ' ἡμῶν; "But the man who was wronging his neighbor pushed Moses aside, saying, 'Who made you a ruler and a judge over us?'"), the aorist participial clause has probably been placed at the end of the sentence to mark it as the "dominant focal element."[50] because of its importance for what Stephen has to say in 7:35 (Τοῦτον τὸν Μωϋσῆν, ὃν ἠρνήσαντο εἰπόντες, Τίς σε κατέστησεν ἄρχοντα καὶ δικαστήν; "This Moses whom they rejected when they said, 'Who made you a ruler and a judge?'").

The clauses introduced by ὥστε in Mark 2:12 (καὶ ἠγέρθη καὶ εὐθὺς ἄρας τὸν κράβαττον ἐξῆλθεν ἔμπροσθεν πάντων, ὥστε ἐξίστασθαι πάντας καὶ δοξάζειν τὸν θεὸν λέγοντας ὅτι Οὕτως οὐδέποτε εἴδομεν "And he stood up, and immediately took the mat and went out before all of them; so that they were all amazed and glorified God, saying, 'We have never seen anything like this!'") may well describe foreground events, too.[51] In contrast, the event described in the postnuclear aorist GA in Acts 24:10 (Ἀπεκρίθη τε ὁ Παῦλος νεύσαντος αὐτῷ τοῦ ἡγεμόνος λέγειν "Paul replied, when the governor motioned to him to speak") would appear to be backgrounded in relation to Paul's response.[52]

---

50  Heimerdinger, *Topic, Focus and Foreground*, 167.

51  A number of modern English versions treat the contents of the clauses introduced by ὥστε as foreground information by translating them in a separate sentence. See, e.g., "They were all amazed and praised God, exclaiming, 'We've never seen anything like this before!'" (NLT)

52  When the event presented with a postnuclear aor. GA occurred before the event described in the main clause, such an order is marked, with added implicatures that may vary (compare Acts 24:10 with Acts 28:25). A similar claim can be made for some postnuclear NPCs that describe events that are out of order (compare Luke 1:12 [καὶ ἐταράχθη Ζαχαρίας ἰδὼν "Zechariah was terrified when he saw him"] with Matt 10:5 [Τούτους τοὺς δώδεκα ἀπέστειλεν ὁ Ἰησοῦς παραγγείλας αὐτοῖς ... "These twelve Jesus sent out after instructing them ..."]). In other instances, however, although the two events are technically out of order, as in Mark 1:31 (ἤγειρεν αὐτὴν κρατήσας τῆς χειρός "lifted her up, having taken her hand"), the purpose of the postnuclear NPC may be to describe "some aspect of the nuclear event" (Levinsohn, *Discourse Features*, §11.1.2), as the NET translates it, "raised her up by gently taking her hand."

Prenuclear subordinate clauses feature in *tail-head linkage*, which, in New Testament Greek, involves the repetition in the prenuclear clause (the "head" of the new sentence[53]) of the main verb and other information that occurred in the previous sentence (the "tail"). Tail-head linkage is sometimes employed immediately before a particularly significant event or speech to highlight it.[54] This repetition may be thought of as a rhetorical device that slows the story down prior to the significant event or speech.

Luke 23:46 (below) provides an example of tail-head linkage. The main verb of 23:46a is εἶπεν. This is repeated in participial form at the beginning of 23:46b, with the rhetorical effect of slowing down the story prior to the climactic event of Jesus' death.

46a   καὶ φωνήσας φωνῇ μεγάλῃ ὁ Ἰησοῦς εἶπεν, Πάτερ, εἰς χεῖράς σου παρατίθεμαι τὸ πνεῦμά μου.
Then Jesus, crying with a loud voice, said, "Father, into your hands I commend my spirit."

46b   τοῦτο δὲ εἰπὼν ἐξέπνευσεν.
Having said this, he breathed his last

## 4. SPECIFIC CONSTRUCTIONS

This section concerns the contribution to grounding made by two constructions: continuative relative clauses and the combination of ἐγένετο and an infinitive plus a temporal expression.

### 4.1 Continuative Relative Clauses

Linguists commonly divide relative clauses into two types: restrictive and nonrestrictive.

A *restrictive* relative clause "serves to delimit the potential referents."[55] In Luke 1:26 (εἰς πόλιν τῆς Γαλιλαίας ᾗ ὄνομα Ναζαρὲθ "to a

---

53  Neither "head" nor "tail" have their usual linguistic meaning here. In particular, "head" does not refer to the syntactic head.
54  For other reasons for employing tail-head linkage, see Levinsohn, *Discourse Features*, §12.1 and Levinsohn, *Narrative*, §3.2.3.
55  Bernard Comrie, *Language Universals and Linguistic Typology*, 2nd ed. (Chicago: University of Chicago Press, 1989), 138.

town in Galilee whose name [is] Nazareth"), for example, the relative clause "delimits the potential referents of 'a city of Galilee.'"[56]

A *nonrestrictive* relative clause "serves merely to give the hearer an added piece of information about an already identified entity, but not to identify that entity."[57] So, in Acts 9:36 (Ἐν Ἰόππῃ δέ τις ἦν μαθήτρια ὀνόματι Ταβιθά, ἣ διερμηνευομένη λέγεται Δορκάς "Now in Joppa there was a disciple named Tabitha, which in Greek is Dorcas"), the relative clause adds a piece of information about a woman who has already been identified as Ταβιθά.

Nonrestrictive relative clauses in Greek are traditionally subdivided into *appositional* and *continuative*.[58] Appositional relative clauses, as their name suggests, stand in apposition to the noun that they modify (as in Acts 9:36 [above]). Continuative relative clauses, in contrast, "typically describe an **event** that involves the referent of the relative pronoun and occurs subsequent to the previous event or situation in which the referent featured."[59] "Characteristically, the information preceding the relative clause is *backgrounded* in relation to what follows."[60]

Acts 1:10–11 (καὶ ἰδοὺ ἄνδρες δύο παρειστήκεισαν αὐτοῖς ἐν ἐσθήσεσι λευκαῖς, οἳ καὶ εἶπαν... "While he was going and they were gazing up toward heaven, suddenly two men in white robes stood by them, who also said ...") provides an example. The continuative relative clause allows the writer to introduce new participants to the discourse and to describe what they did in a single sentence. Pragmatically, this construction also tends to background their appearance to the apostles over against the message that they bring (οὗτος ὁ Ἰησοῦς ὁ ἀναλημφθεὶς ἀφ' ὑμῶν εἰς τὸν οὐρανὸν οὕτως ἐλεύσεται ὃν τρόπον ἐθεάσασθε αὐτὸν πορευόμενον εἰς τὸν οὐρανόν This Jesus, who has been taken up from you into heaven, will come in the same way as you saw him go into heaven").

Acts 11:29–30 (τῶν δὲ μαθητῶν, καθὼς εὐπορεῖτό τις, ὥρισαν ἕκαστος αὐτῶν εἰς διακονίαν πέμψαι τοῖς κατοικοῦσιν ἐν τῇ Ἰουδαίᾳ ἀδελφοῖς·[30] καὶ ἐποίησαν ἀποστείλαντες πρὸς τοὺς πρεσβυτέρους διὰ χειρὸς Βαρναβᾶ

---

56 Levinsohn, *Discourse Features*, §11.2.
57 Comrie, *Language Universals*, 138.
58 G. B. Winer, *A Treatise on the Grammar of New Testament Greek*, trans. W. F. Moulton (Edinburgh: T&T Clark, 1882), 680.
59 Levinsohn, *Narrative*, §10.3.4 (emphasis original).
60 Levinsohn, *Discourse Features*, §11.2 (emphasis original).

καὶ Σαύλου "The disciples determined that according to their ability, each would send relief to the believers living in Judea; ³⁰which they did, sending it to the elders by Barnabas and Saul") ends with a continuative relative clause complex. In the first instance, the continuative relative clause allows the writer to present what the disciples decided to do and the realization of their purpose in a single sentence. Pragmatically, the construction also tends to background their decision (11:29) over against the realization of that decision and, particularly, how they realized it (through Barnabas and Saul). In other words, "So the believers in Antioch decided to send relief to the brothers and sisters in Judea, everyone giving as much as they could" is backgrounded in relation to the foreground events "This they did, entrusting their gifts to Barnabas and Saul to take to the elders of the church in Jerusalem" (NLT).

## 4.2 Ἐγένετο Plus a Temporal Expression

I claim elsewhere that the combination of ἐγένετο and a temporal expression, as in Acts 9:37 (ἐγένετο δὲ ἐν ταῖς ἡμέραις ἐκείναις ἀσθενήσασαν αὐτὴν ἀποθανεῖν "It happened at that time that she became ill and died") "is a device found in the LXX that Luke often uses to background information with respect to the following foreground events ... In particular, it picks out from the general background the *specific circumstance* for the foreground events that are to follow."[61] So, in the above verse, "the temporal expression ἐν ταῖς ἡμέραις ἐκείναις refers to a particular time within the period during which the general background situation of 9:36 [αὕτη ἦν πλήρης ἔργων ἀγαθῶν καὶ ἐλεημοσυνῶν ὧν ἐποίει] held true. The infinitival clause ἀσθενήσασαν αὐτὴν ἀποθανεῖν, which is the subject of ἐγένετο, then presents the specific circumstance that leads to the following foreground events."[62]

In Luke's Gospel, the event that follows ἐγένετο plus a temporal expression is not always presented in an infinitival clause. See, for instance, Luke 17:14 (καὶ ἐγένετο ἐν τῷ ὑπάγειν αὐτοὺς ἐκαθαρίσθησαν "And it happened that, as they went, they were made clean"). The aorist implies that the act of healing (ἐκαθαρίσθησαν) is a foreground event. At the same time, the use of ἐγένετο plus a temporal expression to

---

61  Ibid., §10.3 (emphasis original).
62  Ibid.

introduce it may well have the effect of backgrounding the healing in relation to what follows. This would imply that, as far as Luke is concerned, the healing is less important than the events of 17:15–19.

## 5. SUMMARY AND CONCLUDING COMMENTS

This paper has made the following claims about grounding in narrative.

1.  Because of the nature of narrative, events are assumed to be of a foreground nature unless they are marked in some way. Background information in narrative thus consists of the *nonevents*, together with those events that are *marked* as being of secondary importance (nonthematic).

2.  When considering how the indicative verb forms relate to grounding in narrative, it is useful to distinguish between the natural prominence associated with each tense form and marked uses when the tense-form chosen is judged not to be the default way of portraying the event concerned.

    The *natural* prominence in narrative of the indicative verb forms we have considered is as follows:

    *   Aorists (which portray events as a whole) are the default way of presenting foreground events (unless introduced with γάρ).
    *   Imperfects (which in their default usage portray an event as ongoing) usually present background information, but some events in the imperfect may be foreground.
    *   Perfects, "periphrastic" combinations of a copula and a participial clause, and some pluperfects present background information because of their stative nature.
    *   "True" pluperfects present background information because the events they describe took place *prior* to the theme line events.

    We have noted the following *marked* uses of indicative verb forms:

    *   When an imperfect is used even though it appears not to be the natural way of portraying an event, this has added implicatures such as backgrounding or highlighting.

- Historical presents are usually cataphoric, pointing forward to and giving prominence to what follows.

3. *Prenuclear* subordinate clauses in narrative always background the event concerned in relation to that of the main clause. The status of *postnuclear* subordinate clauses, however, is to be deduced from the context.[63] Prenuclear clauses sometimes feature in *tail-head linkage* immediately before the presentation of a particularly significant event or speech, to highlight it.

4. Two constructions that tend to background information in relation to what follows are *continuative relative clauses* (the information preceding the relative pronoun is backgrounded in relation to what follows) and the combination of ἐthe comand a temporal expression, which picks out from the general background the specific circumstance for the foreground events that are to follow.

Finally, a comment about reported speeches in Mark's Gospel that are introduced with an imperfect speech verb such as ἔλεγεν, even though they appear to have been uttered on a specific occasion. Cross-linguistically, when the theme line of a narrative text consists primarily of nonspeech events, it is common for the majority of reported speeches to be introduced with a form that backgrounds them in relation to theme-line speeches or nonspeech events. One way to indicate this is to present the theme-line events and speeches with perfective aspect, but to introduce those speeches that are backgrounded in relation to the theme-line events with

---

63 The differing status of prenuclear and postnuclear subordinate clauses results from the interaction of two potentially conflicting tendencies:
(1) A tendency for subordinate clauses to be used for less "salient" material (Runge, ch. 7 in this volume).
(2) A tendency for less salient material to precede more salient material.
When a subordinate clause precedes a main clause, the two tendencies coincide, which is why prenuclear subordinate clauses in narrative always background the event concerned in relation to that of the main clause. When a subordinate clause follows a main clause, in contrast, the tendencies are in conflict. In passages such as Acts 28:25 (§3, above), the second tendency is to the fore. In others, the first tendency is to the fore, as in Acts 24:10 (ibid.). In others again, such as Mark 2:12 (ibid.), the two tendencies cancel each other out, so that the events concerned are equally salient.

imperfect aspect.[64] Could it be that Mark is an event-oriented narrative, with reported speeches marked as:

- Default: imperfect[65]
- Prominent, usually cataphoric: historical present
- Theme line: aorist?

## BIBLIOGRAPHY

Alford, Henry. *The Greek Testament*. London: Rivingtons, 1881.

Bailey, Nicholas A. *"Thetic Constructions in Koine Greek."* PhD diss., Vrije Universiteit Amsterdam, 2009.

Barnard, Jody A. "Is Verbal Aspect a Prominence Indicator? An Evaluation of Stanley E. Porter's Proposal with Special Reference to the Gospel of Luke." *FilNeot* 19 (2006): 3–29.

Bhat, D. N. S. *The Prominence of Tense, Aspect and Mood*. Amsterdam: Benjamins, 1999.

Callow, John C. "The Historic Present in Mark." Paper presented at a seminar at SIL. Horsleys Green, UK, 1996.

Callow, Kathleen. *Discourse Considerations in Translating the Word of God*. Grand Rapids: Zondervan, 1974.

Campbell, Constantine R. *Basics of Verbal Aspect in Biblical Greek*. Grand Rapids: Zondervan, 2008.

Comrie, Bernard. *Language Universals and Linguistic Typology*. 2nd ed. Chicago: University of Chicago Press, 1989.

Dormeyer, Florencio, and Florencio Galindo. *Comentario a los Hechos de los Apóstoles: Modelo de Nueva Evangelización*. Estella, Navarra, Spain: Verbo Divino, 2007.

Fanning, Buist. "Greek Presents, Imperfects, and Aorists in the Synoptic Gospels: Their Contribution to Narrative Structuring." Paper presented at the Annual Meeting of the SBL. New Orleans, November 2009.

Fleischman, Suzanne. "Toward a Theory of Tense-Aspect in Narrative Discourse." Pages 75–97 in *The Function of Tense in Texts*. Edited by Jadranka Gvozdanović and Th. A. J. M. Janssen. Amsterdam: North Holland, 1991.

---

64 See Levinsohn, *Narrative*, §7.5.1 for discussion of this point.
65 For discussion of such "markedness reversal," see Suzanne Fleischman, "Toward a Theory of Tense-Aspect in Narrative Discourse," in *The Function of Tense in Texts*, ed. Jadranka Gvozdanović and Th. A. J. M. Janssen (Amsterdam: North Holland, 1991), 77.

Foley, William A., and Robert D. Van Valin. *Functional Syntax and Universal Grammar*. Cambridge: Cambridge University Press, 1984.

Gutt, Ernst-August. *Translation and Relevance: Cognition and Context*. Oxford: Blackwell, 1991.

Heimerdinger, Jean-Marc. *Topic, Focus and Foreground in Ancient Hebrew Narratives*. JSOTSup 295. Sheffield: Sheffield Academic, 1999.

Hopper, Paul J. "Aspect and Foregrounding in Discourse." Pages 213–41 in *Discourse and Syntax*. Edited by Talmy Givón. Syntax and Semantics 12. New York: Academic Press, 1979.

Levinsohn, Stephen H. "Adverbial Participial Clauses in Koiné Greek: Grounding and Information Structure." Paper presented at the International Conference on Discourse and Grammar [DG2008] "Illocutionary Force, Information Structure, and Subordination between Discourse and Grammar." Universeit Ghent, Belgium, 2008. http://www-01.sil.org/~levinsohns/GkParticipialClauses.pdf.

———. "Aspect and Prominence in the Synoptic Accounts of Jesus' Entry into Jerusalem." *FilNeot* 23 (2010), 161–74.

———. "Constituent Order in and Usages of εἰμί - Participle Combinations in the Synoptics and Acts." Paper presented at the International Meeting of the SBL. St. Andrews, Scotland, July 2013. Also presented at the Congress of the International Syriac Language Project. Munich, Germany, August 2013.

———. *Discourse Features of New Testament Greek: A Coursebook on the Information Structure of New Testament Greek*. 2nd ed. Dallas: SIL International, 2000.

———. "Functions of Copula-Participle Combinations ('Periphrastics')." In *The Greek Verb Revisited: A Fresh Approach for Biblical Exegesis*. Edited by Steven E. Runge and Christopher J. Fresch. Bellingham, WA: Lexham Press, forthcoming.

———. "Gnomic Aorists: No Problem! The Greek Indicative Verb System as Four Ordered Pairs." Paper presented at Tyndale House. Cambridge, England, October 2014.

———. *Self-Instruction Materials on Narrative Discourse Analysis*. 2012. http://www-01.sil.org/~levinsohns/narr.pdf.

Longacre, Robert E. *The Grammar of Discourse*. 2nd ed. New York: Plenum, 1996.

———. "Mark 5.1–43: Generating the Complexity of a Narrative from Its Most Basic Elements." Pages 169–96 in *Discourse Analysis and the New Testament: Approaches and Results*. Edited by

Stanley E. Porter and Jeffrey T. Reed. JSNTSup 170. Sheffield: Sheffield Academic, 1999.

Porter, Stanley E. *Idioms of the Greek New Testament.* BLG 2. Sheffield: Sheffield Academic, 1992.

———. "Prominence: An Overview." Pages 45–74 in *The Linguist as Pedagogue: Trends in the Teaching and Linguistic Analysis of the Greek New Testament.* Edited by Stanley E. Porter and Matthew Brook O'Donnell. NTM 11. Sheffield: Sheffield Phoenix, 2009.

Tomlin, Russell S. "Foreground-Background Information and the Syntax of Subordination." *Text* 5 (1–2) (1985): 85–122.

Westfall, Cynthia Long "A Method for the Analysis of Prominence in Hellenistic Greek." Pages 75–94 in *The Linguist as Pedagogue: Trends in the Teaching and Linguistic Analysis of the Greek New Testament.* Edited by Stanley E. Porter and Matthew Brook O'Donnell. NTM 11. Sheffield: Sheffield Phoenix, 2009.

Wilson, Deirdre, and Dan Sperber. *Meaning and Relevance.* Cambridge: Cambridge University Press, 2012.

Winer, G. B. *A Treatise on the Grammar of New Testament Greek.* Translated by W. F. Moulton. Edinburgh: T&T Clark, 1882.

Zegarač, Vladimir. "Relevance Theory and the Meaning of the English Progressive." *UCLWPL* 1 (1989): 19–30.

# CHAPTER 6

# Imperfects, Aorists, Historic Presents, and Perfects in John 11: A Narrative Test Case

PATRICK JAMES

THE GREEK LEXICON PROJECT | FACULTY OF CLASSICS,
UNIVERSITY OF CAMBRIDGE

Before considering the variation in John 11:1–47 between imperfect, aorist, (historic) present, and perfect verb forms, it seems worthwhile to set out my understanding of verbal aspect in Ancient Greek, with illustrative examples from John 11, and of some of the issues in using such a text as a source of linguistic evidence.[1] The following points numbered (1)–(12) have their origin in what I was taught as a first-year undergraduate learning Classical Greek (more or less) *ab initio*[2] and studying Classical Philology and Linguistics. They have

---

[1] I wish to thank the editors of this volume for their invitation to present and forbearance; in particular, Steven Runge for his comments on my draft and Chris Fresch for our initial discussion of the passage. Drs Simon Gathercole and Kim Phillips kindly assisted by providing me with access to certain books

[2] All translations are my own, and I ask that they be read with charity. Their function is to convey my understanding of the Greek for the purposes of this chapter. Translation always involves making decisions and selecting from options. My translation of John 11 was not intended to address every point of interpretation in that passage. In some instances, I am more or less aware of the issues involved, as in the question of how to translate οἱ Ἰουδαῖοι (e.g., 11:8), but I am not in a position to comment on others, such as the nature of the σπήλαιον (11:38). I am aware of the need for further consideration of some points (e.g., the variation between aor., pres., and pf. forms of πιστεύω in 11:15, 26, 27, 40, 42, 45), but, doubtless, not of others.

been developed through my subsequent studies,[3] teaching, and research for the Cambridge Greek Lexicon.[4]

The focus of this test case is an examination of a past-time narrative that consists of finite indicative verb forms. However, an explanation of verbal aspect in Greek is best begun, in my view, with forms and constructions in which there is no temporal contrast and in which past time is not a component. Aspect needs to be disentangled from "tense."[5]

(1) An "action," either as an event as a whole or as it unfolds in progress as a "process," can be situated in any of three "time periods": the past, the present, and the future. The same is true of a "state."[6] I refer to "time periods" in order to avoid the potential

---

The principal authorities were as follows: Bernard Comrie, *Aspect: An Introduction to the Study of Verbal Aspect and Related Problems*, CTL (Cambridge: Cambridge University Press, 1976) and *Tense*, CTL (Cambridge: Cambridge University Press, 1985); John Lyons, *Introduction to Theoretical Linguistics* (Cambridge: Cambridge University Press, 1968), 313–17; L. R. Palmer, *The Latin Language* (London: Faber and Faber, 1954), 265–76; and L. R. Palmer, *The Greek Language* (London: Faber and Faber, 1980), 293, 300–307.

3   What I was taught about the verb in Proto-Indo-European became James Clackson, *Indo-European Linguistics: An Introduction*, CTL (Cambridge: Cambridge University Press, 2007), 114–56.

4   Albert Rijksbaron, *The Syntax and Semantics of the Verb in Classical Greek: An Introduction*, 3rd ed. (Chicago: University of Chicago Press, 2006) has become a standard point of reference. T. V. Evans, *Verbal Syntax in the Greek Pentateuch: Natural Greek Usage and Hebrew Interference* (Oxford: Oxford University Press, 2001), 13–51, is very helpful on recent debates in aspectology and Greek. Another influence has been the research by Maria Napoli, *Aspect and Actionality in Homeric Greek: A Contrastive Analysis*, Materiali linguistici 54 (Milan: FrancoAngeli, 2006).

5   A ready starting point in my studies was Lysias 1.12 (καὶ ἐγὼ τὴν γυναῖκα ἀπιέναι ἐκέλευον καὶ δοῦναι τῷ παιδίῳ τὸν τιτθόν, ἵνα παύσηται κλαῖον "and I used to tell my wife to go away and to give the breast to the infant in order that it might stop crying."), which happens also to open the discussion in Evans, *Verbal Syntax in the Greek Pentateuch*, 13–14. The aor. inf. δοῦναι may be contrasted with the present subjunctive in Lysias 1.10 (ἵνα τὸν τιτθὸν αὐτῷ διδῷ "in order that she might offer"). Another starting point would be the minimal pair of a pf. and an aor. inf. in S. *Ant*. 441–443: (Creon) σὲ δή, σὲ τὴν νεύουσαν εἰς πέδον κάρα, | φῄς, ἢ καταρνῇ μὴ δεδρακέναι τάδε; "You there, you who are bowing your head towards the ground, do you admit, or do you deny, that you have done this?" | (Antigone) καὶ φημὶ δρᾶσαι κοὐκ ἀπαρνοῦμαι τὸ μή. "I admit that I did it and I do not deny it."

6   This is, of course, a simplification in that, as Robert Crellin (ch. 14 in this volume) explains there are pure, anterior, and resultative states and the Greek pf. is not stable throughout the history of the language. See Robert

for confusion presented by the traditional term "tenses." The past, present, and the future are usually defined in relation to the speaker or writer.

(2) Aspect has been prioritized in (1) over the time period in which an event as a whole, a process, or a state is situated. The Greek verb system consists of three stems (imperfective, perfective, and perfect: πιστευ-, πιστευσ-, and πε-πιστευκ-) that are seen in the infinitive, subjunctive, optative, imperative, and participle as well as the indicative. In the indicative, these stems secondarily form "tenses," morphological "packages" of an aspectual stem and an indication of a time period, most obviously in the presence of the augment (ἐ-πιστεύ-ο-μεν past imperfective) or its absence (πιστεύ-ο-μεν present imperfective) and, in more intricate ways, by some of the personal endings (-ο-μεν is not marked for time period, but -α-μεν, whether an aorist or a perfect ending, stands in contrast to the imperfective ending). The future stem and the array of personal endings are complexities that may be left aside for present purposes.

(3) However, not every verb is attested in every combination of time period and aspect. The verb θνήσκω is one that can be used to illustrate the verb system almost in its entirety (as in the following table)[7] and is relevant for the passage under consideration here.

Crellin, "The Greek Perfect Active System: 200 BC–150 AD" (PhD diss., University of Cambridge, 2012). The pf. system in Mycenaean Greek (pf. ptcs. that are neutral for voice) and in Homer is different from that in Classical Greek, which in turn differs from the use of the pf. in post-Classical Greek. The sole modern survivor, βρῆκα (< εὕρηκα), which functions as an aor., illustrates some of how much the system has changed. For that form, see, for example, Basil G. Mandilaras, *Studies in the Greek Language: Some Aspects of the Development of the Greek Language up to the Present*, (Athens: Xenopoulos, 1972), 14.

7   This example was suggested by Plato, *Phaedo* 64a: κινδυνεύουσι γὰρ ὅσοι τυγχάνουσιν ὀρθῶς ἁπτόμενοι φιλοσοφίας λεληθέναι τοὺς ἄλλους ὅτι οὐδὲν ἄλλο αὐτοὶ ἐπιτηδεύουσιν ἢ ἀποθνήσκειν τε καὶ τεθνάναι "For all who happen to engage in philosophy in the true sense of the word run the risk that the rest are not aware that they themselves practice nothing other than both dying and being dead." The illustrative value of this verb is increased by the existence of an active fut. pf. in the fifth century BC and a middle in later authors. The grammarian Ammonius used this in his note on the difference between the aor. and pf., which will be discussed below. Palmer, *Latin Language*, 265, contrasts the pres., aor., and fut. infs. of this verb.

|  | Past | Present | Future |
|---|---|---|---|
| Event | ἔθανεν "He died (on impact)." Cf. John 11:14, 21, and 32. | [7] | θανεῖται "He will die." (not: μέλλει θανεῖν[8] "He is about to die"). Cf. ἵνα ἀποθάνωμεν in John 11:16 of a death in the future "in order that we may die (in the no so distant future)" |
| Process | ἔθνῃσκε "He was dying (of cancer)." | θνῄσκει "He is dying (of cancer)." | μέλλει θνῄσκειν or θανεῖσθαι "He is about to be dying."[9] |
| State | ἐτεθήνκει "He was dead." | τέθνηκε "He is dead." | τεθνήξει or τεθνήξεται "He will be dead." |

8    This box strictly cannot be filled, as is discussed by Klaas Bentein, "Tense and Aspect from Hellenistic to Early Byzantine Greek," *EAGLL* 3:379–82. It has some candidates, such as *Il.* 21.106, which Achilles speaks of Lycaon's imminent and instantaneous death: ἀλλὰ φίλος θάνε καὶ σύ· "All the same, friend, you die too!" The contrasting form would be the imperfective impv.: θνῆσκε "Be dying!"

9    One of my tutors used examples with μέλλω with aor. and pres. infs. in contrast. I have noted the impossibility of the aor. inf. here because the second-century Atticist grammarian Phrynichus condemned the use of μέλλω with an aor. inf. twice in his *Ecloga*: first, (313) ἔμελλον ποιῆσαι, ἔμελλον θεῖναι· ἁμάρτημα τῶν ἐσχάτων εἴ τις οὕτως συντάττει. τετήρηται γὰρ ἢ τῷ ἐνεστῶτι ἢ τῷ μέλλοντι συντασσόμενον, οἷον ἔμελλον ποιεῖν ἢ ποιήσειν. τὰ δὲ συντελικὰ οὐδένα τρόπον ἁρμόσει τῷ μέλλοντι "'I was about to do, I was about to put': It is one of the worst errors, if anyone uses such a construction. For the observation has been made that it is construed either with the present or with the future; for example, 'I was about to be writing' or 'I was intending that I will write.' In no way do the past tenses fit with the future." And, second, (347) ἔμελλον γράψαι: ἐσχάτως βάρβαρος ἡ σύνταξις αὕτη. ἀορίστῳ γὰρ χρόνῳ τὸ ἔμελλον οὐ συντάττουσιν οἱ Ἀθηναῖοι, ἀλλ᾽ ἤτοι ἐνεστῶτι, οἷον ἔμελλον γράφειν, ἢ μέλλοντι, οἷον ἔμελλον γράψειν "'I was about to write' this combination is barbarous in the extreme. For the Athenians do not arrange the future with an aorist tense, but either with a present, as in 'I was about to be writing,' or with a future, as in 'I was intending that I will write.'" Although Phrynichus's reasoning is formulated in terms of tenses (ἐνεστῶτι, μέλλοντι, and τὰ συντελικά or ἀορίστῳ χρόνῳ), not aspects, his observation is generally valid, at least for Classical Attic Greek and his comment here, as elsewhere, seems to be a reaction to the vernacular Greek of his time. See BDF, 174, for μέλλω and, for Phrynichus, see G. C. Horrocks, *Greek: A History of the Language and*

(4) The imperfect and aorist indicative stand in contrast in narrative. Our passage illustrates such a contrast in 11:47 συνήγαγον οὖν οἱ ἀρχιερεῖς καὶ οἱ Φαρισαῖοι συνέδριον καὶ ἔλεγον "So, the high priests and the Pharisees <u>gathered</u> the Sanhedrin together and <u>were saying</u>."

(5) To use a cinematic analogy: the aorist presents the "wide" view of an action as an event either in its entirety or with either its beginning or its end in view (as with ἀπέθανεν "he died" and ἐδάκρυσεν "he wept," 11:14 and 35). By contrast, the imperfect presents the "tight" view of part of an unfolding process with its internal detail and with neither its end nor (usually) its beginning in view.

(6) Speakers and writers of Greek had a choice about whether to present a process in the imperfect or an event in the aorist (both in contrast to a state in the perfect) in past time. I have used "choice" and "to present" deliberately and in contrast to discussions of verbal aspect which are framed in terms of how the action is viewed. The viewpoint could be either (as T. V. Evans rightly regards it)[11] that of the speaker or writer or, as others have formulated the issue, that of a spectator.[12]

(7) The choice between the imperfect and aorist is independent of the duration of the action. Instead, it is a choice between presenting a process in detail or an event in summary. For example, a verb

---

its *Speakers*, 2nd ed. (Chichester: Wiley-Blackwell, 2010), 138–39, and Robert Browning, *Medieval and Modern Greek*, 2nd ed. (Cambridge: Cambridge University Press, 1983), 47–48. Bentein, "Tense and Aspect," summarizes the infinitival periphrases of post-Classical Greek, of which only μέλλω is said to have the fut. inf. as an option in addition to the aor. and pres. infs.

10  Albert Thumb, "On the Value of Modern Greek for the Study of Ancient Greek," *ClQ* 8 (1914): 182, noted that an aspectual distinction became grammaticalized in the future in Modern Greek, as in θὰ γράφω "I will be writing" (a pres. subjunctive in origin) and θὰ γράψω "I will write" (an aor. subjunctive in origin). There are a few traces of such a distinction as early as Homer, such as the pair of futures ἕξω "I will have" (akin to the imperfective stem, ἔχ-ω "I possess") and σχήσω "I will take possession" (akin to the perfective stem, ἔ-σχ-ο-ν "I did possess").

11  Evans, *Verbal Syntax in the Greek Pentateuch*, 50.

12  For an overview of discussions of verbal aspect, see Christopher J. Thomson, ch. 2 in this volume, on the analogy of the set viewpoints of various spectators at a Soviet May Day Parade. Klaas Bentein, "Aspectual Choice and the Presentation of Narrative: An Application to Herodotus' *Histories*," *Glotta* 92 (forthcoming), and "Aspectual Choice with *verba dicendi* in Herodotus' *Histories*," *Emerita* 83 (2015), 221–45, articles which I have not yet seen, employs the term "choice" in relation to verbal aspect.

such as μένω that involves a duration by nature is used both in the aorist, as in John 11:6, and in the imperfect with an indication of the extent of that duration.

> τότε μὲν ἔμεινεν ἐν ᾧ ἦν τόπῳ δύο ἡμέρας
> At that time, he <u>waited</u> in the place where he was for <u>two days</u>.

Here, the aorist is not "punctual." The wait is presented in summary, not in progress, but with a specific duration.

Our passage does not provide an example that would form a minimal pair with this one. However, 11:17 αὐτὸν τέσσαρας ἤδη ἡμέρας ἔχοντα ἐν τῷ μνημείῳ "that he had been in the tomb for four days already" illustrates the alternative that was available in that, in this context, ἔχοντα the present participle (or, rather and henceforth, the participle of the imperfective stem) functions as an imperfect indicative and the extent of the duration is specified by the accusative τέσσαρας ... ἡμέρας "for four days."

The Gospel of John itself provides a closer parallel, such as ἐὰν αὐτὸν θέλω μένειν ἕως ἔρχομαι, τί πρὸς σέ; "If I want him <u>to remain</u> until I come, what is that to you?" (21: 22). Again, a wait is involved, but here it is presented as a process with a definite end (ἕως ἔρχομαι "until I come"). There is no accusative of temporal extent, but a (somewhat empty) phrase such as πάντα τὸν χρόνον "for all the time" could be understood. Since such a phrase in this context has to be nonspecific, it is unlikely to be specified. The important point here is not the duration of the ongoing wait, but the event that will end it (ἕως ἔρχομαι "until I come").

A minimal pair is provided by the end of Acts 28:16 and 30–31:

> [16] ἐπετράπη τῷ Παύλῳ μένειν καθ' ἑαυτὸν σὺν τῷ
> φυλάσσοντι αὐτὸν στρατιώτῃ.
> Permission was granted to Paul to <u>reside</u>
> independently with the soldier who was guarding him.

> [30] ἐνέμεινεν δὲ διετίαν ὅλην ἐν ἰδίῳ μισθώματι καὶ ἀπεδέχετο
> πάντας τοὺς εἰσπορευομένους πρὸς αὐτόν, κηρύσσων τὴν
> βασιλείαν τοῦ θεοῦ καὶ διδάσκων τὰ περὶ τοῦ κυρίου Ἰησοῦ
> Χριστοῦ μετὰ πάσης παρρησίας ἀκωλύτως.
> He <u>resided</u> for two whole years in his own rented
> lodging and he used to welcome all who came to him,

<u>proclaiming</u> the kingdom of God and <u>teaching</u> about
the Lord Jesus Christ, with all frankness and without
hindrance.

The same wait is described, first with an infinitive of the imperfective stem and with no duration specified by an accusative, and second with an aorist indicative (or, rather, the indicative of the perfective stem), an accusative specifying the duration of that wait, and two imperfective participles that specify the details of Paul's ongoing activity during the wait that is presented in summary.

(8) The choice between presentation as a process or as an event as a whole was limited by the nature of certain actions. For example, since the verb "to be" is progressive by nature, it has no aorist, but is readily used in the imperfect: ἤμην (11:15), ἦς (11:21, 32), ἦν (11:1, 2, 5, 18, 30, 32, and 38). By contrast, the verb "to flash"[13] is inherently not a process, but an event which cannot be analyzed further. An iterative function is the obligatory interpretation of an imperfective use, such as "to be flashing," that is, "to flash again and again" or "emit a series of flashes."

(9) This limitation was circumvented at the morphological and lexical levels. For example, an inherently perfective (or "telic") Indo-European root *sleH₂gʷ- underlies the Greek thematic aorist ἔ-λαβ-ον, which is itself the origin of various imperfective aspect forms. Aside from the familiar imperfect, ἐ-λάμβαν-ο-ν, which was formed by the addition of two nasal infixes, two other imperfects existed: ἐ-λαζό-μην (in Homer and various dialects),[14] and ἐ-λαζύ-μην (in the Homeric Hymns and various dialects).[15] The future was originally λήψομαι, without an infix, but this was remodeled as λήμψομαι in the Hellenistic period to align with the present tense forms.

Another example illustrates this phenomenon across languages in the Indo-European family. The inherently perfective root

---

13  I have taken this example from Thomson, ch. 2 in this volume. For a flash or twinkle as a prototypically indivisible event, note 1 Cor 15:52: ἐν ἀτόμῳ, ἐν ῥιπῇ ὀφθαλμοῦ, ἐν τῇ ἐσχάτῃ σάλπιγγι "in an instant, in the flash (or 'glance') of an eye, at the final trumpet blast."

14  There are no instances of the imperfective stem λαμβαν- either in Homer or in the Homeric Hymns.

15  For the details of the Greek forms, see Robert S. P.Beekes and Lucien van Beek, *Etymological Dictionary of Greek*, IEED 10 (Leiden: Brill, 2010), 822 and 828–29.

*leikʷ- is the origin of the Greek thematic aorist ἔ-λιπ-ο-ν, from which imperfective aspect forms were created. In addition to the familiar imperfect ἔ-λειπ-ον (with the e-grade of the root, cf. Gothic leiƕan and Old High German līhan), there was ἐ-λίμπαν-ο-ν (cf. Armenian lkʿ-an-em), with two nasal infixes (attested in compounds with δι-[16] and ὑπ-[17]). A third possibility for creating an imperfective stem is illustrated by Latin imperfective re-linquo "I leave" (perfective re-līqui "I left," re-lictus "having been left") and Sanskrit riṇákti "he/she/it leaves," which involve a single infix.[18] This shows that although the daughter languages faced the same problem, they did not all use the same solution to obtain an imperfective counterpart to perfective verb stems that they inherited.

(10) We may not be able either to determine or to express why an aorist has been used in preference to an imperfect, but it does not follow that there was no reason behind that decision.

(11) It may not be possible to determine the original or current aspectual value of a given form with certainty. For example, it seems likely that there is an aspectual contrast in 11:20 between Martha's immediate action (ὑπήντησεν) and Mary's ongoing condition (ἐκαθέζετο):

ἡ οὖν Μάρθα ὡς ἤκουσεν ὅτι Ἰησοῦς ἔρχεται <u>ὑπήντησεν</u> αὐτῷ·
Μαριὰμ δὲ ἐν τῷ οἴκῳ <u>ἐκαθέζετο</u>
So, when she heard that Jesus was coming, Martha <u>met</u> with him. But Mary <u>continued to sit</u> in the house.

There is no doubt that ὑπήντησεν is an aorist indicative, but scholars disagree about whether ἐκαθέζετο is an imperfect ("She was sitting") or an aorist ("She took her seat"), both in this instance and elsewhere. Friedrich Blass, Albert Debrunner, and Robert Funk noted "ἐκαθέζετο 'sat' ('had sat down') Jn 4:6, 11:20, for which elsewhere ἐκάθητο."[19] Frederick Danker explained John 4:6 (s.v. καθέζομαι 2)[20] as

---

16  Cf. Acts 8:24 D and 17:13 D.
17  Cf. 1 Pet 2:21. LSJ, 1887, s.v. ὑπολιμπάνω cites two Hellenistic papyri with middle forms of this verb.
18  This example is employed by Clackson, Indo-European Linguistics, 151–55. For the details of the Greek forms and their cognates, see Beekes, Etymological Dictionary of Greek, 844–45.
19  BDF, 52.
20  BDAG, 490.

"the impf. w. aor. nuance: 'I sat down'" (as well as the variant reading for [ἐκεῖ] ἐκάθητο in John 6:3 and the reading of Codex Bezae[21] in Luke 22:30), but explains John 11:20 specifically (s.v. 1): "ἐν τῷ οἴκῳ sit, remain at home J[ohn] 11:20" (emphasis original). The only other indicative of this verb in the New Testament (καθ᾽ ἡμέραν ἐν τῷ ἱερῷ ἐκαθεζόμην διδάσκων "every day I used to sit teaching in the temple" Matt 26:55) is certainly an imperfect.

This form certainly can be an aorist in Homer and in Classical Greek, as in the following example:[22]

> ἀκούσαντες δὲ ταῦτα Μαντίθεος καὶ Ἀψεφίων ἐπὶ τὴν ἑστίαν ἐκαθέζοντο, ἱκετεύοντες μὴ στρεβλωθῆναι ἀλλ᾽ ἐξεγγυηθέντες κριθῆναι.
> 
> When Mantitheos and Apsephion heard this [shouts of approval from the council], they sat down at the hearth, making supplication not to be tortured, but to be allowed to provide sureties. (*Andocides* 1.44)

The point must be that Mantitheos and Apsephion sought sanctuary at the hearth (perfective), which involved their spoken

---

21  Codex Bezae has a unique reading καθέζησθε in Luke 22:30, which could be a pres. subjunctive (as in Th. 7.77.4 and Xen. *Cyr.* 4.5.41: ὅποι/ὅπου ἂν καθέζησθε "wherever you sit down"). Other witnesses have κάθησθε (sic) B[(1)] T Δ (a pf. or pres. indic.), καθίσεσθε K Γ (the fut. of καθίζω as in patristic discussions of Matt 19:28, such as [Athanasius] *de sancta trinitate* [page 1277 line 25 of PG Migne 28]; the same form is found in these witnesses at Matt 19:28), or καθίσησθε H (the subjunctive of καθίζομαι). After ἵνα ἔσθητε καὶ πίνητε "in order that you may eat and drink," the context in Luke 22:30 requires a fut. (hence καθήσεσθε "you will sit down" as printed in NA 28, of which καθίσεσθε K Γ may be an itacistic variant), but a third subjunctive in the ἵνα clause might have been expected. The TLG suggests that κάθησθε could be a late pres. subjunctive. A subjunctive function is possible, but not obligatory, in Procopius of Gaza's *Commentary on Isaiah* 30:15 (page 2265 lines 14–16 of PG Migne 87.2): ἐὰν γὰρ κάθησθε, φησίν, ἐν τῷ τόπῳ τῆς Ἱερουσαλὴμ μετανοήσαντες καὶ παυσάμενοι, ... τότε σωθήσεσθε ἐν ἡρεμίᾳ γενόμενοι καὶ ἀναπαύσει "For if you sit down, he says, in the place of Jerusalem, when you have repented and rested, ... at that time you will be restored, having begun to be in gentleness and rest." A. N. Jannaris, *An Historical Grammar: Chiefly of the Attic Dialect as Written and Spoken from Classical Antiquity Down to the Present Time, Founded upon the Ancient Texts, Inscriptions, Papyri and Present Popular Greek* (London: Macmillan, 1897), 463, reports examples of ἐάν with the indic. as early as OG Genesis (38.9) and the New Testament (e.g., Mark 3:11). See also, Ibid., 198–99.

22  LSJ, 851, s.v. καθέζομαι.

supplication rather than that it happened to be the case that they were sitting at the hearth (imperfective) when they heard the council's shouts of approval. Motion towards the hearth is probably the point of the preposition with the accusative in ἐπὶ τὴν ἑστίαν. The preceding section indicates that these two men were among the members of the council when the proposal was made. Flight to the hearth (perfective) was their response to the approval of that proposal.

The problem is that the Greek stem ἑζε/ο- reflects at least two Indo-European origins: an imperfective of a thematic yod present *sed-ie/o- and a perfective reduplicated aorist form *se-sd- (cf. συνήγαγον, 11:47, an aorist whose reduplication is of a different type). Or, the Greek form could reflect the zero grade of the root, $(h_1e\text{-})sd\text{-}$, with the augment and aspiration by analogy.[23]

John seems to have a contrast between the two sisters in mind. Martha went to meet Jesus (perfective), which introduces the next sequence. Meanwhile, on the other hand (Μαριὰμ δὲ ἐν τῷ οἴκῳ ἐκαθέζετο), Mary remained sitting (imperfective) in the house. There is no indication either that Mary was outside the house beforehand or that she was inside, but standing, such that she would take a seat indoors. This creates a cliffhanger, as the audience is left wondering what role Mary will play in the narrative. The effect in John 4:6 seems similar: ὁ οὖν Ἰησοῦς κεκοπιακὼς ἐκ τῆς ὁδοιπορίας ἐκαθέζετο οὕτως ἐπὶ τῇ πηγῇ "in this way Jesus was sitting at the well..."[24] rather than "So, Jesus took a seat at the well."

(12) The variant readings in John 6:3, as mentioned by Danker, bring us to the last preliminary point: some textual variation units involve differences of aspect.[25] In the extract below, which forms the test case for this chapter, the NA 28 text has been presented with the variation units that involve differences of verb form given in the

---

23  See Beekes, *Etymological Dictionary of Greek*, 376, for a full account of the forms, their origins, and their cognates.

24  Although Stephen Levinsohn, *Discourse Features of New Testament Greek: A Coursebook on the Information Structure of New Testament Greek*, 2nd ed., (Dallas: SIL International, 2000), 210, does not explicitly label the form in John 4:6 as an impf., his translation "Jesus ... was sitting" implies that he analyzed it as an impf.

25  Peter Stork, "Aspectual Variant Readings in Herodotus," in *In the Footsteps of Raphael Kühner*, ed. A. Rijksbaron, H. A. Mulder, and G. C. Wakker (Amsterdam: Gieben, 1988), 265–89, provides an exemplary case study on this point.

footnotes.[26] Since it is not my purpose here to determine the content of the original text, the following discussion will concern alternatives presented by the textual tradition, with an awareness that many of the different readings involve changes, such as omissions or additions, that could operate in either direction.

1 ἦν δέ τις ἀσθενῶν, Λάζαρος ἀπὸ Βηθανίας, ἐκ τῆς κώμης Μαρίας καὶ Μάρθας τῆς ἀδελφῆς αὐτῆς.

2 ἦν δὲ Μαριὰμ ἡ ἀλείψασα τὸν κύριον μύρῳ καὶ ἐκμάξασα τοὺς πόδας αὐτοῦ ταῖς θριξὶν αὐτῆς, ἧς ὁ ἀδελφὸς Λάζαρος ἠσθένει.

3 ἀπέστειλαν οὖν αἱ ἀδελφαὶ πρὸς αὐτὸν λέγουσαι· κύριε, ἴδε ὃν φιλεῖς ἀσθενεῖ.

4 ἀκούσας δὲ ὁ Ἰησοῦς <u>εἶπεν</u>· αὕτη ἡ ἀσθένεια οὐκ ἔστιν πρὸς θάνατον ἀλλ᾽ ὑπὲρ τῆς δόξης τοῦ θεοῦ, ἵνα δοξασθῇ ὁ υἱὸς τοῦ θεοῦ δι᾽ αὐτῆς.

5 ἠγάπα δὲ ὁ Ἰησοῦς τὴν Μάρθαν καὶ τὴν ἀδελφὴν αὐτῆς καὶ τὸν Λάζαρον.

6 ὡς οὖν ἤκουσεν ὅτι ἀσθενεῖ, τότε μὲν ἔμεινεν ἐν ᾧ ἦν τόπῳ δύο ἡμέρας,

7 ἔπειτα μετὰ τοῦτο <u>λέγει</u> τοῖς μαθηταῖς· ἄγωμεν εἰς τὴν Ἰουδαίαν πάλιν.

8 <u>λέγουσιν</u> αὐτῷ οἱ μαθηταί· ῥαββί, νῦν ἐζήτουν σε λιθάσαι οἱ Ἰουδαῖοι, καὶ πάλιν ὑπάγεις ἐκεῖ;

9 <u>ἀπεκρίθη</u> Ἰησοῦς· οὐχὶ δώδεκα ὧραί εἰσιν τῆς ἡμέρας; ἐάν τις περιπατῇ ἐν τῇ ἡμέρᾳ, οὐ προσκόπτει, ὅτι τὸ φῶς τοῦ κόσμου τούτου βλέπει·

10 ἐὰν δέ τις περιπατῇ ἐν τῇ νυκτί, προσκόπτει, ὅτι τὸ φῶς οὐκ ἔστιν ἐν αὐτῷ.

11 ταῦτα <u>εἶπεν</u>, καὶ μετὰ τοῦτο <u>λέγει</u> αὐτοῖς· Λάζαρος ὁ φίλος ἡμῶν κεκοίμηται·[27] ἀλλὰ πορεύομαι ἵνα ἐξυπνίσω αὐτόν.

12 <u>εἶπαν</u> οὖν οἱ μαθηταὶ αὐτῷ· κύριε, εἰ κεκοίμηται[28] σωθήσεται.[29]

---

26  Only two of these (11:31 and 33) are discussed by Bruce M. Metzger, *A Textual Commentary on the Greek New Testament*, 2nd ed. (Stuttgart: Deutsche Bibelgesellschaft, 2000), 199, 200.

27  D has κοιμᾶται.

28  Again, D has κοιμᾶται.

29  P75 has ἐγερθήσεται.

13 <u>εἰρήκει</u> δὲ ὁ Ἰησοῦς περὶ τοῦ θανάτου αὐτοῦ, ἐκεῖνοι δὲ ἔδοξαν ὅτι περὶ τῆς κοιμήσεως τοῦ ὕπνου λέγει.

14 τότε οὖν <u>εἶπεν</u> αὐτοῖς ὁ Ἰησοῦς παρρησίᾳ· Λάζαρος ἀπέθανεν,

15 καὶ χαίρω δι᾽ ὑμᾶς ἵνα πιστεύσητε, ὅτι οὐκ ἤμην ἐκεῖ· ἀλλ᾽ ἄγωμεν πρὸς αὐτόν.

16 <u>εἶπεν</u> οὖν Θωμᾶς ὁ λεγόμενος Δίδυμος τοῖς συμμαθηταῖς· ἄγωμεν καὶ ἡμεῖς ἵνα ἀποθάνωμεν μετ᾽ αὐτοῦ.

17 ἐλθὼν οὖν ὁ Ἰησοῦς εὗρεν αὐτὸν τέσσαρας ἤδη ἡμέρας ἔχοντα ἐν τῷ μνημείῳ.

18 ἦν δὲ ἡ Βηθανία ἐγγὺς τῶν Ἱεροσολύμων ὡς ἀπὸ σταδίων δεκαπέντε.

19 πολλοὶ δὲ ἐκ τῶν Ἰουδαίων ἐληλύθεισαν πρὸς τὴν Μάρθαν καὶ Μαριὰμ ἵνα παραμυθήσωνται αὐτὰς περὶ τοῦ ἀδελφοῦ.

20 ἡ οὖν Μάρθα ὡς ἤκουσεν ὅτι Ἰησοῦς ἔρχεται ὑπήντησεν αὐτῷ· Μαριὰμ δὲ ἐν τῷ οἴκῳ ἐκαθέζετο.

21 <u>εἶπεν</u> οὖν ἡ Μάρθα πρὸς τὸν Ἰησοῦν· κύριε, εἰ ἦς ὧδε οὐκ ἂν ἀπέθανεν[30] ὁ ἀδελφός μου·

22 [ἀλλὰ] καὶ νῦν οἶδα ὅτι ὅσα ἂν αἰτήσῃ τὸν θεὸν δώσει σοι ὁ θεός.

23 <u>λέγει</u> αὐτῇ ὁ Ἰησοῦς· ἀναστήσεται ὁ ἀδελφός σου.

24 <u>λέγει</u> αὐτῷ ἡ Μάρθα· οἶδα ὅτι ἀναστήσεται ἐν τῇ ἀναστάσει ἐν τῇ ἐσχάτῃ ἡμέρᾳ.

25 <u>εἶπεν</u>[31] <u>αὐτῇ ὁ Ἰησοῦς· ἐγώ εἰμι ἡ ἀνάστασις καὶ ἡ ζωή· ὁ πιστεύων εἰς ἐμὲ κἂν ἀποθάνῃ ζήσεται,</u>

26 <u>καὶ πᾶς ὁ ζῶν καὶ πιστεύων εἰς ἐμὲ οὐ μὴ ἀποθάνῃ εἰς τὸν αἰῶνα. πιστεύεις τοῦτο;</u>

27 <u>λέγει</u> αὐτῷ· ναὶ κύριε,[32] ἐγὼ πεπίστευκα ὅτι σὺ εἶ ὁ χριστὸς ὁ υἱὸς τοῦ θεοῦ ὁ εἰς τὸν κόσμον ἐρχόμενος.

28 καὶ τοῦτο εἰποῦσα ἀπῆλθεν καὶ <u>ἐφώνησεν</u> Μαριὰμ τὴν ἀδελφὴν αὐτῆς λάθρα εἰποῦσα·ὁ διδάσκαλος πάρεστιν καὶ φωνεῖ σε.

---

30  A, C², Θ, Ψ, and other witnesses have the pluperfect ἐτεθνήκει.

31  Some witnesses, such as ℵ and Θ, add δέ, others, including P75 and Ψ, add οὖν.

32  P66 adds πιστεύω.

29 ἐκείνη δὲ ὡς ἤκουσεν ἠγέρθη[33] ταχὺ καὶ ἤρχετο[34] πρὸς αὐτόν.

30 οὔπω δὲ ἐληλύθει ὁ Ἰησοῦς εἰς τὴν κώμην, ἀλλ᾽ ἦν ἔτι ἐν τῷ τόπῳ ὅπου ὑπήντησεν αὐτῷ ἡ Μάρθα.

31 οἱ οὖν Ἰουδαῖοι οἱ ὄντες μετ᾽ αὐτῆς ἐν τῇ οἰκίᾳ καὶ παραμυθούμενοι αὐτήν, ἰδόντες τὴν Μαριὰμ ὅτι ταχέως ἀνέστη καὶ ἐξῆλθεν, ἠκολούθησαν αὐτῇ δόξαντες[35] ὅτι ὑπάγει εἰς τὸ μνημεῖον ἵνα κλαύσῃ ἐκεῖ.

32 ἡ οὖν Μαριὰμ ὡς ἦλθεν ὅπου ἦν Ἰησοῦς ἰδοῦσα αὐτὸν ἔπεσεν αὐτοῦ πρὸς τοὺς πόδας λέγουσα αὐτῷ· κύριε, εἰ ἦς ὧδε οὐκ ἄν μου ἀπέθανεν ὁ ἀδελφός.

33 Ἰησοῦς οὖν ὡς εἶδεν αὐτὴν κλαίουσαν καὶ τοὺς συνελθόντας[36] αὐτῇ Ἰουδαίους κλαίοντας, ἐνεβριμήσατο[37] τῷ πνεύματι καὶ ἐτάραξεν ἑαυτὸν

34 καὶ <u>εἶπεν</u>· ποῦ τεθείκατε αὐτόν; <u>λέγουσιν</u> αὐτῷ· κύριε, ἔρχου καὶ ἴδε.

35 ἐδάκρυσεν ὁ Ἰησοῦς.

36 <u>ἔλεγον</u> οὖν οἱ Ἰουδαῖοι· ἴδε πῶς ἐφίλει αὐτόν.

37 τινὲς δὲ ἐξ αὐτῶν <u>εἶπαν</u>· οὐκ ἐδύνατο οὗτος ὁ ἀνοίξας τοὺς ὀφθαλμοὺς τοῦ τυφλοῦ ποιῆσαι ἵνα καὶ οὗτος μὴ ἀποθάνῃ;

38 Ἰησοῦς οὖν πάλιν ἐμβριμώμενος[38] ἐν ἑαυτῷ ἔρχεται εἰς τὸ μνημεῖον· ἦν δὲ σπήλαιον καὶ λίθος ἐπέκειτο ἐπ᾽ αὐτῷ.

39 <u>λέγει</u> ὁ Ἰησοῦς· ἄρατε τὸν λίθον. <u>λέγει</u> αὐτῷ ἡ ἀδελφὴ τοῦ τετελευτηκότος Μάρθα· κύριε, ἤδη ὄζει, τεταρταῖος γάρ ἐστιν.

40 <u>λέγει</u> αὐτῇ ὁ Ἰησοῦς· οὐκ <u>εἶπόν</u> σοι ὅτι ἐὰν πιστεύσῃς ὄψῃ τὴν δόξαν τοῦ θεοῦ;

41 ἦραν οὖν τὸν λίθον. ὁ δὲ Ἰησοῦς ἦρεν τοὺς ὀφθαλμοὺς ἄνω καὶ <u>εἶπεν</u>· πάτερ, εὐχαριστῶ σοι ὅτι ἤκουσάς μου.

---

33  P45 and P66, A, C³, and Θ have ἐγείρεται.

34  P45 and P66, A, C³, D, and Θ have ἔρχεται.

35  P75 has δοξάζοντες a ptc. of δοξάζω "think." P66, A C², Θ, and Ψ have λέγοντες.

36  P45, it seems, and D as well as P66 have συνεληλυθότας among other variations in word order and the between αὐτῇ alone or with a preposition (either σύν or μετά).

37  P45 (it seems), D, and others have ὡς ἐμβριμούμενος (or ἐμβριμώμενος, as in P66ᶜ, D, and Θ).

38  W has ἐμβριμῶν. C*, 892ˢ, 1241, and 1424 have ἐμβριμησάμενος.

42 ἐγὼ δὲ ᾔδειν ὅτι πάντοτέ μου ἀκούεις, ἀλλὰ διὰ τὸν ὄχλον τὸν περιεστῶτα εἶπον, ἵνα πιστεύσωσιν ὅτι σύ με ἀπέστειλας. 43 καὶ ταῦτα εἰπὼν φωνῇ μεγάλῃ ἐκραύγασεν·Λάζαρε, δεῦρο ἔξω. 44 ἐξῆλθεν ὁ τεθνηκὼς δεδεμένος τοὺς πόδας καὶ τὰς χεῖρας κειρίαις καὶ ἡ ὄψις αὐτοῦ σουδαρίῳ περιεδέδετο. λέγει αὐτοῖς ὁ Ἰησοῦς· λύσατε αὐτὸν καὶ ἄφετε αὐτὸν ὑπάγειν. 45 πολλοὶ οὖν ἐκ τῶν Ἰουδαίων οἱ ἐλθόντες πρὸς τὴν Μαριὰμ καὶ θεασάμενοι[39] ἃ ἐποίησεν ἐπίστευσαν εἰς αὐτόν· 46 τινὲς δὲ ἐξ αὐτῶν ἀπῆλθον πρὸς τοὺς Φαρισαίους καὶ εἶπαν αὐτοῖς ἃ ἐποίησεν Ἰησοῦς. 47 συνήγαγον οὖν οἱ ἀρχιερεῖς καὶ οἱ Φαρισαῖοι συνέδριον καὶ ἔλεγον· τί ποιοῦμεν ὅτι οὗτος ὁ ἄνθρωπος πολλὰ ποιεῖ σημεῖα;

1 There was a certain person who was ill, Lazarus from Bethany, from the village of Mariam and Martha her sister.

2 Mariam was the woman who anointed the Lord with an ointment and wiped his feet with her hair, whose brother Lazarus was ill.

3 So, the sisters sent to him, saying, "Lord, see the one whom you love is ill."

4 When Jesus heard, he said, "This illness is not towards death, but it is for the glory of God, in order that the Son of God may be glorified through it."

5 (Jesus was loving Martha and her sister and Lazarus.)

6 So, when he heard that he was ill, at that time he waited for two days in the place where he was.

7 Then, after this, he says to the disciples, "Let us go again into Judea."

8 They say to him, "Rabbi, just now the Judeans were seeking to stone you to death, and you are going there again?"

9 Jesus replied, "Are there not twelve hours in the day? If anyone walks by day, he does not stumble because he sees the light of this world.

10 But if anyone walks at night, he stumbles, because the light is not in him."

---

39  P45, P66 and D have ἑωρακότες.

11 He said this, and after this he says to them, "Lazarus our friend is asleep, but I am on my way in order that I may wake him."

12 So, the disciples said to him, "Lord, if he is asleep, he will be restored."

13 (But, Jesus had spoken about his death, but they thought that he was speaking about the sleep of slumber.)

14 So, then, Jesus said to them openly, "Lazarus died 15 and I am glad that I was not there, because of you— that you may believe. But let us go to him."

16 So, Thomas, who is called Didymus, said to his fellow disciples, "Let us go also in order that we may die with him."

17 So, when Jesus came, he found that he had been in the tomb for four days already.

18 (Bethany was close to Jerusalem, at a distance of about fifteen stades.

19 And many of the Judaeans had come out to Martha and Mariam in order to comfort them about their brother.)

20 So, when she heard that Jesus was coming, Martha met with him. But Mariam continued to sit in the house.

21 So, Martha said to Jesus, "Lord, if you had been here, my brother would not have died. 22 [But,] even now, I know that whatever you ask God, God will give to you."

23 Jesus says to her, "Your brother will rise."

24 Martha says to him, "I know that he will rise at the resurrection on the last day."

25 Jesus said to her, "I am the resurrection and the life. Whoever believes in me, even if he dies, will live 26 and everyone who lives and believes in me will not die forever. Do you believe this?"

27 She says to him, "Yes, Lord, I believe that you are the Christ, the Son of God, the one who is coming into the world."

28 And when she had said this, she went away and called for Mariam her sister, saying in secret, "The teacher is here and is calling for you."

29 But that woman, when she heard, got up quickly and was going to him.

30 (Jesus had not yet come into the village, but was still in the place where Martha had met with him.)

31 So, there Judeans who were with her in the house and who were comforting her, when they saw Mariam, that she got up quickly and went out, followed her because they thought that she was going to the tomb in order to weep there.

32 So, Mariam, when she arrived where Jesus was, saw him and fell at his feet, saying to him, "Lord, if you had been here, my brother would not have died."

33 So, Jesus, when he saw her weeping and the Judeans weeping, those who had come with her, he groaned in his spirit and he became troubled.

34 And he said, "Where have you put him?" They say to him, "Lord, come and see."

35 Jesus wept.

36 So, the Judeans were saying, "See how he was loving him."

37 But, some of them said, "Was not this one who opened the eyes of the blind man able to do something in order that this man would not die?"

38 So, Jesus, again groaning in himself, goes to[40] the tomb. There was a cave and a stone rested upon it.

39 Jesus says, "Remove the stone!" The sister of the dead man—Martha—says to him, "Lord, there is already a stench, for he is four-days dead."

40 Jesus says to her, "Did I not say to you that if you believe, you will see the glory of God?"

41 So, they removed the stone. Jesus lifted his eyes upwards and said, "Father, I thank you because you have heard me.

---

40 Perhaps, "into the vicinity of the tomb" would reflect the Greek preposition more closely.

42 I was aware that you always hear me, but for the sake of the crowd that is standing here, I spoke, in order that they may believe that you sent me."
43 And when he had said this, he shouted in a loud voice, "Lazarus, come out!"
44 The dead man came out, bound at his feet and hands with straps, and his face was surrounded with a facecloth. Jesus says to them, "Untie him and let him go."
45 So, many of the Judeans who had come to Mariam and who had seen what he had done believed in him.
46 But some of them went away to the Pharisees and said to them what he had done.
47 So, the high priests and the Pharisees gathered the Sanhedrin together and were saying, "What are we to do[41] because this man does many miraculous signs?"

Not all variation units require consideration. Some alternatives involve readings for which an accidental origin is plausible, such as δόξαντες : δοξαζόντες (11:31), by the addition or subtraction of -ζο-.[42] Other alternations concern meaning rather than aspect, such as λέγοντες for δόξαντες, in which a rationale for the alternation can be proposed, if mechanical errors do not provide a satisfactory explanation.

It is very difficult to draw conclusions about verbal aspect from the additional linguistic data that manuscript variants provide. Some variation units involve alternatives which are likely to be

---

41   See Ridderbos, *Gospel of John*, 408 n. 87, for the likelihood that the pres. indic. has the function of a deliberative subjunctive here.
42   The discussion in Metzger, *Textual Commentary*, 199, lies behind this paragraph. Metzger calls δοξαζοντες "nonsensical." BDAG, 258, gives the meanings in the New Testament as "to influence one's opinion about another so as to enhance the latter's reputation" and "to cause to have splendid greatness." The latter is "a favorite term in J[ohn]" and "while glorifying" would certainly be nonsensical in John 11:31. However, its meaning as reported by LSJ, 444, *s.v.* δοξάζω I, and glossed "think, imagine," "suppose," "expect," "form, hold, or entertain an opinion" would be suitable in the context. Indeed, "while they were supposing that" is not so different from the meaning with δόξαντες "because they thought that." That said, the weight of evidence is against δοξάζω not involving glory in the New Testament and in John in particular.

accidental or mechanical in origin, such as the addition or omission of πιστεύω in 11:27,[43] the transmission of ἀνασυράμενος "having lifted up his clothes" (A) and ἀνασυρόμενος "while lifting up his clothes" (B) in the manuscripts of Theophrastus's *Characters* 11.2 as well as παύονται "they stop"(A) and παύωνται "(whenever) they stop" (B),[44] or, to use Peter Stork's example, which is of great importance for a test case such as this, alternation between the imperfect ἐβασίλευε and the aorist ἐβασίλευσε.[45] However, we cannot, therefore, conclude that the origin of such a change was not deliberate or intentional: accidental errors can be complex and deliberate changes can be slight. A simple alternation, such as the omission or addition of a sigma in ταῦτα δὲ γέγραπται ἵνα πιστεύ[σ]ητε "but these are written in order that you may [start to] believe"(John 20:31), can have significant implications for the interpretation of the whole book.[46]

Other variation units involve alternations that are more likely to be deliberate or intentional because they involve more complex differences, but these too are difficult to assess. A change that seems more likely to be deliberate to a scholar of the Greek text of the New Testament, because it is more involved, may not have seemed so to a native or second language speaker of Greek in the first century. Do alternatives represent corrections to bring what seemed aberrant into line with Greek aspectual usage of the copyist's time (whenever that was)? In any set of alternatives, which, if any, is/are correct, hypercorrect, or substandard? Was the standard for aspectual usage against which changes occurred, or were made, either a consensus of normal vernacular usage or a perceived Classical or even Atticistic norm? Did the copyist responsible for a deliberate alteration "emend" the text correctly? If so, which is the "correct" reading and which the "aberrant" one? Were corrections

---

43  Manuscripts with this addition have an intriguing juxtaposition of a pres. indic., which continues the presents in 11:25-26, and a pf. indic.

44  James Diggle, ed., *Theophrastus: Characters*, CCTC 43 (Cambridge: Cambridge University Press, 2004), 100, prints ἀνασυράμενος "having pulled up his clothes" from A, but παύωνται "(whenever) they stop," which is required after ὅταν "when(ever)," from B. Ibid., 315, rejects the conjecture of an aor. subjunctive, παύσωνται "(whenever) they stop."

45  Stork, "Aspectual Variant Readings in Herodotus," 283-88.

46  See Metzger, *A Textual Commentary*, 219-20.

made systematically? Or, were even those changes that did correct the text made in a haphazard way?

Are there alternatives in the textual tradition that were conceived of as interchangeable and functionally equivalent to each other or does every alternation of verbal form involve either a deliberate correction or a mechanic error? Variation units involving a choice between a perfect indicative and an aorist indicative might be interpreted as reflections of the functional and morphological merger of the perfect and aorist indicative and the loss of their aspectual contrast.[47] Some pairs in John 11 call for consideration as functionally equivalent alternatives, perhaps with different stylistic values; 11:33 has the perfect participle συνεληλυθότας as an alternative to the aorist participle συνελθόντας; 11:45 has as a perfect participle ἑωρακότες as an alternative to an aorist participle θεασάμενοι. The same witnesses (P45, P46, and D) show the same type of alternative, the perfect, in both places. It is not clear whether the functional and morphological syncretism of the perfect and aorist included their participles as well as their indicatives.[48] This line of enquiry about aorist and perfect participles and several other verbal categories is tangential

---

47  See Horrocks, *Greek*, 102, 131–132, 154, 174–178, 245, 302–303, 318, and 330.

48  Ibid., discusses only the pf. and aor. indics. F. T. Gignac, *A Grammar of the Greek Papyri of the Roman and Byzantine Periods: Volume II, Morphology* (Milan: Cisalpino-Goliardica, 1981), 347, provides Byzantine examples of second aor. ptcs. with endings that appear to be those of the pf. ptc., but he also shows that these forms are likely to be the result of the identity of -οντ- and -οτ- in pronunciation. As such, these mixed aor.-pf. forms cannot be used as evidence for the functional and morphological merger of the aor. and pf.

Examples of aor. stems with unequivocally pf. endings, such as those of the feminine in -υι-, have not been reported. Examples of sigmatic or of athematic aor. ptcs. with pf. endings would also provide better evidence.

On the other hand, examples of pf. stems with the endings of the imperfective ptc. were reported from Egyptian inscriptions by Karl Dieterich, *Untersuchungen zur Geschichte der griechischen Sprache von der hellenistischen Zeit bis zum 10. Jahrhundert n. Chr.* (Leipzig: Teubner, 1898), 207. The form κεχορηγηθέντα, a pf. stem with an aor. passive ending, was cited by Edwin Mayser, *Grammatik der griechischen Papyri aus der Ptolemäerzeit; mit Einschluss der gleichzeitigen Ostraka und der in Ägypten verfassten Inschriften, I 2, Laut- und Wortlehre, pt. II, Flexionslehre* (Leipzig: Teubner, 1938), 163.

The conclusion of this discussion is that there is insufficient (morphological) evidence for detecting the functional merger of the pf. and aor. ptcs. and that such variants should be assessed as having their aspectual values and not as functionally interchangeable.

to the focus of this chapter, but it not only serves as a reminder that attention must be paid to alternative reading when studying a given point of a narrative, but also illustrates another area for exploration.

One variation unit is of particular interest in that it concerns the aorist, imperfect, and historic present. John 11:29 has an aorist passive indicative (ἠγέρθη), followed by an imperfect indicative (ἤρχετο). In their stead, one group of witnesses (P45 and P66, A, C³, D, and Θ) have historic present indicatives (ἐγείρεται[49] and ἔρχεται). Here, we may be able to detect one or more comprehensive attempts to "improve" the text by presenting, with historic presents, what others had presented as an event (ἠγέρθη) and a process (ἤρχετο) in past time. We will turn to the question of the effect of the historic present below. For now, we should note the adverb ταχύ and that the historic present interchanges not only with the aorist (ἐγείρεται : ἠγέρθη), which is unsurprising, but also with the imperfect (ἔρχεται : ἤρχετο). The alternation between ἤρχετο and ἔρχεται may simply reflect an attempt to harmonize the choice of verb form with ἔρχεται in 11:38. That is, the copyist's focus may have been on a sense of Johannine style[50] rather than on a choice between verb forms of contrasting aspectual values.

The description of the imperfect and the aorist indicative as in contrast or opposition, point (4) above, raises a crucial question: Which form is the default or unmarked choice in narrative? Or, in the terms of the chapters by Stephen Levinsohn: Which of the imperfect or the aorist indicative is background or offline and which is foreground or mainline?[51]

The answer I first encountered in my studies, in relation to Lysias 1, is that the imperfect is the "basic narrative tense" and that the

---

49  The only (securely transmitted) instance of the HP of this verb in John is 13:4. See John J. O'Rourke, "The Historic Present in the Gospel of John," *JBL* 93 (1974), 586; he counted 12 instances of ἔρχεται as a HP (but none of ἔρχονται). Levinsohn, *Discourse Features*, 210–11, discusses the John 13:4 instance of the HP as highlighting the event (in the aor.) that follows immediately.

50  John has only two instances of ἤρχετο (the other is 8:2, the beginning of the *Pericope Adulterae*) and four of ἤρχοντο (4:30, 6:17, 19:3, and 20:3).

51  See Stephen Levinsohn, "Verb Forms and Grounding in Narrative" (ch. 5 in this volume).

aorist is used to "denote a single completed action."[52] That is, events unfold in the imperfect and events in the aorist are marked. The description of the imperfect as the basic narrative tense may not have been intended as a statement applicable to every narrative in Greek, but it nevertheless suggests that the "tense" that predominates in any given passage is "basic."

Evans presented a contrasting conclusion in his study of verbs in the Greek Pentateuch.[53] The aorist predominates and the imperfect is rare, except in passages that are characterized by free renderings of the *Vorlage* (including historic presents and subordination through participles) and are particularly dramatic sequences. The narratives of the Greek Pentateuch, although Hebrew influence is a plausible factor in relation to the rarity of the imperfect, are a closer point of comparison, especially in less-literal portions, with John 11 in date and language, than a narrative in an Athenian forensic speech of the fifth century BC. The point is essentially the same: the predominant verb form is the default. In the Greek Pentateuch, and as we shall see in John 11, it is the aorist that predominates.

The choice of John 11 as a piece of linguistic evidence was arbitrary, but its choice as a narrative was deliberate. The resurrection of Lazarus is clearly a pivotal narrative in John.[54] It is told at length, unfolds over several days, and involves several changes of scene. It is the seventh of the seven signs in the Gospel of John and the fifth of the seven "I am" sayings. It leads directly into the passion narrative

---

52  The quotations are from the specimen answers to a specimen "Linguistic Structures" examination paper of the spring of 2001 on Lysias 1.11–14. The specimen answer notes that this sequence of impfs. is interrupted by a pres. "to add vividness and emphasis" and that the aor. ἐπυθόμην is used "to highlight the complete understanding that [the speaker] later achieves, and it also marks the fact that this sentence is outside of the narrative sequence." Although not framed in such terms, the final point amounts to associating the aor. with background or offline material. This specimen answer draws on Christopher Carey, ed., *Lysias: Selected Speeches*, CGLC (Cambridge: Cambridge University Press, 1989), 70, who discusses ὕστερον κτλ. [ἐπυθόμην] as "inserted to indicate that the statement of facts unavailable to the speaker at the time is neither inference nor invention" with Lysias frag. XVII.2 and Dem. 54.7 as comparanda.

53  Evans, *Verbal Syntax in the Greek Pentateuch*, 198–219, esp. 216.

54  My appreciation of the passage has been shaped chiefly by Hermann N. Ridderbos, *The Gospel According to John: A Theological Commentary*, trans. John Vriend (Grand Rapids: Eerdmans, 1997), 381–408.

through Caiaphas's entrance and declaration (11:49–53) and it looks forward to the resurrection of Jesus himself.[55] This passage seems a good candidate for an investigation of artful use of the versatility of the Greek verbal system.

As a source of linguistic evidence, the value and interest of this passage has been made clear already in relation to points (4), (7), (11), and (12) above. Several other details that call for further attention will be discussed in passing because they do not fall within the purview of this chapter.[56]

John 11:1 and 2 provide a minimal pair of a periphrastic and a synthetic imperfect:

> $^1$ ἦν δέ τις ἀσθενῶν, ...
> There was a certain person who was ill, ...

> $^2$ ... ὁ ἀδελφὸς Λάζαρος ἠσθένει.
> ... her brother Lazarus was ill.

The use of the first seems to reflect a common method for introducing either a new episode in the main narrative or an embedded narrative with ἦν, τις, and an imperfective participle. John has other examples of the former (4:46 and 5:5),[57] and this feature can be cited from Luke (14:2) and Acts (9:10, 9:36, and 16:1). Luke also has

---

55  In addition to the obvious points of comparison and contrast between the details lingered on in John 20, which is itself some kind of conclusion to the book (20:30-31), and in John 11 (e.g., the cave tomb, the duration of time in that tomb, the need to remove the stone or not in 11:39-41 and 20:1, and the σουδάριον 11:44 and 20:7), the prominence of Thomas is notable (11:16 and 20:24-28; otherwise only in 14:5 and 21:2). He is the only disciple in John 11 who is named and who speaks as an individual (11:16).

56  E.g., the sisters answer Jesus with identical words, but with a slight difference of word order: κύριε, εἰ ἦς ὧδε οὐκ ἂν ἀπέθανεν ὁ ἀδελφός μου. "Lord, if you had been here, <u>my</u> brother would not have died." (11:21) and κύριε, εἰ ἦς ὧδε οὐκ ἄν μου ἀπέθανεν ὁ ἀδελφός "Lord, if you had been here, <u>my</u> brother would not have died." (11:32). For typical word order in Koine Greek and later, and the impact of enclitics (such as μου) on typical word order, see Horrocks, Greek, 108-9, 173, and 277-81.

57  Ridderbos, Gospel of John, 386, cites 5:5 and the opening words of 1 Sam 1:1 (ἄνθρωπος ἦν δέ "There was a person") and Job 1:1 (ἄνθρωπός τις ἦν "There was a certain person"). Bel and the Dragon 2 OG (ἄνθρωπός τις ἦν ἱερεύς "There was a certain person, a priest") and, in particular, Exod 2:1 (ἦν δέ τις ἐκ τῆς φυλῆς Λευι "There was a certain man from the tribe of Levi") should also be noted.

instances in the introductions of embedded narratives, namely the stories narrated by Jesus (16:1, 16:19, and 18:2).[58] As Steven Runge pointed out (pers.comm.), such introductions generally involve a verb of being, as in 11:1, or a verb of motion. The imperfect indicative of a stative verb, such as ἀσθενέω, would have been part of a topic or comment structure, not a thetic or presentational structure and, as such, would not be allowed.

Another piece of illustrative material lies in 11:8: νῦν ἐζήτουν σε λιθάσαι.[59] The population of Jerusalem *were seeking*, but *did not succeed in seeking* (ἐζήτησαν "they sought (to completion)"), *to complete the task of stoning* (to death). There had been attempts at stoning Jesus, but they had come to nothing. Imperfective forms are used for the attempts (διὰ ποῖον αὐτῶν ἔργον ἐμὲ λιθάζετε; "For what deed are you trying to stone me" and περὶ καλοῦ ἔργου οὐ λιθάζομέν σε "We are not trying to stone you in relation to a good deed" in John 10:32–33), but the perfective form in John 10:31 (ἵνα λιθάσωσιν αὐτόν "in order to stone him (to death)") gives the intent of completing the task. An imperfective infinitive, λιθάζειν "to try to stone," in 11:8 would imply that their stoning was less goal-orientated.

Our passage provides a contrasting pair of participles of verbs of speech. In 11:3, ἀπέστειλαν is modified by the imperfective participle, λέγουσαι. In 11:28, ἐφώνησεν is modified by a perfective participle, the second instance of εἰποῦσα, which is not anterior to Martha's use of her voice to call Mary, but contemporaneous in that it conveys the

---

58  For τις in such embedded narratives, cf. instances that, like Luke 16:1 and 16:19, have ἄνθρωπος but employ a different verb, such as Luke 10:30, 14:16, 15:11, 19:12, and 20:9. Several new episodes in Acts are introduced with ἀνὴρ δέ τις "and a certain man" (5:1, 8:9, 10:1) or καί τις ἀνήρ "and a certain man" (14:8).

59  I see that Evans, *Verbal Syntax in the Greek Pentateuch*, 44–45, singled out the impf. (νῦν) ἐζήτουν "just now they were seeking" in his critique of Stanley E. Porter, *Verbal Aspect in the Greek of the New Testament: With Reference to Tense and Mood*, SBG 1 (New York, Lang, 1989), taking it from p. 201. As he demonstrates, the temporal adverb νῦν does not have to situate the action of the verb in present time, as LSJ, 1185, illustrate *s.v.* νῦν I.2 and I.3. BDAG, 681, *s.v.* νῦν 1.b cites John 11:8 among uses of νῦν as a marker "of time in shortly before or after the immediate present" together with John 12:31 (with ἐστι "it is" and ἐκβληθήσεται "he will be thrown out"), 16:5 (with ὑπάγω as a fut. "I am going (or 'will go')"), and 21:10 (with ἐπιάσατε "you caught"), Acts 7:52 (with ἐγένεσθε "you became"), Luke 2:29 (with ἀπολύεις "you dismiss"), and Phil 1:20 (with μεγαλυνθήσεται "he will be made great").

content of Martha's address to Mary, just as λέγουσαι conveys the content of the message from both sisters with ἀπέστειλαν. (The first instance of εἰποῦσα, of course, after καὶ τοῦτο refers back in a summary fashion to the speech act of 11:27, Martha's reply to Jesus). The reasons for the choice of each participle should be sought, although such contrasts are not the immediate concern of this test case. Here, the imperfective participle (11:3) seems to function as a future ("with the intent of saying")[60] and so to involve a temporal rather than an aspectual contrast.

The main body of this test case will concern alternation in finite verbs of speech, which have been presented in underlined type in the extract above. In every instance, the action of the utterance of intelligible sounds is the same, but we find 14 aorists (11:4, 9, 11, 14, 16, 21, 25, 28, 34, [40, 42][61] 41, 43, and 46), 2 imperfects (11:36, 47), 11 historic presents (11:7, 8, 11, 23, 24, 27, 34, 39 twice, 40, and 44), and 1 pluperfect (11:13). As we shall see below, the choice of verbs of speech allows considerable attention to be paid to the use of the historic present in this chapter.

The single verb of speech in the pluperfect may be readily addressed (John 11:11–13):

ταῦτα εἶπεν, καὶ μετὰ τοῦτο λέγει αὐτοῖς·Λάζαρος ὁ φίλος ἡμῶν κεκοίμηται· ἀλλὰ πορεύομαι ἵνα ἐξυπνίσω αὐτόν. εἶπαν οὖν οἱ μαθηταὶ αὐτῷ· κύριε, εἰ κεκοίμηται σωθήσεται. εἰρήκει δὲ ὁ Ἰησοῦς περὶ τοῦ θανάτου αὐτοῦ, ἐκεῖνοι δὲ ἔδοξαν ὅτι περὶ τῆς κοιμήσεως τοῦ ὕπνου λέγει.

He said this, and after this he says to them, "Lazarus our friend is asleep, but I am on my way in order that I may wake him." So, the disciples said to him, "Lord, if he is asleep, he will be restored." (But, Jesus had spoken about his death, but they thought that he was speaking about the sleep of slumber.)

Jesus told his disciples that Lazarus was asleep (11:11). They replied (11:12) that if Lazarus was asleep, he would recover. Then, in

---

60 For the pres., including the imperfective ptc., as a replacement for the fut., see BDF, 168 and 175.
61 Since the aor. indics. in 11:40 and 42 occur in direct speech, they are outside the parameters of this narrative test case. Participles of verbs of speech appear in 11:3 and 32 (imperfective) and in 11:28 (2x) and 43 (perfective).

11:13, the narrator explains Jesus' meaning in his statement in 11:11: Jesus had spoken (at an earlier time) about Lazarus's death. This explanation by the narrator is in contrast to his comment about what the disciples thought at the time (ἔδοξαν) when they said, "If he is asleep, he will recover." This pluperfect εἰρήκει is an example of an anterior past (that is, the past-in-the-past), which is a function of the aorist in Classical Greek (and is illustrated by ὅπου ὑπήντησεν αὐτῷ ἡ Μάρθα "where Martha had met him" in 11:30), but of the pluperfect in Latin. The other pluperfects in this passage have the same function: ἐληλύθεισαν and ἐληλύθει (11:19, 30). This distinction is somewhat similar to that asserted by Ammonius,[62] a Greek grammarian of the first or second century AD, who wrote about similar and different words:

> ἀπέθανε καὶ τέθνηκε διαφέρει. ἀπέθανε μὲν νῦν, τέθνηκε δὲ πάλαι. ὡς περιεπάτησε μὲν ὁ δεῖνα τήμερον, περιπεπάτηκε δὲ πάλαι. (Ammon. Diff. 70)
> "He died" and "He has died" are different. "He died" just now, but "he has died" in the past. For example "someone walked around today, but he has walked around in the past."

The imperfect is conspicuously rare among the verbs of speech in John 11. There are only two instances (36 and 47):

> 36 ἔλεγον οὖν οἱ Ἰουδαῖοι· ἴδε πῶς ἐφίλει αὐτόν.
> So, the Judeans were saying, "See how he was loving him."

> 47 συνήγαγον οὖν οἱ ἀρχιερεῖς καὶ οἱ Φαρισαῖοι συνέδριον καὶ ἔλεγον· τί ποιοῦμεν ὅτι οὗτος ὁ ἄνθρωπος πολλὰ ποιεῖ σημεῖα;
> So, the high priests and the Pharisees gathered the Sanhedrin together and were saying, "What are we to do because this man does many miraculous signs?"

---

62  This passage is cited by Mandilaras, *Studies in the Greek Language*, 20 and 172 n. 20, who considered its applicability to Mark 15:44: ὁ δὲ Πιλᾶτος ἐθαύμασεν εἰ ἤδη τέθνηκεν, καὶ προσκαλεσάμενος τὸν κεντυρίωνα ἐπηρώτησεν αὐτὸν εἰ πάλαι ἀπέθανεν· "Pilate was amazed that he was dead by this time, and summoned the centurion and asked him if he had died already."

The first imperfect coincides with a change of actor, from Jesus to the crowd of Judean mourners. John 11:36–37 could be said to constitute background or offline material. This imperfect does not involve an action that was habitual or incomplete, perhaps by the interruption of their speech.[63] From a traditional point of view, the imperfect here could be used of a repeated action: several members of this group were speaking, not at once and with one voice, but among themselves. This is in contrast to the response (11:37) of a subset of these mourners τινὲς δὲ ἐξ αὐτῶν εἶπαν "but, some of them said,…" in which we should note the departure from the unmarked word order of verb-subject-object.[64] That unmarked order is illustrated by ἔλεγον οὖν οἱ Ἰουδαῖοι "So, the Judeans were saying" in 11:36 and in the majority of sentences in this passage.

The second imperfect may be considered to have the same function, but there is a contextual interpretation that gives it greater significance. The scene is one in which several of the high priests and the Pharisees are speaking. Here, the imperfect stands in contrast to an aorist with the same subject. The event of the assembly of the Sanhedrin is passed over quickly, but the direct speech of the high priests and Pharisees, which continues into 11:48, receives a closer view. The crowd's report of the events of John 11 is mentioned in summary through an aorist (11:46): καὶ εἶπαν αὐτοῖς ἃ ἐποίησεν Ἰησοῦς "and they said to them what he had done." The imperfect ἔλεγον seems to function to mark a cliffhanger here: it sets the scene for the first mention of Caiaphas and his decisive statement introduced by the aorist εἶπεν "he said" (11:49–50), the Evangelist's explanation of it (11:51–52), and the initiation of the passion narrative (11:53).

Alternation between the aorist and the historic present remains to be considered. The nature of this phenomenon has been formulated very neatly by Runge:

> [N]ot only is there a mismatch in the grammaticalized time with the discourse time, but also there is a mismatch in aspect. Most HP actions are perfective in nature, yet they are grammaticalized using an

---

63 For such impfs., and John 8:31 in particular, see Levinsohn, *Discourse Features*, 175.

64 For verb-subject-object word order as typical of Koine and later Greek, see Horrocks, *Greek*, 108–9, 173, and 277–81.

imperfective form. This should not be understood to change the meaning of the verb; rather, it is simply another way in which the HP usage stands out in its context.[65]

While it is clear that the historic present "stands out," there is less clarity and consensus about the reasons for its use.

The treatment of the historic present by Albert Rijksbaron will be used as a starting point, since his description is somewhat more precise than the traditional invocation of "vividness" as an explanation for the use of the historic present at a given point in a narrative. He refers to the "special status" of the historic present and its "special effect, or rather, special effects."[66] The historic present marks "states of affairs that are of decisive importance for the story," "a decisive turning-point in the sequence of events," and "significant events in the course of a person's life."[67] These descriptions are not so different from the assessment of Stanley Porter that the historic present draws added attention to its event.[68] Jesús de la Villa similarly reports that the historic present is "mostly used to focalize a certain event or a series of events within a larger narration."[69] For Rijksbaron, the historic present also "punctuates a narrative."[70] Rijksbaron's terminology recalls allegations of "vividness" when he identifies the "eyewitnesseffect" [sic] of the historic present or a "pseudo-eyewitness" effect on the part of the narrator.[71] This effect is slightly different from the concept of *repraesentatio*,[72] in which the narrator takes on the point of view of the characters in the narrative. That is, the narrative is made present by the narrator for the audience.

---

65  Steven E. Runge, *Discourse Grammar of the New Testament: A Practical Introduction for Teaching and Exegesis* (Peabody MA: Hendrickson, 2010), 128–29, see also 131.

66  Rijksbaron, *Syntax and Semantics of the Verb*, 22.

67  Ibid., 22–25.

68  Stanley E. Porter, *Idioms of the Greek New Testament*, BLG 2 (Sheffield: JSOT Press, 1992), 31.

69  Jesús de la Villa, "Tense/Aspect," *EAGLL* 3:382–89.

70  Rijksbaron, *Syntax and Semantics of the Verb*, 24.

71  Ibid., 23.

72  See, for example, E. C. Woodcock, *A New Latin Syntax* (Oak Park, IL: Bolchazy-Carducci, 2002), 238.

The traditional view,[73] reflected in part by Rijksbaron, that the historic present is used as a "past more vivid" has been challenged by research into its use in premodern English[74] and in New Testament Greek.[75] A particularly relevant criticism is that the verbs that most commonly feature in the historic present do not relate to events in a narrative that deserve to be made to stand out. Most historic presents in the New Testament, and in John specifically, involve verbs of speaking or motion.[76] Indeed, in John 11, only 1 of the 12 historic presents is not a verb of speech: ἔρχεται in 11:38 (also as a variant in

73  See the survey of the grammars in Runge, *Discourse Grammar*, 125–28.

74  See Laurel J. Brinton, *Pragmatic Markers in English: Grammaticalization and Discourse Functions*, TiEL 19 (Berlin: Mouton de Gruyter, 1996), 18–20. In particular, there is an important point for the historical simple present in English, namely that English uses the present progressive, which is imperfective in aspect, for vividness, while the historic simple present is perfective in aspect. See Laurel J. Brinton, "The Historical Present in Charlotte Brontë's Novels: Some Discourse Functions," *Style* 26 (1992): 225, where Comrie, *Aspect*, 77, is cited. Greek, of course, like Latin, had one pres. indic. form that corresponds functionally both with the progressive present and with the simple present of English. Progressive present periphrases are very rare in Classical Greek and in the Koine, even though periphrases involving the ptc. of the imperfective stem and the impf. of εἰμί became more common. See Willem J. Aerts, *Periphrastica: An Investigation into the Use of "einai" and "echein" as Auxiliaries or Pseudo-auxiliaries in Greek from Homer up to Present Day* (Amsterdam: Hakkert, 1965), 26, 53, and 74–75.

75  See Runge, *Discourse Grammar*, 126–28, and Levinsohn, *Discourse Features*, 210–13.

76  See the discussion by Runge, *Discourse Grammar*, 127–28, 136, and 137 n. 45. O'Rourke, "Historic Present in the Gospel of John," 585–586, 587, counted 113 instances of λέγει, 6 of λέγουσι, 1 of φησί, and 1 of φωνεῖ out of a total of 164 HPs. The verb of motion ἔρχεται accounts for a further 12 instances. On page 585 n. 1, he restated the traditional counts for the Synoptic Gospels: 68 verbs of speaking out of 93 HPs in Matt, 72 out of 151 in Mark, and a mere 9 in Luke.

11:29).[77] Such historic presents, as John Callow discussed,[78] are not particularly important and, as such, cannot be considered to represent such "states of affairs that are of decisive importance for the story," "a decisive turning point in the sequence of events," and "significant events in the course of a person's life."

On that basis, Stephen Levinsohn rightly comments[79] that since the historic present is not the default tense for events in a past-time narrative, it must have "added implicatures," and he enlists Callow's claim that the historic present draws attention not to itself, but to the events that follow; with verbs of speech attention is drawn to the speech that follows, not to the fact that words were spoken.[80]

Laurel J. Brinton, drawing on the work of earlier scholars, provides a useful summary of the discourse functions of the historic present in Middle English in contrast to the secondary function of adding "vividness and excitement":[81]

a) to denote "the main actions as against subordinate and less important actions and other attending circumstances";

b) to "introduce a series of events ... and to describe the situation at the beginning of a new phase in the narrative";

c) to move "from one person to another";

d) to end a series of events, or to summarize and round up a foregoing passage; and

e) to introduce direct and indirect speech.

---

77 O'Rourke, "Historic Present in the Gospel of John," 587, states that there are 11 HPs in John 11, but I counted 12 from his catalogue on p. 586 (one of ἔρχεται, nine of λέγει, and two of λέγουσιν). Levinsohn, Discourse Features, 210, cites the HP in John 11:38 as an example of its use to bring an actor who has already been "activated" to the location of the next significant event or interaction. John A. Battle, "The Present Indicative in New Testament Exegesis" (ThD diss., Grace Theological Seminary, 1975), 128, cited this instance as a HP used to signal a change of scene. Since I have not seen Battle, "Present Indicative," I have relied on Runge, Discourse Grammar, 128, for this information.

78 John C. Callow, "The Historic Present in Mark," seminar handout at Horsley Green, UK, 1996, for which I am reliant on Stephen H. Levinsohn, "Verb Forms and Grounding in Narrative" (ch. 5 in this volume).

79 Ibid.

80 See Runge, Discourse Grammar, 137 n. 45.

81 Laurel J. Brinton, Pragmatic Markers in English, 19, and "Historical Discourse Analysis," in The Handbook of Discourse Analysis, ed. Deborah Schiffrin, Deborah Tannen, and Heidi Ehernberger Hamilton (Malden MA: Blackwell, 2001), 143.

We have already seen that the correlation in (e) is self-evidently true in the case of John 11 in particular and in other New Testament narratives. The question of a motive for using λέγει instead of εἶπεν can be considered in light of Callow's assessment. Changes of speaker are a subset of (c). Brinton's (b), (c), (d), and (e) give more precision to Rijksbaron's comment that the historic present "punctuates" and to Brinton's and Runge's own comments about "segmentation" as a function of the historic present.[82] Rijksbaron's terms "decisive importance," "a decisive turning-point," and "significant events" are not dissimilar to (a), which could be reformulated in terms of highlighted events in contrast to mainline and foreground events (for which the aorist seems to be used) again as against offline or background processes and situations.

What conclusions may be drawn from John 11:1–47 in relation to verbs of speech in the aorist and the historic present? The narrative consists of three main conversations (11:7–16, 21–28, and 34–43), which use the historic present to different extents and which will be considered in turn. The first of these begins with λέγει, the second and the third with εἶπεν. The first is closed by εἶπεν, the second and the third by καὶ τοῦτο εἰποῦσα "and when she had said this"(11:28) and καὶ ταῦτα εἰπών "And when he had said this" (11:43).

Of particular interest are juxtapositions of an aorist and a historic present (underlined):

> [11] ταῦτα εἶπεν, καὶ μετὰ τοῦτο λέγει αὐτοῖς· Λάζαρος ὁ φίλος ἡμῶν κεκοίμηται·
> ἀλλὰ πορεύομαι ἵνα ἐξυπνίσω αὐτόν.
> He said this, and after this he says to them, "Lazarus our friend is asleep, but I am on my way in order that I may wake him."

> [34] καὶ εἶπεν· ποῦ τεθείκατε αὐτόν; λέγουσιν αὐτῷ· κύριε, ἔρχου καὶ ἴδε.
> And he said, "Where have you put him?" They say to him, "Lord, come and see."

82 Brinton, "Historic Present," 225–26, and *Pragmatic Markers in English*, 20; Runge, *Discourse Grammar*, 132–33.

In 11:11, ταῦτα εἶπεν is unmarked and, in effect, functions as a closing speech mark. However, the historic present, which reopens Jesus' reply to the disciples, is marked and draws attention to what is said: Jesus will go to "wake" Lazarus. Since there is no change of speaker and, perhaps, there was no significant passage of time, this interruption on the part of the narrator slows the pace of the narrative and adds to the highlighting of what Jesus said next by isolating it. Jesus' teaching moves from "timeless truths" to the specific situation involving Lazarus. Jesus' statement paves the way for the sequence of the disciples' confusion, John's explanation of Jesus' words, Jesus' announcement that Lazarus has died, and of his reaction and its purpose, and, finally his exhortation to depart (a fitting conclusion for this dialogue: ἄγωμεν appears in 11:7, 15, and 16, at the beginning and end of this conversation). In 11:34, the historic present paves the way both for the command in direct speech ἔρχου καὶ ἴδε "come and see" (an echo of John 1:46 and, in part, of 1:39)[83] and for the event of the poignant moment of ἐδάκρυσεν ὁ Ἰησοῦς "Jesus wept" (11:35).

The first conversation makes the least use of the historic present. The historic present marks the transition (11:7) to a dialogue from a narrative (with the exception of εἶπεν in 11:4 and λέγουσα in 11:3). The narrative so far has been scene-setting, but begins in earnest with 11:7. Note also ἔπειτα μετὰ τοῦτο "Then, after this" as markers of transition after the delay of two days. The first reply (11:8) is introduced by the other historic present in this conversation, which is also the first verb of which the disciples are the subject. The disciples are "activated" in Levinsohn's terminology.[84] These could be described as decisive events as far as the commencement of the narrative is concerned. The subsequent changes of speaker are indicated by εἶπεν (11:11, 14, and 16), by εἶπαν (11:12), and by the only instance in John 11 of ἀπεκρίθη (11:9), the Johannine favorite (56 other instances and 15 of ἀπεκρίθησαν).[85]

---

83  The echo is closer if ἴδετε (ℵ, A, C³, and Θ among others) is read in John 1:39.
84  Levinsohn, *Discourse Features*, 210.
85  The characteristic Johannine formula involves two coordinated indics. in contrast to a ptc. and an indic., as in Matt 3:15 ἀποκριθεὶς εἶπεν "He answered and said." Phrynichus, *Ecloga* 78, censured the use of the aor. passive form to mean "answer, reply"; see LSJ, 204, *s.v.* ἀποκρίνω IV.3.

The second conversation, between Martha and Jesus, is certainly a dramatic encounter and makes more use of the historic present, perhaps as a marker of prominence.[86] The second and third statements are presented by historic presents (11:23 and 24) and are sandwiched by aorists (11:21, 25), the second of which introduces the "I am" saying. Martha's two confessions of faith are introduced by historic presents (11:24, 27), which may well be instances of this verb form as a marker of prominence for what follows. The statements of 11:23 and 24 could be described as prominent or decisive, but so could Jesus' words in 11:25–26, which are introduced by aorists. It may well be right to conclude that highlighting of a statement is the function of the historic present in 11:23, 24, and 27 and building anticipation towards a key moment: the "I am" saying in 11:25.

The three historic presents could be said to underline the discontinuities[87] in this second conversation. To some extent, Martha and Jesus talked past each other. Martha did not accept Jesus' claim that he is the resurrection and the life (11:25), but instead professed that he is the Christ (11:27). Her answer to his question τοῦτο πιστεύεις; "Do you believe this?" is not direct and, although it consists of a creedal statement, its content is quite different. Martha accepted Jesus' announcement that Lazarus will rise (11:23), but with the limitation of "at the resurrection on the last day" (11:24). If there is a discontinuity that is underlined by the historic present that introduces Martha's reply, attention is drawn to Jesus' unexpressed timeframe for the resurrection of Lazarus: for Martha the future ἀναστήσεται involves some subsequent date (11:24), but for Jesus it is an immediate future (11:23). The difference may be highlighted by the historic present. That Lazarus will rise imminently because of who Jesus is surely is a key point of the narrative of this sign and "I am" saying. This leaves the first historic present (11:23), which would more readily mark a contrast with 11:21 than with 11:22. Martha implies that Lazarus's death could have been prevented by Jesus, but cannot now be undone. However, there may be a contrast with Martha's statement as

---

86  For the HP as a means of highlighting and marking prominence, see, especially, Runge, *Discourse Grammar*, 130–33.

87  For the HP as a means of underlining a discontinuity already in the narrative, see, especially, Runge, *Discourse Grammar*, 132. Later, ibid., 135, he specifies *thematic discontinuities* as changes in time, location, participants, and actions.

a whole (11:21 and 22), in that, although Martha claims to know that God will grant *whatever* Jesus asks, her subsequent response indicates, her concept of *whatever* did not include the resurrection of Lazarus there and then. If so, the historic present draws out contrasting assumptions and the discontinuities of the conversation between Martha and Jesus.

The third conversation involves clustering or potential "overuse" of the historic present. This conversation follows the only historic present in the chapter that does not involve a verb of speech, namely ἔρχεται in 11:38. This coincides with the significant mention of Lazarus's tomb and burial, which is subsequently described in the imperfect. The aorist is absent after the first statement, apart from εἶπαν (11:37) for the comment of some of the Judeans and εἶπεν for Jesus' prayer (11:41). The larger body of the crowd, as we have seen, is quoted with an imperfect (11:36). The crucial speech act "Λάζαρε, δεῦρο ἔξω." "Lazarus, come out!" involves an aorist ἐκραύγησεν "he shouted" (11:43), to which attention is drawn by the addition of φωνῇ μεγάλῃ "in a loud voice" (which is far from obligatory with this verb). These events and, in particular, Jesus' commands are the climax of this narrative. The dialogue is carried by a series of historic presents (two in 11:39 and one in 11:40). Runge's comment about "the overuse of a device in a series of clauses, like building to a crescendo" seems very appropriate to these historic presents.[88] The final historic present (11:44) ends this series of events and serves to highlight the changes of actors (πολλοί, τινές, the high priests and the Pharisees) and location (the Sanhedrin) that follow (11:45–47). We are left wondering what happened next at Bethany.

The historic present in John 11, then, is a device that highlights statements, in particular, and some actions, by pointing forward to them, draws attention to new speakers and to discontinuities both within conversations and at changes of location and actor. Clustering of historic presents also serves to create a crescendo effect.

The choice between the historic present, aorist, and imperfect indicative is not the only significant variable in this narrative. Some comments about departures from typical verb-subject-object word order have been made already in relation to the imperfect in 11:36–37. The nontypical word order in 11:19, 31–33, 38, and 45 should

---

88  Ibid., 133.

be considered as structural features of the discourse. Further, the range and distribution of particles and conjunctions is noteworthy. Their correlation with aorist and imperfect verb forms calls for attention.

The particle δέ coincides, outside direct speech, with the few imperfect and pluperfect indicatives of this passage. Apart from the use of δέ "and, but" to mark a contrast or an additional piece of information (11:1, 2, 4, 29, 41), this particle occurs with the imperfect ἠγάπα "he was loving" (11:5) and with the pluperfects εἰρήκει "he had said" (11:13), ἐληλύθεισαν "they had come" (11:19), and ἐληλύθει "he had come" (11:30). These are all background items. The two instances with τινές "some people" (11:37 and 46) coincide with changes of subject, but also with changes to a closer view within a group. This leaves ἦν δὲ ἡ Βηθανία "and Bethany was..." (11:18), the first of two background items between the aorists in 11:17 and 20: this one in the imperfect, the second (11:19) in the pluperfect with δέ, as already noted.

The particle οὖν occurs with the imperfect indicative once (11:36) and once with the historic present (11:39). It occurs with aorist indicatives in 13 instances (11:3, **6**, 12, **14**, 16, 17, **20**, **21**, **31**, **32**, 33, 41, 47). The verse numbers in bold are instances of οὖν and an aorist that coincide with a change of tense: after the imperfect in 11:5, after the pluperfect in 11:13, after the imperfect in 11:18, and the pluperfect in 11:19, after a probable imperfect in 11:20, after a pluperfect and an imperfect in 11:30. The others coincide with a change of actor (11:3, 12, 16, 33, 41; cf. 11:20) or scene (11:17; cf. 11:21, 31, 32, 47). In 11:36, οὖν with the imperfect marks a change of actor (after the aorist in 11:35) and in 11:38 οὖν marks a return to the actor of 11:36 and introduces a change from the aorist to the historic present. We should also note the cooccurrence with non-verb-subject-object word order of 11:38. There is considerable back-and-forth between 11:34 and 38, which certainly contains one of the most poignant points of the narrative: ἐδάκρυσεν ὁ Ἰησοῦς ("Jesus wept").

These distributions of particles and changes of verbal aspect may be no more than correlations. We should not conclude that there is a causal relationship in either direction between a particle and a particular aspect of the verb. Instead, it seems that packages of a particle and a verb together mark changes from foreground to background and returns from background to foreground. Since that is so, we should hesitate before assigning the functions of backgrounding and foregrounding to particular aspects in every instance.

This discussion of the alternation of aorists, imperfects, historic presents, and perfects and pluperfects has demonstrated that the aspectual values of these forms are uppermost, not any indication of background or foreground that they might involve. The presence of these particles suggests that the verb forms did not perform the function of marking background and foreground by themselves.

## BIBLIOGRAPHY

Aerts, Willem J. *Periphrastica: An Investigation into the Use of "einai" and "echein" as Auxiliaries or Pseudo-auxiliaries in Greek from Homer up to Present Day*. Amsterdam: Hakkert, 1965.

Battle, John A. "The Present Indicative in New Testament Exegesis." ThD diss., Grace Theological Seminary, 1975.

Bauer, Walter, F. W. Danker, W. F. Arndt, and F. W. Gingrich. *A Greek-English Lexicon of the New Testament and Other Early Christian Literature*. 3rd ed. Chicago: University of Chicago Press, 2000.

Beekes, Robert S. P., and Lucien van Beek. *Etymological Dictionary of Greek*. IEED 10. Leiden: Brill, 2010.

Bentein, Klaas. "Aspectual Choice and the Presentation of Narrative: An Application to Herodotus' *Histories*." *Glotta* 92 (2016), forthcoming.

———. "Aspectual Choice with *verba dicendi* in Herodotus' *Histories*." *Emerita* 83 (2015): 221–45.

———. "Tense and Aspect from Hellenistic to Early Byzantine Greek." *EAGLL* 3:379–82.

Blass, F. and A. Debrunner. *A Greek Grammar of the New Testament and Other Early Christian Literature*. Translated by Robert W. Funk. Revised ed. Chicago: University Of Chicago Press, 1961.

Brinton, Laurel J. "Historical Discourse Analysis." Pages 138–60 in *The Handbook of Discourse Analysis*. Edited by Deborah Schiffrin, Deborah Tannen, and Heidi Ehernberger Hamilton. Malden MA: Blackwell, 2001.

———. "The Historical Present in Charlotte Brontë's Novels: Some Discourse Functions." *Style* 26 (1992): 221–244.

———. *Pragmatic Markers in English: Grammaticalization and Discourse Features*. TiEL 19. Berlin: Mouton de Gruyter, 1996.

Browning, Robert. *Medieval and Modern Greek*. 2nd ed. Cambridge: Cambridge University Press, 1983.

Callow, John C. "The Historic Present in Mark." Seminar handout. Horsleys Green, UK, 1996.

Carey, Christopher, ed. *Lysias: Selected Speeches*. CGLC. Cambridge: Cambridge University Press, 1989.

Clackson, James. *Indo-European Linguistics: An Introduction*. CTL. Cambridge: Cambridge University Press, 2007.

Comrie, Bernard. *Aspect: An Introduction to the Study of Verbal Aspect and Related Problems*. CTL. Cambridge: Cambridge University Press, 1976.

———. *Tense*. CTL. Cambridge: Cambridge University Press, 1985.

Crellin, Robert. "The Greek Perfect Active System: 200 BC–AD 150." PhD diss., University of Cambridge, 2012.

De la Villa, Jesús. "Tense/Aspect." *EAGLL* 3:382–89.

Dieterich, Karl. *Untersuchungen zur Geschichte der griechischen Sprache von der hellenistischen Zeit bis zum 10. Jahrhundert n. Chr.* Leipzig: Teubner, 1898.

Diggle, James, ed. *Theophrastus: Characters*. CCTC 43. Cambridge: Cambridge University Press, 2004.

Evans, T. V. *Verbal Syntax in the Greek Pentateuch: Natural Greek Usage and Hebrew Interference*. Oxford: Oxford University Press, 2001.

Gignac, F. T. *A Grammar of the Greek Papyri of the Roman and Byzantine Periods: Volume 2, Morphology*. Milan: Cisalpino-Goliardica, 1981.

Horrocks, Geoffrey C. *Greek: A History of the Language and its Speakers*. 2nd ed. Chichester: Wiley-Blackwell, 2010.

Jannaris, A.N. *An Historical Grammar: Chiefly of the Attic Dialect as Written and Spoken from Classical Antiquity Down to the Present Time, Founded upon the Ancient Texts, Inscriptions, Papyri and Present Popular Greek*. London: Macmillan, 1897.

Levinsohn, Stephen. *Discourse Features of New Testament Greek: A Coursebook on the Information Structure of New Testament Greek*. 2nd ed. Dallas: SIL International, 2000.

Liddel, Henry George, Robert Scott, Henry Stuart Jones. *A Greek-English Lexicon*. 9th ed. with revised supplement. Oxford: Clarendon, 1996.

Lyons, John. *Introduction to Theoretical Linguistics*. Cambridge: Cambridge University Press, 1968.

Mandilaras, Basil G. *Studies in the Greek Language: Some Aspects of the Development of the Greek Language up to the Present*. Athens: Xenopoulos, 1972.

Mayser, Edwin. *Grammatik der griechischen Papyri aus der Ptolemäerzeit; mit Einschluss der gleichzeitigen Ostraka und der in Ägypten* verfassten Inschriften, I 2, Laut- und Wortlehre, pt. II, Flexionslehre. Leipzig: de Gruyter, 1938.

Metzger, Bruce M. *A Textual Commentary on the Greek New Testament.* 2nd ed. Stuttgart: Deutsche Bibelgesellschaft, 2000.

Napoli, Maria. *Aspect and Actionality in Homeric Greek: A Contrastive Analysis.* Materiali linguistici 54. Milan: FrancoAngeli, 2006.

O'Rourke, John J. "The Historic Present in the Gospel of John." *JBL* 93 (1974): 585–590.

Palmer, L. R. *The Greek Language.* London: Faber and Faber, 1980.

———. *The Latin Language.* London: Faber and Faber, 1954.

Porter, Stanley E. *Idioms of the Greek New Testament.* BLG 2. Sheffield: JSOT Press, 1992.

———. *Verbal Aspect in the Greek of the New Testament: With Reference to Tense and Mood.* SBG 1. New York: Lang, 1989.

Ridderbos, Hermann N. *The Gospel According to John: A Theological Commentary.* Translated by John Vriend. Grand Rapids: Eerdmans, 1997.

Rijksbaron, Albert. *The Syntax and Semantics of the Verb in Classical Greek: An Introduction.* 3rd ed. Chicago: University of Chicago Press, 2006.

Runge, Steven, E. *Discourse Grammar of the Greek New Testament: A Practical Introduction for Teaching and Exegesis.* Peabody MA: Hendrickson, 2010.

Stork, Peter. "Aspectual Variant Readings in Herodotus." Pages 265–89 in *In the Footsteps of Raphael Kühner*, edited by A. Rijksbaron, H. A. Mulder, and G. C. Wakker. Amsterdam: Gieben, 1988.

Thumb, Albert. "On the Value of Modern Greek for the Study of Ancient Greek." *ClQ* 8 (1914): 181–205.

Woodcock, E. C. *A New Latin Syntax.* Oak Park, IL: Bolchazy-Carducci, 2002.

CHAPTER 7

# The Contribution of Verb Forms, Connectives, and Dependency to Grounding Status in Nonnarrative Discourse

STEVEN E. RUNGE

LEXHAM RESEARCH INSTITUTE | STELLENBOSCH UNIVERSITY

## 1. INTRODUCTION

Linguists have recognized a text may be usefully subdivided based on the nature of its contribution to the communicative goals of the discourse. The portions that advance the plot or argument—and thus form the backbone of the discourse—are referred to as the *theme line*.[1] The remainder of the material may be considered *support* for the theme line, offering important background detail and fleshing out concepts. Alternate terminology is used to refer to these two parameters based upon the metaphor chosen to describe the distinction. Thus theme line and support correspond to figure/ground, mainline/offline, and foreground/background,

---

1    For a more complete introduction to the characteristics of theme line and support, see Stephen H. Levinsohn, *Self-Instruction Materials on Non-Narrative Discourse Analysis* (Dallas: SIL International, 2015), 14–16, http://www.sil.org/~levinsohns/NonNarr.pdf.

respectively.[2] Theme line/support will be the preferred terminology throughout this paper.[3] Breeze describes the theme line as presenting "the backbone of the discourse—whether this be the main events of a narrative, the main steps of a procedure, the main points of an argument or the main commands of an exhortation" and the support as providing "all that is necessary as a background for understanding the story, procedure, or argument as a whole."[4] Note how theme line and support differ depending upon the nature of the content (see §1.1 on genre distinctions).

The distinction we have found for differentiating theme line from support concerns the advance or progression of the discourse, based on the writer's goals and objectives. It is rare to find such an overt statement as I have offered, but language describing perfective events as "carrying the narrative forward"[5] or as being "important in the plot progression"[6] suggest an underlying awareness that the elements which advance the discourse toward its intended goal coincide with what is described as theme line or foreground.

---

2    Stephen Wallace, "Figure and Ground: The Interrelationships of Linguistic Categories," in *Tense-Aspect: Between Semantics and Pragmatics*, ed. Paul J. Hopper, TSL 1 (Amsterdam: Benjamins, 1982), 213–16; Helen A Dry, "Foregrounding: An Assessment," in *Language in Context: Essays for Robert E. Longacre*, ed. Shin Ja J. Hwang and William R. Merrifield (Dallas: Summer Institute of Linguistics, 1992), 236–38.

3    Porter uses foreground/background to refer to "planes of discourse" rather than grounding roles, breaking with typical linguistic usage, but he uses mainline/offline in the traditional linguistic sense of the terms. In order to avoid confusion and the freighted association of "offline" with the unimportant, we are adopting the terminology advocated by Breeze and Levinsohn. See Stanley E. Porter, "Prominence: An Overview," in *The Linguist as Pedagogue: Trends in the Teaching and Linguistic Analysis of the Greek New Testament*, ed. Stanley E. Porter and Matthew Brook O'Donnell, NTM 11 (Sheffield: Sheffield Phoenix, 2009), 54–58.

4    Mary Breeze, "Hortatory Discourse in Ephesians," *JOTT* 5 (1992): 314.

5    James Forsyth, *A Grammar of Aspect: Usage and Meaning in the Russian Verb* (Cambridge: Cambridge University Press, 1970), 10. See also Kathleen Callow, *Discourse Considerations in Translating the Word of God* (Grand Rapids: Zondervan, 1974), 54–55; Stephen H. Levinsohn, *Self-Instruction Materials on Narrative Discourse Analysis.* (Dallas: SIL International, 2015), 66, http://www.sil.org/~levinsohns/narr.pdf.

6    Larry B. Jones and Linda K. Jones, "Multiple Levels of Information in Discourse," in *Discourse Studies in Mesoamerican Languages: Discussion*, ed. Linda K. Jones (Dallas: SIL International, 1979), 1:8, http://www.sil.org/resources/archives/8434.

Regarding support/background information, it would be falla-
cious to think of it as unnecessary or unimportant to the discourse.
Dooley and Levinsohn note, "If only the foreground were available,
the resulting representation might be complete in its general outline, but would be sketchy. Background aids in internal and external
contextualization."[7] Or as Breeze puts it, "These different types of
information, which work together to communicate the total message of a discourse, can be distinguished from each other by certain
language-specific surface features, such as tense and aspect markers, verb forms, conjunctions, special particles, and word order."[8]
The support serves the important role of fleshing out the broader
picture of the discourse, but it "is contingent and dependent upon
the theme line events."[9]

## 1.1 Genre Distinctions

As Breeze notes, there are several features of discourse that should
caution us against expecting that theme line and support can be distinguished on the basis of a single feature such as verbal aspect; the
first we will consider is genre. Longacre has developed broad categorizes of genre based on the salience of two parameters, summarized in table 1: Agent orientation and contingent temporal succession. The former describes whether or not a discourse focuses upon
agents throughout as opposed to ideas, arguments, or exhortations;
the latter describes the importance of chronology to the structuring
of the discourse.[10]

---

7   Robert A. Dooley and Stephen H. Levinsohn, *Analyzing Discourse: A Manual
    of Basic Concepts* (Dallas: SIL International, 2001), 41.
8   Breeze, "Hortatory Discourse in Ephesians," 314.
9   Constantine Campbell, *Verbal Aspect, the Indicative Mood, and Narra-
    tive: Soundings in the Greek of the New Testament*, SBG 13 (New York: Lang,
    2007), 116.
10  Robert E. Longacre, *The Grammar of Discourse*, 2nd ed, TLL (New York: Ple-
    num, 1996), 8–9.

Table 1: Broad Categories of Genre[11]

| | | Agent Orientation | |
|---|---|---|---|
| Contingent temporal succession | | + | − |
| | + | Narrative | Procedural |
| | − | Behavioral | Expository |

Thus narrative genre can be distinguished from expository material based on the significant role agents and contingent temporal succession play. Narrative texts are agent-driven and organized primarily chronologically, whereas expository material is not. For the purposes of this paper, I will use the cover term nonnarrative to refer to Longacre's behavioral and expository discourse since these two genres account for most of the New Testament epistolary literature.

So as we begin investigating the relationship of verb forms to grounding roles in nonnarrative, we can speak of theme line and support in the sense of "that which drives the discourse forward" versus "that which does not," but Longacre's parameters direct us to expect that the nature of the material doing the driving in narrative proper will differ compared to the genres found in nonnarrative discourse. As Callow observes, "material which might have a background function in narrative may be thematic in these other types of discourse."[12]

There is a well-documented correlation between grounding and verbal aspect in narrative proper, as Levinsohn and James have demonstrated.[13] The theme line or foreground is predominantly carried forward by past perfective verb-forms (the aor. indic. in Koine Greek), whereas the support predominantly consists of past imperfective and perfect forms (the impf. and plupf. indic. in Koine Greek). Use of the present indicative for theme line events, typically referred to as the "historical present," serves a highlighting function.[14] These are not rules, but general observations. Imperfect

---

11  Ibid.; cited from Dooley and Levinsohn, *Analyzing Discourse*, 4.
12  Callow, *Discourse Considerations in Translating the Word of God*, 56.
13  See chs. 5 and 6 in this volume.
14  See ch. 10 of this volume; also Stephen H. Levinsohn, *Discourse Features of New Testament Greek: A Coursebook on the Information Structure of New Testament Greek*, 2nd ed. (Dallas: SIL International, 2000), 200–214; Steven E.

indicatives may be used at times for theme line actions,[15] whereas the aorist is used for certain support actions.[16] The perfective/imperfective correlation with theme line and support in narrative is prototypical and typological in nature, a useful starting point for understanding the nature of grounding in narrative proper, but certainly not the whole picture.

The strong typological correlation between perfective aspect and narrative theme line/foreground has fostered the sense, particularly within New Testament studies, that grounding roles are somehow monolithically tied to aspect. The claims of Stanley Porter regarding his "planes of discourse" model have only reinforced expectations that grounding is solely based upon verb forms, without apparent consideration for other factors like genre, connectives, and dependency relations.[17] However matters in the nonnarrative genres are not so clear-cut. There is no tidy prototypical correlation between a certain tense or aspect and theme line/support as we find in narrative proper.

A brief survey of linguistic research into grounding shows that— even in narrative—matters are far more complex than the prototypical tendencies lead us to think. Wårvik outlines five conclusions from previous research on grounding in narrative that argue

---

Runge, *Discourse Grammar of the Greek New Testament: A Practical Introduction for Teaching and Exegesis* (Peabody, MA: Hendrickson, 2010), 125–44.

15  "Inchoative verbs of speaking (Levinsohn 2000), mid-speech quotative frames or Wallace's instantaneous imperfect (Runge 2010), and instances like Matt 21:11; 26:5; Mark 6:13; 14:31 where the action was a theme line event, but is portrayed as occurring for some time." Buist M. Fanning, "Greek Presents, Imperfects, and Aorists in the Synoptic Gospels: Their Contribution to Narrative Structuring," in *Discourse Studies and Biblical Interpretation: A Festschrift in Honor of Stephen H. Levinsohn*, ed. Steven E. Runge (Bellingham, WA: Logos Bible Software, 2011), 173–74.

16  E.g., main clauses introduced by γάρ (Matt 14:3, 5; 28:2; Mark 3:10; 6:17, 52; 9:6, 34; Luke 5:9; 8:29; 19:48; 20:19; Acts 8:7–8) and in dependent clauses of imperfective/perfect main clauses (Matt 27:18; Mark 3:21; Luke 5:9; 20:19; Acts 21:29).

17  For a representative overview of Porter's claims about the contribution of verbal aspect to prominence in his planes of discourse model, see Porter, "Prominence."

in favor of building a more complex model of grounding.[18] On her view, grounding is best understood as:

1. Scalar, not binary, "with maximal foregrounding at one end and maximal backgrounding at the other."
2. A cluster concept, "so that foregroundedness vs. backgroundedness of a clause is dependent on several criteria: each of them affects the grounding degree of the clause, but none of them is alone decisive."
3. Contextually dependent: "It is only in relation to other clauses in a text that we can assign a specific degree of foregroundedness vs. backgroundedness to a clause."
4. Representational: Events and actions do not have a real-world grounding value. It "emerges only when a text producer presents them in a certain way in a certain context."
5. Formally marked: Markers typically contribute "toward the same interpretation as the grounding value of the content criteria, but they do not obligatorily support each other."[19]

These complexities do not mean that grounding is unknowable, but caution us against naïvely expecting a one-to-one correlation between a verb form and a specific grounding role.

## 1.2 Distributional Distinctions

Why is it that we do not find the same kind of prototypical, aspect-based grounding distinction between theme line and support in nonnarrative as we have in narrative proper? This section offers tangible answers to this question by highlighting the significant differences between these two types of discourse. The statistics utilized are drawn from searches in the narrative portions of the New Testament (Matthew–Acts) in the OpenText.org Syntactically Analyzed Greek New Testament, a linguistic analysis of features

---

18  Brita Wårvik, "What Is Foregrounded in Narratives? Hypotheses for the Cognitive Basis of Foregrounding," in *Approaches to Cognition Through Text and Discourse*, ed. Tuija Virtanen (Berlin: Mouton de Gruyter, 2004), 100.
19  Ibid.

based on the NA²⁷ text.²⁰ Narrative proper is differentiated from the nonnarrative speeches embedded within narrative based on OpenText.org's category of "Projection."²¹

The finite verbs in narrative proper predominately utilize the indicative mood, a ratio of more than 15:1 compared to nonindicative finite verbs (see table 2). Contrast this with the diversity of finite moods found in nonnarrative discourse, where the ratio of indicative to nonindicative finite verbs decreases to less than 3:1 in Matthew–Acts.

Table 2: Ratio of Indicative to Nonindicative forms in Matthew–Acts

|         | Indicative | Nonindic | Ratio |
|---------|-----------|----------|-------|
| Narrative | 5668 | 365 | 15.52:1 |
| Nonnarr | 5872 | 1920 | 3.05:1 |

This is comparable to the 3.33:1 ratio of indicative to nonindicative found in the balance of the New Testament.²² The wider variation in mood explains why we find no typological counterpart to the role of perfective and imperfective aspect in narrative for determining grounding roles.

Wårvik's "clustering" notion suggests that other features of discourse help readers track shifts in grounding. Bertrand notes that verbal aspect, morphology, and syntax have been fruitfully correlated with grounding roles in narrative discourse.²³ I would add to this list connectives, particularly γάρ and οὖν.²⁴ Levinsohn identifies two

---

20  Stanley E. Porter et al., *The OpenText.org Syntactically Analyzed Greek New Testament: Clause Analysis*, version 2013-04-12T20:32:29Z (Bellingham, WA: Logos Bible Software, 2006).

21  There are 6033 finite verbal clauses in Projected portion of this corpus (which corresponds to narrative proper) and 5964 in the non-Projected or nonnarrative portions.

22  This ratio only considers primary and secondary clauses. Including embedded clauses leads to repeated results due to recursion. The ratio is not intended to be perfect, but illustrative. There are 4890 indicative finite verbal clauses in the corpus of Romans–Revelation, compared to 1468 nonindicative finite verbal clauses.

23  Nicolas Bertrand, "Grounding of Information," *EAGLL* 2:149–50.

24  The term connectives is preferred as a more general term for conjunctions and other adverbs which conjoin sentences, such as narrative τότε and expressions like διὰ τοῦτο. See Stephen H. Levinsohn, "'Therefore' or 'Where-

types of logical connectives that mark intersentential relations in Koine Greek: inferential and logical.[25]

Strengthening connectives (e.g., γάρ and ὅτι) are most associated with support for theme line information. Levinsohn states that they "support a THESIS by introducing a reason, ground or explanation."[26] He considers γάρ "the default strengthening connective, which does NOT indicate a specific logical relation," whereas ὅτι, "[w]hen used as a logical connective, it introduces a reason or evidence for the last assertion (THESIS)."[27] Thus strengthening connectives strongly correlate with support or background information.

The inferential connectives (e.g., διό and οὖν) "introduce a THESIS, CONCLUSION or RESULT which is inferred from the context."[28] Διό typically introduces an expository or hortatory thesis drawn from what precedes, whereas οὖν often marks the resumption of a theme following supportive material.[29] Thus inferential connectives are most often associated with the theme line or foreground of the discourse.

Now if we compare the use of the two connectives primarily associated with marking transitions to support or back to the theme line (γάρ and οὖν, respectively) in narrative against nonnarrative, we find stark contrasts in their distribution, suggesting connectives play a critical role in signaling grounding shifts in nonnarrative. For example, we find γάρ occurs nearly three times as frequently in nonnarrative compared to narrative proper, whereas the ratio for οὖν is inverted in nonnarrative versus narrative.[30] This inversion can be accounted for by the observations of Levinsohn and Buth regarding the propensity in John's gospel to utilize οὖν much as what

---

fore': What's the Difference?," in *Reflections on Lexicography: Explorations in Ancient Syriac, Hebrew, and Greek Sources*, ed. Richard A. Taylor and Craig E. Morrison, PLAL 4 (Piscataway, NJ: Gorgias Press, 2014), 325–43.

25  Levinsohn, *Non-Narrative Discourse*, 37.

26  Ibid.

27  Ibid., 38.

28  Ibid., 37.

29  Ibid., 37–38; Christopher J. Fresch, "The Peculiar Occurrences of οὖν in Septuagint Genesis and Exodus," in *XV Congress of the International Organization for Septuagint and Cognate Studies, Munich, 2013*, ed. Wolfgang Kraus, Martin Meiser, and Michaël van der Meer (Atlanta: Society of Biblical Literature, forthcoming).

30  Fresch, "Peculiar Occurrences."

we might expect in an epistle, signaling distinct steps in the narrative discourse.[31] Consider how excluding John's data for οὖν affects the ratios, bringing it much closer in line with γάρ.

Table 3: Ratio of Usage in Narrative versus Nonnarrative in Matthew–Acts

|  | Γάρ | Οὖν | Οὖν (w/o John) |
|---|---|---|---|
| Narrative | 109 | 216 | 34 |
| Non-Narr | 321 | 137 | 119 |
| Ratio | 2.94:1 | 0.63:1 | 3.5:1 |

These ratios illustrate the increased complexity we find in non-narrative versus narrative. The more regular use of nonindicative moods in nonnarrative, along with more varied use of the tense-forms, demand that writers utilize other means besides aspect to signal transitions in the grounding.[32]

To summarize, the grounding status of information will vary from genre to genre, based on what is most salient. Longacre's "broad categories of genre" offer insight into what is most important in each. Grounding is also representational, despite the strong correlation it might bear with the real world. Contextual factors may lead writers to background an action with respect to another for some reason, exploiting the scalar nature of grounding.[33] Finally, grounding judgments must consider contextual factors besides the tense-form alone.

Grounding roles in discourse fundamentally hinge upon *advancing the flow, based on the writer's goals and objectives.* Support material contributes significantly to the discourse as a whole, but does not advance the discourse. If we compare the flow of discourse with movement toward a destination (the communicative objective of the discourse) we can draw a helpful analogy. The theme line is the road that we must travel upon to reach our destination. We will only

31  Randall Buth, "Ουν, Δε, Και and Asyndeton in John's Gospel," in *Linguistics and New Testament Interpretation*, ed. David A. Black (Nashville: Broadman, 1992), 144–61; Levinsohn, *Discourse Features*, 85–89.
32  Contrast the 265 pf. indics. found in the embedded speeches of the Gospels and Acts versus 8 found in narrative proper.
33  See Levinsohn, *Discourse Features*, 169–96.

make progress while we remain on the road. We may take a side trip along the way and still be driving, but we will not be getting closer to our objective until we return to the theme line. We might even loop back on our path as part of a support side trip, but the theme line is ultimately what carries us toward the writer's objective for the discourse.

In the balance of this paper, this metaphor of directional progress is applied to the charting of discourse using indentation. Descent represents advance or continuation of a theme line. Transitions to support are represented by indentation. As will be seen, extended sections of supportive material may serve as embedded theme lines. With respect to the higher-level theme, the material functions as support; but with respect to itself the support can become its own theme line with supporting material of its own. Movement to the left represents a return to a higher-level theme line, either a brand new one or the resumption of a previous one, as illustrated in example 1.

*Example 1: Phil 2:19–24*

| Theme line | Ἐλπίζω δὲ ἐν κυρίῳ Ἰησοῦ Τιμόθεον ταχέως πέμψαι ὑμῖν, ἵνα κἀγὼ εὐψυχῶ γνοὺς τὰ περὶ ὑμῶν. |
|---|---|
| Support | ²⁰οὐδένα γὰρ ἔχω ἰσόψυχον ὅστις γνησίως τὰ περὶ ὑμῶν μεριμνήσει, |
| Support | ²¹οἱ πάντες γὰρ τὰ ἑαυτῶν ζητοῦσιν, οὐ τὰ Ἰησοῦ Χριστοῦ. |
| Support | ²²τὴν δὲ δοκιμὴν αὐτοῦ γινώσκετε, ὅτι ὡς πατρὶ τέκνον σὺν ἐμοὶ ἐδούλευσεν εἰς τὸ εὐαγγέλιον. |
| Theme line | ²³τοῦτον μὲν οὖν ἐλπίζω πέμψαι ὡς ἂν ἀφίδω τὰ περὶ ἐμὲ ἐξαυτῆς· |
| Theme line | ²⁴πέποιθα δὲ ἐν κυρίῳ ὅτι καὶ αὐτὸς ταχέως ἐλεύσομαι. |

| Theme line | But I hope in the Lord Jesus to send Timothy to you soon, so that I also may be encouraged *when I* know your circumstances. |
| Support | [20] For I have no one like-minded who *will* sincerely be concerned about your circumstances. |
| Support | [21] For they all seek their own interests, not those of Jesus Christ. |
| Support | [22] But you know his proven character, that like a child with a father he served with me for the gospel. |
| Theme line | [23] Therefore I hope to send him at once, as soon as I see my circumstances. |
| Theme line | [24] And I am convinced in the Lord that I myself will arrive shortly also.[34] |

Verse 19 offers the thesis statement about Paul hoping to send Timothy. This is supported by the statement about his like-mindedness in 2:20, which itself is supported by the contrasting portraits of everyone seeking their own interests compared to Timothy's proven character (2:21–22). The οὖν in 2:23 signals the resumption of the theme line of sending Timothy in 2:19, whereas μέν creates an anticipatory rhetorical connection between 2:23 and 2:24.[35] The purpose of this charting strategy is to reflect as closely as possible the advancement of the discourse. The shift to the right at 2:20 represents the suspension of the theme line to introduce important support for 2:19, whereas the movement to the left at 2:23 represents the resumption and advancement of the higher-level theme begun in 2:19. The principles undergirding and directing the analysis above will be outlined below.

---

34  All translations are taken from the Lexham English Bible (LEB) unless otherwise specified.
35  For the use of μέν to create a counterpoint-point set see Runge, *Discourse Grammar*, 74–82.

## 2. VERB FORMS AND GROUNDING STATUS: THEME LINE VERSUS SUPPORT

As the distributional observations suggest, we should not expect a single overarching correlation between certain verb forms and grounding function in nonnarrative. However, several general observations may be made before moving on to connectives and dependency relationships between clauses, though very little can be said without reference to these other factors.

### 2.1 Mood

The nonindicative moods bear a strong correlation with certain grounding roles. Recall Longacre's distinction between behavioral/hortatory and expository discourse, two of his nonnarrative genres. Hortatory discourse typically consists of theme line exhortations with expository material serving as the ground or support for them. Prototypically, hortatory expressions like those using imperative mood are part of the theme line of the discourse, though they may be found in supportive material to reinforce theme line exhortations.[36] This is illustrated in example 2, where the imperative clauses are underlined.

*Example 2: Jas 2:1–4*

| Theme line | Ἀδελφοί μου, μὴ ἐν προσωπολημψίαις <u>ἔχετε</u> τὴν πίστιν τοῦ κυρίου ἡμῶν Ἰησοῦ Χριστοῦ τῆς δόξης; |
|---|---|
| Support | ² ἐὰν γὰρ εἰσέλθῃ εἰς συναγωγὴν ὑμῶν ἀνὴρ χρυσοδακτύλιος ἐν ἐσθῆτι λαμπρᾷ, εἰσέλθῃ δὲ καὶ πτωχὸς ἐν ῥυπαρᾷ ἐσθῆτι, ³ ἐπιβλέψητε δὲ ἐπὶ τὸν φοροῦντα τὴν ἐσθῆτα τὴν λαμπρὰν καὶ εἴπητε· Σὺ <u>κάθου</u> ὧδε καλῶς, καὶ τῷ πτωχῷ εἴπητε· Σὺ <u>στῆθι</u> ἢ <u>κάθου</u> ἐκεῖ ὑπὸ τὸ ὑποπόδιόν μου, ⁴ οὐ διεκρίθητε ἐν ἑαυτοῖς καὶ ἐγένεσθε κριταὶ διαλογισμῶν πονηρῶν; |

---

36  Breeze, "Hortatory Discourse in Ephesians," 314; Levinsohn, *Non-Narrative Discourse*, 16.

| Theme line | My brothers, <u>do not hold</u> your faith in our glorious Lord Jesus Christ with partiality. |
|---|---|
| Support | ² For if someone enters into your assembly in fine clothing with a gold ring on his finger, and a poor person in filthy clothing also enters, ³ and you look favorably on the one wearing the fine clothing and you say, "<u>Be seated</u> here in a good place," and to the poor person you say, "You <u>stand</u> or <u>be seated</u> there by my footstool," ⁴ have you not made distinctions among yourselves and become judges with evil thoughts? |

The passage begins with an exhortation that is supported with a practical example of what holding one's faith with partiality might look like. The illustrative scenario includes two speeches, both of which contain exhortations. Based on the level of embedding of these other imperative verbs (within a speech within the expository illustration), it would be counterintuitive to assert that they possess the same degree of salience within the overall discourse compared to the imperative of 2:1.

Another contextual factor one must take into account is discourse function, such as the use of imperatives as attention-getters (e.g., "Look!" and "Listen!"). When functioning in this way, the imperative directs attention to the proposition that follows and is thus backgrounded (on the difference between "background" and "backgrounded," see §4.2), as in example 3.[37]

*Example 3: Jas 1:17*

| Attention-getter | μὴ πλανᾶσθε, ἀδελφοί μου ἀγαπητοί. |
|---|---|
| Main Clause | ¹⁷Πᾶσα δόσις ἀγαθὴ καὶ πᾶν δώρημα τέλειον ἄνωθέν ἐστιν, καταβαῖνον ἀπὸ τοῦ πατρὸς τῶν φώτων, παρ' ᾧ οὐκ ἔνι παραλλαγὴ ἢ τροπῆς ἀποσκίασμα. |

---

37  See Levinsohn, *Non-Narrative Discourse*, 88; Runge, *Discourse Grammar*, 117–24.

| Attention-getter Main Clause | Do not be deceived, my dear brothers. [17] Every good gift and every perfect gift is from above, coming down from the Father of lights, with whom there is no variation or shadow of change. |
|---|---|

The exhortation μὴ πλανᾶσθε directs attention to the origins of every good gift being from above. The writer might alternatively have more simply asserted that every good gift comes down from above without the call not to be deceived, but this would not have brought about the same effects.

Exhortations may also be conveyed using nonimperatival forms like the hortatory subjunctive (e.g., Rom 13:13; 14:19; 1 Cor 15:32; Gal 5:25; Eph 4:15). Alternatively exhortations may be formed using certain indicative verbs in combination with an infinitive to mitigate its directness, as in example 4.[38]

*Example 4: Rom 12:1*

| <u>Παρακαλῶ</u> οὖν ὑμᾶς, ἀδελφοί, διὰ τῶν οἰκτιρμῶν τοῦ θεοῦ <u>παραστῆσαι</u> τὰ σώματα ὑμῶν θυσίαν ζῶσαν ἁγίαν εὐάρεστον τῷ θεῷ, τὴν λογικὴν λατρείαν ὑμῶν· |
|---|
| Therefore <u>I exhort</u> you, brothers, through the mercies of God, <u>to present</u> your bodies *as* a living sacrifice, holy *and* pleasing to God, *which is* your reasonable service. |

The activity the readers are exhorted to do is actually the dependent infinitive παραστῆσαι. The lexical semantics of the main verb are what indicate the clause is an exhortation rather than the mood. The choice to use this alternative hortatory expression mitigates the directness of Paul's exhortations in 12:1 and 12:3.[39]

---

38  Wårvik, "Foregrounded," 110; Levinsohn, *Non-Narrative Discourse*, 77–78; Bertrand, "Grounding of Information," 150. For a discussion about the relative potency of different forms of exhortation see Levinsohn, *Non-Narrative Discourse*, 79.

39  Breeze, "Hortatory Discourse in Ephesians," 314. Levinsohn notes that such a strategy often adds prominence to the exhortation that follows e.g., 1 Thess 4:1 (We ask and appeal + inf.) or 5:14 (We exhort you + impvs). See

A third observation to be made about the relationship between verbal mood and grounding is the strong association of subjunctive and optative verbs with supportive material when they occur in adverbial subordinate clauses. The hypothetical nature of the information communicated naturally correlates with support rather than theme line material. As Stephen Wallace states in regard to narrative, "What someone asserts as actually happening or having happened is likely to be closer to the center of attention—the foreground—than what did not happen, or might happen, or could happen, or should happen, or perhaps happened, or what someone wants to happen."[40] This observation, if modified to take into account the values of the different nonnarrative genres, corroborates the correlation of irrealis with supportive material. As Grimes notes, the irrealis nonevent "heightens the significance of the real events."[41]

The majority of subjunctive and optative verb forms occur in dependent clauses or are set expressions (e.g., μὴ γένοιτο), so one could more elegantly account for these data by appealing to the typological association of dependent clauses with supportive material (see §4).[42] The contexts where subjunctives and optatives occur in independent clauses are largely limited to hortatory subjunctives, emphatic negation, and prohibitions; in such cases they contribute to the theme line rather than support.[43] In example 5 we see both in action, with the hortatory subjunctive serving as the theme line exhortation, supported by two dependent subjunctive clauses providing motivation for drawing near. The dependent clauses contribute to the grounding of the main clause on which they depend, but not with the same level of salience as the main clause (see §4.2).

---

Levinsohn, *Non-Narrative*, §7.2.1. These initial expressions serve as meta-comments (Runge, *Discourse Grammar*, 101–7.)

40  Wallace, "Figure and Ground," 209.

41  Joseph Evans Grimes, *The Thread of Discourse*, JLSMin 207 (The Hague: Mouton, 1975), 65.

42  See Wallace, "Figure and Ground," 209. Use of subjunctives in secondary (i.e., dependent) clauses is four times more frequent compared to use in primary (i.e., independent) clauses according to the OpenText.org data.

43  Daniel B. Wallace, *Greek Grammar Beyond the Basics: An Exegetical Syntax of the New Testament*, 2nd ed. (Grand Rapids: Zondervan, 1996), 463, 481–83.

*Example 5: Hebrews 4:16*

| |
|---|
| <u>προσερχώμεθα</u> οὖν μετὰ παρρησίας τῷ θρόνῳ τῆς χάριτος, ἵνα λάβωμεν ἔλεος καὶ χάριν εὕρωμεν εἰς εὔκαιρον βοήθειαν. |
| Therefore <u>let us approach</u> with confidence to the throne of grace, in order that we may receive mercy and find grace to help in time of need. |

In summary, there are indeed a few general correlations that can be drawn between verbal mood and grounding in Koine Greek, but they are very limited in their application. The most useful claim concerns the close correlation of imperative verbs with the theme line in nonnarrative, but this is hardly unexpected. Grounding determinations about subjunctives and optatives may be more elegantly subsumed under the principles describing the impact of connectives and dependency relationships on grounding, the topic of sections 3 and 4.

## 2.2 Perfect Indicative

Another general correlation than can be made regarding verbs and grounding in nonnarrative concerns the perfect indicative and supportive information. This form is rarely found in narrative proper: 19 times compared to 355 times in the primary and secondary clauses of Matthew–Acts according to the OpenText.org data. Levinsohn correlates the perfect with support in narrative "since the event concerned often results in a state which holds at the time of the theme-line events."[44] A preliminary study of the perfect in Luke, Romans, and Hebrews found that the overwhelming majority of perfect indicatives served as a ground for a theme line assertion, i.e., were supportive.[45] The use in example 6 is representative of such perfects providing support following a theme line assertion.

---

44  Levinsohn, *Narrative Discourse*, 70.
45  Steven E. Runge, "The Discourse Function of the Greek Perfect" (paper presented at the Annual Meeting of the Society of Biblical Literature, San Diego, CA, November 2014).

*Example 6: Rom 5:2*

| Theme line | Δικαιωθέντες οὖν ἐκ πίστεως εἰρήνην ἔχομεν πρὸς τὸν θεὸν διὰ τοῦ κυρίου ἡμῶν Ἰησοῦ Χριστοῦ, |
|---|---|
| Support | ²δι' οὗ καὶ τὴν προσαγωγὴν <u>ἐσχήκαμεν</u> τῇ πίστει εἰς τὴν χάριν ταύτην ἐν ᾗ <u>ἐστήκαμεν</u>, |
| Theme line | καὶ καυχώμεθα ἐπ' ἐλπίδι τῆς δόξης τοῦ θεοῦ· |
| Theme line | Therefore, *because we* have been declared righteous by faith, we have peace with God through our Lord Jesus Christ, |
| Support | ²through whom also <u>we have *obtained* access</u> by faith into this grace in which <u>we stand</u>, |
| Theme line | and we boast in the hope of the glory of God. |

Having peace with God is the overarching theme here, with the reference to the access we have obtained and in which we stand offering support in a dependent relative clause (see §4) for the preceding assertion. The next theme line statement is offered in the final clause of 5:2.

The remaining instances of perfect indicatives in our test corpus (fewer than 15%) are found on the theme line (embedded or otherwise) and serve a different function: correcting an implied or explicit counterpoint, as in example 7.[46]

*Example 7: Hebrews 8:6*

| Theme line | ⁴εἰ μὲν οὖν ἦν ἐπὶ γῆς, οὐδ' ἂν ἦν ἱερεύς κτλ. ⁶νυνὶ δὲ διαφορωτέρας <u>τέτυχεν</u> λειτουργίας, ὅσῳ καὶ κρείττονός ἐστιν διαθήκης μεσίτης, ἥτις ἐπὶ κρείττοσιν ἐπαγγελίαις νενομοθέτηται. |
|---|---|
| Theme line | ⁴Now if he were on earth, he would not even be a priest ... ⁶But now <u>he has attained</u> a more excellent ministry, by as much as he is also mediator of a better covenant which has been enacted upon better promises. |

---

46  Ibid.

Verse 4 offers a grounding statement as a foil against which a more salient statement is foregrounded, signaled by the use of μέν. The perfect provides a theme-line correction to the implication that, although Jesus is no longer on earth, he is not a priest. On the contrary, the writer asserts that he has obtained a more excellent ministry than any he might have had as an earthly priest. Perfects consistently function to introduce information relevant to an existing situation or proposition, which serves as a basis. Occasionally, the basis itself serves as theme line rather than as support, what I would consider a marked use in contrast to its strong association with supportive material. This latter use of the perfect for theme line corrections appears similar to what Porter asserts to be the "frontgrounding" function of the perfect, but its rarity argues against claiming this as its primary function.[47]

## 2.3 Summary

Mood offers a starting point for grounding judgments in nonnarrative, but little more. Hortatory forms not serving as metacomments or attention-getters are most often on the theme line; furthermore, they can provide secondary exhortations that support a theme line exhortation. They are only rarely found in dependent clauses. Subjunctives not found in dependent clauses are also likely to contribute theme line material. In the case of the indicative, however, its frequent use in both theme line and supportive discourse results in an ambiguity that is best resolved by reference to connectives. These particles offer a much more reliable indicator of grounding status than mood.

For the remainder of the verb forms, two factors offer a better basis for determining grounding status: connectives and dependency relations. Section 3 describes the role certain logical connectives play in signaling transitions from or returns to the theme line. Section 4 describes the contribution of dependency relationships to the marking of relative salience.

---

47　Stanley E. Porter, *Verbal Aspect in the Greek of the New Testament: With Reference to Tense and Mood*, SBG 1 (New York: Lang, 1989), 92–93; Porter, "Prominence," 53–55.

## 3. CONNECTIVES AND GROUNDING

Certain connectives in Greek play a critical role in signaling transitions from theme line to support and back again. Bear in mind that connectives only mark the *beginning* of a unit, constraining how we connect what follows to what precedes. As Levinsohn states, "One cannot tell the **size** of the unit being linked from the connective itself. The Greek connective *gar* 'for' indicates that what follows strengthens the material that immediately precedes it. However, one cannot tell from the presence of *gar* how far the strengthening material will extend."[48] Thus in most cases determinations about the end of a unit will be based in large part upon the markers found at the beginning of the next unit.[49]

### 3.1 Connectives Marking a Shift to Support

In Greek, the sole function of connectives such as γάρ and διότι is to introduce supportive information that strengthens the preceding assertion. Levinsohn states, "Such is the case with Greek sentences introduced by *gar* 'for.' Whatever the genre, their function is to strengthen immediately preceding material (though they can themselves be strengthened and, if the subsequent argument builds upon them, form part of some other theme line)."[50] Thus, γάρ may signal a shift to a brief supportive comment, as in example 8.

*Example 8: Jas 2:13*

| Theme line | ¹²οὕτως λαλεῖτε καὶ οὕτως ποιεῖτε ὡς διὰ νόμου ἐλευθερίας μέλλοντες κρίνεσθαι. |
|---|---|
| Support | ¹³ἡ γὰρ κρίσις ἀνέλεος τῷ μὴ ποιήσαντι ἔλεος· κατακαυχᾶται ἔλεος κρίσεως. |
| Theme line | ¹⁴Τί ὄφελος, ἀδελφοί μου, ἐὰν πίστιν λέγῃ τις ἔχειν ἔργα δὲ μὴ ἔχῃ; μὴ δύναται ἡ πίστις σῶσαι αὐτόν; |

---

48  Levinsohn, *Narrative Discourse*, 85 (emphasis original).
49  For a discussion of boundary features that inform such determinations see Levinsohn, *Discourse Features*, 273-86.
50  Levinsohn, *Narrative Discourse*, 66-67.

| Theme line | [12] Thus speak and thus act as those who are going to be judged by the law of liberty. |
|---|---|
| Support | [13] For judgment *is* merciless to the one who has not practiced mercy. Mercy triumphs over judgment. |
| Theme line | [14] What *is* the benefit, my brothers, if someone says *that he* has faith but does not have works? That faith *is* not able to save him, *is it?* |

Verse 12 contains two exhortations that summarize the action points of the preceding section, supported by a contrasting outlook of judgment for those practicing mercy versus those who do not. Verse 14 introduces a new thesis in the form of a rhetorical question, accompanied by redundant direct address that also marks the transition to a new theme.

Γάρ may also begin an extended section of support as in example 9, which contains six instances of γάρ in succession. Each instance is construed as supportive with respect to what precedes, but forms the theme line for what follows, since it is recursively supported by each new clause introduced by γάρ.[51]

---

51 Steven E. Runge, *High Definition Commentary: Romans* (Bellingham, WA: Lexham Press, 2014), 15–20. I wish to thank Stephen Levinsohn for first bringing this to my attention at the 2003 Annual Meeting of the Society of Biblical Literature in Atlanta.

*Example 9: Rom 1:16–20*

| Theme line | ¹⁴Ἑλλησίν τε καὶ βαρβάροις, σοφοῖς τε καὶ ἀνοήτοις ὀφειλέτης εἰμί κτλ. |
|---|---|
| Support | ¹⁶Οὐ <u>γὰρ</u> ἐπαισχύνομαι τὸ εὐαγγέλιον, |
| Support | δύναμις <u>γὰρ</u> θεοῦ ἐστιν εἰς σωτηρίαν παντὶ τῷ πιστεύοντι, Ἰουδαίῳ τε πρῶτον καὶ Ἕλληνι· |
| Support | ¹⁷δικαιοσύνη <u>γὰρ</u> θεοῦ ἐν αὐτῷ ἀποκαλύπτεται ἐκ πίστεως εἰς πίστιν κτλ. |
| Support | ¹⁸Ἀποκαλύπτεται γὰρ ὀργὴ θεοῦ ἀπ' οὐρανοῦ ἐπὶ πᾶσαν ἀσέβειαν καὶ ἀδικίαν ἀνθρώπων τῶν τὴν ἀλήθειαν ἐν ἀδικίᾳ κατεχόντων κτλ. |
| Support | ²⁰τὰ <u>γὰρ</u> ἀόρατα αὐτοῦ ἀπὸ κτίσεως κόσμου τοῖς ποιήμασιν νοούμενα καθορᾶται κτλ. |
| Theme line | ¹⁴ I am under obligation both to Greeks and to barbarians, both to the wise and to the foolish... |
| Support | ¹⁶ <u>For</u> I am not ashamed of the gospel, |
| Support | <u>for</u> it is the power of God for salvation to everyone who believes, to the Jew first and also to the Greek. |
| Support | ¹⁷ <u>For</u> the righteousness of God is revealed in it from faith to faith... |
| Support | ¹⁸ <u>For</u> the wrath of God is revealed from heaven against all impiety and unrighteousness of people, who suppress the truth in unrighteousness... |
| Support | ²⁰ <u>For</u> from the creation of the world, his invisible *attributes*, both his eternal power and deity, are discerned clearly... |
| Support | |

The embedded theme line concerning the revelation of God's wrath extends through the end of Rom 4. The initial theme line of desiring to visit Rome is finally resumed in 15:22. This represents an extreme case of using γάρ for rhetorical structuring, but γάρ is commonly found introducing large chunks of support.

In cases where the supportive material extends for more than a few clauses, transitions to either a new or previous theme line are prototypically signaled by an inferential connective such as οὖν, as in example 10.[52]

*Example 10: Phil 2:25–28*

| Theme line | ²⁵Ἀναγκαῖον δὲ ἡγησάμην Ἐπαφρόδιτον τὸν ἀδελφὸν καὶ συνεργὸν καὶ συστρατιώτην μου, ὑμῶν δὲ ἀπόστολον καὶ λειτουργὸν τῆς χρείας μου, πέμψαι πρὸς ὑμᾶς, ²⁶ἐπειδὴ ἐπιποθῶν ἦν πάντας ὑμᾶς, καὶ ἀδημονῶν διότι ἠκούσατε ὅτι ἠσθένησεν. |
|---|---|
| Support | ²⁷καὶ <u>γὰρ</u> ἠσθένησεν παραπλήσιον θανάτῳ· ἀλλὰ ὁ θεὸς ἠλέησεν αὐτόν, οὐκ αὐτὸν δὲ μόνον ἀλλὰ καὶ ἐμέ, ἵνα μὴ λύπην ἐπὶ λύπην σχῶ. |
| Theme line | ²⁸σπουδαιοτέρως <u>οὖν</u> ἔπεμψα αὐτὸν ἵνα ἰδόντες αὐτὸν πάλιν χαρῆτε κἀγὼ ἀλυπότερος ὦ. |
| Theme line | But I considered *it* necessary to send to you Epaphroditus, my brother and fellow worker and fellow soldier, but your messenger and servant of my need, ²⁶ because he was longing for all of you and was distressed because you had heard that he was sick. |
| Support | ²⁷ <u>For</u> indeed he was sick, coming near to death, but God had mercy on him and not *on* him only, but also *on* me, so that I would not have grief upon grief. |
| Theme line | ²⁸ <u>Therefore</u> I am sending him with special urgency, in order that *when* you see him again you may rejoice, and I may be less anxious. |

The οὖν in 2:28 signals the original theme of desiring to send Epaphroditus as indicated by the lexical repetition of the verb πέμπω. The intervening clauses of 2:27 offer support for Paul's decision, introduced by γάρ.

To summarize, the use of γάρ marks what follows as supporting what precedes. It strengthens the preceding theme rather than advancing or building upon it. Although γάρ is properly a coordinating particle, it nevertheless constrains a logical dependency upon what precedes. Support may also be signaled by use of logical subordinating particles. Levinsohn observes regarding ὅτι, "when used as a logical connective, it introduces a reason or evidence for the last assertion (THESIS)."[53] On this view, use of the logical, dependent particles ἐπειδή and διότι in Phil 2:26 also introduce support, but with a more specific cognitive constraint compared to γάρ. These logical connectives share a common trait: all signal that what follows is supportive and not elaborating upon the theme of the main clause.

## 3.2 Connectives Marking Return to Theme Line

Inferential connectives contribute to grounding determinations by signaling a return to a theme line following supportive material.[54] The use of οὖν most often signals the resumption of the theme line, whether this be a brand new theme or one that is already established. In contexts where transitions to supportive material result in embedded theme lines with respect to the highest-level theme, continuity of factors (time, place, participants/topic, and kind of action) help readers determine which theme line or part of it is being resumed, though the data are not always unambiguous. This is illustrated in example 11 where Rom 6:12 resumes the suspended theme line from 6:4 following supportive material of 6:5–10 and the intervening summary of 6:11 introduced by οὕτως.

---

53  Levinsohn, *Non-Narrative Discourse*, 38.
54  See Levinsohn, "'Therefore' or 'Wherefore': What's the Difference?"

*Example 11: Rom 6:4–14*

| Theme line | ⁴ συνετάφημεν <u>οὖν</u> αὐτῷ διὰ τοῦ βαπτίσματος εἰς τὸν θάνατον, ἵνα ὥσπερ ἠγέρθη Χριστὸς ἐκ νεκρῶν διὰ τῆς δόξης τοῦ πατρός, οὕτως καὶ ἡμεῖς ἐν καινότητι ζωῆς περιπατήσωμεν. |
|---|---|
| Support | ⁵ Εἰ <u>γὰρ</u> σύμφυτοι γεγόναμεν τῷ ὁμοιώματι τοῦ θανάτου αὐτοῦ, ἀλλὰ καὶ τῆς ἀναστάσεως ἐσόμεθα· ⁶ τοῦτο γινώσκοντες ὅτι ὁ παλαιὸς ἡμῶν ἄνθρωπος συνεσταυρώθη, ἵνα καταργηθῇ τὸ σῶμα τῆς ἁμαρτίας, τοῦ μηκέτι δουλεύειν ἡμᾶς τῇ ἁμαρτίᾳ, |
| Support | ⁷ ὁ <u>γὰρ</u> ἀποθανὼν δεδικαίωται ἀπὸ τῆς ἁμαρτίας. ⁸ εἰ δὲ ἀπεθάνομεν σὺν Χριστῷ, πιστεύομεν ὅτι καὶ συζήσομεν αὐτῷ· ⁹ εἰδότες ὅτι Χριστὸς ἐγερθεὶς ἐκ νεκρῶν οὐκέτι ἀποθνῄσκει, θάνατος αὐτοῦ οὐκέτι κυριεύει· |
| Support | ¹⁰ ὃ <u>γὰρ</u> ἀπέθανεν, τῇ ἁμαρτίᾳ ἀπέθανεν ἐφάπαξ· ὃ δὲ ζῇ, ζῇ τῷ θεῷ. |
| Support | ¹¹ <u>οὕτως</u> καὶ ὑμεῖς λογίζεσθε ἑαυτοὺς εἶναι νεκροὺς μὲν τῇ ἁμαρτίᾳ ζῶντας δὲ τῷ θεῷ ἐν Χριστῷ Ἰησοῦ. |
| Theme line | ¹² Μὴ <u>οὖν</u> βασιλευέτω ἡ ἁμαρτία ἐν τῷ θνητῷ ὑμῶν σώματι εἰς τὸ ὑπακούειν ταῖς ἐπιθυμίαις αὐτοῦ, |

| Theme line | [4] <u>Therefore</u> we have been buried with him through baptism into death, in order that just as Christ was raised from the dead through the glory of the Father, so also we may live a new way of life. |
|---|---|
| Support | [5] <u>For</u> if we have become identified with *him* in the likeness of his death, certainly also we will be *identified with him in the likeness* of *his* resurrection, [6] knowing this, that our old man was crucified together with *him*, in order that the body of sin may be done away with, *that* we may no longer be enslaved to sin. |
| Support | [7] <u>For</u> the one who has died has been freed from sin. [8] Now if we died with Christ, we believe that we will also live with him, [9] knowing that Christ, *because he* has been raised from the dead, is going to die no more, death no longer being master over him. |
| Support | [10] <u>For</u> that *death* he died, he died to sin once and never again, but that *life* he lives, he lives to God. |
| Support | [11] <u>So</u> also you, consider yourselves to be dead to sin, but alive to God in Christ Jesus. |
| Theme line | [12] <u>Therefore</u> do not let sin reign in your mortal body, so that *you* obey its desires, |

The analogy of burial and resurrection symbolized by baptism in 6:4 serves as the ground for the exhortation that follows in 6:11. The use of οὕτως καί correlates how we consider ourselves with our identification in baptism from 6:4. The οὖν in 6:12 signals progression to the next theme line exhortation in the discourse, building upon the preceding one.[55]

Διὰ τοῦτο may also signal the resumption of a specific theme in the absence of other connectives, illustrated in example 12.[56] Here too

---

55  For an introduction to the notion of thematic development see Levinsohn, *Discourse Features*, 71–72; Runge, *Discourse Grammar*, 28–31.

56  See Levinsohn, "'Therefore' or 'Wherefore': What's the Difference?," 336–38. Runge, *Discourse Grammar*, 48–51.

the support introduced by γάρ serves as an embedded theme line, which is in turn supported by 4:14–15.

*Example 12: Rom 4:13–16*

| Support | ¹³ Οὐ γὰρ διὰ νόμου ἡ ἐπαγγελία τῷ Ἀβραὰμ ἢ τῷ σπέρματι αὐτοῦ, τὸ κληρονόμον αὐτὸν εἶναι κόσμου, ἀλλὰ διὰ δικαιοσύνης πίστεως· |
|---|---|
| Support | ¹⁴ εἰ γὰρ οἱ ἐκ νόμου κληρονόμοι, κεκένωται ἡ πίστις καὶ κατήργηται ἡ ἐπαγγελία· |
| Support | ¹⁵ ὁ γὰρ νόμος ὀργὴν κατεργάζεται, οὗ δὲ οὐκ ἔστιν νόμος, οὐδὲ παράβασις. |
| Theme line | ¹⁶ Διὰ τοῦτο ἐκ πίστεως, ἵνα κατὰ χάριν, εἰς τὸ εἶναι βεβαίαν τὴν ἐπαγγελίαν παντὶ τῷ σπέρματι, οὐ τῷ ἐκ τοῦ νόμου μόνον ἀλλὰ καὶ τῷ ἐκ πίστεως Ἀβραάμ (ὅς ἐστιν πατὴρ πάντων ἡμῶν, |
| Support | ¹³ For the promise to Abraham or to his descendants, *that* he would be heir of the world, *was* not through the law, but through the righteousness by faith. |
| Support | ¹⁴ For if those of the law *are* heirs, faith is rendered void and the promise is nullified. |
| Support | ¹⁵ For the law produces wrath, but where *there* is no law, neither *is there* transgression. |
| Theme line | ¹⁶ Because of this, *it is* by faith, in order that *it may be* according to grace, so that the promise may be secure to all the descendants, not only to those of the law, but also to those of the faith of Abraham, who is the father of us all |

The διὰ τοῦτο in 4:16 signals the resumption of the embedded theme of 4:13 by anaphorically referencing a specific proposition, i.e., that the promise came to Abraham and his heirs on the basis of faith.

Likewise, connectives like διό and ὥστε may also signal a return to theme line material within the same development unit of a discourse.⁵⁷ The use of ὥστε with a finite verbal clause constrains what follows to be understood as a result of what precedes as in example 13.

*Example 13: Phil 4:1*

| Theme line | ¹⁷<u>Συμμιμηταί μου γίνεσθε, ἀδελφοί, καὶ σκοπεῖτε τοὺς</u> <u>οὕτω περιπατοῦντας καθὼς ἔχετε τύπον ἡμᾶς·</u> |
|---|---|
| Support | ¹⁸<u>πολλοὶ</u> γὰρ <u>περιπατοῦσιν οὓς πολλάκις ἔλεγον ὑμῖν,</u> <u>νῦν δὲ καὶ κλαίων λέγω, τοὺς ἐχθροὺς τοῦ σταυροῦ</u> <u>τοῦ Χριστοῦ,</u> ¹⁹ <u>ὧν τὸ τέλος ἀπώλεια, ὧν ὁ θεὸς ἡ</u> <u>κοιλία καὶ ἡ δόξα ἐν τῇ αἰσχύνῃ αὐτῶν, οἱ τὰ ἐπίγεια</u> <u>φρονοῦντες.</u> ²⁰ <u>ἡμῶν</u> γὰρ <u>τὸ πολίτευμα ἐν οὐρανοῖς</u> <u>ὑπάρχει, ἐξ οὗ καὶ σωτῆρα ἀπεκδεχόμεθα κύριον</u> <u>Ἰησοῦν Χριστόν,</u> ²¹ <u>ὃς μετασχηματίσει τὸ σῶμα τῆς</u> <u>ταπεινώσεως ἡμῶν σύμμορφον τῷ σώματι τῆς δόξης</u> <u>αὐτοῦ κατὰ τὴν ἐνέργειαν τοῦ δύνασθαι αὐτὸν καὶ</u> <u>ὑποτάξαι αὐτῷ τὰ πάντα.</u> |
| Theme line | ⁴·¹<u>ὥστε</u>, <u>ἀδελφοί μου ἀγαπητοὶ καὶ ἐπιπόθητοι, χαρὰ καὶ</u> <u>στέφανός μου, οὕτως στήκετε ἐν κυρίῳ, ἀγαπητοί.</u> |

---

57  Levinsohn states that new developments typically involve "a change in spatiotemporal setting or circumstances, a change in the underlying subject, or a change to or from a background comment" (*Discourse Features*, 72). See also Levinsohn, "'Therefore' or 'Wherefore': What's the Difference?," 329–30; 334–36.

| | |
|---|---|
| Theme line | [17] Become fellow imitators of me, brothers, and observe those who walk in this way, just as you have us *as* an example. |
| Support | [18] For many live, of whom I spoke about to you many times, but now speak about even weeping, *as* the enemies of the cross of Christ, [19] whose end *is* destruction, whose God *is* the stomach, and *whose* glory *is* in their shame, the ones who think on earthly things. [20] For our commonwealth exists in heaven, from which also we eagerly await a savior, the Lord Jesus Christ, [21] who will transform our humble body *to be* conformed to his glorious body, in accordance with the power that enables him even to subject all *things* to himself. |
| Theme line | [4:1] So then, my beloved and greatly desired brothers, my joy and crown, thus stand firm in the Lord, dear friends. |

Philippians 3:17 offers two exhortations: to become fellow imitators of Paul and to observe those who live similarly so as to follow their example. Verses 18–21 support these exhortations by offering contrasting pictures of how enemies of Christ live compared to those whose commonwealth is in heaven. Introducing the exhortation of 4:1 using ὥστε constrains it to be viewed as a result of the preceding support of 3:18–21, yet still within the larger development unit concerning imitation of those who follow Christ begun in 3:17.

Inferential connectives play an important role within discourse by explicitly signaling a transition from supportive material to a theme line. This might entail the resumption of a previous theme line or the beginning of a new one that draws upon a previous theme. As a class, inferential particles uniquely fulfill this discourse task of shifting back from support. In cases where there is more than one potential theme line, cohesive factors such as continuity of time, place, participants, theme, or discourse topic help to disambiguate which theme line is intended.

# 3.3 Transitions not Marked by Connectives: Asyndeton

Although connectives are a primary means of signaling transitions from one grounding status to another in Koine Greek, there are many contexts where they are not found, referred to as asyndeton.[58] These contexts represent opposite ends of the spectrum: "Asyndeton is found in two very different contexts in nonnarrative text:

- when there is a close connection between the information concerned (i.e., the information belongs together in the same unit)
- when there is no direct connection between the information concerned (i.e., the information belongs to different units)."[59]

The former situation is akin to our use of commas in English, where it serves to simply juxtapose two elements that need no further specification about how they should be related. Levinsohn notes that asyndeton (represented by Ø) is the norm the following relations illustrated in example 14.[60]

*Example 14:*

Orienter – Content: Matt 5:18

| Orienter<br>Content | ἀμὴν γὰρ λέγω ὑμῖν,<br>Ø ἕως ἂν παρέλθῃ ὁ οὐρανὸς καὶ ἡ γῆ, ἰῶτα ἓν ἢ μία κεραία οὐ μὴ παρέλθῃ ἀπὸ τοῦ νόμου, ἕως ἂν πάντα γένηται. |
|---|---|
| Orienter<br>Content | For truly I say to you,<br>until heaven and earth pass away, not one tiny letter or one stroke of a letter will pass away from the law until all takes place. |

---

58  See Levinsohn, *Discourse Features*, 119–25.
59  Ibid., 119.
60  Ibid., 118.

Generic – Specific or vice versa: 1 Cor 7:20–21

| Generic<br>Specific | ἕκαστος ἐν τῇ κλήσει ᾗ ἐκλήθη ἐν ταύτῃ μενέτω.<br>²¹ Δοῦλος ἐκλήθης; μή σοι μελέτω· ἀλλ’ εἰ καὶ δύνασαι ἐλεύθερος γενέσθαι, μᾶλλον χρῆσαι. |
|---|---|
| Generic<br>Specific | Each one in the calling in which he was called—in this he should remain.<br>²¹ Were you called *while* a slave? Do not let it be a concern to you. But if indeed you are able to become free, rather make use of *it*. |

Nucleus – Comment and Nucleus – Parenthesis: Jas 5:1–2

| Nucleus<br><br>Comment | Ἄγε νῦν οἱ πλούσιοι, κλαύσατε ὀλολύζοντες ἐπὶ ταῖς ταλαιπωρίαις ὑμῶν ταῖς ἐπερχομέναις.<br>² ὁ πλοῦτος ὑμῶν σέσηπεν, καὶ τὰ ἱμάτια ὑμῶν σητόβρωτα γέγονεν, |
|---|---|
| Nucleus<br><br>Comment | Come now, you rich people, weep *and* cry aloud over the miseries that are coming upon you!<br>² Your wealth has rotted, and your clothing has become moth-eaten. |

In each instance there is a close connection between the two clauses, but the exact nature is left unspecified. The reader must determine the nature of the relationship in the absence of a connective.

At the other end of the spectrum asyndeton is often used in contexts where there is no close connection between the clauses. Instead we find clustering of what Levinsohn calls boundary features that alert the reader to the transition.[61] Features like metacomments and attention-getters are sufficient to signal the shift to theme line material, as illustrated in example 15.[62]

---

61  For a discussion of other features that may be used to mark a boundary, see ibid., 273–86.
62  For a description of metacomments and direct address, see Runge, *Discourse Grammar*, 117–24.

*Example 15: Jas 1:17*

| | |
|---|---|
| | ¹³μηδεὶς πειραζόμενος λεγέτω ὅτι Ἀπὸ θεοῦ πειράζομαι· ὁ γὰρ θεὸς ἀπείραστός ἐστιν κακῶν, πειράζει δὲ αὐτὸς οὐδένα. ¹⁴ἕκαστος δὲ πειράζεται ὑπὸ τῆς ἰδίας ἐπιθυμίας ἐξελκόμενος καὶ δελεαζόμενος· ¹⁵εἶτα ἡ ἐπιθυμία συλλαβοῦσα τίκτει ἁμαρτίαν, ἡ δὲ ἁμαρτία ἀποτελεσθεῖσα ἀποκύει θάνατον. ¹⁶μὴ πλανᾶσθε, ἀδελφοί μου ἀγαπητοί. μὴ πλανᾶσθε, ἀδελφοί μου ἀγαπητοί. |
| Boundary Feat. | ¹⁷Πᾶσα δόσις ἀγαθὴ καὶ πᾶν δώρημα τέλειον ἄνωθέν ἐστιν, καταβαῖνον ἀπὸ τοῦ πατρὸς τῶν φώτων, παρ' |
| Theme line | ᾧ οὐκ ἔνι παραλλαγὴ ἢ τροπῆς ἀποσκίασμα. |
| | ¹³No one who is being tempted should say, "I am being tempted by God," for God cannot be tempted by evil, and he himself tempts no one. ¹⁴But each one is tempted *when he* is dragged away and enticed by his own desires. ¹⁵Then desire, *after it* has conceived, gives birth to sin, and sin, *when it* is brought to completion, gives birth to death. Do not be deceived, my dear brothers. |
| Boundary Feat. | ¹⁷Every good gift and every perfect gift is from above, coming down from the Father of lights, with whom there is no variation or shadow of |
| Theme line | change. |

Verse 13a describes what God is not characterized by, followed by support in 1:13b–15. Verse 16 begins a theme line related to 1:13, describing what God *is* characterized by, relying upon the natural cohesion of 1:16 with 1:13a for readers to make the connection, plus the metacomment (μὴ πλανᾶσθε) and redundant direct address (ἀδελφοί μου ἀγαπητοί).

These examples make clear that aspect alone cannot determine grounding status in nonnarrative any more than in narrative. There are indeed correlations between certain features of discourse and grounding roles, but there is no one-size-fits-all solution. As Wårvik states, grounding is contextually determined and based upon a clustering of factors.[63]

Another important consideration for identifying shifts in grounding in contexts where there are no connectives present is the shift to a different genre, e.g., a shift from expository to hortatory discourse. In such cases, the change in genre alone is considered sufficient for signaling the change in grounding. Consider the case in example 16, where the shift to imperative mood along with the anaphoric reference of οὕτως in Jas 2:12 indicate that these exhortations are the desired alternative compared to the prohibition of 2:1. The change from the expository material introduced by γάρ in 2:11 to exhortation represents a return to the theme line.[64]

*Example 16: Jas 2:12*

| Support | ¹¹ὁ γὰρ εἰπών· Μὴ μοιχεύσῃς εἶπεν καί· Μὴ φονεύσῃς· εἰ δὲ οὐ μοιχεύεις φονεύεις δέ, γέγονας παραβάτης νόμου. |
|---|---|
| Theme line | ¹²οὕτως λαλεῖτε καὶ οὕτως ποιεῖτε ὡς διὰ νόμου ἐλευθερίας μέλλοντες κρίνεσθαι. |
| Support | ¹¹For the one who said "Do not commit adultery" also said "Do not murder." Now if you do not commit adultery but you do murder, you have become a transgressor of the law. |
| Theme line | ¹²Thus speak and thus act as those who are going to be judged by the law of liberty. |

One must be cautious in making such judgments, since the ordering of theme line and supportive material will vary depending upon whether an inductive or deductive strategy is employed.[65] In this case, the supportive exposition of 2:2-11 supports the

---

63 Wårvik, "Foregrounded," 100.
64 Porter notes that οὕτως may be used inferentially (*Idioms of the Greek New Testament*, 2nd ed., BLG 2 (Sheffield: JSOT Press, 1995), 215). See also Levinsohn, "'Therefore' or 'Wherefore': What's the Difference?," 338 n. 74.
65 See Levinsohn, *Non-Narrative Discourse*, 17-19; for an overview of reasoning styles and their implications for the structuring of discourses, see Stephen H. Levinsohn, "Reasoning Styles and Types of Hortatory Discourse," *JT* 2 (2006): 1-10.

prohibition in 2:1, but also grounds the concluding exhortation of 2:12. The statement introduced by γάρ in 2:13 strengthens what precedes, closing out the unit of 2:1–13.

## 3.4 Summary

Connectives offer the most explicit and unambiguous evidence for determining the grounding relationship of the clause that it introduces to the preceding context. In fact, the connectives described in this section offer a much more reliable means of determining the grounding status of a clause compared to verbal aspect. Classes of connectives play predictable roles in marking grounding. Strengthening connectives like γάρ signal a shift to supportive material, important thematic information that does not advance the discourse. Inferential connectives, on the other hand, as a class signal a shift back to the theme line, whether it be resumption of a previous theme or the beginning of a new one. In cases where no connective is present (asyndeton), other factors such as changes in mood or other boundary features must be taken into consideration.

## 4. GRAMMATICAL DEPENDENCY, RELATIVE SALIENCE, AND GROUNDING[66]

There is another area affecting the grounding status of verb forms that requires a much more nuanced explanation: grammatical subordination. A writer's decision to use a nonfinite verb form (i.e., adverbial participles and infinitives) or a dependent finite verbal clause affects the grounding status of the information conveyed. This section discusses ways in which dependency relationships affect grounding status, structuring, and relative salience.

Although grounding roles primarily concern "that which advances the discourse," the added caveat that it is "based on the writer's goals or objectives" has significant implications for analysis. Recall Wårvik's claim that grounding roles are representational; while certain real-world events and actions naturally correlate with

---

66 This discussion of nonfinite forms only concerns noncomplementary clauses (i.e., adjuncts), those that are not required arguments of the main clause verb.

a given grounding role in a given genre (e.g., events or exhortations to foreground in narrative or hortatory discourse, respectively), it "emerges only when a text producer presents them in a certain way in a certain context."[67] Thus our analysis of the text must respect how the writer has chosen to represent the action or event in a given discourse. These decisions often lack objective, real-world criteria motivating how the events are portrayed. Thus, the writer's choices should be viewed as instructions for the reader regarding how the writer intends the events or discourse to be structured and prioritized in the reader's mental representation of it.

Selection of a dependent verb form or clause places the information conveyed on a fundamentally different track compared to using an independent, finite verbal clause. For example, Wårvik notes advice in ancient writing guides, where students were instructed "to put important things in main clauses and less important things in subordinate clauses, which tallies with the relationship between clause status and grounding as well."[68] This suggests that, all things being equal, dependent clauses should be expected to accomplish different discourse functions compared to independent clauses.

## 4.1 Information Packaging

The writer's choice of a dependent verbal clause over an independent one significantly impacts judgments about the prioritization and structuring of the action within the overall discourse. The principles outlined in figure 2 will serve as our point of departure for what follows:

Finite Independent + Finite Independent = Two Clauses

Finite Independent + Dependent = One Complex Clause

Figure 2

In other words, the writer's selection of a dependent clause where an independent option was available means that readers will

---

67  Wårvik, "Foregrounded," 100.
68  Ibid., 104.

process it as one larger complex rather than as separate, potentially coequal clauses. Omitting a subject in English similarly creates a chaining effect, illustrated in example 17:

*Example 17:*

| I went to work early. I had a lot to do. | I went to work early because I had a lot to do. |
|---|---|

There is a fundamental change in how the same information is packaged. Dependency relationships are an important pragmatic means of structuring and prioritizing information within a discourse. Writers like Paul often exploit grammatical dependency in order to create complex rhetorical structures within discourse, as illustrated in example 18. The indenting of the text depicts the grammatical dependencies of this complex sentence.

*Example 18: Eph 2:1-5*

| Topic Frame | Καὶ ὑμᾶς |
|---|---|
| Ptc Clause | ὄντας νεκροὺς τοῖς παραπτώμασιν καὶ ταῖς ἁμαρτίαις ὑμῶν, |
| Rel Clause | ² ἐν αἷς ποτε περιεπατήσατε κατὰ τὸν αἰῶνα τοῦ κόσμου τούτου, κατὰ τὸν ἄρχοντα τῆς ἐξουσίας τοῦ ἀέρος, τοῦ πνεύματος τοῦ νῦν ἐνεργοῦντος ἐν τοῖς υἱοῖς τῆς ἀπειθείας· |
| Rel Clause | ³ ἐν οἷς καὶ ἡμεῖς πάντες ἀνεστράφημέν ποτε ἐν ταῖς ἐπιθυμίαις τῆς σαρκὸς ἡμῶν, |
| Ptc Clause | ποιοῦντες τὰ θελήματα τῆς σαρκὸς καὶ τῶν διανοιῶν, |
| Rel Clause | καὶ ἤμεθα τέκνα φύσει ὀργῆς ὡς καὶ οἱ λοιποί· |
| Topic Frame | ⁴ ὁ δὲ θεὸς |
| Ptc Clause | πλούσιος ὢν ἐν ἐλέει, διὰ τὴν πολλὴν ἀγάπην αὐτοῦ ἣν ἠγάπησεν ἡμᾶς, |
| Ptc Clause | ⁵ καὶ ὄντας ἡμᾶς νεκροὺς τοῖς παραπτώμασιν |
| Main clause | συνεζωοποίησεν τῷ Χριστῷ |

| Topic Frame | And you, |
|---|---|
| Ptc Clause | being dead in your trespasses and sins, |
| Rel Clause | ² in which you formerly walked according to the course of this world, according to the ruler of the authority of the air, the spirit now working in the sons of disobedience, |
| Rel Clause | ³ among whom also we all formerly lived in the desires of our flesh, |
| Ptc Clause | doing the will of the flesh and of the mind, |
| Rel Clause | and we were children of wrath by nature, as also the rest of *them* were. |
| Topic Frame | ⁴ But God, |
| Ptc Clause | being rich in mercy, because of his great love *with* which he loved us, |
| Ptc Clause | ⁵ and we being dead in trespasses, |
| Main clause | he made *us* alive together with Christ. (Adapted from LEB) |

Exploitation of this complex hierarchy transforms what most translations render as several sentences into a single complex with one key assertion: God made us alive together with Christ. All of the rest of the information in these verses provides important grounding for Paul's main point. Rendering this sentence into multiple clauses in English, while necessary for readability, obscures the writer's choice to package it all as one big idea.

To summarize, the use of dependent forms where independent forms were a viable option should be construed as reflecting the writer's choice about how to package and structure the information. Although largely the same propositional content is conveyed either way, dependency relations bring about certain pragmatic effects that independent clauses would not have achieved. The following sections survey some of these effects.

## 4.2 Relative Salience

Levinsohn claims that "[c]ross-linguistically, the information conveyed in pre-nuclear subordinate clauses is backgrounded in relation to that conveyed in the main clause."[69] Notice that he uses the comparative expression "background**ed**" rather than a declarative "background." Thus, he does not make a claim about grounding so much as about the relative importance of the information vis-à-vis the main clause. Bertrand similarly observes, "Subordination allows an even finer-grained distinction to be made for clauses that do not lie within the narrative assertion but are somewhat backgrounded, since their grammatical subordination mimics their lesser salience within the foreground."[70]

Such would appear to be the case in Koine Greek with the distinction between independent verbal clauses versus dependent ones. The writer's selection of a grammatically dependent form is understood to convey a constraint that an independent verbal clause would not have achieved. To rephrase things into Bertrand's terminology, dependent elements are "somewhat backgrounded" with respect to the main clause on which they depend; "their grammatical subordination mimics their lesser salience within the foreground."[71] This is not to say that the information in the dependent clause is *un*important, but to observe the downgrading of relative importance compared to using a grammatically independent form.

This principle is most clearly manifested in Koine in Levinsohn's claim that "participial clauses that precede their nuclear clause almost always present information that is backgrounded. This means that the information they convey is of secondary importance in relation to that of the nuclear clause. This claim does not hold for participial clauses that follow their nuclear clauses."[72] This backgrounding effect of preverbal anarthrous participles is illustrated in example 19.

---

69  Levinsohn, *Narrative Discourse*, 73.
70  Bertrand, "Grounding of Information," 150.
71  Ibid.
72  Levinsohn, *Discourse Features*, 186.

*Example 19: Rom 8:3*

| Topic Frames | τὸ γὰρ ἀδύνατον τοῦ νόμου, ἐν ᾧ ἠσθένει διὰ τῆς σαρκός, ὁ θεὸς |
|---|---|
| Ptc Clause | τὸν ἑαυτοῦ υἱὸν πέμψας ἐν ὁμοιώματι σαρκὸς ἁμαρτίας καὶ περὶ ἁμαρτίας |
| Main clause | κατέκρινε τὴν ἁμαρτίαν ἐν τῇ σαρκί, |
| Topic Frames | For what *was* impossible for the law, in that it was weak through the flesh, God |
| Ptc Clause | sending his own Son in the likeness of sinful flesh and concerning sin, |
| Main clause | he condemned sin in the flesh. (Adapted from LEB) |

Based on the use of γάρ to introduce this complex clause, the entire clause is construed as conveying support. Within the complex clause, the use of the participle πέμψας constrains the clause to be analyzed as dependent upon the main verb κατέκρινε and thus backgrounded with respect to the main verb. The selection of independent finite verbal clauses for both actions would have resulted in two apparently coequal actions on the basis of syntax, i.e., "God sent his own Son in the likeness of sinful flesh and concerning sin, and condemned sin in the flesh." Use of the participle results in a single hierarchical complex with one element explicitly marked as more salient than the other on the basis of the dependency relationship.

This same principle applies to a lesser degree to dependent finite verbal clauses in Koine, as we have already partially shown in section 2.1 regarding use of nonindicative moods. Greek grammarians have noted this in their classification of such dependent clauses as adverbial based on how it "functions like an adverb in that it modifies a verb."[73] Under this heading Wallace includes infinitival clauses, adverbial participial clauses, "conjunctive clauses" (i.e., those introduced by a dependent conjunction), and relative clauses. The dependency relationship redirects their contribution to the discourse through a specific main clause. This is illustrated in example 20, where καθάπερ constrains the following three clauses to be construed as dependent.

---

73  Wallace, *Greek Grammar*, 662.

*Example 20: 1 Cor 12:12*

| Frame | Καθάπερ γὰρ τὸ σῶμα ἕν ἐστιν |
|---|---|
| Frame | καὶ μέλη πολλὰ ἔχει, |
| Frame | πάντα δὲ τὰ μέλη τοῦ σώματος πολλὰ ὄντα ἕν ἐστιν σῶμα, |
| Main Clause | οὕτως καὶ ὁ Χριστός· |
| Frame | For just as the body is one |
| Frame | and has many members, |
| Frame | but all the members of the body, *although they* are many, are one body, |
| Main Clause | thus also Christ. |

The same propositional content would have been successfully conveyed without καθάπερ (e.g., the body is one and has many members ... so also is Christ), but its role as a basis for a following comparison would not have been forecast, but retroactively inferred. The dependent particle καθάπερ not only adds this constraint, but also collocates the three bases with the main assertion into one complex clause.

To rephrase the claims of this section in terms of figure 2 above, the choice of a dependent clause over an independent finite verbal clause represents the choice to take what might have been understood as equally salient main clauses, on the basis of syntax, and downgrades salience of the dependent elements. This is accomplished by combining what might have been two or more independent clauses into one, complex clause with the dependent action backgrounded with respect to the main clause on which it depends. The claim of background*ing* only concerns its relative prominence or salience with respect to the main verb; it says nothing about its grounding status (i.e., background/foreground or support/theme line, see §4.4). The choice of a dependent form does not affect its grounding status other than connecting it to a finite verbal clause from which its status is derived.

## 4.3 Position

Typological research has demonstrated that there is a meaningful difference between dependent adverbial clauses that precede the

main verb (i.e., preposed) and those that follow or are postposed
with respect to the verb. There are distinct claims for finite adverbial clauses compared to adverbial participial clauses, so each will
be handled in turn, beginning with finite verbal clauses. Diessel has
found that typologically, despite the fact that there are distributional preferences for the location of certain kinds of finite, adverbial
clauses—conditional and temporal clauses tend to precede the verb,
whereas causal and result/purpose clauses tend to follow the verb—
there nevertheless is a meaningful difference in discourse function
based on positioning with respect to the verb.[74] Although the postverbal positioning is almost uniformly attributed to ease of processing based on the new information these adverbial clauses convey,
the same does not hold true for the preverbal ones: "As argued by
Chafe (1984), Thompson (1987), Givón (1990), Ford (1993) and many
others, initial adverbial clauses are commonly used to organize the
information flow in the ongoing discourse; they function to provide
a thematic ground or orientation for subsequent clauses."[75] Thus,
the finite preverbal clauses perform a framing function for the
clause that follows, contextualizing or providing a specific point of
departure for relating what follows to what precedes.[76]

We noted in example 20 above how the dependent connective
καθάπερ constrained the clauses that follow to be construed as dependent upon the main clause, affecting both the packaging of
the information and the relative salience of the component parts.
Yet another effect of this preverbal positioning is constraining these
adverbial clauses to provide a comparative frame of reference for
the main clause. Generally speaking, the postposed adverbial clauses contribute newly asserted information with the rest of the predicate. However, the preposed adverbials generally offer cognitively
accessible information, and thus are not construed as part of the

---

74  Holger Diessel, "Competing Motivations for the Ordering of Main and Adverbial Clauses," *Linguistics* 43 (2005): 455.

75  Ibid. Another function of the preverbal positioning may be to place the information in marked focus; see Knud Lambrecht, *Information Structure and
Sentence Form: Topic, Focus, and the Mental Representations of Discourse Referents*, CSL 71 (Cambridge: Cambridge University Press, 1996), 296.

76  Levinsohn, *Discourse Features*, 7; Runge, *Discourse Grammar*, 93–94; Ran-
dall Buth, "Word Order in the Verbless Clause: A Generative-Functional
Approach," in *The Verbless Clause in Biblical Hebrew*, ed. Cynthia L. Miller,
LSAWS 1 (Winona Lake, IN: Eisenbrauns, 1999), 81.

newly asserted information. Thus, the noticeable difference in their discourse function stems from the information structuring role each plays based on its position with respect to the verb.

Levinsohn makes a similar distinction between the function of participles based on their positioning with respect to the main verb, but it concerns relative saliency: "Cross-linguistically, the information conveyed in pre-nuclear subordinate clauses is backgrounded in relation to that conveyed in the main clause," whereas "post-nuclear subordinate clauses often contain theme-line information (Hwang 1990:69)."[77] Whereas the action of preposed participles

---

77 Levinsohn, *Narrative Discourse*, 73. He adds the following cross-linguistic claim regarding postnuclear subordinate clauses that describe the next theme line event in sequence: "The effect of using such a structure is to highlight the event expressed in the post-nuclear subordinate clause (see sec. 5.4.2)" (ibid). Although placement of theme-line information in postnuclear subordinate clauses for the purpose of foregrounding it with respect to the nuclear clause may be frequent in other languages, it does *not* appear to hold true in Koine Greek. Hwang's examples in support of Levinsohn's claim may be placed into three basic groups. The first consists of initial sentences in a story where innocuous scene-setting information serves as the basis for a foreground assertion to be made about a character, e.g., "The last drops of the thundershower had hardly ceased falling *when the Pedestrian stuffed his map into his pocket, settled his pack more comfortably on his tired shoulders, and stepped out from the shelter of a large chestnut tree into the middle of the road*" (C. S. Lewis, *Out of the Silent Planet* [New York: Simon & Schuster, 1996], 9, [emphasis added]). Such a construct effectively avoids the need for a "once upon a time there was a…" introduction. Its potential uses are very limited.

The second consist of highly accessible information from the preceding discourse making up the main clause, followed by a "when suddenly/ all of a sudden" subordinate clause. The accessible or repeated information accomplishes much the same attention-getting function as found in tail/head linkage constructions, where the accessible information is found in a prenuclear clause rather than the nucleus (see Runge, *Discourse Grammar*, 163–77.) Although these are well-attested in English, I found no evidence for comparable postnuclear foregrounding in the Greek New Testament.

The third is similar to the second, but the subordinate clause information resumes a previously suspended theme line. In this sense, the subordinated information serves as resumptive repetition (see Adele Berlin, *Poetics and Interpretation of Biblical Narrative* [Winona Lake, IN: Eisenbrauns, 1994], 126). Levinsohn offers several examples from modern fiction, e.g., "The party assembled gradually, but, as though by common consent, nothing was said about the pearls until after breakfast, when Oswalt Truegood took the bull by the horns" (Stephen H. Levinsohn, "Preposed and Postposed Adverbials in English," *Work Papers of the Summer Institute of Linguistics, University*

may be fairly independent of the nuclear clausal action, "Participial clauses that follow the nuclear clause may be concerned with some aspect of the nuclear event itself."[78] The dependency relationship still creates a single complex clause, but the postposed participial clauses typically elaborate upon the main clause in some way.[79] This is illustrated in example 21.

_of North Dakota Session_ 36 [1992]: 30). The detective's investigation was suspended earlier due to the lateness of the hour, with the stated expectation of resuming it after breakfast. The subordinated information marks the resumption of this higher-level theme regarding the investigation following an embedded theme line describing the breakfast.

Hwang also cites when "eventline information—the unexpected new information—is given in the postposed _when_-clause" based on what appears to be a reconstructed clause from the Three Little Pigs story (Shin Ja J. Hwang, "Foreground Information in Narrative," _SWJL_ 9 [1990]: 68–69). I could not find this same construction in the original or subsequent translations of this Grimm tale (J. O. Halliwell-Phillipps, _The Nursery Rhymes of England._, 5th ed. [New York: Warne and Co., 1886], 39). It appears the sentence was misquoted or perhaps constructed. Though Levinsohn cites this example favorably and affirms the principle, he offers no examples from, nor applies it to, Koine Greek (Levinsohn, "Preposed and Postposed," 29). The token from the Three Pigs, assuming it is natural, can be accounted for under my third group, marking the resumption of a suspended theme line theme. The description of the pig picking apples before the wolf returns may reasonably be viewed as a transition from the higher-level theme of the pig's interaction with the wolf. The wolf's return is thus not unexpected or foregrounded, it simply signals the resumption of the higher-level theme.

78  Levinsohn, _Discourse Features_, 188. Longacre states, "It appears that the postposed participle is of the same semantic rank as the verb that it follows; that is, it is _consecutive_ on the preceding main verb and continues its function. This applies not only to the indicative forms which are found in narrative but to the imperative forms which are found in hortatory discourse" (Robert E. Longacre, "Mark 5:1–43: Generating the Complexity of a Narrative from Its Most Basic Elements," in _Discourse Analysis and the New Testament: Approaches and Results_, JSNTSup 170 [Sheffield: Sheffield Academic, 1999], 177) (emphasis original).

79  Runge, _Discourse Grammar_, 262.

*Example 21: Phil 2:2–4*

| Main Clause | πληρώσατέ μου τὴν χαρὰν ἵνα τὸ αὐτὸ φρονῆτε, |
|---|---|
| Elaboration | τὴν αὐτὴν ἀγάπην ἔχοντες, |
| Elaboration | σύμψυχοι, |
| Elaboration | τὸ ἓν φρονοῦντες, |
| Elaboration | ³ μηδὲν κατ᾽ ἐριθείαν μηδὲ κατὰ κενοδοξίαν, ἀλλὰ τῇ ταπεινοφροσύνῃ ἀλλήλους ἡγούμενοι ὑπερέχοντας ἑαυτῶν, |
| Elaboration | ⁴ μὴ τὰ ἑαυτῶν ἕκαστοι σκοποῦντες, ἀλλὰ καὶ τὰ ἑτέρων ἕκαστοι. |
| Main Clause | complete my joy, so that you are in agreement, |
| Elaboration | having the same love, |
| Elaboration | united in spirit, |
| Elaboration | having one purpose. |
| Elaboration | ³ doing nothing according to selfish ambition or according to empty conceit, but in humility considering one another better than yourselves, |
| Elaboration | ⁴ each of you not looking out for your own interests, but also each of you *for* the interests of others. (Adapted from LEB) |

The use of finite verb forms in lieu of participles would have resulted in a series of exhortations rather than one exhortation with additional elaborative detail. The close semantic relationship of these actions would have been present in either case, but the canonical version subsumes the addition detail under one overall heading of being likeminded.

In regard to the framing function associated with preposed adverbials, nonfinite verbal clauses behave somewhat differently than finite verbal clauses. While I have chosen to group circumstantial participial clauses as a kind of framing device elsewhere,[80] these clauses are really more of a second cousin once or twice removed compared to finite verbal clauses. This difference may well be attributable to the absence of an explicit semantic relationship with the main clause. Here is an extended quotation from Levinsohn

---

80 Ibid., 243–45.

describing this important difference between the finite and non-finite preposed adverbials:

> It is generally recognized that the events described in adverbial participial clauses relate semantically to their nuclear clauses in a variety of ways. Thus, Funk (1973:669) says, "The circumstantial participle as the equivalent of an adverbial clause may be taken (i.e., inferred from the context) to denote time, cause, means, manner, purpose, condition, concession, or attendant circumstances." However, Robertson (n.d.:1124) points out that "there is a constant tendency to read into this circumstantial participle more than is there. In itself, it must be distinctly noted, the participle does not express time ... These ideas are not in the participle, but are merely suggested by the context." Thus, the function of the adverbial participle is not to specify any of the relationships that Funk lists. "Other more extended but more precise constructions are available for the same purpose: prepositional phrases, conditional, causal, temporal clauses, etc., and finally the grammatical coordination of two or more verbs." (BDF §417)[81]

This lack of an explicit semantic relation makes participial clauses an elegant means of describing attendant circumstances or concurrent action, but weakens their ability to perform a framing function comparable to finite adverbials, which do feature connectives specifying a semantic relationship.

In summary, the position of dependent adverbial clauses indeed affects the nature of their contribution to the discourse. Preverbal adverbials prototypically accomplish a framing function for the main clause that follows, but the degree to which they accomplish this seems directly proportional to the specificity of the semantic relationship to the main verb. By definition, adverbial participial clauses lack an explicit semantic constraint and thus play less of a framing role compared to finite adverbial clauses featuring connectives constraining a specific semantic relation.

---

81  Levinsohn, *Discourse Features*, 186.

This same principle regarding the semantic specificity of the main-clause relations seems also to apply to postposed adverbials. Where participial clauses bear only a loose relation of elaborating upon the main clausal action, finite adverbials are able to accomplish more specific functions based on the semantic specificity provided by the subordinating connective.[82]

## 4.4 Grounding Status

Very little work has been done concerning the impact of grammatical subordination on grounding status, so the principles offered in this section should be regarded as preliminary. They are guidelines for handling prototypical situations, so there may well be contextual circumstances that undermine the applicability of what follows.

First, analyze the complex clause as a complete unit. Although dependent clauses may contribute important information to the discourse, any contribution they make is via the main clause on which it depends. As adverbial modifiers they are indirectly contributing to the overall discourse compared to independent finite verbal clauses which contribute directly. Therefore there is little practical value in analyzing the components of a complex clause since ultimately it is the main clause's grounding status that is determinative. The grounding status of a dependent clause is relative to the main clause and thus cannot be analyzed without regard to the main clause on which it depends.

Although footnote 77 describes certain instances in English were a dependent clause may be construed as more salient than the main clause on which it depends, the grounding status must still be determined for the complex clause as a whole. Such instances are rare in English and seem limited to very specific contexts. There are no

---

82 Another possible implication of the differing degrees of semantic specificity regards relative salience. §4.2 intentionally treated backgrounding as a cline rather than as a binary distinction, but without explicitly stating this. The greater specificity of adverbials introduced with a connective may contribute to them being treated as more salient than participial clauses, though this may merely be coincidental.

comparable claims to be found for Koine Greek in either narrative or nonnarrative genres.[83]

Second, analyze component parts relative to their role within the complex clause. In those instances where a complex clause consists of one or more embedded theme lines, there may be value in analyzing the grounding status of the components within the clause. However, such judgments must be made relative to the dependency relationships of the other parts. This is illustrated in example 22. There is only one main assertion in this overall complex, with all of the other dependent parts providing grounding for it.

*Example 22: Heb 7:20–22*

| Frame of Ref | Καὶ καθ' ὅσον οὐ χωρὶς ὁρκωμοσίας |
|---|---|
| Support | (οἱ μὲν γὰρ χωρὶς ὁρκωμοσίας εἰσὶν ἱερεῖς γεγονότες, |
| Support | [21] ὁ δὲ μετὰ ὁρκωμοσίας διὰ τοῦ λέγοντος πρὸς αὐτόν· |
| Speech | Ὤμοσεν κύριος, καὶ οὐ μεταμεληθήσεται, |
| Speech | Σὺ ἱερεὺς εἰς τὸν αἰῶνα), |
| Frame of Ref | [22] κατὰ τοσοῦτο |
| Main Clause | κρείττονος διαθήκης γέγονεν ἔγγυος Ἰησοῦς. |
| Frame of Ref | And by as much as *this was* not without an oath |
| Support | (for these on the one hand have become priests without an oath, |
| Support | [21] but he with an oath by the one who said to him, |
| Speech | "The Lord has sworn and will not change his mind, |
| Speech | 'You *are* a priest forever' "), |
| Frame of Ref | [22] by so much more |
| Main Clause | Jesus has become the guarantee of a better covenant. |

---

83 Levinsohn (pers. comm.) offers Acts 28:25 and Acts 16:20 as possible examples, where postnuclear GA participial clauses convey what are clearly theme line events, though the motivation for these uses is disputed.

The comparative verbless clause καθ᾽ ὅσον οὐ χωρὶς ὁρκωμοσίας introduces a basis for comparison that will be made in the main clause. This basis is supported by what might be construed as an embedded theme line. This embedded element consists of a counterpoint-point set in 7:20b–21. The statement in 7:20b describing those who became priests without an oath serves as a contrastive foil for the claim in 7:21. This assertion about Jesus becoming a priest on the basis of an oath is substantiated by two reported speeches, one embedded within the other.

This entire complex of verses 7:20b–21 serves as embedded support for the comparative frame of reference in 7:20a, which in turn serves as the basis for the main-clause assertion in 7:22. Another comparative frame of reference begins 7:22, adding degree to the comparison, before we finally reach the main clause. The indenting in the example above reflects the hierarchical grounding of the clause elements. All serve as grounding support for the main statement, and this support even consists of an embedded theme line that itself offers support for the initial verbless comparative clause. Determinations of the grounding status of 7:21 thus must be made relative to the hierarchical relationships it bears with the main clause.

To summarize, determinations about the grounding status of complex clauses should be made for the whole; the contribution of the dependent parts to the overall discourse can only be determined by reference to their contribution to the main clause, never bypassing it. In cases where the complex clause contains embedded theme lines, there may be some value in doing an internal analysis. However, determinations about the grounding status of the dependent parts must be made only within the complex, and relative to the other dependent parts based on the dependency relationships.

## 5. SUMMARY

The factor most determinative in differentiating grounding roles is what advances the plot or progression of the discourse, according to the writer's goals or objectives. The theme line is construed as that which advances it, whereas supportive information does not. The characteristics of these grounding roles will differ from genre to genre based on the value placed on two main features: agent orientation and contingent temporal succession. Discourse is a representational depiction of actions or events according to the writer's goals or objectives, so the writer's assignment of a grounding role to an event involves some measure of interpretation, making such decisions critical to analyzing a discourse.

No single feature of discourse like verbal aspect is sufficient for determining the grounding status of a clause or clause complex. Neither is the grounding status of a clause absolute, but rather relative. The perfective/imperfective correlation with theme line and support in narrative is prototypical and typological in nature, a useful starting point for understanding the nature of grounding in narrative proper, but certainly not the whole picture. Wårvik has demonstrated that the situation is much more complicated than aspect alone; and even more complicated in the nonnarrative genres due in part to the frequent use of nonindicative verb forms.[84]

The increased use of logical connectives (inferential and strengthening) corroborates the notion that factors other than aspect or tense guide judgments about grounding roles outside of narrative proper. Connectives offer the most explicit and consistent basis for grounding judgments across genres, with inferential connectives signaling a shift to the theme line and strengthening connectives signaling a shift to support. Shifts in mood also provide an important basis for grounding determinations. Shifts from exposition back to a hortatory theme line may be accomplished solely on the basis of the shift to a hortatory verb form. Irrealis moods (subjunctive and optative) most often provide support, but this supportive role is generally already indicated by the use of a dependent connective. Finally, of the different Greek aspects that might be expected on the theme line of a nonnarrative discourse, the perfect tense-forms would be the least expected in expository genre. They do occur, but primarily in contexts where an implicit or explicit counterpoint is being corrected.

Another consideration affecting the *relative* grounding status of verb forms is grammatical dependency. The use of dependent forms where independent forms were a viable option should be construed as reflecting the writer's choice about how to package and structure the information. Although largely the same propositional content

---

84 Wårvik, "Foregrounded."

is conveyed either way, dependency relations bring about certain pragmatic effects that independent clauses would not have achieved. Dependency relationships also impact judgments about the relative salience of the clause with respect to the main clause on which it depends. Dependent clauses serve as adverbial modifiers of a main clause rather than independently contributing their content to the discourse. Dependent elements that are preposed prototypically serve a framing function for the main clause, whereas those that are postposed tend to elaborate in some way upon the main clause. Determinations of grounding status of complex clauses should be made for the whole complex based on the fact that the contribution of the subordinated elements is through the main clause. Analysis within the complex clause must account for the internal dependency relations, relative to the main clause.

Much more research needs to be done in nonnarrative genres in order to better understand the interrelationships of the factors described above, as well as to note other mitigating factors I might have overlooked. One of the best means of moving this discussion forward would be sustained analysis of an entire book applying this approach. Preliminary research has been completed on Philippians, Romans, and James, presented in a summary form in the *High Definition Commentary* series, as a basis for a more extended exposition regarding how to chart the flow and structure of discourse. My hope is that the preliminary findings presented in this article will pave the way for others to join in the discussion.

## BIBLIOGRAPHY

Berlin, Adele. *Poetics and Interpretation of Biblical Narrative*. Winona Lake, IN: Eisenbrauns, 1994.

Bertrand, Nicolas. "Grounding of Information." *EAGLL* 2:148–50.

Breeze, Mary. "Hortatory Discourse in Ephesians." *JOTT* 5 (1992): 313–47.

Buth, Randall. "Ουν, Δε, Και and Asyndeton in John's Gospel." Pages 144–61 in *Linguistics and New Testament Interpretation*. Edited by David A. Black. Nashville: Broadman, 1992.

———. "Word Order in the Verbless Clause: A Generative-Functional Approach." Pages 79–108 in *The Verbless Clause in Biblical*

*Hebrew*. Edited by Cynthia L. Miller. LSAWS 1. Winona Lake,
IN: Eisenbrauns, 1999.

Callow, Kathleen. *Discourse Considerations in Translating the Word of God*.
Grand Rapids: Zondervan, 1974.

Campbell, Constantine. *Verbal Aspect, the Indicative Mood, and
Narrative: Soundings in the Greek of the New Testament*. SBG 13.
New York: Lang, 2007.

Diessel, Holger. "Competing Motivations for the Ordering of Main and
Adverbial Clauses." *Linguistics* 43 (2005): 449–70.

Dooley, Robert A., and Stephen H. Levinsohn. *Analyzing Discourse: A
Manual of Basic Concepts*. Dallas: SIL International, 2001.

Dry, Helen A. "Foregrounding: An Assessment." Pages 235–50 in
*Language in Context: Essays for Robert E. Longacre*. Edited by
Shin Ja J. Hwang and William R. Merrifield. Dallas: Summer
Institute of Linguistics, 1992.

Fanning, Buist M. "Greek Presents, Imperfects, and Aorists in
the Synoptic Gospels: Their Contribution to Narrative
Structuring." Pages 157–90 in *Discourse Studies and Biblical
Interpretation: A Festschrift in Honor of Stephen H. Levinsohn*.
Edited by Steven E. Runge. Bellingham, WA: Logos Bible
Software, 2011.

Forsyth, James. *A Grammar of Aspect: Usage and Meaning in the Russian
Verb*. Cambridge: Cambridge University Press, 1970.

Fresch, Christopher J. "The Peculiar Occurrences of ore in Septuagint
Genesis and Exodus." In *XV Congress of the International
Organization for Septuagint and Cognate Studies, Munich, 2013*.
Edited by Wolfgang Kraus, Martin Meiser, and Michaël van
der Meer. Atlanta: Society of Biblical Literature, forthcoming.

Grimes, Joseph Evans. *The Thread of Discourse*. JLSMin 207. The Hague:
Mouton, 1975.

Halliwell-Phillipps, J. O. *The Nursery Rhymes of England*. 5th ed. New
York: Warne and Co., 1886.

Harris, W. Hall III, Elliot Ritzema, Rick Brannan, Douglas Magnum,
John Dunham, Jeffrey A. Reimer, and Micah Wierenga,
eds. *The Lexham English Bible*. Bellingham, WA: Logos Bible
Software, 2012.

Hwang, Shin Ja J. "Foreground Information in Narrative." *SWJL* 9
(1990): 63–90.

Jones, Larry B., and Linda K. Jones. "Multiple Levels of Information in
Discourse." Pages 1:3–28 in *Discourse Studies in Mesoamerican
Languages: Discussion*. Edited by Linda K. Jones. Dallas:

SIL International, 1979. http://www.sil.org/resources/
archives/8434.

Lambrecht, Knud. *Information Structure and Sentence Form: Topic, Focus,
and the Mental Representations of Discourse Referents.* CSL 71.
Cambridge: Cambridge University Press, 1996.

Levinsohn, Stephen H. *Discourse Features of New Testament Greek: A
Coursebook on the Information Structure of New Testament Greek.*
2nd ed. Dallas: SIL International, 2000.

———. "Preposed and Postposed Adverbials in English." *Work Papers
of the Summer Institute of Linguistics, University of North Dakota
Session* 36 (1992): 19–31.

———. "Reasoning Styles and Types of Hortatory Discourse." *JT* 2
(2006): 1–10.

———. *Self-Instruction Materials on Narrative Discourse Analysis.* Dallas:
SIL International, 2015. http://www.sil.org/~levinsohns/narr.
pdf.

———. *Self-Instruction Materials on Non-Narrative Discourse
Analysis.* Dallas: SIL International, 2015. http://www.sil.
org/~levinsohns/NonNarr.pdf.

———. "'Therefore' or 'Wherefore': What's the Difference?" Pages
325–43 in *Reflections on Lexicography: Explorations in Ancient
Syriac, Hebrew, and Greek Sources.* Edited by Richard A. Taylor
and Craig E. Morrison. PLAL 4. Piscataway NJ: Gorgias, 2014.

Lewis, C. S. *Out of the Silent Planet.* New York: Simon & Schuster, 1996.

Longacre, Robert E. "Mark 5:1–43: Generating the Complexity of a
Narrative from Its Most Basic Elements." Pages 169–96 in
*Discourse Analysis and the New Testament: Approaches and
Results.* Edited by Jeffrey T. Reed and Stanley E. Porter.
JSNTSup 170. Sheffield: Sheffield Academic, 1999.

———. *The Grammar of Discourse.* 2nd ed. TLL. New York: Plenum
Press, 1996.

Porter, Stanley E. *Idioms of the Greek New Testament.* 2nd ed. BLG 2.
Sheffield: JSOT Press, 1995.

———. "Prominence: An Overview." Pages 45–74 in *The Linguist as
Pedagogue: Trends in the Teaching and Linguistic Analysis of the
Greek New Testament.* Edited by Stanley E. Porter and Matthew
Brook O'Donnell. NTM 11. Sheffield: Sheffield Phoenix, 2009.

———. *Verbal Aspect in the Greek of the New Testament: With Reference to
Tense and Mood.* SBG 1. New York: Lang, 1989.

Porter, Stanley E., Matthew Brook O'Donnell, Jeffrey T. Reed, and
Randall Tan. *The OpenText.org Syntactically Analyzed Greek*

New Testament: Clause Analysis (version 2013-04-12T20:32:29Z).
    Bellingham, WA: Logos Bible Software, 2006.

Runge, Steven E. Discourse Grammar of the Greek New Testament: A
    Practical Introduction for Teaching and Exegesis. Peabody, MA:
    Hendrickson, 2010.

———. High Definition Commentary: Romans. Bellingham, WA: Lexham
    Press, 2014.

———. "The Discourse Function of the Greek Perfect." Paper
    presented at the Annual Meeting of the Society of Biblical
    Literature. San Diego, CA, November 2014.

Wallace, Daniel B. Greek Grammar Beyond the Basics: An Exegetical
    Syntax of the New Testament. 2nd ed. Grand Rapids:
    Zondervan, 1996.

Wallace, Stephen. "Figure and Ground: The Interrelationships of
    Linguistic Categories." Pages 201–23 in Tense-Aspect: Between
    Semantics and Pragmatics. Edited by Paul J. Hopper. TSL 1.
    Amsterdam: Benjamins, 1982.

Wårvik, Brita. "What Is Foregrounded in Narratives? Hypotheses
    for the Cognitive Basis of Foregrounding." Pages 99–122 in
    Approaches to Cognition Through Text and Discourse. Edited by
    Tuija Virtanen. Berlin: Mouton de Gruyter, 2004.

CHAPTER 8

# Participles as a Pragmatic Choice: Where Semantics Meets Pragmatics

RANDALL BUTH

BIBLICAL LANGUAGE CENTER

## 1. INTRODUCTION

For this conference on the Greek verb I was asked to provide some practical relevance for those who would like an introduction to approaches that are based on pragmatics, information theory, and discourse analysis. Those words can be daunting to someone who would enter this area of study from a traditional theological training. The relationship of participles to finite verbs may provide an appropriate doorway. This paper will lay a foundation for understanding the motives for an author to choose a participle.

Given a choice between a finite verb and a participle, why would an author choose a participle? What benefits are gained? In return, what is the cost to an author, what does the author lose by choosing a participle? These questions are often negotiated at a subconscious level by authors in many languages, both ancient and modern.

There is an underlying principle in all communication that choice implies meaning. Whenever a speaker and listener, or writer and reader interact, they intuitively interpret the explicit content and chosen structures against background assumptions. The broad analysis of those assumptions and their implication for interpretation has developed into a field of study today called Relevance

Theory, which is itself a part of Pragmatics and Discourse Analysis.[1] But this paper is not about Relevance Theory. We will focus on a small piece of the Greek language where authors were making pragmatic choices between participles and finite verbs in almost every sentence.

After discussing participles in general we will also touch on some evidence with participles and historical presents that has a bearing on the questions of tense and aspect in the Greek verb.

## 2. DEFINITION OF A PARTICIPLE FOR THIS PAPER

In Greek, a **participle** is a μετοχή, a *shared* verb form. A participle is a category of adjective that is based on a verb stem[2], whether aorist stem, continuative stem (a.k.a. present and imperfective), perfect stem, or future stem. The verb stems have sets of endings added to the stem form that mark the word for gender (masc., fem., neut.), number (sg., pl., and in very high registers, dual), and case (nom., acc., dat., gen., voc.).

> 1.    Examples of participle forms:
> γράψαντος (act. *sigma* aor., masc./neut. sg. gen.)
> λαβών (act. non-*sigma* aor., masc. sg. nom.)
> ἀποκριθείσης (*theta* aor., sg. fem. gen. [so-called "passive"])
> ἐρχομένην (middle continuative, fem. sg. acc.)
> καθημένῳ (middle non-*omicron* continuative, masc./neut. sg. dat.)
> γεγραμμένων (middle pft., masc./fem./neut. pl. gen.)

---

1    For an introduction, see Deirdre Wilson and Dan Sperber, "Relevance Theory," in *The Handbook of Pragmatics*, ed. Laurence R. Horn and Gregory L. Ward, BHL 16 (Oxford: Blackwell, 2004), 607–32.

2    For this paper, specialized verbal adjectives with a '-τ-' suffix are excluded. So modal adjectives like ποιητέον "needing to be done" will be excluded, along with the other "-τ-" adjectives, like ποιητός -ή -όν "made, cultivated," and δυνατός -ή -όν "strong, capable." Those forms were lexicalized and the structure partially fossilized in the Koine period, and limited in occurrence. Those forms were no longer available as optional replacements for finite verbal clauses in the way that the standard participles could function in Greek.

ἑστηκώς (act. *kappa* pft., masc sg. nom.)

προσκυνήσων (fut., masc. sg. nom.)

# 3. BASIC ASPECTS OF THE PARTICIPLES

The stem of a participle marks its basic aspect category.

An aorist participle marks a **perfective** aspect. The event or state of affairs is presented as an undifferentiated whole, as complete, including the end points. Prototypically, the time of the aorist participle is prior to the main event (that is, antecedent—see ex. 7 below) but it may also be simultaneous to the main verb.

2.    Here are two examples of a simultaneous aorist participle, within the time frame of the main verb or equal to the main verb:

ὁ ὁμόσας (aor. ptc.) ὀμνύει

the oath-taker swears. Matt 23:20[3]

ἀποκριθεὶς (aor. ptc.) εἶπεν

answered he said. Luke 19:40

In the second example the participle is incorporated into the main verb serving as a kind of adverbial modification to the same event.

The **continuative** participle (based on the same stem as a present tense indic. verb) marks **imperfective** aspect[4], where the end points of the action are not in view. Imperfective participles overlap in time with the main verb. However, similarly to the present indicative, continuative participles may look forward to what is coming

3.    Here is a continuative participle in a "futuristic context":

ἀπέστειλεν αὐτὸν εὐλογοῦντα ὑμᾶς

he sent him blessing you [i.e., to bless you]). Acts 3:26

---

3    Unless otherwise indicated, all translations are the author's.

4    Traditionally the continuative participle is called the present participle. However, the participle does not refer to present time at all, but to imperfective aspect. The imperfective aspect is part of the Greek present indicative and the Greek imperfect past indicative. Imperfective participle is an accurate linguistic name for this participle since the participle signals imperfective aspect. However, traditionally the imperfective past tense in Greek is called imperfect so there is potential confusion for learners. As a result, I prefer using a term in English that is not associated with either the present indicative or the imperfect past indicative.

The perfect participle signals an event that has entered a state, a **perfect** aspect. The perfect participle is common with idioms like "knowing" εἰδώς and "standing" ἑστώς, where idiomatically the present indicative of those verbs does not exist with the same lexical meaning.[5] However, in narrative the perfect participle is relatively rare.

4.    Perfect participle, an entered state:
      ὁ τὸ ἓν τάλαντον εἰληφὼς εἶπεν
      the one who had received one talent said. Matt 25:24

The future participle is formed on the future stem and is not really an aspect but a **mood**. The future participle does not refer to an indicative, real future, but to an intended future, a purpose or hoped-for result.

5.    Future participle, an **intended mood** that might happen
      in the future, relative to the main event:
      ὃς ἐληλύθει προσκυνήσων εἰς Ἰερουσαλήμ
      who had come so that he could worship in Jerusalem.
      Acts 8:27

# 4. PARTICIPLES AS SIMPLE REPLACEMENTS FOR FINITE VERBS: VERB PROMINENCE AND PARTICIPLE RANKING

Let us look at some prototypical Greek sentences in order to see the kinds of choices that were available to Greek authors. We will construct sentences in order to make the principles clearer. This is a standard practice in modern linguistic studies; naturally, this assumes that the structures described are readily attested in ancient documents. Constructing our own examples allows us to restrict the variation primarily to the point being illustrated. There will be many examples from attested texts further below after the parameters have been illustrated.

---

5   Compound intransitive verbs with -ἵσταμαι are restricted to the middle. The normal indicative for a noncompounded intransitive "is standing" is a perfect active: ἕστηκα "I am standing, I am in a standing position."

6.   ὁ δὲ Παῦλος ἀφίκετο εἰς Ἱεροσόλυμα ... καὶ προσεκύνησεν ἐν
τῷ ἱερῷ.
Paul arrived in Jerusalem ... and worshiped in
the temple.

Example 6 has two finite verbs ἀφίκετο and προσεκύνησεν. In form, both verbs are aorist indicatives. For a context, it may be accepted as given that both verbs refer to a situational event that is past from the author's perspective and both situations are viewed as completed and as temporally sequential.

In addition, an author may refer to exactly the same situations and use the same vocabulary, but with a different choice of verb form. The following examples will illustrate how the finite verbs may be replaced with participles.

7.   ὁ δὲ Παῦλος ἀφικόμενος εἰς Ἱεροσόλυμα ... προσεκύνησεν ἐν
τῷ ἱερῷ.
Paul, having arrived in Jerusalem, ... worshiped in the
temple.

In example 7 the first finite verb ἀφίκετο has been replaced with an aorist participle ἀφικόμενος (from aor. ἀφικέσθαι, continuative ἀφικνεῖσθαι). The semantic meaning of the two clauses remains the same. The first clause describes a past "entering" and the second clause a past "worshiping." However, the pragmatic effect of example 7 is different from example 6. That different pragmatic effect is the result of the principle that choice implies meaning. In this case the different structure does not change the events referred to, but it changes the presentation of the material. In Greek, example 7 has a structural, thematic crescendo from the first verb to the second. We can look at these examples from a different perspective. We can say that the structural prominence of the verbs in example 6 are equal,[6] while in example 7 the first event has been structurally demoted, that is, the participial clause has become less prominent in relation to the finite verb clause. Practically, choosing to encode one

---

6   It may be claimed that a string of narrative, perfective events, however encoded, has an implied semantic saliency on the end of the real-world string. However, this study is concerned with the function and effect of choosing different structures, not natural semantics.

event with a finite verb and another event with a participle adds a relative ranking scale to their prominence when communicating.

8.    *ὁ δὲ Παῦλος ἀφίκετο εἰς Ἱεροσόλυμα ... προσκυνήσας ἐν
      τῷ ἱερῷ.
      *Paul arrived in Jerusalem, ... having worshiped in
      the temple.

Example 8 attempts to replace the second verb of example 6 with an aorist participle, similar to example 7. However, this does not refer to the same situations as example 6. The referential meaning has changed. The asterisk (*) marks the sentence as unacceptable if the author was trying to communicate the same events as example 6.

Nevertheless, Greek does have a structure that would allow a participle replacement for the second verb.

9a.   ὁ δὲ Παῦλος ἀφίκετο εἰς Ἱεροσόλυμα ... προσκυνήσων ἐν τῷ
      ἱερῷ.[7]
      Paul arrived in Jerusalem ... so that he could worship in
      the temple.

The future participle in example 9a is a possible description of the events in example 6, except that the second verb is no longer presented as a factual event but as an intention.

The potentiality and intentionality of the second event could also be communicated with finite verbs or infinitives.

9b.   ὁ δὲ Παῦλος ἀφίκετο εἰς Ἱεροσόλυμα ... τοῦ προσκυνῆσαι ἐν
      τῷ ἱερῷ.
      Paul arrived in Jerusalem ... to worship in the temple.

9c.   ὁ δὲ Παῦλος ἀφίκετο εἰς Ἱεροσόλυμα ... ἵνα προσκυνήσῃ ἐν
      τῷ ἱερῷ.
      Paul arrived in Jerusalem ... so that he could worship in
      the temple.

Example 9b avoids a full finite verb and may have been more acceptable to New Testament authors than a future participle because they tended to avoid the use of the future participle. The future

---

7    It is doubtful if the present participle would be considered well-formed: *? ὁ δὲ Παῦλος ἀφίκετο εἰς Ἱεροσόλυμα προσκυνῶν ἐν τῷ ἱερῷ. As if meaning to say *? *Paul arrived in Jerusalem for worshiping in the temple.*

participle only occurs 13 times in the New Testament as opposed to 4272 other participles.[8]

Example 9c communicates a situation similar to 9a, but it is structurally heavier, requiring more processing energy of explicit data. Specifying the relationship with ἵνα and using a full finite verb προσκυνήσῃ use more encoding and processing energy. A heavier structure means that the author considered it important to raise the structural importance of the intended event and that the effect was worthwhile even if it required expending more processing energy on the part of the author and audience. While a beginning student may think that all of these sentences require a lot of processing energy, in Relevance Theory terms example 9c requires more processing energy because the relationship is specified and processed rather than implicitly assumed and the relationship of the subjects of the finite clauses must be processed rather than assumed.

10.    ὁ δὲ Παῦλος ... προσεκύνησεν ἐν τῷ ἱερῷ ... ἀφικόμενος εἰς Ἱεροσόλυμα.
Paul ... worshiped in the temple, ... having arrived in Jerusalem.

Example 10 is similar to example 7 but it places the lower ranked participial clause after the main verb as a kind of afterthought. The structure is good Greek, although it is a little more complex for communication because the events are presented out of their natural order.

## 5. PARTICIPLES ADDING CONTENT TO LEXICAL, PHASAL ASPECT: CONTINUING AND ENDING

Continuative participles can be used with particular governing verbs that lexically stipulate a phasal aspect like διατελεῖν ποιῶν "to continue doing" and παύσασθαι ποιῶν "to finish doing". (In earlier dialects the participle was also used occasionally with ἄρξασθαι "to begin doing" for a phasal aspect of beginning a process.)

---

8    The statistics are taken from the Accordance Bible software program (OakTree Software, Inc.).

11.    ὁ δὲ Παῦλος διετέλει βαδίζων εἰς Ἱεροσόλυμα
       Paul was continuing walking (continued to walk) to
       Jerusalem.

12.    ὁ δὲ Παῦλος ἐπαύσατο βαδίζων εἰς Ἱεροσόλυμα
       Paul stopped walking to Jerusalem.

These examples illustrate an additional side to the prominence
and ranking parameters of main verbs and participles. When the
author feels a need for precision about starting, continuing, or stop-
ping, then specific vocabulary items can be chosen to make the aspectual phase explicit. The participle fills in the content of the action while the finite verb marks the phase of the event. One may
say that the author has chosen to make the phasal aspect the most
prominent part of the event complex.

# 6. PARTICIPLES STREAMLINE A COMMUNICATION BUT LEAVE THE SEMANTIC RELATIONSHIP UNSPECIFIED

Consider Matthew 28:19–20:

13.

πορευθέντες οὖν
μαθητεύσατε πάντα τὰ ἔθνη,
βαπτίζοντες αὐτοὺς εἰς τὸ ὄνομα τοῦ πατρὸς καὶ τοῦ υἱοῦ καὶ
τοῦ ἁγίου πνεύματος,
διδάσκοντες αὐτοὺς τηρεῖν πάντα ὅσα ἐνετειλάμην ὑμῖν·
καὶ ἰδοὺ ἐγὼ μεθ᾽ ὑμῶν εἰμι πάσας τὰς ἡμέρας ἕως τῆς
συντελείας τοῦ αἰῶνος.
having-gone, therefore,
make disciples of all nations
baptizing them in the name of the Father and of the Son
and of the Holy Spirit
teaching them to follow all the things that I
commanded you,
and remember ("behold"), I am with you to the end of
the age.

The first participle ranks the idea of "going" under the main verb "make disciples." The "going" naturally precedes the main verb in time and itself becomes part of the command by being syntactically subordinated to the main verb, but the main verb carries the author's choice for prominence.

The second and third participles are also ranked under the main verb but as imperfectives they overlap in time with the main verb "make disciples." While we may want to analyze these participial clauses as stipulating the manner, the "how to" of the main verb, or as generic-specific, the semantic relationship between the participles and the main verb is not specified.

This nicely illustrates the choices of an author. If specific instructions were desired to be equally prominent, **then full finite verbs could have been chosen**.

> 14.    μαθητεύσατε πάντα τὰ ἔθνη,
> [... εὐαγγελίσατε αὐτούς ...]
> ... βαπτίσατε αὐτούς ...,
> καὶ διδάξατε αὐτούς ...
> make disciples ...
> evangelize them ...
> baptize them ...
> and teach them ...

But the author chose to have the verb μαθητεύσατε as structurally and semantically the most prominent, as in example 13 above.[9] Each

---

9    At the conference in Cambridge there was open comment and discussion about whether or not continuative (imperfective, present), post-main-verb participles should be considered "main line, foregrounded events," "demoted, backgrounded events," or something in between. There was consensus that pre-main-verb participial clauses/phrases were prototypically demoted and less prominent in relation to the main verb and typically served as settings and introductory material to the main verb. Thus, as less prominent they are rhetorically backgrounded. Although analyzing events in a text as foregrounded and backgrounded can be a useful technique as a **literary analysis**, I do not think that grounding itself is a broad linguistic feature of **Greek grammar** or **syntax** and the foregrounding question seems to obscure the structural choices that are being made by Greek authors. Grounding appears to be a secondary, analytical construct. This is especially the case if the definition of foreground and background becomes a confluence of semantic features of a particular event rather than syntactic, structural marking. The structural choices need to outweigh subjective analysis. The

of the verbs could have served as a prominent verb on which to hang or arrange the other events. The following two examples help to illustrate the choice of prominence with imperatives and participles.

> 15.   ἐν αὐτῇ δὲ τῇ οἰκίᾳ μένετε ἐσθίοντες καὶ πίνοντες τὰ παρ᾽ αὐτῶν· ἄξιος γὰρ ὁ ἐργάτης τοῦ μισθοῦ αὐτοῦ. μὴ μεταβαίνετε ἐξ οἰκίας εἰς οἰκίαν. (Luke 10:7)
> And remain in the same house, eaing and drinking what they provide,
> for the laborer deserves his wages.
> Do not go from house to house.

Here the context makes it clear that the prominent command is "remain in the same house." The follow up command makes this clear by stating a corollary command in the negative "do not go from house to house." Within this prominent command is a provision and explanation that they are to receive food and drink from their hosts. The eating and drinking could have been encoded as imperatives if this was equally prominent. In fact, Luke 10:8-10 expands on the commands of verse 7 within a generalized framework and includes commands for eating and drinking along with healing and preaching.

> 16.   πλὴν ἀγαπᾶτε τοὺς ἐχθροὺς ὑμῶν καὶ ἀγαθοποιεῖτε καὶ δανίζετε μηδὲν ἀπελπίζοντες. (Luke 6:35)
> But love your enemies, and do good,
> and lend, expecting nothing in return

---

status of foreground and background applied to postverbal participles becomes an analytical label that is subjectively imposed on Greek language signals that are performing other tasks than marking a semantically defined background and foreground. In other words readers and students should be advised to spend time elsewhere than in trying to label participles as foregrounded. Whether or not to call "baptizing" and "teaching" foreground becomes a game of taxonomy. The post-main-verb continuative participles certainly bring in information that may be treated as naturally salient just like other postverbal material. There is a natural information cline in human communication that moves from more-presupposed to more-salient. Post-main-verb participles are typically important and salient, as their postverb position would suggest, yet they are ranked with lower prominence than the main head verbs because they are participles.

The commands at Luke 6:35 summarize the teaching from the previous three verses. The command to love is reinforced with a command to do good. Both are encoded as imperatives and given equal grammatical prominence. However, in the second set of commands, the command to lend is encoded as an imperative while the negative exhortation uses a participle and leaves the "lending" as more prominent. So both structures are illustrated in this one verse, an imperative + imperative of equal prominence, and a more prominent imperative coupled with a following participle.

Another example of prominence chosen through a main verb in relation to a following participle can be given at Matt 3:6.

17.  καὶ ἐβαπτίζοντο ἐν τῷ Ἰορδάνῃ ποταμῷ ὑπ' αὐτοῦ
     ἐξομολογούμενοι τὰς ἁμαρτίας αὐτῶν
     and they were being baptized in the Jordan river by him
     confessing their sins

In the context of Matt 3, the author chose to make "being baptized" more prominent than "confessing sins" through the choice of the finite verb instead of encoding both events with finite verbs in either of two potential orders "ἐβαπτίζοντο ... καὶ ἐξωμολογοῦντο" or "ἐξωμολογοῦντο ... καὶ ἐβαπτίζοντο." One might argue that the choice of the participle allows for a more explicit overlap in time between the two actions, but even if such were the motivation, then either action could have been cited as the framework verb on which a participle was added. The choice of the finite verb from among the two events still gives a relative prominence to one of the two events.

The choices between a participle and a finite verb are different issues than simply "background" and "foreground." For example,

18a.  Περιπατῶν δὲ παρὰ τὴν θάλασσαν τῆς Γαλιλαίας
      εἶδεν δύο ἀδελφούς
      walking along the sea of Galilee
      he saw two brothers

18b.  Περιεπάτει δὲ παρὰ τὴν θάλασσαν τῆς Γαλιλαίας
      καὶ εἶδεν δύο ἀδελφούς
      He was walking along the sea of Galilee
      and he saw two men

The structure in example 18a is found in Matt 4:18. The participle is presented as relatively less prominent than the finite verb. However, another structure was possible, as is seen in example 18b, where both events are presented with finite verbs. The "walking around" in example 18b forms the background to the event "he saw." This is the classic background and foreground relationship that was highlighted by Harald Weinreich back in 1964.[10] So the author had more than one choice, both of which were semantically and syntactically backgrounded to the event of "seeing." Between examples 18a and 18b, we can theorize that the more dependent structure, the participle, is somehow less prominent as well as being the background for the main event. Some questions may arise with a similar structure just a few verses later:

19a.    Καὶ <u>περιῆγεν</u> ἐν ὅλῃ τῇ Γαλιλαίᾳ
        <u>διδάσκων</u> ἐν ταῖς συναγωγαῖς αὐτῶν
        καὶ <u>κηρύσσων</u> τὸ εὐαγγέλιον τῆς βασιλείας
        καὶ <u>θεραπεύων</u> ...
        And he <u>was going around</u> in all of Galilee
        <u>teaching</u> in their synagogues
        and <u>preaching</u> the gospel of the kingdom
        and <u>healing</u> ...

The description at this point in Matthew's narrative deals with backgrounding events under the general umbrella of "walking around the Galilee." The main difference between examples 18a and 19a is that the participles follow the main verb and therefore occur in a more naturally salient position according to the principle of leading from more-presupposed information to less-presupposed. Nevertheless, the participles were not given the status of finite verbs, as can be seen in example 19b.

19b.    Καὶ <u>περιάγων</u> ἐν ὅλῃ τῇ Γαλιλαίᾳ
        <u>ἐδίδασκεν</u> ἐν ταῖς συναγωγαῖς αὐτῶν
        καὶ <u>ἐκήρυσσεν</u> τὸ εὐαγγέλιον τῆς βασιλείας
        καὶ <u>ἐθεράπευεν</u> ...

---

10    Harald Weinreich, *Tempus: Besprochene und erzählte Welt*, SLi 16 (Stuttgart: Kohlhammer, 1964).

> And <u>going around</u> in all of Galilee
> he <u>was teaching</u> in their synagogues
> and <u>was preaching</u> the gospel of the kingdom
> and <u>was healing</u> ...

The participles in 19a are dependent on the main verb of motion. The participles fill in and explain characteristic information rather than raise that information up to an event line in the narrative. The restructuring in 19b shows the difference in choice where the teaching, preaching, and healing are made more prominent by choosing finite verbs. It is actually in the very next verse in the narrative that Matthew describes these generic events with finite verbs. Not only that, but the multiple events were summarized and foregrounded with aorist (perfective) verbs. So the participles in example 19a (Matt 4:23) were used to prepare the way for a foregrounded summary in the next verse (example 20).

20.  Καὶ ἀπῆλθεν ἡ ἀκοὴ αὐτοῦ εἰς ὅλην τὴν Συρίαν·
     καὶ προσήνεγκαν αὐτῷ πάντας τοὺς κακῶς ἔχοντας ποικίλαις
     νόσοις ...
     καὶ <u>ἐθεράπευσεν</u> αὐτούς.
     And his fame went out to all Syria
     and they brought him all those who were ill with various diseases ...
     and he <u>healed</u> them. (Matt 4:24)

The complex relationship of continuative participles after a main verb may be illustrated further with Matt 11:19 (example 21a)

21a.  <u>ἦλθεν</u> ὁ υἱὸς τοῦ ἀνθρώπου <u>ἐσθίων</u> καὶ <u>πίνων</u>,
      The Son of Man <u>came</u> <u>eating</u> and <u>drinking</u>

21b.  <u>ἦλθεν</u> ὁ υἱὸς τοῦ ἀνθρώπου
      καὶ <u>ἤσθιεν</u> καὶ <u>ἔπιεν</u>.
      The Son of Man <u>came</u>
      and he <u>was eating</u> and and he <u>was drinking</u>

The participles in example 21a provide a characterization that contrasts with the characterization of John the Baptist. The eating and drinking, or lack thereof, are not part of the foregrounded narration of the speech. In that sense they fill in backgrounded information like the examples in 21b. However, this information is salient to the context and sits in the postverbal position as unmarked and naturally salient.[11] So the postverbal participles bring salient information, even though they are structurally dependent below the layer of the governing finite verbs. The participles after the main finite verb are adverbial, salient elaboration. But they are not ranked as prominent events like finite verbs, nor are they foregrounded events of narration.

## 7. PROMINENCE IS HELPFUL IN FOLLOWING A MAIN POINT

Recognizing choices of higher prominence and lower prominence can help simplify reading and exegesis. Consider Romans 5:1:

22.   Δικαιωθέντες οὖν ἐκ πίστεως
      εἰρήνην ἔχομεν[12] πρὸς τὸν θεὸν διὰ τοῦ κυρίου ἡμῶν
      Ἰησοῦ Χριστοῦ
      δι’ οὗ καὶ τὴν προσαγωγὴν ἐσχήκαμεν [τῇ πίστει] εἰς τὴν
      χάριν ταύτην
      having-been-acquitted therefore through faith
      we have peace with God through our Lord Jesus Christ
      through whom we have had an entrance through faith
      into this state of grace

The participle refers back to the discussion in Rom 4 and provides the background for the conclusion that is presented in this verse. The conclusion is more prominent because the author chose to make ἔχομεν the main verb. The participle is subordinated and less prominent relative to the main verb. Furthermore, the semantic/logical relationship between the participle and the main verb is not in focus but is assumed.

---

11   It is taken as a given that Matthew intends "Son of Man" as a title to refer to Jesus.

12   The text ἔχομεν (Bc ℵc F G P Ψ 1 6 88 and many) versus subjunctive ἔχωμεν (B* ℵ* A C D K L 049 056 33 69 226) has received considerable discussion. The context (ἐσχήκαμεν) and argument is indicative, so ἔχομεν appears to be the intended word, however a scribe may have written it. The two forms sounded identical in Paul's day (ἔχομεν and ἔχωμεν were both pronounced [ɛ'xomɛn]), so an audience would interpret the word according to its context without further ado.

A finite verb could have been chosen and the semantic relationship could have been clarified if the author chose to make that explicit, as in example 23.

23.  ἐπεὶ οὖν ἐδικαιώθημεν ἐκ πίστεως
     εἰρήνην ἔχομεν πρὸς τὸν θεόν
     Since we have been acquitted through faith
     we have peace with God

But such a choice would change the focus. This illustrates the danger of "doing exegesis" by running a Greek text through a semantic filter into expanded, fully specified propositions in another language. The pragmatic flow of the original presentation is lost.

This may be illustrated from the other direction, too. Consider Romans 6:2:

24a.  οἵτινες ἀπεθάνομεν τῇ ἁμαρτίᾳ, πῶς ἔτι ζήσομεν ἐν αὐτῇ;
      We who have died to sin, how can we still live in it?

24b.  πῶς ἀποθάνοντες τῇ ἁμαρτίᾳ ἔτι ζήσομεν ἐν αὐτῇ;
      How can we, having died to sin, still live in it?

The first example has both dying and living encoded in main finite verb forms. Even though the dying is in a subordinated phrase, a finite verb was chosen rather than a participle. The point about dying is the main argument in verses 2 through 6 so a participle was not chosen. However, later at Rom 6:7 the participle was chosen as more appropriate for a more presupposed item.

25a.  ὁ γὰρ ἀποθανὼν δεδικαίωται ἀπὸ τῆς ἁμαρτίας
      For the one who has died is acquitted from sin.

25b.  ὅστις γὰρ ἀπέθανεν δεδικαίωται ἀπὸ τῆς ἁμαρτίας
      For he who has died, he is acquitted from sin.

The argument about dying had already been made, so subordinating the reference to a participial form allowed for a more streamlined communication at this point.

Nevertheless, when returning to the first person "we" in the next verse (Rom 6:8), the heavier finite verb forms were again chosen.

26.  εἰ δὲ ἀπεθάνομεν σὺν Χριστῷ
     Furthermore, if we died with Christ

The author felt that he was moving on to a new point, reinforced by the δέ, and he chose to avoid a lower-ranked participle in order to preserve a fuller prominence on "having died."

At Romans 3:21–27 the choices of finite verbs and participles help a reader follow the main points.[13]

27.    Rom 3:21–27

3:21 Νυνὶ δὲ χωρὶς νόμου δικαιοσύνη θεοῦ <u>πεφανέρωται</u>
<u>μαρτυρουμένη</u> ὑπὸ τοῦ νόμου καὶ τῶν προφητῶν,
22    δικαιοσύνη δὲ θεοῦ διὰ πίστεως Ἰησοῦ Χριστοῦ εἰς
πάντας τοὺς πιστεύοντας.
   οὐ γάρ <u>ἐστιν</u> διαστολή,
23 πάντες γὰρ <u>ἥμαρτον</u> καὶ <u>ὑστεροῦνται</u> τῆς δόξης τοῦ θεοῦ
   24 <u>δικαιούμενοι</u> δωρεὰν τῇ αὐτοῦ χάριτι διὰ τῆς
   ἀπολυτρώσεως τῆς ἐν Χριστῷ Ἰησοῦ·
   25 ὃν προέθετο ὁ θεὸς ἱλαστήριον διὰ [τῆς] πίστεως ἐν τῷ
   αὐτοῦ αἵματι
εἰς ἔνδειξιν τῆς δικαιοσύνης αὐτοῦ διὰ τὴν πάρεσιν τῶν
προγεγονότων ἁμαρτημάτων 26 ἐν τῇ ἀνοχῇ τοῦ θεοῦ,
πρὸς τὴν ἔνδειξιν τῆς δικαιοσύνης αὐτοῦ ἐν τῷ νῦν καιρῷ, εἰς τὸ
εἶναι αὐτὸν δίκαιον καὶ δικαιοῦντα τὸν ἐκ πίστεως Ἰησοῦ.
3:27 Ποῦ οὖν ἡ καύχησις; <u>ἐξεκλείσθη</u>.
διὰ ποίου νόμου; τῶν ἔργων; οὐχί, ἀλλὰ διὰ νόμου πίστεως.

Now, without law the righteousness of God has been made visible,
   being witnessed by the Law and the Prophets,
and the righteousness of God (is) through the faith of Jesus Christ for all who believe,
for there is no distinction.
for everybody sinned and they fall short of the glory of God,
   being justified freely in his grace through the redemption in Christ Jesus,
   whom God put forward as a propitiation through faith in his blood

---

13 I would like to thank both Stephen Levinsohn and Steven Runge for extended discussions on this passage after the Cambridge conference. The discussions have helped me clarify my positions.

> for indicating his righteousness on account of
> passing over previous sins in the patience of God,
> in order to indicate his righteousness in the pres-
> ent time,
>> so that he might be just and the one justifying the
>> one with faith in Jesus
> So where is boasting? It has been blocked.
> Through what kind of law? of works?
> No, but through a law of faith.

The main argument in Rom 3:21–27ff is that there is no distinction within God's righteousness (between Jew and gentile) and for
that reason no one can boast, which is carried by the main verbs and
the verbless clause (3:22). The participial clauses add salient comments and expansions, but they are not the argument at this point in
the letter. "Being justified" is a side explanation, even though rather
long, including an extended re-characterization of Jesus Christ that
looks ahead to what will be discussed in detail in chapter 4. The participle ranks the clause and explanation under the main clause and
the choice appears purposeful and fitting.

These examples above illustrate how an author's choices help
an audience follow an argument. Participles can be used to rank a
statement relative to a main verb. Participles make the communication lighter, requiring less processing energy in terms of Relevance
Theory. The communication is more streamlined and audiences follow the main points more easily on the first presentation. However,
the condensation of the communication comes with a cost: the relationship between the clauses is no longer specified.

28. The following rules of thumb provide fast processing by
    a Greek audience:
    - Where an author wants to condense a communi-
      cation and to highlight the main point(s), main
      finite verbs can be chosen for natural prominence,
      while participles can be chosen for a lower ranking
      of clauses.
    - Where an author wants to spend extra processing en-
      ergy to specify relationships between clauses, parti-
      ciples are avoided and clauses with main finite verbs
      are chosen, requiring a specified connection.

- Continuative participles after a main verb may play a salient adverbial role of elaboration or characterization of the main finite verb. Nevertheless, the post-verbal participles carry a lower prominence than the main verb.

## 8. PARTICIPLES AND THE HISTORICAL PRESENT

Participles also make a contribution to a general understanding of the Greek historical present and the role that tense (time) and aspect play in the historical present. As a contribution to this conference on the semantics of the Greek verb, the rest of the paper will look at collocations and restrictions between participles and historical present verbs.

The Gospel of Mark has long been noted for a style that multiplies the use of the historical present.[14] We can group the participles that accompany a historical present main verb. I have arranged them into the following categories (some examples fit in more than one list and are listed in each appropriate list):

A) Double historical presents, naturally expecting an aoristic (perfective) interpretation
B) Historical presents, possibly allowing an imperfective interpretation
C) Aorist participles with a historical present
D) Continuative participles with a historical present
E) Historical presents with a participle following the verb

---

14 These are conveniently listed for the Gospel writers by John C. Hawkins, *Horae Synopticae, Contributions to the Study of the Synoptic Problem*, 2nd ed., rev. and supplemented (Oxford: Clarendon, 1909; repr. Grand Rapids: Baker, 1968).

## 8.A. Double Historical Presents, Naturally Expecting an Aoristic (Perfective) Interpretation[15]

Μάρκον 2·18 Καὶ ἦσαν οἱ μαθηταὶ Ἰωάννου καὶ οἱ Φαρισαῖοι νηστεύοντες. καὶ <u>ἔρχονται</u> καὶ <u>λέγουσιν</u> αὐτῷ·
Now John's disciples and the Pharisees were fasting. And people <u>are coming</u> and <u>are saying</u> to him,

Μάρκον 3·13 Καὶ <u>ἀναβαίνει</u> εἰς τὸ ὄρος καὶ <u>προσκαλεῖται</u> οὓς ἤθελεν αὐτός,
And he <u>is going up</u> on the mountain and <u>was calling</u> to him those whom he desired,

Μάρκον 3·20 Καὶ <u>ἔρχεται</u> εἰς οἶκον· καὶ <u>συνέρχεται</u> πάλιν [ὁ] ὄχλος,
Then he <u>is going</u> home, and the crowd <u>is gathering</u> again,

Μάρκον 4·38 καὶ αὐτὸς ἦν ἐν τῇ πρύμνῃ ἐπὶ τὸ προσκεφάλαιον καθεύδων. καὶ <u>ἐγείρουσιν</u> αὐτὸν καὶ <u>λέγουσιν</u> αὐτῷ·
But he was in the stern, asleep on the cushion. And they <u>are waking</u> him and <u>are saying</u> to him,

Μάρκον 5·15 καὶ <u>ἔρχονται</u> πρὸς τὸν Ἰησοῦν καὶ <u>θεωροῦσιν</u> τὸν δαιμονιζόμενον καθήμενον ἱματισμένον καὶ σωφρονοῦντα, τὸν ἐσχηκότα τὸν λεγιῶνα, καὶ ἐφοβήθησαν.
And they <u>are coming</u> to Jesus and <u>are seeing</u> the

---

15  Historical presents have received a double underlining in the examples in Greek and in English. The translations are from the ESV, but the verbs that translate a Greek historical present have been altered to a present progressive in English in order to highlight the rhetorical mismatch of semantics in the Greek. Since English may colloquially use an aoristic present **tense** for a historical present, the English present **progressive** (he is singing) is used rather than the habitual/aoristic present ("he sings") because the English progressive better shows the rhetorical clash of Greek **aspect** as well as the rhetorical clash of **tense** in these Greek contexts. Incidentally, the ESV consistently uses the English simple past (perfective) and not the English past progressive (imperfective) for the Greek historical presents. The translators recognized that the contexts did not support an imperfective understanding. Further discussion on the inability of the aspect-only theory to explain historical presents follows after list B, below.

demon-possessed man, the one who had had the
legion, sitting there, clothed and in his right mind, and
they were afraid.

Μάρκον 5·22 Καὶ <u>ἔρχεται</u> εἷς τῶν ἀρχισυναγώγων, ὀνόματι
Ἰάϊρος, καὶ ἰδὼν αὐτὸν <u>πίπτει</u> πρὸς τοὺς πόδας αὐτοῦ
Then <u>is coming</u> one of the rulers of the synagogue,
Jairus by name, and seeing him, he <u>is falling</u> at his feet

Μάρκον 5·38 καὶ <u>ἔρχονται</u> εἰς τὸν οἶκον τοῦ ἀρχισυναγώγου,
καὶ <u>θεωρεῖ</u> θόρυβον καὶ κλαίοντας καὶ ἀλαλάζοντας πολλά,
They <u>are coming</u> to the house of the ruler of the
synagogue, and Jesus <u>is seeing</u> a commotion, people
weeping and wailing loudly.

Μάρκον 5·40 καὶ κατεγέλων αὐτοῦ. αὐτὸς δὲ ἐκβαλὼν
πάντας <u>παραλαμβάνει</u> τὸν πατέρα τοῦ παιδίου καὶ τὴν
μητέρα καὶ τοὺς μετ' αὐτοῦ καὶ <u>εἰσπορεύεται</u> ὅπου ἦν τὸ
παιδίον.
And they laughed at him. But he put them all outside
and <u>is taking</u> the child's father and mother and those
who were with him and <u>is going</u> in where the child
was.

Μάρκον 6·1 Καὶ ἐξῆλθεν ἐκεῖθεν καὶ <u>ἔρχεται</u> εἰς τὴν πατρίδα
αὐτοῦ, καὶ <u>ἀκολουθοῦσιν</u> αὐτῷ οἱ μαθηταὶ αὐτοῦ. (Possibly
imperfective, but aorist reading is also good.)
He went away from there and <u>is coming</u> to his
hometown, and his disciples <u>are following</u> him.

Μάρκον 7·32 Καὶ <u>φέρουσιν</u> αὐτῷ κωφὸν καὶ μογιλάλον καὶ
<u>παρακαλοῦσιν</u> αὐτὸν
And they <u>are bringing</u> to him a man who was deaf and
had a speech impediment, and they <u>are begging</u> him to
lay his hand on him.

Μάρκον 8·22 Καὶ <u>ἔρχονται</u> εἰς Βηθσαϊδάν. Καὶ <u>φέρουσιν</u>
αὐτῷ τυφλὸν καὶ <u>παρακαλοῦσιν</u> αὐτὸν ἵνα αὐτοῦ ἅψηται.
Three historical presents!
And they <u>are coming</u> to Bethsaida. And some people
<u>are bringing</u> to him a blind man and <u>are begging</u> him
to touch him.

Μάρκον 9·2 Καὶ μετὰ ἡμέρας ἓξ <u>παραλαμβάνει</u> ὁ Ἰησοῦς
τὸν Πέτρον καὶ τὸν Ἰάκωβον καὶ τὸν Ἰωάννην καὶ <u>ἀναφέρει</u>
αὐτοὺς εἰς ὄρος ὑψηλὸν κατ’ ἰδίαν μόνους.
And after six days Jesus <u>is taking</u> with him Peter
and James and John, and <u>is leading</u> them <u>up</u> a high
mountain by themselves.

Μάρκον 10·1 Καὶ ἐκεῖθεν ἀναστὰς <u>ἔρχεται</u> εἰς τὰ ὅρια τῆς
Ἰουδαίας [καὶ] πέραν τοῦ Ἰορδάνου, καὶ <u>συμπορεύονται</u> πάλιν
ὄχλοι πρὸς αὐτόν,
And he left there and <u>is going</u> to the region of Judea
and beyond the Jordan, and crowds <u>are gathering</u> to
him again.

Μάρκον 11·7 καὶ <u>φέρουσιν</u> τὸν πῶλον πρὸς τὸν Ἰησοῦν καὶ
<u>ἐπιβάλλουσιν</u> αὐτῷ τὰ ἱμάτια αὐτῶν, καὶ ἐκάθισεν ἐπ’ αὐτόν.
And they <u>are bringing</u> the colt to Jesus and <u>are
throwing</u> their cloaks on it, and he sat on it.

Μάρκον 11·27 Καὶ <u>ἔρχονται</u> πάλιν εἰς Ἱεροσόλυμα. καὶ ἐν τῷ
ἱερῷ περιπατοῦντος αὐτοῦ <u>ἔρχονται</u> πρὸς αὐτὸν οἱ ἀρχιερεῖς
καὶ οἱ γραμματεῖς καὶ οἱ πρεσβύτεροι
And they <u>are coming</u> again to Jerusalem. And as he was
walking in the temple, the chief priests and the scribes
and the elders <u>are coming</u> to him,

Μάρκον 14·32 Καὶ <u>ἔρχονται</u> εἰς χωρίον οὗ τὸ ὄνομα
Γεθσημανὶ καὶ <u>λέγει</u> τοῖς μαθηταῖς αὐτοῦ·
And they <u>are going</u> to a place called Gethsemane. And
he <u>is saying</u> to his disciples,

Μάρκον 14·37 καὶ <u>ἔρχεται</u> καὶ <u>εὑρίσκει</u> αὐτοὺς καθεύδοντας,
καὶ <u>λέγει</u> τῷ Πέτρῳ· Three!
And he <u>is coming</u> and <u>is finding</u> them sleeping, and he
<u>is saying</u> to Peter,

Μάρκον 14·41 καὶ <u>ἔρχεται</u> τὸ τρίτον καὶ <u>λέγει</u> αὐτοῖς·
And he <u>is saying</u> the third time and <u>is saying</u> to them,

Μάρκον 15·16-17 Οἱ δὲ στρατιῶται ἀπήγαγον αὐτὸν ἔσω
τῆς αὐλῆς, ὅ ἐστιν πραιτώριον, καὶ <u>συγκαλοῦσιν</u> ὅλην τὴν
σπεῖραν. καὶ <u>ἐνδιδύσκουσιν</u> αὐτὸν πορφύραν καὶ <u>περιτιθέασιν</u>

αὐτῷ πλέξαντες ἀκάνθινον στέφανον·

And the soldiers led him away inside the palace (that is, the governor's headquarters), and they called together the whole battalion. And they <u>are clothing</u> him in a purple cloak, and twisting together a crown of thorns, they <u>are putting</u> it on him.

Μάρκον 15·20-22 καὶ ὅτε ἐνέπαιξαν αὐτῷ, ἐξέδυσαν αὐτὸν τὴν πορφύραν καὶ ἐνέδυσαν αὐτὸν τὰ ἱμάτια αὐτοῦ. Καὶ <u>ἐξάγουσιν</u> αὐτὸν ἵνα σταυρώσωσιν αὐτόν. καὶ <u>ἀγγαρεύουσιν</u> παράγοντά τινα Σίμωνα Κυρηναῖον ἐρχόμενον ἀπ' ἀγροῦ, τὸν πατέρα Ἀλεξάνδρου καὶ Ῥούφου, ἵνα ἄρῃ τὸν σταυρὸν αὐτοῦ. Καὶ <u>φέρουσιν</u> αὐτὸν ἐπὶ τὸν Γολγοθᾶν τόπον, ὅ ἐστιν μεθερμηνευόμενον Κρανίου Τόπος.

And when they had mocked him, they stripped him of the purple cloak and put his own clothes on him. And they <u>are leading</u> him out to crucify him. And they <u>are compelling</u> a passerby, Simon of Cyrene, who was coming in from the country, the father of Alexander and Rufus, to carry his cross. And they <u>are bringing</u> him to the place called Golgotha (which means Place of a Skull).

## 8.B. Historical Presents, Possibly Allowing an Imperfective Interpretation

Μάρκον 2·15 Καὶ <u>γίνεται</u> κατακεῖσθαι αὐτὸν ἐν τῇ οἰκίᾳ αὐτοῦ

And as he <u>is reclining</u> at table in his house,

Μάρκον 11·1 Καὶ ὅτε <u>ἐγγίζουσιν</u> εἰς Ἱεροσόλυμα εἰς Βηθφαγὴ καὶ Βηθανίαν πρὸς τὸ ὄρος τῶν ἐλαιῶν, <u>ἀποστέλλει</u> δύο τῶν μαθητῶν αὐτοῦ

Now when they <u>drew</u> near to Jerusalem, to Bethphage and Bethany, at the Mount of Olives, Jesus <u>is sending</u> two of his disciples and <u>said</u> to them,

Μάρκον 11·2 καὶ <u>λέγει</u> αὐτοῖς·

and <u>is saying</u> to them,

Μάρκον 14.13 καὶ <u>ἀποστέλλει</u> δύο τῶν μαθητῶν αὐτοῦ καὶ <u>λέγει</u> αὐτοῖς·

And he <u>is sending</u> two of his disciples and <u>is saying</u> to them,

Μάρκον 15.24 Καὶ <u>σταυροῦσιν</u> αὐτὸν καὶ <u>διαμερίζονται</u> τὰ ἱμάτια αὐτοῦ, βάλλοντες κλῆρον ἐπ᾽ αὐτὰ τίς τί ἄρῃ.

And they <u>are crucifying</u> him and <u>are dividing</u> his garments among them, casting lots for them, to decide what each should take.

Μάρκον 15.27 Καὶ σὺν αὐτῷ <u>σταυροῦσιν</u> δύο λῃστάς, ἕνα ἐκ δεξιῶν καὶ ἕνα ἐξ εὐωνύμων αὐτοῦ.

And with him they <u>are crucifying</u> two robbers, one on his right and one on his left.

List B was added as a foil. None of the examples require an open-ended situation and imperfective interpretation. All of them can be read just like the first list, list A.

The long list A of double historical presents that refer to an otherwise perfective context is quite surprising if one were to believe the claim that the Greek present indicative only marks aspect and not time.[16] Not only do the historical presents contravene the past time by using a traditionally viewed present tense, they also **contravene aspect**, by consistently using present imperfectives in contexts that are contextually bounded as complete and prototypically perfective. In list D below, the participles that are based on the so-called present stem (that is, the continuative, imperfective stem) are regularly and correctly used for marking open-ended, imperfective situations. This confirms what everyone has claimed about the present tense—both indicative and non-indicative—that the present tense system is prototypically imperfective. However, with the historical present structure this prototypical imperfective meaning is flagrantly contravened. Quite obviously, the historical presents

---

16  Primary protagonists for the "aspect-only" view of the Koine Greek verb include Stanley E. Porter, *Verbal Aspect in the Greek of the New Testament: With Reference to Tense and Mood*, SBG 1 (New York: Lang, 1989); Rodney J. Decker, *Temporal Deixis of the Greek Verb in the Gospel of Mark with Reference to Verbal Aspect*, SBG 10 (New York: Lang, 2001); and Constantine Campbell, *Verbal Aspect, the Indicative Mood, and Narrative: Soundings in the Greek of the New Testament*, SBG 13 (New York: Lang, 2007).

are not trying to mark prototypical aspect, since they refer to completed events within their contextual relationships. Thus, rather than support an aspect-only theory of the Greek verb, the historical presents undermine that theory since they are being used against their normal semantics.[17] Rhetorically, they go against the normal imperfective understanding and relationships of the Greek present tense. However, this study goes beyond the historical present and looks at the interaction of participles with the historical present.

## 8.C. Aorist Participles with the Historical Present

Μάρκον 2·4 καὶ μὴ δυνάμενοι προσενέγκαι αὐτῷ διὰ τὸν ὄχλον ἀπεστέγασαν τὴν στέγην ὅπου ἦν, καὶ <u>ἐξορύξαντες</u> <u>χαλῶσι</u> τὸν κράβαττον
And when they could not get near him because of the crowd, they removed the roof above him, and <u>when they had made an opening</u>,[18] they <u>are letting down</u> the bed on which the paralytic lay.

Μάρκον 2·5 καὶ <u>ἰδὼν</u> ὁ Ἰησοῦς τὴν πίστιν αὐτῶν <u>λέγει</u> τῷ παραλυτικῷ
And when Jesus <u>saw</u> their faith, he <u>is saying</u> to the paralytic,

Μάρκον 2·8 καὶ εὐθὺς <u>ἐπιγνοὺς</u> ὁ Ἰησοῦς τῷ πνεύματι αὐτοῦ ὅτι οὕτως διαλογίζονται ἐν ἑαυτοῖς <u>λέγει</u> αὐτοῖς·

---

17　See now, Steven E. Runge, "The Verbal Aspect of the Historical Present Indicative in Narrative," in *Discourse Studies and Biblical Interpretation: A Festschrift in Honor of Stephen H. Levinson*, ed. Steven E. Runge (Bellingham, WA: Logos Bible Software, 2011). Wally V. Cirafesi (*Verbal Aspect in Synoptic Parallels: On the Method and Meaning of Divergent Tense-Form Usage in the Synoptic Passion Narratives*, LBS 7 [Leiden: Brill, 2013] 81–84) does not recognize that the historical presents are aspectually mismatched to their context. He has misunderstood Runge and the difference between semantics and pragmatic function, rendering his criticism of Runge moot.

18　The aorist participles that are used with a historical present receive a single underline and the historical presents receive a double underline in Greek. The translation is the ESV with one modification. The verbs referring to a historical present are altered into English present progressives in order to reflect the imperfective aspect and present time of the Greek. Words that are added to the ESV in order to reflect the Greek have been placed in brackets.

And immediately Jesus, <u>perceiving</u> in his spirit that they thus questioned within themselves, <u>is saying</u> to them,

Μάρκον 2·17 καὶ <u>ἀκούσας</u> ὁ Ἰησοῦς <u>λέγει</u> αὐτοῖς
And when Jesus <u>heard</u> it, he <u>is saying</u> to them,

Μάρκον 3·5 καὶ <u>περιβλεψάμενος</u> αὐτοὺς μετ᾽ ὀργῆς, συλλυπούμενος ἐπὶ τῇ πωρώσει τῆς καρδίας αὐτῶν <u>λέγει</u> τῷ ἀνθρώπῳ·
And he <u>looked</u> around at them with anger, grieved at their hardness of heart, and <u>is saying</u> to the man,

Μάρκον 3·33 καὶ <u>ἀποκριθεὶς</u> αὐτοῖς <u>λέγει</u>·
And he <u>answered</u> them [<u>and is saying</u>],

Μάρκον 4·35 Καὶ <u>λέγει</u> αὐτοῖς ἐν ἐκείνῃ τῇ ἡμέρᾳ ὀψίας <u>γενομένης</u>·
On that day, when evening <u>had come</u>, he <u>is saying</u> to them,

Μάρκον 4·36 καὶ <u>ἀφέντες</u> τὸν ὄχλον <u>παραλαμβάνουσιν</u> αὐτὸν ὡς ἦν ἐν τῷ πλοίῳ,
And <u>leaving</u> the crowd, they <u>are taking</u> him with them in the boat, just as he was.

Μάρκον 5·7 καὶ <u>κράξας</u> φωνῇ μεγάλῃ <u>λέγει</u>·
And <u>crying out</u> with a loud voice, he <u>is saying</u>,

Μάρκον 5·22 Καὶ <u>ἔρχεται</u> εἷς τῶν ἀρχισυναγώγων, ὀνόματι Ἰάϊρος, καὶ <u>ἰδὼν</u> αὐτὸν <u>πίπτει</u> πρὸς τοὺς πόδας αὐτοῦ
Then <u>is coming</u> one of the rulers of the synagogue, Jairus by name, and <u>seeing</u> him, he <u>is falling</u> at his feet

Μάρκον 5·36 ὁ δὲ Ἰησοῦς <u>παρακούσας</u> τὸν λόγον λαλούμενον <u>λέγει</u> τῷ ἀρχισυναγώγῳ·
But <u>overhearing</u> what they said, Jesus <u>is saying</u> to the ruler of the synagogue

Μάρκον 5·39 καὶ <u>εἰσελθὼν</u> <u>λέγει</u> αὐτοῖς·
And when he <u>had entered</u>, he <u>is saying</u> to them,

Μάρκον 5·40 καὶ κατεγέλων αὐτοῦ. αὐτὸς δὲ <u>ἐκβαλὼν</u> πάντας <u>παραλαμβάνει</u> τὸν πατέρα τοῦ παιδίου καὶ τὴν μητέρα καὶ τοὺς μετ᾽ αὐτοῦ καὶ <u>εἰσπορεύεται</u> ὅπου ἦν τὸ παιδίον.

And they laughed at him. But he <u>put</u> them all outside and <u>is taking</u> the child's father and mother and those who were with him and <u>is going in</u> where the child was.

Μάρκον 5·41 καὶ <u>κρατήσας</u> τῆς χειρὸς τοῦ παιδίου <u>λέγει</u> αὐτῇ·

<u>Taking</u> her by the hand he <u>is saying</u> to her,

Μάρκον 6·48 καὶ <u>ἰδὼν</u> αὐτοὺς βασανιζομένους ἐν τῷ ἐλαύνειν, ἦν γὰρ ὁ ἄνεμος ἐναντίος αὐτοῖς, περὶ τετάρτην φυλακὴν τῆς νυκτὸς <u>ἔρχεται</u> πρὸς αὐτοὺς περιπατῶν ἐπὶ τῆς θαλάσσης

And he <u>saw</u> that they were making headway painfully, for the wind was against them. And about the fourth watch of the night he <u>is coming</u> to them, walking on the sea.

Μάρκον 7·1 Καὶ <u>συνάγονται</u> πρὸς αὐτὸν οἱ Φαρισαῖοι καί τινες τῶν γραμματέων <u>ἐλθόντες</u> ἀπὸ Ἱεροσολύμων.

Now when the Pharisees <u>are gathering</u> to him, with some of the scribes who <u>had come</u> from Jerusalem,

Μάρκον 8·1 Ἐν ἐκείναις ταῖς ἡμέραις πάλιν πολλοῦ ὄχλου ὄντος καὶ μὴ ἐχόντων τί φάγωσιν, <u>προσκαλεσάμενος</u> τοὺς μαθητὰς <u>λέγει</u> αὐτοῖς·

In those days, when again a great crowd had gathered, and they had nothing to eat, he <u>called</u> his disciples to him and <u>is saying</u> to them,

Μάρκον 8·12 καὶ <u>ἀναστενάξας</u> τῷ πνεύματι αὐτοῦ <u>λέγει</u>·

And he <u>sighed</u> deeply in his spirit and <u>is saying</u>,

Μάρκον 8·17 καὶ <u>γνοὺς</u> <u>λέγει</u> αὐτοῖς·

And Jesus, <u>aware</u> of this, <u>is saying</u> to them,

Μάρκον 9·5 καὶ <u>ἀποκριθεὶς</u> ὁ Πέτρος <u>λέγει</u> τῷ Ἰησοῦ·

And Peter [<u>answered</u> and] <u>is saying</u> to Jesus,

Μάρκον 9·19 ὁ δὲ <u>ἀποκριθεὶς</u> αὐτοῖς <u>λέγει</u>·

And he <u>answered</u> them [and <u>is saying</u>]

Μάρκον 10·1 Καὶ ἐκεῖθεν <u>ἀναστὰς</u> <u>ἔρχεται</u> εἰς τὰ ὅρια τῆς
Ἰουδαίας [καὶ] πέραν τοῦ Ἰορδάνου, καὶ <u>συμπορεύονται</u> πάλιν
ὄχλοι πρὸς αὐτόν,
And he <u>left</u> there and <u>is going</u> to the region of Judea
and beyond the Jordan, and crowds <u>are gathering</u> to
him again.

Μάρκον 10·23 Καὶ <u>περιβλεψάμενος</u> ὁ Ἰησοῦς <u>λέγει</u> τοῖς
μαθηταῖς αὐτοῦ·
And Jesus <u>looked around</u> and <u>is saying</u> to his disciples,

Μάρκον 10·24 οἱ δὲ μαθηταὶ ἐθαμβοῦντο ἐπὶ τοῖς λόγοις
αὐτοῦ. ὁ δὲ Ἰησοῦς πάλιν <u>ἀποκριθεὶς</u> <u>λέγει</u> αὐτοῖς·
And the disciples were amazed at his words. But Jesus
[<u>answered</u> and] <u>is saying</u> to them again,

Μάρκον 10·27 <u>ἐμβλέψας</u> αὐτοῖς ὁ Ἰησοῦς <u>λέγει</u>·
Jesus <u>looked</u> at them and <u>is saying</u>,

Μάρκον 10·42 καὶ <u>προσκαλεσάμενος</u> αὐτοὺς ὁ Ἰησοῦς <u>λέγει</u>
αὐτοῖς·
And Jesus <u>called</u> them to him and <u>is saying</u> to them,

Μάρκον 11·21 καὶ <u>ἀναμνησθεὶς</u> ὁ Πέτρος <u>λέγει</u> αὐτῷ·
And Peter <u>remembered</u> and <u>is saying</u> to him,

Μάρκον 11·22 καὶ <u>ἀποκριθεὶς</u> ὁ Ἰησοῦς <u>λέγει</u> αὐτοῖς·
And Jesus <u>answered</u> them [and <u>is saying</u>],

Μάρκον 11·33 καὶ <u>ἀποκριθέντες</u> τῷ Ἰησοῦ <u>λέγουσιν</u>·
So they <u>answered</u> Jesus [and <u>are saying</u>],

Μάρκον 12·14 καὶ <u>ἐλθόντες</u> <u>λέγουσιν</u> αὐτῷ·
And they <u>came</u> and <u>are saying</u> to him,

Μάρκον 14·17 Καὶ ὀψίας <u>γενομένης</u> <u>ἔρχεται</u> μετὰ τῶν δώδεκα.
And when it <u>was</u> evening, he <u>is coming</u> with the twelve.

Μάρκον 14·45 καὶ <u>ἐλθὼν</u> εὐθὺς <u>προσελθὼν</u> αὐτῷ <u>λέγει</u>·
And when he <u>came</u>, he <u>went</u> up <u>to</u> him at once and <u>is</u>
<u>saying</u>,

? Μάρκον 14·63 ὁ δὲ ἀρχιερεὺς <u>διαρρήξας</u> τοὺς χιτῶνας αὐτοῦ <u>λέγει</u>·

And the high priest <u>tore</u> his garments and <u>is saying</u>,

Μάρκον 14·67 καὶ <u>ἰδοῦσα</u> τὸν Πέτρον θερμαινόμενον <u>ἐμβλέψασα</u> αὐτῷ <u>λέγει</u>·

and <u>seeing</u> Peter warming himself, she <u>looked</u> at him and <u>is saying</u>,

Μάρκον 15·2 Καὶ ἐπηρώτησεν αὐτὸν ὁ Πιλᾶτος· σὺ εἶ ὁ βασιλεὺς τῶν Ἰουδαίων; ὁ δὲ <u>ἀποκριθεὶς</u> αὐτῷ <u>λέγει</u>·

And Pilate asked him, "Are you the King of the Jews?" And he <u>answered</u> him [and <u>is saying</u>],

Μάρκον 16·2 καὶ λίαν πρωῒ τῇ μιᾷ τῶν σαββάτων <u>ἔρχονται</u> ἐπὶ τὸ μνημεῖον <u>ἀνατείλαντος</u> τοῦ ἡλίου.

And very early on the first day of the week, when the sun <u>had risen</u>, they <u>are going</u> to the tomb.

Μάρκον 16·4 καὶ <u>ἀναβλέψασαι</u> <u>θεωροῦσιν</u> ὅτι ἀποκεκύλισται ὁ λίθος·

And <u>looking up</u>, they <u>are seeing</u> that the stone had been rolled back

The list of aorist participles above with the historical present is remarkable. The participles are all appropriately used to mark perfective aspect, regardless of the governing historical present. The aorist participles all preserve their perfective semantics. This is contrary to the examples of double historical presents in list A.[19]

## 8.D. Continuative Participles with a Historical Present

Μάρκον 1·40 Καὶ <u>ἔρχεται</u> πρὸς αὐτὸν λεπρὸς <u>παρακαλῶν</u> αὐτὸν [καὶ <u>γονυπετῶν</u>] καὶ <u>λέγων</u> αὐτῷ

---

19  The translations provided are from the ESV and partially cover over the facts about the Greek aorist participles. The simple past English translations do in fact reflect a perfective event, while sometimes participles are used in ESV because of the ambiguity inherent in the English language. For example, 16:4 "looking up" reflects a perfective event; the looking up was complete as the Greek makes clear, although this may be expressed in English with a participle.

And a leper <u>is coming</u> to him, <u>imploring</u> him, and <u>kneeling</u> said to him,[20]

Μάρκον 2·3 καὶ <u>ἔρχονται</u> <u>φέροντες</u> πρὸς αὐτὸν παραλυτικὸν
And they <u>are coming</u>, <u>bringing</u> to him a paralytic.

Μάρκον 2·4 καὶ μὴ <u>δυνάμενοι</u> προσενέγκαι αὐτῷ διὰ τὸν ὄχλον ἀπεστέγασαν τὴν στέγην ὅπου ἦν, καὶ ἐξορύξαντες <u>χαλῶσι</u> τὸν κράβαττον ὅπου ὁ παραλυτικὸς κατέκειτο.
(Mark 2:4 is added for excessive completion, though the continuative participle only provides the setting to the verb ἀπεστέγασαν, which is not a historical present)
And when they <u>could not</u> get near him because of the crowd, they removed the roof above him, and when they had made an opening, they <u>are letting down</u> the bed on which the paralytic lay.

Μάρκον 3·5 καὶ περιβλεψάμενος αὐτοὺς μετ᾽ ὀργῆς, <u>συλλυπούμενος</u> ἐπὶ τῇ πωρώσει τῆς καρδίας αὐτῶν <u>λέγει</u> τῷ ἀνθρώπῳ·
And he looked around at them with anger, <u>grieved</u> at their hardness of heart, and <u>is saying</u> to the man,

Μάρκον 5·35 Ἔτι αὐτοῦ <u>λαλοῦντος</u> <u>ἔρχονται</u> ἀπὸ τοῦ ἀρχισυναγώγου
While he <u>was</u> still <u>speaking</u>, there <u>are coming</u> from the ruler's house,

Μάρκον 8·1 Ἐν ἐκείναις ταῖς ἡμέραις πάλιν πολλοῦ ὄχλου <u>ὄντος</u> καὶ μὴ <u>ἐχόντων</u> τί φάγωσιν, προσκαλεσάμενος τοὺς μαθητὰς <u>λέγει</u> αὐτοῖς·
In those days, when again a great crowd <u>had gathered</u>, and they <u>had</u> nothing to eat, he called his disciples to him and <u>is saying</u> to them,

---

20 In List D the ESV translation is marked with a double underline to mark a historical present in the Greek source. These translations of historical presents have been edited from simple past tenses in English into a present progressive in order to reflect the Greek rhetorical style. The ESV translations of the Greek continuative participles are unedited but are marked with a single underline.

Μάρκον 11·27 Καὶ ἔρχονται πάλιν εἰς Ἱεροσόλυμα. καὶ ἐν τῷ ἱερῷ <u>περιπατοῦντος</u> αὐτοῦ <u>ἔρχονται</u> πρὸς αὐτὸν οἱ ἀρχιερεῖς καὶ οἱ γραμματεῖς καὶ οἱ πρεσβύτεροι

And they came again to Jerusalem. And as he <u>was walking</u> in the temple, the chief priests and the scribes and the elders <u>are coming</u> to him,

Μάρκον 13·1 Καὶ <u>ἐκπορευομένου</u> αὐτοῦ ἐκ τοῦ ἱεροῦ <u>λέγει</u> αὐτῷ εἷς τῶν μαθητῶν αὐτοῦ·

And as he <u>came</u> out of the temple, one of his disciples <u>is saying</u> to him,

Μάρκον 14·43 Καὶ εὐθὺς ἔτι αὐτοῦ <u>λαλοῦντος</u> <u>παραγίνεται</u> Ἰούδας εἷς τῶν δώδεκα καὶ μετ᾽ αὐτοῦ ὄχλος μετὰ μαχαιρῶν καὶ ξύλων παρὰ τῶν ἀρχιερέων καὶ τῶν γραμματέων καὶ τῶν πρεσβυτέρων.

And immediately, while he <u>was</u> still <u>speaking</u>, Judas <u>is coming</u>, one of the twelve, and with him a crowd with swords and clubs, from the chief priests and the scribes and the elders.

Μάρκον 14·66 Καὶ <u>ὄντος</u> τοῦ Πέτρου κάτω ἐν τῇ αὐλῇ <u>ἔρχεται</u> μία τῶν παιδισκῶν τοῦ ἀρχιερέως

And as Peter <u>was</u> below in the courtyard, one of the servant girls of the high priest <u>is coming</u>,

The continuative participles (that is, imperfective participles, a.k.a. present participles) are all correctly used to signal open-ended situations by using imperfective aspect. The event of the participle does not include the end-point of its activity and the participle overlaps in time with the event of the main verb. For example, Mark 5:35; 8:1; 11:27; 13:1; 14:43; and 14:66 use participles to describe an open-ended setting in which following events are then narrated that are assumed to be complete and perfective within the stipulated context. Remarkably, none of the imperfective participles refer to bounded, complete contexts in the way that double historical presents in list A do. List C shows that aorist participles with historical presents correctly mark their aspect, and list D shows that continuative participles correctly mark their aspect. But no continuative participles mimic the historical present in mismatching an imperfective verb with a bounded, complete context.

One might possibly argue that the participles in the one case, Mark 1:40 παρακαλῶν and λέγων, can be interpreted to occur after the main verb. But if so, that would make ἔρχεται a completed, perfective imperfective, which reinforces the points being made in this study. However, continuative participles and verbs introducing speech that follow a previous verb can be interpreted as an extension of the situation in the main verb and thus as overlapping the main verb. This is similar to Mark 14:13 "He sent and said/he sends and says."

## 8.E. Historical Presents with a Participle Following the Verb[21]

Μάρκον 1·40 Καὶ <u>ἔρχεται</u> πρὸς αὐτὸν λεπρὸς <u>παρακαλῶν</u> αὐτὸν [καὶ γονυπετῶν] καὶ <u>λέγων</u> αὐτῷ
And a leper <u>is coming</u> to him, <u>imploring</u> him, and <u>kneeling</u> said to him,

Μάρκον 4·35 Καὶ <u>λέγει</u> αὐτοῖς ἐν ἐκείνῃ τῇ ἡμέρᾳ ὀψίας <u>γενομένης·</u>
On that day, when evening <u>had come</u>, he <u>is saying</u> to them,

Μάρκον 6·48 καὶ ἰδὼν αὐτοὺς βασανιζομένους ἐν τῷ ἐλαύνειν, ἦν γὰρ ὁ ἄνεμος ἐναντίος αὐτοῖς, περὶ τετάρτην φυλακὴν τῆς νυκτὸς <u>ἔρχεται</u> πρὸς αὐτοὺς <u>περιπατῶν</u> ἐπὶ τῆς θαλάσσης
And he saw that they were making headway painfully, for the wind was against them. And about the fourth watch of the night he <u>is coming</u> to them, <u>walking</u> on the sea.

Μάρκον 7·1 Καὶ <u>συνάγονται</u> πρὸς αὐτὸν οἱ Φαρισαῖοι καὶ τινες τῶν γραμματέων <u>ἐλθόντες</u> ἀπὸ Ἱεροσολύμων.
Now when the Pharisees <u>are gathering</u> to him, with some of the scribes who <u>had come</u> from Jerusalem,

---

21  Examples with a following λέγων before direct speech have not been included in order to save space: Mark 5:23; 5:35; 10:35; 10:49. Mark 1:40 was included because of other participles after the historical present.

Μάρκον 15·16-17 16 Οἱ δὲ στρατιῶται ἀπήγαγον αὐτὸν
ἔσω τῆς αὐλῆς, ὅ ἐστιν πραιτώριον, καὶ <u>συγκαλοῦσιν</u> ὅλην
τὴν σπεῖραν. 17 καὶ <u>ἐνδιδύσκουσιν</u> αὐτὸν πορφύραν καὶ
<u>περιτιθέασιν</u> αὐτῷ <u>πλέξαντες</u> ἀκάνθινον στέφανον·
And the soldiers led him away inside the palace (that
is, the governor's headquarters), and they <u>are calling</u>
<u>together</u> the whole battalion. And they <u>are clothing</u>
him in a purple cloak, and <u>twisting</u> together a crown
of thorns, they <u>are putting</u> it <u>on</u> him.

Μάρκον 15·24 Καὶ <u>σταυροῦσιν</u> αὐτὸν καὶ <u>διαμερίζονται</u> τὰ
ἱμάτια αὐτοῦ, <u>βάλλοντες</u> κλῆρον ἐπ' αὐτὰ τίς τί ἄρῃ.
And they <u>are crucifying</u> him and <u>are dividing</u> his
garments among them, <u>casting</u> lots for them, to decide
what each should take.

Μάρκον 16·2 καὶ λίαν πρωῒ τῇ μιᾷ τῶν σαββάτων <u>ἔρχονται</u>
ἐπὶ τὸ μνημεῖον <u>ἀνατείλαντος</u> τοῦ ἡλίου.
And very early on the first day of the week, when the
sun <u>had risen</u>, they <u>are going</u> to the tomb.

For the full picture, list E provides cases where a participle follows a historical present. The aorist participles like 4:35; 7:1; 15:17;
and 16:2 are all naturally interpreted in their prototypical perfective
sense. They all occurred prior to the historical present main verb.

On the other hand, the continuative participles at 1:40; 6:48; and
15:24 all overlap or extend from the historical present main verb.
Thus, they, too, are prototypical imperfectives.

The participles preserve and use their aspect exactly as would be
expected. The participles that are used with the historical present
in lists C, D, and E, mark aspect correctly and do not contravene aspectual semantics or expectations.

This situation suggests that the primary reason for using the historical present tense is to contravene tense—to use a present tense
finite verb against the grain, in the past. The examples in list A of
double occurrences of historical presents show that the historical
presents did not bother to signal the relative aspects of serially complete events. The historical present allowed knowledge of the real
world to let the audience conclude that one event was completed before a second perfective event. However, this refusal to mark aspect

occurs only with the finite verb historical presents, does not occur with the continuative (present) participles. When participles are added to the sentence the aspect of the participle is always signaled correctly. Thus, fullest consistency is achieved if the historical present is interpreted as primarily contravening tense for rhetorical effect. The contravention of aspect in the historical presents is a secondary accompaniment. Aspect is always preserved correctly in the rest of the sentence and with participles, so it is the tense side of the historical present that appears to carry the primary rhetorical effect.

Looking from the other direction, if the present tense indicatives were only aspects as some have alleged, and if they were being used simply to contradict aspect, that is, using an imperfective aspect in a contextually complete context, one would expect to find some examples of continuative participles that also contradict the aspect of the situation. After all, list A shows that repeated contraventions of historical present aspect were acceptable and used. But there are no imperfective/continuative participles contravening aspect. **Zero.** Thus, one may conclude that the historical present is a rhetorical effect that is primarily based on a mismatch of time. The mismatch of aspect with a historical present indicative is an accompaniment to the rhetorical and purposeful mismatch of time.[22]

In sum, Greek participles provide a mechanism for signaling relative prominence between clauses in a sentence by allowing the more prominent verb to be recorded as a finite verb.

Participles rank the relative prominence of a clause under a main verb.

---

22 Although aspectual dissonance may be an accompaniment to the dissonance of time in a historical present, it may also be something of a necessary or preferred condition. Albert Rijksbaron commented that the historical present is limited to telic verb phrases (verbs with a natural endpoint) and does not occur with stative verbs: "The historic present is only found with terminative (telic) verbs, not with stative (atelic) verbs" (Albert Rijksbaron, *The Syntax and Semantics of the Verb in Classical Greek: An Introduction*, 3rd ed. [Chicago: University of Chicago Press, 2006], 24 n. 1). It is only with telic verbs that the perception of aspectual incompatibility becomes perceptible.

Participles also preserve their aspectual semantics, even when subordinate to a historical present main verb. (Historical presents rhetorically contravene time, primarily, and aspect, secondarily.)[23]

## BIBLIOGRAPHY

Campbell, Constantine. *Verbal Aspect, the Indicative Mood, and Narrative: Soundings in the Greek of the New Testament.* SBG 13. New York: Lang, 2007.

Cirafesi, Wally V. *Verbal Aspect in Synoptic Parallels: On the Method and Meaning of Divergent Tense-Form Usage in the Synoptic Passion Narratives.* LBS 7. Leiden: Brill, 2013.

Decker, Rodney J. *Temporal Deixis of the Greek Verb in the Gospel of Mark with Reference to Verbal Aspect.* SBG 10. New York: Lang, 2001.

Hawkins, John C. *Horae Synopticae, Contributions to the Study of the Synoptic Problem.* 2nd ed., rev. and supplemented. Oxford: The Clarendon Press, 1909. Repr., Grand Rapids: Baker, 1968.

Porter, Stanley E. *Verbal Aspect in the Greek of the New Testament: With Reference to Tense and Mood.* SBG 1. New York: Lang, 1989.

Rijksbaron, Albert. *The Syntax and Semantics of the Verb in Classical Greek: An Introduction.* 3rd ed. Chicago: University of Chicago Press, 2006.

Runge, Steven E. "The Verbal Aspect of the Historical Present Indicative in Narrative." Pages 191–223 in *Discourse Studies and Biblical Interpretation: A Festschrift in Honor of Stephen H. Levinson.* Edited by Steven E. Runge. Bellingham, WA: Logos, 2011.

Weinreich, Harald. *Tempus: Besprochene und erzählte Welt.* SLi 16. Stuttgart: Kohlhammer, 1964.

Wilson, Deirdre, and Dan Sperber. "Relevance Theory." Pages 607–32 in *The Handbook of Pragmatics.* Edited by Laurence R. Horn and Gregory L. Ward. BHL 16. Oxford: Blackwell, 2004.

---

23  And as an unintended side benefit, it is the relationship of participles with historical presents that reveals the dominant rhetorical feature of historical presents. Historical presents mismatch their semantics to a context, both in time and in aspect, and they do so for rhetorical effect. However, it is the feature of time that is the dominant rhetorical mismatch with historical presents and any accompanying participles are not allowed to mismatch their aspectual semantics.

CHAPTER 9

# Functions of Copula-Participle Combinations ("Periphrastics")

STEPHEN H. LEVINSOHN

SIL INTERNATIONAL

## 1. INTRODUCTION

The term "periphrastic" is used in Classical and New Testament Greek principally to refer to combinations of the copula εἰμί and an anarthrous participle that are judged to be "a *round-about* way of saying what could be expressed by a single verb."[1] The participle may be present (with imperfective aspect) or perfect.[2]

Rijksbaron considers the combination of the participle and εἰμί together as "an 'analytic' or 'complex verb phrase'."[3] Since they can occur in either order and can be separated by other constituents,

---

1   Daniel B. Wallace, *Greek Grammar Beyond the Basics: An Exegetical Syntax of the New Testament* (Grand Rapids: Zondervan, 1996), 647 (emphasis original).

2   Albert Rijksbaron (*The Syntax and Semantics of the Verb in Classical Greek: An Introduction*, 3rd ed. [Chicago: University of Chicago Press, 2006], 128) gives two examples of the copula with an aor. ptc., but writes, "In this puzzling (and rather rare) construction the participle can perhaps best be taken adjectivally." Stanley E. Porter (*Idioms of the Greek New Testament*, BLG 2 [Sheffield: JSOT Press, 1992], 49) reaches a similar conclusion for New Testament Greek. This leads Constantine R. Campbell (*Basics of Verbal Aspect in Biblical Greek* [Grand Rapids: Zondervan, 2008], 118) to write, "Periphrastics in the New Testament involve only the present and perfect participles."

3   Rijksbaron, *Syntax and Semantics*, 126.

however, I shall refrain from using the term "phrase" to refer to the combination.

Definitions of what constitutes a "periphrastic verbal construction" typically refer to the "*combination of a form of the auxiliary verb εἰμί and a participle.*"[4] However, Porter's subsequent assertion, that "it is useful to keep in mind that no elements may intervene between the auxiliary verb and the participle except for those which complete or directly modify the participle (not the verb εἰμί),"[5] implies that such constructions actually consist of εἰμί and a participial *clause*.

Porter would classify Luke 15:1a (Ἦσαν δὲ αὐτῷ ἐγγίζοντες πάντες οἱ τελῶναι καὶ οἱ ἁμαρτωλοὶ "Now all the tax collectors and sinners were coming near him")[6] as periphrastic, since the indirect object αὐτῷ modifies the participle ἐγγίζοντες, while the subject πάντες οἱ τελῶναι καὶ οἱ ἁμαρτωλοὶ follows it.

In contrast, he considers Luke 1:21a (Καὶ ἦν ὁ λαὸς προσδοκῶν τὸν Ζαχαρίαν) not to be periphrastic, as "the grammatical subject is placed between the auxiliary verb and the participle";[7] hence, his translation, "the people were there, expecting Zacharias."[8] However, "most grammarians assume that several words, including part or all of the subject (against Porter 1994:45), *can* intervene."[9] So, since reference had already been made to "the whole assembly of the people" in 1:10, it is unlikely that Luke was positing their presence in 1:21.[10] A rendering such as "the people were waiting for Zechariah" seems much more plausible.

---

4   Porter, *Idioms*, 45 (emphasis original).
5   Ibid., 45.
6   Unless otherwise indicated, translations are taken from the NRSV (adapted, as necessary, to more closely reflect the Greek).
7   Ibid., 46.
8   Ibid., 45–46.
9   Nicholas A. Bailey, "Thetic Constructions in Koine Greek" (PhD diss., Vrije Universiteit Amsterdam, 2009), 199 (emphasis original). See, for example, H. E. Dana and Julius R. Mantey, *A Manual Grammar of the Greek New Testament* (New York: Macmillan, 1957), §203; Maximillian Zerwick, SJ, *Biblical Greek Illustrated by Examples*, English ed. adapted from the 4th Latin ed. by Joseph Smith, SJ [Rome: Biblical Institute Press, 1963], §362.
10  Bailey, "Thetic Constructions," 199 n. 329.

My own research on constituent order of combinations of a copula and a participle in the Synoptics and Acts[11] concluded that the default order in *topic-comment* structures involving the combination was: εἰμί-(subject)-participial clause.

This led me to parse Luke 1:21a as follows:

| Copula | Subject | / | Participial Clause |
|--------|---------|---|--------------------|
| Καὶ ἦν | ὁ λαὸς | / | προσδοκῶν τὸν Ζαχαρίαν |

The subject of the above clause, ὁ λαός, is the topic about which the comment προσδοκῶν τὸν Ζαχαρίαν is made. When a subject is topical, it never carries primary stress in oral English:[12] "Meanwhile the people were WAIting for Zechariah" (NIV).[13]

The same paper went on to discuss the significance of preposing a topical subject to before the copula, as in Luke 5:16 (αὐτὸς δὲ ἦν ὑποχωρῶν ἐν ταῖς ἐρήμοις καὶ προσευχόμενος "But he would withdraw to deserted places and pray").[14] In a later seminar, I also considered the postposing of topical subjects to after the participle, as in Mark 10:32 (καὶ ἦν προάγων αὐτοὺς ὁ Ἰησοῦς "and Jesus was walking ahead of them").[15]

---

11  Stephen H. Levinsohn, "Constituent Order in and Usages of εἰμί: Participle Combinations in the Synoptics and Acts," paper presented at the July 2013 meeting of the International Meeting of the SBL, St Andrews, Scotland, and at the Congress of the International Syriac Language Project in Munich, Germany, August 2013), 11, 3.

12  Knud Lambrecht, *Information Structure and Sentence Form: Topic, Focus, and the Mental Representations of Discourse Referents*, CSL (Cambridge: Cambridge University Press, 1994), 234. See also Matt 26:43; Mark 1:6, 1:33 (NA28), 2:18, 6:52, 14:4 (NA28), 14:40, 15:26; Luke 2:33, 8:40, 9:18 (NA28), 11:1, 12:35, 18:34, 22:69; Acts 12:6, 19:32. Acts 26:26 is discussed in §3. Luke 3:23 (with a discontinuous subject [NA28]) is considered below.

13  The position of the primary accent in Luke 1:21 and 5:17 has been checked against the dramatized recording of the NIV that is available at biblegateway.com//resources/audio and is indicated by capitalization of the stressed syllable.

14  "Most subjects that precede εἰμί signal a switch of topic, though some indicate a renewal of attention, following a discontinuity in the flow of the discourse or in connection with a new point" (Levinsohn, "Constituent Order," 5). Preposed topical subjects are underlined in this paper.

15  "When presenting an **event**, ... postposing the subject typically selects from the cast of active participants the one who is the centre of attention for the next part of the story. It's like saying, 'Fix your attention on this character!'"

*Thetic* constructions do not involve topical subjects. Rather, their subjects are focal as their referents are presented to the scene, as in Luke 5:17 (καὶ ἦσαν καθήμενοι Φαρισαῖοι καὶ νομοδιδάσκαλοι). In oral English, the subject of such constructions carries primary stress: "Pharisees and teachers of the LAW were sitting near by" (NRSV).[16]

Bailey notes that "thetic sentences like that in Luke 5:17 (introducing 'Pharisees and law-teachers') can be judged to be periphrastic on more or less constituent order grounds alone."[17] When a construction is thetic but the subject is placed between the copula and the participle, in contrast, the subject does not feature as an argument in the next clause and/or the participial clause is adjectival.[18] In the case of Luke 8:32 (Ἦν δὲ ἐκεῖ ἀγέλη χοίρων ἱκανῶν βοσκομένη ἐν τῷ ὄρει [NA28]), for instance, GNB treats the participial clause as adjectival: "There was a large herd of pigs nearby, feeding on a hillside"[19] and the herd of pigs does not feature again until the final clause of the sentence (καὶ παρεκάλεσαν αὐτὸν ἵνα ἐπιτρέψῃ αὐτοῖς εἰς ἐκείνους εἰσελθεῖν "and they begged him to let them enter those [pigs]").

A number of grammarians have listed criteria for distinguishing periphrastic participles from those that function as predicate adjectives (e.g., Boyer,[20] Bailey[21] and Johnson[22]). Turner writes, "It is

---

   (Stephen H. Levinsohn, "Constituent Order and 'Emphasis' in the Greek New Testament" [Seminar given at Tyndale House, Cambridge, January 2014], §4) (emphasis original).

16  Lambrecht, *Information Structure*, 234–35. See also Luke 15:1 and Acts 2:5 (Bailey, "Thetic Constructions," 200).

17  Bailey, "Thetic Constructions," 200 (emphasis original).

18  "When the participle is independent, it presumably always follows the thetic subject" (Ibid.).

19  "We can argue that in Luke 8:32 'there' pairs with εἰμί and 'on the hill' with the participial" (Ibid., 205, emphasis original). The same arguments can be applied to the parallel passages (Matt 8:30, Mark 5:11). See also Mark 3:1; Luke 6:43, 12:52, 17:35, 23:53. Matt 27:61 is similar, though Bailey (ibid., 160–61) argues that it is not thetic, because they were introduced to the scene in 27:56. Bailey (ibid., 204) considers Acts 19:14 (NA28) to have narrow focus, answering the question, "Who did this?"

20  Boyer, J. L., "The Classification of Participles: A Statistical Study." *GTJ* 5 (1984), 167.

21  Bailey, "Thetic Constructions," 199–206.

22  "Prototypical periphrastic imperfects ... show an agent, located spatially, in the midst of an activity at a referential time" (Carl E. Johnson, "A Discourse Analysis of the Periphrastic Imperfect in the Greek New Testament Writings of Luke" [PhD diss., University of Texas at Arlington, 2010], 136).

well to note that in true periphrastic tenses the copula keeps very close to the participle."[23] However, Bailey asserts, "Constituent order is usually not very helpful in identifying the periphrastic construction"[24] unless "the subject follows the participle,"[25] as in Luke 5:17 (above). "More important than arguments based on constituent order," he continues, "are ones that explain why a periphrastic form would be used, or not used, in a given context. Such arguments explain the function of forms."[26]

The functions of constructions that are judged to be periphrastic are best determined by comparing them with the equivalent simple ("synthetic"[27]) forms. So, periphrastics with present participles are best compared with simple imperfective forms (presents and imperfects), while periphrastics with perfect participles are best compared with simple perfects and pluperfects. I consider these two types in turn (excluding examples in which the participle precedes the copula, as these are discussed in §4). To avoid prejudging the issue as to which combinations of a copula and a participle are periphrastic and which are not, I shall use the terms copular imperfective and copular perfect.

## 2. SIMPLE AND COPULAR IMPERFECTIVES[28]

Cross-linguistically, if a language has two imperfectives and one of them involves the copula, the norm is for the copular form to be more *stative* than the other.[29] So, for Greek, the combination of a copula and a participle can serve "to emphasize the adjectival

---

23  Nigel Turner, *Grammar of New Testament Greek: Vol.3; Syntax* (T&T Clark, 1963), 89.
24  Bailey, "Thetic Constructions," 199.
25  Ibid., 200.
26  Ibid., 201.
27  Klaas Bentein, "The Periphrastic Perfect in Ancient Greek: A Diachronic Mental Space Analysis." *TPhS* 110 (2012), 171.
28  The following paragraphs are taken more or less verbatim from Levinsohn, "Constituent Order and 'Emphasis,'" §5.
29  In Chinese, for example, "*-zhe*, a stative imperfective ... imposes a stative coloration on non-stative situations" (Carlota S. Smith, *The Parameter of Aspect*, 2nd ed., SLP 43 [Dordrecht: Kluwer, 1997], 77).

[stative] idea inherent in the ptc. rather than the concept of action expressed by the finite verb."[30]

Turner asks, "What possible distinction can there be ... between ἐν τῷ εἶναι αὐτὸν προσευχόμενον and ἐν τῷ προσεύχεσθαι αὐτὸν in Luke 9:18, 29?"[31] The distinction is a stative-active one. The copular form (9:18) implies that Jesus was in a state of prayer without suggesting that he was actually praying when he questioned his disciples (an unlikely scenario!). In contrast, the simple infinitive (9:29) is consistent with him actually praying ("while he was praying"–an action) when the appearance of his face changed.

The copular imperfective is particularly suitable for presenting iterative events,[32] as its stative nature allows the actor to be portrayed as performing the action from time to time during the period envisaged, rather than continuously. So, in Luke 4:44 (καὶ ἦν κηρύσσων εἰς τὰς συναγωγὰς τῆς Ἰουδαίας "So he continued proclaiming the message in the synagogues of Judea"), the copular form is an appropriate way of conveying that Jesus was preaching regularly in the synagogues without suggesting that that was the only thing he was doing during that time.

Both imperfectives occur in Acts 12:5 (ὁ μὲν οὖν Πέτρος ἐτηρεῖτο ἐν τῇ φυλακῇ· προσευχὴ δὲ ἦν ἐκτενῶς γινομένη ὑπὸ τῆς ἐκκλησίας πρὸς τὸν θεὸν περὶ αὐτοῦ [NA28] "While Peter was kept in prison, the church prayed fervently to God for him"). The simple one (ἐτηρεῖτο) is consistent with Peter being kept continuously in the prison. The copular form (ἦν ... γινομένη), being more stative, suggests that, while

---

30  BDAG εἰμί §11.f. "It is usually the descriptive imperfect that uses the periphrastic form" (Archibald Thomas Robertson, *A Grammar of the Greek New Testament in the Light of Historical Research* [New York: Harper, 1931], 888). Chrys C. Caragounis (*The Development of Greek and the New Testament: Morphology, Syntax, Phonology, and Textual Transmission*, WUNT 167 [Tübingen: Mohr Siebeck, 2004], 177) states that, in the New Testament, periphrastics mostly "stress the idea of linearity" and cites Luke 5:17 as an example. *BDF* state (§353), "The reason for periphrasis is the emphasis on duration," but do not indicate whether the duration is stative or active.

31  Turner, *Syntax*, 87.

32  Buist M. Fanning (*Verbal Aspect in New Testament Greek*, OTM [Oxford: Clarendon Press, 1990], 315) refers to the "*customary*, general, or iterative sense" when "the imperfect periphrastic denotes a generalized multiple occurrence or one which is characteristic of a broad period" (emphasis original).

prayer was being repeatedly offered for him, it may not have been continual, around the clock prayer.[33]

In Luke 4:31–32 (καὶ ἦν διδάσκων αὐτοὺς ἐν τοῖς σάββασιν· καὶ ἐξεπλήσσοντο ἐπὶ τῇ διδαχῇ αὐτοῦ "and was teaching them on the sabbath. They were astounded at his teaching"), the copular imperfective precedes the simple one. Commentators disagree as to whether ἐν τοῖς σάββασιν refers to a single Sabbath (the one when the events of 4:33–37 took place) or to several Sabbaths.[34] If the reference is taken as plural, then, as in 4:44, the copular form (ἦν διδάσκων) would be consistent with the iterative nature of Jesus' ministry.[35] In turn, the clause would provide the background for the following statement, and the use of the simple imperfect (ἐξεπλήσσοντο) would imply that the people were amazed whenever he taught (and not just sometimes).[36]

So, when the copular imperfective is used for iterative events, it is of a more stative nature than the simple imperfect. In other words, it is less dynamic than its simple equivalent.[37]

In many other passages, the copular imperfect is used to describe an ongoing state. Acts 18:7 (οὗ ἡ_οἰκία ἦν συνομοροῦσα τῇ συναγωγῇ

---

33 "The word [ἐκτενῶς] has rather the idea that their prayer was *earnest* and *fervent*, than that it was constant" (Albert Barnes, *Notes on the New Testament, III: The Acts of the Apostles* [Glasgow: Blackie, 1846], 217) (emphasis original).

34 Luke uses σάββατον 20 times and 15 of these are singular, which suggests that the plural should be taken literally.

35 BDAG (εἰμί 11e) translates this copular impf., "*He customarily taught*" and cites it as an instance in which "the usage w. the ptc. serves to emphasize the duration of an action or condition." The word "emphasize" is perhaps unfortunate, as the copular form may well be the default way of presenting an iterative event.

36 See also Luke 1:21 (the people were in a state of expectation [copular impf.] and became and continued to be amazed [simple impf.] at his delay). Luke 15:1–2 is similar ("the periphrastic form Ἦσαν ... ἐγγίζοντες is perhaps meant to indicate that the general circumstances of Jesus' ministry rather than one particular incident are in mind" [I. Howard Marshall, *The Acts of the Apostles: An Introduction and Commentary*, TNTC (Leicester: Inter-Varsity Press, 1980), 599]). Mark 1:13 (ἦν ... πειραζόμενος) is also consistent with Satan's temptation being from time to time during the 40 day period.

37 Contrast Johnson, "Discourse Analysis," 53, who places the periphrastic impf. higher on the "Cline of Dynamicity for Greek verbs in Luke's narrative" than the simple impf.

"whose house was next door to the synagogue") is a particularly clear example.[38]

There remain a few tokens at the beginning of pericopes that "report a state of affairs with progressive aspect that functions as background"[39] to later events. The clearest examples are Luke 5:17a (καὶ αὐτὸς ἦν διδάσκων [NA28] "and he was teaching"), 11:14 (Καὶ ἦν ἐκβάλλων δαιμόνιον [NA28] "Now he was casting out a demon"), 13:10 (Ἦν δὲ διδάσκων ἐν μιᾷ τῶν συναγωγῶν ἐν τοῖς σάββασιν "Now he was teaching in one of the synagogues on the sabbath") and 24:13 (Καὶ ἰδοὺ δύο ἐξ αὐτῶν ἐν αὐτῇ τῇ ἡμέρᾳ ἦσαν πορευόμενοι [NA28] "Now on that same day two of them were going").[40] Bailey describes the function of the copular imperfect in these examples as "background-progressive."[41]

In summary, copular imperfectives are used to describe ongoing states, to present iterative events, and to background scene-setting events at the beginning of pericopes. I argue in the next section (§3) that copular perfect forms of ἵστημι are used in the same way.

---

38  I judge the following copular impfs. in Luke-Acts to be describing either an iterative event or an ongoing state: Luke 1:10, 1.22, 2:8 (NA28), 2:33, 2:51, 3:23 (NA28), 4:20, 4:38, 5:16, 5:17b (NA28), 5:29 (NA28), 6:12, 8:32, 8:40, 9:18 (NA28, infinitival), 9:53, 11:1 (infinitival) 13:11, 14:1, 19:47, 21:37, 23:8, 24:32, 24:53 ("The description of them being there continually ... is obviously not to be taken with strict literalness, and therefore need not conflict with the description in Acts 1:12-14 of prayer in the upper room" [Marshall, Luke, 910]); Acts 1:10, 1:13, 1:14, 2:2, 2:5, 2:42, 8:1, 8:13, 9:9, 9:28, 10:24 (NA28), 10:30, 11:5, 12:6, 12:12b, 12:20, 14:7, 16:12, 19:14 (NA28), 21:3, 22:19, 22:20 ("the tenses are descriptive imperfects" [R. C. H. Lenski, The Interpretation of the Acts of the Apostles (Minneapolis: Augsburg, 1961), 913]).

39  Bailey, "Thetic Constructions," 195.

40  Acts 8:28 (ἦν τε ὑποστρέφων καὶ καθήμενος ἐπὶ τοῦ ἅρματος αὐτοῦ [NA28] "and was returning home, sitting in his chariot") may also be a valid example, though it functions in the first instance as background for an event in the simple impf. (καὶ ἀνεγίνωσκεν τὸν προφήτην Ἠσαΐαν "and he was reading the prophet Isaiah"). In addition to this passage and the others listed in this paragraph, Fanning (Verbal Aspect, 314-15) classifies Luke 1:22, 4:20, 24:32; Acts 1:10, 8:1, 12:6 as "progressive... they provide a descriptive narration of a particular occurrence "as it is going on" or denote something which was in process at the time of another occurrence" (emphasis original).

41  Bailey, "Thetic Constructions," 195. Bailey credits this label to Gudmund Björck (Ἦν Διδάσκων: Die periphrastischen Konstruktionen in Griechischen [Uppsala: Almqvist & Wiksell, 1940], 46, 96).

## 3. SIMPLE AND COPULAR PERFECTS

By NT times, tense-aspects exclusively expressed peri-phrastically include "the future perfect and (as already in classical in the passive) the perfect subjunctive (optative), except of course for εἰδῶ (subjunctive of οἶδα)" (BDF §352; see also Dana & Mantey, §203). Besides these, there is a strong preference in classical and lat-er times for using the periphrastic forms instead of the simple perfect and pluperfect indicative forms when the verb is middle or passive; in fact, this is always so for third person plural forms when the stem ends in a consonant or adds σ (Smyth §405, §408). Thus, simple pluperfect forms of middle/ passive indicative verbs are very rare...[42]

I begin by comparing simple and copular pluperfect forms of ἵστημι since, as I noted above, they are used in a similar way to sim-ple and copular imperfects of other verbs.[43] The simple pluperfect is found 14 times in the Greek New Testament,[44] while there are five tokens of the perfect participle with the copula in the past.[45] In par-ticular, both forms are used in John 18.

John 18:15–16 (καὶ συνεισῆλθεν τῷ Ἰησοῦ εἰς τὴν αὐλὴν τοῦ ἀρχιερέως, ὁ δὲ Πέτρος εἱστήκει πρὸς τῇ θύρᾳ ἔξω "and he went with Jesus into the courtyard of the high priest, but Peter was standing outside at the gate") contrasts the actions of the two disciples. Although εἱστήκει portrays the act of standing as ongoing, many English versions translate it with a simple past (e.g., "but Peter had to wait outside at the door" [NIV]).

---

42  Bailey, "Thetic Constructions," 195 n. 317.

43  The discussion of this subsection closely follows that for pres. ptcs. since, as I argued in my seminar paper entitled, "Gnomic Aorists: No Problem! The Greek Indicative Verb System as Four Ordered Pairs" (Seminar given at Tyndale House, Cambridge, England, October 2014), "When no simple imperfective is attested for the verb concerned, as is the case for οἶδα and ἵστημι, then for these and only these verbs, it is not unreasonable to argue with Campbell that the perfect is simply +Imperfective."

44  Matt 12:46, 13:2; Luke 23:10, 35, 49; John 1:35, 7:37, 18:5, 16, 18, 19:25, 20:11; Acts 9:7; Rev 7:11. See also παρίστημι in Acts 1:10.

45  Luke 5:1; John 18:18, 25; Acts 5:25, 16:9 (NA28).

John 18:18 (εἱστήκεισαν δὲ οἱ δοῦλοι καὶ οἱ ὑπηρέται ἀνθρακιὰν πεποιηκότες … καὶ ἐθερμαίνοντο· ἦν δὲ καὶ ὁ Πέτρος μετ' αὐτῶν ἑστὼς καὶ θερμαινόμενος) again presents what the servants and officials were doing as an ongoing action ("and the servants and officials stood around a fire they had made to keep warm" [NIV]). Nonconjunctive καί is then used to add Peter to the scene. Two constituents separate the copula from the participles that parallel εἱστήκεισαν and ἐθερμαίνοντο in the previous sentence. This parallelism, and the stative nature of the sentence, are best captured by the nonperiphrastic rendering in the NASB: "Peter was also with them, standing and warming himself."

Bailey's term "background-progressive"[46] perfectly captures the function of the copular construction in John 18:25a (Ἦν δὲ Σίμων Πέτρος ἑστὼς καὶ θερμαινόμενος "Now Simon Peter was standing and warming himself" [NASB]), as it provides the setting for the next event (εἶπον οὖν αὐτῷ, Μὴ καὶ σὺ ἐκ τῶν μαθητῶν αὐτοῦ εἶ; "They asked him, 'You are not also one of his disciples, are you?'" [25b]).[47]

The focus of the speech of Acts 5:25 (Ἰδοὺ οἱ ἄνδρες οὓς ἔθεσθε ἐν τῇ φυλακῇ εἰσὶν ἐν τῷ ἱερῷ ἑστῶτες καὶ διδάσκοντες τὸν λαόν) is not on the fact that the men are standing, but where they are standing. TEV captures the stative nature of the speech with its rendering, "Listen! The men you put in prison are in the Temple teaching the people!" (emphasis added).

Acts 16:9 (ἀνὴρ Μακεδών τις ἦν ἑστὼς καὶ παρακαλῶν αὐτὸν καὶ λέγων, Διαβὰς εἰς Μακεδονίαν βοήθησον ἡμῖν [NA28]) provides a further example in which more than one participle follows the copula. The focus in the first instance is on who was standing there, which may explain why God's Word to the Nations (GWN) translates what Paul saw as "During the night Paul had a vision of a man from Macedonia. The man urged Paul, 'Come to Macedonia to help us.'" The present participles, however, suggest an iterative interpretation.[48]

I turn now to "true" perfects (i.e., those that contrast with imperfectives). Cross-linguistically, if a language has a three-way contrast between imperfective (present and imperfect) forms, simple

---

46 Bailey, "Thetic Constructions," 195.
47 Luke 5:1 (καὶ αὐτὸς ἦν ἑστὼς παρὰ τὴν λίμνην Γεννησαρὲτ "and he was standing beside the lake of Gennesaret") is similar.
48 "The effect is continuative: there he kept standing, beseeching, and saying, 'Help us!'" (Lenski, Acts, 648).

perfect (present perfect and pluperfect) forms and copular perfect (copula plus perfect participle) constructions, then I would expect them to differ in dynamicity as follows (γράφω is used for illustrative purposes):

- Simple imperfective (most dynamic): portrayed as an ongoing event, as in:
  1 Cor 4:14 (Οὐκ ἐντρέπων ὑμᾶς γράφω ταῦτα "I am not writing this to shame you" [NIV (1984)]);
  John 8:8 (ἔγραφεν εἰς τὴν γῆν "continued writing on the ground" [GWN]).
- Simple perfect: portrayed as a completed event with ongoing (usually stative) results, as in:
  John 19:22 (Ὃ γέγραφα, γέγραφα "What I have written, I have written" [NIV]);
  John 20:31 (ταῦτα δὲ γέγραπται "But these miracles have been written" [GWN]).
- Copular perfect (least dynamic): portrayed as an ongoing state (which results from a completed event), as in John 20:30 (ἃ οὐκ ἔστιν γεγραμμένα ἐν τῷ βιβλίῳ τούτῳ "[which] are not written in this book" [GWN]).[49]

See also the following set of present passive forms with σώζω:

- Simple imperfective (most dynamic), as in 1 Cor 15:2 (δι᾽ οὗ καὶ σῴζεσθε, τίνι λόγῳ εὐηγγελισάμην ὑμῖν εἰ κατέχετε "through which also you are being saved, if you hold firmly to the message that I proclaimed to you").[50]
- Simple perfect, as in Acts 4:9 (ἐν τίνι οὗτος σέσωται "how this man has been healed").

---

49 Bentein ("Periphrastic Perfect in Ancient Greek," 172) claims that "a stative characterization is much less appropriate" in a number of instances. However, he does not address "to what extent the periphrastic and synthetic perfect diverge from a semantic/pragmatic and syntactic point of view" (Ibid., 208).

50 The use of the simple imperfective in Mark 6:56 (καὶ ὅσοι ἂν ἥψαντο αὐτοῦ ἐσῴζοντο "and all who touched it were healed"), rather than the copular equivalent, is consistent with the event being of a foreground nature, rather than a "background-progressive" (see §2).

- Copular perfect (least dynamic), as in Eph 2:8 (τῇ γὰρ χάριτί ἐστε σεσῳσμένοι διὰ πίστεως "For by grace you have been saved through faith").[51]

A complicating factor that needs to be taken into account is that, cross-linguistically, it is common for the third person singular present tense copula to be omitted.[52] This factor appears to influence the distribution of simple and copular perfect forms of γράφω in the Synoptics and Acts, as the simple perfect is used consistently in present tense situations (e.g., καθὼς γέγραπται ἐν νόμῳ κυρίου "as it is written in the law of the Lord" [Luke 2:23]). The only time that a copular form is used with γράφω is when the tense is past (εὗρεν τὸν τόπον οὗ ἦν γεγραμμένον "and found the place where it was written" [Luke 4:17]).[53] This means that, in third person singular present tense situations, the dynamic contrast between simple and copular perfects tends to be lost for the authors concerned (see below for some exceptions).

In John's Gospel, in contrast, the copular perfect form of γράφω is the norm (e.g., καθώς ἐστιν γεγραμμένον "as it is written" [12:14]). The simple form is found only twice in the NA28 text. In 20:31 (cited above), the simple perfect contrasts with the copular form of 20:30 (also cited above). Given that 20:31 "expresses the purpose of the book,"[54] the selection of the simple form suggests that the act of writing is more to the fore than the stative existence of the written form.

The other instance of γέγραπται is in the NA28 text of John 8:17 (καὶ ἐν τῷ νόμῳ δὲ τῷ ὑμετέρῳ γέγραπται ὅτι δύο ἀνθρώπων ἡ μαρτυρία ἀληθής ἐστιν). Again, it is not the stative existence of the written form that is to the fore, but the fact that the testimony of two people

---

51  The "perfect periphrastic construction is most likely intensive," referring to "the state resulting from the act of being saved" (Wallace, Greek Grammar, 575). See also Eph 2:5 (χάριτί ἐστε σεσῳσμένοι "by grace you have been saved").

52  This phenomenon, often referred to as "zero copula," is noted for many languages, including Turkic, Hungarian and Russian.

53  See also Esth 8:8: ὅσα γὰρ γράφεται τοῦ βασιλέως ἐπιτάξαντος καὶ σφραγισθῇ τῷ δακτυλίῳ μου οὐκ ἔστιν αὐτοῖς ἀντειπεῖν "for whatever is written at the king's command and sealed with my ring cannot be contravened."

54  D. A. Carson, The Gospel According to John, PNTC (Grand Rapids: Eerdmans, 1991), 661.

is validated in "your own law." GWN captures the emphasis nicely in its rendering, "*Your own teachings* say that the testimony of two people is true" (emphasis added). (A variant reading has γεγραμμένον ἐστιν, and I suggest in §4 that, when the participle precedes the copula, it is focally prominent.)

Although copular forms of the perfect of γράφω are not used in the Synoptics and Acts when the tense is present, seven other copular perfects are found, in all but one of which the copula is third person singular (the form that is most likely to be omitted).[55] I consider them in turn.

Matt 18:20 (οὗ γάρ εἰσιν δύο ἢ τρεῖς συνηγμένοι εἰς τὸ ἐμὸν ὄνομα, ἐκεῖ εἰμι ἐν μέσῳ αὐτῶν "For where two or three are gathered in my name, I am there among them"). The stative nature of this copular construction is apparent from the second part of the sentence: ἐκεῖ εἰμι ἐν μέσῳ αὐτῶν.

Luke 12:6–7 (οὐχὶ πέντε στρουθία πωλοῦνται ἀσσαρίων δύο; καὶ ἓν ἐξ αὐτῶν οὐκ ἔστιν ἐπιλελησμένον ἐνώπιον τοῦ θεοῦ. ἀλλὰ καὶ αἱ τρίχες τῆς κεφαλῆς ὑμῶν πᾶσαι ἠρίθμηνται "Are not five sparrows sold for two pennies? Yet not one of them is forgotten in God's sight. But even the hairs of your head are all counted"). If the simple perfect in 12:7 is the default way of expressing a perfect in the present, then one effect of using first a copular construction and then a simple perfect is to background the former in relation to the latter (see earlier discussion of John 20:30–31).[56]

Luke 23:15 (καὶ ἰδοὺ οὐδὲν ἄξιον θανάτου ἐστὶν πεπραγμένον αὐτῷ "Indeed, he has done nothing to deserve death"). A legal statement describing Jesus' "not guilty" state.[57]

Acts 21:33 (καὶ ἐπυνθάνετο τίς εἴη καὶ τί ἐστιν πεποιηκώς "he inquired who he was and what he had done").The simple perfect when ποιέω is active is the norm, as in Mark 7:37 (Καλῶς πάντα πεποίηκεν "He has done everything well").[58] Typically, the reference is to events that

---

55  Matt 18:20; Luke 12:6, 23:15; Acts 5:25 (discussed earlier), 21:33, 25:14, 26:26. See also 2 Cor 4:3 (2x); Eph 2:8; Heb 4:2, 7:20.

56  In the parallel passage in Matt 10:30, a copular pf. is used, but the ptc. has been preposed for focal prominence (see §4).

57  J. Reiling and J. L. Swellengrebel, *A Translator's Handbook on the Gospel of Luke* (Leiden, Brill, 1971), 722. See also John 3:21 (ὅτι ἐν θεῷ ἐστιν εἰργασμένα), which NEB renders "that God is in all he does."

58  See also Mark 5:19, 11:17; Luke 1:25, 17:10; John 13:12; 2 Cor 11:25; Heb 11:28.

have just been performed. In contrast, Lenski writes about this verse, "The perfect tense (here periphrastic) implies that what has been done stands indefinitely against the man as his crime."[59]

Acts 25:14 (Ἀνήρ τίς ἐστιν καταλελειμμένος ὑπὸ Φήλικος δέσμιος). Bailey considers "if this is (a) two clauses, where ἐστιν 'is' belongs to the first clause and the participle καταλελειμμένος 'left behind' is the predicate word of a SP [=subsequent predication], or if this is (b) one single clause, where ἐστιν καταλελειμμένος comprises a periphrastic verb form (i.e. one verb phrase)." He continues, "Structure (a) is reflected by 'There is a man who has been left behind as a prisoner by Felix', and (b) by 'A man was left behind by Felix as a prisoner'."[60] Whichever analysis is preferred, what is to the fore is Paul's current state, rather than Felix's act of leaving him behind.

Acts 26:26 (οὐ γάρ ἐστιν ἐν γωνίᾳ πεπραγμένον τοῦτο "for this was not done in a corner"). "Here we have a claim about the public nature of the evidence available for Agrippa and others to consider",[61] where "evidence" is a stative concept.

*Pauline* sentences in which a perfect participle and a present tense copula occur in the same clause also have the state to the fore (see discussion above of Eph 2:8).[62] As for *Hebrews*, 4:2 (καὶ γάρ ἐσμεν εὐηγγελισμένοι καθάπερ κἀκεῖνοι "For we also have had the gospel preached to us, just as they did" [NIV 1984]) refers not so much to the act of having had the gospel preached to them, but to the state of having been evangelized; while in 7:20 (οἱ μὲν γὰρ χωρὶς ὁρκωμοσίας εἰσὶν ἱερεῖς γεγονότες "others became priests without any oath" [NIV]), the copula is probably present because the statement is generic, rather than referring to a particular act.

I conclude that it is indeed the case that copular perfects are less dynamic than their simple equivalents, with the copular form typically used for ongoing states (which result from completed events).

---

59  Lenski, *Acts*, 893.

60  Bailey, "Thetic Constructions," 194.

61  David G. Peterson, *The Acts of the Apostles*, PNTC (Grand Rapids: Eerdmans, 2009), 674.

62  See also 2 Cor 4:3 (εἰ δὲ καὶ ἔστιν κεκαλυμμένον τὸ εὐαγγέλιον ἡμῶν, ἐν τοῖς ἀπολλυμένοις ἐστὶν κεκαλυμμένον "And even if our gospel is veiled, it is veiled to those who are perishing").

## 4. FRONTED PARTICIPLES

When part or all of a participial clause is placed before the copula, the effect is to give it focal prominence, provided its default position is after the copula.[63]

In Acts 2:13 (Γλεύκους μεμεστωμένοι εἰσίν), for example, the participial clause is preposed and, within in it, γλεύκους is preposed to give focal prominence to "filled with sweet wine."[64] As usual in perfect copula constructions, the current state (drunk) is to the fore, rather than the event (filling themselves with sweet wine) that brought them to that state.[65]

---

63  A fronted ptc. never occurs in Mark's Gospel. I have found no commentary that discusses the significance of preposing the ptc. in the passages listed in this section. The question is not addressed by Bentein, either, even though a number of the examples he cites have the ptc. before the copula (Bentein, "Periphrastic Perfect in Ancient Greek," 172, 183, 184, 188, 190, 195–197).

64  "This may be the force of the periphrastic perfect: they are in a state of fullness" (C. K. Barrett, *A Critical and Exegetical Commentary on the Acts of the Apostles*, ICC 34 [Edinburgh: T&T Clark, 1994], 1:125).

65  See also Matt 10:30 (ὑμῶν δὲ καὶ αἱ τρίχες τῆς κεφαλῆς πᾶσαι ἠριθμημέναι εἰσίν [NA28] "And even the hairs of your head are all counted"), about which Leon Morris (*The Gospel according to Matthew*, PNTC [Grand Rapids: Eerdmans, 1992], 264) writes, "The word order ... draws attention to 'all' and thus emphasizes that the Father has complete knowledge of the most insignificant information about each one of his children." However, this observation is true even if the copula is omitted, as in the parallel passage in Luke 12:7, which directs the hearers' attention to the completed act of counting, rather than to the ongoing resultant state (see §3). Other examples in which a pf. ptc. precedes the copula for focal prominence include Luke 1:7 (καὶ ἀμφότεροι προβεβηκότες ἐν ταῖς ἡμέραις αὐτῶν ἦσαν "and both were getting on in years"), John 2:17 (ὅτι γεγραμμένον ἐστίν... "that it was [is] written"), Acts 20:13 (οὕτως γὰρ διατεταγμένος ἦν "for he had made this arrangement"), Acts 25:10 (Ἐπὶ τοῦ βήματος Καίσαρος ἑστώς εἰμι [NA28] "I am now standing before Caesar's court" [NIV]), Rom 13:1 (αἱ δὲ οὖσαι ὑπὸ θεοῦ τεταγμέναι εἰσίν "and those authorities that exist have been instituted by God"), 1 Cor 7:29 (ὁ καιρὸς συνεσταλμένος ἐστίν "the appointed time has grown short"), Gal 2:11 (ὅτι κατεγνωσμένος ἦν "because he stood self-condemned"), Eph 4:18 (ἐσκοτωμένοι τῇ διανοίᾳ ὄντες "being darkened in their understanding"), 2 Pet 3:7 (οἱ δὲ νῦν οὐρανοὶ καὶ ἡ γῆ τῷ αὐτῷ λόγῳ τεθησαυρισμένοι εἰσίν "But by the same word the present heavens and earth have been reserved for fire"), 1 John 4:12 (καὶ ἡ ἀγάπη αὐτοῦ ἐν ἡμῖν τετελειωμένη ἐστίν "and his love is perfected in us"), and 2 John 1:12 (ἵνα ἡ χαρὰ ἡμῶν πεπληρωμένη ᾖ "so that our joy may be complete"). Identificational structures such as Luke 24:38 (Τί τεταραγμένοι ἐστὲ "Why are you frightened?") often end with the verb, anyhow (Stephen H. Levinsohn, *Discourse Features of New Testament Greek: A Coursebook on the Information Structure of*

In Acts 14:7 (κἀκεῖ εὐαγγελιζόμενοι ἦσαν "and there they continued proclaiming the good news"), the copular imperfect is "background-progressive,"[66] with the participle preposed for focal prominence, perhaps because the readers might have expected previous
persecution to cause the apostles to be more circumspect.[67]

In Luke 24:32 (Οὐχὶ ἡ καρδία ἡμῶν καιομένη ἦν [ἐν ἡμῖν] [NA28]
"Were not our hearts burning within us"), the copular imperfect has
an iterative sense—something they kept on experiencing "while he
was talking to us on the road, while he was opening up the scriptures to us" (ὡς ἐλάλει ἡμῖν ἐν τῇ ὁδῷ, ὡς διήνοιγεν ἡμῖν τὰς γραφάς;).[68]

In other copular constructions involving a present participle,
however, the precopular position of the participle may well be
default. Such may be the case, for instance, when a clause would
have begun with the copula had the participle not preceded it, as
in Acts 19:36 (δέον ἐστὶν... "it is necessary...") and 1 Pet 1:6 (εἰ δέον
ἐστὶν... [NA28] "if it is necessary..."). When a clause or sentence begins (apart from any connective) with a third person form of the
copula, the expectation is that it will be thetic or, at least, existential.[69] When a copular clause makes a comment about a third person

---

New Testament Greek, 2nd ed. [Dallas: SIL International, 2000], §4.2). See
also Acts 8:16 (μόνον δὲ βεβαπτισμένοι ὑπῆρχον εἰς τὸ ὄνομα τοῦ... "they had only
been baptized in the name of...").

66  Bailey, "Thetic Constructions," 195. "This implies continued evangelization
over a period of time" (Charles W. Carter and Ralph Earle, The Acts of the
Apostles, Evangelical Commentary [Grand Rapids: Zondervan, 1959], 195).

67  "And still they preached the gospel, despite the setback they had received"
(Marshall, Acts, 234).

68  Although Alfred Plummer (A Critical and Exegetical Commentary on the Gospel According to S. Luke, 5th ed., ICC [Edinburgh: T&T Clark, 1922], 557-58)
writes, "The periphrastic tense ['was burning'] emphasizes the continuance of the emotion," the copular impf. suggests rather that they repeatedly
experienced the emotion and that what is emphasized (by the preposing
of the ptc.) is "burning." Gal 1:23 (μόνον δὲ ἀκούοντες ἦσαν "they only heard it
said", "they knew only what others were saying" [GNB]) is also to be understood iteratively; "It is easy to see how the Judean churches again and again
heard about the man they had never seen" (R. C. H. Lenski, The Interpretation of St. Paul's Epistles to the Galatians, to the Ephesians, and to the Philippians [Minneapolis: Augsburg, 1961], 64). See also Phil 2:26 (ἐπειδὴ ἐπιποθῶν
ἦν πάντας ὑμᾶς καὶ ἀδημονῶν "for he has been longing for all of you, and has
been distressed").

69  Bailey ("Thetic Constructions," 99) states concerning pres. indic. forms of
εἰμί, "In existential sentences, including thetics, initial position is common."
What I am asserting here concerns third person forms, regardless of the

topic, Greek writers therefore have a strong tendency not to begin the clause with the copula.[70] This may well explain the precopular position of δέον in these passages.[71]

The precopular position may also be default for πρέπον (οὕτως γὰρ πρέπον ἐστὶν ἡμῖν πληρῶσαι πᾶσαν δικαιοσύνην "for it is proper for us in this way to fulfill all righteousness" [Matt 3:15])[72] and for ἐξόν (ὃ οὐκ ἐξὸν ἦν αὐτῷ φαγεῖν "which it was not lawful for him to eat" [Matt 12:4]).

## 5. CONCLUSIONS

This paper has argued that combinations of a copula and a participial clause are always more stative than their simple equivalents.[73]

Copular *imperfectives* are used:

- to describe states that are ongoing;
- to present iterative events, with the actor portrayed as performing the action from time to time during the period envisaged, rather than continuously;
- to background scene-setting events at the beginning of pericopes.

These same three uses are also attested for copular perfect forms of ἵστημι, thus confirming that, for this particular verb, "the perfect is simply +Imperfective."[74]

---

tense or mood.

70  See Bailey, ibid. 98–99, for discussion of this point and of provisos about applying the term "postpositive" to copular instances of εἰμί.

71  See also Luke 20:6 (πεπεισμένος γάρ ἐστιν Ἰωάννην προφήτην εἶναι "for they are convinced that John was a prophet"); Acts 1:10 (καὶ ὡς ἀτενίζοντες ἦσαν εἰς τὸν οὐρανὸν "While he was going up toward heaven"), Acts 1:17 (ὅτι κατηριθμημένος ἦν ἐν ἡμῖν "for he was numbered among us"). In addition, some MSS of Luke 15:24 have ἀπολωλὼς ἦν "he was lost." When it is clear from the context that a comment is being made about a third person topic, however, then the ptc. may follow the copula, as in NA28's preferred reading for Luke 15:24: ἦν ἀπολωλώς.

72  See also 1 Cor 11:13.

73  I leave it to the reader to decide whether it is ever appropriate to refer to the combination of a copula and a participial clause in Koine Greek as a *periphrastic* verbal construction.

74  Levinsohn, "Gnomic Aorists," §5.

For verbs with both perfect and simple imperfective forms, in contrast, copular *perfects* differ from simple perfects and imperfectives in dynamicity.

- Simple imperfectives (most dynamic) portray events as ongoing.
- Simple perfects portray events as completed with ongoing (usually stative) results.
- Copular perfects (least dynamic) portray states that result from completed events as ongoing.

However, as in many other languages, the copula is often omitted in third person singular present tense situations. When this happens with the perfect (e.g., with γράφω in the Synoptics and Acts), then the result is a loss of the dynamic contrast between simple and copular perfects.

Finally, the effect of placing part or all of a participial clause before the copula is to give the preposed participle focal prominence, provided its default position is after the copula. The proviso is necessary because the default position for δέον, πρέπον and ἐξόν may be before the copula.

## BIBLIOGRAPHY

Bailey, Nicholas A. "Thetic Constructions in Koine Greek." PhD diss., Vrije Universiteit Amsterdam, 2009.

Barnes, Albert. *Notes on the New Testament, III: The Acts of the Apostles.* Glasgow: Blackie, 1846.

Barrett, C. K. *A Critical and Exegetical Commentary on the Acts of the Apostles.* ICC 34. Edinburgh: T&T Clark, 1994.

Bentein, Klaas. "The Periphrastic Perfect in Ancient Greek: A Diachronic Mental Space Analysis." *TPhS* 110 (2012): 171–211.

Björck, Gudmund. Ἦν Διδάσκων: *Die Periphrastischen Konstruktionen in Griechischen.* Uppsala: Almqvist & Wiksell, 1940.

Boyer, James L. "The Classification of Participles: A Statistical Study." *GTJ* 5 (1984): 163-179.

Campbell, Constantine R. *Basics of Verbal Aspect in Biblical Greek.* Grand Rapids: Zondervan, 2008.

Caragounis, Chrys C. *The Development of Greek and the New Testament: Morphology, Syntax, Phonology, and Textual Transmission.* WUNT 167. Tübingen: Mohr Siebeck, 2004.

Carson, D. A. *The Gospel According to John*. PNTC. Grand Rapids: Eerdmans, 1991.

Carter, Charles W., and Ralph Earle. *The Acts of the Apostles*. Evangelical Commentary. Grand Rapids: Zondervan, 1959.

Dana, H. E., and Julius R. Mantey. *A Manual Grammar of the Greek New Testament*. New York: MacMillan, 1957.

Fanning, Buist M. *Verbal Aspect in New Testament Greek*. OTM. Oxford: Clarendon Press, 1990.

Johnson, Carl E. "A Discourse Analysis of the Periphrastic Imperfect in the Greek New Testament Writings of Luke." PhD diss., University of Texas at Arlington, 2010.

Lambrecht, Knud. *Information Structure and Sentence Form: Topic, Focus, and the Mental Representations of Discourse Referents*. CSL. Cambridge: Cambridge University Press, 1994.

Lenski, R. C. H. *The Interpretation of the Acts of the Apostles*. Minneapolis: Augsburg, 1961.

———. *The Interpretation of St. Paul's Epistles to the Galatians, to the Ephesians, and to the Philippians*. Minneapolis: Augsburg, 1961.

Levinsohn, Stephen H. "Constituent Order in and Usages of εἰμί: Participle Combinations in the Synoptics and Acts." Paper presented at the International Meeting of the SBL. St. Andrews, Scotland, July 2013. Also presented at the Congress of the International Syriac Language Project. Munich, Germany, August 2013.

———. "Constituent Order and "Emphasis" in the Greek New Testament." Seminar given at Tyndale House. Cambridge, England, January 2014.

———. *Discourse Features of New Testament Greek: A Coursebook on the Information Structure of New Testament Greek*. 2nd ed. Dallas: SIL International, 2000.

———. "Gnomic Aorists: No Problem! The Greek Indicative Verb System as Four Ordered Pairs." Seminar given at Tyndale House. Cambridge, England, October 2014.

Marshall, I. Howard. *The Acts of the Apostles: An Introduction and Commentary*. TNTC. Leicester: Inter-Varsity Press, 1980.

Morris, Leon. *The Gospel According to Matthew*. PNTC. Grand Rapids: Eerdmans, 1992.

Peterson, David G. *The Acts of the Apostles*. PNTC. Grand Rapids: Eerdmans, 2009.

Plummer, Alfred. *A Critical and Exegetical Commentary on the Gospel According to S. Luke*. 5th ed. ICC. Edinburgh: T&T Clark, 1942.

Porter, Stanley E. *Idioms of the Greek New Testament*. BLG 2. Sheffield: JSOT Press, 1992.

Reiling, J., and J. L. Swellengrebel. *A Translator's Handbook on the Gospel of Luke*. Leiden, Brill, 1971.

Rijksbaron, Albert. *The Syntax and Semantics of the Verb in Classical Greek: An Introduction*. 3rd ed. Chicago: University of Chicago Press, 2006.

Robertson, Archibald Thomas. *A Grammar of the Greek New Testament in the Light of Historical Research*. New York: Harper, 1931.

Smith, Carlota S. *The Parameter of Aspect*. 2nd ed. SLP 43. Dordrecht: Kluwer, 1997.

Turner, Nigel. *Grammar of New Testament Greek: Vol. 3; Syntax*. Edinburgh: T&T Clark, 1963.

Wallace, Daniel B., *Greek Grammar Beyond the Basics: An Exegetical Syntax of the New Testament*. Grand Rapids: Zondervan, 1996.

Zerwick, Maximillian, SJ. *Biblical Greek Illustrated by Examples*. English ed. adapted from the 4th Latin ed. by Joseph Smith, SJ. Rome: Biblical Institute Press, 1963.

# Linguistic Investigations

CHAPTER 10

# The Historical Present in NT Greek: An Exercise in Interpreting Matthew

ELIZABETH ROBAR

TYNDALE HOUSE, CAMBRIDGE

## 1. HISTORICAL PRESENT CROSS-LINGUISTICALLY

### 1.1 Introduction

The historical present (HP) is the poster child for a language recycling one of its forms to serve an alternative purpose. An HP is a present tense that is used instead of a past tense, when that past tense would not only have been perfectly acceptable, but the semantics of the past tense are still understood to obtain in spite of the present tense form in the text.

### 1.2 Function of HP

Many languages make use of an HP, and every once in a while, scholars seem to be able to explain the motivation. The fundamental insight underlying all such motivations is well put by Suzanne Fleischman in her discussion on the linguistic category of tense:

> For languages that have tense (not all languages do), this category provides a formal, grammatical means of expressing locations in time. But inasmuch as time reference can also be expressed lexically, contextually, or presuppositionally, tense morphology often becomes semantically redundant. Yet since this morphology

is obligatory in tense languages, and since languages moreover seem to strive for functional economy in their use of available resources, there is a strong motivation for recycling tense morphology to do other types of (nontemporal) work in discourse.[1]

## 1.3 Tense Reduction / Kiparsky

The concept of "recycling" tense morphology to do nontemporal work is significant but not entirely new. It was anticipated by those who argued for a form of tense "reduction" or tense "neutralization," such as Kiparsky[2] and Comrie,[3] who recognized that the HP did not have its usual semantic value of present tense and imperfective aspect.

## 1.4 Tenses Used for Nontemporal Work

The nontemporal, "other" types of work that might be performed by an HP are many. In Biblical Hebrew, it has been argued that the HP, or narrative present, has a largely (information) structural role, functioning to mark paragraph continuity.[4] In Modern Conversational English, Wolfson has argued that the alternation of past and HP forms serves to mark boundaries between episodes.[5] The use of tense may be of discourse-pragmatic use, indicating foreground and background.[6] In Premodern English, the HP has been claimed to indicate prominence: whether thematic (more germane to the theme of the narrative than the surrounding text) or

---

1   Suzanne Fleischman, *Tense and Narrativity: From Medieval Performance to Modern Fiction* (London: Routledge, 1990), 19.

2   Paul Kiparsky, "Tense and Mood in Indo-European Syntax," *FL* 4, (1968): 30–57.

3   Bernard Comrie, *Tense*, CTL (Cambridge: Cambridge University Press, 1985), 102.

4   Elizabeth Robar, *The Verb and the Paragraph in Biblical Hebrew: A Cognitive-Linguistic Approach*, SSLL 78 (Leiden: Brill, 2014).

5   Nessa Wolfson, "The Conversational Historical Present Alternation," *Language* 55 (1979): 168–82.

6   Suzanne Fleischman, "Discourse Functions of Tense-Aspect Oppositions in Narrative: Toward a Theory of Grounding," *Linguistics* 23 (1985): 851–82.

evaluative (expressing the narrator's opinion).[7] In Koine Greek, various narrative functions might be served: introducing direct speech, introducing a new character, indicating a change in geographical location.[8]

## 1.5 Definition of the HP

It is important to recognize that this "other work" that can be performed by tenses is, by very nature of being outside the meaning of tense, explicitly nontemporal work. This leads to the (partial) definition of the HP as *the use of the present with identical semantics to the preterite*: by definition not having imperfective or continuing aspect, but very clearly perfective aspect:

> The historical present ... is a real preterit tense. In meaning it is the exact equivalent of a past tense. The action is looked upon as beginning and ending in the time sphere of the past.[9]

> The historical present is so defined in virtue of its substitutability [of present for past tense].[10]

> [O]ne should define the construction simply as the (not necessarily vivid) occurrence of a present tense verb in the narration of a past event where logic would ordinarily dictate the employment of a preterite.[11]

This reflects on the ability of the present tense to be "semantically multivalent," taking on nearly any combination of tense and

7   Otto Jespersen, *A Modern English Grammar on Historical Principles* (London: Allen & Unwin, 1931), 4:19.

8   Buist Fanning, *Verbal Aspect in New Testament Greek*, OTM (Oxford: Clarendon Press, 1991), 231–32; Stephanie Black, "The Historic Present in Matthew: Beyond Speech Margins," in *Discourse Analysis and the New Testament: Approaches and Results*, ed. Stanley E. Porter and Jeffrey T. Reed, JSNTSup 170 (Sheffield: Sheffield Academic Press, 1999), 129–39.

9   J. M. Steadman, Jr., "The Origin of the Historical Present in English," *SPh* 14 (1917): 5.

10  Nessa Wolfson, *CHP, the Conversational Historical Present in American English Narrative*, Topics in Sociolinguistics 1 (Dordrecht: Foris, 1982), 7.

11  L. D. Benson, "Chaucer's Historical Present, Its Meaning and Uses," *English Studies* 42 (1961): 66.

aspect if the context makes it clear.[12] How to explain the HP as a function of the present tense, when in seeming conflict with traditional tense and aspect, has spawned all manner of debate (as with Kiparsky's reduction and Comrie's neutralization). But without embracing any one explanation, we can grasp that the HP functions on a completely *different level* from tense and aspect: not necessarily canceling or overriding tense and aspect, but functioning such that tense and aspect are not applicable.

Runge expresses this same concept with his "processing hierarchy," in which a verbal form may convey semantic function (traditional verbal semantics), or if that seems incongruent with the context, it might convey a processing function (e.g., paragraph boundaries). If this is still incongruent, then the form likely conveys a discourse-pragmatic function: thematic prominence, whether in the form of introducing a new character or location, or highlighting a specific passage.[13]

## 1.6 Vividness

The traditional view is that the HP brings events from the past into the present, as if they were now happening before the reader's eyes, and thus portrays them *vividly*. Jespersen's explanation is most often cited:

> [T]he present tense is used in speaking of the past. This is the case in the "dramatic present" (generally called the "historic present") which is pretty frequent in connected narrative; the speaker, as it were, forgets all about time and imagines, or recalls, what he is recounting, as vividly as if it were now present before his eyes. Very often this present tense alternates with the preterite.[14]

---

12   Cf. Suzanne Fleischman and Linda R. Waugh, eds., *Discourse-Pragmatics and the Verb: The Evidence From Romance* (London: Routledge, 1991).

13   Steven E. Runge, *Discourse Grammar of the Greek New Testament: A Practical Introduction for Teaching and Exegesis* (Peabody, MA: Hendrickson, 2010), 128–33.

14   Jespersen, *Modern English Grammar*, 4:19.

We must juxtapose this with a comment by Wolfson, who has worked extensively with the HP in English:

> The most interesting finding about the attitudes toward the historical present shown in the literature is that although the traditional explanation [of vividness] is generally accepted, not one scholar believes it is accurate as an explanation of the data he himself has worked on.[15]

Such a dismissive comment of vividness as an explanation cannot be said for Koine Greek grammarians, however, which suggests that there may be a grain of truth in it. In fact, we might yet be able to rescue vividness by granting it a more nuanced linguistic dress. If we rechristen vividness as prominence, that is, attracting additional processing time than the surrounding material, we can make some headway as Runge has indicated. The "vividness" is not temporal transport, from the past to the present, but it does arrest the attention and force the reader to evaluate what is happening within the text, whether it be structural prominence or thematic prominence.

## 1.7 Linguistic Evolution and the HP

To understand the HP within a specific language, it it useful to understand the development of the verbal system within the language. Cross-linguistic studies have discovered systematic pathways on which verbal systems evolve, and we can locate the HP within certain portions of those pathways. Scholarly discussions on the origins of the HP refer to the presence or absence of a future form distinct from the present form.

> It seems reasonable to say that the historical present, which indicates past action, could not be used so long as the present form of the verb was used to express general truths (timeless presents), real present actions, and real future actions. Ambiguity or confusion would have arisen. If we argue that the use of a modifying adverb would have made the meaning clear, we shall have

---

15  Wolfson, CHP, the Conversational Historical Present, 22.

to explain why all the Germanic languages did develop a periphrastic future. If this development was not for the sake of clearness, why did each Germanic language separately employ this mode of expressing futurity?

... We have seen also that those Balto-Slavic languages which have a clear form for the future use the historical present with the greatest freedom, and that those languages which had no clear sign for the future and which used the distinction between perfectives, imperfectives, and iteratives to fill up the gaps in the tense system, used the historical present not at all, or only under very restricted circumstances.[16]

Notably, translations from Latin or French (replete with HPs) into Old English consistently *avoided* the HP, presumably because it would have been too confusing, given that future action was expressed by present tense verb forms. But as the English tense system developed (to employ modal forms for distinct future meaning), the HP began to flourish, around the fourteenth century.

As to how the HP developed at all, there is possible evidence in Chaucer that the HP may have developed from aspectual roots.[17] A present may have been used first to slow down the narrative (and build tension) by marking a continuous activity forestalling a climax. Then a present may have been used with durative verbs, not necessarily emphasizing the continuous activity but compatible with the lexical meaning, again leading up to a climactic event. Finally, the present may have been used with durative verbs but explicitly in the absence of continuous activity, still presaging a climactic event. This is a tentative and still hypothetical typological progression, but it opens the possibility that an HP might enter a verbal system through the door of aspect. So perhaps a "young" HP marks aspect indeed, but, as the above definitions demonstrate, a

---

16  Steadman, "Origin of the Historical Present," 42–43.
17  Elizabeth Robar, "From Bitter Sorrow to Exultant Joy: The Verbal System in 1 Samuel 1–2," in *Collected Essays on the Biblical Hebrew Verbal System*, LSAWS (Winona Lake, IN: Eisenbrauns, forthcoming).

"mature" or true HP is generally perfective, functioning semantically as a preterite.[18] There may be a shift in semantic motivation (for continuous action) to pragmatic motivation (in Chaucer, to lead up to a climactic event).

In summary, whatever the development of the HP itself, cross-linguistic parallels suggest that it is tense systems with distinct present and future tenses that have the ability to develop an HP, which, once established, may continue even when the present tense form itself is nearly gone from a language.

## 2. KOINE GREEK

## 2.1 Development of the Present and Future in Greek

In order to discuss the HP in Koine Greek, then, it may be useful to provide but the briefest of sketches of the development of the present tense form in Greek. The athematic verbs, or -μι verbs, are old present forms, retained in Koine Greek in only a few common verbs and continually being replaced by parallel forms in -ω, for example from δίδωμι to δίδω.[19] The thematic verbs may be just as old, but they are far more productive. Within the thematic verbs many suffixes are recognizable, e.g., -ske/o-, -n-, and most especially -ye/o-, now called a semivowel and formerly called the consonantal iota.[20] This suffix is pervasive in forming the present stem, whether from verbs, nouns, or adjectives. Barber has analyzed this suffix most extensively and concludes that, contrary to common belief, it does have semantic content. If the base noun or adjective has an agent or

---

18  In their foundational book, *The Evolution of Grammar: Tense, Aspect and Modality in the Languages of the World* (Chicago: University of Chicago Press, 1994, 147-48), Bybee, Perkins, and Pagliuca mention the HP as a final stronghold for old present tense forms before they disappear from a language altogether. Their brief mention is of the use of the present as a past tense, especially evident in proverbial and folk literature (cf. also Martin Haspelmath, "The Semantic Development of Old Presents: New Futures and Subjunctives Without Grammaticalization," *Diachronica* 15 (1998): 29–62). No comment is made as to how an HP comes into use, only that it seems to continue until its verbal form is lost from the language altogether.

19  A.-F. Christidis, ed., *A History of Ancient Greek: From the Beginnings to Late Antiquity*, (Cambridge: Cambridge University Press, 2007), 615.

20  Ibid., 662.

experiencer, then this became the subject of an intransitive verb. If the base noun or adjective had none, then a default agent role was added and the verb became a (transitive) factitive/causative.[21]

It seems plausible that the -ye/o- suffix became a marker of imperfective aspect that could be attached to make denominative verbs (and possibly deverbative verbs). According to grammaticalization and path theory, that is, observations made from the development of grammatical systems cross-linguistically, then one would expect such a marker to initially be for a specific kind of aspect within imperfectivity, e.g., iterative or progressive.[22] Eventually, it might generalize to generic imperfective aspect, which seems to be what we see in many Koine verbs. Of the many suffixes, it is -ye/o- that generalized the most.

Gradually, the athematic present tense forms disappear, and students no longer have to learn the dreaded -μι verbs.[23] In medieval Greek, however, many new kinds of present tense forms make themselves known. This leaves us, in Koine Greek, with understanding the athematic present forms as old presents and the thematic presents (including -ye/o- forms) also as aging presents. This is particularly evident in the plethora of suffixes included in the thematic presents whose initial semantics (e.g., iterative) have been largely obscured by the natural evolution of the language. We find the HP in both athematic and thematic presents.

Of potentially more significance is the evolution of the future tense in the time of Koine Greek. The aorist subjunctive and future indicative became less and less distinct through paradigm leveling[24] and precipitated the greater use of the present tense for future semantics (along with periphrastic auxiliaries μέλλω and ἔχω).[25] This demise and rebirth of the future reflect the situation that, prior to Koine Greek, there was a clearly distinct future tense. It was

21 Peter Barber, *Sievers' Law and the History of Semivowel Syllabicity in Indo-European and Ancient Greek*, OCM (Oxford: Oxford University Press, 2013), 304–12.
22 Bybee, Perkins, and Pagliuca, *The Evolution of Grammar*; Paul J. Hopper and Elizabeth Closs Traugott, *Grammaticalization*, 2nd ed., CTL (Cambridge: Cambridge University Press, 2003), 125–73, esp. 172.
23 Geoffrey Horrocks, *Greek: A History of the Language and Its Speakers*, 2nd ed. (Chichester: Wiley-Blackwell, 2010), 303.
24 Ibid., 187.
25 Christidis, *History of Ancient Greek*, 626.

semantically unmarked for aspect (it could be used for both perfective and imperfective aspect), though it morphologically had a perfective stem.[26]

This bare outline of the present and future forms in Koine situates it within a cross-linguistic understanding of verbal systems that can develop HP functionality. With the option of a distinct future, the old present tense forms are eligible for use as HPs.

## 3. NEW TESTAMENT > MATTHEW

### 3.1 Program: Motivation and Scope

The two questions this paper will seek to address are: first, given our understanding of the HP, when we encounter it in New Testament Koine Greek, what is the motivation for its use? We know it is an available strategy for many discourse functions, but it is not the only strategy, and the very possibility of alternatives means a choice is required by each author, and, as linguists know, choice implies meaning.

Second, when we encounter an HP, what is the scope of its effect? Does a verb in a speech margin highlight the speech immediately following, or, if in a dialogue, the next response? Does an HP at the beginning of an episode have a different scope from an HP at the end?

### 3.2 Analysis of Matthew

To discover the motivation and scope for the HP, I made a simple clausal and episodic analysis of the Gospel of Matthew, breaking up the Greek text based first on clauses and then on normal categories of change in time, location, actors, and topic, that is, paragraphs and episodes. Once I had a very basic outline, with minimal hierarchy since that is not immediately apparent, I began to seek any discernible role played by the HP in the literary development, either structural or discourse-pragmatic. I will recount how this process unfolded, followed by an evaluation of my initial hypotheses.

---

26  Ibid., 581.

## 3.3 Jesus as New Israel

At first the heavens seemed to open, as I observed a single HP marked the flight to Egypt (2:13), then the return to Israel (2:19) with a detour to Galilee, followed by John the Baptist in the desert of Judah (3:1) and Jesus' arrival at the same. Next was a climactic baptism and temptation scene, with 8 HPs between them. My imagination went wild: were the HPs marking distinct changes in geographical location intended to recapitulate the history of Israel, setting up a parallel between Jesus and Israel? Jesus is the true son of God, who flees to Egypt, then exits Egypt on supernatural prompting, but has to take a different way than expected and ends up in the middle of nowhere (apologies to Galileans!) for a time of maturation. Once ready, he is baptized in the River Jordan and faces the first real temptation: will he trust his God to provide or squirrel away goods for himself as Achan did at Jericho, so long ago? The literary tension is high as the story is rehearsed, but this time with a different ending. Just as John "permitted," ἀφίησιν, Jesus to be baptized, so the devil ends up leaving him, ἀφίησιν, in defeat. Jesus wins two battles: that his will be accomplished in choosing to identify himself with a sinful people, and that he not acquiesce to any of the devil's schemes to reject this identification in favor of his own rights and power as God's own Son. The section concludes in 4:11 with a triple marking: the boundary marker τότε, the HP ἀφίησιν, and the attention getter ἰδού.

Those familiar with scholarship in Matthew know that Matthew indeed uses geography to establish Old Testament parallels, though the most vociferous scholarship prefers to align Jesus with Moses.[27] I hypothesized that Matthew used the HPs consistently to draw together the different geographical movements like beads on a string that would indicate the point-for-point parallel between Jesus' movements and Israel's movements. The initial locations of Israel, Bethlehem, and Judah in the first few verses were not designated with HP's, because they did not fit in with the recapitulation. (Note that, in the examples, HPs are underlined, and direct speech, when quoted, is in a box.)

---

27  Dale C. Allison, Jr., *The New Moses: A Matthean Typology* (Minneapolis: Fortress Press, 1993).

Matt 2:13

Ἀναχωρησάντων δὲ αὐτῶν ἰδοὺ ἄγγελος κυρίου <u>φαίνεται</u> κατ'
ὄναρ τῷ Ἰωσὴφ λέγων· [go to Egypt]

When they had departed, an angel of the Lord
<u>appeared</u> in a dream to Joseph, saying, [Go to Egypt][28]

Matt 2:19

Τελευτήσαντος δὲ τοῦ Ἡρῴδου ἰδοὺ ἄγγελος κυρίου <u>φαίνεται</u>
κατ' ὄναρ τῷ Ἰωσὴφ ἐν Αἰγύπτῳ [saying: return to Israel]

When Herod had died, an angel of the Lord <u>appeared</u>
in a dream to Joseph in Egypt [saying, Return to Israel]

Matt 3:1

Ἐν δὲ ταῖς ἡμέραις ἐκείναις <u>παραγίνεται</u> Ἰωάννης ὁ
βαπτιστὴς κηρύσσων ἐν τῇ ἐρήμῳ τῆς Ἰουδαίας

Now in those days John the Baptist <u>came</u>, preaching in
the desert of Judea

This hypothesis had clear implications for scope: the HP is the
first finite verb in each section, possibly suggesting that the actual
verb was irrelevant with regard to its own semantics, but the HP
opening the episode (and introducing a participant) marked it as
developing this theme of Jesus as the Son of God. The scope for the
HP therefore had to be not the verb or even clause, but rather the
entire literary unit of movement to a new geographic location.

Turning to the double use of ἀφίησιν, which clinched Jesus'
self-identification with Israel on his own terms, the HP was either
the last or nearly last verb in the episode, but the double use suggested the HP was chosen consciously for these specific verbs, to
establish a lexical link: Jesus triumphed over both John the Baptist's
will and over the devil's will. The Israelites were unwilling to trust
God to provide and so complained bitterly about the lack of food
and water. Jesus underwent the same privations, but by choice,
and responded with faith and integrity. If the lexical repetition is

---

28  All translations are the author's own.

intentional,[29] the motivation would seem to be thematic: developing
Jesus as the Son of God who triumphs; and the scope for the HPs is
here first the verb itself, followed by all the implications of that verb
in context.

Matt 3:15

ἀποκριθεὶς δὲ ὁ Ἰησοῦς εἶπεν πρὸς αὐτόν·

> ἄφες ἄρτι,
> οὕτως γὰρ πρέπον ἐστὶν ἡμῖν πληρῶσαι πᾶσαν δικαιοσύνην.

τότε <u>ἀφίησιν</u> αὐτόν.

Jesus answered and said to him,

> Let it be so,
> for thus it is proper to fulfill all righteousness.

Then John <u>consented</u>.

Matt 4:11

Τότε <u>ἀφίησιν</u> αὐτὸν ὁ διάβολος,
καὶ ἰδοὺ ἄγγελοι προσῆλθον
καὶ διηκόνουν αὐτῷ.

Then the devil <u>left</u> him,
and angels came
and began attending to him.

## 3.4 HPs as Distinctively Thematic?

Having come this far in my interpretation, and seeing ahead that
the scene in Gethsemane had the most HPs of all, I began to postulate that the HPs in Matthew traced a theme beginning with identifying Jesus as the Son of God, with anticipatory triumphs of his
will over others', and climaxing with the ultimate triumph of Jesus

---

29　If the lexical repetition were considered coincidental, the instance in 4:11
might signal a transition from climax to dénouement, without thematic
overtones. As will be seen throughout this essay, my own tendency is to propose bold hypotheses, followed by rigorous testing of them. The themes of
the New Testament are bold and paradigm-breaking, which in my opinion
argues for exegetical attempts along similar lines.

in the garden in which he submitted his will to that of his Father's. The drama was not so much his death and resurrection, but his attitude toward them: his willingness to choose that path of pain, sacrifice and humiliating death instead of every privilege to which he was rightfully heir. This would mean the HPs would both function individually but also in concert, together weaving a whole thematic cloth.

The difficulty I encountered was all the text in between. Apart from the baptism/temptation scene (with eight HPs) and Gethsemane (with seven HPs), only two other episodes have more than two: sitting at Jesus' right and left is for whom it has been prepared (three HPs) and rendering to Caesar what is Caesar's (four HPs). Otherwise, thirteen scenes have two HPs and about thirty more have one HP. I tried to fit these into a framework about the kingdom of heaven, characterized by privation and self-denial, and then citizens of that kingdom. The kingdom knows no haste but bides its time, letting the tares grow alongside the wheat until the final harvest. It considers honoring one's parents to demand financial sacrifice, at the expense of one's own interests. It has no room for hardness of hearts, even if this means lifelong struggles in marriage. Its citizens are those who obey, regardless of what they say. It will go to better caretakers than those first chosen. It is not incompatible with, or a substitution for, earthly kingdoms.

I tried, but it was not persuasive. There was no compelling narrative told by those scenes with two HPs. When I ran my data by a true Gospel scholar, I had to conclude my hypothesis was proven false. While the HPs were certainly thematic, meaning, indicating material more directly germane to the overall message of the book than surrounding material, they were not telling a separate narrative or developing a distinct theme within the book, as a kind of discourse *Leitwort* device. Instead, I had to conclude that they were behaving as prototypically expected, as one strategy Matthew employed to indicate his main theme.

From this study, I confirmed the suspicion of scholarship that the HP is one strategy for indicating thematic prominence (among many others, which are beyond the scope of this essay). By identifying the heaviest clusters of HPs in Matthew, one is quickly drawn to the most thematic passages on Jesus as Son of God. Stephanie Black considers the distribution of the HPs in the temptation narrative to lead to a crescendo, as Jesus is tempted more and more fierce-ly. And the HPs in the Gethsemane narrative effectively split the storyline into Jesus on his own and Jesus with his disciples, there-by heightening the tension between his distress and their lack of fervor.[30]

## 3.5 Small Clusters

But what to do with the smaller clusters? Sometimes, as in the dis-cussion on divorce with the Pharisees, two consecutive verbs intro-ducing speech are HPs, as in 19:7–8.

Matt 19:7–8

7 λέγουσιν αὐτῷ·

> τί οὖν Μωϋσῆς ἐνετείλατο
> δοῦναι βιβλίον ἀποστασίου
> καὶ ἀπολῦσαι [αὐτήν];

8 λέγει αὐτοῖς ὅτι

> Μωϋσῆς πρὸς τὴν σκληροκαρδίαν ὑμῶν ἐπέτρεψεν ὑμῖν
> ἀπολῦσαι τὰς γυναῖκας ὑμῶν,
> ἀπ᾽ ἀρχῆς δὲ οὐ γέγονεν οὕτως.
> 9 λέγω δὲ ὑμῖν
> ὅτι ὃς ἂν ἀπολύσῃ τὴν γυναῖκα αὐτοῦ μὴ ἐπὶ πορνείᾳ
> καὶ γαμήσῃ ἄλλην
> μοιχᾶται.

7 They said to him,

> Why, then, did Moses command
> that a ceritificate of divorce be given
> and she be sent away?

8 He said to them that

> On account of the hardness of your hearts Moses
> permitted you
> to divorce your wives,
> but from the beginning it was not so.
> 9 Now I say to you
> that whoever divorces his wive (apart from sexual
> immorality)
> and marries another
> commits adultery.

These seem clear cases in which the HP of speech indicates that the following comment is thematically significant: the Pharisees think they can leverage Moses' permission to divorce against Jesus' hardline stance, but Jesus upends the argument entirely, claiming that Moses' commandment was not an endorsement but a concession, and the spiritually astute and strong enough would recognize this and still reject divorce. This is the flaw in the Pharisees: they think they understand Scripture and confidently proclaim on that basis, but in fact their spiritual blindness and obtuseness have led them astray. From the perspective of grammar, the scope of the HP is indeed the following comment.

In other small clusters, nonadjacent speech verbs are in the HP, as in the discussion with the rich young ruler about what is required to have eternal life, in 19:16–22.

Matt 19:16–22

16 Καὶ ἰδοὺ εἷς προσελθὼν αὐτῷ εἶπεν·

> διδάσκαλε, τί ἀγαθὸν ποιήσω
> ἵνα σχῶ ζωὴν αἰώνιον;

17 ὁ δὲ εἶπεν αὐτῷ·

> τί με ἐρωτᾷς περὶ τοῦ ἀγαθοῦ;
> εἷς ἐστιν ὁ ἀγαθός·
> εἰ δὲ θέλεις
> εἰς τὴν ζωὴν εἰσελθεῖν,
> τήρησον τὰς ἐντολάς.

18 λέγει αὐτῷ·

> ποίας;

ὁ δὲ Ἰησοῦς εἶπεν·

> τὸ οὐ φονεύσεις,
> οὐ μοιχεύσεις,
> οὐ κλέψεις,
> οὐ ψευδομαρτυρήσεις,
> 19 τίμα τὸν πατέρα καὶ τὴν μητέρα,
> καὶ ἀγαπήσεις τὸν πλησίον σου ὡς σεαυτόν.

20 λέγει αὐτῷ ὁ νεανίσκος·

> πάντα ταῦτα ἐφύλαξα·
> τί ἔτι ὑστερῶ;

21 ἔφη αὐτῷ ὁ Ἰησοῦς·

> εἰ θέλεις τέλειος εἶναι,
> ὕπαγε
> πώλησόν σου τὰ ὑπάρχοντα
> καὶ δὸς [τοῖς] πτωχοῖς,
> καὶ ἕξεις θησαυρὸν ἐν οὐρανοῖς,
> καὶ δεῦρο
> ἀκολούθει μοι.

22 ἀκούσας δὲ ὁ νεανίσκος τὸν λόγον
ἀπῆλθεν λυπούμενος·
ἦν γὰρ ἔχων κτήματα πολλά.

16 Then a man came to him and said,

> Teacher, what good must I do
> in order to inherit eternal life?

17 And then he said to him,

> Why do you ask me about what is good?
> There is only one who is good.
> But if you desire
> to enter into life,
> keep the commandments.

18 He said to him,

> Which ones?

And then Jesus said,

> "You shall not murder,"
> "You shall not commit adultery,"
> "You shall not steal,"
> "You shall not bear false witness,"
> 19 "Honor your father and your mother,"
> and "Love your neighbor as yourself."

20 The young man <u>said</u> to him,

> All these I have kept.
> What else is left?

21 Jesus replied,

> If you want to be complete,
> go,
> sell all your possessions
> and give the money to the poor,
> and then you will have treasure in heaven.
> Then come,
> follow me.

22 When the young man heard this message,
he went away in sorrow,
for he had very many possessions.

If one assumes that the HPs direct attention to the immediately following comment, then the young man's question, "which [commands must I keep]?" is highlighted but not Jesus' response, in which he lists six of the Ten Commandments. The young man insists that he has kept them all and asks what he yet lacks. In each case, the young man makes a "countering move" in the dialogue: changing the flow of the conversation from that intended by the previous speaker.[31] In Matthew, such shifts are usually indicated by

---

31  Cf. Robert A. Dooley and Stephen Levinsohn, *Analyzing Discourse: A Manual of Basic Concepts* (Dallas: SIL International, 2001), 4–6.

a form of the allegedly "pleonastic" ἀποκρίθη καὶ εἶπεν/ἔφη,[32] which suggests that the HP here is not purely to mark the countering move, but for another purpose. Following Runge's processing hierarchy, if not semantic nor paragraph-structural, then the most likely purpose is discourse-pragmatic, that is: thematic.

If only the young man's questions are thematic, then the thrust of the passage would be on his lack of knowledge about what eternal life truly entails. If, on the other hand, the question and response are considered together as one unit, and the initiating HP indicates the thematicity of the entire unit (the question and response), then the thrust of the passage would be the centrality of the Ten Commandments to attaining eternal life and the need to free oneself of all earthly concerns that might distract from the kingdom of God.

### a. Developmental Marker δέ

Discourse analysis is helpful here. The use of δέ to introduce Jesus' response in 19:18 signals a new development:

> Δέ is a coordinating conjunction like καί, but it includes the added constraint of signaling a new development (notated "+ development"). Καί, on the other hand, is unmarked for development ("- development"). The use of δέ represents the writer's choice to explicitly signal that what follows is a new, distinct development in the story or argument, based on how the writer conceived of it.[33]

This means that, although Jesus' response might ordinarily be considered to be contained within a single question-and-response unit, it is here signaled as also a new development. Possibly, then, the young man's question ποίας at the beginning of 19:18 stands alone. If so, the thematic point would be the young man's lack of

---

32 Matt 3:15; 4:4; 8:8; 11:4; 11:25; 12:39, 12:48; 13:11, 37; 14:28; 15:3, 13, 15, 23, 24, 26, 28; 16:2, 16, 17; 17:4, 11, 17; 19:4, 27; 20:13, 22; 21:21, 24, 27, 29, 30; 22:29; 24:2, 4; 25:9, 12, 26, 37, 40, 44, 45; 26:23, 25, 33, 66; 27:21, 25; 28:5. This accounts for nearly every instance of ἀποκρίνομαι in Matthew, which should be intriguing to discourse grammarians.

33 Runge, *Discourse Grammar of the Greek New Testament*, 31.

knowledge, not the role of the commandments. This would also explain the term νεανίσκος being first used in 19:20, reflecting a recognition at this point of his youth both in age and understanding. A more confident decision about the unit boundaries may be made after a short digression on the distinction between φημί and λέγω.

## b. Digression on φημί

The lexicons distinguish φημί and λέγω semantically: φημί is "affirm, mean" in addition to "say." In discourse terms, φημί is often used for replies. Given the common meaning "reply" (in every instance in Matthew, excepting only 26:61), it may be suggested that φημί is used to tie a statement to a preceding comment, making a conversational pair.[34]

A simple computer search shows that, in Matthew, φημί often follows an HP.[35] Of the sixteen instances, nine follow an HP, whereas the remaining seven (13:28a; 14:8; 21:27; 22:37; 26:60; 27:11, 65) do not, although 14:8 itself is an HP. In Matthew 4:5-7, the devil tempts Jesus to throw himself down from the temple heights. The devil "says" (HP) to him, "If you are the Son of God, throw yourself down..." and Jesus replies (ἔφη), "Again it is written: 'you shall not test the Lord your God.'"

Matt 4:6-7

6 καὶ λέγει αὐτῷ·

εἰ υἱὸς εἶ τοῦ θεοῦ,
βάλε σεαυτὸν κάτω·
γέγραπται γὰρ ὅτι
    τοῖς ἀγγέλοις αὐτοῦ ἐντελεῖται περὶ σοῦ
    καὶ ἐπὶ χειρῶν ἀροῦσίν σε,
    μήποτε προσκόψῃς πρὸς λίθον τὸν πόδα σου.

7 ἔφη αὐτῷ ὁ Ἰησοῦς·

---

34  Cf. Joseph Henry Thayer, Carl Ludwig Wilibald Grimm, and Christian Gottlob Wilke, *Thayer's Greek-English Lexicon of the New Testament*, (Peabody, MA: Hendrickson, 1996), s.v. φημι.

35  In 4:6-7; 8:7-8; 13:28-29; 17:25-26; 19:20-21; 25:19-21, 23; 26:31-34; 27:22-23 (twice with intervening verbs, in 17:25-26 and 17:22-23).

> πάλιν γέγραπται·
>    οὐκ ἐκπειράσεις κύριον τὸν θεόν σου.

6 He <u>said</u> to him,

> If you are the son of God,
> throw yourself down!
> For it is written that
>    He will command his angels concerning you
>    and they will bear you up on their hands,
>    lest you strike your foot against a stone.

7 Jesus <u>replied</u>,

> It is also written,
>    Do not put the Lord your God to the test.

Discourse is never simplistic, however: ἔφη can also occur with δέ, as in 13:28–29 in the parable of the wheat and the tares. In this case, the response is doubly marked as a reply and as a new development.

Matt 13:27–29

27 προσελθόντες δὲ οἱ δοῦλοι τοῦ οἰκοδεσπότου εἶπον αὐτῷ·

> κύριε, οὐχὶ καλὸν σπέρμα ἔσπειρας ἐν τῷ σῷ ἀγρῷ;
> πόθεν οὖν <u>ἔχει</u> ζιζάνια;

28 ὁ δὲ <u>ἔφη</u> αὐτοῖς·

> ἐχθρὸς ἄνθρωπος τοῦτο ἐποίησεν.

οἱ δὲ δοῦλοι <u>λέγουσιν</u> αὐτῷ·

> <u>θέλεις</u> οὖν
> ἀπελθόντες
> συλλέξωμεν αὐτά;

29 ὁ δὲ <u>φησιν</u>·

> οὔ, μήποτε συλλέγοντες τὰ ζιζάνια
> ἐκριζώσητε ἅμα αὐτοῖς τὸν σῖτον.
> ...

27 When the servants of the master came, they said to him,

> Sir, didn't you sow good seed in your field?
> How, then, <u>did</u> these weeds <u>come about</u>?

28 Then he <u>replied</u>,

> An enemy has done this.

So the servants <u>said</u> to him,

> <u>Do</u> you <u>want</u> us, then,
> to go and
> gather them?

29 But he <u>replied</u>,

> No, lest in gathering the weeds
> you uproot some of the wheat along with them.
> ...

When told of the tares that have appeared, the landowner replies (ἔφη) that an enemy was responsible. When the disciples ask (HP) if they should engage in weeding, the landowner responds (HP, φησίν) in the negative, lest damage be done to the wheat. Each question is a mere prompt for the reply, which is the main point; there is no inherent interest in the questions themselves.

## 3.6 Scope of HP: Discourse Unit

Two factors involved in delimiting a conversational unit are therefore lexical choice (λέγω vs. φημί) and developmental markers (e.g. δέ). Once the units have been delimited, it may be suggested that an introductory HP would refer not only to the immediately following speech, but to the entire conversational unit (if it includes more than the immediately following speech). In 19:18, Jesus' reply is distanced from the initial question with both the absence of φημί (an indicator of a question-answer pair) and the developmental marker δέ, suggesting that the young ruler's question might stand alone as a unit. But in 19:20–21, the use of ἔφη and the absence of any developmental marker suggests that Jesus' reply is to be considered within a question-answer pair. If so, then the thematic point in 19:20–21 is not simply the young man's question, what is necessary beyond the commandments, but also Jesus' reply: to have treasure in heaven requires repudiation of treasure on earth. Matthew does not want to downgrade the commandments as insufficient, but to indicate a yet fuller means of keeping the commandments, to lay up "treasure in heaven."

This leads us to a preliminary definition of the scope of an HP as *the discourse unit which it opens*. When an HP comes at the end (as with ἀφίησιν above), this unit is but the clause itself. When it comes in the middle of a section, that unit may consist only of a single speech unit (as in 19:18) or it may be multiple speech units constituting a larger conversational unit (as in 19:20–21). And when it comes at the beginning of a narrative episode, its scope is the entire narrative episode itself (as in 2:13, 19).

## 4. CONCLUSION

Thus, my conclusion regarding the HP must be that, even in speech margins with λέγω, it is not a stereotyped idiom after all.[36] At least in Matthew, the HP is an editorial device to indicate thematic prominence: an aid to the reader or listener to discern the hierarchy of themes present, and in particular to know which themes are of intrinsic interest to the author himself. It is a simple strategy that does not require additional words, such as discourse-pragmatic adverbs or particles, but instead modifies the form of a verb that is required anyway. It takes advantage of the nature of a narrative in which the tense and aspect are already clear and so do not need to be specified again, which frees up the form of the verb to other, nontemporal and nonaspectual, information.

The scope of the HP is the discourse unit in which it finds itself. I have not defined this extensively but take for granted an understanding that discourse is hierarchically constituted of both consecutive and embedded units. A narrative may be composed of episodes, which may have multiple paragraphs. A paragraph may have multiple clause clusters within it, as well as coordinated single clauses. An understanding of the current discourse is required in order to ascertain which is the smallest unit in which the HP finds itself, and therefore what its scope is.

---

36  Cf. Black, "The Historic Present in Matthew," 126.

If the scope of an HP can be determined, the exegetic value of the HP can be of great interest. Jesus' conversation with the rich young ruler is not about the Ten Commandments; they are mentioned only to be trumped by something greater. And yet, they are in no way dismissed but set in their proper place, as constantly happens throughout Matthew. Caesar has his rights and privileges that rightfully belong to him. Jesus freely acknowledges and endorses this, as long as one sees him as but a shadow of the far greater one who has rights and privileges to which we must, equally, pay far more attention. The HP is intended to make it a bit easier for us to see this: exactly where we, as readers, are to pay the bulk of *our* attention.

# BIBLIOGRAPHY

Allison, Dale C., Jr. *The New Moses: A Matthean Typology.* Minneapolis: Fortress Press, 1993.

Barber, Peter. *Sievers' Law and the History of Semivowel Syllabicity in Indo-European and Ancient Greek.* OCM. Oxford: Oxford University Press, 2013.

Benson, L. D. "Chaucer's Historical Present: Its Meaning and Uses." *English Studies* 42 (1961): 65–77.

Black, Stephanie. "The Historic Present in Matthew: Beyond Speech Margins." Pages 129–39 in *Discourse Analysis and the New Testament: Approaches and Results.* Edited by Stanley E. Porter and Jeffrey T. Reed. JSNTSup 170. Sheffield: Sheffield Academic Press, 1999.

Bybee, Joan, Revere Perkins, and William Pagliuca. *The Evolution of Grammar: Tense, Aspect and Modality in the Languages of the World.* Chicago: University of Chicago Press, 1994.

Christidis, A.-F., ed. *A History of Ancient Greek: From the Beginnings to Late Antiquity.* Cambridge: Cambridge University Press, 2007.

Comrie, Bernard. *Tense.* CTL. Cambridge: Cambridge University Press, 1985.

Dooley, Robert A., and Stephen Levinsohn. *Analyzing Discourse: A Manual of Basic Concepts.* Dallas: SIL International, 2001.

Fanning, Buist. *Verbal Aspect in New Testament Greek.* OTM. Oxford: Clarendon Press, 1990.

Fleischman, Suzanne. "Discourse Functions of Tense-Aspect Oppositions in Narrative: Toward a Theory of Grounding." *Linguistics* 23 (1985): 851–82.

———. *Tense and Narrativity: From Medieval Performance to Modern Fiction.* London: Routledge, 1990.

Fleischman, Suzanne, and Linda R. Waugh, eds. *Discourse-Pragmatics and the Verb: The Evidence From Romance.* Romance Linguistics. London: Routledge, 1991.

Haspelmath, Martin. "The Semantic Development of Old Presents: New Futures and Subjunctives Without Grammaticalization." *Diachronica* 15 (1998): 29–62.

Hopper, Paul J., and Elizabeth Closs Traugott. *Grammaticalization.* 2nd ed. CTL. Cambridge: Cambridge University Press, 2003.

Horrocks, Geoffrey. *Greek: A History of the Language and Its Speakers.* 2nd ed. Chichester: Wiley-Blackwell, 2010.

Jespersen, Otto. *A Modern English Grammar on Historical Principles.* 7 vols. London: Allen & Unwin, 1931.

Kiparsky, Paul. "Tense and Mood in Indo-European Syntax." *Foundations of Language* 4 (1968): 30–57.

Robar, Elizabeth. "From Bitter Sorrow to Exultant Joy: The Verbal System in 1 Samuel 1–2." In *Collected Essays on the Biblical Hebrew Verbal System.* LSAWS. Winona Lake IN: Eisenbrauns, forthcoming.

———. *The Verb and the Paragraph in Biblical Hebrew: A Cognitive-Linguistic Approach.* SSLL 78. Leiden: Brill, 2014.

Runge, Steven E. *Discourse Grammar of the Greek New Testament: A Practical Introduction for Teaching and Exegesis.* Peabody, MA: Hendrickson, 2010.

Steadman, J. M., Jr. "The Origin of the Historical Present in English." *SPh* 14 (1917): 1–46.

Thayer, Joseph Henry, Carl Ludwig Wilibald Grimm, and Christian Gottlob Wilke. *Thayer's Greek-English Lexicon of the New Testament.* Peabody, MA: Hendrickson, 1996.

Wolfson, Nessa. *CHP, the Conversational Historical Present in American English Narrative.* Topics in Sociolinguistics 1. Dordrecht: Foris, 1982.

———. "The Conversational Historical Present Alternation." *Language* 55 (1979): 16882.

CHAPTER 11

# The Function of the Augment in Hellenistic Greek

PETER J. GENTRY

SOUTHERN BAPTIST THEOLOGICAL SEMINARY

## 1. INTRODUCTION

According to the traditional view, the augment is a morpheme prefixed to the verb only in the aorist, imperfect, and pluperfect forms in the indicative modality to mark past tense.[1] This morpheme has two allomorphs: (1) a syllabic morph, and (2) a process morph. The syllabic morph consists simply of the vowel *epsilon* prefixed to the verb. When a compound verb is in question, the *epsilon* is prefixed to the simplex form and is therefore inserted between the adverbial/prepositional prefix(es) and the simplex form of the verb. The process morph entails a lengthening of the vowel, when the verb begins with a vowel instead of a consonant, as indicated in the following synopsis:

| | | |
|---|---|---|
| α | » | η |
| ε | » | η |
| ι | » | ῑ |
| ο | » | ω |
| υ | » | ῡ |
| αι | » | η |

---

1   Robert Beekes, *Etymological Dictionary of Greek*, IEED 10:1 (Leiden: Brill, 2010), 1:365; George Thomson, *The Greek Language* (Cambridge: Heffer & Sons, 1966), 22.

| | | |
|---|---|---|
| αυ | » | ηυ |
| ει | » | η |
| ευ | » | ηυ |
| οι | » | ῳ |
| ᾳ | » | η |
| η, ῑ, ῡ, ω | » | η, ῑ, ῡ, ω |

The process morph augment is unique to Greek. In Proto-Greek (PG), or in Proto-Indo-European (PIE), the putative parent language(s), no syllable may begin with a vowel. Consequently scholars posit that verbs beginning with a vowel at a later time originally began with a laryngeal (e.g., *h1, *h2, *h3). The process morph arose, then, when the syllabic augment (originally h1e-) contracted with the initial vowel of the root resulting in a corresponding long vowel, e.g., for h1es- "be," the augmented forms *h1e-h1es and *h1e-h1s contracted alike to *ēs. Thus "I was" is ā́sam in Vedic and ἦα in Homer. This ε:η relation derived from the verb "be" then became the model or pattern for all verb-initial vowels (as in the above chart) rather than contraction of the augment plus the initial vowel in each verb.[2] Lengthening of the vowel is the highest level of apophony possible in Sanskrit and is called vṛddhi which means "growth" or "increment,"[3] hence the term augment in common usage.[4]

In verbs with an initial r, or an original s or w (digamma) the intervocalic s or w is lost and contraction of syllabic morph and root-initial vowel occurs, respectively *ε-σεχ » εἶχον and *-ε-ϝιδ » εἶδον.[5] The r is doubled as in ρίπτω » ἔρριπτον although not consistently even by the Attic period and afterwards.[6]

---

2   Andrew L. Sihler, New Comparative Grammar of Greek and Latin (Oxford: Oxford University Press, 1995), 485; Sarah R. Rose, "Augment," EAGLL 1:215–16.

3   William D. Whitney, Sanskrit Grammar: Including Both the Classic Language and the Older Dialects of Veda and Brahmana, 2nd ed. (Cambridge: Harvard University Press, 1889).

4   Francine Mawet, Grammaire Sanskrite à l'Usage des Étudiants Hellénistes et Latinistes, LOC 16 (Leuven: Peeters, 2012), 191–92.

5   Cf. Leonard R. Palmer, The Greek Language, Great Languages (London: Faber & Faber, 1980), 294.

6   Friedrich Blass, Albert Debrunner, and Friedrich Rehkopf, Grammatik des neutestamentlichen Griechisch, 18th ed. (Göttingen: Vandenhoeck & Ruprecht, 2001), 11.

Sometimes the syllabic morph is η—the so-called long augment—rather than ε. Beekes plausibly suggests that from cases like ἤθελον « h₁e- h₁dhel- next to present (ἐ)θέλω, long augments arose analogically, e.g., ἠβουλόμην and that all long augments are probably analogical.[7]

Initial diphthongs are sometimes unaugmented. Since ου is never a pure diphthong at the beginning of a verb-form it is never lengthened.[8] Here I avoid use of the term "temporal augment" (unless citing someone) since by this term some scholars mean the process morph while other scholars mean by it the morpheme that indicates past tense regardless of the allomorph used.

It is important to note the rule in Greek that accent is recessive in verbs but may not precede the augment. Thus the augment is frequently accented.

The fact that only Greek, Indo-Iranian, Armenian, and Phrygian have the augment suggests that it was a common innovation developed later than PIE only in the eastern and southern branches of Proto-Indo-European.[9]

## 2. ORIGINS AND USAGE (DESCRIBED DIACHRONICALLY)

Before an attempt is made to interpret the data, a brief overview of the origins of the augment and a history of its usage is given.

### 2.1 Origins

Originally an adverb, *é, or better *h₁e-, meaning "yonder, there » at that time, then," the augment could be prefixed to a verb along with other adverbial prefixes, although it had to be prefixed to the primary stem first and so come between the primary stem and other adverbial prefixes.[10]

---

7   Beekes, *Etymological Dictionary of Greek*, 1:365.

8   Sometimes verbs beginning with ου are given a syllabic augment, e.g., προσεούρουν (Dem. *Con.*, 54.4).

9   Calvert Watkins, "Proto-Indo-European: Comparison and Reconstruction," in *The Indo-European Languages*, ed. Anna Giacalone Ramat and Paolo Ramat (London: Routledge, 1998), 33.

10  Michael Meier-Brügger, *Griechische Sprachwissenschaft*, Sammlung Göschen 2241 (Berlin: de Gruyter, 1992), 1:50–52; Rose, "Augment," 215.

In describing the morphology of the verb in PIE, Hoenigswald, Woodard, and Clackson note, "more loosely attached is the so-called augment *h₁e-, optionally prefixed to past tense indicatives, which survives in a number of descendants."[11] In Sanskrit, Jamison notes, "unlike the perfect both imperfect and aorist prefix the augment, regularly in Classical Sanskrit and optionally (but commonly) in Vedic."[12] In Middle Indic, the augment is found optionally, and seems especially utilized in shorter forms.[13] In Old Persian, the use of the present optative with the augment a- (thus looking like an imperfect optative) to express a repeated action in the past occurs.[14] Although sometimes questioned,[15] the latest research shows Phrygian undoubtedly possessed a preterite (past tense) verb-form with a prefix, the Indo-European "augment" known from Greek, Armenian, and Indo-Iranian.[16] Lastly, Armenian also used the augment to mark past tense verb forms.[17] Colvin provides an illustration:[18]

Gk.    *e-pʰer-on*    Skt.    *a-bʰar-am*    Arm.    *e-ber*

## 2.2 History of Usage

A brief consideration of Sanskrit is helpful before turning to the Greek language. Burrow's description of relations among the present, imperfect, and aorist in Sanskrit is as follows:

> The relation of the present-imperfect on the one hand, and the aorist on the other, can be discussed only in view of the meaning of the three tenses. In Sanskrit this is not at all complicated. The present indicates simply present time, and the imperfect past time in contradistinction to this and no more and no less: *hánti* "he slays," *áhan* "he slew," etc. There exists no trace of an

---

11  Henry M. Hoenigswald, Roger D. Woodard, and James P. T. Clackson, "Indo-European," *CEWAL*, 545.

12  Stephanie W. Jamison, "Sanskrit," *CEWAL*, 689.

13  Idem, "Middle Indic," *CEWAL*, 707, 711.

14  Rüdiger Schmitt, "Old Persian," *CEWAL*, 732.

15  Stephen Colvin, *A Brief History of Ancient Greek*, BHAW (Chichester: Wiley Blackwell, 2014), 18.

16  Claude Brixhe, "Phrygian," *CEWAL*, 785.

17  James P. Clackson, "Classical Armenian," *CEWAL*, 922.

18  Colvin, *Brief History of Ancient Greek*, 18.

"imperfect" sense in Sanskrit of that name, and such a sense, if it is needed, is expressed by the present tense with the addition of the particle *sma*. The aorist in contradistinction to the imperfect expresses a special kind of past time, inasmuch as it is used for describing an action which has just recently been completed: *úd asaú súryo agāt* "yonder sun has risen," etc.[19]

The augment is used only with the imperfect and aorist in Sanskrit. Interesting statistics are provided by Whitney:

a) In RV., the augmentless forms are more than half as common as the augmented (about 2000 and 3300), and are made from the present, perfect, and aorist-systems, but considerably over half from the aorist. Their nonmodal and modal uses are of nearly equal frequency. The tense value of the nonmodally used forms is more often past than present. Of the modally used forms, nearly a third are construed with *mā* prohibitive; the rest have twice as often an optative as a proper subjunctive value.

b) In AV., the numerical relations are very different. The augmentless forms are less than a third as many as the augmented (about 475 to 1450), and are prevailingly (more than four-fifths) aoristic. The nonmodal uses are only a tenth of the modal. Of the modally used forms, about four-fifths are construed with *mā* prohibitive; the rest are chiefly optative in value. Then, in the language of the *Brāhmain* (not including the mantra material which they contain), the loss of augment is, save in occasional sporadic cases, restricted to the prohibitive construction with *mā*; and the same continues to be the case later.[20]

As we shall see, forms with and without the augment occur in the Epic period in Greek as in Vedic and Avestan, but in Classical Greek, the augment appears to be almost a permanent fixture of the aorist.

---

19 Thomas Burrow, *The Sanskrit Language*, rev. ed. (London: Faber & Faber, 1973), 296.
20 Whitney, *Sanskrit Grammar*, 221.

We shall briefly survey five periods or stages in Greek: (1) Mycenaean, (2) Homeric, (3) Classical, (4) Hellenistic, and (5) together—Byzantine and Modern Greek.

In Mycenaean Greek forms of the verb occur consisting only of a primary stem and a secondary ending, e.g., *do-ke* = Hom. δῶκε, *de-ka-sa-to* = Hom. δέξατο. Only one uncertain and debated instance of the augment is known: *a-pe-do-ke* = ἀπ-έ-δωκε, occurring in a temporal dependent clause.[21]

Aorist forms occur in Homer with and without augment. The most recent research, both painstaking and thorough, is that of Egbert Bakker whose conclusions affirm the study of Drewitt published in 1912.[22] Bakker analyzed both the *Iliad* and the *Odyssey*. Of 5795 aorists in the *Iliad*, as an example, he first rules out about 70% where the augment is either required or ruled out by meter. Thus, not all instances can be explained by considerations of meter. He claims that the augment is favored in discourse pertaining to the speaker's "now," in speech introductions, in similes, and in proverbs and general statements. By contrast, the augment is disfavored, avoided, or prohibited in verbs denoting events other than those on the narrative timeline, verbs in ἐπεί-clauses in narrative and in temporal ἐπεί-clauses in discourse, in negated verbs, and in verbs with the distributive-iterative suffix -σκ-. According to Bakker, what these circumstances have in common is a closeness or nearness when the augment is used, while augmentless verbs can equally be explained as denoting events lacking closeness or deixis in space or time. In 2002, a PhD thesis by Frederick James Pagniello entitled "The Homeric Augment: A Deictic Particle" appeared to confirm Bakker's claims.[23] Nicolas Bertrand and Olav Hackstein have developed (in-

---

21  Helmut Rix, *Historische Grammatik des Griechischen: Laut- und Formenlehre*, 2nd ed (Darmstadt: Wissenschaftliche Buchgesellschaft, 1996), 229.

22  J. A. J. Drewitt, "The Augment in Homer" *ClQ* 6 (1912): 44–59, 104–20; Egbert J. Bakker, "Similes, Augment, and the Language of Immediacy," in *Speaking Volumes: Orality and Literacy in the Greek and Roman World*, ed. Janet Watson, MS 218 (Leiden: Brill, 2001), 1–21; idem, *Pointing at the Past: From Formula to Performance in Homeric Poetics*, Hellenic Studies 12 (Washington, DC: Center for Hellenic Studies, 2005).

23  Frederick J. Pagniello, "The Homeric Augment: a Deictic Particle" (PhD diss., University of Georgia, 2002; Rutger Allan assessed Pagniello's thesis in ch. 3 of the present volume.

THE FUNCTION OF THE AUGMENT IN HELLENISTIC GREEK    359

dependently) Bakker's proposal further, arguing that the deictic function of the augment signals foregrounding.[24]

Nonetheless, in spite of prodigious research, Bakker's analysis is not persuasive. First, note that the augment, derived from *é, is generally acknowledged to have had a deictic force originally. But the deictic force is that of a *far*, not a *near* pointer. The same adverbial prefix is found in ἐ-κεῖνος and ἐ-χθές.[25] It ought to indicate something remote, not close or near. Rutger J. Allan's essay, "Tense and Aspect in Classical Greek" (ch. 3 in the current volume), demonstrates convincingly that in each of the augmentless categories provided by Bakker that past tense is obvious and this explains why the augment is unnecessary in such contexts. The history is that an adverb with locative semantic value (there) developed into a temporal semantic value (then).[26] Typologically, Bybee, Perkins, and Pagliuca have shown that the locative rather than the temporal meaning usually undergoes erosion.[27] Cross-linguistically then, the path of development is that first the particle had a spatial meaning, then later a temporal meaning, and finally became bleached semantically and grammaticalized as a marker of past tense. By the Homeric period the spatial meaning has already entirely given way to a temporal meaning, and by the Attic period the particle is grammaticalized simply as a marker of past tense. One cannot have both the spatial and temporal meaning at the same linguistic stage. Note that Bakker's thesis is diametrically opposite to the one debated instance in Mycenaean Greek. According to him, the augment is avoided in temporal ἐπεί-clauses and the one instance where we do have an augment in Mycenaean Greek is a dependent temporal clause—an exact parallel in syntax.

24  Nicholas Bertrand, "Grounding of Information," *EAGLL* 2:150; Olav Hackstein, "The Greek of Epic," in *A Companion to the Ancient Greek Language*, ed. Egbert J. Bakker, BCAW (Chichester: Wiley Blackwell, 2014), 405.

25  Beekes, *Etymological Dictionary of Greek*, 1:397; 2:1632; cf. Eduard Schwyzer, *Griechische Grammatik: Bd. 2, Syntax und syntaktische Stilistik*, HAW 2 (Munich: Beck, 1950), 208–9.

26  Meier-Brügger, *Griechische Sprachwissenschaft*, 1:50; Rose, "Augment," 215.

27  Joan Bybee, Revere Perkins, and William Pagliuca, *The Evolution of Grammar: Tense, Aspect, and Modality in the Languages of the World* (Chicago: University of Chicago Press, 1994), 23–26, 137.

**Excursus on Augment Constrained by Meter:** Each participant in the epic poetry is described by characteristic epithets and phrases. When one shifts from nominative to genitive or dative, the metrical constraints may result in changing the dialect in which the characteristic epithet is expressed. Similarly metrical constraints allow innovations or require archaic forms and so the use or nonuse of the augment may be easily explained.[28]

I am not aware of detailed research for Classical Greek so I shall simply cite the grammar by Smyth:

> In Attic tragedy the augment is sometimes omitted in choral passages, rarely in the dialogue parts (messengers' speeches), which are nearer akin to prose. ...
> In Herodotus the syllabic augment is omitted only in the case of pluperfects and iteratives in σκον; the temporal augment is generally preserved, but it is always omitted in verbs beginning with αι, αυ, ει, ευ, οι, and in ἀγῑνέω, ἀεθλέω, ἀνώγω, ἔρδω, ἐάω, ὁρμέω etc.; in others it is omitted only in some forms (as ἀγορεύω, ἄγω, ἕλκω, ὁρμάω) and in others it is variable (ἀγγέλλω, ἅπτω, ἄρχω, ἐπίσταμαι, ἀνέχομαι); in cases of Attic reduplication the augment is never added, Hdt. omits the augment for the reduplication in the above verbs.[29]

The Ionic dialect of Herodotus appears to preserve something of the original meaning better than Attic. Nonetheless, we can see that the original meaning and usage is generally lost and the morpheme is becoming more or less a permanent fixture of the aorist. This developmental pattern is similar to Sanskrit. As Rose notes, "the augment as a marker of 'past' became compulsory in the classical language."[30] Verb forms without augment in the classical period are

28  Francisco Rodríguez Adrados, *A History of the Greek Language: From Its Origins to the Present*, (Leiden: Brill, 2005), 91–95.
29  Herbert W. Smyth, *Greek Grammar*, 2nd ed. (Cambridge: Harvard University Press, 1956), 147.
30  Rose, "Augment," 216; E. Schwyzer, *Griechische Grammatik: Bd. 1, Allgemeiner Teil, Lautlehre, Wortbildung, Flexion*, HAW 1 (Munich: Beck, 1953.), 650–56.

archaisms, poetic departures from everyday language.[31] We begin to see some forms doubly augmented in the Classical period, like ἔμελλον » ἤμελλον based on analogy to (ἐ)θέλω » ἤθελον.

The Greek of the Hellenistic period, roughly 300 BC to AD 300 is also called *Koine*, from ἡ κοινὴ γλῶσσα, the common language spoken as a *lingua franca* throughout the Graeco-Roman world at that time. As is well known, the main ingredients are Attic and Ionic, although there are influences from other dialects as well (e.g., Doric).

For the Hellenistic period, and especially the papyri, detailed data on the use of the augment may be gleaned from Mayser, *Grammatik der griechischen Papyri aus der Ptolemäerzeit*, Gignac, *A Grammar of the Greek Papyri of the Roman and Byzantine Periods*, Mandilaras, *The Verb in the Greek Non-Literary Papyri* (covering the periods analyzed by Gignac and Mayser together), in addition to Thackeray, *A Grammar of the Old Testament in Greek According to the Septuagint* and Blass-Debrunner-Rehkopf on the Greek of the New Testament.[32]

On the topic of the verb Thackeray notes three features distinguishing Greek of the Hellenistic period from the Classical: (1) the process morph form of the augment almost disappears, (2) the syllabic morph is moved to external position, and (3) reduplication is lost.[33]

Gignac's brief summaries for the papyri of the Roman and Byzantine periods deserve to be cited. For the syllabic morph, he states:

> The syllabic augment is occasionally omitted in compound verbs whose prefix ends in a vowel, but only rarely in compound verbs whose prefix ends in a consonant. In simple verbs, it is occasionally omitted in the

31  Rose, "Augment," 216.
32  Edwin Mayser, *Grammatik der griechischen Papyri aus der Ptolemäerzeit: Band I. Laut- und Worthlehre. II. Teil. Flexionslehre* (Leipzig: de Gruyter, 1938); Francis Thomas Gignac, *A Grammar of the Greek Papyri of the Roman and Byzantine Periods: Volume II. Morphology*, TDSA 55,2 (Milan: Istituto Editoriale Cisalpino – La Goliardica, 1981); Basil G. Mandilaras, *The Verb in the Greek Non-Literary Papyri* (Athens: Hellenic Ministry of Culture and Sciences, 1973); H. St. J. Thackeray, *A Grammar of the Old Testament in Greek According to the Septuagint* (Cambridge: Cambridge University Press, 1909); Blass, Debrunner, and Rehkopf, *Grammatik des neutestamentlichen Griechisch*.
33  Thackeray, *Grammar of the Old Testament in Greek*, 195; Blass, Debrunner, and Rehkopf, *Grammatik des neutestamentlichen Griechisch*, 53–56.

pluperfect and sometimes in other tenses. Conversely, the syllabic augment sometimes appears in moods and tenses of both compounds and simples where no augment is required.[34]

In addition, for the process morph he states:

Temporal augment and/or reduplication is omitted occasionally in both simple and compound verbs beginning with α-, ε-, αι-, or οι-, frequently in verbs beginning with ο-, usually in verbs beginning with ευ-, and normally in verbs beginning with ι-, ει-, and υ-.[35]

Available information for this stage is detailed. For example, from the first to the sixth centuries AD, for the aorist of εὑρίσκω Gignac lists over 26 forms employing ευ and 17 forms employing ηυ and indicates that these data are not exhaustive.[36] Eighty-six pluperfects are found in the New Testament. The syllabic augment is possible in 11 cases where the form is active but occurs only twice and is found in six of seven possible cases where the form is medio-passive.[37] Thus only 8 of 86 instances of the pluperfect are augmented.

We see, then, for the augment, the occasional loss of both process morph and even syllabic morph not only in the papyri, but in the Greek of the Hellenistic period as a whole due to changes in accent, pronunciation of vowels, phonological processes like aphaeresis, etc. Sometimes, especially in the papyri, the augment is falsely transferred to nonindicative moods and nonfinite forms of the verb. We also see forms doubly or even triply augmented. Examples are ἠνώιξαμεν (P.Petr. 2.37, 246/5 BC) and ἠνέῳξα (LXX Gen 8:6, 3 Macc 6:18, NT John 9:17). Through inflation in the language, the force of the adverbial prefix is felt no longer and the form is considered a simplex form. The phenomena of the Hellenistic period, as Gignac notes, are

a step toward a more restricted use of the augment in Modern Greek. Since the past tenses of the indicative were already sufficiently characterized in most verbs

34  Gignac, *Grammar of the Greek Papyri*, 223.
35  Ibid., 233.
36  Ibid., 240–41.
37  William D. Mounce, *The Morphology of Biblical Greek*, (Grand Rapids: Zondervan, 1994), 113–15, 121.

by the endings and/or the stem, the augment was largely a superfluous morpheme, making it particularly
subject to phonological tendencies (e.g., inverse eli-
sion following /ε/ and leveling within the paradigm. In
Modern Greek, the syllabic augment is used generally
only when it bears the accent. It has been incorporated into many verb stem classes, e.g., κατεβαίνω, ξεφεύγω
(ἐξέφ[ε]υγον).[38]

The Medieval and Modern periods are nicely summarized by a
succinct statement from Horrocks:

> The syllabic augment naturally survived more strong-
> ly, but its role too was partially undermined by sound
> change, specifically aphaeresis. In standard Modern
> Greek it therefore survives only when accented, though
> in some dialects it is still retained across the board. It is
> also worth noting that, on the basis of frequently oc-
> curring verb forms augmented at least optionally in
> ['i-], some inherited from antiquity (e.g., ἤθελα ['iθela]
> "I wanted," ἤμελλα ['imela] "I was about to," εἶπα ['ipa]
> "I said," εἶδα ['ida] "I saw"), others arising through var-
> ious analogies in the middle ages (e.g., ἤπια ['ipja] for
> ἔπια ['epja] "I drank," or ἤλεγα ['ileɣa] after εἶπα ['ipa]
> "I said") a number of dialects eventually generalized ἤ-
> ['i-] as the basic form of the syllabic augment. This is
> particularly characteristic of much of the southeastern
> area, many Cycladic varieties, and the speech of east-
> ern Crete. Where the unaccented augment is retained,
> some of these dialects substitute ἐ- [e-], while others
> keep ἠ- [i-] throughout. From late antiquity onwards,
> the practice of using an "internal" augment with com-
> pound verbs (e.g., προσ-έ-βαλον [pros'evalon] "they at-
> tacked") was steadily abandoned in favour of a regular
> "external" augment (e.g., ἐ-πρόσβαλον 'eprozvalon) or no
> augment at all if the initial element began with a vowel.
> This was inevitable, given that word formation using
> the classical prepositions had ceased to be productive

---

38 Gignac, *Grammar of the Greek Papyri*, 225.

and many compound verbs survived only as lexicalized fossils. The true nature of such composition was therefore steadily lost sight of.[39]

The claim, therefore, that the augment is a marker of past tense seems to be called into question by the data on the loss of the augment in the Greek of the Hellenistic and also later periods. It is not entirely surprising that some scholars, like Stanley Porter and Constantine Campbell, have questioned the traditional view regarding the function of the augment.[40] It is at this point that we need to consider the origins and the history of usage of the personal endings. Then we shall be able to put together a proper picture of the whole system marking tense in Greek.

## 3. THE PERSONAL ENDINGS

What many students of Greek never realize is that there is only one set of personal endings for both thematic and athematic verbs. The thematic vowel combines with the personal endings to make the thematic verbs look so different from the athematic conjugation. Detailed discussions for the historical and phonological processes resulting in the forms for each number and person are provided by Sihler.[41]

## 3.1 Primary Personal Endings

| Active | | Medio-Passive | |
|---|---|---|---|
| (ο)μι » ω | (ο)μεν | (ο)μαι | (ο)μεθα |
| (ε)σι » εις | (ε)τε | (ε)σαι » η | (ε)σθε |
| (ε)τι » ει | (ο)ντι » ουσι | (ε)ται | (ο)νται |

---

39  Geoffrey Horrocks, *Greek: A History of the Language and its Speakers*, 2nd ed. (Chichester: Wiley, 2014), 319.

40  Stanley E. Porter, *Verbal Aspect in the Greek of the New Testament with Reference to Tense and Mood*, SBG 1 (New York: Lang, 1989), 208–9; idem, *Linguistic Analysis of the Greek New Testament: Studies in Tools, Methods, and Practice* (Grand Rapids: Baker Academic, 2015), 175–83; Constantine R. Campbell, *Basics of Verbal Aspect in Biblical Greek*, (Grand Rapids: Zondervan, 2008), 36–38; idem, *Advances in the Study of Greek: New Insights for Reading the New Testament* (Grand Rapids: Zondervan, 2015), 114–17.

41  Sihler, *New Comparative Grammar*, 453–79.

## 3.2 Secondary Personal Endings

| Active | | Medio-Passive | |
|---|---|---|---|
| (o)μ » ον | (o)μεν | (o)μην | (o)μεθα |
| (ε)ς | (ε)τε | (ε)σο » ου | (ε)σθε |
| (ε)τ » ε | (o)ντ » ον | (ε)το | (o)ντο |

---

**Excursus:** The factors and phonological processes whereby the combination of thematic vowel and personal ending yields the endings for the thematic verbs cannot be detailed here. Earlier grammarians derived the first pers. c. sg. ending ω from -o- + μι. Jannaris states, "The first person singular of the active voice -ω is the result of dropping the personal ending -μι and the consequent antectasis of the preceding thematic vowel -o- to -ω."[42] Most scholars today derive -ω from -oh2 .[43]

---

Aside from distinction in voice, there are two sets, traditionally labeled primary and secondary based on the distribution of the endings. Primary endings are used in the present and future indicative forms while secondary endings are employed only with the indicative past tenses (imperfect, aorist, and pluperfect) and in the optative. The personal endings for the subjunctive were originally variable, but in Greek, the primary endings became standard.[44]

There is an inversion, however, between traditional terminology and a proper understanding of the development in the language. From a historical-linguistic point of view, the secondary endings are actually original or primary, while the so-called primary endings are *based on* and *developed from* the secondary endings by the addition of ι (*iota*), the *hic et nunc* particle in PIE.[45] Although the first and second pl. endings have the addition of iota in Hittite, they no longer show this in Greek and analysis of the development is

---

42  Antonius N. Jannaris, *An Historical Greek Grammar* (London: Macmillan, 1897), 197.

43  Sihler, *New Comparative Grammar*, 458.

44  Ibid., 453.

45  Hoenigswald, Woodard, and Clackson, "Indo-European," 545; Watkins, "Proto-Indo-European, 60–62.

debated.[46] [The ι (*iota*) as *hic et nunc* particle should not be confused with the *-ye/o-, *-eye/o, *-eH2ye/o particles affixed to verb stems to mark them as frequentative or durative.[47]] Detailed charts from Sihler demonstrate this, followed by a more simplified version from Bubenik.[48]

*3.2.A. Secondary*

|        | PIE  | Vedic   | Avest | Hitt | Grk  | OLat   | Goth  | OCS    | Lith |
|--------|------|---------|-------|------|------|--------|-------|--------|------|
| 1 sg.  | -m   | -m      | -m    | -nun | -ν   | -m     | -ø    |        | -u   |
|        | -m̥   | -am     | -am   | -un  | -α   |        | -u    | -ŭ     | -mi  |
| 2 sg.  | -s   | -s      | -s    | -š   | -ς   | -s     | -s    | -ø     | -si  |
| 3 sg.  | -t   | -t      | -t    | -t   | -ø   | -d     | -ø    | -ø     | -ø   |
|        |      |         |       |      |      |        |       |        |      |
| 1 pl.  | -mĕ̄  | -mā̆     | -ma   | -wen | -μεν | *-mos  | -m(a) | -mŭ    | -me  |
| 2 pl.  | -te  | -ta(na) | -ta   | -ten | -τε  | *-tes? | -Þ    | -te    | -te  |
| 3 pl.  | -nt  | -n(t)   | -n    |      | -ν   | -nt    | -n(a) | [+ nas]| —    |
|        | -n̥t  | -at     | -at   |      |      |        |       |        |      |
|        | -r̥   | -ur     |       |      |      |        |       |        |      |
|        | -ēr  |         |       | -er  |      | -ēre   |       |        |      |

---

46  Sihler, *New Comparative Grammar*, 463–64.

47  Ibid., 491, 503–04; Palmer, *The Greek Language*, 261, 264–66.

48  Sihler, *New Comparative Grammar*, 454; Vit Bubenik, "Verbal System (Tense, Aspect, Mood)," *EAGLL*, 3:483.

## 3.2.B. Primary

|        | PIE   | Vedic    | Avest    | Hitt    | Grk   | OLat   | Goth  | OCS      | Lith  |
|--------|-------|----------|----------|---------|-------|--------|-------|----------|-------|
| 1 sg.  | -oH2  | -āmi     | -ā(mi)   |         | -ω    | -ō     | -a    | -ǫ       | -u    |
|        | -mi   | -mi      | -mi      | -mi     | -μι   | -m     | -m    | -mĭ      | -mi   |
| 2 sg.  | -si   | -si, -ṣi | -hi, -ši | -ši     | -ς    | -s     | -s    | -si, -šĭ | -si   |
|        |       |          |          |         | -εις  |        |       |          |       |
| 3 sg.  | -ti   | -ti      | -ti      | -zi     | -τι   | -t     | -t/Þ  | -tŭ      |       |
|        | -i    |          |          |         | -ι    |        |       | -ø       |       |
|        |       |          |          |         |       |        |       |          |       |
| 1 pl.  | -mos  | -mas(i)  | -maihi   | -weni   | -μες  | *-mos  | -m    | -mŭ      | -me   |
| 2 pl.  | -te   | -tha(na) | -ta      | -teni   | -τε   | *-tes? | -Þ    | -te      | -te   |
| 3 pl.  | -nti  | -nti     | -θa      | -(a)nzi | -ντι  | -nt    | -nd   | [+ nas]tŭ | —    |
|        | -n̥ti  | -ati     | -aiti    |         | *-ατι |        |       |          |       |

## 3.2.C. Simplified Chart

|        | Athematic |           | Thematic  |           |              |
|--------|-----------|-----------|-----------|-----------|--------------|
|        | Primary   | Secondary | Primary   | Secondary | PIE          |
| 1 sg.  | -mi       | -n        | -on       | -ē        | « *-oH       |
| 2 sg.  | -si       | -s        | -es       | -eis      | « *-e h₁i    |
| 3 sg.  | -ti       | -ø        | -e        | -ei       | « *-e        |
| 1 pl.  | -men/s    | -men/s    | -men/s    | -omen/s   | « *-(o)mom (?) |
| 2 pl.  | -te       | -te       | -ete      | -ete      | « *-et(h₁)e  |
| 3 pl.  | -nti      | -n        | -on       | -onti (Doric) | « *-onti |

Andrew Sihler makes an important statement concerning the development of verb forms in Greek:

> It may strike a speaker of modern European language as perplexing that the forms proper to the present indicative would be derived from forms proper to past action or unreal action, but that is the situation not only in PIE but in a large number of the world's languages. A correct appreciation of the relationship of the two sets of endings explains why the optative is marked with

"past tense endings": the endings in question were not specifically past tense, rather they are the GENERIC or UNMARKED endings. It also explains their role in the so-called injunctive forms, ... which are not past tense forms but tenseless ones.[49]

# 4. A HOLISTIC PICTURE: DIACHRONIC AND SYNCHRONIC

With a knowledge of the origins and history of usage of both augment and personal endings, a clearer picture emerges as follows. The augment originates as an adverb having a deictic and spatial semantic value "yonder, there." Clearly this morpheme is prefixed only to verbs. Aorists without augments referred not to specific events but to habitual or generalized matters.[50] Eventually, a temporal sense, "at that time, then," is developed and the spatial sense is eroded. This development is already completed by Homer. When the system of reduced verb marking was abandoned, the augment became grammaticalized as a marker of past tense (e.g., Hom. aor. δίον and ἔδεισα « δείδω). This happened by the Classical period.

Note the development of tense and aspect, first in PIE and then in Greek. At first, tense was marked only by adverbs and conjunctions. In PIE, a present tense was created *secondarily*, by adding the *iota* to the personal endings. The *iota* as *hic et nunc* particle is also found in the present tense of most athematic verbs in terms of reduplication with *iota* (δίδωμι, τίθημι), as well as in some thematic verbs (γίγνομαι » γίνομαι, διδάσκω, πίπτω, τίκτω).[51] Thus the primary personal endings were marked while the secondary endings were originally unmarked. So in the verbal system inherited from PIE by Greek, tense existed as a binary opposition present/nonpresent in addition to aspect. The imperfect was developed from the present.

Uniquely, a future tense developed in Greek as an innovation likely based on a desiderative form in PIE. In the indicative, secondary

---

49  Sihler, *New Comparative Grammar*, 454.
50  Ibid., 484.
51  Cf. Harry A. Hoffner Jr. and H. Craig Melchert, *A Grammar of the Hittite Language: Part I; Reference Grammar*, LANE 1/1 (Winona Lake, IN: Eisenbrauns, 2008), 174.

personal endings are suffixed only to aorist, imperfect, and pluperfect forms, while the primary endings are used for the nonpast
forms. Since the optative is fading from the picture at an early date
and is also distinguished from the indicative forms by the *iota* infix,
by contrast to the primary endings, the secondary endings, originally unmarked, came to be associated with past tense. The feature
of the augment can be construed as a past tense marker attached
to indicative forms in appropriate contexts and then later becoming systematized throughout the imperfect, aorist, and pluperfect
indicatives. The introduction of the augment signals an additional value—which is interpreted here as temporal reference—to the
semantic baggage of indicative forms. Its subsequent grammaticalization does not indicate loss of that value from the usual formal
semantics of the indicative, merely the loss of its connection solely
with the augment.[52] The endings of the verbal forms came to convey
temporal value in addition to person and voice.

In terms of aspect, first there is a binary opposition of perfective
and imperfective. The perfect is a combination of perfective and
imperfective aspect. We end up, then, with three different aspects
in Greek.

Why are there seven verb-forms in the indicative mood and only
three in the nonindicative moods? *The answer is simple*: the forms
in the indicative mark both aspect and tense (the future forms may
mark only tense and not aspect); outside of the indicative they mark
only aspect. Since there are only three aspects, there are only three
verb-forms outside of the indicative.

If we can move to the period of Classical Greek, we arrive at a
situation where the augment and secondary endings are both mandatory and characteristic of the imperfect, aorist, and pluperfect
indicative. As a result we have a redundancy in the language: two
markers of past tense. After coming to this result, Elizabeth Robar
discovered it was already in print.[53]

---

52  Trevor V. Evans, *Verbal Syntax in the Greek Pentateuch: Natural Greek Usage
    and Hebrew Interference*, (Oxford: Oxford University Press, 2001), 49.
53  See ch. 10 in the present volume; John Hewson and Vit Bubenik, *Tense
    and Aspect in Indo-European Languages: Theory, Typology, Diachrony*, CILT
    145 (Amsterdam: Benjamins, 1997), 37. Cf. also Georgios K. Giannakis, "In-
    do-European Linguistic Background." *EAGLL*, 2:221–22.

Note that a matrix of three aspects and three tenses should yield nine forms, but in the indicative we have only seven:

|  | Past | Present | Future |
|---|---|---|---|
| Perfective | Aorist | Present | Future |
| Imperfective | Imperfect | Present | Future |
| Combination | Pluperfect | Perfect | Future Perfect |

Why is this? The answer is again simple: the default for the present tense is imperfective and not perfective aspect.[54] The default for the future tense is perfective. Later in Koine, the periphrastic future allows for aspectual distinction.[55]

Several features of language in general support the conclusion that the augment is a morpheme marking past tense but can also be omitted in Hellenistic Greek.

First, redundancy means that grammatical meaning may be grammaticalized by more than one morpheme or even strategy in a language. From a cross-linguistic perspective, it is unusual to have double markings for aspect, modality, and tense,[56] although examples occur in Italian.[57] In Greek, we have conjugations and forms inherited from PIE, but also constant innovation in the development. Greek inherits the old perfect based on apophony, but consider the variations in forming the so called second perfect which developed alongside the first perfect with double marking (*kappa* and reduplication).

---

54 Imperfective and not perfective aspect is typologically fitting for the present tense. See Bybee, Perkins, and Pagliuca, *The Evolution of Grammar*, 125–75.

55 See also the essay by Amalia Moser, ch. 17 in this volume.

56 Alice C. Harris, and Lyle Campbell, *Historical Syntax in Cross-Linguistic Perspective*, CSL 74 (Cambridge: Cambridge University Press, 1995), 179.

57 Paola Benincà, Adam Ledgeway, and Nigel Vincent, *Diachrony and Dialects: Grammatical Change in the Dialects of Italy*. (Oxford: Oxford University Press, 2014), 149.

## 4.1 So-called Second Perfects

| | | |
|---|---|---|
| 1. Apophony | οἶδα | ειδ- |
| 2. Reduplication | κέκραγα | κραγ- |
| 3. Apophony + reduplication | λέλοιπα | λειπ- |
| 4. Reduplication + aspiration | τέταχα | ταγ- |
| 5. Apophony + reduplication + aspiration | εἴληφα | (σ)λαβ- |
| 6. "Attic" reduplication | ἀκ-ήκ-οα | ακου- |

Double marking, then, is not uncommon in Greek due to the long period of development and use.

Second just as phonemics is an interlocking organization and system of sounds, so grammatical relations and lexical options operate in an interlocking system in a language. Silva illustrated this lexically using research done by Joly:

| be content with | | "love" | | "kiss" | | "impregnate" |
|---|---|---|---|---|---|---|
| ἀγαπᾶν | ↳ | φιλεῖν | ↳ | κυνεῖν | ⇔ | κύειν |
| | | ἀγαπᾶν | | φιλεῖν | | |

Homonymic clash between κυνεῖν and κύειν in the aorist caused φιλεῖν to take the place of κυνεῖν and so ἀγαπᾶν filled in the gap left by φιλεῖν.[58] Similarly in grammar, new strategies are replacing old. For imperfective aspect in past time we find in the Gospel of Luke analytic tense formations like ἦν plus participle alongside simple imperfects (ἦν διανεύων [he was signaling] 1:22, ἐνένευον [he was signaling] 1:62). We find conative *Aktionsart* expressed through the aspect grammaticalized in the imperfect or lexicalized through ζητέω used as a modal verb (ἐζήτουν αὐτὸν οἱ Ἰουδαῖοι ἀποκτεῖναι [the Jews were attempting to kill him] John 5:18). Thus, between Homer and Classical Greek the augment became grammaticalized as a marker of past tense. Perhaps around the same time the secondary endings for person, originally UNMARKED, became associated with past

---

58 Moisés Silva, *Biblical Words and their Meaning: An Introduction to Lexical Semantics*, rev. and exp. ed. (Grand Rapids: Zondervan, 1994), 96.

tense as well, since the optative was marked by the ι (iota) infix.[59] Collapse of the system of 12 vowels and 12 diphthongs to just 6 vowels in the Hellenistic period alongside changes in accent and other factors resulted in the loss primarily of the process morph for augment.[60] Nonetheless, the syllabic augment was largely retained until the Modern period and has not completely disappeared partly because it was taught.[61] It is morphologically part of the past tenses.

Third, diachronic development means that later speakers do not always correctly interpret texts from earlier periods. Leumann has shown that Hellenistic poets did not correctly understand the Greek of Homer in many ways.[62] Thus, even if the augment had a different semantic value in Homer, this has no more influence on the Greek of someone in Palestine in the first century AD than the British rules of 1940 for distinguishing between "shall" and "will" has on an English speaker in Kentucky today.

Alternative theories are not convincing. Campbell argues that the augment is a morpheme marking spatial reference. This is a possible proposal, but not a plausible interpretation of the actual data. The early evidence for development of the future tense and augment does not fit his ideas well.

The exceptional patterns of verbal usage which provide the basis for Porter's theory are better taken as fossilized survivals of an older aspectual structure overlaid by the growing importance of temporal reference. Certainly Porter does not offer a view that comprehensively accounts for development and history of the Greek language as a whole.

---

59  The optative has secondary endings for all forms (present, aorist, perfect) because they were default. Later when these endings were considered markers of past tense, it is the iota infix that remains the exclusive marker of the optative.

60  Francis Thomas Gignac, "The Development of Greek Phonology: The Fifteenth Century BC to the Twentieth Century After Christ," in *Daidalikon: Studies in Memory of Raymond V. Schoder, S.J.*, ed. Robert F. Sutton, Jr. (Wauconda, IL: Bolchazy-Carducci, 1989), 131–37; John W. Wevers, "A Note on Scribal Error." *CJL* 17 (1972): 185–90.

61  Claude Brixhe, "Linguistic Diversity in Asia Minor during the Empire: *Koine* and Non-Greek Languages," in *A Companion to the Ancient Greek Language*, ed. Egbert J. Bakker, BCAW (Chichester: Wiley Blackwell, 2014), 228–52.

62  M. Leumann, *Homerische Wörter* (Basil: Reinhardt, 1950) as summarized by Francisco Rodríguez Adrados, *A History of the Greek Language: From Its Origins to the Present*, (Leiden: Brill, 2005), 96.

This discussion of the augment is not to say that there are not other markers of tense or temporal reference in the language such as adverbs and conjunctions, but these arguments retain the notion that tense is grammaticalized through the augment and personal endings (primary versus secondary).

Constantine Campbell follows Porter in arguing that the forms of the verb in Greek are not marked for tense.[63] One example from Campbell to demonstrate aorists are not past-referring is Mark 1:11:[64]

Mark 1:11 καὶ φωνὴ ἐγένετο ἐκ τῶν οὐρανῶν· σὺ εἶ ὁ υἱός μου ὁ ἀγαπητός ἐν σοὶ εὐδόκησα.

And a voice came from heaven, "You are my beloved Son; in you I am well pleased."

Campbell states: "Suffice to say that no one translates the last clause of this verse, 'in you I was well pleased.' It simply doesn't fit the theological or literary context to read the aorist that way. There are many such instances within the usage of the aorist where this so-called past tense is obviously not past referring."[65]

What is the difference between Campbell's example and 1 Cor 1:21?

1 Cor 1:21 ἐπειδὴ γὰρ ἐν τῇ σοφίᾳ τοῦ θεοῦ οὐκ ἔγνω ὁ κόσμος διὰ τῆς σοφίας τὸν θεόν, εὐδόκησεν ὁ θεὸς διὰ τῆς μωρίας τοῦ κηρύγματος σῶσαι τοὺς πιστεύοντας·

For since in the wisdom of God the world through its wisdom did not know him, God was pleased through the foolishness of what was preached to save those who believe (NIV).

Campbell's examples are unfair and untrue because he does not distinguish semantic meaning and pragmatic effect for them the way he does for the case examples given later in his work. By Campbell's own analysis, there are probably only 10–15 % of instances where the aorist does not seem to be past-referring. Why doesn't he explore this as a result of pragmatic effect rather than as a proof that there is no semantic meaning of past in the other 85%? Bernard

63 Campbell, *Basics of Verbal Aspect*, 36–38.
64 Ibid., 36–37, 89.
65 Ibid., 36.

Comrie, for example, in his foundational work on tense, gives examples of the past in English used for nonpast referring situations: "I just wanted to ask you if you could lend me a dollar."[66] This is a pragmatic effect in English and does not prove that the form is not a past tense.[67]

Later in his work, Campbell provides categories for analyzing verbs and distinguishing semantic meaning from implicature.[68]

1. Semantics
2. Lexeme
3. Context
4. *Aktionsart*

For the category "Lexeme," Campbell's approach to transitivity is based upon whether the action is effective or not and not upon formal categories supplied by the language itself. The category of "Context" is the slippery element in the equation as this category is vague and unprincipled in Campbell's work.

## 5. CONCLUSION

The function of the augment in Hellenistic Greek must be understood from a diachronic perspective which includes a history of both aspect and tense in the verbal system. The system of the verb was originally aspectual that gradually became overlayered with tense as well. The addition of *iota* to morphemes marking only person and voice created the primary endings and present tense. This yielded a present/nonpresent arrangement. Then the creation of a future tense left the set of unmarked personal endings associated only with past tenses in the indicative. An adverbial prefix that originally had a deictic or spatial value developed into a marker with temporal semantic value. By 500 BC this was part of the morphology of the indicative past tenses, especially since apophonic reduction was no longer the sole means of marking the aorist. Within

---

66 Bernard Comrie, *Tense*, CTL (Cambridge: Cambridge University Press, 1985), 19.

67 See also the essay by Christopher J. Fresch, ch. 12 in this volume.

68 Campbell, *Basics of Verbal Aspect*, 55–117, and idem, *Advances in the Study of Greek*, 120–24.

150 years this double marking system deteriorated due to changes in pronunciation of vowels, accent and other phonological phenomena. By Byzantine and Modern times, only the syllabic augment was partially retained owing to education and stress.

## BIBLIOGRAPHY

Bakker, Egbert J. *Pointing at the Past: From Formula to Performance in Homeric Poetics*. Hellenic Studies 12. Washington, DC: Center for Hellenic Studies, 2005.

———. "Similes, Augment, and the Language of Immediacy." Pages 1–24 in *Speaking Volumes: Orality and Literacy in the Greek and Roman World*. Edited by Janet Watson. MS 218. Leiden: Brill, 2001.

———, ed. *A Companion to the Ancient Greek Language*. BCAW. Malden, MA: Wiley Blackwell, 2014.

Beekes, Robert. *Etymological Dictionary of Greek*. 2 vols. IEED 10:1–2. Leiden: Brill, 2010.

Benincà, Paola, Adam Ledgeway, and Nigel Vincent. *Diachrony and Dialects: Grammatical Change in the Dialects of Italy*. Oxford: Oxford University Press, 2014.

Bertrand, Nicolas. "Grounding of Information." *EAGLL* 2:148–50.

Blass, Friedrich, Albert Debrunner, and Friedrich Rehkopf. *Grammatik des neutestamentlichen Griechisch*. 18th ed. Göttingen: Vandenhoeck & Ruprecht, 2001.

Brixhe, Claude. "Linguistic Diversity in Asia Minor during the Empire: *Koine* and Non-Greek Languages." Pages 228–52 in *A Companion to the Ancient Greek Language*. Edited by Egbert J. Bakker. BCAW. Malden, MA: Wiley Blackwell, 2014.

———. "Phrygian." *CEWAL*, 777–88.

Bubenik, Vit. "Verbal System (Tense, Aspect, Mood)." *EAGLL* 3:477–86.

Burrow, Thomas. *The Sanskrit Language*. Rev. ed. London: Faber & Faber, 1973.

Bybee, Joan, Revere Perkins, and William Pagliuca. *The Evolution of Grammar: Tense, Aspect, and Modality in the Languages of the World*. Chicago: University of Chicago Press, 1994.

Campbell, Constantine R. *Advances in the Study of Greek: New Insights for Reading the Greek New Testament*. Grand Rapids: Zondervan, 2015.

———. *Basics of Verbal Aspect in Biblical Greek*. Grand Rapids: Zondervan, 2008.

Chantraine, Pierre. *Morphologie historique du grec*. 2nd ed. Paris: Klincksieck, 1961.

Clackson, James P. "Classical Armenian." *CEWAL* 922–42.

Colvin, Stephen. *A Brief History of Ancient Greek*. BHAW. Chichester: Wiley Blackwell, 2014.

Comrie, Bernard. *Tense*. CTL. Cambridge: Cambridge University Press, 1985.

Dieterich, Karl. *Untersuchungen zur Geschichte der griechischen Sprache von der hellenistischen zeit bis zum 10. jahrhundert n. Chr.* Leipzig: Teubner, 1898.

Drewitt, J. A. J. "The Augment in Homer." *ClQ* 6 (1912): 44–59, 104–20.

Evans, Trevor V. *Verbal Syntax in the Greek Pentateuch: Natural Greek Usage and Hebrew Interference*. Oxford: Oxford University Press, 2001.

Giannakis, Georgios K. *Encyclopedia of Ancient Greek Language and Linguistics*. 3 vols. Leiden: Brill, 2014.

———. "Indo-European Linguistic Background." *EAGLL* 2:212–25.

Gignac, Francis Thomas. "The Development of Greek Phonology: The Fifteenth Century BC to the Twentieth Century After Christ." Pages 131–37 in *Daidalikon: Studies in Memory of Raymond V. Schoder, S.J.* Edited by Robert F. Sutton, Jr. Wauconda, IL: Bolchazy-Carducci, 1989.

———. *A Grammar of the Greek Papyri of the Roman and Byzantine Periods: Volume II. Morphology*. TDSA 55, 2. Milan: Istituto Editoriale Cisalpino – La Goliardica, 1981.

Hackstein, Olav. "The Greek of Epic." Pages 401–23 in *A Companion to the Ancient Greek Language*. Edited by Egbert J. Bakker. BCAW. Malden, MA: Wiley Blackwell, 2014.

Harris, Alice C., and Lyle Campbell. *Historical Syntax in Cross-Linguistic Perspective*. CSL 74. Cambridge: Cambridge University Press, 1995.

Hatzidakis, George N. *Einleitung in die neugriechische Grammatik*. Leipzig: Breitkopf & Härtel, 1892.

Hewson, John, and Vit Bubenik. *Tense and Aspect in Indo-European Languages: Theory, Typology, Diachrony*. CILT 145. Amsterdam: Benjamins, 1997.

Hoenigswald, Henry M., Roger D. Woodard, and James P. T. Clackson. "Indo-European." *CEWAL*, 534–50.

Hoffner, Harry A., Jr., and H. Craig Melchert. *A Grammar of the Hittite Language: Part I; Reference Grammar*. LANE 1/1. Winona Lake, IN: Eisenbrauns, 2008.

Horrocks, Geoffrey. *Greek: A History of the Language and its Speakers*. 2nd ed. Chichester: Wiley, 2014.

Jamison, Stephanie W. "Middle Indic." CEWAL, 700–16.

———. "Sanskrit." CEWAL, 673–99.

Jannaris, Antonius N. *An Historical Greek Grammar*. London: Macmillan, 1897.

Kühner, Raphael. *Ausführliche Grammatik der Griechischen Sprache*. Vol. 2. Hannover: Hahn, 1892.

Leumann, M. *Homerische Wörter*. Basil: Reinhardt, 1950.

Mandilaras, Basil G. *The Verb in the Greek Non-Literary Papyri*. Athens: Hellenic Ministry of Culture and Sciences, 1973.

Mastronarde, Donald J. *Introduction to Attic Greek*. Berkeley: University of California Press, 1993.

Mawet, Francine. *Grammaire Sanskrite à l'Usage des Étudiants Hellénistes et Latinistes*. LOC 16. Leuven: Peeters, 2012.

Mayser, Edwin. *Grammatik der griechischen Papyri aus der Ptolemäerzeit mit Einschluss der gleichzeitigen Ostraka und der in Ägypten verfassten Inschriften: Band I. Laut- und Worthlehre. II. Teil. Flexionslehre*. Leipzig: de Gruyter, 1938.

Meier-Brügger, Michael. *Griechische Sprachwissenschaft*. 2 vols. Sammlung Göschen 2241. Berlin: de Gruyter, 1992.

Mounce, William D. *The Morphology of Biblical Greek*. Grand Rapids: Zondervan, 1994.

Pagniello, Frederick J. "The Homeric Augment: A Deictic Particle." PhD diss., University of Georgia, 2002.

Palmer, Leonard R. *The Greek Language*. Great Languages. London: Faber & Faber, 1980.

Porter, Stanley E. *Linguistic Analysis of the Greek New Testament: Studies in Tools, Methods, and Practice*. Grand Rapids: Baker Academic, 2015.

———. *Verbal Aspect in the Greek of the New Testament with Reference to Tense and Mood*. SBG 1. New York: Lang, 1989.

Psaltes, Stamatios B. *Grammatik der Byzantinischen Chroniken*. FGLG 2. Göttingen: Vandenhoeck & Ruprecht, 1913.

Ramat, Anna Giacalone and Paolo Ramat, eds. *The Indo-European Languages*. London: Routledge, 1998.

Rix, Helmut. *Historische Grammatik des Griechischen: Laut- und Formenlehre*. 2nd ed. Darmstadt: Wissenschaftliche Buchgesellschaft, 1996.

Rodríguez Adrados, Francisco. *A History of the Greek Language: From Its Origins to the Present*. Leiden: Brill, 2005.

Rose, Sarah. "Augment." EAGLL 1:215–18.

Schmitt, Rüdiger. "Old Persian." *CEWAL* 717–41.

Schwyzer, Eduard. *Griechische Grammatik: Bd. 1, Allgemeiner Teil, Lautlehre, Wortbildung, Flexion.* HAW 1. Munich: Beck, 1953.

———. *Griechische Grammatik: Bd. 2, Syntax und syntaktische Stilistik.* HAW 2. Munich: Beck, 1950.Sihler, Andrew L. *New Comparative Grammar of Greek and Latin.* Oxford: Oxford University Press, 1995.

Silva, Moisés. *Biblical Words and their Meaning: An Introduction to Lexical Semantics.* Rev. and exp. ed. Grand Rapids: Zondervan, 1994.

Smyth, Herbert W. *Greek Grammar.* 2nd ed. Cambridge: Harvard University Press, 1956.

Thackeray, H. St. J. *A Grammar of the Old Testament in Greek According to the Septuagint.* Cambridge: Cambridge University Press, 1909.

Thomson, George. *The Greek Language.* Cambridge: Heffer & Sons, 1966.

Watkins, Calvert. 1998. "Proto-Indo-European: Comparison and Reconstruction." Pages 25–73 in *The Indo-European Languages.* Edited by Anna Giacalone Ramat and Paolo Ramat. London: Routledge, 1998.

Watson, Janet, ed. *Speaking Volumes: Orality and Literacy in the Greek and Roman World.* MS 218. Leiden: Brill, 2001.

Wevers, John W. "A Note on Scribal Error." *CJL* 17 (1972): 185–90.

Whitney, William D. *Sanskrit Grammar: Including Both the Classic Language and the Older Dialects of Veda and Brahmana.* 2nd ed. Cambridge: Harvard University Press, 1889.

Woodard, Roger D., ed. *The Cambridge Encyclopedia of the World's Ancient Languages.* Cambridge: Cambridge University Press, 2004.

# CHAPTER 12

# Typology, Polysemy, and Prototypes: Situating Nonpast Aorist Indicatives[1]

CHRISTOPHER J. FRESCH

BIBLE COLLEGE OF SOUTH AUSTRALIA

Consider the following:

> Matt 13:24    Ἄλλην παραβολὴν παρέθηκεν αὐτοῖς
> λέγων· ὡμοιώθη ἡ βασιλεία τῶν οὐρανῶν ἀνθρώπῳ σπείραντι
> καλὸν σπέρμα ἐν τῷ ἀγρῷ αὐτοῦ.

> He presented another parable to them: "The kingdom
> of heaven ὡμοιώθη a person who sowed good seed in
> his field."[2]

> Luke 3:22b    καὶ φωνὴν ἐξ οὐρανοῦ γενέσθαι· σὺ εἶ ὁ
> υἱός μου ὁ ἀγαπητός, ἐν σοὶ εὐδόκησα.

> And a voice came from heaven: "You are my beloved
> son, in you εὐδόκησα."

Aorist verbs such as ὡμοιώθη and εὐδόκησα are problematic for the
typical reader of the Greek New Testament. Many are taught that
the aorist indicative refers to a complete event in the past. These
verbs, however, and others like them, are clearly not past-referring.
Thus, based on instances such as these, one may wonder whether

---

1    I wish to thank Steve Walton, Dirk Jongkind, and Joshua Harper for their
     valuable comments on an earlier version of this paper.
2    Unless otherwise noted, all translations are the author's own.

the aorist indicative truly does encode past temporal reference. In order to arrive at a sound conclusion, it is important to consider not only how the aorist indicative has been treated in Greek scholarship but also, crucially, the wider linguistic issues involved.

## 1. THE AORIST INDICATIVE IN GREEK SCHOLARSHIP

Historically, the Koine Greek verbal system has been regarded as a mixed tense-aspect[3] system. Near the beginning of the twentieth century, this conception was further refined as Greek grammarians realized that the original function of the tense-stems was to signal aspect[4] and that tense, i.e., grammaticalized temporal reference, was restricted to the indicative mood.[5] Understandably, this realignment motivated the grammarians to regard aspect as the primary semantic component of the verb and to regard tense as secondary. This perspective may be seen in Robertson, who writes, "Even in the indicative the time element is subordinate to the kind of action expressed."[6] Similarly, Zerwick states, "In fact, 'aspect' is an essential element of the Greek 'tenses' ... and hence is always distinguished by the form, whereas the time of the actions is expressed in the

---

3    Whether grammatical or lexical aspect or a mix of the two. The historical grammarians often did not make distinctions that are as clear-cut as are currently made between grammatical and lexical aspect. For the purposes of this discussion, I am primarily concerned with whether grammarians have recognized some sort of aspectual distinction central to the tenses rather than whether they have clearly distinguished between the types of aspect.

4    E.g., Robertson writes, "The three tenses (aorist, present, perfect) were first developed irrespective of time." A. T. Robertson, *A Grammar of the Greek New Testament in the Light of Historical Research* (Nashville: Broadman Press, 1934), 824. So also BDF, who state, "The original function of the so-called tense stems of the verb in Indo-European languages was not that of levels of time ... but that of *Aktionsarten* ... or aspects." BDF, §318. See also J. H. Moulton and Nigel Turner, *A Grammar of New Testament Greek: 3, Syntax* (London: T&T Clark, 1963), 59.

5    A helpful survey of historical treatments of the Greek verbal system may be found in Stanley E. Porter, *Verbal Aspect in the Greek of the New Testament, with Reference to Tense and Mood*, 2nd ed., SBG 1 (New York: Lang, 1993), 17–65.

6    Robertson, *Grammar*, 825.

indicative only, and in the other moods is either lacking or secondary."[7] Even earlier, at the turn of the twentieth century, Burton claimed, "The *chief* function of a Greek tense is thus not to denote time, but progress. This latter function belongs to the tense-forms of all the moods, the former to those of the Indicative only."[8] This is largely how the historical grammarians of the past century conceived of the koine verbal system.[9] More recently, many have followed in the tradition of the historical grammarians. For example, Moule states, "Generally speaking, the first question that the Greek writer seems to ask himself is not 'When did (or will) this happen?' but 'Am I conceiving of it as protracted or as virtually instantaneous?'"[10] Mandilaras, who examined the use of the verb in the nonliterary papyri of the Ptolemaic, Roman, and Byzantine periods, writes, "It becomes obvious that (*a*) the tense variation with regard to time is widespread, and (*b*) in the tense-usage of these writers, aspect was their primary consideration, to which precise indication of time was frequently subordinated."[11] Mandilaras never abandons the notion of tense in the indicative, but he does view it as secondary and expendable with respect to aspect. Funk, in his grammar of Hellenistic Greek, notes the fundamental function of the Greek verb as denoting aspect and views explicit temporal reference as isolated to the indicative.[12] On the whole, Greek scholarship has understood the verbal system to be primarily concerned with how the action is conceptualized but has also maintained tense as a crucial, albeit usually secondary, component.

---

7    Maximilian Zerwick, S.J., *Biblical Greek* (Rome: Pontifical Biblical Institute, 1963), §240.

8    Ernest De Witt Burton, *Syntax of the Moods and Tenses in New Testament Greek*, rev. and enl. ed. (Chicago: University Press of Chicago, 1893), 6 (emphasis original).

9    See also Moulton and Turner, *Grammar*, 59–58; William Douglas Chamberlain, *An Exegetical Grammar of the Greek New Testament* (New York: Macmillan, 1941), 67; H. E. Dana and Julius R. Mantey, *A Manual Grammar of the Greek New Testament* (Upper Saddle River, NJ: Prentice Hall, 1957), §167.

10   C. F. D. Moule, *An Idiom Book of New Testament Greek*, 2nd ed. (Cambridge: Cambridge University Press, 1959), 5.

11   Basil G. Mandilaras, *The Verb in the Greek Non-Literary Papyri* (Athens: Hellenic Ministry of Culture and Sciences, 1973), §41.

12   Robert W. Funk, *A Beginning-Intermediate Grammar of Hellenistic Greek*, 3rd ed. (Salem, OR: Polebridge Press, 2013), §0309, §3100.1-2, §311.

Within this framework, the aorist indicative is typically regarded as expressing perfective[13] aspect, i.e., it portrays the event as a complete whole—temporally bounded, and also as expressing past temporal reference. For example, Burton writes, "The Aorist Indicative is most frequently used to express a past event viewed in its entirety, simply as an event or a single fact."[14] Mandilaras' discussion of the aorist indicative explicitly acknowledges the fundamental status of aspect while also evincing a regard for past temporal reference as essential to it, though secondary.[15] De la Villa notes that the prototypical value of the aorist indicative is that of a past tense, that grammatical aspect was "the central category of the verb in Ancient Greek," and that the aorist expresses perfective aspect.[16] Similarly, Napoli writes, "[The aorist's] function is primarily aspectual ... and its temporal value is limited to the indicative form."[17] More could be quoted, but suffice it to say that the conception of the aorist presented here is representative of the majority of Greek scholarship.[18]

Thus, traditional scholarship, since it understands the aorist indicative as the perfective past tense, must somehow account for nonpast occurrences of it, such as those observed in Matt 13:24 and Luke 3:22 above. Generally, nonpast instances have been regarded as exceptions to the rule. Often, one will encounter categories such as the "gnomic aorist" or "proleptic aorist" by which grammarians explain how a past-referring verb can be used in nonpast contexts. Sometimes the discussions of these categories will draw on

---

13  Not to be confused with the perfect tense-form nor with the occasional use of the term "perfective" to denote a perfect-tense meaning (e.g., "perfective present" in BDF, §322).

14  Burton, *Syntax*, §38.

15  Mandilaras, *Verb in the Greek Non-Literary Papyri*, 54, 56, 156–70.

16  Jesús de la Villa, "Tense/Aspect," in *EAGLL* 3:384, 385, 386.

17  Maria Napoli, "Aorist," in *EAGLL* 1:136.

18  See also Herbert Weir Smyth, *Greek Grammar*, rev. Gordon M. Messing (Harvard: Harvard University Press, 1956), §1850–52, §1923; Robertson, *Grammar*, 831–36; Moulton and Turner, *Grammar*, 59–58, 64, 71; Zerwick, *Biblical Greek*, §240–41; Dana and Mantey, *Manual Grammar*, §179; Moule, *Idiom Book*, 10; Funk, *Grammar of Hellenistic Greek*, §787–88; Buist M. Fanning, *Verbal Aspect in New Testament Greek*, OTM (Oxford: Clarendon Press, 1990), §4.3, §4.8; Daniel B. Wallace, *Greek Grammar Beyond the Basics: An Exegetical Syntax of the New Testament with Scripture, Subject, and Greek Word Indexes* (Grand Rapids: Zondervan, 1996), 554–56; John Hewson, "Aspect (and Tense)," in *EAGLL* 1:182.

the aorist indicative's past-referring function. For example, one of the explanations posited by BDF for the gnomic aorist is that "the author had a specific case in mind in which the act had been realized."[19] Zerwick suggests, "The gnomic aorist may have arisen from the expression of a fact of past experience as a guide to present or future judgement."[20] Regarding the proleptic or futuristic aorist, Smyth writes, "The aorist may be substituted for the future when a future event is vividly represented as having actually occurred."[21] Sometimes, however, explanations are provided that do not draw on the aorist indicative's past-referring function at all but seem rather to view the aorist, in these instances, as a timeless perfective. That is to say, the aorist indicative's central aspectual value is maintained while its secondary temporal-referencing component is contextually overridden. Robertson, for instance, writes, "The real 'gnomic' aorist is a universal or timeless aorist and probably represents the original timelessness of the aorist indicative."[22] Similarly, Moulton and Turner suggest, "The present stem in Greek being linear, it would not be suitable for expressing generalities; the timeless tense is therefore used, but the augment denoting past time cannot be jettisoned and has to go with it. We must look rather to the stem than the augment."[23] Wallace also regards the gnomic aorist simply as referring to a timeless fact. He states, "[The gnomic aorist] does not refer to a particular event that *did* happen, but to a generic event that *does* happen."[24] With respect to the future aorist, Robertson writes, "It is a vivid transference of the action to the future ... by the timeless aorist. The augmented form is still used, but the time

---

19  BDF, §333(1). However, BDF also provide an explanation that does not rely on past reference. See n. 23 below.
20  Zerwick, *Biblical Greek*, §256. So also Smyth, *Greek Grammar*, §1931; de la Villa, *EAGLL* 3:384.
21  Smyth, *Greek Grammar*, §1934. So also Moulton and Turner, *Grammar*, 74; Zerwick, *Biblical Greek*, §257; Fanning, *Verbal Aspect*, §4.3.5; Wallace, *Greek Grammar*, 563–64; de la Villa, *EAGLL* 3:384.
22  Robertson, *Grammar*, 836.
23  Moulton and Turner, *Grammar*, 73. So also BDF, §333(1). In addition to the past-time explanation given above, BDF suggest that the gnomic aorist may occur "because the aorist indicative serves for a non-existent perfective present."
24  Wallace, *Greek Grammar*, 562. So also Burton, *Syntax*, §43; Chamberlain, *Grammar*, 77–78; Dana and Mantey, *Manual Grammar*, §181(1); Mandilaras, *Verb in the Greek Non-Literary Papyri*, §352; Fanning, *Verbal Aspect*, §4.3.4.

is hardly felt to be past."[25] Thus, whether appealing to the aorist indicative's past-referring component or recognizing a basic communicative value that is transferable to any temporal context, Greek scholarship, on the whole, has regarded the nonpast instances of the aorist indicative as simple exceptions to its normal role as the perfective past tense.

In recent decades, some scholars have offered an alternative conception of the aorist indicative. Rather than viewing it as a perfective past tense, they argue that, given its use in nonpast contexts, it semantically encodes only perfective aspect, not both perfective aspect and past temporal reference.[26] The basis of this claim is often

25　Robertson, *Grammar*, 846. So also BDF, §333(2); Mandilaras, *Verb in the Greek Non-Literary Papyri*, §350, 169 n. 2.

26　Porter, *Verbal Aspect*, 77–79; Kenneth L. McKay, *Greek Grammar for Students: A Concise Grammar of Classical Attic with Special Reference to Aspect in the Verb*, 2nd ed. (Canberra: Dept. of Classics, Australian National University, 1994), §24.1.3, §24.4; Albert Rijksbaron, "The Discourse Function of the Imperfect," in *In the Footsteps of Raphael Kühner: Proceedings of the International Colloquium in Commemoration of the 150th Anniversary of the Publication of Raphael Kühner's Ausführliche Grammatik der griechischen Sprache, II. Theil; Syntaxe, Amsterdam, 1986*, ed. Albert Rijksbaron, H. A. Mulder, and G. C. Wakker (Amsterdam: Gieben, 1988), 246; Rodney J. Decker, *Temporal Deixis of the Greek Verb in the Gospel of Mark with Reference to Verbal Aspect*, SBG 10 (New York: Lang, 2001), 98–99; Wally V. Cirafesi, *Verbal Aspect in Synoptic Parallels: On the Method and Meaning of Divergent Tense-Form Usage in the Synoptic Passion Narratives*, LBS 7 (Leiden: Brill, 2013), 18–21, 37; Constantine R. Campbell, *Advances in the Study of Greek: New Insights for Reading the New Testament* (Grand Rapids: Zondervan, 2015), 114. However, unlike the others, Rijksbaron does not regard the Greek verbal system as tenseless. It is only the aorist that he regards as not semantically encoded for temporal reference.

"It should be noted that while Campbell does advocate for a tenseless verbal system, he does propose an alternative theory in which proximal distinctions replace temporal reference, i.e., the aorist (and imperfect) indicative marks remoteness rather than past time (Campbell, *Advances in the Study of Greek*, 115–16; Campbell, *Verbal Aspect*, 117–19, 123–24). For critiques of Campbell's proximity-based theory, see Cirafesi, *Verbal Aspect in Synoptic Parallels*, 38–40; Robert Crellin, "Basics of Verbal Aspect in Biblical Greek," *JSNT* 35 (2012): 197–99, 202. For a general critique of remoteness as the core semantic component of a past tense, see John R. Taylor, *Linguistic Categorization*, 3rd ed., OTL (Oxford: Oxford University Press, 2003), 180–81; Lotte Hogeweg, "What's So Unreal about the Past?: Past Tense and Counterfactuals," in *Studies on English Modality in Honour of Frank R. Palmer*, ed. Anastasios Tsangalidēs and R. Facchinetti, Linguistic Insights 111 (Bern: Peter Lang, 2009).

made by appeal to the principle of contrastive substitution. With regard to this, Decker explains,

> Contrastive substitution is a linguistic method that notes either the occurrence of identical forms (in this case, verbal forms) in different contexts or different forms in the same context. If the same verb form can be used in different temporal contexts, and if different verb forms may be substituted in the same time context, and this without changing the temporal reference of the statement, then there is strong evidence that temporal reference is not the proper explanation of the meaning of the form.[27]

Therefore, when applied to the aorist indicative, since the tense-form may occur in past and nonpast contexts, it is claimed that temporal reference is not a semantic component of it. Related to this is the cancelability of implicatures. Porter notes, "Implicatures can be cancelled, whereas the essential meaning cannot."[28] Applying this to the Greek verbal system, Cirafesi argues, "Temporal reference, then, is a cancelable element in the verb and should be understood as a feature that is determined by various co-textual constraints."[29] By this understanding, temporal reference in the Greek verb is a cancelable pragmatic implicature, whereas aspect is the non-cancelable semantic component. Thus, nonpast aorist indicatives are simply regarded as perfectives; they are not problematic since the aorist indicative is not regarded as semantically encoded for temporal reference.[30] This is not too different from some of the historical and modern grammarians mentioned above who view aspect as primary and tense as secondary, the primary distinction being whether temporal reference is regarded as an implicature or

---

27 Decker, *Temporal Deixis*, 34. See also Porter, *Verbal Aspect*, 77–79; Cirafesi, *Verbal Aspect in Synoptic Parallels*, 18. For a critique of this appropriation of contrastive substitution, see Steven E. Runge, "Contrastive Substitution and the Greek Verb: Reassessing Porter's Argument," *NovT* 56 (2014).

28 Porter, *Verbal Aspect*, 104. So also Decker, *Temporal Deixis*, 38, 45. The issues of implicature and cancelability will be discussed in more detail in §3 below.

29 Cirafesi, *Verbal Aspect in Synoptic Parallels*, 19.

30 E.g., see the discussion on and categorization of nonpast aorist indicatives in Porter, *Verbal Aspect*, 217–38.

386 THE GREEK VERB REVISITED

as a semantic component of the Greek verb. Sometimes, however, this version of the traditional perspective can be misunderstood as support for the nontemporal view. Campbell, for example, quotes Rijksbaron arguing that past-temporal reference is not a part of the aorist indicative but is instead a conversational implicature. In his footnote, after citing Rijksbaron, Campbell writes, "See also Hewson, who states that the category of aorist must never be considered as a past tense."[31] By virtue of its placement in this footnote, it is implied that Hewson's claim is in agreement with Rijksbaron and further confirms that past temporal reference is not a part of the meaning of the aorist indicative. This, however, is not the case. Consider Hewson's entire argument:

> The second aorist Indicative forms ... used the secondary inflections, as found in the imperfect *to mark past tense*, the secondary inflections contrasting ... with the primary inflections of the present to establish *the contrast between past and non-past tense in the indicative*. The strong (asigmatic) aorist indicative ... *is doubly marked for past tense*, in the first case by the augment (often omitted, since redundant, in Homer), in the second case by the secondary endings ... It is typical of the forms of the third stage of the chronogenesis [i.e., the indicative], the most complex forms of the system, *that they are often marked for both tense and aspect*. Traditionally, however, the aorist has been taught as a simple past tense, and this leads to gross confusion when other aorist forms (the imperatives, subjunctives, optatives, infinitives, etc.) are observed to represent present or even future time. Anglophone students of Greek may spend a lifetime without ever 'understanding' the aorist, but students and speakers of Slavic languages readily recognize its aspectual nature: that *the aorist indicative is a Perfective past tense*, and that the *other* aorist forms are simply Perfective forms of the other categories of the verb, such as the aorist imperative, the aorist subjunctive, the aorist optative, the aorist infinitive. These

---

31 Campbell, *Verbal Aspect*, 122 n. 30.

forms are not past tenses at all, and the category of aorist must never be considered as a simple preterit, a past
tense.[32]

Hewson is decidedly *not* arguing that past-temporal reference is
not a semantic property of the aorist indicative. In fact, he claims
that it is morphologically encoded for past temporal reference,
states that it is marked for both tense and aspect, and categorizes
it as the perfective past tense. When he writes "the category of the
aorist must never be considered as a simple preterit, a past tense,"
he is referring to the category *as a whole*, beyond the indicative, in
reaction to the aorist, *as a whole*, being taught as a simple past tense
rather than as a perfective with a past-referring semantic component only in the indicative. Hewson's argument does not support
Campbell's claim. In fact, Hewson's argument thoroughly contradicts it.[33]

In what follows, I maintain that the aorist indicative is semantically encoded for both perfective aspect and past temporal reference
(henceforth, +PFV +PAST), albeit with aspect being the prominent
category of the verbal system[34] and temporal reference being a secondary component. By investigating some of the broader linguistic
issues that bear on this discussion, I intend to offer an account of
the aorist indicative and its nonpast uses that explains how the two
may be held together.

## 2. VERBAL SYSTEMS AND LINGUISTIC TYPOLOGY

Perfectives are not unique to Koine Greek. In fact, in Dahl's typological investigation of verbal tense and aspect, wherein he surveyed sixty-four languages from fifteen different language groups,[35]

---

32  John Hewson and Vit Bubenik, *Tense and Aspect in Indo-European Languages: Theory, Typology, Diachrony*, CILT 145 (Amsterdam: Benjamins, 1997), 37–38 (emphasis added).

33  See also Ibid, 43–44, 353–54.

34  Cf. Ellis, ch. 4 in this volume.

35  The language groups are Afro-Asiatic, Altaic, Andean-Equatorial, Australian, Austronesian, Caucasian, Dravidian, Eskimo-Aleut, Indo-European,
Iroquois, Kam-Tai, Mon-Khmer, Niger-Congo, Sino-Tibetan, and Uralic. In-

forty-nine of those languages exhibited a perfective category.[36] In another typological investigation, this one surveying seventy-six languages from twenty-five language groups[37] (only three of the languages surveyed overlap with Dahl's study[38]) — thereby giving typological representation to all of the world's languages — Bybee, Perkins, and Pagliuca found at least forty-eight languages that exhibit a perfective category.[39] One would do well to consider, then, how perfectives tend to function typologically. In other words, one should ask what patterns of use and meaning occur systematically across languages.[40] This is not to say that the perfective in Koine Greek must necessarily mirror perfectives in other languages. As Croft states, "Anyone who does typology soon learns that there is no synchronic language universal without exceptions."[41] However, if

---

do-European was the best represented with twenty-one languages. Östen Dahl, *Tense and Aspect Systems* (New York: Blackwell, 1985), 39–42.

36   Ibid., 183.

37   The language groups are Afro-asiatic, Macro-Algonquian, Andean-Equatorial, Australian, Austroasiatic, Austronesian, Aztec-Tanoan, Caucasian, Macro-Chibchan, Dravidian, Ge-Pano-Carib, Hokan, Indo-European, Indo-Pacific, Khoisan, Na-Dene, Niger-Kordofanian, Nilo-Saharan, Oto-Manguean, Penutian, Salish, Sino-Tibetan, Macro-Siouan, Ural-Ataic, Pidgins/Creoles; Joan L. Bybee, Revere D. Perkins, and William Pagliuca, *The Evolution of Grammar: Tense, Aspect, and Modality in the Languages of the World* (Chicago: University of Chicago Press, 1994), 306–07. There was also an unaffiliated "language group" from which two of the languages surveyed were chosen (311).

38   Alawa, Modern Greek, and Latin. However, I am not clear what specifically is in view by Bybee, Perkins, and Pagliuca's designator "Inuit" and whether it corresponds to the Greenlandic Eskimo surveyed by Dahl.

39   Ibid., 326, 332–33. The smaller percentage in this study, as compared with Dahl's, is likely due to Bybee, Perkins, and Pagliuca listing three separate categories — Perfective, Completive, and Past — though admitting that all three (plus anteriors and resultatives) are related in that "they all describe a situation that is completed prior to some temporal reference point" (52). Since they state that they regarded most completive grams as perfective (54), my count includes every instance of perfective and every instance of completive. Where a single language exhibited both a completive and a perfective, I counted only the perfective.

40   I am drawing here from Croft's second definition of typology, i.e., typological generalization, as "the study of patterns that occur systematically across languages .... The patterns found in typological generalization are language universals." William Croft, *Typology and Universals*, 2nd ed., CTL (Cambridge: Cambridge University Press, 2003), 1.

41   Ibid., 283.

there are consistent patterns of use and meaning cross-linguistically, it is more likely that Koine Greek will follow these trends rather than be a unique exception to them. As Croft goes on to write,

> But a typologist sees not only the exceptions—which, after all, must be possible language types, since they actually exist—but also the highly skewed distribution. In a diachronic perspective, where every language type comes into existence and passes on to another type with different degrees of frequency and stability, and the gradualness of change means all sorts of 'anomalous' intermediate types are found, possibility is much less important than probability.[42]

All things are possible in language, but not all things are probable. Cross-linguistically, it has been demonstrated that perfective verb forms are strongly associated with past temporal reference. Bybee and Dahl state that there is "a universal tendency for there to be a coupling between perfectivity and the past."[43] Dahl elsewhere provides a description for the prototypical perfective verb. He writes,

> A PFV verb will typically denote a single event, seen as an unanalysed whole, with a well-defined result or end-state, *located in the past*. More often than not, the

---

42  Ibid.

43  Joan L. Bybee and Östen Dahl, "The Creation of Tense and Aspect Systems in the Languages of the World," *StudLang* 13 (1989): 83. Regarding the term "perfectivity," while it is often used to denote a completed situation—vs. perfective more generally denoting a complete situation (see Jean-Pierre Desclés and Zlatka Guentchéva, "Universals and Typology," in *The Oxford Handbook of Tense and Aspect*, ed. Robert I. Binnick, Oxford Handbooks [Oxford: Oxford University Press, 2012], 139-40)—Bybee and Dahl regard perfectivity here as a broader category that includes perfectives. They write, "[Perfectivity] is a set of related concepts rather than one single notion. It could thus be called a 'family concept' although 'family of concepts' is perhaps more adequate, as we would argue that the members of the family share a common focus—that is, the prototypical cases are the same" (84). Bybee and Dahl do subsequently state that "notional perfectivity may be manifested in different ways in the grammar, and ... a certain kind of manifestation favors a certain more precise interpretation of it" (84). It is this certain kind of manifestation that is associated with a completed situation (87-88).

event will be punctual, or at least, it will be seen as a single transition from one state to its opposite, the duration of which can be disregarded.[44]

He also states, "There is a strong tendency for PFV categories to be restricted to past time reference.... for all languages it holds that 'past time reference' characterizes prototypical uses of PFV – single, completed events will in the 'typical cases' be located in the past."[45] He further notes that, in his data, there are no unequivocal examples of a situation in which there is no time reference restriction on the PFV.[46] Similar claims are also made by Bybee, Perkins, and Pagliuca. When describing the labels "completive," "anterior," "resultative," "perfective," and "simple past," based on the patterns

---

44  Dahl, *Tense and Aspect Systems*, 78 (emphasis added). Regarding Dahl's conception of prototypical occurrences, see the discussion in n. 45 and §4 below.

45  Ibid., 79. (See also his discussion with regard to PAST on p. 116.) Porter critiques Dahl here for having a traditional understanding of tenses; he also states, "Not only does this formulation seem to be derived from a theory of *Aktionsart* in trying to describe the objective status of the process itself ... but it seems to be formulated around a mentalist view, i.e., trying to reconstruct the psychological conception of time within speakers' minds" (Porter, *Verbal Aspect*, 104). First, regarding Dahl having a traditional understanding of the tenses, Porter is referring to the position that "views the primary usage at the pragmatic level as the controlling feature for defining the semantics of the form, and this estimation is often absolute-tense based" (104; also see the discussion in pp. 102–4). Of course, this critique only holds if temporal reference is, in fact, a pragmatic implicature and not a part of the verbal form's semantics. Porter has not proven this and is therefore assuming the conclusion in his critique of Dahl. Moreover, Dahl is making a typological claim based on a cross-linguistic investigation of sixty-four modern languages. As such, his conclusions are necessarily motivated by information gained from native language speakers; in addition, then, his conclusions are testable and falsifiable (they have not, to my knowledge, been falsified). While this does not undeniably prove that Dahl is correct, it does place him on rather solid ground. Second, Porter's critique that the formulation seems to be derived from a theory of *Aktionsart* appears to ignore that Dahl is describing prototypical usage. He is not claiming that perfective aspect is defined by single, completed events but is rather making the observation, based on empirical evidence, that perfective verb forms are prototypically used for such events. (For more on prototypical usage, see §4 below.) Lastly, the mentalist accusation seems to me unfounded. Dahl is simply remarking on typical use and meaning patterns by native speakers across forty-nine languages that exhibit a perfective category.

46  Dahl, *Tense and Aspect Systems*, 83.

of meaning within their seventy-six languages surveyed, they state, "The meaning labels ... are similar conceptually in that they all describe a situation that is completed prior to some temporal reference point."[47] They claim that, typically, perfective verbs are past-referring, noting that many of the perfectives within their samples are restricted to the past and that the rest are typically used for the past.[48] Moreover, it is evident that they regard this tendency not as pragmatic implicature but as a part of the semantics of typical perfective verb forms just as it is for the simple past. They write,

> The semantic content of simple past and perfective is very similar—they can both be used to signal a completed past action and they are both used in the narration of past sequences of events. The simple past is semantically more general since it can also be used to signal past time for situations viewed imperfectively.[49]

To sum up, then, based on patterns of use across languages, Dahl and Bybee, Perkins, and Pagliuca regard perfective aspect as having a universal tendency to be restricted to the past and perfective verb forms as prototypically encoded (semantically) for past temporal reference.

With respect to verbal system typology, Dahl observes that languages exhibiting a PFV:IPFV [imperfective] split will typically be structured in one of two ways:[50]

---

47  Bybee, Perkins, and Pagliuca, *Evolution of Grammar*, 52.

48  Ibid., 83. Bybee, Perkins, and Pagliuca do note that the temporal notion designated by the perfective is "not one that is reckoned deictically in relation to the moment of speech, but rather that is determined by the viewpoint taken on the situation" and that it instead presents the situation as temporally bounded (83). It is important to note, however, that this is a description of perfective aspect. Their description that perfectives typically signal past time is in relation to perfective grams, i.e., perfective verb form instantiations in their language samples.

49  Ibid. Consider also the straightforward statement "The anterior signals a past action that is relevant to the current moment, while the past and perfective signal only a past action" (86). Also worth consideration is the evidence the authors provide demonstrating that the perfective and simple past both historically develop from the same lexical sources (85–87).

50  Östen Dahl, "The Tense-Aspect Systems of European Languages in a Typological Perspective," in *Tense and Aspect in the Languages of Europe*, ed. Östen Dahl, EALT 20 (Berlin: Mouton de Gruyter, 2000), 17.

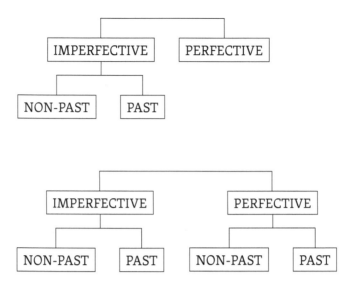

It is important to note that the labels "NON-PAST" and "PAST" specifically refer to morphological encoding.[51] Thus, with regard to the first type, which is more common,[52] the lack of PAST does not necessarily indicate a tenseless perfective verb form but only one that is not morphologically encoded for +PAST. In fact, Dahl writes, "In languages with a distinction between perfective and imperfective verb forms—regardless of the marking relations between them—the perfective forms are in the majority of all cases restricted to past time reference, at least when appearing in asserted main clauses."[53] Regarding this typical structure and the lack of explicit

---

51  See the discussion in Dahl, *Tense and Aspect Systems*, 82–84.
52  Dahl, "Tense-Aspect Systems," 17.
53  Ibid., 16. See also Dahl, *Tense and Aspect Systems*, 189. Dahl does write elsewhere, "In such a system, there would be no 'Past Tense' category comprising both Aorist and Imperfect: Aorist is simply PFV, and the fact that it (normally) has past time reference is in accordance with the general tendencies for that category. Imperfect, on the other hand, would be analysed as a combination of IPFV and PAST. In addition to morphological arguments, such an analysis would be supported by the fact that ... the Aorist is not always restricted to past time reference in all contexts" (82). First, it is crucial to note that Dahl is not specifically referring here to the aorist and imperfect of the ancient Greek verbal system (he does address Classical Greek later, which is discussed below). Second, Dahl is not arguing here in favor of viewing the typical PFV verb as not semantically encoded for past-temporal reference, as there is nothing in his work to suggest such and much to suggest otherwise (such as his argument that past-time morphology for the PFV would be redundant [83]). In fact, a few years later, Dahl wrote with By-

+PAST encoding for the perfective, he elsewhere states, "There is an obvious functional explanation for it: if the mere use of a PFV form entails past time reference, further marking of past time reference is redundant."[54] Thus, in this first type of structure, a perfective verb form entails past time, even if not overtly marked for it. The second type of structure, which is less common, contains two perfective forms, one morphologically encoded for nonpast temporal reference and the other for past temporal reference.[55] To sum up, then, languages that have a PFV:IPFV split, regardless of which of the two structures occurs, will typically exhibit a perfective verb form that signals past time.

\* \* \* \* \*

These typological studies are worth consideration in our conception of the aorist indicative. First, because perfective verb forms tend, cross-linguistically, to be tied to and signal past time, we should, under normal circumstances, expect the aorist indicative to be tied to and signal past time. This past reference should not be viewed as a pragmatic implicature that arises from the verb form's interaction with certain contexts but rather, based on the typological data, as a part of the expected semantic function of the form. Second, languages that have a PFV:IPFV split will typically restrict the PFV verb form to past-time reference. Both of the structures observed by Dahl can account for the Koine Greek verbal system. It could be conceived along the lines of the first structure:

| Imperfective | Perfective (Aorist) |
| --- | --- |
| \| \| | |
| Imperfect  Present | (Typically restricted to past) |

---

bee concerning this type of verbal system that it results "in a system where a gram with the meaning 'perfective past' is opposed to everything else," Bybee and Dahl, "Tense and Aspect Systems," 83. See also Bybee, Perkins, and Pagliuca, *Evolution of Grammar*, 83–84.

54  Dahl, *Tense and Aspect Systems*, 83. On the issue of the Greek augment, see the discussion below. Note that "entail" does not correspond to "implicate." As Levinson writes, "*Implicature* is intended to contrast with terms like *logical implication, entailment* and *logical consequence* which are generally used to refer to inferences that are derived solely from logical or semantic content," Stephen C. Levinson, *Pragmatics*, CTL (Cambridge: Cambridge University Press, 1983), 103–04. Implicatures will be discussed further in §3 below.

55  Dahl, "Tense-Aspect systems," 17.

On the other hand, the aorist indicative may have a perfective partner in the future indicative.[56] If this is the case, then Koine's verbal system exhibits the second structure:

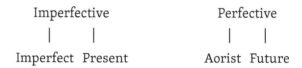

In either case, the aorist fills the same role. It is the perfective past verb form. In the end, considering the typological evidence, either of these structures offers a natural explanation of the aorist indicative. Indeed, it is more probable that Koine Greek is similar to other languages than that it uniquely exhibits a tenseless perfective verb form within a PFV:IPFV structure.

There is one feature of Greek's verbal system that has not been mentioned: the augment. If one regards the augment as a marker of past temporal reference,[57] then there are two options available for approaching the verbal system. The first is to regard the Koine Greek system as exhibiting morphologically marked past and nonpast perfective forms in the aorist and future indicatives, respectively. This would then match Dahl's second structure for languages that have a PFV:IPFV split. The other option, if one does not regard the Greek future as a perfective verb form, is to understand the verbal system as matching Dahl's first structure for languages that have a PFV:IPFV split (thus one PFV form, the aorist, that is restricted to past time) and to regard the augment's affixation to the PFV indicative form as an oddity. This is, in fact, how Dahl views the aorist. He writes,

> Contrary to what we have said about the general tendency in Indo-European, there is a consistent marker of past time reference in [Classical Greek], the so-called

56  Cf. Ellis, ch. 4 in this volume. So also Hewson and Bubenik, *Tense and Aspect*, 353–54.

57  For an argument in favor of the augment as past temporal marker, see Allan, ch. 3 in this volume and Gentry, ch. 11 in this volume. For an argument against, see Stanley E. Porter, *Linguistic Analysis of the Greek New Testament: Studies in Tools, Methods, and Practice* (Grand Rapids: Baker Academic, 2015), 176–83.

augment, i.e. a prefix *e-* which characterizes both the
Aorist and the Imperfect.... The PFV category – the
Aorist – is (in the indicative at least) restricted to past
time reference, but the manifestation of PAST applies
to both PFV and IPFV.[58]

In the end, the aorist fits well, with or without the future, into
universal models of verb systems, filling the role of a perfective verb
form that is prototypically restricted to the past. The augment, if it
does signal past temporal reference, reinforces the temporal component of the aorist indicative. Thus, there is substantial reason to
regard the aorist indicative as a perfective past form with +PFV as
the more central component. This is in line, at least on a basic level,
with the understanding of the historical Greek grammarians.

Given this, one is then faced with the question as to how it can
happen that the aorist can and does occur with nonpast temporal
reference. This is not an issue unique to Greek. Typological investigations must also address how +PFV +PAST verb forms can be used
with nonpast temporal reference. Despite this, linguistic typology
still maintains that perfective verb forms, particularly in those languages that have a PFV:IPFV split, are almost always restricted to
past time reference. Regarding this, Dahl writes,

> For all languages it holds that "past time reference"
> characterizes prototypical uses of PFV – single, com-
> pleted events will in the "typical cases" be located in
> the past. Languages will differ, however, in the extent
> to which they allow uses of PFV with nonpast time ref-
> erence. Also, within one and the same language, the
> "past time reference" restriction may hold with unequal
> force in different contexts.[59]

There are two issues to be considered. One is prototypical use,
which will discussed in §4 below. The other is that languages will, in
varying degrees, allow +PFV verb forms to be used with nonpast reference and that a given language may differ in its allowance based

---

58  Dahl, *Tense and Aspect Systems*, 83.
59  Ibid., 79.

upon context. In addition, Bybee and Dahl argue that, with regard to perfectives, the aspectual properties are dominant relative to the temporal properties.[60] They further state, "It thus happens fairly frequently that perfective categories may have non-past reference in non-indicative moods or (which is often the same thing) certain non-assertive contexts, such as conditional clauses."[61] Thus, there is the notion that, for perfective verb forms, aspect is the dominant category and temporal reference is secondary and therefore may be overridden in certain contexts. This is how many of the historical Greek grammarians and their inheritors regard the Koine Greek verbal system, and with respect to the aorist, they view it as primarily perfective and secondarily past-referring.[62] What the historical grammarians saw in the Greek verbal system and particularly in the aorist is demonstrated by linguistic typology as normal and expected. Thus, for example, in gnomic contexts, it is not problematic for the aorist to be used. Its temporal reference is secondary and the restriction to past time is lifted.

Another issue to consider is how perfectives typically interact with certain verb types. For instance, nonpast aorist indicatives are often instances of stative verbs. Matt 13:24 and Luke 3:22, for example:

> Matt 13:24    Ἄλλην παραβολὴν παρέθηκεν αὐτοῖς λέγων· ὡμοιώθη ἡ βασιλεία τῶν οὐρανῶν ἀνθρώπῳ σπείραντι καλὸν σπέρμα ἐν τῷ ἀγρῷ αὐτοῦ.

> He presented another parable to them: "The kingdom of heaven ὡμοιώθη a person who sowed good seed in his field."

> Luke 3:22b    καὶ φωνὴν ἐξ οὐρανοῦ γενέσθαι· σὺ εἶ ὁ υἱός μου ὁ ἀγαπητός, ἐν σοὶ εὐδόκησα.

> And a voice came from heaven: "You are my beloved son, in you εὐδόκησα."[63]

---

60  Bybee and Dahl, "Tense and Aspect Systems," 84.
61  Ibid.
62  See §1 above.
63  See also some of the examples in Decker, *Temporal Deixis*, 95–98; Campbell, *Verbal Aspect*, 120–21; Porter, *Verbal Aspect*, 226–28.

Bybee, Perkins, and Pagliuca found that not all languages allow perfectives to apply to stative predicates. However, with regard to languages that do allow it, they state, "The effect is usually to signal a present state, not a past one, despite the fact that perfectives are usually past."[64] Thus, when the aorist indicative is used with a stative predicate to communicate a present state, it is behaving exactly as is typologically predicted.[65] However, the aorist indicative may also be applied to stative predicates in order to communicate a past state (e.g., 1 Thess 3:1 – Διὸ μηκέτι στέγοντες εὐδοκήσαμεν καταλειφθῆναι ἐν Ἀθήναις μόνοι. "So, not being able to endure it any longer, *we were happy* to be left in Athens alone."). Given that this is typically a feature of the simple past,[66] this would seem to further confirm that the aorist indicative is encoded for both +PFV and +PAST.

## 3. POLYSEMY

Another issue that must be addressed is whether a verbal category, such as the aorist, may be polysemous (i.e., having two or more related meanings). Some NT scholars argue that semantic meaning is the uncancelable component of a verb form whereas pragmatic meaning is any cancelable meaning. For example, Campbell writes,

> The semantic value is the uncancelable essence of meaning ... that is inherent to the verb form in question.... [Pragmatics] has to do with linguistic performance and implicature, which will vary depending on lexical, stylistic, grammatical and deictic interactions, and thus refers to cancelable features.[67]

This understanding of semantics leads to a monosemous conception of the Greek tense-forms. Since each tense-form is defined by its uncancelable features, only those values that are always present

---

64  Bybee, Perkins, and Pagliuca, *Evolution of Grammar*, 92.
65  The difference, then, between the aorist applied to a stative predicate and the present applied to a stative predicate is to be found in their aspectual values.
66  Ibid., 92, 95.
67  Campbell, *Verbal Aspect*, 24. So also Porter, *Verbal Aspect*, 104; Decker, *Temporal Deixis*, 38, 45; Cirafesi, *Verbal Aspect in Synoptic Parallels*, 19.

in the form are considered a part of the semantic meaning.[68] Thus, because the tense-forms may be used in different temporal contexts, temporal reference is regarded as a cancelable conversational implicature[69] and not as a semantic component. As Decker argues, "If temporal reference is part of the semantic value of the form, then it is not cancelable."[70]

However, this conception of cancelability is problematic in two respects. First, in Gricean pragmatics, from which the concepts of implicature and cancelability come,[71] the cancellation of an implicature is a test that is applied to one particular context. Grice states,

> A generalized conversational implicature can be canceled in a particular case. It may be explicitly canceled, by the addition of a clause that states or implies that the speaker has opted out, or it may be contextually canceled, if the form of utterance that usually carries it is used in a context that makes it clear that the speaker IS opting out.[72]

Following Grice, pragmatic scholarship never conceives of cancelability as comparing the meanings of a form in two different contexts. It is always applied to *one and the same* context in order to test whether there is an implicature. Consider Blakemore's example of an implicature:

(a)    A: Is Anna here?

       B: She's got a meeting.

(b)    Anna is not here

---

68  Cf. Cirafesi, *Verbal Aspect in Synoptic Parallels*, 19 n. 14.
69  In pragmatic linguistics, "conversational implicature" and "implicature" are often used interchangeably.
70  Decker, *Temporal Deixis*, 38. Cf. Campbell, *Verbal Aspect*, 26; Porter, *Verbal Aspect*, 104; Cirafesi, *Verbal Aspect in Synoptic Parallels*, 19.
71  See H. P. Grice, "Logic and Conversation," in *Syntax and Semantics 3: Speech Acts*, ed. Peter Cole and Jerry Morgan (New York: Academic Press, 1975), 57. See also the discussions in Levinson, *Pragmatics*, 100–18; and Katarzyna M. Jaszczolt, "Cancelability and the Primary/Secondary Meaning Distinction," *IPrag* 6 (2009): 260–62.
72  Grice, "Logic and Conversation," 57.

Blakemore states, "The information in (b) is an implicature derived from B's utterance in (a) on the basis of contextual information and the assumption that the speaker is conforming to a general principle or maxim of conversation."[73] As Blakemore demonstrates, this implicature is cancelable by saying, "She's got a meeting but she's here." Thus, comparing the use of a verb form in completely different contexts demonstrates nothing about what is and is not an implicature. Rather, in order to argue that temporal reference is an implicature in the aorist indicative, or the indicative Greek tense-forms more generally, one would have to demonstrate the cancelability of a specific temporal reference within one particular context.[74] However, even if this were possible, it would still not nec-

---

73 Diane Blakemore, *Relevance and Linguistic Meaning: The Semantics and Pragmatics of Discourse Markers*, CSL 99 (Cambridge: Cambridge University Press, 2002), 13. Comrie's example, "It's cold in here," is also helpful in understanding the nature of implicatures. When uttered in a certain context, the recipient deduces the implicature, "Please shut the window." However, when the recipient goes to the window, this implicature may be canceled by the speaker saying, "Please don't close the window, I enjoy the cold." Bernard Comrie, *Tense*, CTL (Cambridge: Cambridge University Press, 1985), 23–24.

74 There is another issue as well. There seems to be some misunderstanding regarding what implicatures are. Compare the descriptions and discussions in Campbell, *Advances in the Study of Greek*, 121; Campbell, *Verbal Aspect*, 24–26; Porter, *Verbal Aspect*, 103–04; and Decker, *Temporal Deixis*, 128, with pragmatic linguistic scholarship, e.g., Kent Bach, "Saying, Meaning, and Implicating," in *The Cambridge Handbook of Pragmatics*, ed. Keith Allan and Kasia M. Jaszczolt, CHLL (Cambridge: Cambridge University Press, 2012), passim; Levinson, *Pragmatics*, 97–118; Jaszczolt, "Cancelability," passim; Grice, "Logic and Conversation," passim; Laurence R. Horn, "Implicature," in *The Handbook of Pragmatics*, ed. Laurence R. Horn and Gregory Ward, BHL (Malden, MA: Blackwell, 2006), passim; Billy Clark, *Relevance Theory*, CTL (Cambridge: Cambridge University Press, 2013), 216–39; Regina Blass, *Relevance Relations in Discourse: A Study with Special Reference to Sissala*, CSL 55 (Cambridge: Cambridge University Press, 1990), 67–72; B. A. Barbara Abbott, "Pragmatics," in *The Routledge Linguistics Encyclopedia*, ed. Kirsten Malmkjær, 3rd ed. (London: Routledge, 2010), 420–21. The same terminology is used, but that is the extent of the similarity. Blakemore's example given above and Comrie's in n73 are the typical forms of implicatures found in pragmatic scholarship. They are unuttered communicative acts that do not match the linguistic content or meaning of what was said nor do they affect the truth-conditional content of the actual utterance. They are retrievable due to situational context and relevance relations. Granted, Porter does seem to realize that there is some difference, as he does write, "I use the term ['implicature'] as it has been applied to the area of tense usage and not solely as it was first used by Grice." Porter, *Verbal Aspect*, 83. However, there

essarily prove that temporal reference is an implicature.[75] This leads to the second issue in how cancelability has been (mis)appropriated in New Testament Greek scholarship. Grice himself did not regard the test of cancelability as a proof for the presence of an implicature. He writes, "Now I think that all conversational implicatures are cancelable, but unfortunately one cannot regard the fulfillment of a cancelability test as decisively establishing the presence of a conversational implicature."[76] From this, one can derive the following: All implicatures are cancelable, but not all cancelable things are implicatures. Thus, aside from the fact that the cancelability test has not been properly applied to the Greek tense-forms, cancelability does not even conclusively demonstrate that a canceled meaning is an implicature.[77]

---

is no special application of implicature to tense usage that differs from the meaning of the linguistic term elsewhere. In the context of Porter's statement, it would seem he is suggesting that his use of implicature is based on Comrie's use in *Tense* and perhaps the use in John Lyons, *Semantics*, vol. 2 (Cambridge: Cambridge University Press, 1977). However, Comrie uses the term throughout his book in the accepted Gricean sense as does Lyons.

75  One reason not addressed in this paper is that implicatures must concurrently satisfy many features (including cancelability) that are not independent of each other (e.g., nondetachability, unable to affect truth-conditional meaning, and calculable). See Mira Ariel, *Defining Pragmatics*, Research Surveys in Linguistics (Cambridge: Cambridge University Press, 2010), 6; Levinson, *Pragmatics*, 119.

76  Paul Grice, *Studies in the Way of Words* (Cambridge: Harvard University Press, 1989), 44. This is noted as well in Jaszczolt, "Cancelability," 267. Cf. Bach, "Saying, Meaning, and Implicating," 60.

77  There also seems to be an unnecessarily harsh line drawn between semantics and pragmatics by those who argue for a tenseless Greek verb. For example, Decker writes, "Only by blurring the line between [semantics and pragmatics] can the traditional explanation be rehabilitated. If the proper domain of semantics is strictly concerned with what the grammatical form means in and of itself, then it would be very difficult to maintain a temporal view of the verb." Decker, *Temporal Deixis*, 153–54 (cf. Campbell, *Verbal Aspect*, 24–25). The issue, though, is that the line between semantics and pragmatics *is* blurry. Knowledge of pragmatic use feeds into semantic knowledge. As Evans comments, "Knowledge of what words mean and knowledge about how words are used are both types of 'semantic' knowledge. This is not to say that I am denying the existence of pragmatic knowledge. Instead, my claim is that semantic and pragmatic knowledge cannot be clearly distinguished ... Semantic and pragmatic knowledge can be thought of in terms of a continuum. While there may be qualitative distinctions at the extremes, it is often difficult in practice to draw a sharp distinction." Vyvyan Evans,

There is cross-linguistic evidence for polysemous verb categories. When considering polysemous syntactic categories in English,
Taylor writes,

> From pastness with respect to the present and the past-
> ness of a historical narrative, the past tense comes to
> be used as a marker of narrativity *tout court*. The past
> tense, however, has at least two other very important
> meanings (or constellations of meanings) in English.
> These have nothing to do with past time, or with narra-
> tivity. Firstly, the past tense indicates the unreality (or

---

*Language and Time: A Cognitive Linguistics Approach* (Cambridge: Cambridge
University Press, 2013), 24. Cf. Vyvyan Evans and Melanie Green, *Cognitive
Linguistics: An Introduction* (Edinburgh: Edinburgh University Press, 2006),
211-13, 367; Jaroslav Peregrin, "The Normative Dimension of Discourse,"
in *The Cambridge Handbook of Pragmatics*, ed. Keith Allan and Kasia M.
Jaszczolt (Cambridge: Cambridge University Press, 2012), 213-14. Similarly,
Langacker writes, "Semantics and pragmatics form a gradation ... with no
precise boundary between the two. But toward either extreme of the scale
lie phenomena that are indisputably either semantic or pragmatic." Ronald W. Langacker, *Cognitive Grammar: A Basic Introduction* (Oxford: Oxford
University Press, 2008), 40. (See also Langacker's discussion in pp. 39-43.)
A harsh divide between semantics and pragmatics actually becomes problematic for those who maintain it. Porter states, "Although implicature does
not dictate tense usage, but to the contrary tense usage governs implicature,
nevertheless, a much-evidenced correlation can be seen between temporal
reference, speaker's conception, and tense usage, related to what Dahl calls
'conventionalization' (*Tense*, 11). Patterns of textual usage readily illustrate
that certain textual conditions become associated with particular tense
forms (e.g., the Aorist in narrative contexts; Present in descriptions), such
that use of the tense form in the textual environment readily implicates the
conventionalized meaning," Porter, *Verbal Aspect*, 104. Conventionalization,
though, is not simply a pattern by which "certain textual conditions become
associated with particular tense forms," nor is conventionalized meaning
"implicated." Consider the rest of what Dahl writes: "What happens when
a conversational implicature is conventionalized may be described as follows: if some condition happens to be fulfilled frequently when a certain
category is used, a stronger association may develop between the condition
and the category in such a way that *the condition comes to be understood as an
integral part of the meaning of the category*." Dahl, *Tense and Aspect Systems*, 11
(emphasis added). When an implicature is conventionalized, it crosses the
blurry border between pragmatics and semantics. Thus, Porter is effectively
arguing here that the tenses are, in fact, encoded with temporal value, by
virtue of the conventionalization of temporal implicatures (so-called).

counterfactuality) of an event or state. Secondly, the past tense can function as a kind of pragmatic softener.[78]

Taylor provides the following examples for the counterfactual use:[79]

1. If I had enough time, ...
2. I wish I knew the answer.
3. Suppose we went to see him.
4. I thought John was married (... but he apparently isn't)[80]
5. (Both speaker and addressee are preparing to go to a concert): But I thought the concert began at 8, doesn't it?

Examples of pragmatic softening:[81]

1. Excuse me, I wanted to ask you something.
    a) More tactful than: Excuse me, I want to ask you something
2. Was there anything else you were wanting?
3. I was wondering if you could help me.

Thus, in English, there are certain contexts in which it is acceptable to use a past tense form even though past temporal reference is not being made. It would be a mistake to attempt to corral these uses under one semantic definition. There is no question that English has a past tense, but it is an accepted convention of English usage to use past tense verbs to accomplish certain effects pragmatically, such as counterfactual meanings and pragmatic softening. As Taylor states, "At issue here is not the existence of past tense forms of verbs ... but rather the contexts of their use."[82]

---

78  Taylor, *Linguistic Categorization*, 177. See also John R. Taylor, *Cognitive Grammar*, OTL (Oxford: Oxford University Press, 2002), §20.2. Cf. Klaas Bentein, "Tense and Aspect from Hellenistic to Early Byzantine Greek," *EAGLL* 3:380.

79  Taylor, *Linguistic Categorization*, 177–78. See also the discussion in Barbara Dancygier and Eve Sweetser, *Mental Spaces in Grammar: Conditional Constructions*, CSL 108 (Cambridge: Cambridge University Press, 2005), 56–61.

80  On this use, Taylor writes, "There are also a number of verbs whose past tense forms, under certain circumstances and with the appropriate intonation, can convey the present-time counterfactuality of a state of affairs represented in a past tense subordinate clause." Taylor, *Linguistic Categorization*, 177.

81  Ibid., 178.

82  Ibid., 180–81.

Similar features may be observed in other languages as well. For example, in French, the *imparfait*, a past imperfective tense, may be used in nonpast contexts. Caudal provides the three following uses:[83]

1. Children preparing to play a game
   a. Tu étais    le gendarme, et moi le voleur.
      You be-IMPF.2sg the policeman and me the thief.
      "You're the cop, and I'm the robber."[84]
2. Politeness
   a. Je voulais    vous parler.
      I want-IMPF.1sg you talk-INF.
      "I wanted to talk to you."
3. Hypocoristic
   a. Oh, mais on avait mal à la papatte!
      Oh, but we have-IMPF.3sg ache at the paw.
      "Oh, but our paw aches!" (with ["Oh My Poor Darling"]
      prosody, speech act is (fictionally) attributed to a
      pet animal)

---

83 Patrick Caudal, "Pragmatics," in *The Oxford Handbook of Tense and Aspect*, ed. Robert I. Binnick, Oxford Handbooks (Oxford: Oxford University Press, 2012), 274–76. Within this discussion, when Caudal refers to the cancellation of a pastness implicature (274–75), it is important to realize that he defines "pastness implicature" here as "the described event does not extend up to speech time." Therefore, he is not suggesting that past temporal reference is a cancelable implicature of the *imparfait* but rather that the notion <event does not extend into the present> is a cancelable implicature. This is clear throughout his discussion on the *imparfait*, especially given that he describes the semantic contribution of the tense as a past imperfective (276). Comrie also distinguishes between past temporal reference and an implicature that the event described no longer holds at the utterance time. Comrie, *Tense*, 24.

84 Regarding this type (termed "preludic" and "ludic"), Caudal states, "It should be highlighted that the above data is not an isolated phenomenon at all, and that similar uses of tense-aspect forms are documented within a substantial number of languages: for instance, the Italian *imperfetto* has related *ludico* uses ... the Spanish *pretérito imperfecto* too ... whereas Dutch has a so-called 'imaginative imperfect.'" Caudal, "Pragmatics," 275. Taylor, not speaking of preludic uses but instead generally of the uses of past tenses cross-linguistically, concludes, "These remarkable cross-language similarities strongly suggest that the past tense needs to be regarded as a polysemous (rather than a homonymous) category." Taylor, *Linguistic Categorization*, 179.

Past tenses expressing nonpast temporal reference are common occurrences. In languages that exhibit such uses, those past tense forms are regarded as polysemous.[85] The fact that the aorist indicative can occur in nonpast contexts in order to express a gnomic idea, a present state, a performative action, or a future event is not evidence that the aorist indicative is not semantically encoded for +PAST. It simply demonstrates that it is polysemous.[86] What I am claiming is not all that different from the historical grammarians. Their intimate knowledge of the Greek language often led them to accurate conclusions even if they did not have the linguistic theory to back it up. The only difference may be that while they viewed these nonpast aorist indicatives as exceptions to the rule, I view them as typologically expected and pragmatically or lexically motivated deviations from the prototypical usage.

## 4. PROTOTYPE CATEGORIES[87]

One may wonder how the aorist, or any perfective past tense, may be described as +PFV +PAST if it is polysemous. The existence of multiple meanings would seem to preclude a default meaning from being posited, and yet, English speakers regard their past tense as

---

85  Comrie also regards past tenses as frequently polysemic, Comrie, *Tense*, 19–21. See also the discussion in Hogeweg, "Past Tense and Counterfactuals," which is a cross-linguistic investigation of the use of past tenses in counterfactuals. Janda notes that grammatical categories generally tend to be polysemous. Laura A. Janda, "Tense, Aspect and Mood," in *Handbook of Cognitive Linguistics*, ed. Ewa Dąbrowska and Dagmar Divjak, HSK 39 (Berlin: de Gruyter, 2015), 623. She also states, "Both the present and the past tense can be used to refer to event-objects that do not belong to the corresponding times" (ibid.). In addition, consider Croft's remark: "Like all grammatical categories, grammatical aspect categories tend to be polysemous within a language and differ in their uses across languages." William Croft, *Verbs: Aspect and Causal Structure* (Oxford: Oxford University Press, 2012), 127.

86  It is also worth noting that the Koine Greek verbal system does not have a perfective present form (cf. Corien Bary, "Aspect in Ancient Greek: A Semantic Analysis of the Aorist and Imperfective" [PhD diss., Radboud University Nijmegen, 2009], 125–26; de la Villa, "Tense/Aspect," 384). Thus, if a Greek speaker wanted to portray an event as perfective in the present, the most reasonable option would be a pragmatic use of the aorist that overrides its past-tense semantic component.

87  I wish to thank John Taylor for interacting with me regarding the content of this section.

a past tense and French speakers regard the *imparfait* as a past imperfective tense, despite accepted nonpast usages in both languages. The reason this occurs is because humans often structure conceptual categories around prototypes.[88] That is, categories are naturally conceived of as having a conceptual prototype that stands at the center of the category and represents certain central features and attributes.[89] Entities are assigned category membership based on their similarity to the prototype—those that are very similar will have a more central status in the category, and those that are less similar will be on the peripheral edges of the category.[90] There are varying degrees, then, by which category members will differ from each other in how well they represent the conceptual center of the category.[91] Thus, with regard to how prototypical categorization applies to the semantics of verbal categories, Boogaart and Janssen write, "Rather than defining aspectual categories by single semantic constraints ... the semantics of aspectual categories is assumed to be organized around a prototype with many language-particular extensions, including extensions in other domains (tense, modality)."[92] This is how the simple past is conceived in English. The prototypical center of the category is the concept of a verb referring to a past complete event. Thus, simple past verbs that accomplish this are regarded as exemplifying the prototype.[93] The nonpast referring occurrences are understood as category members but peripheral ones, since they resemble the prototype in certain respects but are distinct from it and far less normative. As Taylor states, "The more

---

88  See the discussions in Taylor, *Linguistic Categorization*, 41–83; John R. Taylor, *The Mental Corpus: How Language is Represented in the Mind* (Oxford: Oxford University Press, 2012), 186–87; George Lakoff, *Women, Fire, and Dangerous Things: What Categories Reveal about the Mind* (Chicago: University Of Chicago Press, 1987), passim.

89  Taylor, *Linguistic Categorization*, 64. So also John R. Taylor, "Prototype Effects in Grammar," in Dąbrowska, *Handbook of Cognitive Linguistics*, §3. Cf. Comrie, *Tense*, 22.

90  Taylor, *Linguistic Categorization*, 42–46, 53, 65–69. So also Taylor, "Prototype Effects in Grammar," §3; Dahl, *Tense and Aspect Systems*, 4; Comrie, *Tense*, 22.

91  In other words, there are "degrees of representativity." See the discussion in Taylor, "Prototype Effects in Grammar," 563–65.

92  Ronny Boogaart and Theo Janssen, "Tense and Aspect," in Binnick, *The Oxford Handbook of Tense and Aspect*, 817.

93  In this sense, then, the simple past is an example of Taylor's "prototype-as-subcategory." Taylor, *Linguistic Categorization*, 64.

peripheral members of the past tense tend to be instantiated more sporadically and unpredictably than the central members."[94]

Dahl also regards verb categories prototypically. As noted above, based on his survey of sixty-four languages, he regards prototypical perfectives as signaling past temporal reference.[95] He interprets the past tense restriction as a "secondary feature," — it characterizes

---

94  Ibid., 180. While Taylor does not use the descriptor "prototype" in his discussion of the past tense, his reference to the nonpast uses as "peripheral members" and to past temporal reference as the past tense's "central meaning" (176) suggests that he does regard the simple past use as exemplifying the prototype. (Though he was hesitant to use the term "prototype" with respect to central and peripheral uses of some polysemous lexemes [119–20], he has recently done so while noting the flexibility of the concept of "prototype." [See his discussion in Taylor, "Prototype Effects in Grammar," 562–68.]).

There is a slight tension between a polysemous category and positing a prototype. How does one reconcile distinct semantic nodes or centers with prototypical categorization? This is where it is helpful to note, as Taylor does, that the criteria for prototypicality vary depending on what kind of category is in view (Taylor, "Prototype Effects in Grammar," passim; he also made this point to me in a private communication on June 29, 2015). Regarding the topic of this paper, Taylor states, "In the case of tenses/aspects, the dominant criteria for central vs. peripheral senses/uses (or whatever one wishes to call them) would probably be frequency and productivity" (pers. comm., June 29, 2015). With respect to frequency, there is no doubt that the perfective past use of the aorist indicative is extremely more frequent than the nonpast uses. With respect to productivity, there are virtually no restrictions on the perfective past use of the aorist indicative. The nonpast uses, however, are limited lexically (e.g., stative present and performative) and pragmatically (e.g., gnomic) and are only suited to certain contexts of use. Thus, the perfective past use of the aorist indicative appears to clearly emerge as the prototypical center of the category. It would seem that the various semantic nodes of the aorist are organized around the prototype by virtue of the shared, dominant +PFV feature, which motivates the nonpast uses in certain contexts. Thus, by this shared feature alone, there is sufficient resemblance to and extension from the prototype. (This is not to argue that polysemous categories or items must exhibit a shared core meaning—see Taylor, Linguistic Categorization, 108—but simply an observation that this happens to be the case with the aorist.) Since they do not share the +PAST feature, though, the peripheral members stand at a distance from the prototypical center. That this is the case seems all the more likely given the ancient Greeks' conception of the verbal system, wherein the aorist was conceived as a past undetermined tense (discussed below).

95  Dahl, Tense and Aspect Systems, 79.

the prototypical occurrences, but it may not always hold.[96] The perfective feature is dominant.[97] This typological generalization characterizes the aorist indicative. It is encoded for both +PFV and +PAST. Prototypically, both semantic components are featured — it is the perfective past tense. However, perfective aspect is dominant.[98] Past-temporal reference is secondary and will hold much of the time but it can be overridden for use in certain nonpast contexts. The nonpast uses can all be understood as resembling the prototype and as extensions from it, in that they retain the dominant feature, perfective aspect, and are meaningfully motivated by it.

This kind of prototypical conception is evident in the systematized categorization of the ancient Greeks themselves. For instance, Dionysius Thrax, who is credited as the author of *Techne Grammatike*,[99] assigns past tense to the aorist (as well as the imperfect, perfect, and pluperfect) and pairs it with the future.[100] The Stoics arranged the verbal system according to tense and aspect, regarding the present and imperfect as present and past incomplete, the perfect and pluperfect as present and past complete, and the future and aorist as the future and past undetermined.[101] The fact that

---

96  Ibid., 79-80. Curiously, Dahl's discussion on secondary meanings in his first chapter (10-11) does not appear to match the description given here. In his first chapter, he states that secondary meanings are normally represented by a subset of the prototype (10), which would not seem to allow him to regard the past-restricted perfective as a prototype. In any case, I find his discussion on and conclusion regarding perfectives to be much more consistent with how prototypes are typically described.

97  Ibid., 9, 23.

98  This is expected given that Greek is an aspect-prominent language; see Ellis, ch. 4 in this volume.

99  R. H. Robins, *A Short History of Linguistics*, 4th ed., LLL 6 (London: Longman, 1997), 37.

100  Ibid., 44; Jean Lallot, "Tense (*khrónos*), Ancient Theories of," *EAGLL* 3:§2.

101  Robins, *A Short History of Linguistics*, 36; Porter, *Verbal Aspect*, 21; J. Pinborg, "Classical Antiquity: Greece," *CurTL* 13 (1975):, 94; Jean Lallot, "Aorist (*aóristos*), Ancient Theories of," *EAGLL* 1:137; Lallot, "Tense (*khrónos*), Ancient Theories of," 378. However, Campbell states, "Haberland argues that the Stoics understood the aorist as, by itself, not contributing anything to temporal reference." Campbell, *Verbal Aspect*, 123. This is an incorrect assessment. First, not only do Robins, Porter, Pinborg, and Lallot state otherwise, but Pinborg presents four scholars' systems (including his own) representing the Stoic conception of the Greek verb, and all categorize the aorist as a past tense (Pinborg, "Classical Antiquity: Greece," 92–94). Second, this is not quite what Haberland claims. He writes, "Taken by itself,

this is how the ancient Greeks themselves arranged their own verbal system demonstrates that they prototypically conceived of the tense-forms as encoding both aspect and temporal reference and therefore regarded the aorist as the perfective past tense.

Porter, however, critiques the Stoics' arrangement of their verbal system, since it cannot account for variations of use. He states,

> Though the Stoics are to be commended for their attention to both temporal content and kind of action conveyed by verbs, and for their attempt to elucidate tense categories through apparent formal oppositions ... the exact nature of the system has apparently eluded them. Most obviously, the Stoics have failed to develop

---

the aorist (or the aorists, since for the Stoics, the future was as much of an aorist as the aorist of the past, which *we* call the aorist *simpliciter*) do [*sic*] not contribute anything to time reference." Hartmut Haberland, "A Note on the 'Aorist,'" in *Language and Discourse: Test and Protest: A Festschrift for Petr Sgall,* ed. Jacob Mey, LLSEE 19 (Amsterdam: Benjamins, 1986), 176. It is clear that Haberland is conceiving of "aorist" as including *both* the aorist and future tenses (which he claims is the Stoic conception, but the Stoics likely paired the aorist and future together simply owing to morphological resemblance [see Lallot, "Tense," 378]). If one conflates the aorist and future into one category as Haberland does, then the inevitable result will of course be a nontemporal category (this is made even more clear in his following discussions on the "aorist" in pp. 177, 180–81), but Campbell does not make this distinction, which leads to a misunderstanding of what Haberland is arguing. In addition, Haberland is not making a definitive claim. He writes, "This attempt to do justice to the Scholiast's remark about the 'indefiniteness' of the aorist is of course rather mechanical (in addition to being speculative): moreover, with regard to the meaning of the tenses involved, our analysis is not necessarily more correct." Haberland, "A Note on the 'Aorist,'" 178. I am sympathetic with Haberland's attempt to clarify the scholiast's comments on the aorist, as they can be difficult to understand (they can be found in Alfredus Hilgard, ed., *Grammatici Graeci: Scholia in Dionysii Thracis - Artem Grammaticam* [Leipzig: Teubner, 1901], 249–51). However, I believe that the context of the scholiast's comments indicates that he is speaking of indefiniteness with reference to temporal *structure* (i.e., aspect) rather than temporal *reference*. This is also the conclusion of Lallot who explains that while the perfect and pluperfect were defined by their "quantity of pastness," the aorist was understood as the past tense that was undefined in this respect, i.e., it does not specify "the temporal distance separating the related facts from the moment of utterance." Lallot, "Aorist," 137. Of course, there is also the issue of whether the scholiast's remarks even represent the Stoic conception of the aorist (on this, see n. 102).

a complete system that elucidates all the verbal forms and functions ... Their categories make no reference to past-referring Presents or Perfects, present-referring Imperfects and Pluperfects, as well as non-Indicative usage.[102]

Porter wants a verbal system that can account for *every* possible use, but this is simply not how humans conceive of grammatical categories.[103] Certainly, the Stoics would have been aware that they could use the aorist indicative with nonpast temporal reference or the aorist nonindicative forms without any explicit temporal reference. The fact that their verbal system was arranged prototypically

---

102  Porter, *Verbal Aspect*, 21. After stating "the Stoics have failed to develop a complete system that elucidates all the verbal forms and functions," Porter writes, "(especially such an important form as the Aorist, where it is defined in terms of ἄρτι and πάλαι [see Pinborg, 'Antiquity,' 92; Haberland, 'Note,' 175-76])." This is misleading. First, the aorist is not defined in terms of ἄρτι and πάλαι. Haberland writes, "The aorist is explained as being equivalent to a perfect *when combined* with a time adverbial like ἄρτι 'just now,' while with a time adverbial like πάλαι 'long ago,' it is said to be equivalent to a pluperfect." Haberland, "A Note on the 'Aorist,'" 175 (emphasis added). Similarly, Pinborg states, "[Stephanos] says that it is uncertain whether the aorist should be determined by *palai* ('long ago') as to effect a pluperfect, or with *arti* ('recently') as to effect a perfect." Pinborg, "Classical Antiquity: Greece," 92. This is a crucial distinction to make. The aorist is decidedly not defined in terms of ἄρτι and πάλαι. Rather, when occurring *with* the time adverbials, it is defined in terms of either perfect (with ἄρτι) or pluperfect (with πάλαι). Thus, these aorists are regarded as maintaining their past-temporal value and, by virtue of the time adverbials, gaining a completive aspectual value. Second, the definitions come from a scholium commenting on *Techne Grammatike* that Haberland guesses was likely composed in the sixth century AD (Haberland, "A Note on the 'Aorist,'" 174). Thus, not only is the author, Stephanos, a speaker of sixth century Greek, but he also does not necessarily represent the Stoic conception of the verbal system. As Pinborg states, "It is a difficulty that Stephanos takes the aorist in opposition to perfect/pluperfect, as this does not agree very well with the Stoic system of distinctions. But Stephanos' words here are not explicitly ascribed to the Stoa and might reflect the later system of the grammarians, who distinguished 1 future, 1 present and 4 past tenses." Pinborg, "Classical Antiquity: Greece," 92. Cf. Haberland, "A Note on the 'Aorist,'" 175.

103  See the discussions in Taylor, *Linguistic Categorization*, 170-84; 200-20; Lakoff, *Women, Fire, and Dangerous Things*, 58-67; Taylor, *Cognitive Grammar*, 9-10.

and did not account for the nonpast occurrences evinces that such uses were regarded as peripheral category members that did not exemplify the prototype.

## 5. CONCLUSION

In sum, given the typological evidence, the existence of polysemous past tenses cross-linguistically, and the use of prototypes in humans' conceptions of categories, there is substantial reason to regard +PFV and +PAST as semantic components of the aorist indicative. This is not to say that the two are held with equal weight. As discussed above, in a perfective past verb form, such as the aorist, perfective aspect will typically be the dominant component and the past-temporal reference will be secondary. On account of this and on account of the fact that verb forms may be polysemous, the use of the aorist indicative in nonpast contexts does not therefore indicate that the verb is not semantically encoded for +PAST. It simply confirms the secondary status of temporal reference and indicates that the aorist indicative is a polysemous category. This account of the aorist indicative finds further validation in that it is largely in agreement with the conception of the tense form posited by the historical grammarians and their inheritors.

Scholars such as McKay, Porter, Decker, and Cirafesi were right to push against some of the more time-oriented approaches to the Greek verbal system. While I believe they went too far and erred in their timeless conception of the system, I appreciate and commend their focus on aspect as the most central component of the verb. Indeed, I find many of their descriptions of nonpast aorists satisfying, as they do not attempt to force them into a temporal mold but rather allow its perfective aspect the explanatory power it deserves.

For the New Testament scholar, the important takeaway is that nonpast aorist indicatives are a part of natural Greek idiom, similar to what we see occurs in English and many other languages. When they occur, their past temporal reference restriction has been lifted for communicative and pragmatic purposes. The crucial feature of the nonpast aorist indicative, not unlike the prototypical aorist indicative, is its perfective aspect and how it portrays and interacts with its predicate.[104]

## BIBLIOGRAPHY

Abbott, Barbara. "Pragmatics." Pages 418–26 in *The Routledge Linguistics Encyclopedia*. Edited by Kirsten Malmkjær. 3rd ed. London: Routledge, 2010.

Ariel, Mira. *Defining Pragmatics*. Research Surveys in Linguistics. Cambridge: Cambridge University Press, 2010.

Bach, Kent. "Saying, Meaning, and Implicating." Pages 47–67 in *The Cambridge Handbook of Pragmatics*. Edited by Keith Allan and Kasia M. Jaszczolt. CHLL. Cambridge: Cambridge University Press, 2012.

Bary, Corien. "Aspect in Ancient Greek: A Semantic Analysis of the Aorist and Imperfective." PhD diss., Radboud University Nijmegen, 2009.

Bentein, Klaas. "Tense and Aspect from Hellenistic to Early Byzantine Greek." *EAGLL* 3:379–82.

Blakemore, Diane. *Relevance and Linguistic Meaning: The Semantics and Pragmatics of Discourse Markers*. CSL 99. Cambridge: Cambridge University Press, 2002.

Blass, F., and A. Debrunner. *A Greek Grammar of the New Testament and Other Early Christian Literature*. Translated by Robert W. Funk. Revised ed. Chicago: University Of Chicago Press, 1961.

Blass, Regina. *Relevance Relations in Discourse: A Study with Special Reference to Sissala*. CSL 55. Cambridge: Cambridge University Press, 1990.

Boogaart, Ronny, and Theo Janssen. "Tense and Aspect." Pages 803–28 in *The Oxford Handbook of Tense and Aspect*. Edited by Robert I. Binnick. Oxford Handbooks. Oxford: Oxford University Press, 2012.

Burton, Ernest De Witt. *Syntax of the Moods and Tenses in New Testament Greek*. Rev. and enl. ed. Chicago: University Press of Chicago, 1893.

---

104 For how this works out in the New Testament, the historical grammarians are often an excellent source, especially those that do not attempt to fit the nonpast aor. indics. into a past time mold. See also Bary, "Aspect in Ancient Greek."

Bybee, Joan L., and Östen Dahl. "The Creation of Tense and Aspect Systems in the Languages of the World." *StudLang* 13 (1989): 51–103.

Bybee, Joan L., Revere D. Perkins, and William Pagliuca. *The Evolution of Grammar: Tense, Aspect, and Modality in the Languages of the World*. Chicago: University of Chicago Press, 1994.

Campbell, Constantine R. *Advances in the Study of Greek: New Insights for Reading the New Testament*. Grand Rapids: Zondervan, 2015.

―――――. *Verbal Aspect, the Indicative Mood, and Narrative: Soundings in the Greek of the New Testament*. SBG 13. New York: Lang, 2007.

Caudal, Patrick. "Pragmatics." Pages 269–305 in *The Oxford Handbook of Tense and Aspect*. Edited by Robert I. Binnick. Oxford Handbooks. Oxford: Oxford University Press, 2012.

Chamberlain, William Douglas. *An Exegetical Grammar of the Greek New Testament*. New York: Macmillan, 1941.

Cirafesi, Wally V. *Verbal Aspect in Synoptic Parallels: On the Method and Meaning of Divergent Tense-Form Usage in the Synoptic Passion Narratives*. LBS 7. Leiden: Brill, 2013.

Clark, Billy. *Relevance Theory*. CTL. Cambridge: Cambridge University Press, 2013.

Comrie, Bernard. *Tense*. CTL. Cambridge: Cambridge University Press, 1985.

Crellin, Robert. "Basics of Verbal Aspect in Biblical Greek." *JSNT* 35 (2012): 196–202.

Croft, William. *Typology and Universals*. 2nd ed. CTL. Cambridge: Cambridge University Press, 2003.

―――――. *Verbs: Aspect and Causal Structure*. Oxford: Oxford University Press, 2012.

Dahl, Östen. *Tense and Aspect Systems*. New York: Blackwell, 1985.

―――――. "The Tense-Aspect Systems of European Languages in a Typological Perspective." Pages 3–25 in *Tense and Aspect in the Languages of Europe*. Edited by Östen Dahl. EALT 20. Berlin: Mouton de Gruyter, 2000.

Dana, H. E. and Julius R. Mantey. *A Manual Grammar of the Greek New Testament*. Upper Saddle River, NJ: Prentice Hall, 1957.

Dancygier, Barbara and Eve Sweetser. *Mental Spaces in Grammar: Conditional Constructions*. CSL 108. Cambridge: Cambridge University Press, 2005.

Decker, Rodney J. *Temporal Deixis of the Greek Verb in the Gospel of Mark with Reference to Verbal Aspect*. SBG 10. New York: Lang, 2001.

Desclés, Jean-Pierre, and Zlatka Guentchéva. "Universals and Typology." Pages 124–154 in *The Oxford Handbook of Tense and Aspect*. Edited by Robert I. Binnick. Oxford Handbooks. Oxford: Oxford University Press, 2012.

Evans, Vyvyan. *Language and Time: A Cognitive Linguistics Approach*. Cambridge: Cambridge University Press, 2013.

Evans, Vyvyan and Melanie Green. *Cognitive Linguistics: An Introduction*. Edinburgh: Edinburgh University Press, 2006.

Fanning, Buist M. *Verbal Aspect in New Testament Greek*. OTM. Oxford: Clarendon Press, 1990.

Funk, Robert W. *A Beginning-Intermediate Grammar of Hellenistic Greek*. 3rd ed. Salem, OR: Polebridge Press, 2013.

Grice, H. P. "Logic and Conversation." Pages 41–58 in *Syntax and Semantics 3: Speech Acts*. Edited by Peter Cole and Jerry Morgan. New York: Academic Press, 1975.

Grice, Paul. *Studies in the Way of Words*. Cambridge: Harvard University Press, 1989.

Haberland, Hartmut. "A Note on the 'Aorist.'" In *Language and Discourse: Test and Protest; A Festschrift for Petr Sgall*. Edited by Jacob Mey, 173–84. LLSEE 19. Amsterdam: Benjamins, 1986.

Hewson, John. "Aspect (and Tense)." *EAGLL* 1:181–83.

Hewson, John, and Vit Bubenik. *Tense and Aspect in Indo-European Languages: Theory, Typology, Diachrony*. CILT 145. Amsterdam: Benjamins, 1997.

Hilgard, Alfredus, ed. *Grammatici Graeci: Scholia in Dionysii Thracis – Artem Grammaticam*. Leipzig: Teubner, 1901.

Hogeweg, Lotte. "What's So Unreal about the Past?: Past Tense and Counterfactuals." Pages 181–208 in *Studies on English Modality in Honour of Frank R. Palmer*. Edited by Anastasios Tsangalidēs and Roberta Facchinetti. Linguistic Insights 111. Bern: Lang, 2009.

Horn, Laurence R. "Implicature." Pages 3–28 in *The Handbook of Pragmatics*. Edited by Laurence R. Horn and Gregory Ward. BHL. Malden, MA: Blackwell, 2006.

Janda, Laura A. "Tense, Aspect and Mood." Pages 616–633 in *Handbook of Cognitive Linguistics*. Edited by Ewa Dąbrowska and Dagmar Divjak. HSK 39. Berlin: de Gruyter, 2015.

Jaszczolt, Katarzyna M. "Cancelability and the Primary/Secondary Meaning Distinction." *IPrag* 6 (2009): 259–89.

Lakoff, George. *Women, Fire, and Dangerous Things: What Categories Reveal about the Mind*. Chicago: University Of Chicago Press, 1987.

Lallot, Jean. "Aorist (*aóristos*), Ancient Theories of." *EAGLL* 1:137–38.

———. "Tense (*khrónos*), Ancient Theories of." *EAGLL* 3:377–79.

Langacker, Ronald W. *Cognitive Grammar: A Basic Introduction*. Oxford: Oxford University Press, 2008.

Levinson, Stephen C. *Pragmatics*. CTL. Cambridge: Cambridge University Press, 1983.

Lyons, John. *Semantics*. Vol. 2. Cambridge: Cambridge University Press, 1977.

Mandilaras, Basil G. *The Verb in the Greek Non-Literary Papyri*. Athens: Hellenic Ministry of Culture and Sciences, 1973.

McKay, Kenneth L. *Greek Grammar for Students: A Concise Grammar of Classical Attic with Special Reference to Aspect in the Verb*. 2nd ed. Canberra: Dept. of Classics, Australian National University, 1994.

Moule, C. F. D. *An Idiom Book of New Testament Greek*. 2nd ed. Cambridge: Cambridge University Press, 1959.

Moulton, J. H. and Nigel Turner. *A Grammar of New Testament Greek: 3, Syntax*. London: T&T Clark, 1963.

Napoli, Maria. "Aorist." *EAGLL* 1:136–37.

Peregrin, Jaroslav. "The Normative Dimension of Discourse." Pages 209–26 in *The Cambridge Handbook of Pragmatics*. Edited by Keith Allan and Kasia M. Jaszczolt. Cambridge: Cambridge University Press, 2012.

Pinborg, J. "Classical Antiquity: Greece." *CurTL* 13, (1975): 69–126.

Porter, Stanley E. *Linguistic Analysis of the Greek New Testament: Studies in Tools, Methods, and Practice*. Grand Rapids: Baker Academic, 2015.

————. *Verbal Aspect in the Greek of the New Testament, with Reference to Tense and Mood*. 2nd ed. SBG 1. New York: Lang, 1993.

Rijksbaron, Albert. "The Discourse Function of the Imperfect." Pages 237–54 in *In the Footsteps of Raphael Kühner: Proceedings of the International Colloquium in Commemoration of the 150th Anniversary of the Publication of Raphael Kühner's Ausführliche Grammatik der griechischen Sprache, II. Theil; Syntaxe, Amsterdam, 1986*. Edited by Albert Rijksbaron, H. A. Mulder, and G. C. Wakker. Amsterdam: Gieben, 1988.

Robertson, A. T. *A Grammar of the Greek New Testament in the Light of Historical Research*. Nashville: Broadman Press, 1934.

Robins, R. H. *A Short History of Linguistics*. 4th ed. LLL 6. London: Longman, 1997.

Runge, Steven E. "Contrastive Substitution and the Greek Verb: Reassessing Porter's Argument." *NovT* 56, (2014): 154–73.

Smyth, Herbert Weir. *Greek Grammar*. Revised by Gordon M. Messing. Harvard: Harvard University Press, 1956.

Taylor, John R. *Cognitive Grammar*. OTL. Oxford: Oxford University Press, 2002.

———. *Linguistic Categorization*. 3rd ed. OTL. Oxford: Oxford University Press, 2003.

———. *The Mental Corpus: How Language is Represented in the Mind*. Oxford: Oxford University Press, 2012.

———. "Prototype effects in grammar." Pages 562–78 in *Handbook of Cognitive Linguistics*. Edited by Ewa Dąbrowska and Dagmar Divjak. HSK 39. Berlin: de Gruyter, 2015.

Villa, Jesús de la. "Tense/Aspect." *EAGLL* 3:382–89.

Wallace, Daniel B. *Greek Grammar Beyond the Basics: An Exegetical Syntax of the New Testament with Scripture, Subject, and Greek Word Indexes*. Grand Rapids: Zondervan, 1996.

Zerwick, Maximilian, S.J. *Biblical Greek*. Rome: Pontifical Biblical Institute, 1963.

CHAPTER 13

# Perfect Greek Morphology
# and Pedagogy

RANDALL BUTH

BIBLICAL LANGUAGE CENTER

The morphology of the Greek perfect has a complexity that iconically matches its complex semantics. Greek marks the perfect with
a reduplication and, in the active, a *kappa*. It also has two indicatives, one with primary endings ("perfect," in Greek: παρακείμενος)
and one with secondary endings and an augment (pluperfect, in
Greek: ὑπερσυντέλικος).

A session at the Annual Meeting of the Society of Biblical
Literature in November 2013 was devoted to the semantics of the
Greek perfect tense. Unfortunately, in discussing the semantics of
the perfect, morphology was only addressed in passing and dismissed as irrelevant. Even though my research interests tend to be
motivated more by pragmatics, I would like to point out how the
morphology of the Greek perfect has something to contribute to the
discussion of the semantics of the perfect within New Testament
circles. A complex morphology leads us to at least question proposals that assume a single, simplex meaning of the perfect category
in Greek.

Most grammarians recognize that Greek has three aspectual systems, an imperfective (the so-called "present"), a perfective (the so-
called "aorist"), and a *perfect*. (The future is really more of a mood
and a tense than an aspect.)

For most Greek verbs the perfective aspect (hereafter interchangeable with aorist aspect), has a particular stem. These can
be divided into aorists formed by a *sigma* added to the imperfective stem, and others. (The "other" category is older but will not be

discussed in this paper.) For all the aorists, the *same* stems are used for both active and middle voice, not active only or middle only. This will become an issue when we look at the perfect stem. An additional item is important: the simple *sigma* morpheme is the sole marker of these *sigma*-aorist stems and the lack of *sigma* marks the imperfective stem of these verbs.

*Example 1: Active and middle use the same stem.*

Aorist

     Act.   λῦ-σ-αι "to untie" [with active endings]

     Mid.  λύ-σ-ασθαι "to untie oneself" [with middle endings]

     Both active and middle aorists have the same stem.

Imperfective ("present")

     Act.   λύ-ειν "to be untying" [with active endings]

     Mid.  λύ-εσθαι "to be untying oneself" [with middle endings]

     Both active and middle imperfectives have the same stem.

For comparison, an example of a non-*sigma* aorist is also provided.

*Example 2: Active and middle use the same stem.*

Aorist

     Act.   λαβ-εῖν "to take" [with active endings]

     Mid.  λαβ-έσθαι "to take for oneself" [with middle endings]

     Both active and middle aorists have the same stem.

Imperfective

     Act.   λαμβάν-ειν "to be taking" [with active endings]

     Mid.  λαμβάν-εσθαι "to be taking for oneself" [with middle endings]

     Both active and middle imperfectives have the same stem.

(There is an additional middle voice [the so-called "*theta-passive*"] in the aorist and future system, λυθῆναι//λυθήσεσθαι, that we can ignore for our discussions since it does not parallel either the perfect or the imperfective systems.)

When we turn to the perfect system we find two incongruities.

First incongruity:

The active and middle voices use two different stems.

The *kappa* is used only for the actives. The middle does not use a *kappa*. This difference between active and middle stems is different from the aorist and the imperfective systems, where the actives and middles use the same stem.

Second incongruity:

There are *two* separate, morphological markers of the perfect stems.

a) There is a reduplicated prefix used in both the active and the middle.
b) The active has the reduplication and a *kappa*. Again, this double morphology is different from the aorist and imperfective aspectual system.

One may ask how such a double system developed in the perfect system and why such a double system developed.

In the 19th century Greek scholars were surprised to find out that the *kappa* perfect does not seem to go back to Proto-Indo-European. It is an early-Greek innovation within Indo-European.[1] This raises the question about the development of the perfect in general. Where did it come from?

There are three morphological layers to the development of the Greek perfect. The first stage of a Proto-Indo-European perfect was probably a vowel-shift perfect that has left some remnants in Greek.

---

1    E.g., "Daß die x-Bildung, wie ἕστηκε, wenn sie auch nach ihren hauptsäch-lichsten Typen bereits im Urgriechischen bestand, eine umfängliche For-menkategorie erst auf griech. Boden geworden war, ist nicht zu bezweifeln." ("There is no room to doubt that the *kappa*-development, like ἕστηκε, if it already existed in its most basic characteristics in earliest Greek, first became a generalized Form-category within Greek itself.") Karl Brugmann *Grundriss der Vergleichenden Grammatik der Indogermanischen Sprachen, Zweiter Band, Wortbildungslehre (Stammbildungs- und Flexionslehre). Zweite Hälfte* (Strassburg: Trübner, 1892), 1232.

Semantically, the first perfects were stative and intransitive. This is widely recognized.[2]

*Example 3*

|   | | |
|---|---|---|
| a. | (root *ϝιδ) | seeing |
|   | ϝοῖδα | know [have seen] |
| b. | πείθομαι | being convinced |
|   | πέποιθα | convinced |
| c. | -κτειν- | kill/killing |
|   | -κτον- | killed[3] |

In addition, we can note the confluence of the middle voice of some present and aorist verbs being joined with the active form of the perfect. The old stative perfects became associated with middle voice as middle voice developed, even though they used active morphology, e.g., πέποιθα "I am convinced, believe," but in the present as a middle voice πείθομαι.

As a second stage, reduplication is attested systematically in Eastern Indo-European (as an Eastern Indo-Iranian-Greek isogloss according to Bridget Drinka[4]) so it, too, is a proto-Greek feature of the perfect.[5]

---

2  See Bridget Drinka, "The Development of the Perfect in Indo-European, Stratigraphic evidence of Prehistoric Areal Influence," in *Language Contacts in Prehistory: Studies in Stratigraphy; Papers from the Workshop on Linguistic Stratigraphy and Prehistory at the Fifteenth International Conference on Historical Linguistics, Melbourne, 17 August 2001*, ed. Henning Anderson, AST 239 (Amsterdam: Benjamins, 2003), 77–105. "Abundant evidence has been assembled to indicate that the oldest reconstructible value of the perfect was intransitive and stative" (82).

3  The LXX uses a perfect with an -α- vowel, e.g., οὐκ ἀπέκταγκά σε.

4  Drinka, "Development of the Perfect," 78–79, 89–90, 94–97.

5  The vowel of the perfect reduplication contrasts with the -ι- vowel of some present tense reduplications: cf. δέδωκα (perfect δε-) versus δίδωμι (present δι-). There is no necessity to posit the incorporation of an additional morpheme -ε- in the perfect reduplication. Simple disambiguation is a sufficient explanation. The -ι- vowel is one of the signs of the imperfective aspect and present tense, as seen, for example, in words like βαίνειν "to be going" from a root βη/βα.

Reduplication must be considered to have developed after the vowel-shift perfect. Why? If the reduplication had preceded the vowel shift as a marking device, the rare and restricted vowel shift would never have arisen on common verbs. The examples of vowel shifting need to be seen as fossil forms from the first stage of perfect marking. Vestigial forms in a few common verbs are often seen in languages around the world, where frequent usage helps common verbs to resist the systematic application of new morphological features.

At the last stage, active transitivity entered the perfect semantic system and it was paralleled morphologically with regularization of the *kappa* perfect actives. The *kappa* perfect was limited to the active endings.

We must inquire about any semantic background associated with the two morphological developments, first with reduplication and second with the *kappa* perfect (active only). In several languages there appears to be a connection between doubling a word and a frequentive-iterative meaning, as if in a pidgin I said "he went went" to mean "he frequently went," i.e., "he used to go." A doubling of a word can be morphologized into a tighter form that partially doubles the word. This tighter morphology can become a reduplication prefix. Bybee, Perkins, and Pagliuca have suggested the following semantic trajectory as a cross-linguistic pattern for morphologizing duplication into a reduplication morpheme:[6]

*Example 4: A proposed trajectory of morphologizing reduplication cross-linguistically*

iterative → continuative → progressive →

                                        imperfective → intransitive

iterative → frequentative → habitual →

The reduplication marker mimics a doubled verb and at the same time the semantics develop along the trajectory. Such a suggestion links reduplication with imperfectivity. However, Greek does two things differently. One, the Greek perfect appears to have started

---

6    Joan Bybee, Revere Perkins, and William Pagliuca, *The Evolution of Grammar: Tense, Aspect, and Modality in the Languages of the World* (Chicago: University of Chicago Press, 1994), 172.

out as a stative. This would imply going one step further along a trajectory from intransitive to stative. Two, early Greek is starting out at the end of the trajectory, not the beginning. Thus, there is probably some prehistory to the Greek language that we are simply missing. The exact history, of course, does not affect the reality of Greek having an aspect that is marked by reduplication that includes an open-ended semantic.

The second morphological marker, the *kappa* perfect, was not part of Indo-European but is a development within Greek itself. It appears to be related to an old, fossilized aorist, a *kappa* aorist. By old, of course, we mean from before the attested history of Greek, from before Mycenaean Linear B. Sara Kimball has summarized this nicely: "Although the aorists ἔθηκα, ἔδωκα, and perhaps ἧκα are found as early as Mycenaean, the perfects τέθηκα and δέδωκα, as Wackernagel[7] pointed out, are resultative, clearly recent, and found only in the classical period."[8]

The *kappa* aorist is tied to the *kappa* perfect. Kimball again:[9]

> It seems clear that any explanation for the origin of the -κ-perfect ... should explain it in Greek terms as a Greek innovation; ... and it should explain why the distribution of the -κ- in the perfect parallels the distribution of the -κ- in the aorists, even though perfects and aorists did not usually influence each other.
>
> There is, of course, one point of contact between the perfect and the aorist: the alphathematic endings -α, -ας, -ε, shared by the active perfect, the sigmatic aorist and the κ-aorist. This suggests that the κ-perfect may have arisen through the reinterpretation of the - κ- of the aorists as part of the endings while alphathematic inflection was being established.

I think that the link between the *kappa* aorists and the *kappa* perfect is clear. Both the *kappa* aorist and the *kappa* perfect are limited to the active. There is no *kappa* aorist middle *ἐθηκάμην and there

---

7   Jacob Wackernagel, "Studien zum Griechischen Perfektum," *Kleine Schriften* (Göttingen: Vandenhoek & Ruprecht, 1953), 1002–3.

8   Sara Kimball, "The Origin of the Greek κ-Perfect," *Glotta* 69 (1991): 146.

9   Ibid., 148.

is no *kappa* perfect middle *\*τέθηγμαι*. The *kappa* aorists are old and apparently vestigial, remnants from some older process that only remains in some very common words like the finite actives of δοῦναι ("give") and θεῖναι ("put.") This means that Greek speakers imported an aorist morphological marker into the perfect stem. Both the *kappa* aorist and the *kappa* perfect are asymmetrical and break the normal pattern in the present and aorist where the active and middle use the same stem. Such an anomalous restriction cannot be ascribed to coincidence.

The connection between the *kappa* aorist and the *kappa* perfect is important. The aspect of *kappa* aorists is perfective, not imperfective. The *kappa* perfect imported a morphological pattern from a perfective.

So the *kappa* perfect has two, fused etymologies. It has a *perfective etymology* that is congruent with the *kappa* aorist, and it has an apparent *frequentive etymology* that was connected to reduplication. However, please understand, we are not claiming that etymology determines meaning; it is merely a history of where the form or meaning has come from. The meaning of the Greek perfect is not frequentative—it is *continuing an achieved state*. Greek πεποίηκα, "I have done it," is a perfective that marks an on-going relevance. This complex semantic category is iconically mimicked by the complex morphology.

How can we best capture this? Previously I have described the perfect with two features {+perfective, +imperfective}.[10] This has the advantage of allowing the Greek three-aspect system to be described with only two labels, perfective and imperfective. However, this statement may be misleading, because only a restricted subset of imperfective is intended. The imperfective aspect normally includes verbs whose internal semantics allow for change and progressive action. However, the ongoing relevance of the perfect tense does not refer to a changing or developing situation. It is open-ended, but it is static. It is not progressive, "in the process of doing," like

---

10  Randall Buth, "Verbs Perception and Aspect: Greek Lexicography and Grammar, Helping Students to Think in Greek," in *Biblical Greek Language and Lexicography: Essays in Honor of Frederick W. Danker*, ed. Bernard Taylor et al. (Grand Rapids: Eerdmans, 2004), 191–92.

prototypical imperfectives. We have a choice to make in our meta-linguistic labeling.

We can give up elegance by stipulating three aspects based on three features: one aspect with {+perfective}, one with {+imperfective}, and one with a {+perfect} semantic feature. Notice that I did not use "stative" as the term for the definition of the third aspect. I am uncomfortable with the idea of using the term *stative* in the aspectual descriptions, because stative is a lexical, semantic feature of certain verbs rather than a subjective, deictic, morpho-syntactic aspect category.

We can describe perfects more elegantly with two features {+perfective} and {+imperfective}. Imperfect is defined as "open-ended," including statives. We can add support to the stative character of the imperfective feature in the perfect with another iconic relationship. The perfect middles use a set of endings without any linking vowel. The perfect middle only uses -μαι -σαι -ται -μεθα -σθε -νται.

Which verbs use those endings in the present tense? (The so-called "present tense," of course, is part of the imperfective system in Greek.) Verbs that are lexically stative use those endings,

> like κεῖμαι κεῖσαι κεῖται, "lying down"
> and κάθημαι κάθησαι κάθηται, "sitting"
> and δύναμαι δύνασαι δύναται, "being able."

So in the perfect middle, the continuing state is mimicked in the morphology.

So I will stay with the abstract analysis of the Greek perfect as {+perfective, +imperfective} as long as one allows the definition of "imperfective" to be a subset definition of "continuing relevance."[11]

Using features like +perfective and +imperfective to describe the Greek perfect has cross-linguistic support. D. N. S. Bhat categorizes languages according to whether they have a prominence of tense, mood, or aspect in the verb system and he claims that this has a potential affect on any perfect they may have.[12]

The notion of Perfect:

---

11  There is a natural ordering to the features. The perfective feature precedes the imperfective relevance feature so that the relevance can be ongoing and is not ended by the perfective feature.

12  D. N. Shankara Bhat, *The Prominence of Tense, Mood, Aspect*, SLCS 49 (Amsterdam: Benjamins, 1999), 170.

1. Temporal view: past event with current (present) relevance
2. Aspectual view: completed (perfective) event with continuing (imperfective) relevance
3. Modal view: realis event with irrealis relevance (something needs to be done)

By the way, I would add that Greek has a kind of modal perfect adjective/participle with ποιητέον.

Greek is an aspectually prominent language. But Greek is more complicated than Bhat's category. In the indicative, Greek has two perfects, and they are placed within a temporal framework. The Greek perfect indicative has a current/present relevance and the pluperfect has an anterior perfective situation with current relevance to a past reference time. I should probably add at this point that the *augment* that optionally marks the pluperfect is a temporal morphological marker. Renaming the augment as a "remote proximity" marker simply uses a spatial metaphor for something that is not related to locational space.[13] Let me explain this in English: "He was standing" is not farther away geographically than "he is standing." Calling the Greek augment a remoteness marker means that the remoteness *metaphor* requires a definition and that definition is *time* related. In plain English, the augment is a past marker. (By the way, the Greeks themselves claimed this 2000 years ago.)

Some support on the semantics for the Greek perfect can be brought from Robert Crellin's 2012 dissertation:[14]

> The aspect of the perfect active [is] dependent on whether the subject participant can be presented as being either in or having entered a state: if it can, the perfect active stem will not necessarily carry past time

---

13  This argues against the terminology developed by Stanley E. Porter, *Verbal Aspect in the Greek of the New Testament: With Reference to Tense and Mood*, SBG 1 (New York: Lang, 1989), and followed in popularizations like Constantine Campbell, *Basics of Verbal Aspect in Biblical Greek* (Grand Rapids: Zondervan, 2008), 19: "Remoteness is not temporal remoteness, there are other kinds of remoteness besides temporal remoteness such as logical remoteness," and "Remoteness: The spatial quality of distance. Used as a spatial replacement for past tense" (136).

14  Robert Crellin, "The Greek Perfect Active System: 200 BC–AD 150," (PhD diss., University of Cambridge, 2012), 3.

reference, whereas if it cannot, it will in almost all circumstances do so.

I think that this complexity is a reasonable generalization and that Greek morphology iconically reflects the history of that complexity. The Greek perfect is not a simple stative, the Greek perfect is not a simple perfective, and the Greek perfect is not a simple imperfective. Only a complex semantics does justice to the synchronic use of the perfect in Classical and Koine Greek, and that complexity is iconically mimicked by the complex anomalous morphology.

The question now becomes, how do we teach this? I will argue that the complexity of the perfect blocks a potential reliance on a simple rule but it leads to a simple method to conceptualize and teach the perfect.

We must start with a cognitive linguistic approach and ask how the Greeks themselves would have learned the perfect. (Cognitive Linguistics gives due consideration to how something would be categorized in a brain and how it might be learned.)

Before a child can conceptualize a perfect they will need to pair up and link many specific words to specific situations. For example, somewhere around one year old they will hear their excited parents saying things like ἕστηκεν "she is standing [perfect morphology]" and ἕστηκας "you are standing [perfect morphology]." Of course, the child will not know that this is "'you are in a state of standing,' *kappa* perfect second person active, used for a present state." But by three to seven years old they will distinguish ἕστηκα from words like ἐκαθήμην οὐκ εἱστήκειν ἀλλὰ νῦν ἕστηκα καὶ οὐ κάθημαι "I was sitting, I was not standing [pluperfect morphology] but now I am standing [perfect morphology] and I am not sitting." Equally important and more surprising for those thinking about Greek rules, the child will use the present ἵστημι only in situations where they are setting something up, that is, in transitive situations with an object to set up. ἵστημι does not mean, "I am standing"; it means, "I am setting it up." And situations like an intransitive "I am standing up" only use a middle ἀνίσταμαι. The same unpredictable, semantic dissonance occurs in the simple past situations. "I set up the glass" is ἕστησα τὸ ποτήριον.

These relationships will be cemented into the networking of a child's brain along with words like οἶδα, and as they get to school-age, πέποιθα.

The idiosyncrasies of perfect lexical items must be learned at the center of one's language learning, and they will become the core of the mappings between morphological forms and meanings.

Many verbs must be learned in order to internalize the scale of meanings that are mentioned by Crellin. This will provide a better grasp and truer perception of the perfect than a generalized rule of any kind. Internalizing the various kinds of perfects within communicative frameworks not only mimics the cognitive framework of first-language learners, it is the only guarantee of building the system correctly within second-language learners and ourselves.

Common perfect verbs include prototypical transitive perfect verbs. These are easy to do in the classroom and can be differentiated from aorists and from presents.

For example,

> ὁ μαθητὴς ἔθηκεν τὸ βιβλίον ἐκεῖ,
> μετὰ ταῦτα ἔθηκεν τὸ βιβλίον ἐκεῖ,
> μετὰ ταῦτα τέθεικεν αὐτὸ ὧδε καὶ ἔτι κεῖται ὧδε.

The student placed the book there,
afterward he placed the book there,
afterward he has placed the book here and it is still lying here.

This is a prototypical situation and good for getting the prototypical pieces of the system in place. Here is another:

> John 11:34 καὶ εἶπεν· ποῦ <u>τεθείκατε</u> αὐτόν; λέγουσιν αὐτῷ· κύριε, ἔρχου καὶ ἴδε

And he said, "Where have you placed him?" They say to him, "Sir, come and see."[15]

The middle perfects may have a tendency toward more stativity, except of course, for something like ἴαται τὸν νεανίσκον "He has healed the young man," where the perfect middle is transitive and governs an accusative complement.

---

15  Author's translation.

One of the reasons that New Testament Greek metalinguistics has been in a turmoil is that the language has not been learned well enough from a cognitive linguistics perspective. Thousands of instantiations have not been internalized so that Greek users have the correct core language from which to be evaluating all of the proposals, terms, and discussions. This is a blemish on our field and it does create not a little aporia for upcoming generations.

What our field needs is a way of making sure that students, that is ourselves, have internalized the irregular and core vocabulary of our language. That means making sure that we internalize the 200–300 "funky verbs" whose semantics and morphology are not predictable from rules. Otherwise, we are only viewing the texts through a coarsely gridded metalanguage.

Common verbs include:

ἀπολώλεκα αὐτά    I have destroyed the things

ἀπόλωλα            I am lost, in a lost state

Here we have two perfect actives for the same word: one transitive active, with *kappa*, and one intransitive active.

In the imperfective present, ὧδε ἀπόλλυμαι is middle for intransitive "I am being destroyed here." (Luke 15:17). Compare Matthew 8:25: κύριε, σῶσον, ἀπολλύμεθα "we are dying." The present tense is used, not the perfect, because the event is not complete. The perfect includes a completed state, and would have been a despairing statement of hopelessness, or potentially humorous in the same context: ἀπολώλαμεν "we're dead already" (cf. Num 17:27 LXX). Plutarch's account of the report of Pan's death used the perfect because Pan had already died—he was not in the process of dying: Πᾶν ὁ μέγας τέθνηκεν "Pan the Great is dead!" (Plut., Περὶ τῶν Ἐκλελοιπότων Χρηστηρίων 17, [Def. orac. 419E]). Again, the perfective component within perfect events is typical of perfects versus presents. Again, this can be seen in basic verbs like ἐλήλυθα, "I have come" (i.e., "I am *in a state of having arrived*," not ἔρχομαι "I am in the process of coming, but not yet there"), etc. (This is especially telling against Campbell's "imperfective" interpretation of the perfect.)

Both irregular morphology and some unpredictable semantics need to be internalized as part of core language. The universal rule of grammar, followed by all children, is: "We do it like that because that's the way they do it."

As long as our field does not seriously accept the challenge of internalizing Greek, we may continue to generate more smoke than fire, more heat than light. We need to work in classrooms with these common verbs and be using them thousands of times, so that they are read automatically with correct semantics (not consciously parsed) when reading in first century authors like Paul, Luke, Plutarch, and Josephus. Three years of seminary is insufficient, of course. But learning Greek to second-language fluency must also become part of the wider academia if we value true access to the original language literature.

## BIBLIOGRAPHY

Bhat, D. N. Shankara. *The Prominence of Tense, Mood, Aspect.* SLCS 49. Amsterdam: Benjamins, 1999.

Brugmann, Karl. *Grundriss der Vergleichenden Grammatik der Indogermanischen Sprachen, Zweiter Band, Wortbildungslehre (Stammbildungs- und Flexionslehre), Zweite Hälfte.* Strassburg: Trübner, 1892.

Buth, Randall. "Verbs Perception and Aspect: Greek Lexicography and Grammar, Helping Students to Think in Greek." Pages 177–98 in *Biblical Greek Language and Lexicography: Essays in Honor of Frederick W. Danker.* Edited by Bernard Taylor, John A. L. Lee, Peter R. Burton, and Richard E. Whitaker. Grand Rapids: Eerdmans, 2004.

Bybee, Joan, Revere Perkins, and William Pagliuca. *The Evolution of Grammar: Tense, Aspect, and Modality in the Languages of the World.* Chicago: University of Chicago Press, 1994.

Campbell, Constantine. *Basics of Verbal Aspect in Biblical Greek.* Grand Rapids: Zondervan, 2008.

Crellin, Robert, "The Greek Perfect Active System: 200 BC–AD 150." PhD diss., University of Cambridge, 2012. Repr. as *The Syntax and Semantics of the Perfect Active in Literary Koine Greek.* Malden, MA: Wiley-Blackwell, forthcoming.

Drinka, Bridget. "The Development of the Perfect in Indo-European: Stratigraphic evidence of Prehistoric Areal Influence." Pages 77–105 in *Language Contacts in Prehistory: Studies in Stratigraphy; Papers from the Workshop on Linguistic*

*Stratigraphy and Prehistory at the Fifteenth International Conference on Historical Linguistics, Melbourne, 17 August 2001.* Edited by Henning Anderson. AST 239. Amsterdam: Benjamins, 2003.

Kimball, Sara E. "The Origin of the Greek κ-Perfect." *Glotta* 69 (1991): 141–53.

Porter, Stanley E. *Verbal Aspect in the Greek of the New Testament: With Reference to Tense and Mood.* SBG 1. New York: Lang, 1989.

Wackernagel, Jacob. "Studien zum Griechischen Perfektum." Pages 1000–21 in *Kleine Schriften.* 2 vols. Göttingen: Vandenhoek & Ruprecht, 1953.

CHAPTER 14

# The Semantics of the Perfect in the Greek of the New Testament[1]

ROBERT CRELLIN

FACULTY OF CLASSICS, UNIVERSITY OF CAMBRIDGE

## 1. INTRODUCTION

The perfect in the Greek of the New Testament (and in Koine Greek more generally) is well known for resisting straightforward analysis within a clear aspectual framework. The fundamental problem is that, although bearing the label perfect, the range of use of the Greek perfect in this period is very broad. Studies of the perfect in the post-Classical period have not in recent years been as many as those for the classical period,[2] although the situation in the New

1  May I express my thanks to the participants of the conference "Linguistics and the Greek Verb' for their helpful comments and questions following my presentation of an earlier version of this paper, as well as to the faculty of Örebro Theological Seminary, Sweden, where a much earlier version of this paper was presented."
2  Recent studies on the Homeric and Classical Greek perfect include Martin Haspelmath "From Resultative to Perfect in Ancient Greek," in *Nuevos Estudios Sobre Construcciones Resultativos*, ed. Leza Iturrioz and Luis José, Función 11-12 (Guadalajara: Universidad de Guadalajara, 1992), 187–224; C. M. J. Sicking and P. Stork "The Synthetic Perfect in Classical Greek," in *Two Studies in the Semantics of the Verb in Classical Greek*, ed. C. M. J. Sicking and P. Stork, MS 160 (Leiden: Brill, 1996), 119–298; Eva-Carin Gerö and Arnim von Stechow, "Tense in Time: The Greek Perfect," in *Words in Time: Diachronic Semantics from Different Points of View*, ed. Regine Eckardt, Klaus von Heusinger, and Christoph Schwarze, TiLSM 143 (Berlin: de Gruyter,

Testament has received more attention.[3] Following the taxonomy of Bybee et al.,[4] the perfect in the post-Classical period may be found denoting the following tense-aspectual categories:

- ANTERIOR, i.e., "a past action with current relevance," e.g., πεποίηκα "I have done."[5]

1. ὕπαγε εἰς τὸν οἶκόν σου πρὸς τοὺς σοὺς καὶ ἀπάγγειλον αὐτοῖς ὅσα ὁ κύριός σοι <u>πεποίηκεν</u> καὶ ἠλέησέν σε.

   Go to your house to your people and tell them what the Lord <u>has done</u> for you, and how he had mercy on you. (Mark 5:19)[6]

- Resultant state, i.e., a state resulting from an event taking place prior to reference time, e.g., ἐλήλυθα, "I have come."

---

2003), 251–94; Dag Trygve Triuslew Haug, "Aristotle's Kinesis/Energeia-Test and the Semantics of the Greek Perfect," *Linguistics* 42 (2004): 387–41; idem, "From Resultatives to Anteriors in Ancient Greek: On the Role of Paradigmaticity in Semantic Change," in *Grammatical Change and Linguistic Theory: The Rosendal Papers*, ed. Thórhallur Eythórsson, Linguistics Today 113 (Amsterdam: Benjamins, 2008), 285–305; Sander Orriens, "Involving the Past in the Present: The Classical Greek Perfect as a Situating Cohesion Device," in *Discourse Cohesion in Ancient Greek*, ed. Stéphanie Bakker and Gerry Wakker, ASCP 16 (Leiden: Brill, 2009), 221–39; Klaas Bentein, "The Periphrastic Perfect in Ancient Greek: A Diachronic Mental Space Analysis," *TPhS* 110 (2012): 171–211.

3    Studies include K. L. McKay, "On the Perfect and other Aspects in New Testament Greek." *NovT* 23 (1981): 289–329; Stanley E. Porter, *Verbal Aspect in the Greek of the New Testament*, SBG 1 (New York: Lang, 1989); Buist Fanning, *Verbal Aspect in New Testament Greek*, OTM (Oxford: Oxford University Press, 1990); Trevor V. Evans, "Another Ghost: The Greek Epistolary Perfect," *Glotta* 75 (1999): 194–221; Constantine Campbell, *Verbal Aspect, the Indicative Mood, and Narrative*, SBG 13 (New York: Lang, 2007); and Robert Crellin, "The Greek Perfect through Gothic Eyes: Evidence for the Existence of a Unitary Semantic for the Greek Perfect in New Testament Greek." *JGL* 14 (2014): 5–42. K. L. McKay, "The Use of the Ancient Greek Perfect Down to the End of the Second Century AD," *BICS* 12 (1965): 1–21 and idem, "On the Perfect and Other Aspects in the Greek Non-Literary Papyri," *BICS* 27 (1980): 23–49 have a focus outside of the New Testament. Trevor V. Evans, *Verbal Syntax in the Greek Pentateuch: Natural Greek Usage and Hebrew Interference* (Oxford: Oxford University Press, 2001) examines the verb system in the Greek Pentateuch.

4    Joand L. Bybee, Revere D Perkins, and William Pagliuca, *The Evolution of Grammar* (Chicago: University of Chicago Press, 1994), 61.

5    Ibid.

6    The Greek text used is NA[28]; unless otherwise specified, all translations are the author's.

2. οὐκ <u>ἐλήλυθα</u> καλέσαι δικαίους ἀλλ᾽ ἁμαρτωλοὺς εἰς μετάνοιαν.
I <u>am</u> not <u>come</u> to call the righteous but sinners to repentance." (Luke 5:32 ASV)

- State concurrent with the reference time of the clause with no reference to any prior event,[7] as in the following example of ἤλπικα "I have hope."

3. ἔστιν ὁ κατηγορῶν ὑμῶν Μωϋσῆς, <u>εἰς ὃν ὑμεῖς ἠλπίκατε</u>.
Your accuser is Moses, on whom your hopes are set. (John 5:45 NIV)[8]

Uses of the perfect without apparent reference to prior terminating event can be paralleled outside of the New Testament, as in the following example of the perfect of σπουδάζω "be zealous, eager":

4. ... πρὸς δὲ τὸ γενομένης ὀργῆς ἢ διαβολῆς ἢ στάσεως διδάξαι καὶ πραῦναι καὶ μεταθεῖναι <u>τοὺς ἠγνοηκότας</u> ὁλοσχερῶς ἀστοχοῦσιν[9] ...
but when anger, or slander, or insurrection actually occur, [the Carthaginians] completely fail to teach, or calm down, or change <u>those who are ignorant</u>. (Plb. 1.67.5)

5. πέμψαντες πρὸς Ἰούδαν ἐδήλουν αὐτῷ ὅτι λαβεῖν <u>ἐσπούδακε</u> Τιμόθεος τὸ χωρίον εἰς ὃ συνεπεφεύγεσαν.
... [they] sent to Judas and informed him that Timotheus <u>was eager</u> to take the land to which they had fled. (Jos. A.J. 12.330)

---

7   Of course, all states must in principle start at some time. However, so much would also be true of a state described by a present tense. The question is whether or not a perfect predicate by virtue of its being a perfect predicate must assert something about this start point.

8   According to the views outlined by Haug and McKay, whereby the perfect first instantiates the predicate via an aorist, this example should denote that the event of hoping started prior to reference time. Accordingly, there would be no difference between this and change of state predicates as at 48. The presence of the preposition εἰς "to, into," suggesting a dynamic situation, might be taken to support this. However, εἰς in the New Testament has in several places a purely locative function. Furthermore, on several occasions εἰς is used with πιστεύω "believe" where it is not necessarily obvious that it is a dynamic situation that is being described, e.g., John 9:35, 12:44, 14:1, 16:9; Rom 10:10; and Jas 2:19. Finally, it is striking that three ancient versions, namely the Vulgate, Gothic, and Old Syriac (Curetonian), all translate ἠλπίκατε without any explicit past reference. For discussion of this example in the Gothic case, see Crellin, "Greek Perfect through Gothic Eyes," 33–34.

9   This example is quoted and discussed in Robert Crellin, "The Greek Perfect Active System: 200 BC–AD 150" (PhD diss., University of Cambridge, 2011), 211; all classical texts are from LCL.

The capacity of the perfect in certain circumstances to express present-only time reference has led some to suggest that the perfect's semantics are devoid of time reference.[10] Consider the following statement from Porter:

> It is appropriate to assert that the Perfect grammaticalizes the state or condition of the grammatical subject as conceived by the speaker. Whether a previous event is alluded to or exists at all is a matter of lexis in context and not part of aspectual semantics.[11]

Porter does not give an account of the specific lexical circumstances under which past time reference is made by a perfect form, although it is true to say that the interaction of perfect and lexical semantics can have important implications for the interpretation of the perfect. Nor indeed does Porter elaborate on what exactly is meant by "state or condition." McKay, however, provides a more fulsome explanation. As part of his summary of the meaning of the perfect from Homer to the Roman period he describes the usage of the perfect as follows (emphasis original):

- *State* or *condition*, normally, if not always, of the *subject*:
  a) in verbs of action—a state usually arising from a prior action or series of actions. This state may be that of responsibility for having performed the action(s) or of a characteristic established by the action(s)
  b) in verbs whose present denotes a state—a state usually arising from the aoristic operation of that verb, resulting either in a continuing state or a subsequent state.

---

10 An intensive force has often been ascribed to some present-only perfects. However, it is often difficult to know in a particular case whether or not this sense is really present (cf. Haug, "Aristotle's Kinesis/Energeia-Test," 394) and consequently I will not attempt to deal with this phenomenon in this paper. Another problem of the perfect is its apparent capacity to detransitivize, i.e., to reduce the number of arguments projected by the verbal head by one. Thus for example ἕστηκε is the perfect active of ἵστημι "make to stand," yet the subject is not someone who is making another stand, but rather is standing himself. There is unfortunately not space to address this problem here. For an integration of this phenomenon into a semantic description of the Greek perfect, see Crellin, "Greek Perfect Active System," 82–179.

11 Porter, *Verbal Aspect*, 259.

c) in verbs of emotion, etc.—a state of continued feeling which usually implies greater intensity than the present.[12]

Notably, however, McKay also allows for the existence of what he calls "category" perfects "where the *state* or condition has continued only as *historical* reputation." Yet it is questionable to what extent "historical reputation" may be meaningfully regarded as a state or condition.

Finally, Campbell analyzes the perfect as aspectually imperfective, based on the distributional evidence that both the perfect and the present occur frequently in discourse, "The demonstrable facts about the usage of the perfect indicative within discourse signify that the most likely aspectual value of the perfect is that of imperfectivity."[13]

Campbell's understanding of the perfect as a kind of imperfective leads to some somewhat novel and perhaps surprising interpretations in the case of dynamic verbs, such as at 2 Tim 4:7, where the Greek perfects are rendered by Campbell as present continuous forms in English, as in example 6.

6. τὸν καλὸν ἀγῶνα ἠγώνισμαι, τὸν δρόμον τετέλεκα, τὴν πίστιν τετήρηκα.
I am fighting the good fight, I am finishing the race, I am keeping the faith. (2 Tim 4:7. Campbell's trans.)[14]

So does the perfect in this period have a unified semantic description? Some suggest not.[15] However, if it does, what does it basically denote?

---

12  McKay, "Use of the Ancient Greek Perfect," 17. For the intensive use see n. 10 above.
13  Campbell, *Verbal Aspect*, 186.
14  Ibid. For critiques of Campbell's views see Robert Crellin, "Basics of Verbal Aspect," *JSNT* 35 (2012): 196–202 and Stanley E. Porter, "Greek Linguistics and Lexicography," in *Understanding the Times: New Testament Studies in the 21st Century; Essays in Honor of D. A. Carson on the Occasion of His 65th Birthday*, ed. Andreas J. Köstenberger and Robert W. Yarbrough (Wheaton, IL: Crossway, 2011), 19–61.
15  E.g., Haug, "From Resultatives to Anteriors," 302.

## 2. EVENT AND SITUATION STRUCTURE

In this paper I will present a proposal for a unified semantic description of the perfect which I believe takes account of the majority of
phenomena which are attested. However, in order to do this we
need to reconsider how events are represented in language. In doing
this I adopt the semantic aspectual framework outlined by Klein.[16]
I am therefore concerned with the truth conditions associated with
the perfect.

Many have tended to think of tense and aspect as a property of
verbs.[17] However, more recent consensus has it that these are properties of propositions realized as predicates,[18] e.g.:

7. Mary made a cake.

This is a proposition with a subject Mary, and with a predicate,
"made a cake." The proposition can exist independent of time, i.e.,
<make a cake>. This event has its own time structure, which we
shall term its situation structure, which has a set of times associated with it (TSit). In this case the event has a beginning (when the
event of making a cake starts), a middle (when the making of the
cake happens), or an end (when the cake is made). This is diagrammatically represented at Figure 1.

16  Wolfgang Klein, "The Present Perfect Puzzle," *Language* 68 (1992): 525–52,
    and idem, *Time in Language*, Germanic Languages (London: Routledge, 1994).
    This approach has been incorporated in approaches for describing tense
    and aspect in Russian in Alla Paslawska and Arnim von Stechow, "Perfect
    Readings in Russian," in *Perfect Explorations*, ed. Artemis Alexiadou, Monica
    Rathert, and Arnim von Stechow, IE 2 (Berlin: Mouton de Gruyter, 2003),
    307–62; and for Ancient Greek in Gerö and von Stechow, "Tense in Time."
17  Thus Zeno Vendler, "Verbs and Times," *PhR* 66 (1957): 143–60, although he
    is sensitive to differences induced by the different properties of particu-
    lar predicates.
18  Carol Tenny and James Pustejovsky, "A History of Events in Linguistic The-
    ory," in *Events as Grammatical Objects: The Converging Perspectives of Lexical
    Semantics and Syntax*, (Stanford, CA: Center for the Study of Language and
    Information, 2000), 6.

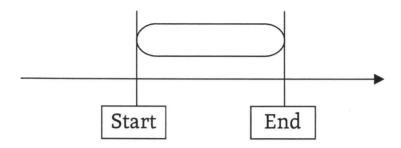

Figure 1. Predicate <make a cake>

Different kinds of events or situations can be distinguished according to their time structure.[19] These can be distinguished on the basis of telicity, that is, the presence of a set end point, durativity, namely duration for more than one conceptual moment, and homogeneity, the capacity to divide a given event into multiple, albeit smaller, instances of the same event type.[20] This latter category can be further analyzed into a "strong" homogeneity, where an eventuality is infinitely subdividable into events of the same character, and "weak" homogeneity, where an eventuality is subdividable only to a certain granularity. In what follows, I am concerned only with "strong" homogeneity.[21]

Accordingly, the following kinds of eventuality may be distinguished:

---

19  See e.g., Vendler, "Verbs and Times," 143–60.

20  For discussion of different event types and their properties, with references, see Tenny and Pustejovsky, "History of Events," 5.

21  For this distinction and definitions of the two types, see Tenny and Puste-jovksy, "History of Events," 5; Gillian Catriona Ramchand, *Aspect and Predication: The Semantics of Argument Structure* (Oxford: Clarendon Press, 1997), 123–24; David R. Dowty, *Word Meaning and Montague Grammar: the Semantics of Verbs and Times in Generative Semantics and in Montague's PTQ*, SLL 7 (Dordrecht: Kluwer, 1979), 166; and Barry Taylor, "Tense and Continuity" *Ling&P* 1 (1977): 199–220. Ramchand, *Aspect and Predication*, 123–24, explains as follows:

> Stative verbs ... have completely homogeneous reference in the sense that one cannot distinguish any change, gradual or otherwise, occurring as a part of the eventuality. The difference [with activities] ... is that the divisibility of "running" is limited by a certain level of granularity. At some point, if the divisions get small enough, a subevent of running can no longer be distinguished as "running" per se, as opposed to "walking" or "jumping" or "moving the foot."

1. Activity, e.g., swimming: no set endpoint, nonhomogeneous, durative;

2. Accomplishment, e.g., building a house: set endpoint, non-homogeneous, durative;

3. Achievement, e.g., recognizing a friend: set endpoint, non-homogeneous, nondurative (i.e., no conceptual duration);

4. State, e.g., sitting on the mat: no set endpoint, homogeneous, and nondurative.[22]

5. Complex events: change of state, e.g., <the banana rot>: accomplishment which leads to a state (being rotten). This state has no set endpoint (see figure 2).

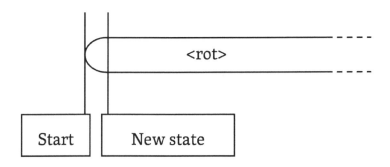

Figure 2. Change of state predicate

## 3. TENSE AND ASPECT

However, the sentence <Mary make a cake> is not well formed. It needs also to be given properties of tense and aspect, which are in Greek (and English) usually ascribed to the sentence through the verb.

---

22 The nondurativity of states needs some qualification; it is true that states may have duration. Indeed, Vendler, "Verbs and Times," 146–47 asserts that they do. Thus it is possible to say "I loved her for a long time." However, duration is not a necessary inference from the statement "I love her." This is simply a statement that a state of loving holds at the present moment, and is a feeling that may be lost at any time. The statement "I love her" does not make a claim, per se, on the future. This is different from specifically durative states, such as "staying," which do carry such an expectation. Thus if I say, "I'm staying," and then immediately leave, I will not be understood to have spoken truly in my statement.

Crucial to Klein's semantic definition of tense and aspect is Topic Time (which Klein abbreviates to TT, and which I abbreviate to TTop). This is "the time for which, on some occasion, a claim is made."[23] Within this framework, tense concerns the relationship of TTop to Utterance Time (which Klein abbreviates to TU, and which I abbreviate to TUtt).[24] The past tense asserts that TTop precedes TUtt, the future that TUtt precedes TSit and the present tense that TSit includes TUtt. By contrast, aspect relates TTop to TSit.

Consider the following example:

8. I was washing up the dishes at ten o'clock.

This sentence contains the predicate <wash up the dishes>. TTop, ten o'clock then bears a relationship of priority with respect to TUtt. This is a relationship of tense. The tense of this sentence is "past," because TTop precedes TUtt. The aspect of this sentence is the relationship that the predicate "washing up the dishes" holds to TTop, which is ten o'clock.

The event described by this predicate has a relationship to TTop, which for this predicate is defined as ten o'clock. Specifically, TTop, ten o'clock, is located in time during the event <wash up the dishes>. In other terms it may be said that TSit properly includes TTop.[25] This is an aspectual relationship. There are two principal aspects in languages with aspect, imperfective and perfective·

- Perfective: TTop includes TSit[26]
- Imperfective: TSit properly includes TTop[27]

Accordingly, the aspect of the predicate <wash up the dishes> in 43 is imperfective.

The perfective aspect can also be used to define TTop, e.g.:

---

23  Klein, "Present Perfect Puzzle," 535.

24  Ibid., 536.

25  Set A is said to properly include set B if B is a subset of A, and A is unequal to B; see Herbert B. Enderton, *Elements of Set Theory* (San Diego: Elsevier, 1977), 85.

26  Corien Bary, "Aspect in Ancient Greek: A Semantic Analysis of the Aorist and Imperfective" (PhD diss., Radboud Universiteit Nijmegen, 2009), 78, and Klein, *Time in Language*, 118. By contrast, Klein, "Present Perfect Puzzle," 537, defines perfective as "TTop including end of TSit and beginning of time after TSit."

27  Klein, "Present Perfect Puzzle," 537. Bary, "Aspect," 78, expresses imperfective in these terms as TTop being a nonfinal subset of TSit.

9. I was washing up when I caught sight of a pigeon.

Here the event described by "I caught sight of a pigeon" determines TTop for the event described by "I was washing up."

## 4. TENSE AND ASPECT IN GREEK

Ancient Greek (as Modern Greek) is a language that marks both tense and aspect. In Greek the "aorist" stem forms convey perfective aspect, while the "present" stem forms (i.e., present and imperfect) convey imperfective. In the indicative tense is also marked, and may be distinguished between past and nonpast. Here the aorist (perfective) and imperfect (imperfective) denote past tense, while the present and future mark nonpast.[28] Consider the following examples:

10. ἐγερθεὶς δὲ ὁ Ἰωσὴφ ἀπὸ τοῦ ὕπνου <u>ἐποίησεν ὡς προσέταξεν αὐτῷ ὁ</u> <u>ἄγγελος κυρίου</u> καὶ παρέλαβεν τὴν γυναῖκα αὐτοῦ...
When Joseph woke from sleep, <u>he did as the angel of the Lord commanded him</u>: he took his wife... (Matt 1:24 ESV)

11. ἔτι <u>αὐτοῦ λαλοῦντος</u> ἰδοὺ νεφέλη φωτεινὴ <u>ἐπεσκίασεν αὐτούς</u> ...
While he was still speaking, behold a bright cloud covered them... (Matt 17:5 NIV)

The aorist predicate in 10 can be represented diagrammatically as follows at Figure 3:

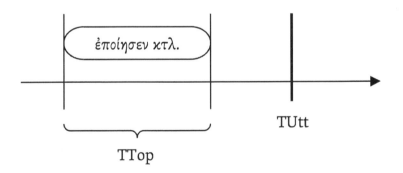

Figure 3. Aorist predicate at Matt 1:24

---

28  For the view that the aorist and imperfect are not restricted to past tense use, see Porter, *Verbal Aspect*, 211–38. For the use of past tenses in irrealis, see Eva-Carin Gerö, " 'Irrealis' and Past Tense in Ancient Greek." *Glotta* 77 (2001): 178–97.

In the second example, the aorist predicate ἐπεσκίασεν αὐτούς determines TTop for the participle predicate ἔτι αὐτοῦ λαλοῦντος, i.e.:

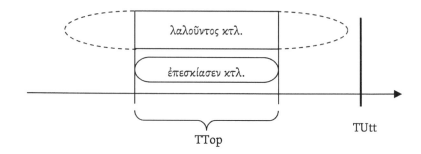

Figure 4. Aorist and participle predicates at Matt 17:5

## 5. PROBLEM OF THE PERFECT IN TERMS OF TENSE AND ASPECT

We can now put the problem of the perfect in the tense and aspectual terms that we have been introducing. On the one hand, it sometimes behaves like an imperfective. Leaving aside TTop for the time being, the problem is that a perfect predicate appears to bear at least three kinds of relationship to TUtt. First, where the perfect is formed to a state predicate, TSit may include TUtt:

12. = 3.
    ἔστιν ὁ κατηγορῶν ὑμῶν Μωϋσῆς, <u>εἰς ὃν ὑμεῖς ἠλπίκατε</u>.
    Your accuser is Moses, <u>on whom your hopes are set</u>. (John
    5:45, NIV)[29]

---

29  According to the views outlined by Haug and McKay, who favor an interpretation of the perfect whereby there is first an instantiation of the predicate via an aorist, this example should denote that the event of hoping started prior to reference time. Accordingly, there would be no difference between this and change of state predicates as at 13. The presence of the preposition εἰς "to, into," suggesting a dynamic situation, might be taken to support this. However, εἰς in the New Testament has in several places a purely locative function. Furthermore, on several occasions εἰς is used with πιστεύω "believe" where it is not necessarily obvious that it is a dynamic situation that is being described, e.g., John 9:35, 12:44, 14:1, 16:9; Rom 10:10; and Jas 2:19.

This is diagrammatically represented in Figure 5.

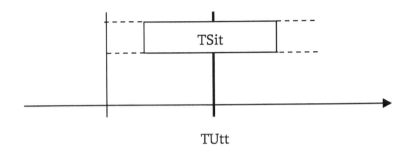

Figure 5. Perfect of a State Predicate

Alternatively, if the predicate describes a change of state, the temporal duration of the poststate includes TUtt, as in the next example, diagrammatically represented in Figure 6:

13. οὐκ ἐλήλυθα καλέσαι δικαίους ἀλλ’ ἁμαρτωλοὺς εἰς μετάνοιαν.
I am not come to call the righteous but sinners to repentance." (Luke 5:32, ASV)

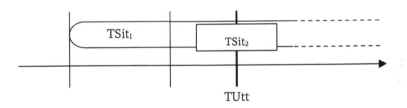

Figure 6. Perfect of a change of state predicate

However, in predicates that neither describe a state nor change of state on the part of the subject, TSit precedes TUtt, as in the following example, represented diagrammatically at Figure 7:

14. οὕτως καὶ ὑμεῖς, ὅταν ποιήσητε πάντα τὰ διαταχθέντα ὑμῖν, λέγετε ὅτι δοῦλοι ἀχρεῖοί ἐσμεν, ὃ ὠφείλομεν ποιῆσαι πεποιήκαμεν.

---

Finally, it is striking that three ancient versions, namely the Vulgate, Gothic, and Old Syriac (Curetonian), all translate ἠλπίκατε without any explicit past reference. For discussion of this example in the Gothic case, see Crellin, "Greek Perfect through Gothic Eyes," 33–34.

So you also, when you have done all that you were commanded, say, "We are unworthy servants; <u>we have only done
what was our duty.</u>" (Luke 17:10, ESV)

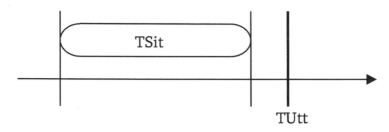

Figure 7. Perfect of a predicate not describing or
giving rise to a state for the subject

In this case, the relationship of TSit to TUtt is parallel to that
of aorist predicates, as may be seen by comparing Figure 7 with
Figure 3.

In sum, therefore, the problem of the perfect may be said to be
the following: How can one predict which particular reading a perfect predicate is going to generate, and is there a single semantic
description that captures all observed patterns?

So far we have deliberately left TTop out of consideration. Could
bringing this in help? Recall that TTop is the set of times for which a
claim is being made. Klein posits that for any event there exists a set
of times after the event itself has terminated, the posttime of that
event, and which we will henceforth term TPostSit.[30] He then provides a definition of the English perfect in terms of TTop and TSit,
such that TTop is in the posttime of TSit; see figure 8:

---

30  Klein, "Present Perfect Puzzle," 538. Klein is careful to state that "posttime
is not defined by what is the case at TSit, nor by what is the case after TSit:
it is just the time after TSit."

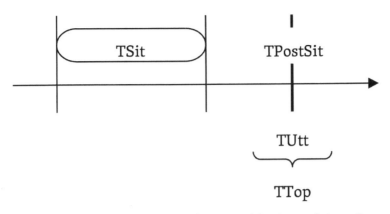

Figure 8. Representation of Klein's proposal for the English perfect

Note the contrast with Klein's definition of the perfective, namely that TTop includes TSit: while the perfect presents the event in terms of the time period after TSit, the perfective makes no reference to this, and refers only to the time interval of the situation itself, TSit.

This description, applied to the Greek perfect, goes some way to resolving the problems, since it is sufficiently flexible to embrace the behavior of the perfect of both change of state predicates and predicates which do not describe or give rise to a state for the subject. Specifically, in change of state predicates, TPostSit is taken to be the TSit of the poststate described by the predicate, while in predicates without state or change of state TPostSit is simply the situation that pertains after the event has terminated.[31] Thus Figure 8 may be taken to represent examples like 14, while Figure 9 may be taken as representing examples like 13.

---

31  These two ways of interpreting TPostSit may be said to correspond to Parsons' target and result states respectively, see Terence Parsons, *Events in the Semantics of English: A Study in Subatomic Semantics*, CurSL 19 (Cambridge: MIT Press, 1990), 234–35.

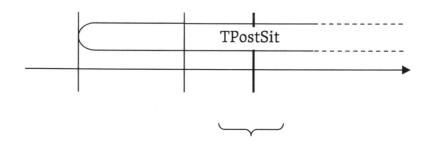

Figure 9. Change of state predicates under Klein's framework

However, Klein's proposal still cannot account for state predicates where TSit includes TTop and TUtt, as in example 12.

Gerö and von Stechow, whose focus is the Classical Greek perfect rather than that in post-Classical Greek, propose to analyze the Greek perfect as an Extended-Now (XN). They observe the following:

> When the present perfect is used in Greek, it frequently seems to be the case that the event denoted by the VP [Verb Phrase] either continues after the speech time or that it at least continues up to the speech time (in an inclusive way). In terms of an XN-analysis, the speech time can be seen as a final subinterval of an interval which reaches into a contextually or lexically determined past ...[32]

It is beyond the scope of the present article to assess the validity of this proposal for Classical Greek. However, for the Greek found in the New Testament, it is at least not the whole story. It is true that it does account for uses of the perfect such as that in example 15, where the event described by the predicate ἐμὲ πρῶτον ὑμῶν μεμίσηκεν starts in past time and continues up to and including TUtt.

15. Εἰ ὁ κόσμος ὑμᾶς μισεῖ, γινώσκετε ὅτι <u>ἐμὲ πρῶτον ὑμῶν μεμίσηκεν</u>. "If the world hates you, know that <u>it has hated me before it hated you</u>. (John 15:18 ESV)

This may be represented diagrammatically per Figure 10.

---

32  Gerö and von Stechow, "Tense in Time," 274.

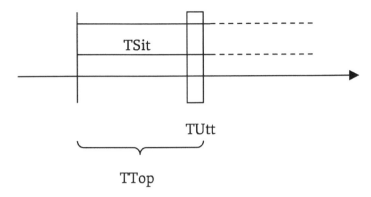

Figure 10. Representation of John 15:18 under
Gerö and Stechow's XN framework

The XN analysis fails to account, however, for the fact that certain kinds of perfect predicate describe events which are not included in TTop. Thus with ἀκούω, examples such as the following are frequent:

16. τότε ὑπέβαλον ἄνδρας λέγοντας ὅτι <u>ἀκηκόαμεν αὐτοῦ λαλοῦντος</u> <u>ῥήματα βλάσφημα εἰς Μωϋσῆν καὶ τὸν θεόν.</u>

Then they secretly instigated men who said, "<u>We have heard</u> <u>him speak blasphemous words against Moses and God.</u>" (Acts 6:11 ESV)

Here the event of hearing described by the predicate ἀκηκόαμεν αὐτοῦ λαλοῦντος ῥήματα βλάσφημα κτλ must have occurred and terminated well before TUtt, since it is asserted in the immediately preceding verses that Stephen, the subject of the predicate in question here, was speaking in such a way that his accusers could not argue with him. However, it is hard to find examples in the New Testament of events where the event of hearing continues up to and includes reference time.[33] There are similarly no clear examples with ποιέω "I

---

33  The perfect of ἀκούω occurs at John 4:42, 5:37, 18:21; Acts 6:11, 6:14; Rom 15:21; 1 John 1:1, 1:3, 1:5, 4:3, in all of which the event of hearing terminates prior to TTop.

do, make."[34] Indeed, there are occasions where it comes very close to a perfective reading:[35]

17. τρὶς ἐρραβδίσθην, ἅπαξ ἐλιθάσθην, τρὶς ἐναυάγησα, <u>νυχθήμερον ἐν τῷ βυθῷ πεποίηκα</u>

Three times I was beaten with rods. Once I was stoned. Three times I was shipwrecked; <u>a night and a day I was adrift at sea</u>; (2 Cor 11:25 ESV)

Yet on an XN analysis one should expect the perfect of all predicate types to be able in principle to include TTop.[36] The XN approach, therefore, does not appear adequate to provide a comprehensive

---

34  Thus Mark 5:19, 11:17; Luke 1:25, 17:10; John 12:18, 12:37, 13:12, 18:18; Acts 3:12, 21:33; 2 Cor 11:25; Heb 11:28; Jas 5:15. The only possible exceptions to this are Mark 7:37 καλῶς πάντα πεποίηκεν, καὶ τοὺς κωφοὺς ποιεῖ ἀκούειν καὶ [τοὺς] ἀλάλους λαλεῖν. "He has done all things well. He even makes the deaf hear and the mute speak." (ESV) and 1 John 5:10 ὁ μὴ πιστεύων τῷ θεῷ ψεύστην πεποίηκεν αὐτόν, ὅτι οὐ πεπίστευκεν εἰς τὴν μαρτυρίαν ἣν μεμαρτύρηκεν ὁ θεὸς περὶ τοῦ υἱοῦ αὐτοῦ. "Whoever does not believe God has made him a liar, because he has not believed in the testimony that God has borne concerning his Son." (ESV). The first case can easily be taken as a summary of Jesus' miracles to-date. The present tense predicates that follow can then be taken as generalizing Jesus' ministry. The second case does not have any past referring context in the same way. However, it is noteworthy that the implicit event by which the predicate ψεύστην πεποίηκεν αὐτόν comes about is homogeneous and atelic, namely μὴ πιστεύων τῷ θεῷ. Perhaps then the predicate ψεύστην ποιεῖν αὐτόν could be taken as a homogeneous and atelic synonym for μὴ πιστεύων τῷ θεῷ, whose perfect is therefore also homogeneous and atelic. Support for this reading comes from the Vulgate which translates πεποίηκεν in this predicate with the present tense *facit*.
35  Parallel to this use may be considered Heb 11:28 and Jas 5:15.
36  Gerö and von Stechow, "Tense in Time," are actually unclear on the issue of whether or not the time of the event described by the predicate is asserted to be included in TTop (which they refer to as reference time). On the one hand they assert , "Let us use the abbreviation XN(t,n) for 't is a time interval that extends up to n (and possibly includes n)'"(p. 275). This statement suggests that n may or may not be included in t. However, they later assert, "Recall that XN(t', t) means that t is a final subinterval or point of t" (p. 280). This statement, contrary to the previous one, suggests that t' is in fact included in t. This latter is confirmed by the statement (also p. 280) that, "An XN rather stretches the reference time into an indefinite past," suggesting that the period of time denoted by XN includes reference time, since it must include it in order to stretch it.

description of the perfect, at least for the data in the New Testament and of the post-Classical period more generally.[37]

An alternative solution is proposed by Haug in reference to the Homeric and Classical Greek perfect:

> ... the perfect denotes a present state resulting from a former event that can be expressed by the VP in the aorist. The perfect, therefore, has a double reference: a present state and a past event that culminated. But, as we would expect in such situations, pragmatic factors can put emphasis on the state or on the event.[38]

In the earlier stages of the language, where the perfect is generally not found with atelic nonstate predicates, the state in question is the target state of the predicate, whether the target state described by the predicate itself in the case of change of state predicates, or a derived target state in the case of atelic state predicates. However, in the later language, the perfect is increasingly applied to predicates that do not give rise to a state for the subject. In these cases the interpretation of "state" is that of Parsons' result state,[39] defined as follows:

> For every event e that culminates, there is a corresponding state that holds forever after. This is "the state of e's having culminated," which I call the "Resultant state of e" or "e's R-State." If Mary eats lunch, then there is a

---

37  From the corpus of post-Classical authors (Polybius, Plutarch, Appian, and Josephus) investigated for Crellin, "Perfect Active System," it is hard to find convincing cases where the event described by a perfect predicate does not give rise to a state for the subject that continues at TTop. A possible case could be considered Jos. A.J. 12.338, with the perfect προσβέβληκα from προσβάλλω "attack." Indeed, Whiston translates with an English past continuous form, "were attacking" (www.perseus.tufts.edu ad loc.). However, it seems better to take the verb as meaning "make an assault, attack," per LSJ προσβάλλω II.1. In this case the perfect would refer to the fact that an assault had been made, with the assault terminating before TTop. A TLG search of the same corpus for the phrase ἐκ πολλοῦ χρόνου "a long time since" did not yield any predicates not describing or giving rise to a state of the subject.

38  Haug, "Aristotle's Kinesis/Energeia-Test," 395–96.

39  Ibid., 409–410.

state that holds forever after: The state of Mary's having eaten lunch.[40]

Parsons' proposal is not unproblematic. Not least significant is the issue that the positing of a state after every event that culminates weakens considerably the notion of what statehood involves, to the point where one wonders whether they really are the same notion. This causes problems specifically with the Greek perfect in later periods, where, as Haug notes, as the perfect is applied to atelic predicates, there emerges an ambiguity as to which state to derive, whether the target or result state.[41] Haug observes, however, that the issue is lexically resolved, citing σιγάω "be silent" and ἀκούω "hear," where in the former case the perfect produces a target state reading, while in the latter case the perfect produces a result state reading.[42] However, it is not specified precisely what semantic features lead to the correct reading in each case.

A further issue with Haug's proposal is its requirement for a prior event to be realized.[43] This Haug frames by applying the perfect to a predicate which has already had the aorist applied to it.[44] Yet this is problematic in the case of examples where there can have been no prior event.[45] In an attempt to address these concerns, I previously proposed the following formulation:

> The perfect of a predicate P denotes a property of the subject S as a function of S existing at or beyond a

---

40 Parsons, *Events*, 234–35, quoted by Haug, "Aristotle's Kinesis/Energeia Test," 398.
41 Haug, "Aristotle's Kinesis/Energeia Test," 410–11.
42 Ibid., 410.
43 Ibid. 409–10.
44 This is also a feature of McKay's proposal in McKay, "Use of the Ancient Greek Perfect," 17. Fanning, *Verbal Aspect*, 119–20 has something similar in his summary of perfect semantics: "The perfect in NT Greek is a complex verbal category denoting in its basic sense, a state which results from a prior occurrence."
45 The perfect ἀνακεχώρηκα, from ἀναχωρέω "withdraw" at Plb. 2.11.16, discussed at Crellin, "Greek Perfect through Gothic Eyes," 8, may be considered a particularly problematic case.

terminal point of the event as determined by the event structure of P.[46]

In order to address the problematic nature of Parsons' R-states, this proposal picks up and modifies Smith's participant property notion of the perfect,[47] so that in cases where a true state follows from TSit, the property is interpreted as this. Yet this is not a requirement, so that events that do not give rise to a state for the subject can be interpreted simply in terms of a participant property.

While this formulation removes the requirement for event realization, with the perfect simply reading off a state from the event structure described by the predicate, it still carries the requirement of the imposition of a terminal point onto this event structure. While for events that naturally terminate or include such a terminal point this is unproblematic, for state predicates this is less than ideal, since the assertion of such a terminal point by the perfect is not undisputable in all such cases, as at example 12 above. A further difficulty with this formulation is that it does not specify the characteristics of the property described by the perfect predicate in terms of event structure.

# 6. PROPOSAL FOR THE SEMANTICS OF THE GREEK PERFECT

The issue of the semantics of the Greek perfect has been clouded by various authors referring to three different things as "states": pure states, result states, and the situation pertaining after an event.[48] This leads to issues of ambiguity regarding the derivation

---

46 Ibid., 14. This is a development of the proposal put forward in Crellin, "Greek Perfect Active System," 280–85.

47 Carlota S. Smith, *The Parameter of Aspect*, 2nd ed., SLP45 (Dordrecht: Kluwer, 1997), 107, gives the following definition of the semantics of the English perfect: "Perfect sentences ascribe to their subjects a property that results from their participation in the prior situation." Haug, "Aristotle's Kinesis/Energeia-Test," 396–97 discusses Smith's proposal in the context of the Greek perfect of earlier periods. For further discussion see Crellin, "Greek Perfect Active System," 280–285 and idem, "Greek Perfect through Gothic Eyes," 15.

48 Thus Parsons, *Events*, 234–45, describes result states as "target states," and post-situations as "result states." He is followed in this by Haug, "Aristotle's Kinesis/Energeia-Test," 398–405. Porter, *Verbal Aspect*, 259, and McKay, "Use

of the correct state in different circumstances. There is the further
question of what Smith's participant property amounts to in event
structure terms, and what it might have in common with true states.
We need a notion defined in event structure terms that is capable
of capturing the properties that pure states, result states, and the
participant property notion share with one another.

This is, in fact, not as difficult as it might at first seem, since these
concepts share the fact that they are homogeneous and atelic. This
is clear in the case of pure and result states.[49] In purely event structure terms, the participant property may also be viewed in this way,
since it is both unchanging (i.e., homogeneous), insofar as the property of having done something never ceases to hold (at least while
the subject continues to exist), and atelic, insofar as it has no set
terminal point. This eventuality would have many of the properties
of Parsons' R-State.[50] There is an important difference, however, between what I am proposing and Parsons' proposal. The participant
property described by the perfect in cases where the predicate does
not give rise to a state for the subject is a secondary eventuality derived by the perfect itself, and is not part of the original predicate.
As such I do not identify (post)states and the participant property.
Rather I am saying that both may be regarded as eventualities that
share two properties of event structure, namely homogeneity and
atelicity. States are distinguished from the participant property by
the fact that the former are part of the prescribed event structure of
the situation described by the original predicate, while the latter is a
secondary derived category, defined purely in terms of the situation
described by the predicate.[51]

---

of the Ancient Greek Perfect," 17, do not distinguish kinds of state, but assert that the perfect describes the "state or condition of the subject," where
the precise relationship between "state" and "condition" is, as far as I can
see, not explained.

49  I.e., Parsons' target states.
50  It might a priori seem implausible to regard such a participant property as
an eventuality, in the Neo-Davidsonian sense, at all. However, its eventual-
ity-hood is suggested by examples like the following: "I have made a chair,
and I'm glad about that." In this example "that" refers back not just to the
making of the chair, but to the fact that this is now a fact about him or her.
51  In this respect Porter, Verbal Aspect, 259, may be said to be correct, namely
that past reference on the part of the perfect is not part of its own semantic
description, but rather a consequence of its interaction with "lexis in context."

I therefore propose the following semantic description of the Greek perfect:

> The perfect of a predicate derives a homogeneous atelic eventuality from the predicate for the grammatical subject and includes Topic Time in the Situation Time of this derived homogeneous atelic eventuality.

This proposal has the potential to resolve the issues that other formulations have had. Crucially, it is able to derive the correct kind of result with the correct temporal entailments regarding the event described by the predicate. Thus, for predicates that do not give rise to a state for the subject, events like "Mary made a cake," the only means that the perfect has of deriving a homogeneous atelic eventuality from the predicate is by asserting that a participant property holds at TTop, namely the property of having once done the event described by the predicate. This in turn requires that in these cases the eventuality described by the predicate be realized. Thus this kind of perfect is readily interpreted as experiential, familiar from English, as at 14 above.[52]

By contrast, for predicates describing states and changes of state, our formulation correctly predicts that two readings should be available: either (1) the state described by the predicate holds at TTop, without necessarily requiring prior event realization, or (2) the state no longer holds at TTop, but once did, and the participant property of this state now holds at TTop. Example 12, with ἤλπικα, is an example of the first interpretation. Example 18, by contrast, is a case of the second type, where the state does not hold at TTop, and should be analyzed per Figure 8:

---

52 If the participant property is a homogeneous and atelic eventuality, it might be wondered why the adverbial ἔτι "still" does not combine with perfects that describe such an eventuality. (For this discussion, see Haug, "Aristotle's Kinesis/Energeia-Test," 397–98, who cites Östen Dahl, *Tense and Aspect Systems* [Oxford: Blackwell, 1985], 133ff.) I suggest that this is because adding this notion to such predicates would be tautological: unlike natural states, the participant property cannot cease. This is to say that once I have made a chair, by virtue of the fact that traveling in time is not possible, it is not possible for me to change this fact about me.

18. καὶ ἔρχονται πρὸς τὸν Ἰησοῦν καὶ θεωροῦσιν τὸν δαιμονιζόμενον καθήμενον ἱματισμένον καὶ σωφρονοῦντα, <u>τὸν ἐσχηκότα τὸν λεγιῶνα</u>, καὶ ἐφοβήθησαν.

And they came to Jesus and saw the demon-possessed man, <u>the one who had had the legion</u>, sitting there, clothed and in his right mind, and they were afraid. (Mark 5:15 ESV)

Note that this is a genuine ambiguity in pure state predicates, and is not lexically resolved, given examples such as the following:

19. ... <u>δι' οὗ καὶ τὴν προσαγωγὴν ἐσχήκαμεν</u> [τῇ πίστει] εἰς τὴν χάριν ταύτην <u>ἐν ᾗ ἑστήκαμεν</u>...

... Through him we have also obtained access by faith into this grace in which we stand, and we rejoice in hope of the glory of God... (Rom 5:2 ESV)

Here, in contrast to example 18 where it is the post-situation that holds at TTop, the perfect of ἔχω "have" is used to assert that the state described by the predicate, not the postsituation, holds at TTop.[53]

Finally, our proposal is sufficiently flexible to encompass the XN perfects that are attested, since the eventuality derived by the perfect is constrained only in terms of homogeneity and telicity, that is to say that is must be homogeneous and atelic. It is not, however, constrained in terms of durativity, and thus may be durative or nondurative according to the specifications of the particular predicate. Thus at 15 the predicate is durative because of the adjunct phrase πρῶτον ὑμῶν referring to a time span prior to TUtt. By the same token, if the arguments of the predicate refer to entry into the state described, the perfect is also capable of expressing this, as demonstrated in example 19.

Furthermore, our proposal is able to predict where XN perfects should not occur, specifically where the predicate describes a non-homogeneous event, since in this case TSit is not homogeneous and cannot include TTop. Rather, the perfect must derive a homogeneous and atelic participant property that can be included in

---

53  Indeed, at 2 Cor 2:13 it appears that the perfect of ἔχω is used in past narrative. However, see A. T. Robertson, *A Grammar of the Greek New Testament in the Light of Historical Research*, 3rd ed. (New York: Hodder & Stoughton, 1919), 900–902, for alternative approaches to this verse.

TTop. This provides an explanation for why there are no clear cases of predicates headed by the perfect of ἀκούω "hear" and ποιέω "do, make" with XN readings.

## 7. SEMANTIC RELATIONSHIP AND MERGER WITH THE AORIST

It is clear that many of the entailments of perfects of examples 14 and 18 are not far from those of the aorist, namely that an event in the denotation of the verb started and finished prior to TUtt. The difference is that in the case of the perfective, TTop includes TSit and is prior to TUtt, while in the case of the perfect, TTop includes TUtt and is itself properly included in TPostSit. However, it is clear that it would only take a small semantic shift for the semantics of the perfect and aorist to merge, i.e., for TTop to move backwards to include TSit rather than be included in TPostSit.[54] Indeed, the following examples suggest that this change is already underway in the period of the writing of the New Testament:[55]

> 20.καὶ ἀνέβη ὁ καπνὸς τῶν θυμιαμάτων ταῖς προσευχαῖς τῶν ἁγίων ἐκ χειρὸς τοῦ ἀγγέλου ἐνώπιον τοῦ θεοῦ. καὶ <u>εἴληφεν</u> ὁ ἄγγελος <u>τὸν λιβανωτὸν</u> καὶ ἐγέμισεν αὐτὸν ἐκ τοῦ πυρὸς τοῦ θυσιαστηρίου...

---

54  This proposal is not far, in principle, from that of McKay, "Use of the Ancient Greek Perfect," 11, who proposes that the semantic change undergone by the perfect was "along the lines of an increasingly conscious implication of the past and present time relationship in the essential state idea of the perfect." Robertson, *Grammar*, 898–99, describes a similar process.

55  Fanning, *Verbal Aspect*, 302–3, includes these examples in his list of those "which the grammars generally agree should be labeled aoristic." He also includes 2 Cor 2:13 quoted at p. 452 n. 54 above. However, in the case of Rev 5:7 and 8:5, Robertson, *Grammar*, 899 invokes "a vivid dramatic colloquial historical perfect," presumably akin to the historical present. Citing Moulton's support, he appears to take πέπρακεν in Matt 13:46 in the same way, noting that it occurs in a vivid parable (ibid., 900). In the case of Rev 8:5, it is hard to see why the event of seizing the censer should be given particular prominence, while in Matt 13:47 one can see why the event of selling everything for the sake of buying the pearl might be emphasized. However, it is hard to see why in these examples one would use the perfect to do this, in preference to the historic present, since the latter would unambiguously place focus on the event of selling, as opposed the postevent situation, as would be the case if the perfect had its former semantic value. (My thanks to Steve Runge for these references.)

... and the smoke of the incense, with the prayers of the saints, rose before God from the hand of the angel. Then the angel <u>took the censer</u> and filled it with fire from the altar... (Rev 8:4-5 ESV)

21. εὑρὼν δὲ ἕνα πολύτιμον μαργαρίτην ἀπελθὼν <u>πέπρακεν πάντα ὅσα εἶχεν</u> καὶ ἠγόρασεν αὐτόν.

Who, on finding one pearl of great value, went and <u>sold all that he had</u> and bought it. (Matt 13:46 ESV)

I suggest the reason for such a development is that in change of state predicates and predicates that do not give rise to a state for the subject there is a potential conflict of interest between the event occurring before TTop, and the postsituation. It is not hard to imagine that in certain instances the former would have more pragmatic value, and in such cases TTop would appear to be shifted backwards. If repeated over a long enough period of time, this change could have become encoded as the "meaning" of the perfect.

## 8. CONCLUSION

To conclude, we set out to provide a semantic description of the Greek perfect capable of taking account of its problematic phenomena, namely that it is apparently able to convey anterior, resultative, and pure state in a single form. Using Klein's semantic framework as a reference point, giving a description of tense and aspect of predicates in terms of Situation Time (TSit), Topic Time (TTop) and Utterance Time (TUtt), I surveyed the various existing views on the perfect in the Greek of the New Testament. I then proposed a description of the semantics of the perfect adopting Klein's semantic aspectual framework, whereby the perfect derives a homogeneous atelic eventuality from the predicate and includes TTop within the TSit of this eventuality. Where a predicate itself describes a state for the subject (state predicates and change of state predicates), the perfect may simply return this state. By contrast, where a predicate does not describe or give rise to a state for the subject, the perfect derives a homogeneous atelic eventuality for the subject, a property of the subject based on the subject having previously participated in the event described by the predicate. This is readily interpreted as experiential in many situations. This latter interpretation is also available for state and change-of-state predicates, so that all instances of the perfect are in principle capable of anterior denotation. I ended by suggesting that it is the semantic development of the perfect from including TTop in the posttime of the predicate (TPostSit), to including TSit of the event described by the predicate that led to its eventual merging with the aorist and ultimate demise.

# BIBLIOGRAPHY

Bary, Corien. "Aspect in Ancient Greek: A Semantic Analysis of the Aorist and Imperfective." PhD diss., Radboud Universiteit Nijmegen, 2009.

Bentein, Klaas. "The Periphrastic Perfect in Ancient Greek: A Diachronic Mental Space Analysis." *TPhS* 110 (2012): 171–211.

Bybee, Joan L., Revere D. Perkins, and William Pagliuca. *The Evolution of Grammar*. Chicago: University of Chicago Press, 1994.

Campbell, Constantine. *Verbal Aspect, the Indicative Mood, and Narrative: Soundings in the Greek of the New Testament*. SBG 13. New York: Lang, 2007.

Crellin, Robert. "Basics of Verbal Aspect." *JSNT* 35 (2012): 196–202.

———. "The Greek Perfect Active System: 200 BC–AD 150." PhD diss., University of Cambridge, 2012.

———. "The Greek Perfect through Gothic Eyes: Evidence for the Existence of a Unitary Semantic for the Greek Perfect in New Testament Greek." *JGL* 14 (2014): 5–42.

Dahl, Östen. *Tense and Aspect Systems*. Oxford: Blackwell, 1985.

Dowty, David R. *Word Meaning and Montague Grammar: The Semantics of Verbs and Times in Generative Semantics and in Montague's PTQ*. SLL 7. Dordrecht: Kluwer, 1979.

Enderton, Herbert B. *Elements of Set Theory*. San Diego: Elsevier, 1977.

Evans, Trevor V. "Another Ghost: The Greek Epistolary Perfect." *Glotta* 75 (1999): 194–221.

———. *Verbal Syntax in the Greek Pentateuch: Natural Greek Usage and Hebrew Interference*. Oxford: Oxford University Press, 2001.

Fanning, Buist. *Verbal Aspect in New Testament Greek*. OTM. Oxford: Oxford University Press, 1990.

Gerö, Eva-Carin. "'Irrealis' and Past Tense in Ancient Greek." *Glotta* 77 (2001): 178–97.

Gerö, Eva-Carin, and Arnim von Stechow. "Tense in Time: The Greek Perfect." Pages 251–94 in *Words in Time: Diachronic Semantics from Different Points of View*. Edited by Regine Eckardt, Klaus von Heusinger, and Christoph Schwarze. TiLSM 143. Berlin: de Gruyter, 2003.

Haspelmath, Martin. "From Resultative to Perfect in Ancient Greek." Pages 187–224 in *Nuevos Estudios Sobre Construcciones Resultativos*. Edited by Leza Iturrioz and Luis José. Función 11–12. Guadalajara: Universidad de Guadalajara, 1992.

Haug, Dag Trygve Truslew. "Aristotle's Kinesis/Energeia-Test and the Semantics of the Greek Perfect." *Linguistics* 42 (2004): 387–418.

———. "From Resultatives to Anteriors in Ancient Greek: On the Role of Paradigmaticity in Semantic Change." Pages 285–305 in *Grammatical Change and Linguistic Theory: The Rosendal Papers*. Edited by Thórhallur Eythórsson. Linguistics Today 113. Amsterdam: Benjamins, 2008.

Josephus. *Jewish Antiquities*. Translated by Henry St. J. Thackeray et al. 9 vols. LCL. Cambridge: Harvard University Press, 1930–1965.

Klein, Wolfgang. "The Present Perfect Puzzle." *Language* 68 (1992): 525–52.

———. *Time in Language*. Germanic Linguistics. London: Routledge, 1994.

McKay, K. L. "On the Perfect and Other Aspects in New Testament Greek." *NovT* 23 (1981): 289–329.

———. "On the Perfect and Other Aspects in the Greek Non-Literary Papyri." *BICS* 27 (1980): 23–49.

———. "The Use of the Ancient Greek Perfect down to the End of the Second Century AD." *BICS* 12:1–21.

Orriens, Sander. "Involving the Past in the Present: The Classical Greek Perfect as a Situating Cohesion Device." Pages 221–39 in *Discourse Cohesion in Ancient Greek*. Edited by Stéphanie Bakker and Gerry Wakker. ASCP 16. Leiden: Brill, 2009.

Parsons, Terence. *Events in the Semantics of English: A Study in Subatomic Semantics*. CurSL 19. Cambridge: MIT Press, 1990.

Paslawska, Alla, and Arnim von Stechow. "Perfect Readings in Russian." Pages 307–62 in *Perfect Explorations*. edited by Artemis Alexiadou, Monica Rathert, and Arnim von Stechow. IE 2. Berlin: Mouton de Gruyter, 2003.

Polybius. *The Histories*. Translated by W. R. Paton. 6 vols. LCL. Cambridge: Harvard University Press, 2010–2012.

Porter, Stanley E. "Greek Linguistics and Lexicography." Pages 19–61 in *Understanding the Times: New Testament Studies in the 21st Century; Essays in Honor of D. A. Carson on the Occasion of His 65th Birthday*. Edited by Andreas J. Köstenberger and Robert W. Yarbrough. Wheaton, IL: Crossway, 2011.

————. *Verbal Aspect in the Greek of the New Testament.* SBG 1. New York: Lang, 1989.

Ramchand, Gillian Catriona. *Aspect and Predication: The Semantics of Argument Structure.* Oxford: Clarendon Press, 1997.

Robertson, A. T. *A Grammar of the Greek New Testament in the Light of Historical Research.* 3rd ed. New York: Hodder & Stoughton, 1919.

Sicking, C. M. J., and P. Stork. "The Synthetic Perfect in Classical Greek." Pages 119–298 in *Two Studies in the Semantics of the Verb in Classical Greek.* Edited by C. M. J. Sicking and P. Stork. MS 160. Leiden: Brill, 1996.

Smith, Carlota S. *The Parameter of Aspect.* 2nd ed. SLP 45. Dordrecht: Kluwer, 1997.

Taylor, Barry. "Tense and Continuity." *Ling&P* 1 (1977): 199–220.

Tenny, Carol, and James Pustejovsky. "A History of Events in Linguistic Theory." Pages 3–33 in *Events as Grammatical Objects: The Converging Perspectives of Lexical Semantics and Syntax.* Stanford, CA: Center for the Study of Language and Information, 2000.

Vendler, Zeno. "Verbs and Times." *PhR* 66 (1957): 143–60.

CHAPTER 15

# Discourse Function of
# the Greek Perfect

STEVEN E. RUNGE

LEXHAM RESEARCH INSTITUTE | STELLENBOSCH UNIVERSITY

## 1. INTRODUCTION

The Greek perfect tense-form has been an enigma for many years. Scholars have generally sought to describe it in terms of its semantic meaning, or its translation value. However the interplay of this complex aspect with lexical semantics—not to mention issues of diachrony and voice—have resulted in a Gordian knot that continues to resist simplistic untangling. This paper takes a different tack by asking a more basic question: What is the discourse function of the Greek perfect? What does it *do* in discourse?

There is a characteristic mentioned in most every description of the perfect, both in New Testament studies and in the broader linguistic literature, but still receives little consideration: relevance. Here is how Comrie first introduces the notion in differentiating the perfect from perfective aspect: "The term 'perfect' refers to a past situation which has present relevance, for instance the present result of a past event *(his arm has been broken)*."[1] His chapter devoted to the perfect describes "various kinds of perfect all consistent with

---

1    Bernard Comrie, *Aspect: An Introduction to the Study of Verbal Aspect and Related Problems*, CTL (Cambridge: Cambridge University Press, 1976), 12 (emphasis original).

the general characterization of perfectness as the present relevance of a prior situation."[2]

Although it may seem incorrect to describe an aspect in such temporal, tense-like terms, Bhat—building on Comrie's initial claim—has demonstrated that the relevance constraint is found across language types:

> Notice that the definition of the notion of perfect that is generally given provides us only with a "temporal" (or tense-oriented) view of the notion. We can also have aspectual and modal definitions of this notion, as shown below:
>
> The notion of perfect:
>
> 1. Temporal view: past event with current (present) relevance
> 2. Aspectual view: completed (perfective) event with continuing (imperfective) relevance
> 3. Modal view: realis event with irrealis relevance (something needs to be done).[3]

According to Bhat, the notion of the perfect is necessarily dependent on temporal chronology. Even in aspect-prominent languages such as Greek where tense is not prominent there is nevertheless some logically preceding activity or state which the perfect correlates to the current discourse situation. Bhat's conception of the perfect combining perfective and imperfective aspect is echoed by New Testament grammarians. Blass describes the perfect as combining the aorist (perfective) and the present (imperfective, non-past), or the pluperfect as aorist (perfective) plus imperfect (imperfective, past).[4] Wallace also claims a combination: "The aspect of the perfect and pluperfect is sometimes called *stative, resultative, completed,* or *perfective-stative.* Whatever it is called, the kind of action portrayed (in its unaffected meaning) is a combination of the external and internal aspects: The *action* is presented *externally*

---

2   Ibid., 14.
3   D. N. Shankara Bhat, *The Prominence of Tense, Aspect, and Mood,* SLCS 49 (Amsterdam: Benjamins, 1999), 170.
4   Friedrich Blass, *Grammar of New Testament Greek,* trans. Henry St. John Thackeray (London: Macmillan, 1898), 198.

(summary), while the *resultant state* proceeding from the action is presented *internally* (continuous state)."[5]

Also of significance is Bhat's elaboration on what the present relevance of the perfect means practically. More than simply introducing a state of affairs, the perfect constrains the reader to view the information as particularly relevant to the immediate context of the discourse. Orriens makes a more specific claim by means of a spatial representation of the perfect, stating that it is "concerned with marking a *reciprocal* (or: *bilateral*) relationship between a completed past S[tate]o[f]A[ffairs] and the moment of speech. By this I mean that a speaker, when using a perfect in discourse, simultaneously refers to a completed past SoA and explicitly links this SoA to the moment of speech. By doing this he directly involves the SoA in the present communicative context."[6]

He goes on to contrast the reciprocal nature of the perfect with the unidirectional or unilateral direction of the aorist, described in figure 1 below. Whereas the aorist only looks back on a completed state of affairs, the relevance constraint of the perfect is manifested by the explicit link from the state of affairs to the present discourse context.[7]

---

5   Daniel B. Wallace, *Greek Grammar Beyond the Basics: An Exegetical Syntax of the New Testament*, 2nd ed. (Grand Rapids: Zondervan, 1996), 573 (emphasis original).

6   Sander Orriens, "The Greek Perfect as a Situating Cohesion Device," in *Discourse Cohesion in Ancient Greek*, ed. Stéphanie J. Bakker and G. C. Wakker, ASCP 16 (Leiden: Brill, 2009), 225 (emphasis original).

7   Ibid.

Aorist:

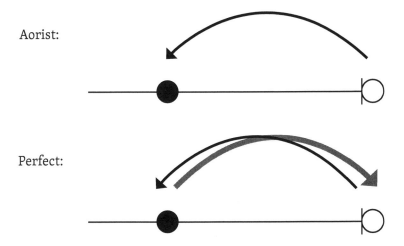

Perfect:

Figure 1: Orriens's Spatial Conception of the Perfect

Another factor that must be accounted for is the logical or temporal location of the action or state of affairs in the perfect with respect to the reference time of the discourse. Horrocks offers the following description:

> The perfect, considered purely as an aspect, involves the postulation of a "viewing point" from which a given "event," having previously taken place, is seen to be already completed. This is the essence of the perfect aspect, which entails the notion of continuing relevance for the earlier event at the later viewing point ... The viewing point may then be located objectively in time. In the case of a past perfect, the event is earlier than a viewing point that is in the past with respect to the time of utterance (i.e., the event is anterior to the past-time viewing point). In the case of a future perfect, the event is earlier than a viewing point that is in the future with respect to the time of utterance (i.e., the event is anterior to the future viewing point, but still itself potentially in the future). In the case of the present perfect, there can be no present viewing point distinct from the time of utterance (the present is the present), and the event is simply earlier than "now." In each case, the time reference of an aspectually perfect-tense form

is determined by the location not of the viewed event but of the viewing point with respect to the time of utterance.[8]

Note that even though the perfect is an aspect, it nevertheless has a logical temporal ordering that cannot be ignored and that is present in every tense-form.[9] For states of affair that are atelic (i.e., lack a clear ending), the state that results still logically precedes the viewing point.

The perfect indicative's connection of a completed state of affairs to the present reference time of the discourse is the most concrete description I have found to describe the practical impact of the relevance constraint. It is also consistent with the dual or combinative descriptions offered by the older grammarians, notwithstanding their misguided efforts to associate the action with the subject or the object.[10] The perfective aspect captures the state of affairs, whereas the imperfective component implicates an ongoing connection to the present discourse context.

Horrocks makes a comparable claim concerning current relevance at reference time of the discourse, but adds that the continued relevance "is easily downgraded, and the grammaticalized temporal focus then shifts immediately to the event itself, with the result that what was the viewing point becomes instead the temporal reference point for the location of that event ... In this way the perfect may come to be understood not just as an alternative to the simple past when continued relevance at the time of utterance is to be emphasized but also, through confusion of the aspectual viewing point with the temporal reference point (natural in the case of the present perfect), as a general alternative to the simple past in all contexts."[11] In either case, use of the perfect explicitly establishes a connection between some logically anterior state of affairs and the reference time of the discourse, as portrayed by Orriens in figure 1. It is plausible that the overlapping use of the aorist and the perfect

---

8   Geoffrey Horrocks, *Greek: A History of the Language and Its Speakers*, 2nd ed. (Chichester: Wiley, 2014), 176.

9   See Thomson, ch. 2 n. 13 in this volume and the discussion of figure 2; see also Crellin, ch. 14 in this volume and the discussion of figure 10.

10  On the combinative view of the perfect, see Ellis, ch. 4 in this volume.

11  Horrocks, *Greek*, 177.

in the Koine period inevitably led to a bleaching of the relevance constraint in some instances.

The balance of this paper considers the use and function of perfect indicative verbs from three books of the New Testament: Luke's gospel, Romans, and Hebrews. Representative examples will be discussed, but all instances of perfect indicative verbs will be considered. The principles outlined here provide a basis for future research into nonindicative forms of the perfect and uses in the balance of the New Testament.

## 2. PERFECTS PRECEDING THAT TO WHICH THEY ARE RELEVANT

Discourse is necessarily linear, and the state of affairs conveyed by the perfect is logically anterior to the discourse context to which it is relevant. It is thus not surprising to find this logically anterior information iconically *preceding* the context to which it is relevant. Ordered in this way the reader processes the relevant information before encountering the salient proposition to which it relates. This is illustrated by Luke 14:22, where the perfect is relevant to what follows. In Luke 14:17-20 the master has ordered his servants to call those invited to his banquet, yet all decline his invitation. He then commands in 14:21 that the poor, crippled, blind, and lame be invited.

Luke 14:22

καὶ εἶπεν ὁ δοῦλος· Κύριε, γέγονεν     And the slave said, "Sir, what
ὃ ἐπέταξας, καὶ ἔτι τόπος ἐστίν.     you ordered <u>has been done</u>, and
                                     there is still room."[12]

The perfect in 14:22a constrains the reader to expect that this situational information is somehow relevant to what follows. Inviting all the sick and infirm is expected to have filled the banquet hall. Reporting the fulfilled command provides relevant background for the more salient report that there is yet room, and for the master sending out the servants yet again in 14:23.

---

12  All English translations are from the Lexham English Bible unless otherwise specified.

Similarly in Luke 7:33 and 34 the perfects introduce information relevant to the clause which immediately follows.

Luke 7:33–34

| | |
|---|---|
| <u>ἐλήλυθεν</u> γὰρ Ἰωάννης ὁ βαπτιστὴς μὴ ἐσθίων ἄρτον μήτε πίνων οἶνον, καὶ λέγετε· Δαιμόνιον ἔχει· <u>ἐλήλυθεν</u> ὁ υἱὸς τοῦ ἀνθρώπου ἐσθίων καὶ πίνων, καὶ λέγετε· Ἰδοὺ ἄνθρωπος φάγος καὶ οἰνοπότης, φίλος τελωνῶν καὶ ἁμαρτωλῶν. | For John the Baptist <u>has come</u> not eating bread or drinking wine, and you say, "He has a demon!" The Son of Man <u>has come</u> eating and drinking, and you say, "Behold, a man who is a glutton and a drunkard, a friend of tax collectors and sinners!" |

The two perfect clauses describe the manner in which John the Baptist and Jesus came, setting the stage for a contrast to be drawn between them. Despite the two extremes of their ministry, the Pharisees found grounds for rejecting both. The salient part of the contrast is not how they came, but how they were received. This material in turn supports the preceding assertions of 7:31–32 based on its introduction by γάρ. Use of the perfect constrains the reader to view the manner in which each came as relevant to the response. The salience of the perfect's information cannot be understood without reference to the more-salient element to which it is relevant.[13]

The only clear example from Romans is found in 11:20, where the Gentiles who have been grafted in figuratively by virtue of their faith are contrasted with the unbelieving Jews who have been broken off for their unbelief. The perceived security of those standing by faith in 11:20a is undermined in the very next clause.

Romans 11:20

| | |
|---|---|
| καλῶς· τῇ ἀπιστίᾳ ἐξεκλάσθησαν, σὺ δὲ τῇ πίστει <u>ἕστηκας</u>. μὴ ὑψηλὰ φρόνει, ἀλλὰ φοβοῦ· | Well said! They were broken off because of unbelief, but you <u>stand firm</u> because of faith. Do not think arrogant thoughts, but be afraid. |

---

13  Other instances where the perfect indicative precedes the clause to which it is relevant are Luke 8:10, 20, 49; 19:46.

The use of the perfect here stands in contrast to a comparable figurative use of the same lemma in the present in Romans 3:31 to describe an ongoing activity, and the many uses in the aorist to describe completed actions. The perfect adds the additional constraint of current relevance to the state of affairs of standing: that it will not last. Use of the aorist would not have evoked this constraint of current relevance.

Three of the five instances from Hebrews of perfect indicatives preceding the relevant context are found in frames of reference, subordinate clauses which provide situational information to orient the main clause on which it is grammatically dependent. In each case, the state of affairs described in the perfect is marked as relevant to the action in the main clause.

Hebrews 2:14

ἐπεὶ οὖν τὰ παιδία <u>κεκοινώνηκεν</u> αἵματος καὶ σαρκός καὶ αὐτὸς παραπλησίως μετέσχεν τῶν αὐτῶν ἵνα διὰ τοῦ θανάτου καταργήσῃ τὸν τὸ κράτος ἔχοντα τοῦ θανάτου τοῦτ' ἔστιν τὸν διάβολον.

Therefore, since the children <u>share</u> in blood and flesh, he also in like manner shared in these same things, in order that through death he could destroy the one who has the power of death, that is, the devil.

Hebrews 2:18

ἐν ᾧ γὰρ <u>πέπονθεν</u> αὐτὸς πειρασθείς δύναται τοῖς πειραζομένοις βοηθῆσαι.

For in that which he himself <u>suffered</u> when he was tempted, he is able to help those who are tempted.

Hebrews 7:11

Εἰ μὲν οὖν τελείωσις διὰ τῆς Λευιτικῆς ἱερωσύνης ἦν ὁ λαὸς γὰρ ἐπ' αὐτῆς <u>νενομοθέτηται</u> τίς ἔτι χρεία κατὰ τὴν τάξιν Μελχισέδεκ ἕτερον ἀνίστασθαι ἱερέα καὶ οὐ κατὰ τὴν τάξιν Ἀαρὼν λέγεσθαι.

Thus if perfection was through the Levitical priesthood, for on the basis of it the people <u>received the law</u>, what further need is there for another priest to arise according to the order of Melchizedek and not said to be according to the order of Aaron?

In Hebrews 2:14, the fact that the children have shared in flesh and blood provides the basis for Jesus also sharing in these same things when he came to destroy the devil. Similarly, the fact that Jesus had suffered is the basis for him being able to help us when we are tempted, making him the well-qualified high priest described in 2:17. In Hebrews 7:11 the fact that God's law was delivered through the priesthood suggests that there is no need for another priest to arise. Had these same actions been encoded using aorist tense-forms, there would have been no explicit relevant connection to the main clause, only an implicit one.

Note also that the major translations use a simplex verb to translate each of these instances rather than a perfect form, suggesting that there is a mismatch in the scope of acceptable usage of the perfect in Koine Greek compared to English. Commenting in an email to the author, on the common practice of translating aorist verbs using the English perfect, Levinsohn observes: "The difference, I think, is that in Greek, what is relevant is typically a state that results from the preceding perfective or completive event. In English, as the M[at]t 27:4 examples indicate, there is no need for the events in the perfective to produce an actual resultant state."[14] This mismatch in respective usage of the perfect must be taken into account when describing the usage found in Greek. The fact that a simple perfective may be used in English translation, or vice versa, does not ameliorate its function to signal current relevance in either language.

## 3. PERFECTS THAT FOLLOW THAT TO WHICH THEY ARE RELEVANT

Fully one-third of the perfect indicatives *follow* the clause to which they are relevant in Luke, over half follow in Hebrews, and over 80% follow in Romans. Since the anterior action does not iconically precede that to which it is relevant, perfects that follow are most often placed in a dependency relationship of some kind. These relationships help readers make the proper relevance connection back to the main clause on which they depend.

---

14  Pers. comm., September 20, 2014.

Perfects are commonly found in *subordinate clauses*, such as those introducing Old Testament quotations relevant to some preceding assertion. For example, Luke 3 first describes John the Baptist's ministry in 3:2–3 before backfilling the relevant quotation from Isaiah in 3:4. Ordering it in this way necessitates that the relevant quotation from Isaiah must follow.

Luke 3:4

² ἐπὶ ἀρχιερέως Ἄννα καὶ Καϊάφα, ἐγένετο ῥῆμα θεοῦ ἐπὶ Ἰωάννην τὸν Ζαχαρίου υἱὸν ἐν τῇ ἐρήμῳ. ³ καὶ ἦλθεν εἰς πᾶσαν περίχωρον τοῦ Ἰορδάνου κηρύσσων βάπτισμα μετανοίας εἰς ἄφεσιν ἁμαρτιῶν,

² in the time of the high priest Annas and Caiaphas, the word of God came to John the son of Zechariah in the wilderness. ³ And he went into all the surrounding region of the Jordan, preaching a baptism of repentance for the forgiveness of sins,

⁴ ὡς γέγραπται ἐν βίβλῳ λόγων Ἡσαΐου τοῦ προφήτου· Φωνὴ βοῶντος ἐν τῇ ἐρήμῳ· Ἑτοιμάσατε τὴν ὁδὸν κυρίου, εὐθείας ποιεῖτε τὰς τρίβους αὐτοῦ.

⁴ as it is written in the book of the words of the prophet Isaiah, "The voice of one crying out in the wilderness, 'Prepare the way of the Lord, make his paths straight!

The grammatical subordination of the perfect clause using ὡς or καθώς (e.g., Luke 2:23, Rom 3:4, Heb 4:3) is commonly used to connect relevant quotations to some preceding situation. Structuring considerations explain the frequent presence of the perfect following that to which they are relevant in subordinate clauses.[15]

The next example connects an existing state of affairs—sluggishness—to the current discourse situation of correcting or chastising his readers for their immaturity. The preceding verses (Heb 5:7–10) describe how Jesus learned obedience and was perfected based on his suffering, whereas the verses that follow (5:12–14) assert that the readers have had ample opportunity to have matured, yet have not.

15  Examples of quotations introduced by perfects which follow that to which they are relevant include Rom 2:24; 3:4, 10; 4:17; 8:36; 9:13, 33; 10:15; 11:8, 26; 12:19; 14:11; 15:3, 9, 21. Examples of the same from Hebrews include 4:3, 7; 8:5; 13:5.

Hebrews 5:11

Περὶ οὗ πολὺς ἡμῖν ὁ λόγος καὶ δυσερμήνευτος λέγειν ἐπεὶ νωθροὶ γεγόνατε ταῖς ἀκοαῖς

Concerning this we have much to say and it is difficult to explain, since you have become sluggish in hearing.

The perfect explicitly correlates the underlying state of affairs that has caused the immaturity with the current discourse situation about having much to say. Use of an aorist or imperfect would describe the past state of sluggishness without implicating its continuance. Similarly, a present tense-form would denote the present state, but without any reference to its preexistence. The perfect uniquely offers a combination of the two.

This next example illustrates the use of relative clauses to subordinate the perfect. The clause to which the perfect is relevant governs the relative just as observed in the other subordinate clauses above.

Luke 4:18

Πνεῦμα κυρίου ἐπ' ἐμέ, οὗ εἵνεκεν ἔχρισέν με εὐαγγελίσασθαι πτωχοῖς, ἀπέσταλκέν με κηρύξαι αἰχμαλώτοις ἄφεσιν καὶ τυφλοῖς ἀνάβλεψιν, ἀποστεῖλαι τεθραυσμένους ἐν ἀφέσει

"The Spirit of the Lord is upon me, because of which he has anointed me to proclaim good news to the poor. He has sent me to proclaim release to the captives, and recovery of sight to the blind, to send out in freedom those who are oppressed

Although this is a quotation from the Septuagint, it illustrates an important point. There are two finite verbs following the relative pronoun ὅς; both ultimately modify the assertion that the Spirit of the Lord is upon the speaker. However, only the second verb is a perfect; the first is an aorist. Nevertheless, both are rendered in the translation as English perfects. Based on the principle that choice implies meaning, the choice to render only one Greek verb a perfect suggests a prioritization of the information in the relative clauses. Both provide background information for the governing clause, but only ἀποστέλλω is explicitly connected to the present situation using the perfect. The sending is what has the ongoing relevance, not the anointing. Thus there is exegetical significance attached to the use of the perfect that is not attached to the aorist in this context.

Another example of perfects occurring in relative clauses which are relevant to the matrix clause is found in Romans 5:2. There are actually two perfects in the verse, and 5:1 is supplied for context.

Romans 5:1–2

Δικαιωθέντες οὖν ἐκ πίστεως εἰρήνην ἔχομεν πρὸς τὸν θεὸν διὰ τοῦ κυρίου ἡμῶν Ἰησοῦ Χριστοῦ, ² δι᾽ οὗ καὶ τὴν προσαγωγὴν ἐσχήκαμεν τῇ πίστει εἰς τὴν χάριν ταύτην ἐν ᾗ ἑστήκαμεν, καὶ καυχώμεθα ἐπ᾽ ἐλπίδι τῆς δόξης τοῦ θεοῦ·

Therefore, having been declared righteous by faith, we have peace with God through our Lord Jesus Christ ² through whom also we have obtained access by faith into this grace in which we stand, and we boast in the hope of the glory of God (translation modified).

The matrix clause uses a present tense-form to describe the status of peace we have with God as a result of having been declared righteous by faith. The means by which this peace has come about is backfilled following the main proposition in a series of relative clauses about Jesus Christ. The first relative clause describes the access we have obtained, and is rendered quite naturally using an English perfect based on the overlapping usage here between Greek and English. The same cannot be said for the next perfect in 5:2b, which is most often translated using a simple present in English. The perfect correlates the state of affairs with the current discourse context of having peace with God.

Dependency relations may also be established logically through the use of γάρ. Levinsohn states, "The presence of γάρ constrains the material that it introduces to be interpreted as *strengthening* some aspect of the previous assertion, rather than as distinctive information."[16] The use of γάρ thus provides the same kind of anaphoric redirection of the perfect's relevance constraint as subordinate

16  Stephen H. Levinsohn, *Discourse Features of New Testament Greek: A Coursebook on the Information Structure of New Testament Greek*, 2nd rev. ed. (Dallas: SIL International, 2000), 91 (emphasis original).

clauses, but the dependency relation is logical rather than explicitly grammatical. In Luke 12:30, there are two clauses which offer strengthening material for the exhortation about "these things" i.e., not worrying about what you will eat or drink.

Luke 12:29–30

| | |
|---|---|
| καὶ ὑμεῖς μὴ ζητεῖτε τί φάγητε καὶ τί πίητε, καὶ μὴ μετεωρίζεσθε, ταῦτα γὰρ πάντα τὰ ἔθνη τοῦ κόσμου ἐπιζητοῦσιν, ὑμῶν δὲ ὁ πατὴρ <u>οἶδεν</u> ὅτι χρῄζετε τούτων. | And you, do not consider what you will eat and what you will drink, and do not be anxious. For all the nations of the world seek after these things, and your Father <u>knows</u> that you need these things. |

Although 12:30b is introduced by δέ rather than γάρ, it is nevertheless part of the strengthening material begun in 12:30a: the nations seek these things, and your Father knows you need them. The shift from strengthening material back to the theme line of the discourse occurs in 12:31 with the exhortation to seek his kingdom and these things will be added.[17]

Another instance of logical subordination using γάρ is Hebrews 3:3, where the writer supports the assertion made in 3:2 that Jesus is worthy of consideration based on his faithfulness just as Moses was faithful. This comparison sets the stage for asserting in 3:3 that Jesus is worthy of greater honor than Moses.

---

17 Other perfects which follow the clause to which they are relevant include Luke 1:22; 2:23; 4:6, 10, 18a; 9:36; 10:11; 11:13, 44; 12:7; 17: 2; 21:5, 20; 23:34; 24:29.

Hebrews 3:3

| | |
|---|---|
| ¹Ὅθεν, ἀδελφοὶ ἅγιοι, κλήσεως ἐπουρανίου μέτοχοι, κατανοήσατε τὸν ἀπόστολον καὶ ἀρχιερέα τῆς ὁμολογίας ἡμῶν Ἰησοῦν, ²πιστὸν ὄντα τῷ ποιήσαντι αὐτὸν ὡς καὶ Μωϋσῆς ἐν τῷ οἴκῳ αὐτοῦ. ³ πλείονος γὰρ οὗτος δόξης παρὰ Μωϋσῆν ἠξίωται καθ᾽ ὅσον πλείονα τιμὴν ἔχει τοῦ οἴκου ὁ κατασκευάσας αὐτόν | ¹Therefore, holy brothers, sharers in a heavenly calling, consider Jesus, the apostle and high priest of our confession, ²who was faithful to the one who appointed him, as Moses also *was* in his household. ³For this one is considered worthy of greater glory than Moses, inasmuch as the one who builds it has greater honor than the house. |

The writer merely juxtaposes Jesus and Moses in 3:2, creating the impression that they are equals in regard to their faithfulness. This delays the introduction of the important distinction made in 3:3 in regard to the honor that each receives. The perfect connects the logically anterior state of affairs regarding Jesus' greater worthiness to the present situation. Such discourse considerations often require that the perfect follow rather than precede, which correlates with the perfect so frequently occuring in subordinate clauses.

Another example of such logical subordination using γάρ is found in Romans 7:2. The preceding verse asserts that the law only has authority over a person as long as they are alive, framed as a rhetorical question. Romans 7:2 offers a practical example of this principle by contrasting the resulting state of affairs for a married woman when her husband is alive versus dead.

Romans 7:2

| | |
|---|---|
| ἡ γὰρ ὕπανδρος γυνὴ τῷ ζῶντι ἀνδρὶ δέδεται νόμῳ· ἐὰν δὲ ἀποθάνῃ ὁ ἀνήρ, κατήργηται ἀπὸ τοῦ νόμου τοῦ ἀνδρός. | For the married woman is bound by law to her husband while he lives, but if her husband dies, she is released from the law of the husband. |

Paul drives home his point in 7:3 by considering the legal ramifications of being with another man in each of these situations. We see again that the Greek perfects are not rendered into English using perfects in the major translations, but using imperfectives. The Greek perfect correlates a logically anterior state of affairs (being bound or released) with the present discourse context. All of the verbs in 7:1 are present tense-forms, whereas the perfects in 7:2 capture both the state of affairs and its current relevance.

## 4. PERFECTS ON THE THEME LINE OF THE DISCOURSE

The placement of perfects either just before that to which they are relevant, or following in a dependency relation, accounts for two-thirds of the usage observed in Luke, nearly all of the instances in Romans, and about three-quarters of the instances in Hebrews. We will consider the remainder of examples from Luke first, and then move on to those in Romans and Hebrews. This remaining third of perfect indicatives in Luke are found in the second part or "turn" of an embedded speech.

### 4.1 Theme Line Perfects in Embedded Speeches

Most dialogues are composed of paired speeches: an initial statement or question, and a response of some kind.[18] The second turn may be a response to the preceding turn, or to a narrative situation. In some cases the perfect clause is the only clause in the speech. In each instance, the perfect indicative adds information relevant to a preceding speech or situation. Since the information conveyed by the perfect is logically anterior to that which it is relevant, having it follow might theoretically present a problem for readers processing the discourse. In the absence of alternatives, readers and hearers seem quite willing to infer that these speech-initial perfects contribute information relevant to the preceding context.

Li, Thompson, and Thompson describe various motivations for such usage, many of which are attested in English and other

---

18  Stephen H. Levinsohn, *Self-Instruction Materials on Narrative Discourse Analysis* (Dallas: SIL International, 2015), http://www.sil.org/~levinsohns/narr.pdf.

languages.[19] They conclude that these functions are better explained as pragmatic effects of use in a given context than as typologically distinct, since the perfect is still fulfilling the expected function of marking the content as relevant to the current reference time of the discourse. The perfects beginning the second turn of a speech pair in Luke all offer climactic theme line pronouncements relevant to some aspect of the preceding situation. These occurrences stand in contrast to the more frequent use in supporting material. The limitations of reported speech disallow either anterior positioning or placement in a dependency relation as observed elsewhere in the context of monologue or narrative proper.

Perfects in the second speech-turn in Luke most often *counter* some aspect of the preceding speech or situation, though countering should not be construed as its meaning.[20] In English the perfect can introduce relevant information that serves as a negative response. For instance, if I were asked if I needed a ticket I could say, "I have purchased one, thanks." Use of the perfect constrains the information to be viewed as relevant to the present discourse context, i.e., to the open question. This countering usage can account for each of Jesus' responses to Satan's temptations in Luke 4. There are no explicit refusals by Jesus. Rather the quotations introduced using perfect indicatives are construed as introducing information relevant to Satan's temptations.

Luke 4:4

| καὶ ἀπεκρίθη πρὸς αὐτὸν ὁ Ἰησοῦς· | And Jesus replied to him, "It <u>is</u> |
| <u>Γέγραπται</u> ὅτι Οὐκ ἐπ' ἄρτῳ μόνῳ | <u>written</u>, 'Man will not live on |
| ζήσεται ὁ ἄνθρωπος. | bread alone.' " |

The quotation of Deuteronomy 8:3 provides the basis for Jesus' resisting Satan's temptation, and is pragmatically understood as a refusal to comply. Use of a different tense-form would not have evoked the same constraint on the information. The perfect's relevance constraint leads to the interpretation of Jesus' reply as a

---

19  Charles N. Li, Sandra A. Thompson, and R. McMillan Thompson, "The Discourse Motivation for the Perfect Aspect: The Mandarin Particle LE," in *Tense-Aspect: Between Semantics and Pragmatics*, ed. Paul J. Hopper, TSL 1 (Amsterdam: Benjamins, 1982), 19–44.

20  Ibid., 39–40.

climactic rejection of Satan's offer. The same may be said of Jesus'
next two responses in 4:8 and 4:12.

The perfects in the parable of the narrow door from Luke 13 are
doubly embedded; an embedded speech recounts a narrative that
contains embedded speeches. Each of the master's responses to
those calling is a perfect, marking the information as relevant. Just
as with the temptation of Jesus, there is no explicit rejection of the
request. Rather the master's response that he does not know them is
construed as a refusal to open the door.

Luke 13:25–27

| | |
|---|---|
| ἀφ' οὗ ἂν ἐγερθῇ ὁ οἰκοδεσπότης καὶ ἀποκλείσῃ τὴν θύραν, καὶ ἄρξησθε ἔξω ἑστάναι καὶ κρούειν τὴν θύραν λέγοντες· Κύριε, ἄνοιξον ἡμῖν· καὶ ἀποκριθεὶς ἐρεῖ ὑμῖν· Οὐκ οἶδα ὑμᾶς πόθεν ἐστέ. | When once the master of the house has gotten up and shut the door, and you begin to stand outside and knock on the door, saying, 'Lord, open the door for us!' And he will answer and say to you, 'I do not know where you are from!' |
| ²⁶τότε ἄρξεσθε λέγειν· Ἐφάγομεν ἐνώπιόν σου καὶ ἐπίομεν, καὶ ἐν ταῖς πλατείαις ἡμῶν ἐδίδαξας· | ²⁶Then you will begin to say, 'We ate and drank in your presence, and you taught in our streets!' |
| ²⁷ καὶ ἐρεῖ λέγων ὑμῖν· Οὐκ οἶδα πόθεν ἐστέ· ἀπόστητε ἀπ' ἐμοῦ, πάντες ἐργάται ἀδικίας. | ²⁷And he will reply, saying to you, 'I do not know where you are from! Go away from me, all you evildoers!' |

Although οἶδα is a diachronic fossil of sorts, it appears to have retained the relevance constraint of the perfect. The master's lack of
knowledge implicates his intention not to honor the request.

Other instances of perfects in second turns of a speech present
some interesting exegetical implications. A number of them are
Jesus' declarations of healing or forgiveness. The use of ἀφέωνται in
Luke 5:20, 23, and 7:28 accomplishes the action as it is spoken, i.e., it
is a performative verb. The others simply provide relevant information for processing the preceding event. In all cases the use of the
perfect is consistent with the typological expectation of relevance to
the current context. Readers relate this speech-initial information

as relevant to the preceding context in the absence of an alternative option later in the speech.

Consider Jesus' interaction with the sinful woman at Simon's house in Luke 7. He has just drawn a series of comparisons between how this woman has treated him compared to Simon's treatment as his host. The implication of 7:39 is that Jesus was not viewed as a prophet based on his allowing the woman to anoint his feet. There has been no request for forgiveness, just a correlation made between the amount of forgiveness with degrees of love; one who is forgiven much will love much. Jesus' statement in 7:47 contains a declaration of forgiveness based on the great love she has shown.

Luke 7:47–50

οὗ χάριν, λέγω σοι, ἀφέωνται αἱ ἁμαρτίαι αὐτῆς αἱ πολλαί, ὅτι ἠγάπησεν πολύ· ᾧ δὲ ὀλίγον ἀφίεται, ὀλίγον ἀγαπᾷ.

For this reason I tell you, her sins—which were many—have been forgiven, for she loved much. But the one to whom little is forgiven loves little."

[48] εἶπεν δὲ αὐτῇ· Ἀφέωνταί σου αἱ ἁμαρτίαι.

[48] And he said to her, "Your sins are forgiven."

[49] καὶ ἤρξαντο οἱ συνανακείμενοι λέγειν ἐν ἑαυτοῖς· Τίς οὗτός ἐστιν ὃς καὶ ἁμαρτίας ἀφίησιν;

[49] And those who were reclining at the table with *him* began to say among themselves, "Who is this who even forgives sins?"

[50] εἶπεν δὲ πρὸς τὴν γυναῖκα· Ἡ πίστις σου σέσωκέν σε· πορεύου εἰς εἰρήνην.

[50] And he said to the woman, "Your faith has saved you. Go in peace."

The perfect in 7:47 serves as a climactic theme line pronouncement, and the presence of the metacomment λέγω σοι adds further prominence to it.[21] The supporting ὅτι attributes her forgiveness to the amount of love she has shown. Thus, the forgiveness described in the perfect of 7:47 provides a climactic pronouncement, either of a new status or a description of what had already occurred. The same holds true for the comment to the woman in 7:48.

---

21  Steven E. Runge, *Discourse Grammar of the Greek New Testament: A Practical Introduction for Teaching and Exegesis* (Peabody, MA: Hendrickson, 2010), 101–2.

The perfect in 7:50 is far less open to debate about a preexisting status. Based on the woman's gestures and Jesus' assessment of them, they have apparently played a significant role in her forgiveness. There has been no mention of faith in the conversation. Furthermore, ἡ πίστις has been placed in marked focus before the verb for the sake of emphasis. Based on the context, the perfect is understood as backfilling relevant information that attributes her salvation (and perhaps forgiveness) to her faith, rather than her outpouring of love. On this view, her expressions of love simply manifest the faith she already had. It was her faith that saved her as opposed to something else.

This section has presented examples of the perfect in the second portion of a speech in response to a preceding turn or state of affairs. The constraints of dialogue do not allow for it either to precede or to be explicitly dependent upon that to which it is relevant. The reader accommodates this situation by inferring that the perfect marks the information as relevant to what precedes. The typological function of marking relevant information is still present. Other examples of perfects found in the second portion of a speech pair are Luke 5:32; 8:48; 10:9; 13:12; 17:10; 22:57, 60; and 24:46.

## 4.2 Theme Line Perfects in Nonnarrative Contexts

All of the instances of perfects occurring on the theme line of the narrative discourse were found in embedded speeches responding to a previous speech or situation. All had the pragmatic effect of countering some aspect of the preceding speech or situation. The fact that it could not be construed as dependent upon or preceding that to which it is relevant meant that they were unambiguously identifiable. But what about theme line perfects occurring outside of narrative proper? If they occur, what basis is there for unambiguously identifying them? This was the dilemma I sought to address by adding data from Romans and Hebrews to my preliminary analysis of Luke's usage.

As it turned out, there is only one unambiguous instance in Romans, found in 11:5. There were other instances a perfect occurred in a theme line argument, but they were embedded theme lines that in turn were supporting an overarching theme line (see Rom 3:21 and 13:2). Romans 11 begins by asking whether God has forsaken his people, followed by a quotation in 11:3–4 from 1 Kings 19:18 describing the preservation of a remnant who had not bowed their knee to Baal. The perfect verb in 11:5 serves to answer the opening rhetorical question in 11:2 about God forsaking Israel.

Romans 11:5

² οὐκ ἀπώσατο ὁ θεὸς τὸν λαὸν αὐτοῦ ὃν προέγνω. ἢ οὐκ οἴδατε ἐν Ἠλίᾳ τί λέγει ἡ γραφή, ὡς ἐντυγχάνει τῷ θεῷ κατὰ τοῦ Ἰσραήλ; κτλ.

² God has not rejected his people, whom he foreknew! Or do you not know, in *the passage about** Elijah, what the scripture says—how he appeals to God against Israel...

⁴ ἀλλὰ τί λέγει αὐτῷ ὁ χρηματισμός; Κατέλιπον ἐμαυτῷ ἑπτακισχιλίους ἄνδρας, οἵτινες οὐκ ἔκαμψαν γόνυ τῇ Βάαλ. ⁵ οὕτως οὖν καὶ ἐν τῷ νῦν καιρῷ λεῖμμα κατ' ἐκλογὴν χάριτος γέγονεν·

⁴ But what does the divine response say to him? "I have left for myself seven thousand people who have not bent the knee to Baal." ⁵ So in this way also at the present time, there is a remnant selected by grace.

The information conveyed by the perfect serves to reframe the opening question. It is not an all-or-nothing proposition when it comes to God's faithfulness. Paul infers here that God has indeed been faithful, but it is the preservation of a remnant rather than the whole nation.

In contrast to Romans, there are about a dozen clear examples in Hebrews where the perfect is operating on the theme line of the discourse rather than providing supporting information. The correlation with a preceding proposition is sometimes explicitly marked, as in Hebrews 8:6 by the use of a counterpoint-point set using μέν/δέ. Hebrews 8:4 asserts that if Jesus were on earth that he would not be eligible to serve as a priest. This proposition serves as a foil for the assertion in 8:6 that Jesus has attained something better.

Hebrews 8:6

νυνὶ δὲ διαφορωτέρας τέτυχεν λειτουργίας ὅσῳ καὶ κρείττονός ἐστιν διαθήκης μεσίτης ἥτις ἐπὶ κρείττοσιν ἐπαγγελίαις νενομοθέτηται

But now he has attained a more excellent ministry, by as much as he is also mediator of a better covenant which has been enacted upon better promises.

The perfect works in concert with the μέν/δέ set to constrain the reader to correlate these contrasting propositions. This tense-form correlates the existing state of affairs with the present discourse context: Jesus' inability to serve as an earthly priest. An aorist would simply have described the acquisition of the more excellent ministry without explicitly marking its current relevance. The presence of μέν alone correlates the statement, but the addition of the perfect increases the rhetorical impact of the contrast.

In other cases of theme line perfects in Hebrews, the correlation with a preceding foil or counterpoint is achieved using conventional cohesion devices like lexical repetition. For example, in the opening verses of Hebrews 1 the author compares the things said to the angels with the things said to the Son. After describing the superior status of the Son in 1:2–4, the question is asked in 1:5 about which of the angels God told (aor.) that he had begotten them or that they were his son. Another assertion is made in 1:6 regarding the angels worshiping God's Son, suggesting a hierarchy. Then in 1:7 we learn what is actually said about the angels by God in contrast to what he says about the Son in 1:8–12. Thus far we see that the angels are told to worship the Son (1:6) and that they have different roles, but the assertion in 1:13 goes one step further.

Hebrews 1:13

| | |
|---|---|
| πρὸς τίνα δὲ τῶν ἀγγέλων <u>εἴρηκέν</u> ποτε Κάθου ἐκ δεξιῶν μου ἕως ἂν θῶ τοὺς ἐχθρούς σου ὑποπόδιον τῶν ποδῶν σου | But to which of the angels <u>has he</u> ever <u>said</u>, "Sit down at my right hand, until I make your enemies a footstool for your feet." |

This verse essentially restates the same question from 1:5, but this time using a perfect indicative rather than an aorist. Instead of just noting that each are told different things, the verse asserts that what the Son is told is reserved only for the him and not for the angels.

Another example utilizing repetition is found in Hebrews 7:6 in the description of Melchizedek. An alternate referring expression is used to characterize him as the one not tracing his descent from the Levites to reinforce the irony of Abraham paying a tithe and

being blessed. The point is made in 7:5 that it is the Levites who collect tithes, not others.

Hebrews 7:4-6
But see how great this man *was*, to whom Abraham the patriarch
gave a tenth from the spoils! ⁵ And indeed those of the sons of
Levi who receive the priesthood have a commandment to collect
a tenth from the people according to the law, that is, from their
brothers, although they are descended from Abraham.

| | |
|---|---|
| ⁶ ὁ δὲ μὴ γενεαλογούμενος ἐξ αὐτῶν <u>δεδεκάτωκεν</u> Ἀβραὰμ καὶ τὸν ἔχοντα τὰς ἐπαγγελίας <u>εὐλόγηκεν</u> | ⁶ But the one who did not trace his descent from them <u>collected tithes</u> from Abraham and <u>blessed</u> the one who had the promises. |

Instead of Abraham blessing others (see Gen 12:3), he is the one
being blessed. Instead of his descendants receiving tithes, they figuratively pay them (pf. δεδεκάτωται) through Abraham (Heb 7:9).
Hebrews 7:5 serves as a foil to create an expected outcome, whereas
the perfects in 7:6 and 7:9 counter this expectation.

There are only two instances found in my corpus of theme line
perfects that could not be construed as countering a previous assertion as in the preceding examples. These are the assertions
in Hebrews 11:17 and 11:28 about actions that were done by faith.
Abraham offering up Isaac uses προσενήνοχεν, which does more than
than the simple reporting of an aorist verb. Although this action is
elaborated upon in 11:18-19, these verses provide supporting information to the one theme line assertion. The same can be said for the
account of Moses keeping the Passover in 11:28. The only theme line
assertion here is that by faith he kept (pf. πεποίηκεν) the Passover.
The other portion of the sentence is a subordinate purpose clause,
leaving nothing else for the perfect to be relating to. It nevertheless
accomplishes its core task of correlating an existing action or state
of affairs with the present discourse context, marking it as relevant.
With so many of the other actions in this chapter being reported in
the aorist, the choice of the perfect should not be quickly dismissed.
Other examples of theme line perfects include Hebrews 5:5; 7:22; 8:6,
13; 9:18, 26; and 12:5.

## 5. APPARENT EXCEPTIONS

There are a few tokens from the chosen corpus that appear in an unmarked dependency relation with what precedes. In Luke, both are in speeches that begin with exhortations using imperatives, and a perfect follows without any explicit marker of dependence. Further, the perfect is the final clause of the speech. Therefore the only viable option available to the reader is to construe the perfect as relevant to what precedes. Levinsohn has found that strengthening material following exhortations is often not overtly marked.[22] The change in mood from imperative to indicative makes the explicit marking unnecessary. Readers accommodate the shift, construing the information as intended to strengthen the exhortations. And just as in Luke 7:50 above, ἡ πίστις precedes the verb placing it in marked focus. The emphasis placed on faith and the relevance constraint of the perfect both suggest this information is important for processing what precedes.

Luke 17:19

| καὶ εἶπεν αὐτῷ· Ἀναστὰς πορεύου· | And he said to him, "Get up |
| ἡ πίστις σου <u>σέσωκέν</u> σε. | and go your way. Your faith <u>has saved</u> you." |

Luke 18:42

| καὶ ὁ Ἰησοῦς εἶπεν αὐτῷ· | And Jesus said to him, "Regain |
| Ἀνάβλεψον· ἡ πίστις σου <u>σέσωκέν</u> | your sight! Your faith <u>has saved</u> |
| σε. | you." |

The perfect is in an unmarked dependency relation with the imperatives, providing information particularly relevant to what precedes.

The same holds true for the remaining perfects that end a short speech turn, but are not the initial clause in it. In Luke 17:14 Jesus commands ten lepers to go and show themselves to the priests, implicating this as the key action to their subsequent healing. In the healing of the blind man in Luke 18:41, there is only the request to be healed which precedes, and no action on the blind man's part. Based on the fact that the perfects conclude Jesus' speeches, the relevance

---

is understood to relate to the preceding clauses or situation. Nevertheless, all these examples uphold the typological expectation of relevance observed in the more prototypical uses.

There were no such exceptions among the perfects in Hebrews, but a few were found in Romans. Two occur in metacomments—what form critics have termed disclosure formulas—where Paul comments on what he is about to say. Romans 14:14 begins with οἶδα καὶ πέπεισμαι (I know and am convinced), drawing extra attention to the assertion that follows that nothing is inherently unclean. Such usage is in keeping with the perfect's core meaning of summarizing a state of affairs and correlating it with the present context. It casts his comments about cleanness as a settled conviction rather than as some new epiphany. The same could be said of the perfect in Romans 6:16, which also occurs in a metacomment: οὐκ οἴδατε ὅτι ᾧ παριστάνετε ἑαυτοὺς (Don't you know that to whomever you present yourselves). This cognitive state of affairs is nearly always found in the perfect.

The one remaining example is found in Romans 14:23, and occurs immediately following hortatory material as was the case in Luke. The exhortations are underlined in the example below.

Romans 14:20–23
Do not destroy the work of God on account of food. All *things are* clean, but *it is* wrong for the person who eats and stumbles in the process. ²¹ *It is* good not to eat meat or to drink wine or *to do anything* by which your brother stumbles or is offended or is weakened. ²² The faith that you have, have with respect to yourself before God. Blessed *is* the one who does not pass judgment on himself by what he approves.

| | |
|---|---|
| ²³ ὁ δὲ διακρινόμενος ἐὰν φάγῃ κατακέκριται, ὅτι οὐκ ἐκ πίστεως· πᾶν δὲ ὃ οὐκ ἐκ πίστεως ἁμαρτία ἐστίν. | ²³ But the one who doubts is condemned if he eats, because he does not do so from faith, and everything that is not from faith is sin. |

This section has several main assertions with accompanying expositional material. The prohibition against destroying God's work on account of food is substantiated by 14:20b–21. The exhortation in 14:22a about how to have our faith is essentially extended by a quasi-exhortation at the end of the verse regarding the one not passing judgment being blessed. Romans 14:23 offers expositional material supporting the preceding assertion, a corollary of sorts about the person. There is room for debate about this example, but the usage seems to be in keeping with the perfect being used in expositional material following exhortations that is not explicitly marked using either logical or grammatical subordination.

## 6. AREAS FOR FURTHER RESEARCH

The usage of the perfect indicative in Luke, Romans, and Hebrews has been shown to correlate logically anterior states of affairs with the current discourse situation. However, little has been said about the grounding status of the information conveyed by the perfect. Most of the perfects recount supportive information, such as the tokens found in dependency relations with what precedes. A minority clearly convey theme line information, such as the perfects in the second part of speech-pairs recounting pronouncements of Jesus, and the few tokens from Romans and Hebrews. This calls into question the prominence marking claims of Porter and possibly Campbell.

Both scholars treat the information conveyed by the perfect as more prominent than the surrounding information. This stands in contrast to the findings here that most perfects offer expositional support for a more salient element. Porter's view often promotes supporting information to a level more prominent than the theme line/foreground assertion to which it is relevant. Statements like the following unambiguously represent the perfect as though it is inherently more salient than the others: "The result is that the perfect gives 'the appearance of something precisely more emphatic than the aorist. The perfect awakes therefore the impression as though it were more pertinent' (Waarde, 27, 29)."[23] Campbell's claims

---

23  Stanley E. Porter, *Verbal Aspect in the Greek of the New Testament: With Reference to Tense and Mood*, SBG 1 (New York: Lang, 1989), 258. Elsewhere his description of the "more marked" perfect focuses attention on it rather than the following verb to which it is relevant: "The most convincing examples [demonstrating the perfect's markedness] virtually always have the more heavily marked form preceding the less heavily marked, reinforcing the scheme of markedness according to the semantic hierarchy of tense forms.

of "heightened proximity" leading to "intensive" and "prominent" implicatures of the perfect also treat them as though they are more relevant than that to which they relate.[24] He states, "The concept of prominence is here taken to refer to the degree to which an element stands out from others in its environment. Thus, prominence is here roughly synonymous with *stress*."[25] He also uses emphasizing glosses in his translations to capture the "heightened proximity" conveyed by the tense-form.[26] Such claims likely only apply to perfects used on the theme line of the discourse, not the supporting ones.

A second area deserving further investigation is the corollary to the previous one: the willingness of exegetes to treat perfects as indifferent from aorists. From a diachronic standpoint, it is true that the perfect eventually passes out of Koine use in favor of the aorist. But this should not be construed to mean that there is no exegetical differentiation between them. Current research in Classical Greek has demonstrated that aorist vs. perfect is the meaningful choice available to the author, not present vs. perfect.[27] The displacement of the perfect by the aorist might well be attributable to *decreasing precision* in marking relevant material, the kind we find in American English. Increasingly we observe use of the simple past in contexts where a past perfect might have been expected.

---

This is an understandable progression whereby the less heavily marked forms is used in support of the more heavily marked." (Ibid, 251)

24 Constantine Campbell, *Verbal Aspect, the Indicative Mood, and Narrative: Soundings in the Greek of the New Testament*, SBG 13 (New York: Lang, 2007), 206–7.

25 Ibid., 206 (emphasis original).

26 Campbell adds the underlined words to his glosses to capture the heightened proximity, e.g., "we truly believe and know," "among you now stands one you do not even know," "they had actually seen," "I have carefully prepared." Ibid., 201–7.

27 Orriens, "Greek Perfect as a Situating Cohesion Device"; Arjan Amor Nijk, "The Rhetorical Function of the Perfect in Classical Greek," *Philologus* 157 (2013): 237–62.

| Past Perfect to Mark Relevance | Simple Past with Relevance Inferred |
|---|---|
| (1) I have lost my penknife. Could you help me find it, please? | (2a) I lost my penknife. Could you help me find it, please? |
| | (2b) I lost my penknife, but I think I know where it is. |

The reader is able to infer from both (1) and (2) that the loss of the penknife is relevant. However, use of the perfect in (1) explicitly marks the first statement as relevant, creating the expectation that something more will be said about it. In the case of the simple past in (2), no such relevance expectation exists. Rather in (2a) the fact that the information is relevant to what follows can only be inferred after the fact based on the request for help. In (2b) the lost knife is construed as theme line information based on the additional comment made about finding it. Alternatively, the perfect may have suffered from overuse, where its prototypical function of "expressing present relevance of a past action, especially a resultant state" gives way to a "functional merger" by the fourth century AD.[28]

## 7. ADDENDUM

The essays in this volume on the perfect by Crellin and Buth offer significant insights into the important impact that voice (act. vs. middle/passive) and lexical semantics (telicity and valence) have on judgments about the semantics conveyed by the perfect. Porter has claimed that the perfect is stative, which is true of many perfects that only ever occur in the middle voice, and that are inherently stative in their lexical semantics. Others are judged to be stative based on being intransitive. However, there are numerous instances that are not stative in the traditional linguistic sense, i.e., the telic activity verbs. These latter have been called anteriors or simply perfects. Porter, Fanning, and Campbell have each captured important pieces of the puzzle, but none fully assemble them into the whole.

---

28 Horrocks, *Greek*, 102, 177.

Our hope is for the essays on the perfect in this volume to provide a more complete though composite picture.


# BIBLIOGRAPHY

Bhat, D. N. Shankara. *The Prominence of Tense, Aspect, and Mood*. Amsterdam: Benjamins, 1999.

Blass, Friedrich. *Grammar of New Testament Greek*. Translated by Henry St. John Thackeray. London: Macmillan, 1898.

Campbell, Constantine. *Verbal Aspect, the Indicative Mood, and Narrative: Soundings in the Greek of the New Testament*. SBG 13. New York: Peter Lang, 2007.

Comrie, Bernard. *Aspect: An Introduction to the Study of Verbal Aspect and Related Problems*. CTL. Cambridge: Cambridge University Press, 1981.

Horrocks, Geoffrey. *Greek: A History of the Language and Its Speakers*. 2nd ed. West Sussex, UK: John Wiley & Sons, 2009.

Levinsohn, Stephen H. *Discourse Features of New Testament Greek: A Coursebook on the Information Structure of New Testament Greek*. 2nd rev. ed. Dallas: SIL International, 2000.

Li, Charles N., Sandra A. Thompson, and R. McMillan Thompson. "The Discourse Motivation for the Perfect Aspect: The Mandarin Particle LE." Pages 19-44 in *Tense-Aspect: Between Semantics and Pragmatics*, edited by Paul J. Hopper. Amsterdam: Benjamins, 1982.

Nijk, Arjan Amor. "The Rhetorical Function of the Perfect in Classical Greek." *Philologus* 157, no. 2 (2013): 237–62.

Orriens, Sander. "The Greek Perfect as a Situating Cohesion Device." Pages 221-239 in *Discourse Cohesion in Ancient Greek*, edited by Stéphanie J. Bakker and G. C. Wakker. Amsterdam: Brill, 2009.

Porter, Stanley E. *Verbal Aspect in the Greek of the New Testament: With Reference to Tense and Mood*. SBG 1. New York: Peter Lang, 1989.

Runge, Steven E. *Discourse Grammar of the Greek New Testament: A Practical Introduction for Teaching and Exegesis*. Peabody, MA: Hendrickson, 2010.

Wallace, Daniel B. *Greek Grammar Beyond the Basics*. 2nd ed. Grand Rapids: Zondervan, 1996.

CHAPTER 16

# Greek Prohibitions

MICHAEL AUBREY

FAITHLIFE CORPORATION

## 1. INTRODUCTION

The question of aspect and prohibitions in Ancient Greek has been subject to much debate.[1] In recent decades, there seems to be a real sense for many scholars that the conclusions of the past are dramatically misguided. Daniel Wallace, for example, devotes substantial space to arguing against the idea that the basic, or in his

---

1   My purpose here is not to provide a complete literature survey of the question. There are a number of recent discussions of the question for those who are interested: Douglas S. Huffman, *Verbal Aspect Theory and the Prohibitions in the Greek New Testament*, SBG 16 (New York: Lang, 2014) provides a monograph length discussion. Others such as Fanning and Fantin have also given substantive attention: Buist Fanning, *Verbal Aspect in New Testament Greek*, OTM (Oxford: Oxford University Press, 1990), 325–88; Joseph Fantin, *The Greek Imperative Mood: A Cognitive and Communicative Approach*, SBG 12 (New York: Lang, 2010), 91–95. I would highly recommend Fantin's (albeit brief) discussion as the best summary. While Huffman provides the largest and most detailed account of prohibitions, he adopts a rather flawed view of the history of Greek grammar that colors his readings of old grammars and grammatical discussions. In his view, the STOP DOING X/DO NOT START X usages are artifacts of what he calls, "*Aktionsart* Theory." He views this so-called theory as inherently flawed as compared to the modern "Aspect Theory," following Stanley Porter (*Verbal Aspect and the Greek of the New Testament: With Reference to Tense and Mood*, SBG 1 [New York: Lang, 1989]). Like Porter, Huffman's conception of *Aktionsart* is an anachronism. He reads a definition of *Aktionsart* from the late 20th century back into the 19th and early 20th centuries. This methodological failure at the beginning of his work complicates the analysis that follows. Thankfully, however, it does not negate the book's value; it is an extremely useful collection of data.

terms, "unaffected," meaning of the imperfective and perfective prohibitions is STOP DOING X and DO NOT START X, respectively, lamenting,

> Grammarians' hypotheses about the unaffected meaning of a particular morpho-syntactic element (such as genitive case, present tense, etc.) are supposed to be based on a decent sampling of the data and with a proper linguistic grid to run it through. Older works tended to obscure the unaffected meaning because the data on which they based their definitions were insufficient. For example, the idea that the present prohibition means, *in essence*, "stop doing" is in reality a *specific usage* that cannot be applied universally. An abstract notion of the present prohibition first needs to be found, one that is both distinctive to the present prohibition and able to explain most of the data.[2]

And elsewhere in a separate discussion, he notes again,

> For over eighty years, students of the NT assumed a certain view about the semantics of commands and prohibitions. This view is often traced to a brief essay written in 1904 by Henry Jackson. He tells of a friend, Thomas Davidson, who had been struggling with commands and prohibitions in modern [sic] Greek:[3]

To a large degree, he is not wrong. For any number of topics, biblical scholars have had a tendency to reduce linguistic structure to a handful of simplistic rules. Another well-known example of this would be the supposed "once and for all aorist."[4] This tendency to

---

2  Daniel Wallace, *Greek Grammar beyond the Basics: An Exegetical Syntax of the New Testament With Scripture, Subject, and Greek Word Indexes* (Grand Rapids: Zondervan, 1997), 3.

3  Ibid., xiv.

4  Specifically, this is the problematic idea that the aorist refers to events as a single point and the building of theological framework around that idea; see Frank Stagg, "The Abused Aorist," *JBL* 91 (1972): 222–31.

reduce complex grammatical phenomenon to a simple rule is what is at play here.[5]

All of this is a very striking perspective on the broader perception of claims put forward by grammarians. Douglas Huffman takes pains to demonstrate that in the original discussions of the STOP DOING X and DO NOT START X usages, both advocates and critics of the usages clearly acknowledge that the point of contention is not about the basic meaning of imperfective and perfective prohibitions. Instead, the debate is about the possible existence of specific meanings that can be expressed by imperfective and perfective prohibitions.[6] He goes on to comment,

> "Curiously then, despite all the nuancing from both the nay-sayers … and the proponents themselves …, after this post-turn-of-the-century discussion in *The Classical Review* … the *Aktionsart* understanding of the distinction between the two main Greek prohibition constructions quickly becomes the accepted rule in NT Greek studies. By the end of the twentieth century,

---

5    William Varner in his recent commentary on James provides an interesting illustration of this, stating,

> Recent discussions on the broader subject of verbal aspect have emphasized that the ceasing of an action that is already in progress is not the nature of the action addressed by the use of a negated present tense imperative. While this could be the case, such a kind of action (*Aktionsart*) should be determined only from a close examination of the context in which the command is found. A better approach to this subject is found by recognizing that the present tense of the imperative mood is intended to convey a general rather than a more specific prohibition. (*James*, EEC [Bellingham, WA Lexham Press, 2014], 445)

Now Varner is certainly correct that treating cessation as the single basic meaning of imperfective prohibitions is problematic, but caution is necessary in how far to go in the other direction. Varner appears to want to make the observation about aspect and prohibitions in terms of specificity equally basic. Making an overarching claim about imperfective prohibitions as always being general cannot be sustained either. There is certainly a strong correlation between general commands with the imperfective aspect and specific commands with the perfective aspect, but the data do not support so strong a generalization as Varner presents (see Fanning, *Verbal Aspect*, 325–88).

6    Huffman, *Verbal Aspect Theory*, 14–21.

scholars ... boldly declare the distinction as a universal rule for Greek."[7]

For Huffman, the probable source of the quick acceptance by New Testament scholarship of this observation as universal truth is a result of the influence of James H. Moulton's discussion of it in his *Prolegomena*.[8] That seems likely, though my reading of Moulton leads me to believe that this was not Moulton's intent. While Moulton might be the origin, I believe it more likely that the overgeneralization of specific usages into universal rules here is the result of the same process that Stagg observed from the Greek aorist.

> Careful grammarians make it clear that the "punctiliar" idea belongs to the writer's manner of presentation and not necessarily to the action itself. Some grammars actually misrepresent the matter, holding that at least in the indicative mood the aorist has to do with the action which itself is punctiliar. From this follow the ill-advised arguments of exegetes or theologians that because the aorist is used, the reference has to be a single action or even a "once-and-for-all" action. It is this line of argument that is false and needs to be challenged; the action may be momentary, singular, or "once and for all," but it is not the use of the aorist that makes it such.[9]

In the same vein, I propose that both the STOP DOING X and DO NOT START X meanings are not the meaning of the imperfective and perfective prohibitions, but that they are, nevertheless, usages that naturally arise from a particular set of linguistic conditions. The goal of this study is to determine what those conditions are. Even though an imperfective prohibition does not inherently mean STOP DOING X or a perfective prohibition does not inherently mean DO NOT START X, it does not follow, as we shall see, that there is no relationship between the aspect and the semantic

---

7  Ibid., 21.
8  James H. Moulton, *A Grammar of New Testament Greek: Prolegomena*, 3rd ed. (Edinburgh: T&T Clark, 1906), 123–26.
9  Stagg, "Abused Aorist," 222.

expression. The defender of the generalization in *The Classical Review* way back in 1905, Walter Headlam, says it well:

> My [original] statement of it [the generalization] was made for the sake of dealing with two passages, in a paper where I had many other things to say and no room to mention even the qualifications that were in my mind; and there are still cases which I am not prepared at present to account for by more than tentative explanations. And the rule itself was somewhat clumsily expressed. It will be more safely stated thus:
>
> When the meaning is *Do not as you are doing, Do not continue doing so*, and this meaning is to be conveyed by the verb alone and unassisted, then μή must be followed by the present imperative.
>
> When the meaning is *Beware of doing this in future time*, and this meaning is to be conveyed by the verb alone, then μή must be followed by the aorist subjunctive.
>
> I do not say that μὴ ποίε or μὴ λέγε always mean *Do not thus any longer*; but that to express that meaning by the verb alone you must use μὴ ποίε or μὴ λέγε; though the same meaning may be conveyed by μὴ δράσῃς ἔτι or μὴ εἴτῃς πέρα.[10]

This expression of the generalization is the opposite of what it has become. It is not that the imperfective prohibition means STOP DOING X. Instead, the meaning STOP DOING X requires an imperfective prohibition if the speaker desires to express it with a single verb. That's a significantly less outrageous claim.

Following a brief discussion of some theoretical perquisites, my analysis comes in two sections. The first examines imperfective and perfective prohibitions in terms of the types of predicates they appear with. The second section then focuses on how negation interacts with the propositions contained in prohibitions for each aspect. I show that, in particular, negation scope can have significant influence over the propositional content of prohibitions in both aspects. The questions at hand are: What motivates the STOP DOING X and DO NOT START X expressions? Can we distinguish a relationship

---

10  Walter Headlam, "Greek Prohibitions," *ClR* 19 (1905), 30–36.

between these two meanings and other observations about commands/prohibitions? What patterns do prohibitions demonstrate in relation to predicate types? And finally, what patterns do prohibitions demonstrate in terms of negation scope?

The data for these two sections come from a variety of sources, including the SBL Greek New Testament, Holmes's edition of the Apostolic Fathers, Rahlfs's and Hanhart's edition of the Septuagint, the Niese edition of Josephus, Borgen et al.'s text of Philo, the Old Testament Pseudepigrapha edited by Heiser and Penner, the New Testament Apocrypha collected and edited by Brannan, and where necessary, the Perseus Project's larger corpus of Greek texts.[11]

## 1.1 Theoretical Prerequisites: Grammatical Categories and Semantic Scope

The approach to language structure that I follow below is grounded in a set of cognitive concepts built into the basic nature of all human categorization. I take the stance that to talk about *true* language universals is to talk about communication and cognition. For my purposes here, the central claim is that the language universal categories of PREDICATE and ARGUMENT share an iconic relationship with the language specific lexical categories of verb and noun.[12] The categories PREDICATE and ARGUMENT are universal categories

---

11  Peder Borgen, Kåre Fuglseth, and Roald Skarsten. *The Works of Philo: Greek Text With Morphology* (Bellingham, WA: Logos Bible Software, 2005); Rick Brannan, *Greek Apocryphal Gospels, Fragments and Agrapha: Texts and Transcriptions* (Bellingham, WA: Logos Bible Software, 2013); Gregory R. Crane, ed., *Perseus Digital Library* (Tufts University), http://www.perseus.tufts.edu; Michael W. Holmes, ed., *The Apostolic Fathers: Greek Texts and English Translations*, 3rd. ed. (Grand Rapids: Baker Academic, 2007); Michael W. Holmes, ed., *The Greek New Testament: SBL Edition* (Bellingham, WA: Logos Bible Software, 2010); Benedikt Niese, ed., *Flavii Iosephi Opera Recognovit*, 7 vols. (Berlin: Weidmannos, 1888–1895); Ken Penner and Michael Heiser, eds., *Old Testament Greek Pseudepigrapha with Morphology* (Bellingham, WA: Logos Bible Software, 2008); Alfred Rahlfs and John Hanhart, *Septuaginta: Editio altera* (Stuttgart: Deutsche Bibelgesellschaft, 2006).
12  I say this fully aware that not all languages conclusively have both of these two categories. Not all languages necessarily have the categories noun and verb, but all languages still make some sort of distinction between predicate and argument, even if it is not a distinction grounded in a lexical classification or a parts-of-speech system.

because they derive from the fundamental cognitive-communicative concepts of predication and reference. Without an ability to assert, affirm, or deny propositions, there is no language or communication. Likewise, without an ability to refer to people, places, or things symbolically, we cannot make propositions about objects in the world. These two concepts, PREDICATE and ARGUMENT, are emergent from the embodied reality of human experience of participants and actions/events.[13]

The concepts of predication and reference form the groundwork for semantic and syntactic structure.[14] Language structure, then, has as its foundation the following semantic oppositions presented in Table 1.[15]

Table 1. Universal Oppositions Underlying Clause Structure

| Predicate +Arguments | Nonarguments |
|---|---|

---

13  I take the position, following Cognitive Linguistics, that our experience of embodiment and interactions with each other and with objects in the world motivate both the semantic and syntactic structure of language (Robert Langacker, *Foundations of Cognitive Grammar* [Stanford, CA: Stanford University Press, 1987]; George Lakoff, *Women, Fire, and Dangerous Things: What Categories Reveal about the Mind* [Chicago: University of Chicago Press, 1987]; George Lakoff and Mark Johnson, *Philosophy in the Flesh: The Embodied Mind and Its Challenge to Western Thought* [New York: Basic Books, 1999]; John Taylor, *Linguistic Categorization*, 3rd ed., OTL [Oxford: Oxford University Press, 2003]).

14  The particular framework I am working within here is Role and Reference Grammar (RRG). While RRG does not place itself within the same range of frameworks subsumed within Cognitive Linguistics in the same way that Cognitive Grammar or Construction Grammar are, the framework still builds on the same research that grounds those frameworks (Robert D. Van Valin and Randy J. LaPolla, *Syntax: Structure, Meaning, and Function*, CTL [Cambridge: Cambridge University Press, 1997], 28). Role and Reference Grammar is, in a rather real sense, a cousin of Construction Grammar, one that bridges the gap between European and West Coast Functionalism. For the term West Coast Functionalism, see Christopher S. Butler, María de los Ángeles Gómez-González, and Susana M. Doval-Suárez, *Dynamics of Language Use: Functional and Constrastive Perspectives*, P&B NS 140 (Amsterdam: Benjamins, 2003), 2–5.

15  Van Valin and LaPolla, *Syntax*, 25.

This diagram involves an ambiguity, however. The term ARGU-MENT can refer to either a semantic or syntactic entity. The distinction is relatively small, but important because of the question of precedence. Table 1 deals with semantic arguments. It is the semantic distinctions above that motivate the syntactic categories shown in Table 2.[16]

Table 2. Semantic Units and Syntactic Units of the Layered Structure of the Clause

| Underlying semantic element(s) | Syntactic unit |
|---|---|
| Predicate | Nucleus |
| Argument in semantic representation of predicate | Core argument |
| Nonarguments | Periphery |
| Predicate + Arguments | Core |
| Predicate + Arguments + Nonarguments | Clause (= Core + Periphery) |

The units in the right column represent the syntactic layers and components of the clause. The syntactic nucleus is motivated by the semantic predicate. Syntactic arguments are motivated by semantic arguments. Syntactic peripheries are motivated by nonargument entities. These may be defined as temporal and spatial entities (e.g., in the house, tomorrow, etc.), cognitively motivated by our embodied experience in the world as both spatial and temporal. The core of a clause is motivated by the predication, composed of a predicate and its arguments, and the clause, by the proposition, composed of a predicate and its arguments together with nonarguments. All of these build into a layered structure, as shown below in Figure 1 below.[17]

---

16  Robert D. Van Valin, Jr., *Exploring the Syntax-Semantics Interface* (Cambridge: Cambridge University Press, 2005), 5.

17  This is a simplified presentation of syntactic structure, but it provides the relevant details for our purposes and concisely brings together both the syntactic and semantic elements from table 2 above. For a more complete discussion of syntax and semantics in RRG, see Van Valin, *Exploring the Syntax Semantics Interface.*

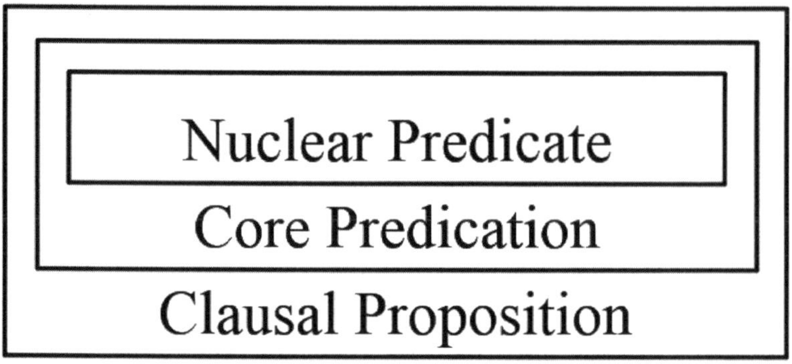

```
┌─────────────────────────────────────────┐
│  ┌───────────────────────────────────┐  │
│  │  ┌─────────────────────────────┐  │  │
│  │  │                             │  │  │
│  │  │     Nuclear Predicate       │  │  │
│  │  │                             │  │  │
│  │  └─────────────────────────────┘  │  │
│  │        Core Predication           │  │
│  └───────────────────────────────────┘  │
│           Clausal Proposition            │
└─────────────────────────────────────────┘
```

Figure 1. Layered Structure of the Clause

Each of these layers is significant for understanding how the syntactic structure of the clause relates to the grammatical categories like tense, aspect, modality, negation, and others, most of which are highly relevant for how we understand and interpret imperatives. Each of the three layers in figure 1 collocates with particular grammatical categories in terms of their semantic scope. The semantic scope of grammatical category refers to the portion of the syntactic structure to which it applies. Some grammatical categories only affect the semantics of the nuclear predicate alone. Other grammatical categories affect the semantics of the core predicate. Still others affect the meaning of the entire clause and its proposition. Some of these grammatical categories—those relevant to the discussion here are marked in bold—and the extent of their scope are presented in Table 3 below.

Table 3. Grammatical Categories and the Layered Structure of the Clause[18]

| Semantic-Syntactic Unit | Grammatical category |
|---|---|
| Nuclear Predicate | **Aspect** |
| | **Negation** |

---

18  For discussion of the scope of the nonbold categories, see Van Valin, *Exploring the Syntax-Semantics Interface*, 8–30.

| Core Predication | **Deontic modality** |
| --- | --- |
| | Event Quantification |
| | **Negation** |
| Clausal Proposition | **Epistemic modality** |
| | **Negation** |
| | Tense |
| | Evidentiality |
| | **Illocutionary Force** |

Each of these categories shares a scope relationship with the larger clause. Note that aspect only appears in the nuclear predicate and illocutionary force only over the clausal proposition, but there are two types of modality—each with its own scope. Further, negation can have scope over any of the three layers of the clause. Aspect has the narrowest domain of scope, limited to the nuclear predicate. What does this mean? Consider example 1.

1. a. I <u>was pouring</u> some water (progressive).
   b. I <u>poured</u> some water (perfective).

This example presents a distinction between the English past progressive and past perfective aspects. The former is unbounded or uncontained in its internal temporal structure. The latter is bounded/contained in its internal temporal structure. Note that in both cases, the aspect only affects the predicator/verb. Neither the semantics of the progressive nor the perfective has any effect on the participants: the agent argument, "I," and the patient argument, "some water."

Modality, depending on its type, may have scope over the core predication (the verb and one or more arguments) or over the entire clausal proposition. Deontic modality is limited to the core predication and refers to the ability or obligation of a participant, while epistemic modality has scope over the whole clausal proposition, referring to a proposition's existential status (e.g., probability, possibility, or necessity). We find both in example 2 below, with the scope of the modality marked in bold text and the grammatical morpheme of the modality underlined.

2. a. **John <u>should</u> play** the piano for Anne (deontic).
   b. **John <u>might</u> play the piano for Anne** (epistemic).

Observe, in example (2a), the obligation expressed by the auxiliary "should" only affects the subject "John" in terms of the obligation placed upon him to carry out the action. The auxiliary has no influence over Anne or the piano. That they are not within its scope demonstrates that deontic modality cannot have scope over the entire clause. On the other hand, for sentence in example (2b) the auxiliary "might" has an effect over the entire clause. The auxiliary can be read in relation to Anne, John, the piano, or even the action of playing itself (vs. some other verb, like "breaking," for example).

Since negation is even more complicated, I want to first look briefly at illocutionary force. This category includes clause types like questions, declaratives, commands, admonitions, and prohibitions. All these subsume the entire clause in their scope. If the clause is a command or a question, as in the example 3 sentences below, then the entire clause is a command or question, not merely a portion of it.

3. a. Give Mary her new bicycle (command).
   b. Did you give Mary her new bicycle? (question).

For our purposes, we are interested in those types of illocutionary force that also interface with the Greek imperative mood, particularly with commands and prohibitions.[19]

Finally, negation can, for a given clause, have scope over any one of these three layers. While most people think of negation simply in terms of negating a clause, when we look closely at particular instantiations and examples, we quickly find this is not the case. Consider the three sentences in example 4 below. Each is provided with the negated sentence and a context for clarifying the speaker's intended meaning.

4. a. **John did not eat lunch.** He is starving now (clausal proposition).

---

19 Other possible types of illocutionary force that may appear with the imperative mood are: requests and admonitions—many of Wallace's various specific usages of the imperative are types of illocutionary force (*Greek Grammar*, 485–93).

b. John did **not** eat **lunch.** He ate earlier and wasn't hungry at noon (core predication).

c. John **was unable to eat** lunch. He was fed lunch through an IV (nuclear predicate).

Each one of these three sentences has a negator that affects a different part of the clause. In sentence (4a), the entire clause is negated: the proposition "John ate lunch" is false in every respect. The scope or effect of the negator is narrower in sentence (4b) the object of the verb is the negated element, but not the clause and not the verb: John did eat, but it was not lunch.[20] Finally, in sentence (4c) only the nuclear predicate is negated. In English, nuclear negation is only done with derivational affixes (e.g. de- or un-).[21] Sentence (4c) conveys that John did receive lunch, but that he did not perform the action of the verb. The negation does not have scope over *John* and does not have scope over *lunch*, but is constrained to the verb phrase *able to eat*. Note that in all three sentences, at least for English, scope is only made explicit via situational or linguistic context.

# 1.2 Imperatives and Propositional Semantics[22]

For propositional semantics, I adopt Role and Reference Grammar's version of Vendler's classification of verbs. RRG modifies the model in light of the work of David Dowty and Carlotta Smith.[23] I follow the

---

20 Note in English the position of the negator is not affected by scope. This is not true of all languages.

21 English cannot use the *not* negator for nuclear negation. For that reason, I have had to change the verb to "able" rather than "eat." Other languages do not necessarily have this restriction.

22 The summary below is adapted from Michael G. Aubrey, "The Greek Perfect and the Categorization of Tense and Aspect: Toward a Descriptive Apparatus for Operators in Role and Reference Grammar" (MA Thesis, Trinity Western University, 2014), 12–15.

23 David Dowty, *Word Meaning and Montague Grammar: The Semantics of Verbs and Times in Generative Semantics and in Montague's PTQ*, SLL 7 (Dordrecht: Reidel, 1979); Carlotta Smith, *The Parameter of Aspect*, 2nd ed., SLP 43 (Dordrecht: Kluwer, 1997). These kinds of distinctions among predicates have received a number of different labels. Perhaps most prominent among them has been the term *Aktionsart*, German for "action type." Other terms that have gained some credence among linguists are "actionality" (a term that is essentially an Anglicized version of the German word *Aktionsart*), "lexical aspect" (Mari Olsen, "A Semantic and Pragmatic Model of Lexical

terminology decisions of Emma Pavey and Christopher Butler and refer to these classes as "predicate classes."[24] This captures the important fact that these are kinds of predications, not lexemes, and is thus a transparent label.[25] The original Vendlerian classes (state, achievement, accomplishment, activity) are provided in 5 with representative English predicates.[26]

5. a. States: *be sick, be dead, know, believe*
   b. Achievements: *pop, explode, shatter* (the intransitive versions)
   c. Accomplishments: *melt, freeze, dry* (the intransitive versions); *learn*
   d. Activities: *march, walk, roll* (the intransitive versions); *swim, think, write*

The distinctions among these types are rather clear, at least in their prototypical realizations. States and activities are atelic. Achievements and accomplishments involve a change of state, and thus are inherently telic. States differ from activities by their static nature compared to the dynamic nature of activities. Achievements are instantaneous and accomplishments are not.

---

and Grammatical Aspect," [PhD diss., Northwestern University, 1994]), and "situation aspect." The final term was proposed by Smith (*Parameter of Aspect*) as a label that attempts to capture both the inherent semantics of the category and also its relationship to aspect. When referring to the distinction between perfective and imperfective, which we might label as "aspect proper," Smith prefers the term "viewpoint aspect."

24  Emma Pavey, *The Structure of Language: An Introduction to Grammatical Analysis* (Cambridge: Cambridge, 2010); Christopher S. Butler, *Structure and Function: A Guide to Three Major Structural-Functional Theories*, 2 vols., SLCS 63–64 (Amsterdam: Benjamins, 2003).

25  The traditional term *Aktionsart* has a complex history in Greek grammar as far back as the 1870s with work in Indo-European that conflated aspect and *Aktionsart* together into a single category, beginning with Georg Curtius's use of the term *Zeitsart* (Georg Curtius, *The Greek Verb: Its Structure and Development*, trans. Augustus S. Wilkins and Edwin B. England, 2nd ed. [London: Murray, 1883]). This adds additional difficulty for using this term, since it involves the history of Greek grammar over the past 150 years that has developed independent of mainstream linguistics.

26  These examples are taken from Van Valin, *Exploring the Syntax-Semantics Interface*, 32.

RRG adds two classes. The first is Smith's "semelfactive."[27] These are instantaneous achievements, but with no change of state. Consider the achievement, "The balloon popped." Such a predicate denotes change in the state of the balloon. However, a sentence like "The candle flickered" does not express a similar change. The candle participates in a particular state of affairs (flickering), but remains unchanged afterward. The other addition is a complex type formed from activity predicates, called "active achievements."[28] This class may be formed by taking an activity predicate and adding an endpoint. Active achievements tend to be verbs of motion, consumption, and creation as shown in 6.

6.  a. The soldiers marched in the park.     Activity
    a'. The soldiers marched to the park.    Active achievement
    b. Dana ate fish.                        Activity
    b'. Dana ate the fish.                   Active achievement
    c. Leslie painted for several hours.     Activity
    c'. Leslie painted Mary's portrait.      Active achievement

We can derive all these clauses from four features: [± static], [± dynamic], [± telic], [± punctual]. The basic division involves static and nonstatic. Van Valin states,

> [This] distinguishes verbs which code a "'happening" from those which code a "non-happening." In other words, with reference to some state of affairs, one could ask, "what happened?" or "what is happening?" If for example, a sentence like *Bob just ran out the door* could be the answer to this question, then the verb *run* is [-static]. On the other hand, a sentence like *John knows Bill well* could not be the answer to this question,

---

27  Smith, *Parameter of Aspect*, 29.
28  There is some inconsistency in the terminology here. Active achievements were previously labeled "active accomplishments," a term used as recently as Van Valin, *Exploring the Syntax-Semantics Interface*. It has since been revised to "active achievement" in Pavey (*Structure of Language*, 100–101) on the basis that the final change of state involved in the class is an instantaneous one. The examples in (6) below are taken from Van Valin, *Exploring the Syntax-Semantics Interface*, 33, but have been revised according to this shift in terminology.

because nothing is taking place. Hence, *know* is a [+static] verb.[29]

The "happening" test helps us draw a distinction between states and the other five types. That is, states do not happen; they simply exist. The other features are less dramatic, marking more nuanced contrasts between the five classes, shown in 7.[30]

7.  a. State:              [+static], [−dynamic], [−telic], [−punctual]
    b. Activity            [−static], [+dynamic], [−telic], [−punctual]
    c. Accomplishment      [−static], [−dynamic], [+telic], [−punctual]
    d. Semelfactive        [−static], [±dynamic], [−telic], [+punctual]
    e. Achievement         [−static], [−dynamic], [+telic], [+punctual]
    f. Active              [−static], [+dynamic], [+telic], [−punctual]
       achievement

All six basic predicate classes also have in addition a complex causative form.[31] Noncausatives predicates are provided below in example 8 together with their causative alternative.

8.  a. Tucker was terrified.              State
    a'. Pierre terrifies Tucker.          Causative state
    b. Dave walked around the park.       Activity
    b'. Dave walked his dog in the park.  Causative activity
    c. The door opened abruptly.          Accomplishment
    c'. Rachel opened the door slowly.    Causative accomplishment
    d. The car crashed into the barrier.  Achievement
    d'. Dave crashed the car into the     Causative achievement
        barrier.

---

29  Ibid., 33.
30  The inclusion of the feature [± dynamic] in the presentation exists entirely for the distinction of active achievements from accomplishments, which share the features [+telic] and [−punctual]. Otherwise, [± dynamic] is redundant in terms of minimal distinguishability of features (ibid.).
31  The addition of causatives to the system is unique to Role and Reference Grammar, but has potential for valuable insight. Causativity has not played a role in the discussions of predicate/*Aktionsart* classes for Ancient Greek (e.g., Fanning, *Verbal Aspect*; Olsen "Semantic and Pragmatic Model"; and Mari Napoli, *Aspect and Actionality in Homeric Greek: A Contrastive Analysis* [Milan: FrancoAngeli, 2006]).

| | |
|---|---|
| e. The soldiers marched to the park. | Active achievement |
| e'. The captain marched the soldiers to camp. | Causative active achievement |
| f. The lightning flashed in the night. | Semelfactive |
| f'. Henry flashed his headlights at another car. | Causative semelfactive |

Causativity contributes an additional argument to the syntax. This reflects an increase in the number of participants in the proposition.

Finally, central to this typology are a number of morphosyntactic tests for the classification of a predicate as a state, activity, accomplishment, achievement, semelfactive, or active achievement. These tests are an important theoretical mechanism for language description in RRG since they aim to provide language-internal criteria for the status of a given predicate. Discussion of these tests is beyond the scope of the current project, but a thorough discussion is available in the standard RRG resources as well as several works related to Ancient Greek.[32]

## 2. ASPECT, NEGATION, AND PREDICATE TYPES IN PROHIBITIONS

To the best of my knowledge, there has been no thoroughgoing analysis of prohibitions and aspect that attempts to organize the data in terms of the event-types being prohibited—much less in terms of the scope of the negation, which follows in the next section.[33] The following is a survey of my data with a variety of verbs. These are organized, first, by the aspect of the imperative and then by the classification of the predicate types. Semelfactives (instantaneous predicates that involve no change of state) are excluded, as I have

---

32  See for example: Van Valin and LaPolla, *Syntax*, 82–130; Fanning, *Verbal Aspect*, 126–97; Peter Stork, *The Aspectual Usage of the Dynamic Infinitive in Herodotus* (Groningen: Bouma's Boekhuis, 1982), 29–38; Olsen, "Semantic and Pragmatic Model," 25–58; Napoli, *Aspect and Actionality*, 32–44.

33  Fanning provides some discussion. However, he deals with predication types in relation to prohibition as secondary in his analysis.

no data for prohibitions being used with a semelfactive. I take as already established the generalization that there is a correlation between the imperfective aspect with general commands/prohibitions and the perfective aspect with specific commands/prohibitions.[34]

## 2.1 Imperfective Prohibitions

Imperfective prohibitions involve an imperfective verb in the imperative mood preceded by the negator μή. For the sake of clarity and the ability to maintain fairly concise discussions, I have separated out each of the types of predicates: states, activities, active achievements, accomplishments, and achievements. The various types of causatives represent a unique case and I discuss them as a group. When I view a given example as being a prospective instance for the meaning STOP DOING X, I translate it accordingly.[35]

### 2.1.1 State Predicates

State predicates fairly clearly allow for the STOP DOING X reading and also the regular negation readings. The latter almost invariably refer to states of affairs that may exist iteratively or habitually. Similarly, these iterative or habitual readings consistently appear in general admonition contexts.

9. Εἷς δὲ μὴ πιστευέσθω μάρτυς
   Do not believe a single witness (Jos., A.J. 4.219)

10. μὴ δὲ μερίμνα πῶς Περσῶν ἄρξεις
    Do not be concerned with how the Persians rule (Sib. Or. 5.440–1)

Here in examples 9 and 10, we see this in action. In the prohibition from Josephus, the speaker directs the audience toward regular and appropriate legal practice for the testimony of witnesses. Example 10, again is also a general prohibition, referring to the

---

34  See Fanning, *Verbal Aspect*, 325–88. I also must reiterate that *correlation* does not mean that an imperfective imperative must then necessarily be a general command/prohibition or that a perfective one must be a command/prohibition. There is, however, an important pattern that Fanning shows to be motivated by the nature of each aspect.

35  In the survey that follows, all translations are my own.

general state of concern the audience should have for how other nations rule.

With state predicates, especially, the STOP DOING X usage is particularly clear when the imperfective prohibition refers to a specific situation. Thus in example 11, Jesus speaks to his disciple, Thomas, after appearing to him in the upper room, just after Thomas questions Jesus' resurrection.

11. μὴ γίνου ἄπιστος ἀλλὰ πιστός.
Stop doubting, but believe (John 20:27).

Contextually, Thomas's already existing and currently ongoing state of doubt is widely acknowledged. Jesus seeks that it should cease now that he is physically present with them. Another good example where the already existing state is directed to end can be found in the Shepherd of Hermas in example 12.

12. ἐθαύμαζον δὲ ἐγὼ ... λέγει μοι ὁ ποιμήν· Μὴ θαύμαζε εἰ τὸ δένδρον ὑγιὲς ἔμεινε τοσούτων κλάδων κοπέντων
I was surprised ... The shepherd said to me, "Stop being surprised that the tree remained sound after so many branches were chopped off" (Herm. Sim. 8.1.5).[36]

Here again, the state of the person being spoken to in the prohibition is explicitly clear: the author is experiencing surprise at the events and the shepherd commands him to stop.[37] The past context involves a situation where the narrator (the audience of the prohibition) is already in a state of surprise as he watches the branches of the tree being chopped off.

Finally, there are also some state predicates in prohibitions that are ambiguous, exemplified in 13 and 14. Both of these clauses present prohibitions of specific states rather than general ones. However, it is not clear that the state being prohibited is one that the audience was already in. The imperfective prohibition in John 5:28 comes at a point mid-monologue for Jesus and we have no access to the experiences or feelings of his disciples. One possibility for why

---

36 A similar instance is available in T.Levi 2.9.

37 The English translation here with "stop being" might sound awkward to some with a state predicate such as "surprise," This is not a result of the Greek, but because the English progressive aspect generally avoids collocation with state predicates.

the author chose the imperfective here rather than the normal perfective used for specific commands/prohibitions would be to imply to the reader that the disciples in listening to Jesus expressed surprise at his words.

13. μὴ θαυμάζετε τοῦτο
    Do not be astonished at this (John 5:28).

14. καὶ μὴ πιστεύετε αὐτῷ, ὅτι οὐ μὴ δύνηται ὁ θεὸς παντὸς ἔθνους καὶ βασιλείας τοῦ σῶσαι τὸν λαὸν αὐτοῦ ἐκ χειρός μου καὶ ἐκ χειρὸς πατέρων μου
    And do not trust him, because no God of any nation or kingdom is able to save his people from my hand and from the hands of my ancestors (2 Chron 32:15).

Likewise, here in 14, the representative of King Sennacherib is telling the people of Jerusalem not to trust Hezekiah, but it is not definite whether or not the representative believes that the people are currently in a state of trust in Hezekiah or not. Here the linguistic choice of the imperfective prohibition over the perfective prohibition might have been made on the assumption that the people of Jerusalem did trust their king.

### 2.1.2 Activity Predicates

Recall that activity predicates are dynamic, but they lack explicit and definable endpoints. For that reason, they are not telic. They do, however, involve duration. We find similar patterns with activity predicates as we do with state predicates. General prohibitions do not appear to allow for the STOP DOING X reading. Thus in Sirach 5:9, the author is making a general prohibition against a particular behavior.

15. μὴ πορεύου ἐν πάσῃ ἀτραπῷ
    Do not walk in every direction (Sir 5:9)

16. ὀργίζεσθε καὶ μὴ ἁμαρτάνετε·
    Be angry and do not sin (Eph 4:26)

Ephesians 4:26 in example 16 likewise presents a general prohibition against a behavior. The author is not prohibiting a specific, referential act of sin, but any sin, generally.

Activity predicates, like states, also provide clear instances of the STOP DOING X usage. In example 17, Jesus walks into the house of Jairus, whose daughter had died before Jesus arrived. Everyone is in mourning, weeping for the dead girl (ἔκλαιον δὲ πάντες καὶ ἐκόπτοντο αὐτήν).

17. <u>Μὴ κλαίετε</u>, οὐ γὰρ ἀπέθανεν ἀλλὰ καθεύδει.
<u>Stop weeping</u>—she isn't dead; she's asleep (Luke 8:52).

In the midst of this scene, Jesus walks into the house and his first words are: Μὴ κλαίετε. Contextually speaking, "stop weeping" is the clear interpretation here.[38]

Similar examples exist outside the New Testament. Consider 3 Baruch 16.1 in example 18 below.

18. Τάδε λέγει κύριος· <u>Μή ἐστε σκυθρωποί</u>, καὶ <u>μὴ κλαίετε</u>, μηδὲ ἐάσατε τοὺς υἱοὺς τῶν ἀνθρώπων·
Thus says the Lord, "<u>Stop being sorrowful</u> and <u>stop weeping</u>, but also do not leave the children of humanity alone (3 Bar. 16.1).

The larger context of this prohibition involves three groups of angels coming before the archangel Michael. The third group of angels comes before him in 3 Baruch 13, wailing and weeping. They have been watching over the unrighteous of humanity who have no good in them and they beg Michael to have them given a different task (3 Bar. 13.3–5). Michael tells them to wait until he has heard from the Lord. The Lord's response then comes in 16.1 above. God commands them to cease their sorrow and weeping and he commands them not to leave the people they are watching.[39]

---

38 Huffman's (*Verbal Aspect Theory and the Prohibitions*, 141) view that the proper interpretation should be, "Do not be weeping," feels like special pleading here. The main problem with Huffman's approach is that he assumes various uses of aspect in prohibitions (stop doing/do not start, general/specific, etc.) as competing theories of aspect and imperatives rather than contextualized realizations from the interface of multiple grammatical categories. Nevertheless, his work is incredibly useful as a compendium of prohibitions in the New Testament and their possible interpretations.

39 While it is not relevant to our purpose here, the use of the perfective imperative for the third prohibition rather than the normal perfective subjunctive is striking.

Examples 17 and 18 both involve prohibitions of specific activities, but prohibitions with activity predicates in specific contexts do not inherently require the STOP DOING X usage—just as we saw with state predicates. For example, the king of Syria going to battle against Ahab, king of Israel, and Jehoshaphat, king of Judah, gives orders to his men in 3 Kingdoms 22:29 using a imperfective prohibition and activity predicate.

> 19. <u>Μὴ πολεμεῖτε</u> μικρὸν καὶ μέγαν ἀλλ᾽ ἢ τὸν βασιλέα Ισραηλ μονώτατον.
> <u>Do not engage</u> in battle with the small or great, but only the king of Israel (3 Kingdoms 22:31 / 1 Kgs 22:31).

The context demonstrates that this is a very specific prohibition, but it is also quite clear that the STOP DOING X usage is improbable here, perhaps even impossible.

*2.1.3 Accomplishment Predicates*

There are few prohibitions in the imperfective aspect that are also accomplishment predicates. Accomplishments are predicates where the event is presented by the speaker/author as a durational change of state. My data appear to involve general prohibitions rather than specific ones. Both these facts are likely a limitation of the data rather than a significant grammatical generalization. I provide two examples from the Septuagint below in 20 and 21. The first, from the Psalms, cannot be explicitly connected to a specific event or situation in the world. It appears in the context of a petition to the Lord for his judgment. The predicate κραταιούσθω is an accomplishment because becoming strong is a progressive change of state with inherent duration.

> 20. ἀνάστηθι, κύριε, <u>μὴ κραταιούσθω</u> ἄνθρωπος
> Rise up, Lord, humanity <u>must not grow strong/must stop growing strong</u> (Psa 9:20)

This example is ambiguous as to the STOP DOING X usage. It seems either would be possible contextually. The question rests upon whether the idea that humanity has already begun to grow strong is a reasonable implicature to derive from 9:19: "For the poor will not be forgotten in the end; the perseverance of the poor will not experience ruin forever."

21. Κατὰ τὰς ὁδοὺς τῶν ἐθνῶν <u>μὴ μανθάνετε</u>
According to the ways of the nations, <u>do not learn</u> (Jer 10:2).

The act of learning, here, inherently implies a durational period where knowledge is gained over time and is thus an accomplishment. The prohibition involves an implicature that communicates that there is another way of learning that the audience should be participating in. The STOP DOING X usage is not a possible interpretation of this prohibition. This prohibition appears at the beginning of a speech from the Lord through Jeremiah. The preceding context provides no interpretive cues for the audience to conclude that the people of Judah had been learning from the nations. The lack of a specific ongoing act of learning precludes the STOP DOING X usage.

### 2.1.4 Active Achievement Predicates

I noted in the introduction that active achievement predicates share similarities with activity predicates and achievement predicates. Traditionally, these sorts of predicates have been labeled accomplishments because they have both duration and an endpoint. However, their temporal structure is distinct from accomplishments. For an accomplishment, the duration and the arrival at the endpoint go hand in hand. If a person "learns math for an hour," then at any given point during that hour the person can be said to have learned math. That is, the change of state that causes the endpoint itself has inherent duration. For an active achievement, however, the change of state that causes the endpoint is presented by the speaker/author as instantaneous.[40] Thus, if a person "walks to the park," that person might walk for an hour or for five minutes and be no more in the park than he was when he began walking, but the change of state from "not in the park" to "in the park" is presented without duration. The duration only refers to the walking rather than the arrival.

---

40 Whether or not it is instantaneous in objective reality is not relevant. It only matters that it is subjectively conceived as instantaneous linguistically.

Example 22 is an active achievement in the same way. For the
person who wrote the sign, the act of writing is, itself, an activity
without an endpoint.

22. Μὴ γράφε· Ὁ βασιλεὺς τῶν Ἰουδαίων
Do not write: "The king of the Jews" (John 19:21)

Had he stopped writing half way through the sign with, "The
king of," or simply spent the entire day writing the word, "king," repeatedly, we would not be able to say that he wrote, "The King of
the Jews." However, the completed statement, since it is specific and
referential, functions as an endpoint for the proposition. In addition, this very specific command in 70 is not a good candidate for the
STOP DOING X usage because the sign's writing had already been
completed at the time of speech. The Jewish leaders had seen the
contents of the sign and at this point, it would have been incoherent
for them to command Pilate, "Stop writing, 'The king of the Jews.'"

One tendency we see with active achievement predicates in prohibitions is that they demonstrate a general preference for specific
situations rather than general ones. This is likely the result of the
fact that for transitive active achievements (usually predicates of
creation or consumption), a prerequisite is that the object is necessarily specific and referential.[41] Example 23 is one of the more complicated instances of this.

23. ἐὰν δέ τις ὑμῖν εἴπῃ· Τοῦτο ἱερόθυτόν ἐστιν, μὴ ἐσθίετε δι' ἐκεῖνον
τὸν μη νύσαντα καὶ τὴν συνείδησιν·
But if someone says to you, "This is sacrificed meat," Do not
eat [it] for the sake of the one who informed you and their
conscience (1 Cor 10:28)

On the one hand, this looks like a general prohibition. That could
suggest that the implicit object "sacrificed meat" is nonreferential.
The larger context of this clause makes two things clear. First, Paul
is establishing a *specific* hypothetical situation: "But if someone says
to you, 'This is sacrificed meat'" So in a sense we have a general command being given for a specific situation. Second, the missing object
in the prohibition itself should be treated as a definite, in terms of

41 Consider: "He wrote literature" (nonspecific, nonreferential activity) vs.
"He wrote Moby Dick" (specific, referential active achievement).

the mental representation Paul intends to create for the audience. That is to say, Paul views "it" as sufficiently referential in the discourse from the previous clause that he can drop it out and does not need to make it explicit. For that reason, the prohibition itself must be viewed as involving both activity-like duration (eating) and also an endpoint (the dropped referential object). Finally, it needs to be noted that while there are people at Corinth who have been eating food sacrificed to idols, the hypothetical situation presented here prevents this prohibition from being interpreted as an instance of the STOP DOING X usage. In fact, across my corpus of data, I have no clear examples of the STOP DOING X usage with an imperative involving a general command.

Example 24 provides an example of prohibition in a specific context with an active achievement.

24. ἐπεὶ πεφώραται πάντα ἐκεῖνα τῷ πατρί σου, <u>μὴ παραγίνου πρὸς</u>
<u>αὐτόν</u>, ἂν μή τινα πορίσῃ παρὰ τοῦ Καίσαρος δύναμις
Since all those things have been discovered by your father,
<u>do not come to him</u> [Herod], unless you can obtain some
authority from Caesar (Jos., B.J. 1.620)

Here the mother of Antipater has written a warning to her son that his father Herod the Great has discovered Antipater's plot against him and commands him not to come home. This prohibition is not a probable instance of the STOP DOING X usage because the writer of the prohibition, Antipater's mother, has no way of knowing whether he has yet begun his journey from Rome yet or not.[42]

### 2.1.5 Achievement Predicates

Recall that achievements are predicates that refer to changes of state that the speaker/author wants to present as instantaneous. Standard English examples are predicates like *shatter* or *pop*, where the duration is so quick that it is linguistically practical to refer to these situations as instantaneous. Other types are achievement predicates that involve a speaker conceiving of an event as the arrival at a terminal point or the crossing of a boundary. These event

---

42  If anything, it is probable that the clause assumes that Antipater is still in Rome, considering the difficulty of delivering a letter to a person in the midst of travel from Rome to Palestine.

conceptualizations may also be blended together in some manner. In Luke 21:21, a specific situation, we find that entering a city combines the boundary crossing and terminal point conceptualizations together in example 25.

> 25. οἱ ἐν ταῖς χώραις <u>μὴ εἰσερχέσθωσαν</u> εἰς αὐτήν
> Those in the fields <u>must not enter</u> into it [the city]
> (Luke 21:21).

The use of the imperfective aspect could perhaps refer to ongoing unavailability of Jerusalem to those in the fields. The STOP DOING X usage is not an available reading here. Nor is it possible with the general prohibition in example 26.

> 26. γονέωνἀγαθῶν, ὁ δὲ μὴ μέλλων ἄγεσθαι παρθένον <u>μὴ ζευγνύσθω</u>
> συνοικοῦσαν ἄλλῳ νοθεύσας μηδὲ λυπῶν τὸν πρότερον
> αὐτῆς ἄνδρα·
> <u>Do not</u> let a man who does not intend to marry a virgin <u>join together</u> with a woman living with another man, corrupting her and grieving her former husband. (Jos., A.J. 4.244)

The context of this prohibition involves Josephus's summation of the Jewish law in his history of the Jewish people. The achievement predicate "join together" conceptualized the event of sexual relations as instantaneous.[43]

My final example of a prohibition with an achievement predicate is, perhaps, the most notable. Here in example 27 is an instance of the STOP DOING X usage with a predicate that inherently lacks duration. Both the textual context and the cultural context make it clear that Peter, to whom this prohibition is directed, has been calling these foods unclean. Indeed, the entire point of the discourse here in Acts 10 is the cessation of a particular behavior that alienates gentiles from the gospel.

---

43  Note, also, that examples like this demonstrate that predicate types (*Aktionsart*) do not objectively refer to the external nonlinguistic world. Rather the speaker/author presents a conceptualization of an event with duration as if it were instantaneous. The verb ζεύγνυμι cannot be used to express duration.

27. Ἃ ὁ θεὸς ἐκαθάρισεν, σὺ <u>μὴ κοίνου</u>.

What God has made clean, you <u>must stop calling unclean</u> (Acts 10:15).[44]

This example is important because it demonstrates that the STOP DOING X usage and its association with imperfective aspect is not also constrained by predicate types that inherently express duration. Here rather than involving the cessation/prohibition of an event/action in progress, the imperfective aspect functions to signal habituality.

### 2.1.6 Causative Predicates

Causative predicate types are not entirely distinct from the others, since they are a complex type. There are causative states, causative activities, causative accomplishments, causative active achievements, and causative achievements. Each normal type has a causative alternative. Some are more difficult to test for, especially in a corpus. For example, the difference between a causative state and causative accomplishment is subtle, as in example 28.

28. <u>μὴ παροργίζετε</u> τὰ τέκνα

<u>Do not make</u> your children <u>angry</u> (Eph 6:4)

Is this clause best interpreted as a causative state (cause your children to be angry) or a causative accomplishment (cause your children to become angry). The English rendering above might suggest the causative accomplishment view, but the related noun (παροργισμός) is clearly a state. Deciding between causative state and causative accomplishment would hinge upon the nature of the derivational morpheme -ίζω together with the types of words it forms into causative verbs.[45] Moreover, the author of Ephesians is not prohibiting making one's children angry while implying

---

44  See also Acts 11:9. Arguably, this predicate could be treated as a state. BDAG provides the gloss, "consider/declare (ritually) unclean" (552), which is a difficult glossing to account for semantically—declaration being a fundamentally different type of situation than consideration in terms of the elaboration of events. Making a decision based on the various occurrences in the corpus is practically impossible.

45  Unfortunately, to the best of my knowledge, there is no comprehensive study of Greek causative derivational morphology.

that making someone else's children angry is perfectly acceptable. Rather he is simply making an absolute prohibition about anger and one's children.

Example 29 is a clear causative state (cause X to have Y) from the Apostolic Fathers.

> 29. μὴ ἀφορμὰς <u>δίδοτε</u> τοῖς ἔθνεσιν
> <u>Do not give</u> any opportunity to the pagans (Ign. *Trall.* 8.2)

Here the speaker prohibits the audience from being the agent who causes a transference of opportunity, such that the pagans (τοῖς ἔθνεσιν) have opportunity. The context is a general one and does not refer to a specific situation to prohibit. Instead, Ignatius is warning against certain behaviors that would give cause for non-Christians to blaspheme God.

Finally, in example 30, we have an instance of a prohibition with a causative activity predicate.

> 30. Ἄρατε ταῦτα ἐντεῦθεν, <u>μὴ ποιεῖτε</u> τὸν οἶκον τοῦ πατρός μου οἶκον ἐμπορίου.
> Get rid of these things! <u>Do not make/Stop making</u> my father's house a marketplace! (John 2:16)

This instance is a potential use of the STOP DOING X usage. Arguably, the rendering "do not make" does not make sense because the people had already done that. The temple court was already in use as a marketplace; Jesus is demanding the cessation of that situation. If this interpretation is the correct one, it is evidence of the STOP DOING X usage with causative predicates. It also functions as further evidence of the correlation between the STOP DOING X usage and prohibitions that refer to specific situations—the opposite of what is expected for imperfective imperatives.

### 2.1.7 *Preliminary Observations*

Before moving on to how perfective prohibitions interact with predicate types, it might be worthwhile here to briefly recap the patterns encountered above. We can distinguish two generalizations for imperfective prohibitions: one for predicate types and one for the general vs. specific distinction. In terms of predicate types, there seems to be a correlation between the STOP DOING X usage and predicate types involving duration. Any of the predicate types can be used with the STOP DOING X usage, but achievements only do so in contexts that involve habitual or iterative events. This should not be surprising considering the natural relationship between the imperfective aspect and temporal duration. For the distinction between general vs. specific commands, the STOP DOING X usage consistently patterns with specific prohibitions. This is notable in as much as the normal expectation is for imperfective aspect to correlate with general commands/prohibitions. In the final summary of the predicate types below, we will discuss both these patterns in more detail and attempt to provide some explanation for what we are seeing in the data.

## 2.2 Perfective Prohibitions

Prohibitions in the perfective aspect diverge from the imperfective in that the normal expectation is for the mood to be subjunctive rather than imperative. Beyond that the pattern is similar with the negator μή being used for the prohibition. The scope of the negation is still contextually determined rather than morphosyntactically marked. As before the data is organized by predicate type, beginning with states.

One thing that becomes apparent rather quickly, both with state predicates and the others that follow is that it is far more difficult to distinguish contexts where the perfective prohibition's DO NOT START X usage is the probable function. There is much less semantic distinction between DO NOT DO X and DO NOT START X. This arises from the fact that the latter falls within the domain of the former. In contexts where the prohibited situation has not been initiated, DO NOT DO X subsumes DO NOT START X. Nevertheless, there are some generalizations that we can make and many of them are closely tied to the semantics of particular types of predicates.

### 2.2.1 State Predicates

State predicates, lacking both dynamicity and change in their semantic content, do not lend themselves to agent initiation, since initiation inherently implies change, if not also dynamicity. The prohibition of a state is more likely to have absolute connotations: STATE

X IS PROHIBITED. Example 31 provides an instance of this in a context with a specific prohibition.

> 31. καὶ <u>μὴ θαυμάσῃς</u> εἰ δύναται μιμητὴς ἄνθρωπος γενέσθαι θεοῦ
> And <u>do not be surprised</u> when a person is able to become an imitator of God (Diogn. 10.4)

Here, the prohibition is specific because it functions within a metacomment on the actual discourse on faith and imitating God. Still, the same applies to general prohibitions as well, as with the prohibition in Luke 12:11.

> 32. ὅταν δὲ εἰσφέρωσιν ὑμᾶς ἐπὶτὰς συναγωγὰς καὶ τὰς ἀρχὰς καὶ τὰς ἐξουσίας, <u>μὴ μεριμνήσητε</u> πῶς ἢ τί ἀπολογήσησθε ἢ τί εἴπητε·
> When they bring you before the synagogues, the rulers, and the authorities, <u>do not be anxious</u> about how you should defend yourselves or what you should say (Luke 12:11).

As before, the static nature of the predicate does not fit well with the dynamicity of the DO NOT START X conceptualization. These two instances are representative for the rest of the corpus.

### 2.2.2 Activity Predicates

Activity predicates, being dynamic, fit better with the DO NOT START X conceptualization. However, unlike the STOP DOING X usage for imperfective prohibitions, it is difficult to refer to an explicit usage, since usually a simpler DO NOT DO X conceptualization also fits sufficiently well. For example, in Jeremiah 42:7 either understanding is feasible. A command to not start building houses or sowing seeds fits well with the larger context in which the Rechabites are explaining to Jeremiah that their ancestor Jonadab had commanded them to maintain a nomadic lifestyle.

> 33. καὶ οἰκίαν οὐ <u>μὴ οἰκοδομήσητε</u> καὶ σπέρμα οὐ <u>μὴ σπείρητε</u>
> And you <u>must not start building</u> houses and you <u>must not start sowing</u> seed (Jer 42:7).

On the other hand, we see easily that "do not start building" and "do not start sowing" could easily be replaced "do not build" and "do not sow." Granted, distinguishing English translations is not an adequate criterion for deciding, but that is the central problem.

No definitive language internal criterion seems to present itself within the data.

Nevertheless, one hypothesis worth testing involves the perfective prohibitions relationship to general and specific commands. I noted previously in the discussion of imperfective prohibitions that there is a clear tendency for the STOP DOING X usage to prefer specific rather than general situations. The opposite might be at play here, too. Normally, we expect a perfective for specific commands/prohibitions. Perhaps one motivation for choosing a perfective verb in a nonspecific or general prohibition would be in order to take advantage of the DO NOT START X conceptualization. Of course, this does not mean that perfective prohibitions involving specific circumstances cannot also involve the DO NOT START X conceptualization.

Other occurrences that also fit this pattern are provided in examples 34 and 35.

34. μὴ πορευθῇς ταῖς ὁδοῖς τῆς ἀδικίας
    Do not walk in the way of the unrighteous (Tob 4:5)

35. μὴ φάγῃς πᾶν ἀκάθαρτον
    Do not eat anything unclean (Judg 13:4).

Each of these prohibitions fits with the DO NOT START X conceptualization, at least, with the caveats already stated and the limits of our ability to draw firm conclusions. Both clauses involve a contrast between an explicit prohibited action and an implicit encouraged one: Where one walks (the path of the righteous vs. unrighteous) and what one eats (clean vs. unclean). Still, despite that contrast, the prohibited place for walking and the prohibited kind of eating are nonspecific and nonreferential. The prohibitions are general in their nature with the specifics established elsewhere in the texts.

### 2.2.3 Accomplishment Predicates

Perfective prohibitions of accomplishment predicates are difficult to find in my corpus. The following is the only defendable example I have been able to find.

36. Ἐὰν δὲ καὶ ἐκκακῶν τις πλουτίσῃ, ὡς Ἡσαῦ ὁ πατράδελφός μου,
<u>μὴ ζηλώσητε</u>
And though a man become rich by evil means, even as Esau,
the brother of my father, <u>do not become jealous</u> (T.Gad 7.4).

The problem here is that it isn't clear whether the preferred
rendering should be a state (do not be jealous) or an accomplishment (do not become/grow jealous). Contextually, the situation involves watching another person grow more and more wealthy by
evil means and for this reason, I lean toward the accomplishment
reading, where jealousy is presented as a change of state with duration parallel to the durational change of state implicit in becoming
wealthy. Like the activity predicates above, the DO NOT START X
conceptualization is at least plausible here, but again, there is no
sufficient means of demonstrating it conclusively.

### 2.2.4 Achievement Predicates

Achievement predicates, those that conceptualize an event as an instantaneous change of state, appear in abundance. Because achievement predicates inherently lack duration and the perfective aspect
cannot be used to convey iterative semantics, achievements do not
collocate well with the DO NOT START X conceptualization. Thus,
the prohibition against murder in example 37 is quite unlikely to
have the meaning "do not start murdering."

37. Μὴ φονεύσῃς
Do not murder (Mark 10:19).

On the other hand, Headlam's explicit formulation of the generalization technically is not grounded in event initiation (which implies duration), but rather the prohibition of a future or prospective
event, in his own words, "When the meaning is *Beware of doing this
in future time*, and this meaning is to be conveyed by the verb alone,
then μή must be followed by the aorist subjunctive."[46] The question
is whether or not a clause like Mark 10:19 is referring to the prohibition of a prospective event or the prohibition of an event absolutely:
"Do not do this at all."

---

46  Headlam, "Greek Prohibitions," 31.

Example 38 perhaps makes more sense in terms of the prospective prohibition reading.

38. μὴ λάβῃς γυναῖκα ἀλλοτρίαν
Do not take a foreign wife (Tob 4:12).

Here, the prohibited event can conceivably be conceptualized as prospective. Tobias is about to begin a search for a wife among his relatives. Tobit, his father, warns him with a perfective prohibition not to take a wife who is a foreigner. Examples like this one are important for the question above regarding absolute prohibitions vs. the prohibition of a prospective event for example (37). While Mark 10:19 could be argued to be ambiguous, Tobit 4:12 is much more clearly prospective in nature since the recipient of the prohibition has never married. Regardless of whether we take the more contemporary DO NOT START X phrasing or Headlam's prospective prohibition, it is of note that the examples above are instances of perfective prohibitions in nonspecific/general contexts, where we would normally expect an imperfective prohibition.[47]

### 2.2.5 Active Achievement Predicates

Active achievement predicates have duration followed by an instantaneous change of state. These are often verbs of motion to an endpoint or verbs of production or consumption. Because they involve duration, the DO NOT START X conceptualization is a feasible reading of the text.

39. μὴ ἐπέλθῃς ἐκεῖ, ἔκκλινον δὲ ἀπ᾽ αὐτῶν καὶ παράλλαξον.
Do not go there, instead turn away from them and pass by (Prov 4:15)

40. μὴ προσέλθῃς αὐτῷ ἐν καρδίᾳ δισσῇ
Do not come to him with a divided heart (Sir 1:28).

Examples 39 and 40 each involve situations where the speaker of the prohibition wants the audience to refrain from doing something

---

47 To reiterate my position stated at the beginning of this section (Aspect, Negation, and Predicate Types in Prohibitions), I take the generalization for aspect and imperatives involving general (imperfective) and specific (perfective) commands as already shown in Fanning, *Verbal Aspect*, 325–88.

that has not yet taken place, paralleling what we have seen with the rest of the dynamic predicate types thus far. In each case, the speaker is not prohibiting the entire clause, but only a portion of it. Proverbs 4:15 evokes the image of two alternative paths at a fork in the road (cf. 4:14): one for the wicked and one for the righteous (4:18). Likewise, Sirach 1:28 implies a contrast between a united and a divided heart and prohibits the latter.

### 2.2.6 Causative Predicates

Finally, with causative predicates we find much of the same for perfective prohibitions. Causatives behave like other dynamic predicates rather than like states. Unfortunately, the data I have for causative predicates fails to suggest any kind of meaningful criteria for distinguishing the DO NOT START X conceptualization from a simple prohibition. There is little difference in usage with causatives compared to the above predicate types. A couple of illustrative examples are provided in 41 and 42. The first, from Acts of Pilate 15:5, is situated in a context where the priests are questioning Joseph of Arimathea about the disappearance of Jesus' body from the tomb where Joseph had buried him.

> 41. καὶ σὺ οὖν <u>μὴ κρύψῃς</u> ἀφ' ἡμῶν ἕως ῥήματος.
> And you, therefore, <u>do not hide</u> so much as a word from us (Acts Pil. 15:5).

The purpose of the prohibition is to dissuade Joseph from lying to them. Contextually, the DO NOT START X meaning fits here since, at the beginning of the interrogation, the speakers are prohibiting the initiation of hiding information—any and all information. Example 42 differs in that the prohibition is limited to a particular constituent of the clause rather than the clause—the beginning of the clause and also the larger context intimates that those who do obey can be led into Jerusalem. Nevertheless, the DO NOT START X meaning still fits rather well.

> 42. τοὺς δὲ μὴ ἀκούοντάς σου, <u>μὴ εἰσαγάγῃς αὐτοὺς</u> ἐκεῖ [=εἰς Ἰερουσαλήμ].
> Those who do not obey you, <u>do not lead them</u> there [=into Jerusalem] (4 Bar. 8.3).

Example 42 fits well the DO NOT START X conceptualization within the broader definition involving some form of future reference, since the initiation of leading people, whether spouses who follow the Lord or spouses who do not, has not yet begun. The commands/prohibitions here about whom to lead come before the beginning of the event.

## 2.3 Summary

The above survey of imperfective and perfective data for predicate types demonstrates patterns. For the imperfective aspect, we noted two generalizations: one related to predicate types and one related to the specific prohibitions. First, while all predicate types allow for the STOP DOING X usage, achievements only do so in contexts that involve habitual or iterative events. We can account for this by observing that the STOP DOING X usage is tied to the incomplete and durational character of the imperfective aspect. In turn, when the usage is realized with a predicate type that inherently lacks duration, such as achievements, the aspect must contribute the entire durational character by itself. The combination of achievement predicate semantics in conjunction with the imperfective aspect causes a given clause to be realized in terms of an instantaneous event that repeatedly takes place (e.g., "What God has made clean, you must stop calling unclean").

Second, the STOP DOING X usage shows a consistent tendency to appear in prohibitions that are contextually specific situations, where the prohibition was not universal or generic in its scope, but instead had a distinct referent. Referentiality is the linguistic category that grounds the general versus specific generalization for prohibitions. A general prohibition is nonreferential; no individual event or situation functions as the reference for the prohibition. A specific prohibition is necessarily a referential prohibition because it points to a particular instance of something that should be prohibited. My data falls in line with Fanning's observation that the imperfective aspect is normally the preferred aspect for nonreferential prohibitions (i.e., general prohibitions).[48] At the same time, my data show that the STOP DOING X usage is more likely to appear in referential prohibitions.[49] This is striking, but not unexpected, since commanding a person to cease something implies specific knowledge of that individual's actions and behavior. I would suggest a speaker's desire to use the STOP DOING X usage is one motivation for deviating from the expected perfective subjunctive for a referential/specific prohibition and using an imperfective imperative instead.

Prohibitions with the perfective aspect exhibit fewer clear-cut distinctions. This is because, as I noted a few times above, it is extremely difficult to distinguish between a simple prohibition (DO NOT DO X) and the proposed DO NOT START X construction. Still, it was clear in my data that the DO NOT START X meaning does not collocate with state predicates, likely as a result of the nondynamic nature of states. Further, I explored the possibility above that the DO NOT START X conceptualization seemed more common in contexts that were nonreferential. If this is true—and it does appear the case in my data—then the DO NOT START X conceptualization is, in a sense, a contextual motivation for a speaker to select a perfective subjunctive to express a general prohibition in the same way that the STOP DOING X usage is for specific prohibitions in the imperfective aspect.

## 3. LAYERS OF SCOPE AND NEGATION

In a simple and practical sense, negation scope is simply asking the question, "What portion of a clause is being negated?" My goal here is to provide some elaboration of how negation works in

---

48 The observation itself is actually much older than Fanning's work, but his *Verbal Aspect* is a useful reference because of its breadth and detail of discussion, dedicating an entire chapter to the topic of the use of aspect in commands and prohibitions. Equally important, however, is his survey of the relationship between reference and aspect in general without reference to the particular issues of commands and prohibitions (*Verbal Aspect*, 179–85).

49 In fact, the only instance I have of the STOP DOING X usage with a general or nonreferential prohibition is from the Psalms, which could be argued to also be specific for its original context and purpose.

conjunction with the generalizations I have noted in the analysis above. Essentially, this is a descriptive account of the interface between aspect, negation, and command-type illocutionary force that results in the creation of prohibitions.[50] The structure of the description here is organized on the basis of the degree of grammaticalization. Aspect and mood, being marked in the verb morphology, are the most grammaticalized categories and so I use them together as the primary point of organization.

Recall from the introduction that the grammatical categories tend to have scope over one of three layers of the clause, the clausal proposition, the core predication, and the nuclear predicate. The diagram of these three layers is presented again below in figure 2.

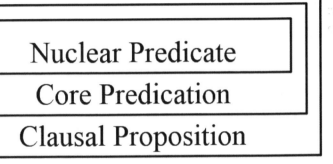

Figure 2. Layered Structure of the Clause

Aspect has scope over the nuclear predicate only, but negation might have scope over any of these layers. However, the aspect of the prohibition also influences which layers of scope are possible for negation. With the imperfective prohibitions (imperfective with the imperative), negation may have scope over any of these three layers of the clause, but with perfective prohibitions, only the clausal proposition and the core predication seem to be possible options for the scope of the negating element (μή for the imperative and subjunctive moods).

---

50  My research here functions as a small piece of a larger effort to work toward a full-scale descriptive reference grammar of New Testament and Koine Greek oriented toward linguists and translators.

In this section, I make two important claims. First, the STOP DOING X usage is inherently tied to the scope of negation for imperfective prohibitions. This relationship is derived from the nature of semantic scope for both aspect and negation. Secondly, the DO NOT START X conceptualization cannot be correlated with any particular layer of negation scope. This is significant because, despite the fact that the phenomena of aspect in prohibitions seem parallel, it demonstrates that the STOP DOING X and DO NOT START X are fundamentally distinct in their motivation and realization.

## 3.1 Imperfective Aspect with the Imperative Mood

In imperfective prohibitions when the negation has scope over the entire clausal proposition, the whole clause, including its arguments and its adjuncts, is negated. Such prohibitions have a tendency to be absolute in nature, as in example 43, which cannot mean that it is perfectly acceptable for the audience to make other people's children angry. The scope of the negator encompasses the entire clause.

43. μὴ παροργίζετε τὰ τέκνα
Do not make your children angry (Eph 6:4)

44. καὶ ἐάν τις ἐπαινῇ ὑμᾶς ὡς ἀγαθούς, <u>μὴ ἐπαίρεσθε, μηδὲ</u>
<u>μεταβάλλεσθε</u>, μήτε εἰς τέρψιν, μήτε εἰς ἀηδίαν.
And if anyone praises you as good, <u>do not be proud [lit.</u>
<u>lifted up]</u> and <u>do not be affected</u>, either to delight or disgust
(T.Dan 4.3).

The same is true in example 44 from the pseudepigraphical Testament of the Twelve Patriarchs. Here we have Dan, the son of Jacob and Bilhah exhorting his family not to be proud or affected by other people's words. Again the negation covers the entire proposition. The two prepositional phrases μήτε εἰς τέρψιν, μήτε εἰς ἀηδίαν establish the comprehensive scope of the prohibition.

The conceptualization of clausal scope negation with the imperfective aspect is represented in Figure 3 below. The largest circle denotes clausal proposition scope, the middle circle refers to core predication scope where constituents like subject and object arguments reside, and the smallest circle to nuclear predicate scope, which is limited to the predicate itself. The bidirectional arrow refers to the imperfective aspect, signifying the unboundedness of its internal temporal structure.

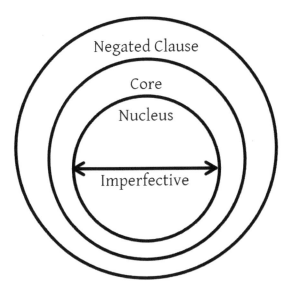

Figure 3. Negation with Scope over the Clausal Proposition (Imperfective)

The two examples above, 43 and 44, both involve this type of scope. The negation encompasses the entirety of the clause. The entire clause is affected: the event, its internal temporal structure, and also the participants. The negation is absolute and comprehensive in nature.

We have also seen instances of negation where the scope is limited to a smaller portion of the clause, such as when an event is negated only with reference to particular participant rather than absolutely. A good example of this was observed in our discussion of imperfective prohibitions with state predicates, provided again below in example 45.

45. Εἷς δὲ μὴ πιστευέσθω μάρτυς
    Do not believe a single witness (Jos., A.J. 4.219)

The negation in this clause only has scope over the number of witnesses to be believed. The speaker/writer does not want to prohibit belief itself—there are others who should still be believed. The larger context involves Josephus describing the legal requirements for witnesses in order to establish a sufficient burden of proof. A single witness is insufficient as a burden of proof. Multiple separate witnesses are viewed as and assumed to be a more reliable guide for determining the facts than a single witness alone would.

There is a similar instance of negation scope in 2 Clement, which I provide in example 46.

46. μὴ φοβεῖσθε <u>τοὺς ἀποκτέννοντας ὑμᾶς καὶ μηδὲν ὑμῖν</u>
<u>δυναμένους ποιεῖν</u>
Do <u>not</u> fear <u>those who kill you and can do nothing else</u>
(2 Clem. 5.4).

Here we have a command from Jesus to Peter from an unknown source.[51] Jesus is exhorting Peter to be more concerned about spiritual death than physical death. Do not fear those who can only kill, but rather fear the one who "has power to cast both soul and body into fiery hell." Here again the purpose of the negation is not to prohibit fearing absolutely, but to prohibit fearing of a particular and specific participant. This narrows the scope of the negation from the clause to the core, as in Figure 4 below.

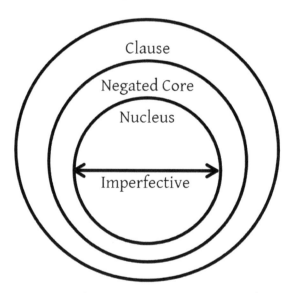

Figure 4. Negation with Scope over the Core Predicate (Imperfective)

---

51   See Holmes, *Apostolic Fathers*, 112 n. 9. This particular saying has a parallel in Matt 10:28.

With core negation, the proposition itself remains intact since the negation pertains only to an argument rather than the verb. At least this is the normal account for indicative clauses (i.e., "John didn't bring pizza; he brought soup" means the event of bringing still happened). Because prohibitions are nonindicative, the relationship between negation and the proposition is more complicated. Commands and prohibitions involve situations that are desired by the speaker/writer that may or may not exist. They project a particular declarative state of affairs onto their recipient. If Rachel were to say to John, "Do not bring pizza; bring soup," then Rachel's desired expectation is that when John arrives at the door with soup, he could say, "I brought soup, not pizza." The scope of core negation with nonindicative clauses places an expectation on the desired event, such that the predication still takes place but with different participants.

In the case of example 45 above, belief itself is not prohibited. The audience of the prohibition is still completely free to believe witnesses. The question is how many there are. The prohibition projects a state of affairs where "I do not believe just one witness" would be true. Similarly, in example 46, the speaker of the prohibition is not concerned with people being afraid, but that their fear has the proper source. In both cases, significant portions of the proposition that is desired by the speaker/writer are left intact and are not affected by the negation.

Finally, I propose that negation with scope solely over the nuclear predicate provides the best explanation for the existence of the STOP DOING X usage. I would go so far as to argue that *both* the nature of scope for negation and the nature of scope of the imperfective aspect work together to communicate the STOP DOING X usage. Recall from the introductory discussion of scope that aspect as a grammatical category only has scope over the nuclear predicate. It does not have scope over the individual arguments or other peripheral constituents of the clause. Thus in our example clause, repeated here as example 47, whether the perfective aspect is used or the progressive aspect is used, the participants (the speaker "I" and "some water") are unaffected by the temporal structure.

47. a. I <u>was pouring</u> some water (progressive)
    b. I <u>poured</u> some water (perfective).

Regardless of the aspect chosen, the basic event and its proposition remain. Each sentence (a) and (b) entails the other.[52] Now, the difference between a perfective aspect, on the one hand, and a progressive (English) or imperfective (Greek) aspect on the other is dependent upon the internal temporal structure presented by the speaker. By presenting an event as incomplete or in progress, it then becomes at least possible to end the event part way through without full completion. It appears that Greek takes advantage of this fact for the expression of a particular contextualized meaning by means of a combination of aspect, negation, and modality. Fundamentally, then, in a clause such as example 48, it is the temporal structure of the aspect that is being negated. The speaker has "παράτασις, duration, continuation in mind" and desires its cessation.[53] When this is the context for a sentence, each of these three elements has a grammatical corollary: duration/continuation (imperfective aspect), desire (modality, i.e., imperative), and cessation (negation). Bringing these three together creates a semantic expression that is more than merely the sum total of its constituent parts.

48. μὴ γίνου ἄπιστος ἀλλὰ πιστός.
Stop doubting, but believe (John 20:27).

The context of this clause provides clarity that the STOP DOING X usage is the correct interpretation. Thomas had heard from the other disciples that Jesus was alive and had appeared to them, rejecting the idea with grand declarations. Then Jesus appears before Thomas in 20:26 and commands him to stop doubting here in 20:27. The duration of Thomas's doubt is at the forefront of Jesus' mind and he commands its cessation. Effectively, what we have with the STOP DOING X usage in terms of negation scope is something that perhaps looks like Figure 5 below.

---

52  At least, this is true for these two particular sentences. Entailment and aspect may be a more complicated affair in other situations, particularly when telicity is involved—which is not the case here with this particular sentence pair. For a full discussion of aspect and entailment, see Olga Borik and Tanya Reinhart, "Telicity and Perfectivity: Two Independent Systems," in *Proceedings of LOLA 8 (Symposium on Logic and Language)*, ed. László Hunyadi, György Rákosi, and Enikő Tóth (Debrecen, Hungary, 2004), 13–34.

53  To adopt a turn of phrase from J. P. Louw, "On Greek Prohibitions," *Acta Classica* 2 (1959), 46.

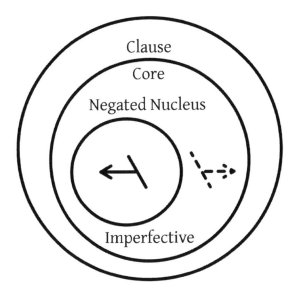

Figure 5. Negation with Scope of the Nuclear Predicate (Imperfective)

In this diagram, the negation is narrowed to the internal temporal structure of the nuclear predicate. The imperfective aspect is necessary for the STOP DOING X usage because the alternative choice, the perfective, lacks internal temporal structure entirely in its conceptualization.[54] The imperfective aspect is a necessary element for the negation scope.

Another striking example is 1 Timothy 5:23 below in example 49. Clauses where the negator is μηκέτι rather than merely μή are particularly helpful in seeing the pattern.

49. μηκέτι ὑδροπότει, ἀλλὰ οἴνῳ ὀλίγῳ χρῶ διὰ τὸν στόμαχον καὶ τὰς πυκνάς σου ἀσθενείας

End your sobriety, instead use a little wine for your stomach and your frequent health issues (1 Tim 5:23).

Other discussions of prohibitions, such as those of Huffman or Boyer,[55] have difficulty with 1 Timothy 5:23 as a candidate for meaning STOP DOING X because of the verb ὑδροπότει, typically glossed

---

54 Perfect imperatives notwithstanding.
55 Huffman, *Verbal Aspect Theory*, 158; James L. Boyer, "A Classification of Imperatives: A Statistical Study," *GTJ* 8 (1987) 35-54.

as "drink water." The argument goes that it is absurd for Paul to command Timothy to stop drinking water. However, this difficulty feels contrived and results from an insufficient understanding of compounding and the resulting semantics. Like most constructional processes, compounding tends to result in a final meaning that is more than the sum of its parts.[56] For this particular verb, the incorporation of the noun ὕδωρ into the verb πίνω creates a meaning more specific than "drink water," which an examination of other occurrences bears out. This verb is nearly always used in contexts that explicitly contrast with the drinking of alcohol.[57] Sobriety is an emergent semantic property that arises from the combination of these two disparate lexical elements in conjunction with the shared knowledge of the world.[58] Fundamentally, this verb seems to be less

---

56  The seminal article demonstrating this fact is Charles J. Fillmore, Paul Kay, and Mary Catherine O'Connor, "Regularity and Idiomaticity in Grammatical Constructions: The Case of Let Alone," *Language* 64 (1988): 501–538. More recently, see for an introductory overview of the nature of constructions: Adele E. Goldberg, *Constructions at Work: The Nature of Generalization in Language*, Oxford Linguistics (Oxford: Oxford University Press, 2006).

57  These include: Hdt., *Hist.* 1.71.3, Luc. *Bis acc.* 16, Dan 1:12 LXX; Plato, *Resp.* 561c; Plut., *Para.* 19, and Xen., *Cyr.* 6.2.26. The last of these is the most striking for determining the meaning of this compound verb. What is notable about this instance of the verb is that is appears in contrast not only with the drinking of wine, but also in contrast with the transitive verb πίνω with the accusative object ὕδωρ:

"As for wine, everyone should bring only enough to last until we can grow accustomed to sobriety (ὑδροποτεῖν). For most of the journey, wine will be unavailable. Even if we take a large quantity, all the wine we can carry will be insufficient. To avoid falling ill when we suddenly find ourselves out of wine, this is what we must do: we must immediately begin to drink water (πίνειν ὕδωρ) at our meals, for by so doing we shall not greatly change our manner of living" (Xen., *Cyr.* 6.2.26–27).

The thrust of the speaker's argument is that they should start drinking water (πίνειν ὕδωρ) at meals now in order to slowly transition away from wine so that when they are forced to be sober (ὑδροποτεῖν), they will not need to endure miserable withdrawal symptoms.

Finally, there are two instances in the verb that appear merely in highly ascetic contexts are: Luc., *Macr.* 5 and App., *Pun.* 11. While neither of these contrast explicitly with the drinking of alcohol, the sobriety sense still fits.

58  On emergence, embodiment and their importance to cognitive science, see Raymond J. Gibbs, *Embodiment and Cognitive Science* (Cambridge: Cambridge University Press, 2006); Francisco J. Varela, Evan Thompson, and Eleanor Rosch, *The Embodied Mind: Cognitive Science and Human Experience* (Cambridge, MA: MIT Press, 1991).

about literal drinking of water and more a euphemistic means of referring to alcoholic sobriety. In that context, Paul's command to Timothy makes the most sense as an instance of the STOP DOING X usage. Timothy has been abstaining from alcohol and Paul wants him to stop for health reasons.

The cognitive and grammatical processes involved in the formation of the verb ὑδροπότει are precisely parallel to those involved in the formation of the STOP DOING X usage. As I have already stated, nuclear scope negation does not happen in Greek independent of a particular aspect, a particular mood, and a particular mental representation on part of the speaker—he has an ongoing event in mind and desires its cessation.[59] This mental representation, in turn, functions to provide explanation for an additional fact that I find in my data: the STOP DOING X usage only appears with specific, referential events. It does not appear possible to use the construction with general, nonreferential contexts. This makes sense logically. One wonders how someone would stop doing something nonreferentially.[60]

## 3.2 Perfective Aspect with the Subjunctive Mood

The perfective aspect's relationship to negation scope is dramatically simpler. Unlike the imperfective aspect and the STOP DOING X usage, there is no clear correlation between negation scope and the perfective aspect's DO NOT START X expression. It appears that for the perfective aspect negation in Greek functions much the same as it does in English—clause scope negation and core scope negation are possible options, but nuclear scope negation is only possible with derivational morphology—the α-privative prefix, for

---

59 It is an open question in my mind as to whether or not the imperative mood is a necessary element of the construction or whether it is possible for nuclear scope negation to arise solely with a negator and the imperfective. In such a situation, the cessation of the event would not be a command/prohibition, but a statement of fact. In theory, such a construction might appear with a past imperfective indic. verb that still functions in the narrative as a foregrounded event in the storyline rather than as background context. As a construction, this seems plausible, but I have not searched the data.

60 On the other hand, logic has never stopped language from doing fascinating things before. The fact that this construction is tied to an irrealis modality makes the question of referentiality more flexible.

example.[61] This not surprising given the lack of temporal structure of the Greek perfective aspect.

Independent of the possibility of nuclear scope negation with perfective imperatives in Greek, the evidence is against the DO NOT START X meaning from involving such negation. Consider the following examples.

50. μὴ διαβιβάσῃς ἡμᾶς τὸν Ιορδάνην.
    Do not make us cross over the Jordan (Num 32:5)

Example 50 here and example 51 diverge from one another in their negation scope. Example 50 involves a situation where the negation has scope over the entire clause. The speakers of the prohibition are the people of the Israelite tribes of Gad and Reuben. They do not want to cross over the Jordan because they find the land of the western bank to be better for their way of life. The scope of μὴ falls over the entire clause because the speakers want to prohibit the entire proposition. While it is possible that they would find other river crossings to be acceptable, there is not an alternative river within the context that they could cross instead. Without a contextual contrast, the necessary interpretation is that the entire clause is being negated, both the verb and its arguments.[62] We can represent clausal negation scope with perfective prohibitions with Figure 6 below.

61  It deserves to be emphasized at this point that is not uncommon for individual aspects to interact with imperatives in general and prohibitions in particular in different ways. Some languages do not allow the perfective aspect to be used with prohibitions at all—constraining aspect and negation in a much more extreme manner than what we seen in Greek. See, for example, John Forsyth, *A Grammar of Aspect: Usage and Meaning in the Russian Verb*, Studies in the Modern Russian Language, Extra Volume (Cambridge: Cambridge University Press, 1970).

62  One could argue that there could be a contrast between the tribes of Gad and Reuben and the other ten that would convey narrow scope negation. If that were the case, however, we would see the speakers' position of the pronominal constituent ἡμᾶς in a syntactic position in front of the verb in order to mark it as contrastive rather than in its default postverbal position.

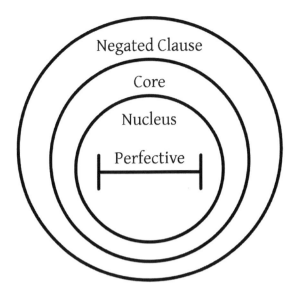

Figure 6. Negation with Scope over the Clausal Proposition (Perfective)

Conversely, example 51 provides an excellent example of how core negation scope functions with perfective prohibition with a clear contrast provided between two alternatives.

51. μὴ ἐπέλθῃς ἐκεῖ, ἔκκλινον δὲ ἀπ' αὐτῶν καὶ παράλλαξον.
Do not go there; instead turn away from them and pass by (Prov 4:15)

This clause appears within a proverb that relies on a LIFE AS A JOURNEY metaphor in 4:10–19. The speaker is warning the audience of two possible roads of travel. There are those roads of lawlessness where the ungodly set up camp. They are dark and dangerous roads. There are also the roads of the just and righteous that are well lit with daylight. The speaker, here in 4:15, prohibits the audience from traveling the roads of the ungodly and instead gives them an alternative: turn away, pass them by, and travel the roads of the righteous. The context makes it clear: only specific roads are being prohibited and not merely the traveling of roads more generally. The prohibition projects a state of affairs where the recipient could say, "I did not go there; I went elsewhere." The scope of the negator falling upon ἐκεῖ, which in turn refers back to ὁδοὺς ἀσεβῶν (roads of the ungodly) and ὁδοὺς παρανόμων (roads of lawlessness) in 4:14. As such the negation scope can be represented in Figure 7 in the core rather than the clause below.

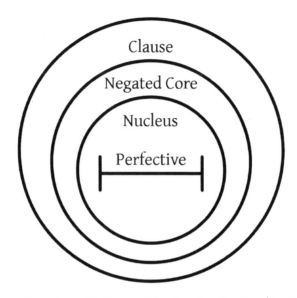

Figure 7. Negation with Scope of the Core Predication (Perfective)

As I said before, there is no evidence for nuclear scope negation with perfective prohibitions. Unlike the STOP DOING X construction, the DO NOT START X meaning cannot be correlated in any way with negation scope. Recall the following two causative prohibitions from examples 41 and 42 above, repeated here as examples 52 and 53. The first of these involves negation over the entire clause; the second over only the pronominal object αὐτούς.

52. καὶ σὺ οὖν <u>μὴ κρύψῃς</u> ἀφ᾽ ἡμῶν ἕως ῥήματος.
    And you, therefore, <u>do not hide</u> so much as a word from us (Acts Pil. 15.5).

Here, the prohibition is absolute and comprehensive. The prohibition encompasses the entire proposition and forbids any and all hiding of information.

53. τοὺς δὲ μὴ ἀκούοντάς σου, <u>μὴ εἰσαγάγῃς</u> <u>αὐτοὺς</u> ἐκεῖ [=εἰς Ἰερουσαλήμ].
    Those who do not obey you, do <u>not</u> lead <u>them</u> there [=into Jerusalem] (4 Bar 8.3).

Fourth Baruch 8.3 contrasts with the prohibition in example 52 in that the overt accusative argument αὐτούς is locus of the prohibition.[63] This prohibition appears in a message from the Lord to his people through Jeremiah. Specifically, it fits within a discourse of instructions regarding what the Jews should do with Babylonian spouses: gather them by the Jordan and say to everyone, "Let those who desire the Lord leave the works of Babylon behind" (4 Bar. 8.2). The spouses who obey (οἱ ἀκούοντες) and leave behind the works of Babylon may be brought into Jerusalem. The spouses who do not obey, must not be brought there. These two examples (52–53) are important evidence that both clause and core negation are possible with the meaning DO NOT START X. Granted, that does not rule out the possibility that there are instances of nuclear scope negation with perfective prohibitions. Unfortunately, my analysis has not provided any guidance for either what they would look like semantically or how one would go about searching for them. For that reason, Figure 8 leaves it as an open question.

---

63 Note also that this pronoun is resumptive from the fronted noun phrase in the left-detached position of the sentence. This is evidence that negation scope is a distinct phenomenon from the focus domain of information structure. Most of the time negation scope will parallel the focus domain of a given clause. Here, however, the resumptive pronoun is necessarily topical and thus by definition cannot be within the focus domain.

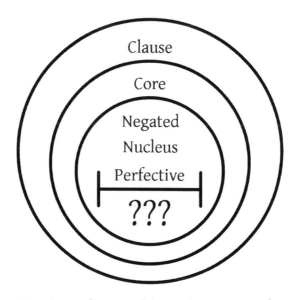

Figure 8. Negation with Scope of the Nuclear Predicate (Perfective)

## 4. CONCLUSION: PROHIBITIONS AS COMPLEX CONSTRUCTIONS

Language is fundamentally constructional in nature. Individual formal elements involve their own semantic expression and when multiple forms come together, more complex meanings arise, meanings that are greater than the constituent pieces. That is precisely what we have seen with Greek prohibitions. Neither the STOP DOING X meaning nor the DO NOT START X meaning is a defining characteristic of what an imperfective or perfective prohibition is. Instead in both cases, aspect, negation, modality, and referentiality all come together in formation of each of them.

On the basis of my analysis, I propose the following formal criteria for expression.

The STOP DOING X construction requires:

- Imperfective aspect
- Imperative mood
- Nuclear-scope negation*
- A specific, referential event*

The DO NOT START X construction requires:

- Perfective aspect
- Subjunctive mood
- Negation of any scope*
- A nonspecific, nonreferential event (?)

The criteria marked by asterisks are proposals that I have argued for in the analysis presented above. The idea of nuclear scope negation being a prerequisite for the STOP DOING X construction is, perhaps, the most novel proposal here. However, I view the idea as compelling because of how well it fits with the nature of the imperfective aspect and also because of the lack of clear data evincing alternative negation scopes, particularly core negation.[64] The fact that my data only consisted of instances of the STOP DOING X construction with referential events suggests that the construction is a particular type of divergence from the standard usage of the imperfective imperative for general commands and prohibitions.

The DO NOT START X construction was more ambiguous in its usage. Its semantics in particular contexts were clear, however. For one, there is clear evidence that negation scope does not play a role in its formation. Clear instances of both clause and core negation are quite common. Additionally, the larger textual contexts in which the construction appears tends to involve nonreferential events. This almost feels like a logical necessity, since referentiality *tends* to be tied to existence either in the world or, at the very least, in the discourse for the mental representation of the audience. My data, at best, demonstrates a *preference* for nonreferential events. This preference could be related to the fact that this construction often seems to function prospectively, where the speaker is desiring to prevent a potential event from occurring.[65] Still, this relationship between the DO NOT START X construction and referentiality is

---

64  It deserves to be emphasized that the claim does not mean that it would be impossible for a Koine Greek speaker to say, with core negation, perhaps "Stop going *to Tarsus*" with negation scope over the core argument, but rather that such a meaning would be expressed with a periphrastic construction rather than with a single imperfective prohibition.

65  This might suggest that Jo Willmott's analysis of such clauses as preventative rather than prohibitive is correct (*The Moods of Homeric Greek*, CCS [Cambridge: Cambridge University Press, 2008], 96).

the most tenuous in terms of its relationship to the language data. It represents an opportunity for future research moving forward.

## BIBLIOGRAPHY

Aubrey, Michael G. "The Greek Perfect and the Categorization of Tense and Aspect: Toward a Descriptive Apparatus for Operators in Role and Reference Grammar." MA Thesis, Trinity Western University, 2014.

Borgen, Peder, Kåre Fuglseth, and Roald Skarsten. *The Works of Philo: Greek Text With Morphology*. Bellingham, WA: Logos Bible Software, 2005.

Borik, Olga and Tanya Reinhart. "Telicity and Perfectivity: Two Independent Systems." Pages 13–34 in *Proceedings of LOLA 8 (Symposium on Logic and Language)*. Edited by László Hunyadi, György Rákosi, and Enikő Tóth. Debrecen, Hungary, 2004.

Boyer, James L. "A Classification of Imperatives: A Statistical Study." *GTJ* 8 (1987): 35–54.

Brannan, Rick. *Greek Apocryphal Gospels, Fragments and Agrapha: Texts and Transcriptions*. Bellingham, WA: Logos Bible Software, 2013.

Butler, Christopher S. *Structure and Function: A Guide to Three Major Structural-Functional Theories*. 2 vols. SLCS 63–64. Amsterdam: Benjamins, 2003.

Butler, Christopher S., María de los Ángeles Gómez-González, and Susana M. Doval-Suárez. *Dynamics of Language Use: Functional and Contrastive Perspectives*. P&B NS 140. Amsterdam: Benjamins, 2005.

Crane, Gregory R., ed. Perseus Digital Library. Tufts University. http://www.perseus.tufts.edu

Curtius, Georg. *The Greek Verb: Its Structure and Development*. 2nd ed. Translated by Augustus S. Wilkins and Edwin B. England. London: Murray, 1883.

Dowty, David. *Word Meaning and Montague Grammar: The Semantics of Verbs and Times in Generative Semantics and in Montague's PTQ*. SLL 7. Dordrecht: Reidel, 1979.

Fanning, Buist. *Verbal Aspect in New Testament Greek*. OTM. Oxford: Oxford University Press, 1990.

Fantin, Joseph. *The Greek Imperative Mood in the New Testament: A Cognitive and Communicative Approach*. SBG 12. New York: Lang, 2010.

Fillmore, Charles, Paul Kay, and Mary Catherine O'Connor. "Regularity and Idiomaticity in Grammatical Constructions: The Case of Let Alone." *Language* 64 (1988): 501–538.

Forsyth, James. *A Grammar of Aspect: Usage and Meaning in the Russian Verb.* Studies in the Modern Russian Language, Extra Volume. Cambridge: Cambridge University Press, 1970.

Gibbs, Raymond W. *Embodiment and Cognitive Science.* Cambridge: Cambridge University Press, 2006.

Goldberg, Adele E. *Constructions at Work: The Nature of Generalization in Language.* Oxford Linguistics. Oxford: Oxford University Press, 2006.

Headlam, Walter. "Greek Prohibitions." *ClR* 19 (1905): 30–36.

Holmes, Michael W., ed. *The Apostolic Fathers: Greek Texts and English Translations.* 3rd ed. Grand Rapids: Baker Academic, 2007.

———, ed. *The Greek New Testament: SBL Edition.* Bellingham, WA: Logos Bible Software, 2010.

Huffman, Douglas S. *Verbal Aspect Theory and the Prohibitions in the Greek New Testament.* SBG 16. New York: Lang, 2014.

Lakoff, George. *Women, Fire, and Dangerous Things: What Categories Reveal about the Mind.* Chicago: University of Chicago Press, 1987.

Lakoff, George, and Mark Johnson. *Philosophy in the Flesh: The Embodied Mind and Its Challenge to Western Thought.* New York: Basic Books, 1999.

Langacker, Ronald. *Foundations of Cognitive Grammar.* Stanford, CA: Stanford University Press, 1987.

Louw, J. P. "On Greek Prohibitions." *Acta Classica* 2 (1959): 43–57.

Moulton, James Hope. *A Grammar of New Testament Greek: Prolegomena.* 3rd ed. Edinburgh: T&T Clark, 1908.

Napoli, Maria. *Aspect and Actionality in Homeric Greek: A Contrastive Analysis.* Milan: FrancoAngeli, 2006.

Niese, Benedikt. *Flavii Iosephi Opera Recognovit.* 7 vols. Berlin: Weidmannos, 1888–1895.

Olsen, Mari. "A Semantic and Pragmatic Model of Lexical and Grammatical Aspect." PhD diss., Northwestern University, 1994.

Pavey, Emma. *The Structure of Language: An Introduction to Grammatical Analysis.* Cambridge: Cambridge, 2010.

Penner, Ken, and Michael Heiser. *Old Testament Greek Pseudepigrapha with Morphology.* Bellingham, WA: Logos Bible Software, 2008.

Porter, Stanley. *Verbal Aspect in the Greek of the New Testament: With Reference to Tense and Mood.* SBG 1. New York: Lang, 1989.

Rahlfs, Alfred, and John Hanhart, eds. *Septuaginta: Editio altera.* Stuttgart: Deutsche Bibelgesellschaft, 2006.

Smith, Carlotta. *The Parameter of Aspect.* 2nd ed. SLP 43. Dordrecht: Kluwer, 1997.

Stagg, Frank. "The Abused Aorist." *JBL* 91 (1972): 222–31.

Stork, Peter. *The Aspectual Usage of the Dynamic Infinitive in Herodotus.* Groningen: Bouma's Boekhuis, 1982.

Taylor, John. *Linguistic Categorization.* 3rd ed. OTL. Oxford: Oxford University Press, 2003.

Van Valin, Robert D., Jr. "An Overview of Role and Reference Grammar." 2010. http://linguistics.buffalo.edu/people/faculty/vanvalin/rrg/RRG_overview.pdf

———. *Exploring the Syntax-Semantics Interface.* Cambridge: Cambridge University Press, 2005.

Van Valin, Robert D., Jr., and Randy J. LaPolla. *Syntax: Structure, Meaning, and Function.* CTL. Cambridge: Cambridge University Press, 1997.

Varela, Francisco J., Evan Thompson, and Eleanor Rosch. *The Embodied Mind: Cognitive Science and Human Experience.* Cambridge, MA: MIT Press, 1991.

Varner, William. *James.* EEC. Bellingham, WA: Lexham Press, 2014.

Wallace, Daniel B. *Greek Grammar Beyond the Basics: An Exegetical Syntax of New Testament Greek With Scripture, Subject, and Greek Word Indexes.* Grand Rapids: Zondervan, 1996.

Willmott, Jo. *The Moods of Homeric Greek.* CCS. Cambridge: Cambridge University Press, 2007.

Xenophon. *Cyropaedia.* Translated by Walter Miller. 2 vols. LCL. New York: MacMillan, 1914.

CHAPTER 17

# Tense and Aspect after the
New Testament[1]

AMALIA MOSER

NATIONAL AND KAPODISTRIAN UNIVERSITY OF ATHENS

## 1. INTRODUCTION

The aim of this paper is to show that the knowledge of the history of Greek after the New Testament and the knowledge of its outcome, i.e., Modern Greek, can provide the tools for a better understanding of some of the linguistic problems presented by New Testament Greek. No linguist, of course, could claim that this knowledge is indispensable. From Saussure onwards, it has been established that languages can and should be studied synchronically, as structured systems. It is becoming more and more obvious to linguists, however, that familiarity with the history of a language can enrich one's understanding of a specific period considerably. This insight is usually limited to the history of the language leading up to the period under investigation; here it is maintained that subsequent developments can be equally important for our understanding.

---

1  This paper owes a lot to everyone who participated in the *Linguistics and the Greek Verb* conference at Tyndale House in Cambridge and who made me see in a fresh light a subject on which I have been working for more than two decades. Particular thanks go to the organizers and editors, Chris Fresch and Steven Runge, who honored me with an invitation to this interesting and lively meeting. Chris Fresch's careful review of the paper and constructive comments contributed to its great improvement; any remaining flaws are entirely my own responsibility.

The testing ground for this claim will be aspect and its relationship to *Aktionsart* and tense. The paper starts with a brief overview of the Modern Greek verbal system in comparison to the Classical Greek verb (§2), will continue with a brief discussion of a theoretical approach to tense and aspect and its application to Modern Greek (§3), and proceed retrospectively, examining the situation in Early, Classical, and New Testament Greek in the light of the Modern Greek data (§4).

## 2. THE GREEK VERB: MODERN VS. CLASSICAL

Greek is almost universally assumed to have preserved the basic structure of its verbal system intact over at least three millennia. This idea will be challenged further down. Nevertheless, table 1, which contains a contrastive presentation of the active indicative in Classical and Modern Greek, does indeed show a remarkable similarity. In the case of the verb πείθω "persuade" there is little change even in the phonology. This is indicated in table 2, which is a transcribed version of table 1: the diphthong has been monophthongized and the *theta* changed from an aspirated stop to a fricative; incidentally, both changes were probably complete by the time of the New Testament.

Table 1: Classical vs. Modern Greek

|  | *Classical Greek* | *Modern Greek* |
|---|---|---|
| *Present* | πείθ-ω | πείθ-ω |
| *Imperfect* | ἔ-πειθ-ον | έ-πειθ-α |
| *Aorist* | ἔ-πεισ-α | έ-πεισ-α |
| *Future* | πείσ-ω | θα πείθ-ω |
|  |  | θα πείσ-ω |
| *Perfect* | πέ-πεικ-α | έχω πείσ-ει |
| *Past Perfect* | ἐ-πε-πείκ-ειν | είχα πείσ-ει |
| *Future Perfect* | πε-πεικ-ώς ἔσομαι | θα έχω πείσ-ει |

Table 2: Classical vs. Modern Greek (phonemically transcribed)

| | Classical Greek | Modern Greek |
|---|---|---|
| Present | peit\u02b0-o | piθ-o |
| Imperfect | e-peit\u02b0-on | e-piθ-a |
| Aorist | ep<u>eis</u>-a | e-pis-a |
| Future | p<u>eis</u>-o | θa piθ-o<br>---<br>θa p<u>is</u>-o |
| Perfect | pe-p<u>eik</u>-a | exo p<u>is</u>-i |
| Past Perfect | e-pe-p<u>eik</u>-ein | ixa p<u>is</u>-i |
| Future Perfect | pe-p<u>eik</u>-os esomai | θa exo p<u>is</u>-i |

The changes most relevant to the topic of this paper are visible in table 1: two new future forms have replaced the single Ancient Greek future and periphrases have replaced the synthetic perfects. It is important to note that the perfect stem has disappeared completely.

There have been some losses in the verbal system as a whole, indicated in tables 3 and 4, which present an overview of the active and mediopassive forms of the verb respectively:

Table 3: The Modern Greek active voice

| | Indicative | Subjunctive | Descendants of the Participle |
|---|---|---|---|
| Present | πεί<u>θ</u>-ω | να πεί<u>θ</u>-ω | πεί<u>θ</u>-οντας |
| Imperfect | έ-πειθ-α | | |
| Aorist | να πεί<u>σ</u>-ω | να πεί<u>σ</u>-ω | |
| Future | θα πεί<u>θ</u>-ω<br>θα πεί<u>σ</u>-ω | | |
| Perfect | έχω πεί<u>σ</u>-ει | να έχω πεί<u>σ</u>-ει | έχοντας πεί<u>σ</u>-ει |
| Past Perfect | είχα πεί<u>σ</u>-ει | | |
| Future Perfect | θα έχω πεί<u>σ</u>-ει | | |

Table 4: The Modern Greek passive voice

| | Indicative | Subjunctive | Descendants of the Participle |
|---|---|---|---|
| Present | πείθ-ομαι | να πείθ-ομαι | (πειθ-όμενος, -η, -ο) |
| Imperfect | πειθ-όμουν(α) | | |
| Aorist | πείσθ-ηκα/ πείστ-ηκα | να πεισθ-ώ/ πειστ-ώ | |
| Imperfective Future | θα πείθ-ομαι | | |
| Perfective Future | θα πεισθ-ώ/ πειστ-ώ | | |
| Perfect | έχω πεισθ-εί/ πειστ-εί | να έχω πεισθ-εί/ πειστ-εί | (πε)πεισμένος, -η, -ο έχοντας πεισθ-εί/πειστ-εί |
| Past Perfect | είχα πεισθ-εί/ πειστ-εί | | |
| Future Perfect | θα έχω πεισθ-εί/ πειστ-εί | | |

In brief, the losses of the paradigm can be described as follows:

- The optative is completely extinct, a development that was to be expected, since it was already weakened by the Classical period, when it had a predominantly syntactic function;
- The infinitive has disappeared, replaced by clauses introduced by the complementizers ότι and να;
- Most participles are gone, their function now taken over by dependent clauses.[2]

---

2  The changes in the participial system can be summarized as follows: the aor. and fut. ptc. have been lost, with the former preserved in certain more or less fixed expressions; the act. pres. ptc. has lost all its adjectival characteristics (inflection and gender specification) and has become a verbal adv. (converb), while its mediopassive counterpart is rarely used with certain deponent verbs, mostly in the higher registers; and finally the mediopas-

The only gain for the system is the emergence of the two future forms, the outcome of a long, slow development from a volitional periphrasis: θέλω πεῖσαι/πείθειν > θέλω ἵνα πείσω/πείθω > θέλω νὰ πείσω/πείθω > θὲ νὰ πείσω/πείθω > θὰ πείσω/πείθω. The significance of this development is sadly overlooked in most of the literature. The emergence of these forms introduced the aspectual distinction into the future, a rather uncommon phenomenon cross-linguistically.[3] Another development frequently overlooked is the loss of the perfect stem. Most analyses of Modern Greek assume that the tense and aspect system has retained its original tripartite distinction based on the three stems. This view is adopted even in studies by staunch structuralists, like Mirambel[4] and Seiler,[5] despite the predilection of Structuralism for binary oppositions. I believe that the morphological loss of one of the three stems, a change of immense magnitude in an otherwise remarkably conservative morphology, cannot be insignificant.[6] Phonological change cannot be blamed for this loss, though it often is, because, if anything, it made the difference between perfect and aorist more pronounced.[7] To this should be added that the new periphrasis does not emerge until the thirteenth century, leaving almost ten centuries in which the language functions perfectly well without a perfect.

The loss of the perfect stem, therefore, strongly suggests the loss of the classical category perfect, whether this was an aspect or something else. This issue is taken up in Section 3, after a brief discussion of the definition of aspect and the controversy surrounding its potential distinction from *Aktionsart*.

---

sive pft. ptc. is extremely productive, formed even by verbs that do not have a mediopassive voice (e.g. ανθίζω "bloom"—*ανθίζομαι–ανθισμένος "in bloom").

3   See e.g Östen Dahl, *Tense and Aspect Systems* (Oxford: Blackwell, 1985) and Joan Bybee, Revere Perkins, and William Pagliuca, *The Evolution of Grammar: Tense, Aspect, and Modality in the Languages of the World* (Chicago: University of Chicago Press 1994), 81–87.

4   André Mirambel, *La langue grecque moderne: Description et analyse* (Paris: Klincksieck, 1959).

5   Hansjakob Seiler, *L'aspect et le temps dans le verbe néo-grec* (Paris: Les belles lettres, 1952).

6   The conservatism of Greek morphology extends beyond the verb, to the inflectional system of the noun and adjective and to productive morphology.

7   Compare the pronunciation of pairs of forms like πέφευγα–ἔφυγον (AGr pepʰeuga-epʰugon—MGr pefevya-efiyon).

## 3. *AKTIONSART* AND ASPECT

### 3.1 Aktionsart

*Aktionsart* (also known as *actionality* or *lexical aspect*) and *aspect* (also referred to as *grammatical aspect* or *viewpoint aspect*) are both concerned with the internal temporal structure of situations, albeit in different ways.

*Aktionsart* is the internal temporal constituency of situations, inherent in the meaning of verbs/predicates. It refers to characteristics such as duration, homogeneity, completion, etc. The most widely-used categorization is Vendler's;[8] he uses the criteria of telicity and homogeneity to distinguish four categories: states, activities, achievements, and accomplishments. Table 5 is based on his classification.[9]

Table 5: Vendler's verb classes

| telicity<br>homogeneity | homogeneous | nonhomogeneous |
|---|---|---|
| atelic | **states**<br>*know*<br>*believe*<br>*have*<br>*love* | **activities**<br>*run*<br>*walk*<br>*swim*<br>*read* |
| telic | **achievements**<br>*recognize*<br>*find*<br>*lose*<br>*die* | **accomplishments**<br>*paint a portrait*<br>*run a mile*<br>*bake a cake*<br>*read a book* |

---

8    Zeno Vendler, "Verbs and Times," *PhR* 66 (1957), 143–60. Mourelatos's hierarchical categorization ends up with the same four categories, but stresses the importance of a binary distinction between states and dynamic situations; Alexander Mourelatos, "Events, Processes and States," *Ling&P* 2 (1978), 415–34.

9    See also the discussion in Christopher J. Thomson, ch. 2 in this volume.

## 3.2 Aspect

According to Comrie's definition, "aspects are different ways of viewing the internal temporal constituency of a situation".[10] The basic aspectual opposition is that between perfective and imperfective. The best description of the opposition is probably the following, which explains the essentially subjective nature of the category; it is a matter of choice by the speaker:

> Another way of explaining the difference between perfective and imperfective meaning is to say that *the perfective looks at the situation from outside*, without necessarily distinguishing any of the internal structure of the situation, whereas *the imperfective looks at the situation from inside*, and as such is crucially concerned with the internal structure of the situation.[11]

The opposition is expressed in Greek, both Ancient and Modern, by the aorist stem for the perfective and the present stem for the imperfective, and it embodies the difference between sentences such as the following, which can be used to refer to the same event:

Χτες όλη την ημέρα διάβασα ένα βιβλίο.
Χτες όλη την ημέρα διάβαζα ένα βιβλίο.

"All day yesterday I read a book".

In Modern Greek the freedom of choice is almost limitless. It is true that the implicatures that arise make one or the other aspect more likely to be used in different contexts or to express different nuances. The example above, for instance, would probably be used in its perfective form if a speaker wanted to emphasize that it was the only constructive thing that he or she did the whole day and in the imperfective if the emphasis was on the continuity of the situation throughout the day. Nevertheless, this is certainly not a rule that has to be followed and the choice is indeed up to the speaker.

---

10  Bernard Comrie, *Aspect: An Introduction to the Study of Verbal Aspect and Related Problems*, CTL (Cambridge: Cambridge University Press, 1976), 3.
11  Ibid., 3–4 (emphasis added).

It is generally acknowledged that the imperfective is subdivided as follows, according to Comrie:[12]

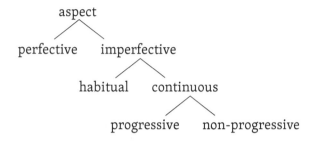

While the [±PROGRESSIVE] opposition is not realized morphologically in Modern Greek, the imperfective is systematically used to express habituality:

Το καλοκαίρι διάβαζα τουλάχιστον ένα βιβλίο την εβδομάδα.

"In the summer I used to read at least one book per week".[13]

## 3.3 The Necessity of the Distinction

There have been strong voices against the *Aktionsart*-aspect distinction from opposite theoretical positions. Cognitive linguists, especially Langacker,[14] consider it pointless, since according to their approach everything is a matter of construal, and therefore subjective. Verkuyl,[15] a formal semanticist, considers it perfectly legitimate, but claims that *Aktionsart* classes are strictly ontological and irrelevant to linguistics; the aspectuality of the sentence is produced compositionally on the basis of two features, [±ADD TO] and [±SQA],[16] which are independent of *Aktionsart*.

---

12  Ibid., 25.
13  See also the discussion in Christopher J. Thomson, ch. 2 in this volume.
14  E.g., Ronald W. Langacker, *Foundations of Cognitive Grammar, Volume II: Descriptive Application* (Stanford: Stanford University Press, 1991).
15  Henk J. Verkuyl, *A Theory of Aspectuality: the Interaction between Temporal and Atemporal Structure*, CSL (Cambridge: Cambridge University Press, 1993), 3-32.
16  SQA: Specified quantity of A, where A = argument(s) of the verb. [ADD TO] concerns the possibility of incremental development of situations.

I believe the distinction to be both possible and necessary. The main reason is that the freedom of choice provided by aspect is rarely complete in practice and the constraints in most languages derive from *Aktionsart*. Despite this frequently attested lack of clear boundaries between the two categories, the distinction remains important on theoretical grounds as well as for the practical purposes of analysis. As Aarts points out, "The well-motivated setting up of discrete categories of form classes is logically prior to claiming that gradience obtains between them."[17]

The *Aktionsart*-aspect distinction is perhaps best understood in terms of subjectivity: *Aktionsart* can be said to be objective in that it concerns inherent characteristics of the situation (duration, homogeneity, etc.); aspect can be seen as subjective in that it expresses the point of view chosen by the speaker. This, too, is a controversial issue; Bache,[18] who argues for the distinction, was the first to point out a weakness in the subjectivity criterion: While it works for the basic aspectual distinction between perfective and imperfective, it does not apply to the others. The progressive does not normally combine with states or achievements, while the habitual expresses an objective characteristic of events: regular repetition or periodicity. He suggests that the definition on the basis of subjectivity is inadequate; another solution to this problem, however, is to exclude both the progressive and the habitual from the prototypical category of aspect. For the habitual, there is good cross-linguistic evidence: There are several non-Indo-European languages that use a distinct form for this category.[19] The progressive, on the other hand, is unquestionably aspectual in nature, but is constrained by *Aktionsart*. In previous research they were arranged on a continuum of subjectivity on which [±IMPERFECTIVE] is at the subjective end, *Aktionsart* at the objective end, and habitual and progressive in between.[20]

---

17  Bas Aarts, *Syntactic Gradience: the Nature of Grammatical Indeterminacy* (Oxford: Oxford University Press, 2007), 207.

18  Carl Bache, "Aspect and Aktionsart: Towards a Semantic Distinction," *JL* 18 (1982): 57–82.

19  Dahl, *Tense and Aspect Systems*, 79–84.

20  Amalia Moser, "Aktionsart, Aspect and Tense: A Study on the Nature of Grammatical Categories," in *Major Trends in Theoretical and Applied Linguistics*, ed. Nikolaos Lavidas, Thomaï Alexiou, and Areti-Maria Sougari (London: Versita, 2013), 99–121.

More importantly perhaps from the point of view of this paper, subjectivity can serve as a means to assess aspectual systems and to order them on a similar gradient. Modern Greek would be very close to the subjectivity end. Its aorist-present stem opposition expresses the basic [±PERFECTIVE] distinction—all but a negligible number of verbs have both stems and the choice between them is generally free, with a few exceptions. Their value for an explanation of the history of aspect is far from negligible; this will be taken up in Section 4 below.

## 3.4 Perfect, Future, Tense, and Aspect

Comrie chooses to treat the perfect in his book on aspect, succumbing to the traditional view of it as a third aspect, although as he points out, "It is an aspect in a rather different sense from the other aspects treated so far."[21] Accepting its usual definition as a form that connects a present state to a prior situation, he distinguishes four types: *resultative, experiential, persistent situation,* and *recent past,* as exemplified respectively by the following:

> Bill has gone to America.
> Bill has been to America.
> We've lived here for years.
> Bill has just arrived.[22]

The Modern Greek present perfect has only two of these functions: *experiential* and *resultative*. It is interesting that in the latter case, it is no more resultative than the aorist, which can always replace the perfect in this function, although the reverse does not hold. Interestingly, these two uses are the ones least closely connected with the present; in fact, the use of the perfect instead of the aorist may carry an implicature of greater distance, given that it cannot express recent past.

According to earlier research,[23] the Modern Greek present perfect can probably be best analyzed as an anterior in the present

---

21  Comrie, *Aspect*, 52.
22  Ibid., 56.
23  Amalia Moser, "Tense, Aspect and the Greek Perfect," in *Perfect Explorations*, ed. Artemis Alexiadou, Monika Rathert, and Arnim von Stechow, Interface Explorations 2 (Berlin: de Gruyter, 2003), 235–52; Αμαλία Μόζεραχαι

sphere in the sense of Declerck.[24] Anteriority is of course a feature of tense rather than aspect. If this analysis is correct, then, the Modern Greek perfect is categorically different from the Ancient Greek one; this would explain the temporal gap between the disappearance of the synthetic forms and the rise of the modern periphrases mentioned in Section 2 above. This analysis, moreover, has the advantage of accounting for the perfect system as a whole: The past perfect is universally accepted as a true, cross-linguistically prototypical pluperfect, designating an event anterior to another event in the past, while the future perfect expresses anteriority in the future. The attribution of anteriority to the entire perfect system accounts for the fact that its periphrases are formed with a fossilized form of the aorist, i.e., perfective infinitive, when they could easily have imperfective counterparts (*ἔχω πείθει).

The two future periphrases, on the contrary, have a perfective and an imperfective form. This is significant both for tense and for aspect. The domain of aspect expands to cover the future, a development that signals the increased significance of aspect for the system. It also signals a greater significance of tense: the verb gains symmetry in all three tense domains.

If the analysis delineated above is correct, the Modern Greek verbal system displays the following image with respect to tense and aspect:

Table 6: The Modern Greek Tense System

| Tense (absolute)    Aspect | Imperfective | Perfective |
|---|---|---|
| Present | πείθω | (πείσω) |
| Past | έπειθα | έπεισα |
| Future | θα πείθω | θα πείσω |

---

Σπυριδούλα Μπέλλα, "Παρελθόν, παρόν, οριστικότητα και παρακείμενος," in 60 Διεθνές Συνέδριο Ελληνικής Γλωσσολογίας, Ρέθυμνο 18-20 Σεπτεμβρίου 2003, ed. Αλέξης Καλοκαιρινός et al. (Ρέθυμνο: Πανεπιστήμιο Κρήτης, 2003).

24  Renaat Declerck, Tense in English: its Structure and Use in Discourse (London: Routledge, 1991).

| Tense (absolute-relative: anterior) Aspect | Imperfective | Perfective |
|---|---|---|
| Present | – | ἔχω πείσει |
| Past | – | είχα πείσει |
| Future | – | θα ἔχω πείσει |

Even if the analysis of the Modern Greek verbal system proposed above is not accepted in its entirety, it seems clear that the system attributes more or less equal importance to aspect and tense. This is already a considerable difference from Classical and New Testament Greek, where the predominance of aspect seems incontestable.[25] The contention of this paper is that the nature of aspect itself has changed over the centuries. It is at this point that a retrospective examination can be of help.

# 4. A RETROSPECTIVE LOOK AT GREEK ASPECT

This section concentrates on the basic aspectual opposition as expressed by the aorist and present stems of the verb, preceded by a brief overview of the evolution of the perfect. In both cases, the vantage point will be that of a native speaker of Modern Greek and of the differences that this speaker perceives, based on the uses that seem unusual or even unnatural, all of which exclusively concern perfects, imperfects, and infinitival complements. The section will close with an explanation of the anomalies of the Modern Greek system as relics of earlier stages in its evolution.

## 4.1 The Perfect

According to most analyses, the classical perfect had a variety of meanings, which are possible to group into two broad categories: state and state resulting from a previous action. It seems certain

---

25  See e.g., Eduard Schwyzer and Albert Debrunner, *Griechische Grammatik: auf der Grundlage von Karl Brugmanns Griechischer Grammatik, Zweiter Band; Syntax und Syntaktische Stilistik* (Munich: Beck, 1950); and Buist Fanning, *Verbal Aspect in New Testament Greek*, OTM (Oxford: Clarendon Press, 1990).

that the latter is more recent;[26] one of the most widespread theories about the reasons for the disappearance of the synthetic perfect is that it was precisely this development that made it redundant, since the resultative meaning could be expressed by the versatile aorist.[27]

This view is supported by the fact that from the late classical period onwards the perfect is found more and more frequently to co-occur with aorists:

ἀντέκρουσέ τι καὶ γέγονε οἷον οὐκ ἔδει; πάρεστιν Αἰσχίνης.

"A regrettable incident is reported. Aeschines in evidence." (Dem. Cor., 198 [Vince & Vince])

This explanation of the disappearance of the synthetic perfect also finds support in current views about the Proto-Indo-European verbal system: The consensus nowadays is that the perfect signaled a state, the aorist a dynamic situation which was either telic or instantaneous and the present a dynamic situation which was either atelic or durative or both.[28] The acquisition by the perfect of a resultative meaning is supposed to have disrupted this tripartite system. The mere change in the nature of what continues to be a state, however, seems rather an inadequate trigger for a loss as major as that of one of the three stems.

It is of significance that these stems are often supplied by different verbs, along with ablaut and the later affixal formation:

ὁρῶ - εἶδον - ὄπωπα "see"
λείπω - ἔλιπον - λέλοιπα "leave"
λύω - ἔλυσα - λέλυκα "untie"

---

26 See e.g., D. B. Monro, *A Grammar of the Homeric Dialect*, 2nd ed. (Oxford: Clarendon Press, 1891), 31-32 Pierre Chantraine, *L'histoire du parfait grec* (Paris: Champion, 1927), 4-20; Schwyzer, *Grammatik*, 248-69; Yves Duhoux, *Le verbe grec ancien: Éléments de morphologie et de syntaxe historiques*, BCLL 61 (Louvain: Peeters, 1992), 406-26.
27 Chantraine, *L'histoire du parfait*, 146-90.
28 See e.g., Andrew L. Sihler, *New Comparative Grammar of Greek and Latin* (Oxford: Oxford University Press, 1995). William Randall and Howard Jones, "On the Early Origins of the Germanic Preterite Presents," *TPhS* 113 (2015), 137-76, postulate the existence of an even earlier PIE unreduplicated stative, which would be the ancestor of both the pft. and the preterite presents.

The fact that in Homer we encounter not only perfects but even
aorists with a clearly present meaning, which correspond to modern presents and are often found side by side with a morphological
present, is also of interest:

ὡς δ' ὅθ' ὑπὸ φρικὸς Βορέω <u>ἀναπάλλεται</u> ἰχθὺς
θῖν' ἐν φυκιόεντι, μέλαν δὲ ἑ κῦμ' <u>ἐκάλυψεν</u>

"and as beneath the ripple of the North Wind a fish
<u>leaps up</u> on the seaweed-strewn sand of a shallow,
and then the black wave <u>hides</u> it" (*Iliad*, xxiii, 692–693
[Murray])

It is at this point that the theoretical distinction between
*Aktionsart* and aspect reveals its explanatory value. The descriptions of the Ancient Greek perfect and the postulated meaning of
the three stems in Proto-Indo-European all involve notions that
clearly belong to the category not of aspect but of *Aktionsart*. Since,
according to the prevalent view, Proto-Indo-European tense was introduced into the system at a later stage, the uses of perfects and
aorists with a present meaning become easy to explain: The former
are only found with state verbs and the latter with punctual/telic
verbs. This is not to say that these categories of verbs are consistently expressed by the corresponding stem; the epic is a multilayered
text in terms both of dialects and, crucially, of phases of the history
of the language. This type of use is best explained as a relic of one
of the earliest periods. Some relics of this situation with respect to
the perfect can be seen in the *perfecta praesentia* of Classical Greek
(πέφυκα "be [by nature]", δέδια "be afraid", οἶδα "know", etc.).

The meaning of state as a result of prior action necessarily as-
sociates the perfect with the past, without discarding its present
dimension. As the classical period progresses, the perfect's developing relationship with the past becomes more pronounced. Its dual
nature is perhaps more evident in this passage than anywhere else:

<u>οὔ ποτε γέγονεν</u>, οὔτ' ἐγίγνετο, οὔτ' ἦν ποτε, <u>οὔτε νῦν</u>
<u>γέγονεν</u> οὔτε γίγνεται οὔτε ἔστιν, οὔτ' ἔπειτα γενήσεται,
οὔτε γενηθήσεται, οὔτε ἔσται.

"<u>it neither has become</u> nor became nor was <u>in the past</u>,
<u>it has neither become</u>, nor is it becoming nor is it <u>in</u>

<u>the present</u>, and it will neither become nor be made to become nor will be in the future" (Pl., *Parm.* 141e [Fowler])

A side effect of this development is a growing interchangeability association with the aorist, which brings its meaning closer to that of the perfective aspect.

Contrary to the widespread view that the synthetic perfect is almost extinct in Hellenistic times and is only used consistently by the Atticists, recent study has shown that it is quite frequent in the New Testament.[29] The purely stative meaning, however, seems to be very rare.[30] The results of a large number of studies show that its use, especially its distribution with respect to the aorist, is rather complex and there is some difficulty in delineating the domain of each. Fanning, for instance, points out that, "A fourth category of the perfect, over which there is some dispute, is the use of the tense as an equivalent to the aorist: that is, as a simple narrative tense to report past occurrences without attention paid to their present consequences. ... But the question remains whether this aoristic use of the perfect appears in the NT."[31] The following passage from John with the constant juxtaposition of the perfect and the aorist seems to give a positive answer to this question:

δόξασόν σου τὸν υἱόν, ἵνα ὁ υἱὸς δοξάσῃ σέ, καθὼς <u>ἔδωκας</u>(aor.) αὐτῷ ἐξουσίαν πάσης σαρκός, ἵνα πᾶν ὃ <u>δέδωκας</u>(perfect) αὐτῷ δώσῃ αὐτοῖς ζωὴν αἰώνιον. ... ἐγώ σε ἐδόξασα ἐπὶ τῆς γῆς τὸ ἔργον τελειώσας ὃ <u>δέδωκάς</u>(perfect) μοι ἵνα ποιήσω ... νῦν ἔγνωκαν ὅτι πάντα ὅσα <u>δέδωκάς</u>(perfect) μοι παρὰ σοῦ εἰσιν· ὅτι τὰ ῥήματα ἃ <u>ἔδωκάς</u>(aor.) μοι <u>δέδωκα</u>(perfect) αὐτοῖς, καὶ αὐτοὶ ἔλαβον καὶ ἔγνωσαν ἀληθῶς ὅτι παρὰ σοῦ ἐξῆλθον

---

29  Robert Crellin, "The Greek Perfect Active System: 200 BC–AD 150," PhD diss., University of Cambridge, 2012) reveals the interesting interaction between the pf. and the *Aktionsart* of the verb; see also his discussion in ch. 14 of this volume.

30  Although Stanley Porter, *Verbal Aspect in the Greek of the New Testament*, SBG 1 (New York: Lang, 1989), 245–49, analyzes the pf. as still having a basic meaning of state, regardless of whether it is the result of a past action or not. It is interesting that, as Chris Fresch pointed out, in the very passage that I use below as an example of the perfect's predominantly aoristic nature, ἔγνωκαν clearly denotes a state.

31  Fanning, *Verbal Aspect*, 299–300.

"Glorify your Son so that the Son may glorify you, since you have given him authority over all people, to give eternal life to all whom you have given him. ... I glorified you on earth by finishing the work that you gave me to do ... now they know that everything you have given me is from you; for the words that you gave to me I have given to them, and they have received them and know in truth that I came from you." (John 17:1-2, 4, 7-8)[32]

It is possible to find explanations for the alternation of perfect and aorist;[33] the variation alone, however, indicates that a change is in progress and this is borne out by subsequent developments.[34] The important fact from the point of view taken here is the eventual loss of the perfect stem, which, as pointed out above, must signal the loss of the category it expressed. Not only is the new periphrasis based on a perfective form, but it does not appear until around the 13th century AD. The gap of several centuries makes it possible that, despite the label allotted to it, the new periphrasis is not necessarily an exponent of the original category.

## 4.2 Imperfective vs. Perfective

Imperfects that feel inappropriate to modern speakers always correspond to aorists in Modern Greek, and complements with an imperfective (traditionally labeled present) infinitive correspond to the perfective (traditionally called aorist) subjunctive. In earlier

---

32  All translations of the Greek New Testament are taken from the NRSV.

33  Chris Fresch rightly pointed out that all perfects in this passage "aside from the last one ... occur in relative clauses and provide information that leads into and is picked up on by the main verb, which would be an expected use of a resultative/stative." It is true that it is usually possible to find an explanation for the choice of one or the other form; my argument is based on the fact that there is no consistency in these choices. The reversal in the last sentence of this particular passage, for instance, seems to me to be a case in point, even if a different explanation is possible.

34  See the discussion in Geoffrey Horrocks, *Greek: A History of the Language and Its Speakers* (Oxford: Wiley, 2010), 174-78, where the merger of the aor. and the pf. are explained mainly as a result of the ease with which the perfect's retrospective viewing of an event from the vantage point of the present can be "downgraded" to that of a simple past tense.

research,[35] these cases were systematically investigated in historians of the Classical, Hellenistic, and early Byzantine period. The choice of historical texts was partly due to their uninterrupted flow during these periods, which afforded the opportunity to compare instances of a single prose genre across time, and partly to the nature of the genre as prose and narrative. The results of this investigation showed that in all the cases where an imperfect sounded inappropriate in the modern rendition of the ancient text, it was an imperfect of a nonstative durative verb, i.e., an activity or an accomplishment. The choice of aspect was thus shown to be constrained by *Aktionsart*. This example from Thucydides shows clearly how verbs with different *Aktionsarten* are treated differently within the same sentence:

εἰ δὲ μή, Μυτιληναίοις εἰπεῖν ναῦς τε παραδοῦναι$_{[+perf]}$ καὶ
τείχη καθελεῖν$_{[+perf]}$, μὴ πειθομένων δὲ πολεμεῖν $_{[-perf]}$.

"but if not, the generals were to order the Mytileneans
to deliver up their ships and pull down their walls, and
if they disobeyed, go to war" (Thucydides, 3.3 [Smith])

Sometimes there seem to be other considerations, also connected to inherent characteristics of the action, such as iterativity, which can sometimes be a result of plural subjects, as in the following example:

κατὰ οὖν μεταπύργιον προσέμισγον πρὸς τὰς ἐπάλξεις, εἰδότες
ὅτι ἐρῆμοί εἰσι, πρῶτον μὲν οἱ τὰς κλίμακας φέροντες, καὶ
προσέθεσαν· ἔπειτα ψιλοὶ δώδεκα ξὺν ξιφιδίῳ καὶ θώρακι
ἀνέβαινον, ὧν ἡγεῖτο Ἀμμέας ὁ Κοροίβου καὶ πρῶτος
ἀνέβη· μετὰ δὲ αὐτὸν οἱ ἑπόμενοι, ἓξ ἐφ' ἑκάτερον τῶν
πύργων, ἀνέβαινον.

"so they came up to the battlement at a space between
two towers, knowing that the battlements were deserted. First came the men with the ladders, who set them
against the wall; next came twelve light-armed men,

---

35  Amalia Moser, "Aktionsart, Aspect and Category Change in the History of Greek," in *Language Variation and Change: Tense, Aspect and Modality in Ancient Greek*, ed. Klaas Bentein et al. (Leiden: Brill, forthcoming).

with dagger and corslet only, who <u>mounted </u>the ladder. These were led by Ammeas son of Coroebus, who was the first to <u>ascend</u>, and after him his followers <u>ascended</u>, six men going against each of the adjoining towers". (Thucydides, 3.22.3 [Smith])

As was to be expected, and as can be seen in figure 1, these uses diminish as we proceed to late Classical, Hellenistic, and Early Byzantine historians, even the Atticists, with the notable exception of Procopius, who seems to have been conscious of this subtle but distinctive feature of Classical Attic. The vertical axis indicates the number of uses of the imperfective which would be unacceptable in Modern Greek usage. The horizontal axis presents in chronological order nine historians: Herodotus, Thucydides, Xenophon, Polybius, Diodorus, Arrian, Eusebius, Theodoretus, and Procopius. The results are based on a random sample of 10,000 words of each author.

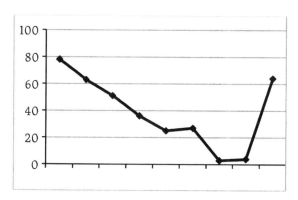

Figure 1: "Different" uses of the imperfective in the historians (Herodotus, Thucydides, Xenophon, Polybius, Diodorus, Arrian, Eusebius, Theodoretus, and Procopius)

In the New Testament, such uses are almost nonexistent, with the exception of some imperfects of verbs of saying; this group of verbs is still more flexible than others in Modern Greek narrative contexts. It is interesting that many of the aorists that have been discussed in the literature as deviant, and which are indeed difficult to explain since they appear where imperfects would be expected in Classical Greek, sound perfectly normal for native speakers of Modern Greek. The following passage is a case in point:[36]

ὡς οὖν ἤκουσεν ὅτι ἀσθενεῖ, τότε μὲν <u>ἔμεινεν</u>_(aor.) ἐν ᾧ ἦν τόπῳ δύο ἡμέρας

"after having heard that Lazarus was ill, <u>he stayed</u> two days longer in the place where he was" (John 11:6)

The problem that this aorist would pose for Classical Greek is that it is used for a situation of considerable duration. In Modern Greek the actual duration would be irrelevant; the choice is free and in this context the unmarked choice would be the aorist, because the event is simply reported, without any intention on the part of the speaker of foregrounding any particular facet of its internal constituency. The same holds for the following use:

Ὁ οὖν Ἰησοῦς οὐκέτι παρρησίᾳ περιεπάτει ἐν τοῖς Ἰουδαίοις, ἀλλὰ ἀπῆλθεν ἐκεῖθεν εἰς τὴν χώραν ἐγγὺς τῆς ἐρήμου, εἰς Ἐφραὶμ λεγομένην πόλιν, κἀκεῖ <u>ἔμεινεν</u>_(aor.) μετὰ τῶν μαθητῶν

"Jesus therefore no longer walked about openly among the Jews, but went from there to a town called Ephraim in the region near the wilderness; and <u>he remained</u> there with the disciples." (John 11:54)

For a similar reason, the imperfect (οὐκέτι) περιεπάτει would be awkward in Modern Greek, where it would be expressed either by an aorist (δεν περιόδευσε ἄλλο) or periphrastically, with the verb σταματῶ or παύω (σταμάτησε να περιοδεύει).

On the contrary, the imperfects ἤρχοντο, ἔλεγον in the following passage would be the normal choice, since they function as habituals:

στέφανον ἐξ ἀκανθῶν ἐπέθηκαν αὐτοῦ τῇ κεφαλῇ καὶ ἱμάτιον πορφυροῦν περιέβαλον αὐτὸν καὶ <u>ἤρχοντο</u> πρὸς αὐτὸν καὶ <u>ἔλεγον</u>· χαῖρε ὁ βασιλεὺς τῶν Ἰουδαίων.

---

36 See the discussion in Patrick James, ch. 6 in this volume.

"[And the soldiers wove ] a crown of thorns and put it on
his head, and they dressed him in a purple robe. <u>They
kept coming</u> up to him, <u>saying</u>. 'Hail, King of the Jews!'"
(John 19:2)

It is in such cases, then, that a knowledge of Modern Greek can
prove useful: Uses that are puzzling compared to their Classical
counterparts can be justified more easily if seen as part of the long-
term evolution of the system; knowing how the system ended up, it
is possible to see here the symptoms of a tendency toward a stronger expression of aspect as a subjective category and hence a truly
subjective choice, unconstrained by *Aktionsart*.

This is not to say that discussions of the reasons of the author's
choice are pointless; on the contrary, it is only through the detailed
analysis of these early manifestations that the mechanism of change
can be understood.

My contention, then, is that the Greek verbal system underwent
a major change, starting from the expression of *Aktionsart* distinctions and gradually moving to the expression of both aspect and
tense. Change in progress is already evident in Homer, becomes
more pronounced in the Classical period, and very much so in
Hellenistic Greek. In Classical Greek we find the two stems (aor. and
pres.) assuming a much more aspectual character, but still subject
to *Aktionsart* considerations. At the same time, the perfect seems
to be hovering between two tenses (present and past) and two as-
pects/*Aktionsarten* (state/durative and perfective). In the Koine already the aorist-present aspectual opposition is far less dependent
on *Aktionsart*, and eventually attains almost complete freedom in
Modern Greek. I believe that it is exactly this shift toward the establishment of the binary [±PERFECTIVE] opposition as the main
building block of the verbal system that caused the ultimate loss
of the perfect. A third aspect had no place in this system, while an
*Aktionsart* distinction was even more inappropriate.[37] As for tense

---

37  The introduction, during the Hellenistic period, of the progressive, can be
seen as a symptom of the shift toward an aspectual system. However, although its presence in the New Testament is prolific (see, e.g., Καὶ ἰδοὺ δύο ἐξ
αὐτῶν ἐν αὐτῇ τῇ ἡμέρᾳ <u>ἦσαν πορευόμενοι</u> εἰς κώμην "Now on that same day two
of them <u>were going</u> to a village." [Luke 24:13]), it does not survive the period,
and was accordingly not analyzed in this paper. For a recent analysis of its

distinctions, the present, past, and future tenses were perfectly adequate. In fact, the weakest of the three, the future, was strengthened through the development of periphrases, which had the added bonus of allowing for the growing aspectual distinction to be expressed in the domain of the future. I would like to stress again the importance of the fact that the perfect was not to be replaced by the modern periphrases for about ten centuries to come, and then only in some dialects; crucially, however, from the 19th century onwards, these periphrases were included in the grammars of what became the official language of the newly founded state. The overhaul of the tense and aspect system was almost complete in early Byzantine and certainly by late Byzantine times, although there are still a few remnants of the old order in the modern language. These are the modern exceptions to the freedom of aspectual choice mentioned in Section 2:

a) all the verbs that do not have perfective forms denote states (though not all states are without perfective forms)

b) the perfective forms of some of the state verbs, apart from the normal perfective function, can be used to signal entry into the state:

κοιμήθηκε τρεις ώρες
"he slept for three hours"
κοιμήθηκε στις τρεις
"he slept (fell asleep) at three"

c) while all achievement verbs have imperfective forms, they can only be used with the normal, nonhabitual, imperfective meaning when they are construed as background to another situation, i.e., as progressives

## 5. CONCLUSIONS

In this paper it was argued that a good knowledge of the structure of Modern Greek can prove useful for the study of New Testament Greek. Modern Greek provides what is so far the final outcome of the changes that have taken place over the intervening centuries

---

rise and fall see Αθανάσιος Γιάνναρης, Οι περιφράσεις είμί/είμαι + Μετοχή στην Ελληνική: Διαχρονική προσέγγιση, (PhD diss., University of Athens, 2007).

and may thus explain some of the seemingly random deviations from the norm, which is determined to a great extent by what we know about Classical Greek, and at the same time reveal the path of change that has led to the current situation in the language.

The domain of verbal aspect and tense was used as an example of the merits of such an approach. It has been well established in the literature that the use of the verbal forms in the New Testament and the Koine can differ rather substantially from their use in Classical Greek, often in very puzzling ways. I tried to show that the uses that deviate from the classical norm sound, as a rule, perfectly normal to the ears of the speaker of Modern Greek; this surely indicates that in the New Testament we see the beginning of a change that led to the Modern Greek aspectual system. The analysis of the change that I proposed was based on my own explanation, which is by no means uncontroversial: On the one hand it rests on a specific theoretical approach to aspect, one that admits a distinction between aspect and *Aktionsart* based on subjectivity; on the other hand it maintains that Modern Greek has a binary [±PERFECTIVE] aspectual opposition, virtually impervious to *Aktionsart* differences, while the [+PERFECTIVE] perfect has a basic meaning of anteriority in the past, present, and future. The history of the verbal system was thus explained as a shift from the expression of *Aktionsart* toward the expression of aspect and tense.

The principle of the proposal, however, remains the same, regardless of whether the specific analysis is convincing or not: The product of the historical developments that followed the period in which the New Testament was composed gives us a very good indication of whether what seems as a deviant use is indeed an individual digression from the norm, which should be analyzed to reveal its purpose, or whether it is simply a new way of expression, on its way to standardization.

This does not invalidate the kind of analysis that insists on such unusual occurrences; on the contrary, this type of investigation is indispensable for a proper understanding of the process and possibly the reasons for change. One of the most fascinating aspects of historical linguistics is precisely the quest for the first slight shift toward something new.

# BIBLIOGRAPHY

Aarts, Bas. *Syntactic Gradience: The Nature of Grammatical Indeterminacy*. Oxford: Oxford University Press, 2007.

Bache, Carl. "Aspect and Aktionsart: Towards a Semantic Distinction." *JL* 18 (1982): 57–82.

Bybee, Joan, Revere Perkins, and William Pagliuca. *The Evolution of Grammar: Tense, Aspect, and Modality in the Languages of the World*. Chicago: University of Chicago Press 1994.

Chantraine, Pierre. *L'histoire du parfait grec*. Paris: Champion, 1927.

Comrie, Bernard. *Aspect: An Introduction to the Study of Verbal Aspect and Related Problems*. CTL. Cambridge: Cambridge University Press, 1976.

Crellin, Robert. "The Greek Perfect Active System: 200 BC–AD 150." PhD diss., University of Cambridge, 2012.

Dahl, Östen. *Tense and Aspect Systems*. Oxford: Blackwell, 1985.

Declerck, Renaat. *Tense in English: Its Structure and Use in Discourse*. London: Routledge, 1991.

Demosthenes. *Orations, Volume 2: Orations 18–19: De Corona, De Falsa Legatione*. Translated by C.A. Vince and J.H. Vince. LCL. Cambridge: Harvard University Press, 1926.

Duhoux, Yves. *Le verbe grec ancien: Éléments de morphologie et de syntaxe historiques*. BCLL 61. Leuven: Peeters, 1992.

Fanning, Buist. *Verbal Aspect in New Testament Greek*. OTM. Oxford: Clarendon Press, 1990.

Γιάνναρης, Αθανάσιος. Οι περιφράσεις εἰμί/εἴμαι + Μετοχή στην Ελληνική: Διαχρονική προσέγγιση. PhD diss., University of Athens, 2007.

Homer. *Iliad*. Translated by A.T. Murray. Revised by William F. Wyatt. 2 vols. LCL. Cambridge: Harvard University Press, 1924–1925.

Horrocks, Geoffrey. *Greek: A History of the Language and its Speakers*. 2nd ed. Chichester: Blackwell, 2010.

Langacker, Ronald W. *Foundations of Cognitive Grammar, Volume II: Descriptive Application*. Stanford: Stanford University Press, 1991.

Mirambel, André. *La langue grecque moderne: Description et analyse*. Paris: Klincksieck, 1959.

Monro, D. B. *A Grammar of the Homeric Dialect*. 2nd ed. Oxford: Clarendon Press, 1891.

Moser, Amalia. "Aktionsart, Aspect and Category Change in the History of Greek." In *Language Variation and Change: Tense, Aspect and Modality in Ancient Greek*. Edited by Klaas Bentein et. al. Leiden: Brill, forthcoming.

―――. "Aktionsart, Aspect and Tense: A Study on the Nature of Grammatical Categories." Pages 99-121 in *Major Trends in Theoretical and Applied Linguistics*. Edited by Nikolaos Lavidas, Thomaï Alexiou, and Areti-Maria Sougari. London: Versita, 2013.

―――. "Tense, Aspect and the Greek Perfect." Pages 235-52 in *Perfect Explorations*. Edited by Artemis Alexiadou, Monika Rathert, and Arnim von Stechow. Interface Explorations 2. Berlin: de Gruyter, 2003.

Μόζερ, Αμαλία, και Σπυριδούλα Μπέλλα, "Παρελθόν, παρόν, οριστικότητα και παρακείμενος." In 60 Διεθνές Συνέδριο Ελληνικής Γλωσσολογίας, Ρέθυμνο 18-20 Σεπτεμβρίου 2003. Edited by Αλέξης Καλοκαιρινός et al. Ρέθυμνο: Πανεπιστήμιο Κρήτης, 2003.

Mourelatos, Alexander. "Events, Processes and States." *Ling&P* 2 (1978), 415-34.

Plato. *Cratylus, Parmenides, Greater Hippias, Lesser Hippias.* Translated by Harold North Fowler. LCL. Cambridge: Harvard University Press, 1926.

Porter, Stanley. *Verbal Aspect in the Greek of the New Testament*. SBG 1. New York: Peter Lang, 1989.

Randall, William, and Howard Jones. "On the Early Origins of the Germanic Preterite Presents." *TPhS* 113 (2015), 137-76.

Schwyzer, Eduard, and Albert Debrunner. *Griechische Grammatik: auf der Grundlage von Karl Brugmanns Griechischer Grammatik, Zweiter Band; Syntax und Syntaktische Stilistik.* HAW 2. Munich: Beck, 1950.

Seiler, Hansjakob. *L'aspect et le temps dans le verbe néo-grec.* Paris: Les belles letters, 1952.

Sihler, Andrew L. *New Comparative Grammar of Greek and Latin.* Oxford: Oxford University Press, 1995

Thucydides. *History of the Peloponnesian War.* 4 vols. Translated by Charles Forster Smith. LCL. Cambridge: Harvard University Press, 1919-1923.

Vendler, Zeno. "Verbs and Times." *PhR* 66 (1957), 143-60.

Verkuyl, Henk J. *A Theory of Aspectuality: the Interaction between Temporal and Atemporal Structure.* CSL. Cambridge: Cambridge University Press, 1993.

CHAPTER 18

# Motivated Categories, Middle Voice, and Passive Morphology

RACHEL AUBREY

CANADA INSTITUTE OF LINGUISTICS
TRINITY WESTERN UNIVERSITY

## 1. INTRODUCTION

It is standard practice for students of New Testament Greek to learn the -(θ)η- inflectional forms of the aorist verb as the passive voice in Greek, treating the form as though it functions solely as a passive marker. Yet when -(θ)η- shows a nonpassive function, such cases are taken as exceptions to the rules. As deviant uses, they require further labeling: "passive in active sense" or "passive in form but active in meaning."[1] This practice ignores two significant points regarding the nature of language: (1) the semantic diversity of voice forms as a cross-linguistic pattern;[2] and (2) the myriad ways in which humans

---

1   J. Gresham Machen, *New Testament Greek for Beginners* (New York: Macmillan, 1923), 61 (§116); A. T. Robertson, *A Grammar of the Greek New Testament in the Light of Historical Research*, 4th ed. (Nashville: Broadman, 1934), 811–12.

2   Masayoshi Shibatani, "Voice," in *Morphology: An International Handbook on Inflection and Word-Formation*, ed. Geert Booij et al., HSK 17.2 (Berlin: Walter de Gruyter, 2004), 2:1145–65; Masayoshi Shibatani, ed., *Passive and Voice*, TSL 16 (Amsterdam: Benjamins, 1988); Talmy Givón, *Bio-Linguistics: The Santa Barbara Lectures* (Amsterdam: Benjamins, 2002); Tasaku Tsunoda and Taro Kageyama, *Voice and Grammatical Relations: In Honor of Masayoshi Shibatani*, TSL 65 (Amsterdam: Benjamins, 2006).

create motivated categories that are semantically diverse but crucially connected.[3]

For (1), what grammarians typically label as middle and/or passive markers actually represent multifunctional, semantically diverse categories, cross-linguistically expressing a variety of event types.[4] Greek -(θ)η- morphology is consistent with these cross-linguistic trends; it is both synchronically and diachronically polysemous. As an inflectional form, -(θ)η- expresses both *voice* (middle-passive) and *aspect* (aorist perfective).[5]

For (2), these various functions of -(θ)η- are not an arbitrary list of accidental features, but show resemblances to one another as semantically related types. The traditional template for grammatical voice expects all voice oppositions to conform to a set of syntactic rules in an active-passive contrast. Yet ignoring the cross-linguistic patterns that arise in voice morphology distorts our expectations of how -(θ)η- ought to behave in relation to its fellow voice categories, prompting grammarians to devise further rules and subcategories to account for what is perceived as erratic behavior.

What is needed is a framework that accounts for the deeper regularities in -(θ)η- usage, not limited to its passive usage, that can clarify the relations and distinctions in its other patterns also. A cognitive linguistic approach brings to bear the human conceptual and experiential motivations that help to identify a semantic basis for

---

3   Ronald Langacker, *Essentials of Cognitive Grammar* (Oxford: Oxford University Press, 2013); Eve Sweetser, *From Etymology to Pragmatics: Metaphorical and Cultural Aspects of Semantic Structure*, CSL 54 (Cambridge: Cambridge University Press, 1990).

4   Suzanne Kemmer, "Human Cognition and the Elaboration of Events: Some Universal Conceptual Categories," in *The New Psychology of Language: Cognitive and Functional Approaches to Language Structure*, ed. Michael Tomasello (London: Erlbaum, 2003) 2:89–118; Masayoshi Shibatani, "Passives and Related Constructions: A Prototype Analysis," *Language* 61 (1985), 821–48; Shibatani, *Passive and Voice*; Martin Haspelmath, *Transitivity Alternations of the Anticausative Type*, Institut für Sprachwissenschaft Arbeitspapiere NS 5 (Cologne: Universität zu Köln, 1987).

5   Andrew L. Sihler, *New Comparative Grammar of Greek and Latin* (Oxford: Oxford University Press, 1995), 563–64; José Luis García Ramón, "From *Aktionsart* to Aspect and Voice: On the Morphosyntax of the Greek Aorists with -η- and -θη-," in *The Greek Verb: Morphology, Syntax, and Semantics: Proceedings of the 8th International Meeting of Greek Linguistics, Agrigento, October 1–2, 2009*, ed. Annamaria Bartolotta, BCLL 128 (Leuven: Peeters, 2014), 149–82.

-(θ)η- morphology and views its semantic scope alongside the rest of the Greek voice system.[6] Instead of an exclusively passive form with random deviants, -(θ)η- is better understood as a diachronically and synchronically motivated form with multiple functions, all of which fit within the semantic scope of the middle domain.[7]

## 1.1 Traditional Approaches and the Trouble with -(θ)η-

For grammatical voice studies, analysis and explanation tend to focus on the formal oppositions and grammatical rules that create syntactic structure. Describing -(θ)η- is a matter of linking its form to its morphosyntactic function—the role it plays among the elements in the system.[8] If a link consistently holds between -(θ)η- morphology and passive syntax, then this pattern is attributed to an underlying morphosyntactic rule in the grammar where the -(θ)η- inflection marks a passive syntactic function within the grammatical voice set.

This form-function pairing constitutes its role in the system: -(θ)η-, defined as passive morphology, ought to correspond to a passive function in the syntax.[9] This expectation shapes not just what we do with its canonical realization, i.e., those instances that fit the rules; but it crucially shapes what we do with those that do *not* fit the rules. When -(θ)η- does not live up to expectation, the traditional response is to dismiss such cases as exceptions, suggesting they

6   Ronald W. Langacker, *Foundations of Cognitive Grammar, Volume 2: Descriptive Application* (Stanford, CA: Stanford University Press, 1991); Ronald W. Langacker, "Dimensions of Defocusing," in Tsunoda, *Voice and Grammatical Relations*, 115–38.

7   Rutger J. Allan, *The Middle Voice in Ancient Greek: A Study in Polysemy*, ASCP 11 (Amsterdam: Gieben, 2003); Carl W. Conrad, "New Observations on Voice in the Ancient Greek Verb," https://pages.wustl.edu/files/pages/imce/cwconrad/newobsancgrkvc.pdf.

8   M.H. Klaiman, *Grammatical Voice*, CSL 59 (Cambridge: Cambridge University Press, 1991), 23–31.

9   Roy Harris, "Language as Social Interaction: Integrationalism versus Segregationalism," in *Integrational Linguistics: A First Reader*, ed. Roy Harris and George Wolf, LCLib 18 (Oxford: Pergamon, 1998), 10.

have somehow skirted the rules and taken on an active role: "passive in form but active in meaning."[10]

Although -(θ)η- may appear well behaved at first glance, it shows much more variety than the syntactic rules would lead us to anticipate. Describing -(θ)η- according to a set of voice rules not only affects how we see the category, but how we deal with departures from those rules. Deviations from the norm appear random and without motivation or reason. Further, there is no room for such cases in a syntactic system, so they are pushed aside, deemed as puzzling, illogical, or hardly discernable from their active counterpart.[11]

But the problem remains. None of these cases fit the conditions for membership in the passive voice category (-(θ)η- form tied to passive syntax). What is to be done, for instance, with unexpected cases of -(θ)η- wherein the subject does the action as in examples 1–6?

(1) πρὸς ἀλλήλους γὰρ <u>διελέχθησαν</u> ἐν τῇ ὁδῷ τίς μείζων
for on the way <u>they had argued</u> with one another who was the greatest (Mark 9:34)[12]

(2) τότε <u>ἠγέρθησαν</u> πᾶσαι αἱ παρθένοι ἐκεῖναι καὶ ἐκόσμησαν τὰς λαμπάδας ἑαυτῶν
Then all those bridesmaids <u>got up</u> and trimmed their lamps (Matthew 25:7)

(3) ταῦτα δὲ αὐτοῦ <u>ἐνθυμηθέντος</u>
As he was <u>considering</u> these things (Matt 1:20)

(4) καὶ <u>ἐμνήσθησαν</u> τῶν ῥημάτων αὐτοῦ
And they <u>remembered</u> his words (Luke 24:8)

(5) <u>ἐξηράνθη</u> ὁ χόρτος
The grass <u>withers</u> (1 Peter 1:24)

(6) καὶ τοῦτο εἰπὼν <u>ἐκοιμήθη</u>
when he had said this, <u>he died</u> (Acts 7:60)

---

10  Matthew Baerman, et al., eds., *Deponency and Morphological Mismatches*, PBA 145 (Oxford: Oxford University Press, 2007); Stratton L. Ladewig, "Defining Deponency: An Investigation into Greek Deponency of the Middle and Passive Voices in the Koine Period" (PhD diss., Dallas Theological Seminary, 2010), 103–63.

11  Cf., e.g., Ladewig, "Defining Deponency," 134.

12  Unless otherwise indicated, all translations are mine.

Syntactic rules, such as the passive for -(θ)η-, are expected to account for syntactic structure and stipulate linguistic behavior.[13] Cases like these appear to have taken on the syntactic trappings of the active (i.e., the subject does action, or there is a direct object in the clause).

Applying labels such as "deponent" or "passive in active sense" creates a sense of legitimacy in the midst of the inconsistencies in its behavior, giving scholars occasion to invent new subcategories and further rules to justify their existence as leaks in the system.[14] When -(θ)η- appears in a clause with an agent subject, it is described as having exchanged one meaning for another, as a mismatched form-function pairing.[15] Lists and charts are drawn up in descriptive analysis to illustrate this exchange.[16]

Figure 1 illustrates the standard conception of voice with a tripartite division of the aorist.

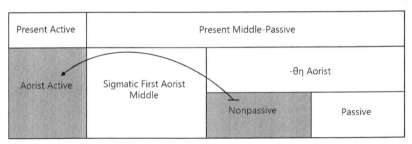

Figure 1. Traditional Conception of Voice (Tripartite Divide in the Aorist)

For the present and perfect verbal paradigms, one set of inflectional forms represents the active while another set represents the

13  Matthew Baerman, "Morphological Typology of Deponency," in Baerman, *Deponency and Morphological Mismatches*, 3.

14  Nikolaos Lavidas and Dimitra Papangeli, "Deponency in the Diachrony of Greek," in Baerman, *Deponency and Morphological Mismatches*, 97–126.

15  Rather than the expected passive function, it appears to have an active one instead. This is often described as a mismatch or tension between voice form and voice function (see Ladewig, "Defining Deponency," 185). Their assigned grammatical role (-[θ]η- matched to passive syntax) does not match how they are actually used in real-world contexts (-[θ]η- matched to nonpassive syntax).

16  H. E. Dana and Julius R. Mantey, *A Manual Grammar of the Greek New Testament* (New York: Macmillan, 1955), 163; Baerman, "Morphological Typology of Deponency," 2; Ladewig, "Defining Deponency," 123–24.

middle-passive. These middle-passive forms are capable of expressing either middle or passive semantics. Context is considered key
to their interpretation. The three distinct morphological markers
of the aorist paradigm, on the other hand, are understood to correspond to a tripartite division of active, middle, and passive voice.
One set of inflectional forms exists for the active. Nonactive sigmatic (i.e., first aorist) forms (-σαμην, -σω, -σατο) are taught as middle
morphology attached to middle voice. While -(θ)η- is considered a
fully distinct category, signifying a passive voice that exists apart
from either active or middle.

Nonpassive cases of -(θ)η- are considered active in meaning, requiring us to regard the form via a split conception. From a linguistic and logical standpoint, such deviant cases necessitate it leaping
over categorical lines, bypassing the middle, and landing itself in
the active instead. Ergo, we are led to conclude: -(θ)η- is surely passive ... except when it's not.

Rather than questioning the validity of categorizing -(θ)η- as a
distinct passive, the traditional approach suggests that the trouble
lies with -(θ)η- itself, ceding its use to the grammatical rules. This
persuades us to regard -(θ)η- as somewhat of a degenerate category,
defined, at least in part, by its deviant behavior.[17] It is either homog-
enized to fit the rules, or it falls apart into collected lists that do not
fit with one another or the rest of the system.[18]

## 1.2 Dynamic model: Beyond Discrete Categories

Understanding the broader patterns that arise in voice phenomena
across languages enables us to shift perspective and see the system

---

17  K. L. McKay, *Greek Grammar for Students: A Concise Grammar of Classical Attic
with Special Reference to Aspect in the Verb* (Canberra: Dept. of Classics, Australian National University, 1974), 136.

18  We find verbs that take -(θ)η- marking like καταγω (BDAG, 516), πλαναω
(BDAG, 822), σεβαζομαι (BDAG, 917) listed as either deponent or "passive in
active sense," their entries in the lexicon signifying their exceptional status.
In such cases, the verbs are often taught as actives and students learn them
in lists as exceptions to the voice canon (e.g., William D. Mounce, *Basics of
Biblical Greek Grammar*, 3rd ed. [Grand Rapids: Zondervan, 2009], 152). As a
result, understanding -(θ)η- is largely a matter of being able to distinguish
its true passive sense on the one hand, versus recognizing all those exceptional cases that diverge from it on the other.

in a new light. These cross-linguistic patterns alter expectations in regard to voice categories, allowing us to reconsider the supposed deviance of -(θ)η- and investigate its usage as a semantically motivated form. Rather than a single form-function set with illogical exceptions, considering the experiential and conceptual motivations that come in to play allows a more accurate description of its patterned activity.

The tripartite divide in the aorist, as in figure 1 above, may be appealing. It provides each morphological form with a distinct voice function (active, middle, passive + deponent). But it offers a misleading account since it runs counter to the nature of grammatical voice in language, both from a typological stance and in the diachronic development of voice morphology in Greek, especially with respect to the origins of -(θ)η- and its gradual spread over time.

Voice categories are better understood as waypoints along a semantic continuum. This prototype model of categorization points to the relational character of meaning in language; it is inextricable from human behavior and the interpretive process; it does not come divided up into discrete boxes.[19] Voice categories are not produced through rules that create discrete sets but through the action of analogy.

Prototype categories assign membership based on a perception of similarity to other members in the category.[20] Membership is gradable and exists on a continuum rather than a dichotomy. Category members demonstrate degrees of likeness and difference with reference to a central prototype. Members can be counted as better or worse instances of a category, more central or marginal, core or borderline. The category prototype, the most typical member, serves as a reference point for ascribing new members, each of which may be closer to or further from the prototype based on similarity to it. These are often termed "family resemblance patterns"

---

19  Michael R. Walrod and Jamin R. Pelkey, "Four Faces, Eight Places: Elaborate Expression, Emergent Meaning, and Translation as Discourse Art," *JT* 6 (2010): 11–26.

20  For an overview of prototype categorization and its role in language, see George Lakoff, *Women, Fire, and Dangerous Things: What Categories Reveal about the Mind* (Chicago: University of Chicago Press, 1987), 5–57; Dirk Geeraerts, *Theories of Lexical Semantics* (Oxford: Oxford University Press, 2010), 183–203.

where categories take on a radial structure with clusters, or networks, of related meanings, as members relate to the prototype in different ways.[21]

Though it may seem complex, the prototype model makes a very basic claim: Language reflects the nature of those who use it.[22] Language categories are grounded in and arise from how humans understand and interpret their circumstances. Grammar itself is concerned with structuring and symbolizing the many ways we interpret events via our cognitive capacities for perception, attention, and categorization. Here, the categorizing process is a deeply meaningful one for a very simple fact: The structure of language reflects our fundamental experience of making sense of the world in and through our use of language.

Accepting a dynamic view of categories alters expectations for voice. Instead of clear distinctions between voice types, we expect a more gradient scale with gradual shifts in meaning and no definite boundaries. Instead of categories that contrast with respect to one feature, we expect a complex interplay of competing motivations to underlie the categorization of an event.[23]

---

21  Laura A. Janda, "Cognitive Linguistics," *Glossos* 8 (2006): 13–18.

22  Joan Bybee, *Language, Usage and Cognition* (New York: Cambridge University Press, 2010), 1–13.

23  Yet this complexity need not dissuade us, since the patterns that arise in language are the very same kinds of patterns that are fundamental to our body-based nature. The factors involved in the categorization of -(θ)η- are not different in kind from those we already use in daily interactions in the world. This recognition—that language reflects our general cognitive abilities—opens up investigations into -(θ)η-, suggesting that it is not illogical but deeply motivated, and that it is not beyond our ability to understand, but rises from what we already find familiar. This engages us in our ability to see patterned variation across complex phenomena—even if all types do not share a uniform feature. As we engage in the world so we engage in language. We are continuously synthesizing vastly different experiences into patterned interactions, noticing likeness and differences among events as a constant comparison of unequal things. People are analogy makers by trade; pattern recognition permeates the whole of our thinking and doing. Metaphor, as a conceptual connection or mapping from one domain of experience to another, helps us to understand abstract concepts in terms of our body-based experiences. Our embodied interactions provide a rich backdrop of source domains from which we may reason abstractly (George Lakoff and Mark Johnson, *Metaphors We Live By* [Chicago: University of Chicago, 1980]; Raymond W. Gibbs, ed., *The Cambridge Handbook of Metaphor and Thought* [Cambridge: Cambridge University Press, 2008]).

What this means for -(θ)η- is that instead of a single defining function, it is more likely to be used for multiple related senses. Its functions are varied and arise through the communicative process. As speakers see similarities among different types of events, they categorize them together under one formal expression.

Since there are only so many grammatical forms available in a given language, it makes sense that a single morphological form would be used for more than one function.[24] Placing Greek morphology into cross-linguistic context bears this out. Grammatical polysemy (one form; multiple meanings) is manifest across languages and voice morphology in Greek as well as cross-linguistically is no exception to this pervasive pattern.

One pattern that arises in voice phenomena is that passive morphology commonly grows up as an extended, or secondary function, from other existing markers and continues to retain its multifunctional use. Through diachronic spread, a single form begins with one function but then adopts a number of others as it is employed in new contexts for related ideas. From a synchronic standpoint (a slice of the language at one period), a marker of passive voice, such -(θ)η- in the Koine period, may include the passive function within its scope, but it is likely to show a number of other related functions as well.

The -(θ)η- form was initially adopted into the aorist paradigm in Greek to express events that involved a change of state. This included events like the spontaneous type in which a nonvolitional participant undergoes a change of state without involvement from an external force. This could be a physical change (ἐμίγη "mingled," ἐάγη "broke"), a mental change (ἐδάη "learned," i.e., "got informed"), or a change in location/posture (ἐάλη "crouched," ἐκ ... ῥύη "flowed out").[25]

This initial semantic type enabled -(θ)η- to extend to a semantically similar type—the prototypical passive. For this type, -(θ)η- provided the means for speakers to focus attention onto the participant who undergoes a change of state, i.e., the patient. The difference between a spontaneous event and a passive event is that the passive includes the external force that induces the event (i.e., the agent) in

---

24  Suzanne Kemmer, *The Middle Voice*, TSL 23 (Amsterdam: Benjamins, 1993), 5.
25  García Ramón, "From *Aktionsart* to Aspect and Voice," 149, 163.

its conception, while the spontaneous type does not. This is the difference between the spontaneous: "The balloon burst" in contrast to the passive: "The balloon was popped by Leah." In this type, -(θ)η- was used with transitive, two-participant verbs (ἔτυψε "strike someone") to express a passive reading (ἔτυπη "was struck").[26]

Typically, the passive is recognized in contrast to an active transitive clause. In a prototypical active like "Micah hit the punching bag," the agent as grammatical subject initiates or supplies the force for the event but is unaffected by it; no change of state is profiled for Micah. Instead, it is the patient or object receiving the action that undergoes the change. In the passive alternation, "The punching bag was hit by Micah," the most salient entity (the patient) is promoted to grammatical subject. Micah's role as agent is downplayed and supplied in an oblique phrase, often called a "by-phrase" (ὑπό + GEN.), to reflect its lowered salience.

If we consider the spontaneous event types and the passive type together, then we already have a clear semantic pattern arising in -(θ)η- in Homeric Greek, since these two types were well-established patterns using -(θ)η- morphology by this period; -(θ)η- expressed events in which a nonvolitional participant undergoes a change of state. In this way, -(θ)η- matched a limited spectrum within the wider semantic space of the middle domain. In Homer and later in Classical and Hellenistic Greek, -(θ)η- was used alongside the sigmatic (first aorist) middle forms. For the aorist paradigm, these two forms (sigmatic and -[θ]η-) were used in tandem to divide up the semantic scope of the middle-passive voice accomplished by the present and perfect paradigms.

The sigmatic middle was employed for middle types that had a more agent-like participant as the focus of attention. These events included middles like reflexives, reciprocals, and perceptions, among others. The -(θ)η- form was employed for those middle events that had a more patient-like participant as the focus of attention. These included the spontaneous events mentioned above as the semantic origin of the category, and also expanded into the passive.

The division of labor in the aorist paradigm between more agent-like (receiving sigmatic middle marking) and more patient-like (with -(θ)η-) continued in Homer, but it was not static. The

---

26  Ibid., 169.

-(θ)η- form began a slow process of encroaching in the opposite direction into the semantic domain originally reserved for the sigmatic aorist middle form (see §4). From Homeric to Classical and into Hellenistic, -(θ)η- slowly expanded in two directions: (1) enveloping the semantically and syntactically passive events, and (2) encroaching on and gradually displacing sigmatic middles as the marking of choice for certain middle event types.[27]

This diachronic picture illustrates semantic gradience in voice categories. Figure 2 plots these middle types in the sigmatic and -(θ)η- forms alongside the active on a semantic continuum.

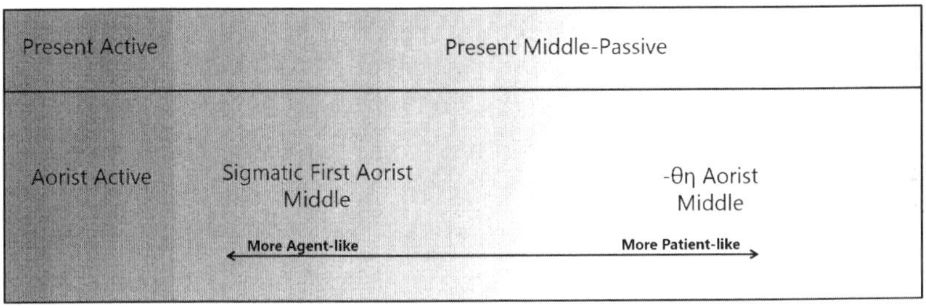

Figure 2. Semantic Continuum of Voice

At one end of the spectrum, the active voice is used to express the most transitive, most agent-like events. Example (7) illustrates a prototypical active transitive in which an agent (subject) volitionally performs an action. The patient (object) undergoes the affects of the action. In this conception, the patient (object) is the most affected participant while the agent (subject) is typically unaffected.

(7) Prototypical transitive
καὶ λαβόντες οἱ γεωργοὶ τοὺς δούλους αὐτοῦ ὃν μὲν ἔδειραν,
ὃν δὲ ἀπέκτειναν, ὃν δὲ ἐλιθοβόλησαν
And the tenants seized his slaves, one they beat,
another they killed, and another they stoned
(Matt 21:35)

At the other end of the spectrum, the passive voice represented in (8) also involves two participants, but in this case, the patient, as the most affected entity (i.e., undergoes a change of state) is encoded as grammatical subject.

---

27  Allan, *Middle Voice*, 147, 156.

(8) Passive

ἀπὸ τῶν τριῶν πληγῶν τούτων <u>ἀπεκτάνθησαν</u>

By three plagues a third of <u>humanity was killed</u>

(Rev 9:18)

The active and passive are mirror images, expressing the same kind of event: an agent does something to cause a change of state in a patient. But the passive shifts the spotlight from the agent (in the active) onto the patient so that what happens to him is the most salient part of the event. Changing its syntactic expression shifts attention from the initiator of the action onto the most affected participant. This end of the spectrum involves the most patient-like events: The grammatical subject is nonvolitional and fully affected.

If these event types represent two extremes from the most transitive, most agent-like events down to the least transitive, most patient-like events, then the intervening portions of the continuum represent the scalar semantic patterns in voice. These gradient shifts in meaning occur on a scale from more agent-like to more patient-like events. This represents the middle domain: Those events that show a lowered transitivity. Each event type may be plotted along the continuum, with the prototypical voice members (active, middle, passive) representing waypoints along the scale.

The path from prototypical active transitive event to prototypical passive involves a decreasing level of agency and an increasing level of subject affectedness. Yet the reason we have plotted voice categories on a semantic continuum from more agent-like to more patient-like is that even active events can show some level of subject affectedness. Consider, especially, the case of the active intransitive (single participant) event, such as ὁρμάω "rush/run." Like the prototypical transitive, the subject initiates the action, but this event type still involves a lowered transitivity and higher subject affectedness since the single participant is both an initiating force as well as experiencing the affects of the action. It is difficult to think of any intransitive event in which the subject is not, in some way, experiencing the effects of the event. The morphological expression may be formally active, but because of the lowered transitivity, it represents a departure from the most agent-like, most transitive event.

The feature of subject-affectedness offers a critical starting point for discussing voice since it is a generally accurate parameter.

Yet voice types involve interplay of other factors as well. We must also consider: (1) which participant initiates the action and which is affected by it, (2) lexical semantics, (3) number of participants, and (4) adjustments in the scope of attention that alternations in voice confer onto different participants.

This offers a preliminary overview, painting a picture of middle voice with broad brushstrokes and providing a glimpse of the voice landscape. As a general conception, this puts us in a better position to investigate -(θ)η- marking patterns more specifically. A more detailed look at the diachronic development of -(θ)η- follows in section 2, where we consider the kinds of event types included within its scope with respect to typological patterns as well as its diachronic development in the Greek voice system.

Section 3 takes the variety of event patterns in section 2 and considers the semantic connections among them. Though the primary focus remains on -(θ)η- morphology, the principles outlined are applicable to the rest of the middle system.

The -(θ)η- form is better understood as sharing a division of labor in the middle domain with the sigmatic middle forms than as an exclusively passive marker with defective, deponent exceptions. It marks the same set of middle event types subsumed within the semantic middle domain with respect to the other middle-passive morphology in the present and perfect paradigms. This investigation of the semantic types culminates in a semantic map of the middle domain, allowing us to locate the role of -(θ)η- with respect to the rest of the middle system. But before we do so, we consider the variety of event types expressed in -(θ)η-, especially with respect to cross-linguistic patterns for voice morphology and how this plays out in Greek.

# 2. SYNCHRONIC VARIETY AND DIACHRONIC DEVELOPMENT

In traditional approaches, -(θ)η- is described as a marker of a distinct passive voice in Greek. The challenges of this approach to -(θ)η- is that it shows far more variety in its use, appearing in a host of constructions that diverge from the passive in a number of ways. Labels such as "pseudo-reflexive" (for verbs like ἐκοιμήθην "fall asleep") or "pseudo-passive" (for verbs like ἐφοβήθην "became afraid") are employed to describe these discrepancies from the passive function.[28]

Typological research in this regard offers insight into cross-linguistic patterns in voice phenomena, highlighting ways in which languages show similarity as well as difference in their organizing categories. One recurring theme in language after language is that morphemes that are labeled as passive markers (because they are used to express passive syntax) are also employed for other functions as well, including reflexives, reciprocals, motion, collectives, spontaneous events, and potential passives among others.[29]

For instance, most of the so-called "pseudo-passives" in -(θ)η- are better explained as fitting into the spontaneous process type in which the subject changes state without an external cause. Cross-linguistically and in Greek, this event type includes autonomous actions that can occur without external force[30] (such as ἐφάνη or ὤφθη "appear/become visible," ἐκρύβη "be hidden" and καταποντισθῇ "sink,") along with physiological processes that arise naturally (such as ἐπαλαιώθη "grow old," ἐπωρώθη "become hard," ἐπληθύνθη "increase," ἐξηράνθη "dry up").

Related to this type are the "pseudo-reflexives." These are better understood as collective events in which plural agents perform an action (συνάχθητε "gather together"), reflexives in which an agent performs an action on himself (ἐβαπτίσθη "wash"),[31] body motion in which the subject changes location (ἐπορεύθη "go"),[32] or mental processes in which a subject experiences mental/emotional change (ἐφοβήθη "become frightened").

This kind of synchronic variety in -(θ)η- is not just a random assortment of types, but is integrated with its diachronic development (i.e., how it originated and developed over time), and thus is best

---

28  Albert Rijksbaron, *The Syntax and Semantics of the Verb in Classical Greek*, 3rd ed. (Chicago: University of Chicago Press, 2002), 160–61; Allan, *Middle Voice*, 2.

29  For a discussion of passive markers and their multifunctionality across languages, see Martin Haspelmath, "The Grammaticalization of Passive Morphology," *StudLang* 14 (1990), 32–37; Givón, *Bio-Linguistics*, 207–14; Shibatani, "Passives and Related Constructions," 825–30.

30  Shibatani, "Passives and Related Constructions," 827; Haspelmath, "Transitivity Alternations of the Anticausative Type," 15–17.

31  Cf. Luke 11:40.

32  Haspelmath, "Transitivity Alternations of the Anticausative Type," 27; Kemmer, *Middle Voice*, 53.

considered in light of its diachronic history.[33] If diachronic change is directly involved in shaping the synchronic system, i.e., the nature of the system at one stage of the language,[34] then the synchronic variety in -$(\theta)\eta$- and its diachronic development are two sides of the same coin, so much so that they shed light on the same data.[35]

Multifunctional morphology, like -$(\theta)\eta$-, gains new functions over time. In early stages, a form might mark function A, but later extend to include function B. But these assimilations are not arbitrary such that a category becomes a grab bag of disparate elements. Rather, functional similarity motivates the extension from old (established usage) to new (unestablished use). New senses arise through adaptive experimentation in communicative contexts, extending what is a known use to what is a new but similar use via association, semantic connection, and analogy.

Moreover, the historical order that new senses are added offers insight into *how* they are related. As changes occur along a similar path in many languages, we have a better view of how grammatical forms develop.[36] This applies to passive morphology cross-linguistically. Passive morphemes in Indo-European (IE) and non-IE languages arise secondarily from middles and a variety of other source domains, such as statives, reflexives, causatives, and impersonals.[37] A form in a given language may begin with one use, such as reflexive, and then expand to other functions, becoming more and more abstract over time as it includes an ever-growing set of senses within its domain. The synchronic polysemy of an element reflects a chain of related uses and extensions over time. As each new sense is

---

33  Allan, *Middle Voice*, 126–28; García Ramón, "From *Aktionsart* to Aspect and Voice," 149–82.

34  Sweetser, *From Etymology to Pragmatics*, 9–10; Johanna Nichols, "Diversity and Stability in Language" in *The Handbook of Historical Linguistics*, ed. Brian D. Joseph and Richard D. Janda, BHL (Malden, MA: Blackwell, 2003), 283–310; Joan Bybee and Clay Beckner, "Language Use, Cognitive Processes, and Linguistic Change," in *The Routledge Handbook of Historical Linguistics*, ed. Claire Bowern and Bethwyn Evans (London: Routledge, 2015), 503–18.

35  Sweetser, *From Etymology to Pragmatics*, 18–22.

36  For a fuller discussion of the historical order in which event types were added within the scope of the -$(\theta)\eta$- marking pattern, see §3.

37  Haspelmath, "Passive Morphology"; Givón, *Bio-Linguistics*, 207–14; Shibatani, "Passives and Related Constructions," 821–48.

added, we see how two very different functions (such as reflexives and passives) are included within the scope of a single form.

Before considering the history of -(θ)η-, we must first examine its origins in Proto-Indo-European (PIE). The earliest stages of IE languages, such as Greek, Latin, and Sanskrit, reflect a voice opposition inherited from the PIE verb, that of the active and middle.[38] This implies, in spite of its descriptive priority in most grammatical voice studies, the active-passive alternation is neither the oldest contrast nor the primary voice distinction in the classical languages.

For Greek, there are separate verbal paradigms for active and middle. There never was a distinct passive inflection in PIE, nor originally in its daughter languages. This is not to suggest that the passive construction was impossible but that it was one of the functions served by the middle. The middle included within its scope events that were more volitional (such as reflexives) as well as those events in which a nonvolitional subject undergoes a change of state. This may be an autonomous change: burst/break (intransitive spontaneous process) or it may be brought about by an external cause: be broken (by someone) (passive).[39]

The -(θ)η- form was initially integrated into the Greek aorist from a stative suffix in PIE, *-eh$_1$-, a derivational morpheme denoting state predicates.[40] Initially, -(θ)η- was just -η-. Both the aorist (θ)η and the future (θ)ησ- were later developments added to the original -η- aorist form.[41] Because -(θ)η- was integrated early on, we

---

38  Sihler, *New Comparative Grammar*, 448.

39  Jacob Wackernagel, *Lectures on Syntax: With Special Reference to Greek, Latin, and Germanic*, trans. David Langslow (Oxford: Oxford University Press, 2009), 160; Oswald Szemerényi, *Introduction to Indo-European Linguistics* (New York: Oxford University Press, 1996), 283; Sihler, *New Comparative Grammar*, 448; Robert S.P. Beekes and Michiel Arnoud Cor de Vaan, *Comparative Indo-European Linguistics: An Introduction*, 2nd ed. (Amsterdam: Benjamins, 2011), 256; Leonid Kulikov, "Passive and Middle in Indo-European: Reconstructing the Early Vedic Passive Paradigm," in *Passivization and Typology: Form and Function*, ed. Werner Abraham and Larisa Leisiö, TSL 68 (Amsterdam: Benjamins, 2006), 62–91.

40  Though some debate exists whether it was a stative marker or originally a fientive one. See Allan, *Middle Voice*, 132 n. 241; and García Ramón, "From *Aktionsart* to Aspect and Voice," 155–57 for further discussion.

41  Though different forms, the -η- and -(θ)η- lack a functional contrast (García Ramón, "From *Aktionsart* to Aspect and Voice," 152–53). See Allan, *Middle Voice*, 126–41 for a helpful discussion of the morphological distribution of

find it in Homer to denote the same event types as -η-; I use the full -(θ)η- label in this discussion.

Originally a marker of state predicates, -(θ)η- developed through a process of grammaticalization. A derivational morpheme not attached to any specific verbal stem[42] grew into a fully productive inflectional form expressing both *aspect* (aor. perfective) and *voice* (middle-passive semantics). As a stative, -(θ)η- was initially restricted to two predicate types, both involving states: telic-transformative predicates[43] ands state predicates.[44]

The telic-transformative type interacted with the -(θ)η- form in two ways, depending on a verb's transitivity. For intransitive (one-participant) verbs, -(θ)η- redundantly marked what the aorist stem already marked: the achievement of a state, as in ἐπάγη "got stuck." For these, the root aorist and the -(θ)η- aorist expressed a change of state, while the perfect denoted the final state. The present referred to the progressive reaching of the state (or of multiple subjects reaching a state).[45] The -(θ)η- form in these cases consistently denoted a spontaneous process for the event.

Transitive verbs functioned differently. The second participant in the syntax allowed for a second opposition. The -(θ)η- form could detransitivize the event to express either the canonical passive meaning or a spontaneous process. For transitive verbs, such as ἀνοίγω, "I open [something]," -(θ)η- could denote either a passive in which the agent is present or a spontaneous event in which a change took place autonomously without an agent.[46] This is a difference between a book being opened (ἠνοίχθη) *by someone* as in Rev 20:12 (passive) and the earth opening (ἠνοίχθη) and devouring Dathan in

---

42  Early examples include φανη "became visible," ἐτέρση "became dry," θαρσησε "became bold." See García Ramón, "From *Aktionsart* to Aspect and Voice," 157–60 for a more extensive discussion.

43  Telic-transformatives are activities that involve a change of state.

44  States are nondynamic properties, like "be," "love" / "hate," "be dry" / "wet"; García Ramón, "From *Aktionsart* to Aspect and Voice," 162.

45  Ibid., 163.

46  In this second pattern, -(θ)η- is used as a contrast to causatives (transitives) to encode the noncaused spontaneous counterpart. The causative is expressed in the active while the noncaused version is expressed in -(θ)η-, as in σαλεύω, "I shake [something]" vs. ἐσαλεύθη "[something] shook."

the forms in Homer and Classical Greek. For a discussion of the future form see ibid., 178–202.

LXX Psalm 105:17 [Eng. 106:17] (spontaneous). In this type, the passive reading of the -(θ)η- aorist stands in opposition to the transitive sigmatic first aorist (either active or middle). The subject in the -(θ)η- is more like a prototypical patient (a nonvolitional participant that goes through a change of state) and the subject in the sigmatic aorist is more like a prototypical agent (a volitional participant who brings about an event).[47] However, regardless of the transitivity of these telic-transformatives, -(θ)η- historically communicated a change in state for the subject.

The other event type, states, provided a second source for -(θ)η- aorists, usually with state verbs with no preexisting aorist paradigm. The use of -(θ)η- provided them with a way to develop one. A good example of a verb still pervasive in the Koine is φαίνειν, "to shine" in the present stem. Originally, it lacked an aorist; its stativity conflicted with the semantics of the root aorist. The -(θ)η- provided a way for the verb to fill out the paradigm: φανῆναί "to become visible." In this verb class, the present stem denoted a state, while the aorist, provided via -(θ)η-, denoted an ingressive expression, entry into a state.[48]

What is of specific interest for the development of the -(θ)η- form is its exclusive integration into Greek within the aorist and not the present stem. This draws out semantic differences in aspect and its interaction with -(θ)η- and predicates types. The aorist perfective aspect correlated well with telicity—endpoint to the action; conveying the action as complete. The present stem involves imperfective aspect, or noncomplete events; no telicity (endpoint) is involved in its conception. This is a difference between perfective aorist ἐπλήσθη "became full" and imperfective present πίμπλαντο "was becoming full."[49]

When -(θ)η- was first integrated into the aorist, it involved not just a change or affectedness for the subject, but a complete change of state. If we look back at the two predicate types involved, this includes the telic-transformative lexemes as well as the state predicates. It is this relationship between change-of-state/telicity with

47  Ibid., 169–70.
48  Ibid., 172. See also Allan, *Middle Voice*, 126–77; Conrad, "New Observations."
49  See García Ramón "From *Aktionsart* to Aspect and Voice," 154 for further discussion and examples.

the perfective aspect of the aorist that defines the -(θ)η- in contrast with the other middle inflectional forms. The aorist perfective aspect aids in this process because it expresses the fulfillment of that change, so that the new state is fully reached or totally complete. If a middle form is used in the present stem (imperfective), it indicates that the subject is undergoing change but it does so as a progressive reaching of the state so that the change is not fully reached. This is a difference between ἐτήκετο "it was melting" in the imperfect and ἐτάκη "it melted" in the aorist. When used with the -(θ)η- aorist stem, the change is fully complete.

This diachronic development establishes that the passive function of -(θ)η- grew up as one of the semantic extensions of the domain, but that -(θ)η- morphology remained multifunctional and spreading, never restricted to a uniquely passive function. A variety of patterns, relations, and connections begin to emerge when we recognize that passive syntax is not the defining feature of -(θ)η-. The picture that emerges within its use resembles more of a widening diffusion through a network of related types than of a sharp, one-to-one distinction, a variety of connections and relations rather than a single form-function pairing.

In fact, if grammatical voice were restricted to a search for only those forms that mark a single voice function, such as expecting passive morphology to correlate with passive syntax in the strictest sense, the number of languages that meet such a requirement becomes very small indeed. Numerous languages, including Greek and English, would be excluded from evincing voice categories at all.[50] The irony here is that within the traditional approach the very origin of -(θ)η- usage, the spontaneous event type, is not considered a true member of the -(θ)η- category. There are a host of categories and distinctions presupposed in analysis that do more to skew our understanding than clarify the kinds of distinctions languages actually make. The active-passive binary illustrates this well in the case of -(θ)η-.

---

50 Shibatani, "Voice" 1146; Masayoshi Shibatani, "On the Conceptual Framework for Voice Phenomena," *Linguistics* 44 (2006): 219.

## 2.1 Cross-Linguistic Variety in Voice Distinctions

Many languages express voice oppositions that are not based upon the active-passive contrast, do not resemble it, and are in fact typologically distinct from it.[51] Instead they show other voice divisions, both in semantic contrast and formal expression. Typological research calls attention to the diversity of voice distinctions that languages express, highlighting trends and patterns in voice phenomena across the world's languages. Ultimately research in this area makes two very simple claims: (1) Different languages express different voice distinctions, and (2) we cannot rely upon one type of voice system to define all others. This is precisely because languages reflect a variety of voice types that evince very different categories from those found in the active-passive contrast.[52]

Understanding the variety of semantic event types helps us recognize that not all languages encode events in comparable voice categories. One set of languages may subsume a series of event types under a single form while in another set of languages each of these event types might be expressed by different forms. In the former, categorizing them under one expression shows their semantic relatedness, whereas in the latter categorizing them separately reflects their differences.[53]. Preferring one model over another diverts our attention and distorts our expectations for how a given system ought to be organized.

The intuition among Greek scholars that voice categories in English do not really fit those in Greek reflects this fact. English exhibits a contrast between active and passive voices,[54] while Greek represents a typologically distinct contrast, active and middle.[55] One key difference between the two is that the former is *derived*, i.e.,

51  Klaiman, *Grammatical Voice*, 44–109.
52  Patrick Farrell, *Grammatical Relations*, OSSM 1 (Oxford: Oxford University Press, 2005); Robert M. Dixon and Alexandra Y. Aikhenvald, eds., *Changing Valency: Case studies in Transitivity* (Cambridge: Cambridge University Press, 2000); Robert M. Dixon, *Ergativity* CSL 69 (Cambridge: Cambridge University Press, 1994).
53  Kemmer, *Middle Voice*, 28.
54  Robert M. Dixon, *A Semantic Approach to English Grammar*, OTLing (Oxford: Oxford University Press, 2005), 61; Randolph Quirk, *A Comprehensive Grammar of the English Language* (New York: Longman, 1985), 159–71.
55  Kemmer, *The Middle Voice*, 1, 16–20.

traced from a source, while the latter is *basic*, i.e., not traced from a source.[56]

A defining trait of the active-passive derived system is that the passive entails a structural remapping from the basic active voice to a nonbasic (hence, derived) configuration. Passives redraw the participants in the clause so that the object of a transitive active is reconfigured as the subject of the passive. Given the examples "Micah hit the punching bag" and "The punching bag was hit by Micah" we can note the differences. In the active, the subject has the semantic role of agent (doer) while the object has the semantic role of patient (receiver). This alternation relies on a change of the subject in relation to the verb. The subject is assigned a new semantic role; it goes from agent in the active ("<u>Micah</u> hits") to patient ("<u>The punching bag</u> was hit by Micah") in the passive. We can call this the syntactic passivization process. Note, however, this operation requires basic transitive clauses. All passives must have an active counterpart. Thus, there cannot be passive-only verbs within this type of voice system. The passive category can only arise derivationally from the basic configuration. All passives have an active as their source.

The active-passive derived system contrasts with the middle system. Middle systems have a division between two voice types, but the alternation differs: middles are not derived like the syntactic passive. Middle voice entails no reconfiguration of arguments from a basic to a nonbasic structure. The choice between active and middle does not rely on semantic role alternation for the clause participants. A verb like αἱρέω "take" versus αἱρέομαι "choose," provides no reason to consider one more basic than the other; the semantic roles remain the same in both voices and the difference exists in the lexical semantics of the verb itself. In each, the subject plays the same role: agent, the one who performs the action. Likewise, in the active ἅπτω "light a fire" and middle ἅψωνται "touch something," the subject remains in the same role.

This typological principle impacts the kinds of relations we ought to expect between middle forms and the existence of active counterparts. Instead of expecting all -(θ)η- verbs to have an active (source) counterpart as would be the case in an English-like derived system, some verbs will inflect for one voice and not the other

---

56  Klaiman, *Grammatical Voice*, 23–24.

because they are not derived by a syntactic process from the active. A given verb marked with the -(θ)η- inflection does not presuppose an active source as its basis. In fact, one recurring theme in languages with middle systems is the presence of middle-only verbs (*media tantum*), verbs without a contrasting active counterpart since there is no active basis from which they have been derived.[57] Both voices are basic with no need for a derivational process. This is what we find in Greek, both -(θ)η- only (often called *passiva tantum*) and middle-only (*media tantum*) verbs appear in the Greek voice system. The middle voice, as expressed by -(θ)η- morphology and other middle-passive morphology, is basic, i.e., not derived via a morphosyntactic process from the active, and must be understood in its own right apart from passivization.[58]

Thus the middle voice system in Greek shows far more similarity to the middle systems of other languages than to the active-passive system of English. Such system-to-system solidarity spans across genetic lines. Voice systems from unrelated language families show affinity in their expression of semantic contrasts, though formal expression varies from one to the next.[59] Without a doubt, it is helpful to know that other languages make similar voice distinctions as those in Greek. These include classical languages such as Sanskrit, as well as modern European languages (Romance, Slavic, and Germanic, though English is an exception), and even non-IE languages such as Kanuri (Nilo-Saharan), Fula (Niger-Congo) and Tamil (Dravidian).[60] As a cross-linguistic pattern found in many languages that are genetically and geographically diverse, it is remarkable how the same set of middle senses are repeated across languages. From Russian to Turkish, and from French to Guugu Yimmidhirr, languages bear compelling resemblance to one another in the event types that are encoded in the middle voice. A brief inventory of the types may help us to see the parallels. Middle semantics across

---

57  Ibid., 44–45.
58  Maldonado, Ricardo. "Middle as a Basic Voice System," in *Studies in Role and Reference Grammar*, ed. Lilian Guerrero, Sergio Ibáñez, and Valeria Balloro (Mexico City: UNAM, 2009), 69–111.
59  Kemmer, *Middle Voice*. 16–20.
60  Klaiman, *Grammatical Voice*, 58.

languages include the following situation types. The middle marker in each lexeme is underlined.[61]

- Grooming/body care: Latin *lavor* "wash"; Bahasa Indonensia *berdandan* "get dressed"; Greek λύομαι "bathe," κνάομαι "scratch"
- Motion: German *sich verbeugen* "bow," Hungarian *emel-ked-* "rise, get up", Old Norse *ganga-sk* "go, leave," Greek τρέπομαι "turn" (intrans.); τάνυμαι "stretch oneself out," πορεύομαι "go, walk"
- Indirect reflexive (subject is a beneficiary of action): Turkish *ed-in* "acquire"; Changana (Niger-Congo, SE Bantu) *ku ti-tekela* "take for oneself," Greek: δέχομαι "receive, accept," ἐργάζομαι "work at, make, perform"
- Reciprocal: Latin *amplecto-r* "embrace"; Bahasa Indonesia *ber-gumul* "wrestle," Greek μάχομαι "fight, quarrel with," ἀμιλλάομαι "contend with"
- Cognition (experience a mental state): Mohave (Hokan, Yuman) *mat* iθa:ν "be angry"; Hungarian *ban-kod-* "grieve, mourn"; Greek πείθομαι "obey," φοβέομαι "fear"
- Speech acts: Sanskrit krpa-*te* "lament"; Pangwa –*i*-lumba "admit one's guilt," εὔχομαι "vow, pray, boast," Greek ἀποκρίνομαι "I answer"
- Spontaneous process: Changana *ku-ti-milela* "sprout"; Turkish *dinl-en* "recover"; Greek θερομαι "become warm," καίομαι "burn" (intrans.), ἀπόλλυμαι "die, perish"
- Passives: Kanuri *t-uruk-in* "I am seen," Greek βάλλομαι (ὑπό) "I am being hit (by)"

# 3. CONCEPTUAL PROTOTYPES AND THE NATURE OF VOICE

Section 2 noted the variety of event types expressed within voice morphology, especially in regard to the diachronic origins of -(θ)η-morphology and its development within the Greek voice system. We saw it grew up as a marker of middle voice in the aorist paradigm,

---

61  See Kemmer, *Middle Voice*, 16–20 and Allan, *Middle Voice*, 43 for further examples.

alongside the sigmatic first aorist middle marker, providing a semantic division of labor for the two inflectional sets. The sigmatic aorist primarily marked those events that involved a more agentive subject, while -(θ)η- was the preferred marker of choice for those event types that involved a more patient-like subject. These included the spontaneous events (such as mental process, spontaneous process, motion, and collective motion) as well as passive event types.

The remainder of the article examines the semantic event types marked by -(θ)η-, noting the similarities and differences among them. Once we describe each type in turn, we can step back to consider them as a whole by sketching out a semantic map of their relationship as a network of interconnected types. As we will see, -(θ)η- need not be distinguished as a separate passive voice marker, but is best represented with the rest of middle voice morphology in Greek.

Middle voice morphology, both in the present and aorist paradigms, involves a semantic continuum rather than a dichotomy. In this continuum, middle voice includes both middle and passive semantics in its scope. This means the event types we discuss below are also applicable to all middle voice morphology in Greek; each event type applicable to -(θ)η- morphology is also applicable to the rest of the middle voice. They show an overlap in their semantic scope.

Before examining each type in detail, we must draw on certain parallels from our embodied experience to describe the connections between how we conceive events and how we express them in language. Voice distinctions in language find their conceptual basis in how we see and categorize events and the participants that interact within them.

We start with a few conceptual notions that furnish a foundation for talking about voice distinctions. Some of our most fundamental conceptual patterns arise from our embodied experience of movement and interactions in space. These *conceptual schemas* are cognitive processing patterns that help us to engage in the world by taking all our vastly different experiences we have in the course of a day and understanding them through recurring elements. These patterns and processes help us to comprehend two basic themes in events, *participants* and *relationships*. For relationships, two schemas are pertinent: one and two-participant relations.[62] Some relationships involve one focused participant, which can occupy a location (κάθημαι "sit"), or change that location (πνίγομαι "drown," ἐβυθίσθην "sink"). A single participant may exhibit a stable property (ξηρός "dry") or undergo a change (ξηραίνομαι "dry up, become dry"). A person can experience a state (κοίμησις "sleep") or experience that state change (διεγείρομαι "wake up").

Figure 3 illustrates these single-participant schemas. These relationships may be static, where the participant is in a static location, state, or experience, as illustrated in the left column. Conversely, they may also be dynamic, where the participant goes through a dynamic process that involves changing location, property, or experience, as illustrated on the right.[63]

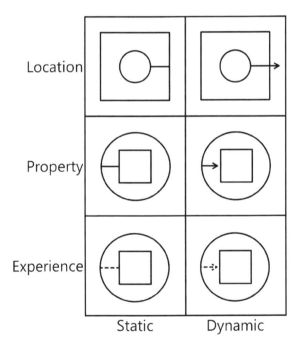

Figure 3. Types of Event Conceptualization

---

62 Langacker, "Dimensions of Defocusing," 116–17.
63 Figures in this section are adapted from Langacker, "Dimensions of Defocusing," 115–37. In this figure, the circles represent locations; squares are properties; solid lines are physical changes; and dashed lines are mental or psychological changes.

Either type (static or dynamic) can be conceptualized as taking place without the involvement of an outside force. Conversely, a dynamic version of these prototypes may also be conceptualized as part of a more elaborate two-participant relation representing common types of causation. The double arrows in figure 4 indicate exertion from an external force that induces a change of state in the second participant. This may be a physical change of state/property (a), a change in location (b), or a change in mental/emotional experience (c).

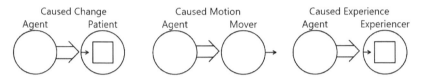

Figure 4. Two-participant caused change[64]

Relational schemas like these presuppose that participants relate together within a given event. Because of this, we can talk about *participant roles*. Participant roles have to do with how participants are involved in an event. The more active participant, the agent, is the energy source, the one who induces a change in other participants. In figure 4 the mover in (a) is a participant that changes location. A prototypical patient in (b) undergoes a change of state. Experiencers in (c) involve a cognitive or emotional change of state.

Conceptual schemas shape our thinking and avail themselves of expression in language. They are readily accessible as the prototypes for fundamental grammatical categories. As such, conceptual schemas mediate between situations in the world and their grammatical expression in language. Our body-based understanding of physical objects supplies the category prototype for the linguistic category of nouns. And our body-based understanding of causation/physical force supplies the prototype for the linguistic category of active transitive events.

For the prototypical transitive, the agent is the starting point or energy source and the patient is the endpoint or energy goal, as in example (9).

---

64  Adapted from Langacker, "Dimensions of Defocusing," 117.

(9) οἱ στρατιῶται τοῦ πρώτου <u>κατέαξαν</u> τὰ σκέλη
The soldiers <u>broke</u> the legs of the first man (John 19:32).

This transitive type provides the basis for most two-participant events in language. It arises through our embodied experience of physical force and energy transfer, where humans, as agents in the world, act on other entities by physical contact. A volitional participant (agent) causes a change of state in another participant (patient). This is called the *prototypical transitive event*.[65]

As a prototype category, this basic two-participant relation provides a framework for organizing knowledge about the world and understanding different event types in our shared human experience. Because of this, it is primarily concerned with the *construal process*, or how we think about events. Fortunately, the construal process is dynamic; we can think about a single event from a variety of different perspectives and express them in language accordingly.

For instance, given the default active clause in (9), we can construe the event in different ways. One strategy focuses attention on the man with the broken legs by expressing the same event within a passive clause: "The legs of the first man were broken by the soldiers." Another strategy focuses attention on how the soldiers worked in a group to carry out the action: "The soldiers together broke the legs of the first man." Each expression changes how we see the event. Within the grammatical resources of a given language, the same situation can be coded in multiple ways with alternate grammatical devices that reflect how a speaker conceives an event.

Each grammatical structure has conceptual content and imposes different imagery on the event. In this way, coding and construal become interdependent processes.[66] A situation's construal determines whether a linguistic structure may code it. And in turn, linguistic structures embody conventional imagery and thus impose a certain construal on the situation they encode.

The construal process is inevitably present in all language use, reflecting the fact that language provides various means (via grammatical structures) for categorizing events and their participants in

---

65   It is best understood as an experiential gestalt because it involves a cluster of properties that we understand as a patterned whole (Lakoff, *Women, Fire, and Dangerous Things*, 54–55).

66   Langacker, *Foundations of Cognitive Grammar*, 294.

varying ways. Speaking entails choice; every utterance construes an event in some manner, imposing an interpretation on the content involved. As soon as people begin to speak, they are participating in a meaningful construal process. Each linguistic expression involves an interpretive act. A speaker chooses a way in which to view an event, adopting it for the purpose of expression, and suggesting it to their audience by means of linguistic expression.[67]

Voice alternations enter the picture here. Voice changes offer a grammatical means to express different events' conceptualizations. It is a tool, one among many supplied within the grammatical resources of a language, for interpreting events in different ways. Specifically, voice involves two principal motivations in the construal process. One involves the energy flow for the event and the other regards the focus of attention we give to different elements within it.

For the first, every event involves some type of energy transfer.[68] For the prototypical transitive event, there are two participants, an energy source and an energy endpoint. Consider a person kicking a ball. The person, as the energy source, makes contact with the ball, as energy endpoint. Energy is transferred from the person's foot to the ball. The ball (patient) receives the energy and undergoes a change of state as a result—in this case, a change in location. As it receives the energy, the ball flies through the air from one location to another farther away. In our event conception, no change is profiled for the prototypical agent (energy source). The agent is left unaffected by the event. As the energy endpoint, the patient is the one who receives the energy transfer and is altered by it. We can follow the energy transfer from the agent (as subject) to the patient (as object) and watch the affect play out on the patient participant.

This basic event type is typically coded in the prototypical active transitive clause so that we mentally scan it from cause to effect, from energy source (agent subject) to energy endpoint (patient object). This pattern reflects the nature of our body-based experience with causation: In a cause-effect relationship, someone does

---

67 Arie Verhagen, "Construal and Perspectivization," in *The Oxford Handbook of Cognitive Linguistics*, ed. Dirk Geeraerts and Hubert Cuyckens (Oxford: Oxford University Press, 2007), 48–81.

68 I.e., they must be a change of state. Bare states, such as "I live here," lack change and energy transfer.

something that causes something else to happen; then we see the consequences of this action take place in the world.

Two key points regarding the prototypical active transitive clause are important to remember for our discussion of voice alternations. The basic alignment involves two fully distinct participants playing two fully distinct roles in the event.[69] The subject as the energy source plays the part of the volitional agent who causes the event to take place and who does not experience a change of state within it. The object as the energy endpoint plays the part of the nonvolitional patient who receives the energy transfer and experiences a change of state because of it. The schema in figure 5 provides a picture for what we may refer to in our voice discussion as the active transitive prototype.

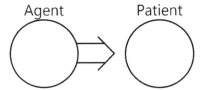

Figure 5. Prototypical Transitive

The second motivation for voice construal involves a visual metaphor in terms of the scope of attention. All languages provide structural schemas for one- and two-participant clauses. Each schema highlights one participant as the primary focus of attention. In an agent-oriented system like Greek, this focus is conferred on the most agent-like participant as the event's source of energy.[70] When the template is metaphorically extended to nonagentive interactions, the more agent-like participant (e.g., an experiencer or mover) is naturally chosen as the focus of attention and the energy source. The more patient-like participant becomes the secondary focal point.

As we saw in example (9) above with the soldiers breaking the man's legs, we can shift attention to different aspects of an event. These shifts in attention give rise to voice alternations. In a two-participant event, such as the active transitive prototype, there is

69  Suzanne Kemmer, *Middle Voice*, 50–51. Åshild Næss, *Prototypical Transitivity*, TSL 72 (Amsterdam: Benjamins, 2007), 28.
70  Langacker, "Dimensions in Defocusing," 123.

generally a primary focal participant and a secondary focal participant.[71] Our attention is divided between two participants playing two distinct roles. One is portrayed as the energy source, or starting point, for the event, while the other plays the role of energy endpoint. The main spotlight on stage for our visual and mental attention shines on both participants. When the action begins, that is, when the agent does something, the spotlight is on the energy source. We follow the arc of the action and see its affects play out on a distinct patient. The spotlight of our focus shifts to see what affect it has on this separate participant.

But if a speaker chooses to narrow the focus for an event to just one participant, then the spotlight is no longer split or shifting between two. The natural consequence of this is that the single participant becomes the most salient for the event and has our undivided attention. In contrast to the two-participant event, we can already see how just changing the number of participants shifts the center of attention for an event.

Departures from the prototypical transitive event with respect to the interplay of these two parameters give rise to voice alternations. Voice thus involves two kinds of motivation for how we construe events in different ways:

- Adjustments in the *energy source* and *energy endpoint* for the event[72]
- Adjustments in the *scope of attention*. Specifically middle voice involves a narrowing of scope.
- The natural consequence of shifting the center of attention in an event is a change in the relative *salience of participants*.

Situations that deviate from the transitive prototype with respect to these two parameters are often encoded by marked voice

---

71  Ibid., 119.

72  The terminology employed in cognitive linguistics is generally "trajector" (TR) and "landmark" (LM). The trajector is the starting point for the event, or the initiating figure. The landmark is the energy goal or endpoint for the event, the one who receives the energy transfer and is changed by it (Langacker, *Foundations of Cognitive Grammar*, 304–29). In a basic active clause, the subject is the TR as the primary, most salient figure in the relation. The object is LM as secondary figure, as the second-most prominent participant.

constructions. The active supplies the basic voice type, while middle marking indicates that an event departs from the basic transitive prototype in some way.[73] We will see these voice parameters play out in each middle event type discussed below. Though our focus is primarily on -(θ)η- marked verbs, the semantic patterns in -(θ)η- are applicable to the rest of the middle voice system in Greek.

In the transitive prototype, the default primary figure is the agent as the energy source for the relation. But the passive construction confers the primary focus of attention on the patient instead, giving the event a new focus and a new starting point for mentally accessing it. Selecting the patient as the participant in the spotlight increases its relative salience for the relationship.

In example (10) below, the passive voice encoded with -(θ)η- morphology represents the most patient-like event on the semantic continuum from agent-like to patient-like event types. The primary focal point is on the participant that undergoes a change of state and is not volitionally involved in the event at all.

(10) μὴ ἔχοντος δὲ αὐτοῦ ἀποδοῦναι ἐκέλευσεν αὐτὸν ὁ
κύριος <u>πραθῆναι</u>
as he could not pay, his lord ordered him to <u>be sold</u>
(Matthew 18:25)

The patient in focus is the servant who owes the master money, activated from the previous verse. The conceptual content evoked in a passive event is still the same type of event as the active transitive prototype. The agent is irrelevant. *Who* sold him is not so salient as the fact that he was sold. Our attention is on the patient, indicating that the discourse relevance of the agent is low and becomes blurred in the background of the event conception. The agent is still the initiating entity and the patient is still the one who receives the energy transfer and experiences a change of state from it. But the key element that is changed in the passive conception is shifting the spotlight to the patient, so that the agent is blurred in the shadows.

The passive exemplifies but one alternate construal based on shifting the focus of attention from the agent in the active to the patient in the passive. However, another alternate construal is

---

73  Ibid.125; Næss, *Prototypical Transitivity*, 17; Shibatani, "Conceptual Framework," 217–69.

achieved by changing the energy flow for the event. This choice in the energy source and energy endpoint, i.e., choosing which participant plays the starting point or the final endpoint for the energy transfer in the event may also diverge from the active transitive prototype. As we will see, -(θ)η-, as a marker of middle semantics, is used to encode two kinds of deviation from the prototypical active pattern—one for energy transfer and one for the focus of attention.

In the discussion that follows, I break up the event types into two smaller sets, those that are more patient-like and thus closer to the traditional passive voice type, and those that are more agent-like and thus closer to the active transitive prototype.

## 3.1 Alternations in Voice: More Patient-Like Events

In its original integration into Greek, -(θ)η- was initially restricted to five middle event types within the wider potential semantic range of the middle: spontaneous processes, motion, collective motion, and passives. All five lean toward the more patient-like end of the spectrum. But as -(θ)η- developed further within Classical and into Hellenistic Greek, it expanded its scope to express other middle events as well: reflexives, reciprocals, etc. These types are the more agent-like middle events; we will get to these in section 3.2. Events in sections 3.1 share a property with the passive type: They all include a marked choice in the focus of attention that departs from the prototypical active. But, unlike the passive, which presents the same two-participant relation as the active transitive, this set of middle events includes just one participant.

### 3.1.1 Spontaneous Process

Recall from figure 4 above that an external cause brings about a change to a second participant. It may be a change in location, change in state, or change in experience. In each case, the focus of attention is on the agent, as the energy source and starting point, causing a change of state in the patient, as energy endpoint. The active is used to express caused events of this nature.

Examples (11) and (12) involve the active voice used for an event where an agent (energy source) performs an action that induces a change of state in the patient (energy endpoint). In the first example, eating the scroll makes the stomach bitter. In the second, he [Jesus] causes the money to spill out. The syntactic expression in each reflects this two-participant-caused relation. The energy source is encoded as subject, while the energy endpoint is encoded as object.

(11) Active Caused Change
Λάβε καὶ κατάφαγε αὐτό [τὸ βιβλαρίδιον], καὶ <u>πικρανεῖ σου</u>
<u>τὴν κοιλίαν</u>.
Take and eat it [the scroll], and it will <u>make your</u>
<u>stomach bitter</u> (Rev 10:9).

(12) καὶ τῶν κολλυβιστῶν <u>ἐξέχεεν</u> τὰ κέρματα καὶ τὰς
τραπέζας ἀνέστρεψεν
And he <u>made</u> the moneychanger's money <u>spill out</u> and
he overturned their tables (John 2:15).

Now consider examples (13) and (14) where a voice change, from active to middle -(θ)η-, alters the event conception. The same verbs are used but the perspective of the event shifts.

(13) Middle Spontaneous Change
ὅτε ἔφαγον αὐτό, <u>ἐπικράνθη</u> ἡ κοιλία μου.
When I ate it, my stomach <u>grew bitter</u> (Rev 10:10).

(14) καὶ πρηνὴς γενόμενος ἐλάκησεν μέσος, καὶ <u>ἐξεχύθη</u>
πάντα τὰ σπλάγχνα αὐτοῦ.
And falling headlong, he burst open in the middle and
all his internal organs <u>spilled out</u> (Acts 1:18).

Here, -(θ)η- expresses an event in which a single focused participant undergoes a change of state with no external cause involved in the event. The omission of cause results in a shift in attention. The patient, the one who undergoes a change of state, is the focus and starting point for mentally accessing the event. This narrowing of scope to one participant heightens the salience of that participant. The syntactic expressions in (13) and (14) signal the patient is the primary concern. Each is expressed as an intransitive clause with a single focused participant. The grammatical subject plays the role of patient, the one who undergoes a change of state. The energy source and energy endpoint are conflated into one participant—the energy is entirely internal.

This is why the spontaneous event type cross-linguistically includes events usually conceived as lacking an external force, such as growing, rusting, rotting, and other physiological changes in nature.[74] But keep in mind, as we have seen in the examples above, that spontaneous processes may also be formulated using active voice to express a causative version of the same state of affairs. Almost all spontaneous processes in Greek have a causative active counterpart:

- κραταιόω [Active: "make strong"; -(θ)η- : "become strong"]
- μεθύσκω [Active: "make drunk"; -(θ)η- : "become drunk"]
- πωρόω [Active: "make hard"; -(θ)η- : "become hard"]
- ὁράω [Active: "make visible"; -(θ)η- : "appear/become visible"]

In contrast, the passive event implies the presence of an external cause that brings about the event—even if it is not syntactically expressed. Although the passive type often involves events that come about by external cause,[75] no strict and clearly delineated line is possible. At times, it is difficult to tell if an external source is implied or if it is construed more like a one-participant event that is brought about spontaneously. This kind of ambiguity is illustrated in example (15).

(15) καὶ ὁ οὐρανὸς ἀπεχωρίσθη ὡς βιβλίον ἑλισσόμενον.
And the sky was split apart like a rolled up scroll
(Rev 6:14).

Deciding to interpret this clause as a spontaneous process versus a passive relies on the prominence the reader gives the supernatural context of the Revelation narrative. Natural events that "just happen"—earthquakes, floods, etc.—are taken as spontaneous processes, but a supernatural narrative like Revelation opens up the possibility for the passive reading.

In contrast to the active transitive prototype, -(θ)η- narrows the scope of attention so that the onstage focus is on the patient participant—the one who undergoes a change of state. In turn, this shift in attention heightens its salience so that it becomes the primary figure in the event. The spotlight remains on the patient, without sharing attention with an agent. For the passive type, the patient is the primary focus of attention with the agent still inducing external

---

74  Kemmer, *Middle Voice*, 142.
75  Haspelmath, "Transitivity Alternations," 15.

force. Now, what happens to the patient is the most salient part of the event for the discourse.

For the spontaneous type, the conceptual content (or kind of event) is altered. Rather than an agent causing a change, the spontaneous type presents an event that takes place without external force. The starting point for the action is the patient. Because our attention is not divided between two participants (as is the case in the active transitive), our focus naturally falls on the single participant left. As both energy source and endpoint, the energy for the event is internal.

The spontaneous type can be contrasted to the active by means of a schematic illustration. In figure 6, a two-participant active relation is shown in contrast to the one-participant -(θ)η- event.

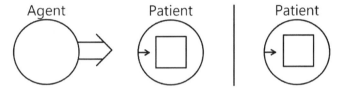

Figure 6. Caused Change versus Spontaneous Change

The active examples in (11) and (12) correspond to the figure on the left in which an agent (energy source) triggers a change in the patient (energy endpoint). The spontaneous types in (13) and (14) correspond to the figure on the right. There is no external cause; no agent is present. Instead, a single focused participant with an internal energy source undergoes a change of state.

The schema in figure 6, contrasting two-participant and one-participant events, is also applicable to the next four types of middle events with -(θ)η-. The only alteration is the participant role that the single participant plays in the event. This participant role change arises from the verb's lexical semantics. If it is a mental process then the participant has an experiencer role—the one who undergoes a mental or emotional change. If the event involves motion, then the single participant plays a mover—the one who undergoes a change in location or posture. This recurring pattern in -(θ)η- usage accomplishes the same adjustments in focus and salience in the motion, collective motion, and mental process types as it does in the spontaneous type.

### 3.1.2 Motion

Motion events involve either a change in location (go, come, leave, return) or a change in body posture (stand up, sit down, turn around). In the active two-participant event, an agent (energy source) causes a mover to change location or posture (energy endpoint). As the energy source for the event and the starting point for construal, the agent is the external cause that brings the event about. The mover is construed as the energy endpoint, the one that is made to move. This conceptualization is illustrated in examples (16) and (17).

> (16) Active Caused Motion
> σὺ <u>ἔστρεψας</u> τὴν καρδίαν τοῦ λαοῦ τούτου ὀπίσω.
> You <u>turned</u> the heart of this people back (3 Kgdms 18:37).

> (17) ὅτε ἐπλήσθησαν αἱ ἡμέραι τοῦ καθαρισμοῦ αὐτῶν
> κατὰ τὸν νόμον Μωϋσέως, <u>ἀνήγαγον</u> αὐτὸν εἰς Ἱεροσόλυμα
> παραστῆσαι τῷ κυρίῳ
> When the days of their purification were complete
> according to the Law of Moses, they <u>brought</u> him to
> Jerusalem to present him to the Lord (Luke 2:22).

Example (16) is a change in posture, while (17) references a change in location. Note ἐπλήσθησαν in (17) is a -(θ)η- verb expressing a spontaneous process in which the activity of purification came to an end. It is thus a telic event, a fully achieved or complete change of state, as is in keeping with the perfective aspect and the historical origins of the category.

In contrast to the active conception of caused motion, -(θ)η- marking expresses a single participant who moves without external cause. The mover is the primary figure for the event, its energy source and energy endpoint. As an event involving internal energy, the one who induces the change is also the one who undergoes the change. This motion middle event type is provided in examples (18) and (19). The same verbs are used as in the active events, but here the grammatical subject is the one who experiences the change in location or posture.

> (18) Middle Body Motion
> ταῦτα εἰποῦσα <u>ἐστράφη</u> εἰς τὰ ὀπίσω, καὶ θεωρεῖ τὸν Ἰησοῦν ἑστῶτα
> After saying these things, she <u>turned around</u> and saw Jesus
> standing there (John 20:14).

(19)Ἡμεῖς δὲ προελθόντες ἐπὶ τὸ πλοῖον <u>ἀνήχθημεν</u> ἐπὶ τὴν Ἄσσον
Going on ahead, <u>we set sail</u> for Assos (Acts 20:13).

Because no external force induces the change, no agent subject is needed. Thus, the scope of attention narrows from two-participants down to one, resulting in greater salience for the single participant mover. Its syntactic expression reflects this shift in attention. This -(θ)η- marked event appears in an intransitive clause with a grammatical subject that plays the role of mover.

### 3.1.3. Collective Motion

A second type of caused motion is collective motion. It occurs when an agent moves multiple participants en masse. In the active causative version, the agent is the energy source and causes a group to change location as the energy endpoint. In (20), Joseph is energy source and the food that he gathers is the endpoint. Likewise, example (21) involves an agent (God) and a mover (people) but in this case it is two people who are joined together in marriage to become one.

(20) Caused Collective Motion
καὶ <u>συνήγαγεν</u> πάντα τὰ βρώματα τῶν ἑπτὰ ἐτῶν, ἐν οἷς ἦν ἡ εὐθηνία ἐν γῇ Αἰγύπτου.
And he <u>gathered together</u> all the food from the seven years in which there was an abundance in the land of Egypt (Gen 41:48).

(21) ὃ οὖν ὁ θεὸς <u>συνέζευξεν</u> ἄνθρωπος μὴ χωριζέτω.
Therefore what God has <u>joined</u> no human must separate (Matt 19:6).

Collective motion expressed using -(θ)η- is similar, but the examples in (22) and (23) have no external agent that brings about the collective event. In each case, the motion is conceptualized as taking place spontaneously by internal energy. The focus of attention is on what happens to the crowd, downplaying the salience of an external force by omitting any kind of agent in the syntactic expression. The energy endpoint from the caused active event becomes the energy source in the -(θ)η- collective event, making the mover the primary figure in the conception.

(22) Collective Motion
Καὶ διαπεράσαντος τοῦ Ἰησοῦ ἐν τῷ πλοίῳ πάλιν εἰς τὸ πέραν <u>συνήχθη</u> ὄχλος πολὺς ἐπ᾽ αὐτόν.
And after Jesus had crossed over in the boat to the other side, a large crowd <u>gathered</u> to him (Mark 5:21).

(23) ἐγένετο δὲ παροξυσμὸς ὥστε <u>ἀποχωρισθῆναι</u> αὐτοὺς ἀπ᾽ ἀλλήλων, τόν τε Βαρναβᾶν παραλαβόντα τὸν Μᾶρκον ἐκπλεῦσαι εἰς Κύπρον.
There was a sharp disagreement, so they <u>separated</u> from each other and Barnabas took along Mark and sailed to Cyprus (Acts 15:39).

### 3.1.4. Mental process

In the active transitive prototype, an agent (energy source) causes a change in the patient (energy endpoint). In mental events, this is maintained, but it metaphorically extends the physical domain to include psychological (cognition/emotion) events. In examples (24) and (25), an agent causes a mental experience, disturbance, or change in the experiencer. In (24), the Jews, as energy source, mentally stir up the crowd (energy endpoint), causing a change in their state of mind.

(24) Active Caused Experience
οἱ ἀπὸ τῆς Ἀσίας Ἰουδαῖοι θεασάμενοι αὐτὸν ἐν τῷ ἱερῷ συνέχεον πάντα τὸν ὄχλον καὶ <u>ἐπέβαλον</u> ἐπ᾽ αὐτὸν τὰς χεῖρας.
The Jews from Asia who had seen him in the temple <u>stirred up</u> the entire crowd (Acts 21:27).

(25) καὶ μὴ <u>λυπεῖτε</u> τὸ πνεῦμα τὸ ἅγιον τοῦ θεοῦ
And do not <u>grieve</u> the Holy Spirit of God (Eph 4:30).

In contrast, -(θ)η- mental events express a spontaneous mental change of state in the experiencer. By shifting the focus to the experiencer and omitting an explicit external force, attention is undivided and the spotlight shines on the single participant going through a mental change.

(26) Middle Mental Process
γενομένης δὲ τῆς φωνῆς ταύτης συνῆλθε τὸ πλῆθος καὶ
<u>συνεχύθη</u>
At this sound, the crowd gathered together and <u>became
confused</u> (Acts 2:6)

(27) <u>ἐλυπήθησαν</u> σφόδρα
They were extremely <u>depressed</u> (Matt 17:23)

In examples (26) and (27), the experiencer is brought forward by profiling the energy source or starting point for the event not as an external cause but as an internal change. The experiencer alone is in view. One becomes confused in (26) and one becomes depressed in (27).

From the spontaneous process middle through the motion middles and mental processes, the use of -(θ)η- marking reflects a change in the conception of the event, specifically a conceptual shift away from the active transitive prototype in which an agent (energy source) does something to cause a change in the patient (energy endpoint). What motivates middle marking in each of these events is their deviation from the prototypical active with respect to two parameters. The shift from a two-participant relation in the active to one-participant in the -(θ)η- event (1) conflates the energy source and energy endpoint roles onto a single focused participant. The energy is internally induced; and (2), it narrows the scope of attention so that the spotlight is not divided between two participants but is focused on one. Our attention naturally lands on the single participant that is left, i.e., the one that undergoes some kind of change—be that physical state, mental experience, or motion. What happens to it is the primary matter of concern.

Each syntactic expression reflects conceptual content. In the active caused event type, the experiencer/mover/patient is expressed as syntactic object—the secondary focus of attention. But in the -(θ)η- middle event, these same participants become the syntactic subject—the primary focus of attention. In the resulting intransitive predication, the subject does not play the role of agent as in the active, but plays the role of experiencer, mover, or patient. Their participant role does not change, just their heightened salience in the discourse.

## 3.2. Alternations in Voice: More Agent-Like Events

In section 3.1, we encountered events in which the primary figure is more like a prototypical patient, not playing the role of an external cause or instigator, but undergoing a change of state. These more patient-like primary figures do not initiate a change in others, but experience the change of state themselves. But for section 3.2, the primary figure in the event is more agentative, playing a volitional role in the activity, causing a change to take place. Each event type still deviates from the active transitive prototype because the change that is profiled in the event does not happen to a distinct patient, but occurs on the agent that brings about the event in the first place. In this way, the primary focal point and the energy source for the event is also the energy endpoint as well. The source/endpoint roles are a single, conflated participant.

Recall from the preliminaries to section 3 that although the more agent-like middle events are well within the middle domain, historically they did not receive -(θ)η- marking, which was initially restricted to events with a more patient-like participant. But -(θ)η- did not remain static in its semantics; instead it began a process of expansion to event types that had previously been exclusive to the sigmatic (first aorist) middle. Through its growth in Classical and Hellenistic Greek, -(θ)η- began a process of gradually replacing the sigmatic aorist form for middle events.[76]

Over time it came to encode events with more agency in their conception, such as reflexives, reciprocals, and mental activities, which involve a more prototypical agent as the primary figure. In Classical and Hellenistic Greek, -(θ)η- is sporadically used within this more agent-like set of middles as it gradually encroached on the sigmatic aorist form. This means that the majority of middle verbs in this set have sigmatic middle forms rather than -(θ)η- forms, -(θ)η- marked verbs are still present. While they are in the minority here, they do illustrate this gradual process of change as more and more verbs receive -(θ)η- aorist marking in the middle domain.

This places Classical and Hellenistic Greek as transitional periods for -(θ)η-. As the sigmatic middle slowly loses ground to the -(θ)η- in these periods, it eventually disappears in later Greek.

---

76  García Ramón, "From *Aktionsart* to Aspect and Voice," 149–82.

-(θ)η- becomes the sole middle marker in the aorist, encompassing all the middle-passive events types within its scope. We end up in Modern Greek with the aorist verbal paradigm showing the same middle-passive marking as we see in the present and perfect paradigms in Hellenistic, in which one form spans the scope of the middle domain from the more agent-like events all the way down to the more patient-like events.[77]

In examining the more agent-like middle events, we begin with the direct reflexive type since it is the typical event type people think of when they conceive of the middle category.

### 3.2.1. Direct Reflexive/Grooming Verbs

Formal changes in voice marking are motivated by differences in the conceptualization of events, indicating some kind of conceptual distinction. For direct reflexives, the energy source and endpoint are conflated in a single participant. The agent who causes the event is also clearly the patient changed by the action. We see this role conflation in events like (28) and (29) where the action is performed on the self. The same participant who causes the event is also affected by it.

> (28) ὁ δὲ Φαρισαῖος ἰδὼν ἐθαύμασεν ὅτι οὐ πρῶτον ἐβαπτίσθη πρὸ τοῦ ἀρίστου.
> The Pharisee, when he saw, was astounded that he did not first <u>wash</u> before the meal (Luke 11:38).

> (29) τότε ὁ Παῦλος παραλαβὼν τοὺς ἄνδρας τῇ ἐχομένῃ ἡμέρᾳ <u>ἁγνισθεὶς</u> εἰσῄει εἰς τὸ ἱερόν σὺν αὐτοῖς
> Then Paul took the men, and the next day, <u>having purified himself</u>, he entered the temple with them (Acts 21:26).

---

77  While little study has been done on middle voice in Medieval Greek, by the time we arrive at Modern Greek, -(θ)η- morphology is used for the expression of reflexive meaning far more extensively than in the Koine (e.g., Κοιτάχτηκε στον καθρέφτη, "She looked at herself in the mirror"), according to David Holton et al., *Greek: A Comprehensive Grammar of the Modern Language*, 2nd ed. RCG (London: Routledge, 2012), 282–83. For further discussion on Modern Greek see Linda Joyce Manney, *The Middle Voice in Modern Greek*, SLCS 48 (Amsterdam: Benjamins, 2000).

In Greek and cross-linguistically, verbs in this type often include grooming, dressing, bathing, and other kinds of body care. The agent performs an action that produces an effect or a change on oneself. It may be a partial change as in wiping one's nose, or brushing one's hair; or it may involve more of a complete change of state—from unclean to clean. This role conflation is depicted in figure 7 by means of an arrow to a single focused participant that plays double roles (AG/PAT) in the event.

Unlike the active transitive prototype, with its distinct agent causing a change in a distinct patient, the direct reflexive middle has no second participant. Instead, the ultimate endpoint for the event is the energy source. This narrows the scope of attention so that instead of two participants in a transitive active clause, we end up with a single focused participant in an intransitive middle clause. By removing a separate patient participant, our attention naturally rests on the remaining participant. The syntactic subject plays the role of agent and patient.

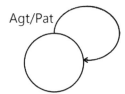

Agt/Pat

Figure 7. Direct Reflexive/Grooming Verbs[78]

Most often in the Koine period direct reflexives are expressed with sigmatic middle marking. Thus, νίψαι appears in the sigmatic middle for washing oneself (Matt. 6:17) as opposed to its use in the aorist active to express washing someone else (John 13:14 "I have washed your feet"). Again, the verb κείρω is used in the sigmatic middle for cutting one's hair/getting a hair cut (Acts 18:18) while its use in the active expresses shearing sheep (Acts 8:32).

Verb like ἀναζώννυμι "bind up the loins/get oneself ready" are extended metaphorically from the physical domain to the mental sphere as in 1 Peter 1:13 (with a sigmatic middle) to express an idiom

---

78  Figures in §3.2 are adapted from Kemmer, *Middle Voice*, 52–128.

"binding up the loins of the mind, get one's mind ready, be alert."[79] Such metaphorical extensions illustrate that though we discuss these types as discrete and segmented, they are actually extended in and through one another and multiply connected. Metaphor pervades their use. It is because of this that one verb may not fit into the bounds of a single type but span across many in its various uses and extensions.

Be aware these event types have only a virtual existence—a tool in aiding our understanding and supplying the imagery to help us conceive relations and distinctions that arise via voice morphology. These types don't exist as discrete grammatical objects out in the linguistic universe. Their existence is dynamic, bound up in shared meaning and interpretation, existing in and through cognitive processing activity and communicative interactions.

### 3.2.2. Reciprocal Events

Reciprocal events involve two participants whose energy source/ endpoint and agent/patient roles are conflated on both participants. The agent (source) does something to affect the patient (endpoint); simultaneously the patient does something to affect the agent. Both participants play the part of starting point and endpoint for the energy transfer. While the active transitive prototype profiles two fully distinct roles, for reciprocal middle events that distinction is lost. In a slightly different manner compared to direct reflexives, this narrows our attention from two distinct participants with distinct roles down to two participants sharing both roles. The spotlight does not shine on the agent before shifting to see what happens on the patient. Rather, the narrowed attention puts the spotlight on the interaction between both participants. Figure 8 illustrates the role conflation of reciprocal events, which includes verbs that naturally involve mutual exchange, such as kissing, hugging, fighting, and conversing.[80]

---

79  BDAG, 62. The physical domain supplies a rich backdrop of meaning to extend to the cognitive domain. See the discussion of the Mind-is-a-Body Metaphor in George Lakoff and Mark Johnson, *Philosophy in the Flesh: The Embodied Mind and Its Challenge to Western Thought* (New York: Basic Books, 1999), 248.

80  Kemmer, *Middle Voice*, 102–8.

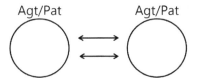

Figure 8. Reciprocal Events

(30) Reciprocal Events
οἱ δὲ ἐσιώπων, πρὸς ἀλλήλους γὰρ <u>διελέχθησαν</u> ἐν τῇ ὁδῷ τίς μείζων.
They were silent with each other because <u>they had argued</u> on the way about who was the greatest (Mark 9:34).[81]

Other reciprocal middles that do not show a -(θ)η- form in New Testament usage include verbs like μάχομαι "fight, quarrel with" and ἀγωνίζομαι "fight, struggle" which appear with sigmatic middle marking. Both of these events share the same conceptual imagery in figure 8, with both participants simultaneously playing agent and patient (energy source/endpoint).

### 3.2.3. Mental Activity

Mental activities are similar to direct reflexives and reciprocals in that all involve a volitional participant who experiences a change in the process expressed by the verb. The difference is that within the mental domain, the effect on the participant is psychological rather than physical. The use of the experiencer label in figure 9 reflects this fact.

Mental activities are similar to mental processes. Both have an experiencer undergoing a mental change rather than a physical one. They differ in that the mental activity type tends to involve participants who are more agent-like with more volitional involvement in the event. The difference between the two types (mental activity and mental process) runs along a continuum of volitionality, so that mental processes tend to involve a participant that is less volitional

---

81  See Allan, *Middle Voice*, 168 for a discussion of the history of this verb in Homer and in Classical Greek and its early adoption of a -(θ)η- form.

and more patient-like, while mental activities tend to include a participant that is more agent-like.

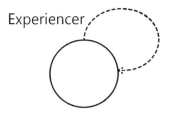

Experiencer

Figure 9. Intransitive Mental Activity

The dotted arrow in figure 9 indicates that within the mental activity type no distinct secondary figure is affected by the action. This also reflects its deviation from the active transitive prototype in which an agent causes a change in a distinct patient. Within mental activity middles, the change caused by the event does not alter a distinct entity but stays within the sphere of the one who started it. Rather than dividing the spotlight between two participants, it shines on just one focused entity. What happens to this single participant is put into sharp focus for the discourse. The experiencer is mentally altered by his involvement in the event.

This kind of mental activity is illustrated in example (31) in which -(θ)η- is used to mark a mental event in an intransitive (single participant) clause. The experiencer is both the starting point as well as the affected endpoint.

(31) Mental Activity Middle
Ὤμοσεν κύριος, καὶ οὐ <u>μεταμεληθήσεται</u>
The Lord swore an oath and <u>will</u> not <u>change his mind</u>
(Heb 7:21)

The mental activity middle type is not limited to a single participant but can also be used with events that involve a second participant, as in figure 10. In a two-participant mental activity, an experiencer directs his mental energy to a stimulus and in turn a mental event is brought about in the mind of the experiencer, so that he is cognitively changed in the course of the event.[82]

---

82 Kemmer, *Middle Voice*, 129.

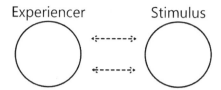

Figure 10. Transitive Mental Activity

Though there are two participants, this type still departs from the active transitive prototype in that it profiles a change *not* in the secondary participant (stimulus), but in the primary participant (experiencer). Within the transitive prototype, the agent causes a change to take place in the patient. There is no profiled change that occurs in the agent. But for mental events expressed in -(θ)η- and other middle marking, the opposite is true. The profiled change occurs in the primary figure (experiencer) instead. The stimulus, as the secondary figure, remains unchanged.

In example (32), Peter (experiencer) is cognitively affected by his involvement in the event. He remembers the words spoken by Jesus. And in (33) Joseph makes a decision to dismiss Mary. Even though there are two participants in these examples, the most salient participant is the one who experiences the mentally altered state, as the energy endpoint for the event.

> (32) καὶ ἐμνήσθη ὁ Πέτρος τοῦ ῥήματος Ἰησοῦ εἰρηκότος
> And Peter <u>remembered</u> the statement Jesus had spoken
> (Matt 26:75).
>
> (33) ἐβουλήθη λάθρα ἀπολῦσαι αὐτήν
> He (Joseph) <u>planned</u> to dismiss her (Mary) quietly
> (Matt 1:19)

Sometimes, mental activity middles may arise from metaphoric extension from another middle type. One example of this is στρέφω, which is used within the motion event type to express physical/bodily turning. The active voice expresses a causative event: "he turns someone else around." The middle (expressed with a sigmatic aorist), on the other hand, expresses the spontaneous single participant event: "he turns around." This sense is found in Matthew 7:6: "do not throw your pearls before swine, or they will trample them under foot and <u>turn</u> (στραφέντες) and maul you." In this motion event, a physical turning of the body is in view.

But this motion type is then extended from the physical domain into the psychological, so στρέφω also fits into the mental activity type. Consider a metaphorical use like Matthew 18:3: "Truly I tell you, unless you <u>turn</u> (στραφῆτε) and become like children, you will never enter the kingdom of heaven." This use is more about an attitude of the mind. Jesus isn't suggesting that his disciples need to physically turn around and that this will get them into heaven, but he is addressing their attitude toward life and faith—urging them to mentally turn or change their outlook. In this way, a verb like στρέφω fits both motion and mental activity middle types. This kind of metaphorical extension occurs throughout the middle network.

Two further types within the mental domain are speech act middles and perception middles. Both types also involve the interplay of the experiencer and stimulus roles. As such, the schema in figure 10 applies just as much to these two as it does to the mental activity middle. In the perception and speech act types, we find the very same patterns repeated as in the mental activity type. The only difference is the lexical semantics of the verbs: speech and perception.

### 3.2.4. Speech Act

In speech acts, an experiencer makes a verbal statement: a question, a prayer, or a reply. The focus is on the experiencer as the energy source for the event. The second participant plays the role of stimulus since there is no change of state profiled for this participant in the event. Instead, the effect, or energy endpoint of the event, is ultimately visited back on the one who started it.

In the middle voice version of this event one figure plays both energy source and endpoint for the event. Conflating these energy roles onto one participant highlights its salience for the discourse as the one who experiences the cognitive affect of the action. -(θ)η-marked verbs appear in examples (34) with an indirect object and in (35) with a direct object.

> (34) Speech Act Middle
> καὶ οὐκ ἴσχυσαν <u>ἀνταποκριθῆναι</u> πρὸς ταῦτα.
> And they were not able <u>to reply</u> to these things
> (Luke 14:6)

(35) <u>δεήθητε</u> οὖν τοῦ κυρίου τοῦ θερισμοῦ ὅπως ἐκβάλῃ
ἐργάτας εἰς τὸν θερισμὸν αὐτοῦ
Therefore <u>ask</u> the lord of the harvest to send out
workers into his harvest fields (Matt 9:38).

Most speech acts are expressed using the sigmatic middle aorist (such as αἰτήσασθε "ask, demand, plead"), but there are a few
prominent exceptions that have adopted -(θ)η- marking, such as
ἀποκρίνομαι. Its active form from Classical means "separate, select,
distinguish," but its use in the New Testament is exclusively as a
speech act verb within the middle domain.[83]

Likewise, the verb δέομαι in (35) is actually a speech act that does
not appear in sigmatic middle aorist but only occurs in -(θ)η-. This
fact may be due to its original meaning "lack, need, want," which
shows an emotional or physical affectedness for the primary figure.
The semantic extension to the speech act type here in the asking
sense may be due to the pragmatic implication that when one needs
help, one usually asks for it.[84]

### 3.2.5. Perception

The perception event type fits within the cognitive domain as well.
These designate events that involve the perceptual senses like see,
taste, touch, and smell. The experiencer perceives an object through
the bodily senses and is mentally altered by the experience. In the
-(θ)η- marked events in (36) and (37), the primary figure plays the
role of experiencer of the cognitive event. This perception middle
type may involve events that are more volitionally controlled by the
experiencer or ones that involve a more patient-like figure who is
more passively involved.

Again, in the perception middles the experiencer is both energy
source and energy endpoint for the event with the effect of narrowing the scope of attention. The one who experiences the perception
is the most salient and is of primary concern for the discourse.

---

83  It occasionally appears as a first aor. mid. form ἀπεκρινάμην, but most fre-
quently takes -(θ)η- ἀπεκρίθη as a speech act (BDAG, 113). See Allan, *Middle Voice*, 105–11 for further discussion of speech act middles.
84  Ibid., 108.

(36) Perception Middle
ὠσφράνθη τὴν ὀσμὴν τῶν ἱματίων αὐτοῦ
He <u>smelled</u> the scent of his garment (Gen 27:27).

(37) ὡς τρισόλβιοι κεῖνοι βροτῶν, οἳ ταῦτα <u>δερχθέντες</u> τέλη
μόλωσ᾽ ἐς Ἅιδου· ζῆν ἔστι, τοῖς δ᾽ ἄδοντι πάντ᾽ ἐκεῖ κακά᾽.
As especially lucky are those among mortals who,
<u>having seen</u> these [mysteries], will pass to Hades. For
them is a life beyond; for everyone else there is evil
there.
(Plut., *Adol. poet. aud.* 4)

Most perception verbs in the middle domain receive a sigmatic
aorist, reflecting their more volitional involvement, but there are
some expressed in -(θ)η-, such as the form in (37).

The verb, δερχθέντες shifts semantically in Classical from the
Homeric use of "fix one's eyes, look at" to more of a sense of "seeing."
This shift provides some semantic motivation for why the lexeme
may have adopted the -(θ)η- form when other perception middles
had not done so yet. The event of "seeing" suggests a bit less volitionality and control on the part of the experiencer, placing it closer
to the patient-like end of the transitivity scale compared to other
perception verbs that involve a more agent-like participant, such as
γεύομαι ("taste"), θεάομαι ("observe, look at"), ἅπτω ("touch"), all of
which utilize sigmatic middle aorist forms in New Testament use.
In this way, δερχθέντες reflects a more patient-like involvement for
the primary figure, resembling the mental process middle type.[85]

The middle event types in section 3.2 are events in which the primary focal participant is more like a prototypical agent. They involve the same two parameters as the middles in section 3.1: energy
source/endpoint and scope of attention. For the energy transfer in
these event types, the energy source is also the ultimate energy endpoint. Conflating these roles onto one participant narrows the scope
of attention compared to shifting between two distinct participants
and two distinct roles in the active transitive. This primary focal
point is the participant who is affected by the energy of the event
as its final endpoint. This participant becomes the most salient in
the event conception. In its syntactic expression, the conflation of

---

85  See ibid., 159 for further discussion.

energy source/endpoint onto one participant is expressed as grammatical subject to show its primary status. If there is a second participant, it functions as the object of the clause.

## 4. SEMANTIC MAP

One of the aims for section 3 has been to take the variety of event types expressed using -(θ)η- and sketch out the semantic connections among them that illustrate motivations for voice-marking patterns. One way to do this is to create a semantic map. Semantic maps help us to take a step back in order to consider the larger picture. They articulate the semantic space for the middle domain as a whole and illustrate how -(θ)η- morphology fits in among the other middle types. In the semantic map in figure 11 the boxes represent semantic middle types with lines showing semantic connections among them.

The event types on the map are arranged in terms of transitivity, decreasing as one moves from left to right. The semantic distinctions in sections 3.1 and 3.2 are distributed over the map as a continuous space so that those events whose primary figure is more agent-like are toward the left side; those with a more patient-like primary figure are toward the right. This gives us a scalar portrait of transitivity. Instead of regarding transitivity strictly in binary terms of whether or not there is a direct object present, we can more accurately describe it as a semantic scale, in which events can be more or less transitive, and closer to or farther from the transitive prototype.

For -(θ)η- marking patterns, its original five types are on the lower right of the map. In those types, the profiled event generally focuses on one-patient participant. The motion, collective motion, mental process, and spontaneous process types step away from the prototypical transitive event in two ways. First, they change the energy transfer for the event so that the energy source and energy endpoint are conflated in that one participant. The energy is internal without an external force (agent) in the event's conception; and second, narrowing from two participants to one heightens the salience of the remaining focused participant in the conception. This narrowing of scope sharpens focus onto the patient participant experiencing the change of state.

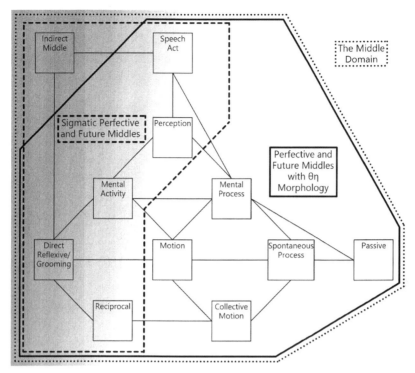

Figure 11. Semantic Space of the Greek Middle Morphology[86]

This second parameter, narrowing the scope of attention, also applies to the passive event type. For passives, there are still two distinct participants with distinct roles in the event—one as agent (energy source) and one as patient (energy endpoint). But the on-stage spotlight shifts from the naturally salient agent to the less salient patient by promoting the patient to the subject position. While the patient is brought into clear focus, the agent fades into the background.

In each of these -(θ)η- types, the formal syntactic expression reflects these semantic departures from the transitive prototype. The event is now scanned sequentially with a focus on the patient (or mover, experiencer) undergoing a change of state. The spontaneous

---

86  Adapted from ibid., 156. See also the semantic map for the distribution of sigmatic mid. aor. and -(θ)η- aor. in Homer (ibid., 147) compared to the map of their distribution in Classical (ibid., 156). We see -(θ)η- extending its roots from Homer through Classical to Hellenistic as it includes more middle types within its scope.

types (mental process, motion, collective motion, and spontaneous process) are expressed with intransitive syntax and -(θ)η- morphology (if in the aorist paradigm, or other middle morphology if in the present stem) to reflect the conceptual distinction. Likewise, the passive type gives the patient nominative case marking usually reserved for the agent, reflecting its new status as the primary figure. The agent is defocused and either left unexpressed or coded in an oblique by-phrase.

Middle event types closer to the transitive prototype are farther left on the map, including direct and indirect reflexives, reciprocals, mental activities, speech acts, and perception middles. These more resemble a prototypical agent volitionally controlling and causing the event. This is the area of the map where we might find a two-participant (transitive) event as well with both the energy source (agent) and energy endpoint (patient). The more agent-like middle types also depart from the active transitive prototype, where the agent (energy source) causes a change of state to a distinct patient (energy endpoint). There is no change in the agent. The event's energy endpoint is only in the patient. But the middle types on the left of the map show a marked step away from the prototypical transitive in terms of both energy transfer and scope of attention.

With respect to energy source and endpoint, these events either profile a single focused participant as both the source of energy and its endpoint (as in mental intransitives or direct reflexives), or, if they do include a second participant, tend to play a stimulus role rather than a prototypical patient role because they do not go through a change of state in the conception of the event. Instead, the energy source and energy endpoint are conflated into one participant. The one who began the event is also the one affected by it. Our attention is no longer divided between a distinct energy source and endpoint, but is trained on a single participant. This narrows the scope of attention and heightens the salience of the affected agent in the event.

This indicates a semantic motivation for voice alternations so that when an event is conceived as closer to the prototypical transitive, it is more likely to be categorized within active voice and receive active coding in its expression. If an event shows a marked departure from the transitive prototype, then it is more likely to be categorized within the middle domain encoded with middle morphology to reflect the conceptual distinction.

One apparent exception to the semantic transitivity continuum is the presence of the passive function all the way on the right side, despite the fact that it entails the very same elements as the prototypical transitive in terms of energy source and energy endpoint. A distinct agent (energy source) induces a change of state in a distinct patient (energy endpoint). This is where recognizing the second voice parameter is key. The passive type legitimately fits with the rest of the middle events with respect to attention and the salience of participants. All middle event types, including the passive type, focus undivided attention on the affected participant by assigning it the syntactic role of subject. What would have been the less salient participant in the active transitive conception of the event is promoted to the most salient participant. The agent is downgraded and no longer salient for the discourse. In contrast, although the more agent-like middles shine the spotlight on the agent—the one who induces the action, this same participant is also the affected participant, the energy endpoint for the event.

In terms of the division of labor within the aorist middle paradigm discussed earlier, we can see this reflected in the map. Those middle types on the left that are more agent-like are typically expressed by the sigmatic first aorist form, while the more patient-like middle types on the right side of the map are expressed by -(θ)η- morphology in the aorist. Usage of the sigmatic middle form is confined to the more agent-like middles. It does not encroach upon the area dominated by the -(θ)η- form.

The situation is different within the -(θ)η- usage. We see a gradual diachronic expansion to both the left and to the right from its starting point on the semantic map. -(θ)η- originally encoded spontaneous events (like spontaneous process, mental process, body motion, and collective motion) and then expanded down the transitivity scale to include passives. But it also extended its reach over time up the transitivity scale to mark the intermediate middle types like the motion events that play a key role in this process. The motion middles are the most volitional of the original -(θ)η- uses, providing a semantic bridge to expand to other types that involve a volitional primary figure, including grooming events (a volitional agent performs an action on the body), and mental activities (volitional thought processes like "consider," "decide," and "change one's mind"). Mental processes do the same, extending to other cognition middles, all of which involve a relationship in which an experiencer apprehends a stimulus and experiences a cognitive change in the process. Some of these cognitive middles involve a primary figure that is more volitional (perceptions like "look at," "gaze") while others are more patient-like (perceptions like "see").

-(θ)η- spreads in this way through metaphor and analogy, where one event is like another in some aspect. We don't expect it to leap across types and jump over lines to include a type like the direct or indirect reflexive in its scope without first including the intervening types. We would not expect to find, for instance, -(θ)η- marking spontaneous processes and direct reflexives without including the motion events within its scope as well.

Because -(θ)η- has just begun encroaching upon the direct reflexive (grooming) type by the Hellenistic period (its extension is more of a sporadic one, limited to a few cases), this explains why there are no clear examples of its further spread into the indirect reflexive type. The indirect reflexive is semantically farther away from other types and closer to the semantic transitive prototype since it is a two-participant relation that involves both a distinct agent and distinct patient. The only difference is that the primary figure (energy source) also plays the role of beneficiary or recipient of the action— as the ultimate energy endpoint for the event.

The diachronic path for -(θ)η- shows its spread from one type to another through semantic similarity and from one contiguous space to another. The semantic map is iconic in this way. It reflects what we know to be true about semantic proximity.

## 4.1. Final Remarks: How Do We Think about -(θ)η- and Middle Voice?

In our discussion of -(θ)η- morphology, section 1 showed that the apparent deviance of -(θ)η- resulted from its miscategorization as a distinct passive marker, ostensibly classifying its perceived active uses as exceptions or deponent. Exploring the semantic motivation for the category, placing it in cross-linguistic context and reviewing its place within the middle system, exposes a more unified and linguistically plausible account. Section 2 illustrated the variety of events in -(θ)η- with respect to its synchronic use and diachronic development. This section noted the difference in voice systems across languages, with special attention to derived active-passive systems and basic active-middle systems. Greek fits into a cross-linguistic type whereby the primary voice distinction is between the active and middle, just like a great many other languages with middle systems. Greek fits the patterns found in language after language; the same semantic event types are marked within middle voice. Each of the middle types discussed in section 3, including the passive event type, fit into this cross-linguistic pattern observed in middle voice systems. Section 3 began a process of pointing out the semantic connections among these various middle event types and considered the conceptual distinctions that motivate their middle marking patterns.

Voice distinctions are ultimately concerned with how humans conceive the nature of events and categorize those events in language, particularly with respect to the kind of event construed and how the participants relate to one another in it. This suggests that when we find -(θ)η- in a text, we must consider the interpretive parameters that motivate its use. The choice of voice marking options, such as the choice to encode an event in -(θ)η- or other middle morphology, implicates an intentional conceptual distinction in how a speaker/writer sees an event. Specifically, this choice involves two key adjustments:

- Adjustments in the *energy source* and *energy endpoint* for the event
- Adjustments in the *scope of attention*. Middle voice involves a narrowing of scope.
- The natural consequence is a change in the *relative salience of participants*.

Middle voice merges the energy source and energy endpoint into one participant. Instead of shifting between two participants to see the effects of the action, the middle gives undivided attention to the energy endpoint. This effectively increases its salience for the event construal. What happens to the affected participant is the most salient for our understanding of the event.

For middle events, we can ask two questions: What kind of energy transfer is involved? Which participant is the primary focus of attention? Middle morphology encodes the conceptual notion of shift in focus. Middle voice indicates a marked choice for which the participant is brought into the spotlight for the event. In the active transitive prototype, the agent is the primary figure while the patient, as the affected entity, is secondary. The middle, in contrast, shines a spotlight on the affected entity, heightening its salience by defocusing other participants in the event.

With respect to -(θ)η- aorist morphology specifically, its predominant use in New Testament texts lies in its original five functions: the spontaneous event types and the passive type. The primary focus for these events is the participant who undergoes a change of state—whether this is mental, physical, or with respect to location/ posture. For the spontaneous events—mental process, motion, collective motion, and spontaneous process—-(θ)η- places undivided attention on a single participant who is both energy source and energy endpoint in contrast to a two-participant relation. Encoding the primary figure as the subject of the clause reflects its heightened salience for the discourse. In this intransitive syntactic expression, the subject plays the role of patient, experiencer, or mover; no external force is involved in the change of state.

These spontaneous event types are often mistaken as active since the subject is doing the action. This is especially true with the motion middles in which a person, as an animate and volitional actor gets up/sits down/walks/etc. But these -(θ)η- event types are not motivated by a single syntactic parameter. As we have seen, being both energy source and endpoint disallows them from functioning as actives. Further proof is found in that the active counterpart for these -(θ)η- verbs is causative in nature. The active voice profiles the active transitive prototype in which an agent (energy source) causes a change of state in a separate patient (energy endpoint).

The relationship between the active voice and -(θ)η- spontaneous verbs is not a question of whether the subject does the action but a conceptual divide between a causative and a noncausative event. Treating these middles as deponents ignores this central semantic motivation for -(θ)η- marking. The conceptual content for the type of event evoked (caused vs. spontaneous) changes and shifts the audience's attention to the patient, not the naturally more salient agent.

The other dominant use of -(θ)η- marking is the passive function. In this event type, the conceptual content remains the same as the transitive active prototype, where an agent (energy source) induces a change of state in a patient (energy endpoint). But in the passive -(θ)η- type, the essential difference is that the audience's attention is shifted from the naturally more salient agent as primary figure to the patient. Here, the process for mentally scanning the event is the opposite of the active, which we scan from cause to consequence. In the passive, it is reversed: from consequence to cause. Its syntactic expression reflects this shift in focus, giving the patient the status of primary figure and defocusing the agent into the background as an oblique phrase.

Because -(θ)η- morphology spread from the original five to more transitive middle event types as well, this means we may find -(θ)η- instances in other middle types too. If -(θ)η- appears in a reciprocal event, direct reflexive, mental activity, perception, or speech act, we should not construe it as functioning as an active, but instead as -(θ)η- continuing to extend itself throughout the rest of the middle domain. In these instances, the motivation for selecting -(θ)η- is the same as for the sigmatic (first aorist) middle marking—to express a marked departure from the active default for the energy endpoint of the event. In these middle types, the endpoint ultimately confers back on the agent (energy source) who started it, so that the agent experiences some kind of affect from the action. This affect may be physical or mental—such as in the mental activity type in which -(θ)η- and other middle morphology is used to profile a mental experience that results in a mental change for the experiencer.

Having looked at the middle event types that span a semantic continuum from more agent to more patient-like events, we can revisit the troublesome -(θ)η- verbs from section 1. Consider ἠγέρθησαν from Matthew 25:6: "Then all the bridesmaids <u>got up</u> and trimmed their lamps." This is a motion -(θ)η- that shifts primary attention to the mover who undergoes a change in location. Or, διελέχθησαν in Mark 9:34: "they had argued with one another." This is a use of -(θ)η- extending to the reciprocal middle type. The -(θ)η- uses in 1 Peter 1:24 (ἐξηράνθη "the grass withers") and in Acts 7:60 (ἐκοιμήθη "he died") are both exemplary examples of the spontaneous process middle. The primary figure in the conception of the event undergoes a change of state.

Changing our categorization of -(θ)η- from the analogous English counterpart (passive) to a typologically attested middle form alters our view of Greek voice. Instead of seeing it as a passive marker with defective active outliers in an active-passive system, -(θ)η- is rightly treated as marking the less-transitive middle events—including passives—within a larger transitivity continuum in an active-middle system. The middle share of the space divides the labor across two morphological forms in the aorist and future compared to one in the present and perfect.

In Hellenistic Greek, -(θ)η- is used predominantly within its original five types, marking those events that shift the focus of attention to the more patient-like participant. The sigmatic middle aorist morphology predominantly marks the other middle types, which involve a more agent-like primary figure. Within the aorist stem, the morphology is meaningfully split into two sets based on the semantic representation of the event type. The middle morphology in the present stem is not split into two sets, middle and passive, because one set of forms encompass the whole range of middle types from the right-hand side of the semantic map (with passives and spontaneous processes) to left side of the map (including direct and indirect reflexives).

In each case of middle marking—whether in the present middle-passive, the aorist sigmatic or -(θ)η- morphology—the middle encompasses a semantic continuum in which events show a departure from the prototypical transitive clause. The labels active, middle, and passive do not describe discrete categories, but rather waypoints along a continuum of descending transitivity. Some middle events are more agent-like and closer to the transitive prototype, while others lie farther down the scale, with a primary figure that is closer to a prototypical patient. In each case, the middle event involves a departure from the default active in some way, providing the means for linguistically encoding a change in the conception of the event. Each middle type involves a shift in energy transfer and where our attention (reader or audience) is directed.

# BIBLIOGRAPHY

Allan, Rutger J. *The Middle Voice in Ancient Greek: A Study in Polysemy.* ASCP 11. Amsterdam: Gieben, 2003.

Baerman, Matthew. "Morphological Typology of Deponency." Pages 1–19 in *Deponency and Morphological Mismatches.* Edited by Matthew Baerman, Greville G. Corbett, Dunstain Brown, and Andrew Hippisley. PBA 145. Oxford: Oxford University Press, 2007.

Baerman, Matthew, Greville G. Corbett, Dunstain Brown, and Andrew Hippisley, eds. *Deponency and Morphological Mismatches.* PBA 145. Oxford: Oxford University Press, 2007.

Beekes, Robert S. P., and Michiel Arnoud Cor de Vaan. *Comparative Indo-European Linguistics: An Introduction.* 2nd ed. Amsterdam: Benjamins, 2011.

Bybee, Joan L. *Language, Usage and Cognition.* New York: Cambridge University Press, 2010.

Bybee, Joan, and Clay Beckner. "Language Use, Cognitive Processes, and Linguistic Change." Pages 503–18 in *The Routledge Handbook of Historical Linguistics.* Edited by Claire Bowern and Bethwyn Evans. London: Routledge, 2014.

Conrad, Carl W. "New Observations on Voice in the Ancient Greek Verb." https://pages.wustl.edu/files/pages/imce/cwconrad/newobsancgrkvc.pdf.

Dana, H. E. and Julius R. Mantey. *A Manual Grammar of the Greek New Testament.* New York: Macmillan, 1955.

Dixon, Robert M. *Basic Linguistic Theory: Methodology.* Oxford: Oxford University Press, 2010.

———. *Ergativity.* CSL 69. Cambridge: Cambridge University Press, 1994.

———. *A Semantic Approach to English Grammar.* OTLing. Oxford: Oxford University Press, 2005.

Dixon, Robert M., and Alexandra Y. Aikhenvald, eds. *Changing Valency: Case Studies in Transitivity.* Cambridge: Cambridge University Press, 2000.

Farrell, Patrick. *Grammatical Relations.* OSSM 1. Oxford: Oxford University Press, 2005.

García Ramón, José Luis. "From *Aktionsart* to Aspect and Voice: On the Morphosyntax of the Greek Aorists with -η- and -θη-." Pages 149–82 in *The Greek Verb: Morphology, Syntax, and Semantics: Proceedings of the 8th International Meeting of Greek Linguistics,*

*Agrigento, October 1-2, 2009*. Edited by Annamaria Bartolotta. BCLL 128. Leuven: Peeters, 2014.

Geeraerts, Dirk. *Theories of Lexical Semantics*. Oxford: Oxford University Press, 2010.

Gibbs, Raymond W., ed. *The Cambridge Handbook of Metaphor and Thought*. Cambridge: Cambridge University Press, 2008.

Givón, Talmy. *Bio-Linguistics: The Santa Barbara Lectures*. Amsterdam: Benjamins, 2002.

Harris, Roy. "The Integrationist Critique of Orthodox Linguistics." Pages 15-26 in *Integrational Linguistics: A First Reader*. Edited by Roy Harris and George Wolf. LCLib 18. Oxford, Pergamon, 1998.

———. "Language as Social Interaction: Integrationalism versus Segregationalism." Pages 5-14 in *Integrational Linguistics: A First Reader*. Edited by Roy Harris and George Wolf. LCLib 18. Oxford, Pergamon, 1998.

Haspelmath, Martin. "The Grammaticalization of Passive Morphology." *StudLang* 14 (1990): 25-72.

———. *Transitivity Alternations of the Anticausative Type*. Institut für Sprachwissenschaft Arbeitspapier NS 5. Cologne: Universität zu Köln, 1987.

Holton, David, Peter Mackridge, Irene Philippaki-Warburton, and Vassilios Spyropoulos. *Greek: A Comprehensive Grammar of the Modern Language*. 2nd ed. RCG. London: Routledge, 2012.

Hopper, Paul J. "Emergent Grammar." *BLS* 13 (1987): 139-57.

Hopper, Paul J. and Sandra Thompson. "Transitivity in Grammar and Discourse." *Language* 52 (1980): 251-99.

Janda, Laura A. "Cognitive Linguistics," *Glossos* 8 (2006): 1-60.

Jelf, William. *A Grammar of the Greek Language*. 4th ed. 2 vols. London: Parker, 1866.

Kemmer, Suzanne. "Human Cognition and the Elaboration of Events: Some Universal Conceptual Categories" Pages 89-118 in *The New Psychology of Language: Cognitive and Functional Approaches to Language Structure; Vol. 2*. Edited by Michael Tomasello. London: Erlbaum, 2003.

———. *The Middle Voice*. TSL 23. Amsterdam: Benjamins, 1993.

Kiparsky, Paul. "Lexical Morphology and Phonology." Pages 3-91 in *Linguistics in the Morning Calm*. Edited by Yang In-Seok. Seoul: Hanshin, 1982.

Klaiman, M. H. *Grammatical Voice*. CSL 59. Cambridge: Cambridge University Press, 1991.

Kühner, Raphael, and Bernhard Gerth. *Satzlehre*. 3rd ed. Part 2, vol. 1 of *Ausführliche Grammatik der griechischen Sprache*. Hannover; Leipzig, 1898. Repr., Munich: Hueber, 1963.

Kulikov, Leonid. "Passive and Middle in Indo-European: Reconstructing the Early Vedic Passive Paradigm." Pages 62–81 in *Passivization and Typology: Form and Function*. Edited by Werner Abraham and Larisa Leisiö. TSL 68. Amsterdam: Benjamins, 2006.

Ladewig, Stratton, L. "Defining Deponency: An Investigation into Greek Deponency of the Middle and Passive Voices in the Koine Period." PhD diss., Dallas Theological Seminary, 2010.

Lakoff, George. *Women, Fire, and Dangerous Things: What Categories Reveal about the Mind*. Chicago: University of Chicago Press, 1987.

Lakoff, George, and Mark Johnson. *Metaphors We Live By*. Chicago: University of Chicago Press, 1980.

———. *Philosophy in the Flesh: The Embodied Mind and Its Challenge to Western Thought*. New York: Basic Books, 1999

Langacker, Ronald W. "Dimensions of Defocusing." Pages 115–37 in *Voice and Grammatical Relations: In Honor of Masayoshi Shibatani*. Edited by Tasaku Tsunoda and Taro Kageyama. TSL 65. (Philadelphia: Benjamins, 2006).

———. *Essentials of Cognitive Grammar*. Oxford: Oxford University Press, 2013.

———. *Foundations of Cognitive Grammar, Volume 2: Descriptive Application*. Stanford, CA: Stanford University Press, 1987.

Lavidas, Nikolaos, and Dimitra Papangeli. "Deponency in the Diachrony of Greek." Pages 97–126 in *Deponency and Morphological Mismatches*. Edited by Matthew Baerman Greville G. Corbett, Dunstan Brown, and Andrew Hippisley. PBA 145. Oxford: Oxford University Press, 2007.

Machen, J. Gresham. *New Testament Greek for Beginners*. New York: Macmillan, 1923.

Maldonado, Ricardo. "Middle as a Basic Voice System." Pages 69–109 in *Studies in Role and Reference Grammar*. Edited by Lilian Guerrero, Sergio Ibáñez, and Valeria Balloro. Mexico City: UNAM, 2009.

Manney, Linda Joyce. *The Middle Voice in Modern Greek*. SLCS 48. Amsterdam: Benjamins, 2000.

McKay, K. L. *Greek Grammar for Students: A Concise Grammar of Classical Attic with Special Reference to Aspect in the Verb*. Canberra: Dept. of Classics, Australian National University, 1974.

Mounce, William D. *Basics of Biblical Greek Grammar*. 3rd ed. Grand
      Rapids: Zondervan, 2009.

Næss, Åshild. *Prototypical Transitivity*. TSL 72. Amsterdam:
      Benjamins, 2007.

Nichols, Johanna. "Diversity and Stability in Language." Pages
      283–310 in *The Handbook of Historical Linguistics*. Edited by
      Brian D. Joseph and Richard D. Janda. BHL. Malden, MA:
      Blackwell, 2003.

Quirk, Randolph. *A Comprehensive Grammar of the English Language*.
      New York: Longman, 1985.

Rijksbaron, Albert. *The Syntax and Semantics of the Verb in Classical
      Greek: An Introduction*. 3rd ed. Chicago: University of Chicago
      Press, 2002.

Robertson, A. T. *A Grammar of the Greek New Testament in the Light of
      Historical Research*. 4th ed. Nashville: Broadman, 1934.

Shibatani, Masayoshi. "On the Conceptual Framework for Voice
      Phenomena." *Linguistics* 44 (2006): 217–69.

———. "Passives and Related Constructions: A Prototype Analysis."
      *Language* 61 (1985): 821–48.

———. "Voice." Pages 1145–1165 in *Morphology: An International
      Handbook on Inflection and Word-Formation; Volume 2*. Edited by
      Geert Booij, Christian Lehmann, Joachim Mugdan, Wolfgang
      Kesselheim, and Stavros Skopeteas. HSK 17.2. Berlin: de
      Gruyter, 2004.

———, ed. *Passive and Voice*. TSL 16. Amsterdam: Benjamins, 1988.

Sihler, Andrew L. *New Comparative Grammar of Greek and Latin*.
      Oxford: Oxford University Press, 1995.

Smyth, Herbert Weir. *Greek Grammar*. Revised by Gordon M. Messing.
      Cambridge: Harvard University Press, 1956.

Sweetser, Eve. *From Etymology to Pragmatics: Metaphorical and Cultural
      Aspects of Semantic Structure*. CSL 54. Cambridge: Cambridge
      University Press, 1990.

Szemerényi, Oswald. *Introduction to Indo-European Linguistics*. New
      York: Oxford University Press, 1996.

Taylor, John. *Linguistic Categorization*. 3rd ed. Oxford: Oxford
      University Press, 2003.

Tsunoda, Tasaku and Taro Kageyama. *Voice and Grammatical Relations:
      In Honor of Masayoshi Shibatani*. TSL 65. Amsterdam:
      Benjamins, 2006.

Verhagen, Arie. "Construal and Perspectivization." Pages 48–81. In
      *The Oxford Handbook of Cognitive Linguistics*. Edited by Dirk

Geeraerts and Hubert Cuyckens. Oxford: Oxford University Press, 2007.

Wackernagel, Jacob. *Lectures on Syntax: With Special Reference to Greek, Latin, and Germanic.* Translated by David Langslow. Oxford: Oxford University Press, 2009.

Wallace, Daniel. *Greek Grammar beyond the Basics: An Exegetical Syntax of the New Testament.* Grand Rapids: Zondervan, 1996.

Walrod, Michael R. and Jamin R. Pelkey. "Four Faces, Eight Places: Elaborate Expression, Emergent Meaning, and Translation as Discourse Art." *JT* 6 (2010): 11-26.

Winer, George B. *A Treatise on the Grammar of New Testament Greek: Regarded as a Sure Basis for New Testament Exegesis.* Translated by W. F. Moulton. 3rd ed. Edinburgh: T&T Clark, 1882.

CHAPTER 19

# Envoi

GEOFFREY HORROCKS

FACULTY OF CLASSICS, UNIVERSITY OF CAMBRIDGE

## 1. INTRODUCTION

It is a great honor to have been invited to contribute a concluding
chapter to this important new collection of articles dealing with the
forms, meanings, and uses of ancient Greek verbs. They are focused
around the theme of tense and aspect and I very much hope that
the volume as a whole will attract the attention not only of students
of the New Testament but of those with wider interests in ancient
Greek, including linguists who study tense and aspect from a general theoretical or typological perspective. There is much here that is
new, intellectually challenging, and corrective of received wisdom,
and the work will surely help to shape our future thinking about
issues of tense and aspect, both in Greek and beyond.

First, however, a very few words about what this chapter is not.
It will not provide a summary of the book's contents, which readers
will access and process for themselves. Nor will it attempt an evaluation of individual chapters, which is properly the task of independent reviewers in learned journals. Rather I shall outline in general
terms the key issues that have been addressed and taken forward
here, while attempting, *en passant*, to identify one or two topics that
invite further thought and clarification, or whose analysis points
the way toward future research and refinement.

I begin with some general observations about method and terminology, and then move on to consider a number of specific advances

with respect to the analysis and understanding of Greek. Since relevant Greek examples are cited throughout this book, I have made the perhaps surprising decision not to repeat any of them in this chapter, but to try to encapsulate what really matters in Greek by using carefully chosen English examples to reinforce key points *without* opening the door to the kind of interpretative disagreements that analyses of decontextualized material excerpted from texts in a "dead" language all too easily generate.

## 2. GENERALITIES

It is a truism that, while all languages (probably) have ways of expressing aspectual notions, at least optionally, native speakers of languages that have not *grammaticalized* viewpoint aspect typically have great difficulty in coming to terms with languages that have, and that even speakers of one aspect-prominent language (e.g., Russian) can find some of the usages of another (e.g., Modern Greek) confusing. This provides a clear warning that any abstract analysis of (tense and) aspect, whether universal or language-specific in scope, will need (1) to focus on the implications of being *required* by the grammar of a language to make aspectual choices and (2) to bear in mind the more contingent or purely conventional facets of speakers' choices in this domain.

One major virtue of this collection is that the importance of both these issues is recognized from the outset. Living with a grammaticalized opposition that *forces* an aspectual choice when you use a verb (the future indicative is one major exception in Ancient Greek) is not at all the same thing as being *able* to make aspectual distinctions as and when you think you might need to. While almost every ancient Greek verb form is built to a stem that conveys determinate aspectual information, the English past tense, for example, has no inherent aspectual value at all, and the same form can be interpreted in different ways in different contexts, compare, for example, "she swept the floor every day/all day/in ten minutes; used to sweep and was sweeping" are available to mark habituality or progressiveness overtly, but only on a facultative basis.

It is also emphasized here (see in particular the second and third sections) that pragmatic and conventional factors merit just as much attention as formal semantic ones. The former type have to do with things like the perceived appropriateness of a particular choice of aspect in a particular context. It is, for example, unclear whether imperfective or perfective aspect is the more "natural" choice when describing a single protracted action/activity with no natural termination (cf. "she ran till noon") or the open-ended repetition of a particular event (cf. "she came every Wednesday"), and default preferences may easily shift over time, as they clearly have in the history of Greek. It is equally important to appreciate that the use of particular tense/aspect choices to "signpost" elements of a discourse in some way, e.g., as foregrounded vs. backgrounded, may have as much to do with convention as with their inherent or prototypical semantic values, cf. the shift to the present tense (nonprogressive) in "I was in the Rose and Crown last Monday night when this idiot comes in and says …"

Another crucial issue is the long-term disinclination of those who study Greek in different institutional environments to communicate effectively with one another, or indeed with linguists who have a more general interest in grammatical and semantic categories that happen to have instantiations in Greek. It is still not unusual, for example, for Classicists to have no real sense of the evolution of the language in postclassical periods (whether ancient, medieval, or modern), or for New Testament scholars largely to ignore what was happening more generally to Greek in the Roman period, or for Hellenists collectively to lack any clear theoretical or typological perspective when framing their analyses of specifically Greek phenomena. This volume, by contrast, is characterized throughout by the openness of its contributors to the value of information and insights derived from work in linguistic theory and linguistic typology, and to the importance of scholarship conducted right across the spectrum of Greek studies. As a consequence, the argumentation in its different chapters is more incisive, and the analyses more grounded and more compelling, than would otherwise ever have been possible. Nothing, after all, breeds cant and gibberish more rapidly than a closed circle of devotees who are certain they have all the answers.

Finally, the study of aspect has long been bedeviled by problems arising from a proliferation of technical terminology and an often-wild inconsistency in the use of particular terms. The net result has been simply to compound an already prevailing state of confusion. Thanks to the willingness on the part of the contributors to this book to listen, learn, and then make use of emerging terminological norms, these problems are largely absent and the reader is free to focus on substantive issues such as the validity of particular ways of resolving the core problems of definition or of analyzing Greek data in terms of the categories proposed.

(A)telicity, for example, the quality of having or not having an inherent endpoint, is generally, and correctly, seen as a defining property of whole predicates (and/or the situations they denote) rather than of verbs, whose lexical aspectual character (or *Aktionsart*) might instead be described, at the level of highest generality, as either "terminative" or "nonterminative": thus "wash" in isolation denotes a nonterminative activity, but "washes cars for a living" is atelic and "washes the cars in half an hour" is telic.

A more precise description of lexical aspectual character is often hard to pin down in specific cases: e.g., "love" is routinely taken to denote a state, and stative verbs normally reject progressive forms (cf. *"I'm knowing that ..."), but "I'm loving my time as an intern here" is fine. It is interesting, in passing, to compare this slipperiness of aspectual character in languages like English, which do not grammaticalize viewpoint aspect, with the corresponding (relative) stability in languages like Greek, that do. One particularly clear example is the resistance of Greek throughout its history to the secondary use of nonterminative activity verbs as terminative causatives, i.e., there are no acceptable translation equivalents of sentences such as "Achilles smashed Hector's body into pieces." The nature of this connection, which is typologically very well grounded, is clearly worth further consideration.

Such difficulties with the notion of aspectual character notwithstanding, the specifically *lexical* contribution to the aspectual interpretation of verb forms is regularly, and very helpfully, kept distinct here from the purely subjective choice that speakers of aspect-prominent languages are obliged to make between perfective forms (marked in Greek by the aorist stem) and imperfective forms (marked in Greek by the present stem).

I shall have more to say on this last topic below. For the present, however, I would just like to express the hope that the important consolidation of good terminological practice seen in this volume will in due course become the basis for a much more general acceptance of the relevant terminological conventions among Greek linguists in the future.

## 3. SPECIFICS

Having addressed some important general points, I turn now to the principal gains for our interpretation and understanding of Greek. Any reader, having worked through the chapters of this book, will surely be convinced that, while viewpoint aspect is indeed an essentially "temporal" category, it is one that has little or nothing to do with the *actual* temporal properties of the situation described, whether in terms of its location in time or of its duration/punctuality; even momentary events, after all, may be viewed imperfectively, cf. "he only coughed for a split second, but while he was coughing ..." It is instead a matter of the grammatically obligatory, but always subjective, choice of a speaker or writer to describe a given eventuality with either a perfective or an imperfective verb form that requires his/her audience to view that eventuality, respectively, either as "bounded" (i.e., with a beginning and end in time, thus focusing on its completeness and by implication eliding its middle) or "unbounded" (i.e., without a beginning or end in time, thus focusing on its incompleteness and by implication its undelimited middle).

It is important to note here that a fully grammaticalized aspectual opposition of the kind seen in Greek, in which the majority of verb forms participate, will necessarily involve a very high level of generality and abstractness in the "meanings" of the contrasting stems. By contrast, discretionary lexical or periphrastic options for the expression of aspect-like notions, as in English, almost always have more precise values, simply because they are designed to make specific readings explicit to the exclusion of others. It is misleading, therefore, to impose a set of values of the second kind on forms of the first type, even if something along these lines has to be done, *faute de mieux*, when faced with the task of translating from Greek into English.

Furthermore, it is clearly the case that lexical aspectual character and viewpoint aspect interact, with subtly different consequences for the interpretation of the very general notions of bounded and unbounded. For example, the perfective forms of a lexically terminative verb are normally understood to indicate that the action described has reached its natural endpoint (cf. the default reading of "the cheese melted," implying that there is no more melting to be done), while those of a nonterminative verb most naturally indicate that the action has merely stopped at some arbitrary point (cf. "Sarah ran along the beach" [e.g., as far as the pier but no further]). Nonetheless, the fact that the vast majority of Greek verbs, regardless of their lexical aspectual character, have both perfective and imperfective stems (the relatively small number of exceptions are mostly stative) demonstrates beyond doubt that these two aspectual notions are indeed fundamentally different and very largely independent of one another.

Equally importantly, a careful reader could have little doubt that the basic function of the augment in Classical Greek, as in early Postclassical Greek for the most part, was as an obligatory comarker, along with secondary endings, of past time reference in indicative verb forms. The prehistory and earlier history of this prefix remain matters of speculation, and while the text of Homer, for example, reveals a significantly different ratio of augmented vs. unaugmented forms in speeches compared with narrative, it is not at all self-evident what this actually shows. Whatever the truth of the matter for earlier times, the grammaticalized augment in its classical function was largely redundant, and unaccented augments were later lost in many medieval dialects, as also in standard Modern Greek.

It is also made abundantly clear that the conventionalized use of augmented, normally past-referring, aorists in a specified set of nonpast contexts is in practice no more surprising, or indeed destabilizing of the tense/aspect system, than e.g., the "future" use of the past tense (cf. "if she came tomorrow/in future ...") or the present progressive (cf. "I am applying for the job next week") in English. This state of affairs has never been used as an argument for denying that the English past tense basically refers to the past or that the progressive present tense basically refers to the present, and correspondingly, there is no good reason to suggest that nonpast uses of the aorist indicative somehow undermine its core function as a past perfective.

In each of the relevant types of sentence the aorist is used to describe nonpast eventualities that are naturally viewed perfectively. Many instances involve reference to the present time, which is not normally or readily associated with perfectiveness (e.g., "I write

books" is not a description of my current activity, which would
have to be expressed using the imperfective/progressive). But this
particular time/aspect combination *is* required in performative utterances (e.g., "I name this ship 'Bellerophon'"), in making certain
kinds of suggestion (e.g., "why don't we call your wife?"), and in
eyewitness reporting (e.g., "Suarez gets the ball, sweeps past the
defender, shoots, and scores!!") Given that the aorist was aspectually appropriate in such situations but temporally misleading, and
that the present was temporally appropriate but aspectually misleading, the emergence of a competition between the two forms in
these contexts is completely predictable. Each requires an element
of compromise *vis-à-vis* its normal usage, but there is always a contextual cue for the listener/reader to suppress the unwanted component of meaning.

The remaining type is the so-called "gnomic" aorist, used both
in genuine expressions of popular wisdom (cf. "too many cooks
spoil the broth") and in generic descriptions (cf. "on arrival they unpack the contraband and sell it to gullible locals"). This has a close
relationship with the so-called "future" aorist used in conditional
apodoses (cf. "if I confess, my wife loses everything"), and both of
these involve an extended use of the "perfective present" already
discussed. What these last types share is the notion of temporal indefiniteness, i.e., the events described are not real events occurring
at actual times, but potential/hypothetical events that could occur
at *any* time. In each case, one potential time is selected as a reference point, and the event is then imagined as occurring at that time,
which is treated as present relative to that reference point. Thus
the sentences above might be paraphrased as follows: "(at any time
you like) too many cooks spoil the broth (at that time)," "on arrival
(at any time they choose) they unpack the contraband, etc. (at that
time)," and "if I confess (at any time in the future), my wife loses everything (at that time)." In other words, in these unreal, i.e., atemporal and future/hypothetical, domains, the relevant occurrence is
conceptualized in such a way as to require the use of a perfective
present, even though the event in question never takes place in the
actual, real-world present.

Last but by no means least, defining the role of the perfect tense
within the Greek tense/aspect system clearly remains the major issue it has always been, and it is no surprise that many of the chapters

in this book deal, exclusively or in part, with the form, status, meaning, and use of the perfect. While it would be misleading to suggest that the problem of the perfect has at last been cracked, some very significant strides have been taken in this collection.

It was noted earlier that grammaticalized aspectual meanings are necessarily rather general and abstract because of the near-universal availability of contrasting perfective and imperfective stems regardless of lexical aspectual character. By this criterion, the perfect looks like a reasonable contender for consideration as another aspect, since any meaning shared by all perfect forms (apart, perhaps, from a few lexicalized fossils) will clearly have to be quite abstract if it is to achieve compatibility with verbs of all lexical characters. Previous attempts to describe the perfect as a verb form denoting a state of the subject, an acquired state of the subject, or a past action of the subject with continuing relevance have all run into difficulty precisely because each covers only a subset of cases; and forming an overarching pseudocategory, comprising stative perfects, nacto-stative perfects (i.e., denoting result states), experiential perfects etc., is really no more than an acknowledgement of defeat.

But if we simply understand the Greek perfect to require an eventuality to be understood as homogeneous, nonterminative, and continuing at least up to a temporal reference point (usually the present), and then allow any further characterization of that eventuality, together with the exact nature of the subject's participation in it, to be determined by lexical factors, this definition could indeed apply equally well to the perfects of all verbs. Thus a verb meaning "hope," for example, whose present tense describes a state of the subject at the present moment, would have a perfect with the meaning "in the past I entered a state of hopefulness that now persists"; correspondingly, a change-of-state verb meaning "die" would have a perfect meaning "in the past I died and (so) entered a state of death that now persists"; and nonstative activity verbs meaning e.g., "run" or "write" would have perfects that mean "in the past I had a run and now carry this property with me," and "in the past I wrote (something) and now carry this property with me."

This approach, however, is not without its difficulties. The characterization of the perfect above in fact involves a recasting of the *lexical* aspectual character of the relevant verb rather than a different way of "viewing" its core aspectual character, uniformly conceived. Note in particular that the perfect often requires the role of the subject to be reinterpreted as something more passive or experiential: e.g., in "I am writing/wrote a book" the individual denoted by the subject is clearly an agent, but in "I have written a book" s/he is primarily the carrier of a property. The Greek perfect therefore stands outside the core aspectual opposition of perfective vs. imperfective, which has no impact on aspectual character, and instead has features in common with English-style refinements and modifications of aspectual character such as progressive "be X-ing" and habitual "used to X" on the one hand (= specifications of imperfective type), and the corresponding perfect "have X-ed" on the other (= a recasting of aspectual character). It is, in other words, a facultative option that may be deployed for clarity and explicitness rather than a true third choice in the grammaticalized system of viewpoint aspect. There are, it should be noted, no contexts in ancient Greek that *require* the use of a perfect in an aspectual role (the temporary increased frequency of perfect infinitives in indirect speech in the Hellenistic and Roman periods is motivated by temporal rather than aspectual factors, namely the need to be able to mark reported speech as past with respect to the time of the main verb). By contrast, in the absence of a perfect (or future) form the choice between a perfective or an imperfective stem is unavoidable.

   In general, there is a close correlation typologically between a relatively labile conception of lexical aspectual character (normally associated with various optional means of refinement, specification, and modification) and the absence of a grammaticalized perfective/imperfective opposition. Correspondingly, such oppositions of aspectual viewpoint are routinely correlated with a relatively fixed conception of lexical aspectual character and the absence of optional means for its refinement, specification, or modification. "Perfectness," of course, is a partial exception in that it is distinguished from most other such modifications in not being straightforwardly (re)interpretable as a subtype of perfective or imperfective. It might, then, be fair to see the perfective/imperfective contrast of Ancient Greek as the product of a gradual grammaticalization of earlier sets of modifiers of aspectual character into two opposed categories displaying the expected levels of generality and abstractness; hence, for example, the great variety of present/imperfective and, to a lesser extent, aorist/perfective stem types seen in Greek. Despite the semantically distinctive character that prompted its survival as an independent category, the perfect does not sit comfortably in such a system (there is nothing strictly comparable in Slavic, for example), and it is no surprise that what is already a relatively rare tense form in Classical Greek eventually disappears altogether from early Medieval Greek (other than as a stylistically marked equivalent of the aorist in literary registers). The reintroduction of a perfect in the modern period is almost certainly due to long-term contact with Romance, a process that began with innovative pluperfects in the 12th–14th centuries and then took several more centuries to inspire the creation of parallel "present" forms.

## 4. CONCLUSION

I hope that all those who read this book will get as much pleasure, enlightenment, and stimulation from its contents as I did. Despite a largely shared framework of theoretical assumptions and academic debate, there is no party line on display here. Different writers have felt free, within the agreed parameters, to take different positions on many of the core issues. Such disagreement and discussion among those who seek to advance knowledge rather than promote dogma is, of course, at the heart of all good research: hypotheses must first be formulated in a manner that allows them to be tested, and honest testing will almost always reveal inadequacies that lead to further analysis and refinement—and sometimes to entirely novel ways of approaching the problems in question.

The authors of the essays in this book and the editors of the volume as a whole are to be congratulated on their commitment to achieving, through constructive dialogue and debate, a better understanding of the complexities of tense and aspect in Greek. Though many of the central issues are inherently difficult to grasp and analyze, their resolution is critical to the establishment of optimal, or at least the most appropriate, readings of our texts. Those who work their way through this collection will be much better equipped to approach the Greek language with heightened sensitivity to the semantic and pragmatic implications of choices made among available verb forms. With luck, some may even be inspired to take the debate forward themselves.

# Contributors

RUTGER J. ALLAN (Vrije Universiteit, Amsterdam)

MICHAEL AUBREY (Faithlife Corporation)

RACHEL AUBREY (Canada Institute of Linguistics, Trinity Western University)

RANDALL BUTH (Biblical Language Center)

ROBERT CRELLIN (Faculty of Classics, Cambridge)

NICHOLAS J. ELLIS (BibleMesh)

BUIST FANNING (Dallas Theological Seminary)

CHRISTOPHER J. FRESCH (Bible College of South Australia)

PETER J. GENTRY (Southern Baptist Theological Seminary)

GEOFFREY HORROCKS (Faculty of Classics, Cambridge)

PATRICK JAMES (The Greek Lexicon Project; Faculty of Classics, Cambridge)

STEPHEN H. LEVINSOHN (SIL International)

AMALIA MOSER (National and Kapodistrian University of Athens)

CHRISTOPHER J. THOMSON (University of Edinburgh)

ELIZABETH ROBAR (Tyndale House, Cambridge)

STEVEN E. RUNGE (Lexham Research Institute; Stellenbosch University)

# Subject/Author Index

## A

ablaut, 151, 551
abstract, 10, 16, 35, 96, 113–14, 423, 487,
    570n23, 577, 627, 630, 633–34
    abstract schema, 96, 113
accent, 309n13, 255, 363, 372, 375, 631
accusative, 26, 189, 190, 193, 274, 426,
    528n57, 533
active. *See* voice
adjunct, 253n66, 452, 522
adverbial(s) 72, 355, 359, 374, 409n102,
    451n52
    adverbial modifier/clause, 3, 72,
        174, 174n47, 235, 253, 258–60,
        264–65, 265n82, 269, 275, 286,
        290
agent, agentive. *See* participant roles
Aktionsart, xxi, 9, 11, 18–19, 19n21,
    28–34, 28n66, 29n71, 31n81, 36,
    39–41, 45, 47, 47n176, 49, 63n218,
    82n2, 93n28, 103, 371, 374, 380n4,
    390n45, 486n1, 488, 488n5, 497n23,
    498n25, 500n31, 540, 543–44, 546–47,
    552, 553n29, 555, 558, 560, 629. *See
    also* predicate class
    Aktionsart vs. aspect, 28–34,
        497n23, 498n25, 544–48, 552, 555,
        558, 560. *See also* aspect
analytic, 282n9, 307, 371
anterior, 89, 206, 208, 388n39, 390,
    391n49. *See also* perfect: anterior
aorist, 8, 11, 13n2, 39, 41, 44, 46, 60,
    63, 72–73, 81n1, 82–84, 86, 88n16,
    89–97, 95n33, 99–100, 102n50,
    103–04, 107, 110, 112–13, 136, 138–39,
    144, 148, 151, 153n34, 155–56, 166–67,
    167n16, 169, 171–72, 173n43, 175,
    178–79, 181, 184, 184n2, 185n5,
    186, 186n6, 187n9, 188–93, 188n9,
    188n10, 201–04, 201n44, 202n48,
    203n49, 204n52, 207–09, 207n61,
    213, 214n85, 215–18, 224–25, 274–75,
    277–78, 285, 290–92, 291n15, 296,
    296n18, 300, 300n19, 302, 304, 336,
    307n2, 353, 356–58, 360, 362, 365,
    368–71, 372n59, 373–74, 379–80,
    380n4, 382–87, 383n23, 384n26,
    385n30, 392n53, 393–97, 397n65,
    399, 401n77, 404, 404n86, 406n94,
    407–10, 408n101, 409n102, 411n104,
    416–19, 421–22, 426, 532n8, 433, 439,
    439n28, 440, 440n29, 442, 447–48,
    453, 453n55, 455, 459–62, 465–66,
    468–69, 478–79, 482–83, 487, 487n4,
    489–90, 516, 540–45, 542n2, 548–58,
    553n30, 554n34, 563–73, 578–81,
    585–86, 602–04, 608–11, 610n83,
    613n86, 614–15, 618–20, 629–32, 635
    empiric aorist, 94, 94n31, 99–100,
        99n44, 100n47
    gnomic aorist, 83–84, 86, 90–93,
        90n21, 93n28, 95–96, 95n32,
        97n37, 99–100, 100n47, 382–83,
        383n23, 396, 404, 406n94, 632
    kappa aorist, 421–22
    nonpast referring aorist, 379–11
    proleptic/futuristic aorist, xx,
        382–83, 632
    root aorist, 103–04, 104n64, 579–80
    sigmatic/sigma aorist, 202n48,
        274 ex 1, 386, 416–17, 421, 567–68,
        572–73, 575, 580, 586, 602, 604,

606, 608, 610–11, 613n86, 615, 619–20

thematic aorist, 104n64, 190–91

-θη- aorist, 153n34, 202n48, 214n85, 274 ex 1, 417, 563–20

apophony, 354, 370–71

argument (syntactic/semantic), 39, 47n174, 48, 93, 253n66, 310, 433n10, 452, 491, 491n12, 492–93, 495, 501, 522, 525, 530, 533, 535n64, 546n16, 583

aspect:

aspect stem, 133–35, 138–41, 143–47, 145n25, 150–54, 158

combinative, 133–36, 141–44, 143n24, 146–47, 150–54, 156–67, 159, 462, 462n10. See also perfect

perfective-imperfective, 11, 18, 20–27, 23n36, 23n37, 23n38, 30–36, 39–46, 48, 48n179, 51, 59–67, 69, 72n239, 73, 91–94, 125–26, 131–36, 138–44, 145n25, 146–59, 167, 186, 188n10, 190–91, 193, 206, 207n61, 211n74, 224–27, 268, 175, 281, 281n9, 290, 291n15, 292, 295–96, 302–05, 316–17, 331, 334–37, 369–70, 370n54, 391–95, 392n53, 416–18, 422–27, 423n11, 438–39, 459, 462, 487–88, 488n5, 489–90, 495, 498n23, 502, 502n34, 513–15, 517n47, 519–21, 526, 529, 534–5, 542, 545–50, 554–60, 581, 628–35

imperfective, 23n35, 61, 71, 83, 139–40, 158, 168, 270, 187, 189, 190n14, 202n48, 205, 207, 207n60, 210, 225n16, 274, 275n4, 294–96, 307, 311–14, 315n43, 317, 323–24, 370n54, 371, 403, 403n83, 405, 419n5, 420, 440, 472, 502–06, 510, 511–13, 522–29, 529n59, 534, 534n64

perfective, 25n45, 37, 42n146, 59, 67n223, 94n30, 101n49, 102, 112, 112n93, 138–39, 148, 153n34, 156,

180, 277n6, 285, 291, 300, 335, 382–97, 382n13, 388n39, 389n43, 390n45, 404–08, 404n86, 406n94, 407n96, 410–11, 416, 443, 446, 453, 466, 458, 495, 505n39, 513–17, 525, 529–34, 530n61, 535, 548, 553, 560, 564, 579–81, 598. See also completive

and procedural character, 48–70, 626–35

as time-relational, 34–38

review of, in NT studies, 38–48

verbal, xix–xxv, 1–4, 7–11, 13–28, 70–73

See also habitual and progressive

asyndeton, 249–50, 253

augment, xxi, 2–3, 81–90, 83n4, 84n6, 87n12, 87n13, 88n15, 88n16, 89n18, 90n20, 134, 136, 138, 140–41, 144, 146–47, 149–53, 154–57, 186, 193, 353–64, 355n8, 368–75, 383, 386, 393n54, 394, 394n57, 395, 416, 424, 631

auxiliary, 39, 82n3, 126–27, 126n8, 130, 308, 336, 496

**B**

Bache, Carl, 16n14, 19, 20n24, 25, 25n44, 25n47, 25n48, 27n55, 28, 28n66, 29, 29n69, 31, 31n86, 31n88, 32, 32n89, 32n90, 32n91, 33, 33n101, 34, 41, 43, 43n150, 43n151, 45n166, 46, 48n178, 63, 63n219, 547, 547n18

Bhat, D. N. S., 124n4, 128, 128n9, 129n11, 131, 133n15, 137, 137n18, 143n23, 148, 148n28, 154, 170n29, 423–24, 423n12, 459–60, 459n3

boundedness, bounded vs. unbounded, 23, 34n107, 51, 67, 69–70, 70n233, 92–94, 125–26, 128, 134, 295, 302, 382, 391n48, 495, 523, 630

**C**

Campbell, Constantine R., xxii, xxii (n8), 1–2, 10, 11n7, 13n1, 13n2, 14n3, 14n4, 14n5, 16, 16n11, 16n13, 17–18, 17n25, 18n19, 22n32, 23n38, 29n71,

38-39, 44-46, 44n158, 44n160,
45n162, 45n165, 45n166, 45n167,
46n169, 46n170, 46n171, 48, 60n214,
61n216, 63n218, 69-70, 69n230,
72-73, 72n240, 72n242, 142, 142n22,
166n9, 223n9, 295n16, 307n2,
315n43, 364, 364n40, 372-74, 373n63,
374n68
cancelability, cancelable/noncan-
celable, 17, 17n17, 332, 385, 385n28,
397-400, 399n73, 400n75, 403n83
Carson, D. A., xix-xx, xix, 1n1, 15n10,
318n54
cataphoric, 171-72, 180-81
causation, causative/noncausative,
336, 500-02, 500n31, 511-12, 518-19,
532, 574, 576-79, 579n46, 588-91,
594-04, 607-08, 614, 618-19, 629
change of state, 52, 54, 56n204,
103-04, 104n59, 104n64, 432n8,
437, 440n29, 441, 443-44, 447,
451, 454-55, 498-99, 499n28, 501,
506-07, 509, 516-17, 571-74, 576,
578-79, 579n43, 580-81, 587-90,
590n68, 591, 593-02, 604, 609,
612-15, 618-19, 633
cognitive, cognitive framework, 2,
92, 96-97, 96n35, 102n51, 106n68,
110n86, 122-23, 132, 158, 243, 260,
425-27, 481, 491-93, 492n13, 492n14,
528n58, 529, 546, 570, 570n23, 586,
588, 592n72, 605, 605n79, 607-10,
616
Comrie, Bernard, 9, 9n5, 16n13, 17n18,
19, 19n22, 23n38, 25-29, 25n48,
26n50, 27n55, 27n56, 28n60, 28n61,
30n79, 31-32, 34, 36, 36n120, 39-42,
42n146, 44n156, 45-46, 45n165,
47n176, 58n209, 63n219, 64, 73n244,
73n245, 105n66, 110, 111n87, 126n7,
176n55, 177n57, 185n2, 211n74, 330,
330n3, 332, 374, 374n66, 399n73,
400n74, 403n83, 404n85, 405n89,
405n90, 458-59, 458n1, 545-46,
545n10, 548, 548n21

clausal proposition, 495-96, 521-22,
531
climax, 58-59, 59n211, 59n212, 63, 65,
216, 334, 340, 340n29
code, encode, 1, 13, 15, 16, 87, 98-99,
109, 129-30, 132, 148, 166, 168,
172n41, 277, 277n6, 279, 282-83, 287,
380, 384-85, 384n26, 387, 391-93,
392n53, 397, 401n77, 404, 407-08,
410, 454, 466, 499, 573, 579n46, 582,
584, 589-90, 592-95, 602, 614-15,
617-18, 620
completion, completive, 21-22, 24-25,
36-37, 40, 42, 59-60, 62, 67, 69,
91-94, 107n71, 128, 156-57, 204, 206,
209, 275, 277, 295, 300n19, 301-05,
317, 320, 321n65, 324, 357, 379,
388n39, 389n43, 390-91, 405, 407,
424, 427, 459-62, 465-66, 508, 519,
526, 544, 580-81, 598, 604, 630. *See
also* aspect-perfective
complex clause, 254-69
complex event. *See* change of state
conative, 61, 371
conceptual, conceptualize, 29, 32, 52,
55, 69, 92-93, 95, 96n37, 98, 98n40,
102, 102n51, 381, 391, 405, 425, 436-
37, 510, 510n43, 514-20, 522, 527, 564,
569, 570n23, 585-90, 593, 597-99,
601, 603, 606, 614-15, 617-19, 632
conditional clause, 85, 95, 260, 264,
396, 632
connectives, 3, 221, 225, 227-28, 232,
238-53, 260, 265, 268, 322
γάρ, 171-72, 179, 225n16, 227-29,
239-46, 253, 258, 464, 469-71
διό, 228, 246
διότι, 239, 243
μέν, 231, 231n35, 238
οὖν, 217, 227-29, 231, 242-45
ὅτι, 228, 243
construe, construal, 50n189, 57,
58n207, 58n210, 59n212, 63-66,
63n219, 68, 92-94, 92n26, 92n27,
94n30, 96n37, 109, 110n86, 187n9,

240, 256, 258, 260, 265, 267–68, 357, 369, 473–74, 476, 479–80, 483–84, 546, 559, 589, 590–91, 593, 596, 598, 617, 619

constituent order, 307, 309–11, 309n11, 309n14, 316, 530n62

continuative, continuous, 32, 68, 102, 111, 111n90, 142, 176–78, 180, 274–75, 275n4, 277, 279–80, 282n9, 285–90, 295, 300–05, 316n48, 331, 334–35, 420, 422–24, 433–34, 459–62, 526, 545–46, 633

contrastive substitution, 385, 385n27

copula. *See* periphrastic (copula-participle) combinations

core predication, 493, 495, 497, 521–22, 532

counterfactual, 83, 85, 95–96, 97n37, 402, 402n80, 404n85. *See also* realis/irrealis

**D**

dative, 274, 360

δέ developmental marker, 346ff

Decker, Rodney J., 1, 10, 14n5, 17n15, 17n17, 39n125, 63n218, 295n16, 384n26, 385, 385n27, 385n28, 396n63, 397n67, 398, 398n70, 399n74, 400n77, 410

definiteness, 408n101, 446n36, 508–09, 632

deixis, deictic, 28, 28n62, 28n63, 36n114, 40–45, 42n146, 84, 87, 87n12, 89, 96n37, 358–59, 368, 374, 391, 397, 423

dependency relations, 221, 225, 236, 238, 243, 253, 255–56, 258, 262, 267–69, 466, 469–70, 472–73, 480, 482. *See also* subordination

deponency, 3, 542n2, 567–69, 568n18, 575, 616, 618

derived, derivational, 20, 31, 104n64, 148, 354, 359, 365, 367, 447–48, 450–52, 454, 497, 511, 529, 578–79, 582–84, 617

diachronic, 3, 85, 100, 101n48, 101n49, 108, 110n86, 355, 368, 372, 374, 389, 458, 474, 483, 564–65, 573, 575–77, 581, 585, 615–17

direct discourse, 84–85, 88

duration, durative, 21, 24, 27n55, 32–33, 39, 42, 49, 51, 51n193, 53, 55, 58n207, 61n216, 66–67, 69, 72, 188–90, 204n55, 312n30, 313n35, 334, 366, 436–37, 437n22, 411, 452, 504, 506–07, 509–11, 510n43, 513, 516–17, 519, 526, 544, 547, 551, 555, 557–8, 630. *See also* predicate class

dynamicity:
dynamicity in discourse, 166, 167n14, 173, 313, 313n37, 317–18, 320, 324
dynamicity in predicate type, 51, 55n203, 56n205, 59n211, 71, 432n8, 434, 440n29, 498–500, 500n30, 504, 513–14, 518, 520, 544n8, 551, 579n44, 587–88. See also *predicate types*

**E**

energy transfer (energy source, energy endpoint), 588–20, 590n68, 592n72

epsilon augment. *See* augment

event vs. nonevent, 164–65, 173, 179, 235

eventuality, 25n48, 436, 436n21, 450–52, 450n50, 451n52, 454, 630, 633. *See also* predicate class

extension (from a prototype), 83, 95n32, 96, 113–14, 405, 407, 577, 581, 605, 406n94

**F**

Fanning, Buist, xix (n3), xx, xxii, xxii (n8), 1–2, 7, 11n7, 13n1, 14–18, 14n5, 15n7, 15n8, 15n10, 16n13, 17n15, 17n18, 18n19, 23n38, 30n77, 38–39, 41–48, 41n139, 42n145, 42n146, 43n147, 43n152, 44n161, 45n168, 46n173, 47n176, 47n177,

48n178, 48n182, 49n187, 50–51,
50n188, 51n191, 53n199, 55n202
55n203, 56n205, 58, 58n208, 59n211,
59n213, 60n214, 61n216, 66n222,
67, 67n224, 67n225, 69–70, 69n229,
73, 142, 142n21, 142n22, 166n13,
167n20, 168n22, 171n36, 225n15,
312n32, 314n40, 331n8, 382n18,
383n21, 383n24, 448n55, 453n55,
484, 486n1,488n5, 500n31, 501n32,
501n33, 502n34, 517n47, 519, 520n48,
550n25, 553, 553n31
finite/nonfinite, 3, 88n16, 185, 207,
227, 227n21, 227n22, 247, 253–54,
253n66, 258–60, 263–65, 273–74,
274n2, 276–90, 304–05, 312, 339,
362, 422, 468
focus, focus domain, 31–32, 34, 41–44,
92–93, 173n43, 260n75, 286–87,
310n19, 316, 453n55, 462, 476, 480,
482n23, 533n63, 571–72, 587, 589,
590–97, 599–04, 607, 609, 612–15,
617–20, 630
foreground/background, 2–3, 89,
89n18, 92, 163–65, 167–75, 168n22,
172n41, 173n46, 175n51, 177–80,
180n63, 203, 204n52, 209, 213,
217–18, 221–26, 222n3, 228–29, 233,
238, 247n57, 254, 256–57, 259, 261,
262n77, 265n82, 282n9, 283–86,
313–14, 314n40, 316, 317n50, 319, 323,
330, 359, 463, 468, 482, 529n59, 557,
559, 593, 613, 619, 628
background vs. backgrounded,
256–59
frame, framing function, 255n15,
255–56, 258–60, 263–64, 266–67,
269, 465, 471, 477
frequentive, 420, 422
future, 18, 32, 38–39, 82n3, 88, 88n16,
93, 99, 110n86, 123–24, 128, 130n12,
136, 138–39, 144, 147–48, 148n31,
148n32, 150, 153n34, 154–56, 185–87,
186n7, 187n9, 188n10, 190, 192n21,
206n59, 207, 207n60, 215, 274–79,

315, 333–37, 365, 368–72, 374, 383,
386, 394–95, 404, 407, 408n101,
409n102, 416–17, 438–39, 461, 490,
516, 519, 540–43, 542n2, 548–50,
553, 559–60, 578, 579n41, 620, 627,
631–32, 634

G
gender, 274, 542n2
generic, genericity, 83, 90–100,
93n28, 96n34, 98n40, 336, 368, 383,
519, 632. *See also* generic-specific
generic-specific, 178, 180, 245–46, 250,
258, 260, 264–65, 281, 285, 320
genitive, 274, 360, 487, 572
genitive absolute (GA) 172–73,
173n43, 175, 175n52, 266n83
genre, discourse, 164, 222–25, 229,
232, 235, 239, 252, 254, 266–69, 555.
*See also* narrative/nonnarrative
procedural, 224
expository, 224, 228, 232–33, 252,
268
behavioral, 224, 232
grammaticalization, 18n19, 28, 40, 70,
101n48, 105n66, 108, 129–35, 135n16,
158–59, 209, 336, 359, 368, 370–71,
373, 380, 462, 521, 579, 627
grounding status, 163–81 (narrative),
221–69 (nonnarrative), 281n8, 482.
*See also* foreground/background

H
habitual, 26, 39, 71, 89, 89n18, 96n34,
155, 209, 291n15, 368, 420, 502, 511,
513, 519, 546–47, 557, 627, 634
highlighting, 87, 88n15, 114, 164, 172,
176, 179–80, 203n49, 213–16, 224,
261n77, 289, 291n15, 332, 337, 345,
591, 609
historical present (HP), 3, 125, 125n5,
166–67, 170–72, 180–81, 203n49,
209–12, 211n74, 211n76, 212n77,
215n86, 215n87, 218, 224, 274,
290–96, 291n15, 296n17, 296n18,

300–06, 301n20, 303n21, 305n22, 329–51, 453n55

homogeneity, 436–37, 436n21, 446n34, 450–52, 451n52, 454, 544, 633

Horrocks, Geoffrey, 3, 30n80, 112, 113n97, 149n33, 187n9, 202n47, 205n56, 209n64, 336n23, 363, 364n39, 461–62, 462n8, 462n11, 484n28, 554n34, 626

**I**

illocutionary force, 495–96, 496n19, 521

immediacy, 41, 83–85

imperative, 87, 88n16, 127, 129, 135, 139–40, 142, 186, 187n8, 232–33, 234n39, 236, 252, 262n78, 282–83, 386, 480, 488n5, 490, 494, 496, 496n19, 497, 501, 502n34, 505n38, 509, 512–13, 517n47, 520–22, 526, 527n54, 529n59, 530, 530n61, 534–35

imperfect (impf.), 11, 17, 46n169, 61, 63, 65, 84, 88n16, 89, 89n18, 95, 95n33, 98, 158, 166–69, 168n22, 170n28, 172, 179–81, 184, 188–92, 193n24, 201, 203–09, 204n52, 206n59, 209n63, 211n74, 216–18, 224, 225n15, 275n4, 310n22, 311, 312n30, 312n32, 313–14, 313n35, 313n36, 313n37, 314n38, 314n40, 315–17, 322, 322n68, 353, 356–57, 365, 368–71, 384n26, 386, 392n53, 393–95, 403n84, 407, 409, 423, 439, 439n28, 459, 468, 540–42, 550, 554–57, 581. *See also* aspect: imperfective

imperfective. *See* aspect

implicature, 99, 108–09, 169–70, 172, 175n52, 179, 212, 374, 385, 385n28, 386, 390n45, 391, 393, 393n54, 397–400, 399n73, 399n74, 400n75, 403n83, 483, 506–07, 545, 548

inceptive, 58n207, 72. *See also* result state

indicative/nonindicative, 1, 3, 13, 14n3, 15, 38–39, 38n124, 46n169, 73, 73n245, 83, 85, 87, 87n13, 88n15,

88n16, 93, 95, 95n32, 96n37, 97, 112, 123, 127, 129–30, 133–44, 147, 150, 154–59, 192n21, 200n41, 201n43, 206, 211n74, 214n85, 227n22, 275, 322n69, 336, 353, 356, 362, 365, 368–70, 374, 379–87, 383n23, 384n26, 385n30, 393–97, 399, 404, 406n94, 407, 409–11, 411n104, 424, 434, 439, 462–66, 464n13, 472–73, 478, 480, 482, 489, 525, 529n59, 540–42, 627, 631

infinitive, 38n124, 53n198, 129, 135–36, 139–40, 142, 176, 185n5, 186n7, 187n9, 188n9, 190, 206, 234, 234n39, 253, 278, 312, 386, 403, 542, 549, 554, 634

inflectional marking, morphology, 133–34, 147, 149–51, 154, 563–64, 568, 579, 581, 586

ingressive, 82, 91, 580

irregular stems/verbs, 139, 150–54, 427

Isačenko, A. V., 19–22, 21n29, 22n33, 22n34, 23, 23n35, 23n38, 23n40, 24, 24n41, 24n42, 27, 34, 41, 46

iterative, 39, 63, 82, 89, 89n18, 93–94, 96, 96n34, 102, 106–07, 312–14, 312n32, 313n35, 314n38, 316, 322–23, 334, 336, 358, 360, 420, 502, 513, 516, 519

**L**

Levinsohn, Stephen H., 2–3, 122n1, 163, 164n4, 166n8, 167n21, 168n22, 170n28, 170n31, 170n33, 170n34, 171n36, 171n37, 172n39, 173n43, 173n44, 174n47, 175n52, 176n54, 177n56, 177n59, 177n60, 181n64, 193n24, 203, 203n49, 203n51, 209n63, 211n75, 212, 212n77, 212n78, 214, 214n84, 221n1, 222n5, 223, 223n7, 224, 224n11, 224n14, 225n15, 227–28, 227n24, 227n25, 229n31, 229n33, 232n36, 233n37, 234n38, 234n39, 236, 236n44, 239, 239n48, 239n49, 239n50, 240n51, 242n52, 243, 243n53, 243n54, 245n55, 245n56, 247n57, 249–50, 249n58, 252n65,

256-57, 257n69, 257n72, 260n76, 261, 261n77, 262n78, 263, 264n81, 266n83, 288n13, 307, 309n11, 309n14, 310n15, 311n28, 321n65, 323n74, 345n31, 466, 469, 469n16, 472n18, 480, 480n22

lexical aspect. *See* Aktionsart; predicate type

lexical core, 132-35, 133n14, 138-41, 146-47, 147n26, 149, 149n33, 151-53

Longacre, Robert E., 163n1, 164n3, 166-68, 166n10, 166n12, 167n14, 173-74, 173n43, 173n45, 174n49, 223-24, 223n10, 229, 232, 262n78

**M**

mainline/offline, 166, 203, 204n52, 209, 213, 221, 222n3. *See also* foreground/background; grounding status

markedness, marked-unmarked, 23n38, 73, 73n244, 88n15, 89, 89n17, 97-98, 103-04, 144, 147, 150, 154-55, 164, 167-69, 167n16, 173, 175, 179, 181, 181n65, 186, 203-04, 209, 214, 226, 238, 249, 258, 260n75, 286, 337-39, 346, 348, 367-69, 371-74, 386-87, 393-94, 421, 439, 465, 476-77, 480, 482, 483n23, 513, 521, 557, 579, 586, 592-94, 599, 614, 618-19, 629, 635

McKay, Kenneth L., 1, 8, 8n3, 10, 14n3, 15n5, 85n8, 90n21, 91n23, 92, 92n25, 107n73, 108n78, 109n83, 110n85, 111n90, 112, 112n95, 384n26, 410, 431n3, 432n8, 433-34, 434n12, 440n29, 448n44, 449n48, 453n54, 568n17

metacomment, 235n39, 238, 250, 250n62, 251, 475, 481, 514

Mɪ verb paradigm, 135, 139-40, 145n25, 149-50, 149n33, 153-54, 335

middle-passive. *See* voice

minimal marking tendency, 97-98

modal, modality, 32, 43, 85, 95, 127, 133, 139-41, 148, 274n2, 334, 353, 357,

370-71, 405, 424, 459, 494-96, 526, 529n60, 534

deontic modality, 495-96

epistemic modality, 85, 97n37, 495-96

mood, 1, 3, 8, 13, 18, 38, 44, 73, 87, 87n14, 123-24, 124n3, 126-44, 135n16, 135n17, 139n19, 148, 150, 154, 158-59, 227, 229, 276, 322n69, 362, 369, 380-81, 396, 416, 423, 480, 488-89, 496, 502, 513, 521-22, 529, 529n59, 534-35. *See also* indicative/nonindicative

mood-discourse grounding, 232-36, 238, 252-53, 258, 268

**N**

narrative/nonnarrative, 3, 28n63, 46, 84, 86, 88-89, 89n17, 89n18, 163-81, 184, 193, 203-06, 204n52, 206n58, 207n61, 209-18, 276, 277n6, 284, 330-34, 341-42, 350, 358, 401, 401n77, 472-74, 476-82, 529n59, 553, 555, 556, 596, 631

narrative grounding status, 163-81

narrative superstructure, 164-65, 164n6

nonnarrative grounding status, 221-69

negate, negation, 84, 89, 111n90, 235, 282-83, 349, 358, 473, 486n1, 488n5, 490, 494-96

negation scope, 490-91, 496-97, 497n20, 497n21, 501-02, 513, 520-35, 529n59, 530n61, 533n63, 535n64

nominative, 274-75, 360, 614. *See also* participial clause: nominative participial clause (NPC)

nominative absolute, 173n43

**O**

obligatory, 83-85, 129, 135-36, 159, 190, 192n21, 216, 330, 630-31

Ω verb paradigm, 139-40, 145-50, 149n33, 153-54

optative, 38n124, 87, 87n14, 88n16, 93,
   96, 96n34, 127, 129, 135, 139, 141–42,
   144, 186, 235–36, 268, 315, 356–57,
   365, 367, 369, 372, 372n59, 386, 542

**P**

participant roles:
   agent/agentive, 31, 62, 109, 164,
      164n3, 223–24, 267, 310n22, 335–
      36, 495, 512–13, 567, 571–74, 576,
      579–80, 583, 588–94, 596–608,
      611–16, 618–20, 634
   experiencer, 336, 588, 591, 597,
      600–01, 606–11, 613, 616, 618–19
   mover, 588, 591, 597–01, 613, 618–19
   patient, 495, 571–74, 580, 583, 586,
      588, 590–97, 600–08, 610–16,
      618–20
   stimulus, 607–09, 614, 616
participle, 3, 38n124, 123, 129, 131,
   135–36, 139–40, 142, 158, 158n35,
   173n43, 174–75, 174n47, 186, 186n6,
   189–90, 196n35, 202, 202n48, 204–
   07, 207n60, 211n74, 214n85, 253,
   257–58, 261, 262n78, 263–64, 273–06
   (participles as pragmatic choice),
   307–24, 371, 424, 440, 541–42, 542n2,
   543n2. *See also* periphrastic (copula-participle) combination
   anarthrous, 257–58, 307
   circumstantial, 263–64
   continuative, 275, 275n4, 277,
      279–80, 281n9, 285, 290, 295,
      300–05, 301n20, 316n48
   as pragmatic choice,
   substantival, 123, 158
participial clause, 172–73, 173n43,
   173n46, 172–76, 179, 255–58, 260,
   262–65, 265n82, 266n83, 277, 279,
   281, 281n9, 289, 309–10, 321, 323n73,
   324
   nominative (NPC), 174, 175n52
passive. *See* voice
past, xxi, 3, 13, 17, 28, 32, 44, 48n179,
   51, 62, 72, 72n242, 73n244, 83, 85–89,
   85n8, 86n12, 87n14, 87n25, 88n16,

89n17, 89n18, 89n19, 91, 93–100,
   95n32, 95n33, 96n34, 96n37, 102–03,
   105, 105n66, 109, 111–14, 112n93,
   124–26, 128–31, 143, 158n35, 168, 185–
   88, 203, 208, 211–12, 224, 275n4, 277,
   291n15, 295, 300n19, 301n20, 304,
   315, 318, 329–33, 335n18, 353, 355–57,
   359–60, 362, 364–65, 367–74, 372n59,
   (nonpast aorists) 379–11, 424–25,
   424n13, 431, 432n8, 433, 438–39,
   439n28, 441, 444, 446n34, 446n36,
   447, 447n37, 450n51, 452n53, 454n54,
   458–62, 468, 483–84, 495, 529n59,
   540–42, 548–50, 552–53, 553n30,
   554n34, 558–60, 627, 631, 633–34
   past/nonpast distinction, 134–36,
      138–42, 144–48, 148n31, 149–58,
      153n34, 158n35, 369, 392, 439
perfect, xxii, xxii (n8), 1–3, 10, 18,
   18n19, 25, 25n45, 36, 36n120, 37,
   43, 46n169, 67–69, 81–83, 88n16,
   100–14, 123, 132, 136, 138, 142–44,
   142n22, 156, 158, 166–67, 170, 172,
   179, 184, 184n2, 185n5, 185n6, 186,
   186n6, 186n7, 184n2, 188, 192n21,
   201n43, 202, 202n48, 218, 224,
   225n16, 236–38, 268, 274, 276, 307,
   307n2, 311, 315n43, 317n49, 318n51,
   321n64, 321n65, 323–24, 356–57,
   369–71, 372n59, 380n4, 382n13, 407,
   408n101, 409, 409n102, 416–28
   (morphology), 458–85 (semantics),
   458–85 (discourse), 527n54, 540–43,
   548–54, 558–60, 567, 572, 575, 579,
   603, 620, 632–35
   anterior (current relevance),
      18n19, 36, 69, 102–03, 108, 185n6,
      424, 431, 454–55, 461–63, 466,
      471–73, 482, 484, 548–50, 560
   continuative, 102, 111, 111n90, 142,
      420
   existential, 102, 105n66, 110–11
   experiential, 102, 105–06, 105n66,
      111–12, 451, 454, 548, 633–34

intensive, 102, 107, 107n73, 318n51,
433n10, 434n12, 483
persistent situation, 34n107, 105,
105n66, 111, 111n90, 548
recent past, 102, 111–12, 548
resultative-stative, 102, 104n64,
109, 113
totalizing-iterative, 102, 106–07,
420
perfective. *See* aspect
periphrastic (copula-participle)
combination, 170, 172, 179, 307–24
pervasive, 129, 135–36, 145n25, 159, 335,
571, 580
pleonastic, 346
pluperfect, 18, 46n169, 142–43, 166,
170, 172, 173n46, 179, 195n30, 207–
08, 217–18, 224, 311, 315, 317, 353, 360,
362, 365, 369, 370, 407, 408n101,
409, 409n102, 416, 424, 459, 635
Porter, Stanley E., xix–xxii, xix (n1),
xix (n3), xxii (n8), 1–2, 1n1, 7, 11n7,
13n1, 14–19, 14n3, 14n4, 14n5, 15n6,
15n7, 15n8, 15n10, 16n13, 17n15, 17n17,
17n18, 18n19, 22, 22n32, 23n38,
24, 24n43, 38–48, 40n129, 40n130,
40n131, 40n132, 40n133, 41n136,
41n137, 40n138, 42n144, 44n160,
46n173, 47n176, 49n188, 60n214,
61n216, 69, 69n227, 69n231, 70–71,
71n235, 73, 103n53, 112, 112n95,
142n20, 142n22, 163n1, 166, 166n10,
166n11, 167, 167n15, 167n16, 168,
171, 171n35, 206n59, 210, 210n68,
222n3, 225, 225n17, 227n20, 238,
238n47, 252n64, 295n16, 307n2, 308,
308n4, 331n8, 364, 364n40, 372–73,
380n5, 384n26, 385, 385n27, 385n28,
385n30, 390n45, 394n57, 396n63,
397n67, 398n70, 400n74, 401n77,
407n101, 408–10, 409n102, 424n13,
431n3, 433, 433n11, 434n14, 439n28,
449n48, 450n51, 482, 482n23, 484,
486n1, 553n30

pragmatic, 3, 17n17, 35, 63, 63n218,
73n243, 81n1, 99, 108, 125n5, 159,
177–78, 255–56, 269, 273–74, 277–87,
296n17, 317n49, 330, 332, 335, 337,
346, 350, 373–74, 385, 390n45,
391, 393, 397–98, 398n69, 399n74,
401n77, 402, 404, 404n86, 406n94,
410, 416, 447, 454, 473, 476, 610, 627,
635. *See also* semantic vs. pragmatic
predicate, 30, 58n207, 72, 310, 320,
397, 397n65, 411, 432n7, 432n8, 435–
55, 440n29, 446n34, 446n36, 447n37,
451n52, 490–95, 497–27, 497n23,
500n31, 503n43, 511n44, 517n47, 534,
544, 578–80, 629
predicate class:
accomplishment, 49, 51, 53, 55,
55n203, 59–63, 66, 437, 498,
499n28, 500, 500n30, 502,
506–07, 511, 515–16, 544
achievement, 49–51, 55, 56n205,
57–58, 58n207, 58n210, 63, 72, 437,
498–502, 507–11, 513, 516–17, 519,
544, 547, 559, 579
active achievement, 499–502,
499n28, 500n30, 507–09, 508n41,
517–18
activity, 29–30, 32, 49–50, 54–55,
55n202, 58, 62, 437, 459, 465,
498–501, 504–09, 508n41, 512, 514,
516, 555, 628–29, 632–33
semelfactive, 58n209, 499–502
state, 11, 18n19, 24–25, 34, 36, 44,
49, 50n189, 51–58, 51n193, 51n194,
53n199, 556n204, 558n207, 67–69,
70n233, 72, 72n242, 101n49,
102–04, 102n50, 102n51, 103n53,
104n59, 104n64, 105n66, 106n68,
107, 107n78, 108n78, 109, 112–13,
112n93, 142, 156, 170, 185–88,
185n6, 276, 313–14, 313n36, 314n38,
317, 318n51, 319–21, 321n64,
321n65, 323–24, 389–90, 397, 402,
404, 422–25, 427, 431–34, 432n7,

432n8, 437, 437n22, 440–44,
440n29, 447–52, 447n37, 448n44,
450n48, 450n49, 451n52, 453n54,
454–55, 459–60, 462, 466, 468,
484, 498–03, 499n28, 503n37,
504–07, 509, 511–13, 516–18, 520,
523, 544, 544n8, 547–48, 550–52,
553n30, 558–59, 571–74, 576,
578–79, 579n43, 579n44, 580–81,
585, 587–91, 590n68, 593–604,
608–09, 612–15, 618–19, 629, 633.
*See also* result state; stative;
Aktionsart
preposed/postposed dependent elements, 173n43, 174, 259–65, 261n77,
269, 309, 309n14, 309n15, 319n56,
321–24, 323n70
present time/tense, xx, 3, 11, 13, 13n2,
32, 39, 41, 67–68, 73, 81n1, 82–84,
84n6, 85, 88n15, 88n16, 92–95,
93n28, 97–100, 102–03, 102n51, 105,
105n66, 111, 111n90, 112–13, 112n93,
123–25, 131, 134, 141–44, 150, 154–55,
157–58, 174, 185–87, 185n5, 186n7,
187n9, 188n9, 188n10, 192n21, 193,
200n41, 201n43, 204n52, 207n60,
211n74, 274–76, 275n4, 281n9, 307,
307n2, 311, 316–20, 322, 322n69,
324, 355–57, 365, 367–68, 370,
372n59, 374, 380n4, 382n13, 383,
383n23, 386, 393–94, 397, 401,
402n80, 403n83, 404, 404n85,
404n86, 406n94, 407, 409, 416–17,
419, 419n5, 422–23, 425–27, 432n7,
433–34, 433n10, 437n22, 438–39, 444,
446n34, 447, 453n54, 458–62, 465,
468–69, 472, 483, 487, 488n5, 490,
540–42, 542n2, 545, 548–50, 552, 554,
558–60, 567, 572, 575, 580–81, 586,
603, 614, 620, 628–29, 631–35. *See
also* historical present
preterite, 331–32, 335, 356, 551n28
procedural character/class. *See*
predicate class

processing effort, processing hierarchy, 169, 279, 289, 332–33, 346, 472,
474, 480, 586
productive, productivity, 145, 145n25,
149, 149n33, 335, 363, 406n94, 543n2,
543n6, 579
profile, 52, 52n196, 54, 56, 70n233,
102n51, 572, 601–02, 605, 608–09,
612, 614, 618–19
progressive, 25, 44, 48n179, 51, 50,
63–64, 125–26, 131, 170, 190, 211n74,
291n15, 296n18, 336, 420, 422, 495,
503n37, 525, 546–47, 558n37, 559, 627,
629, 631–32, 634
    background-progressive, 314,
    314n40, 316, 317n50, 322
prohibition, 3, 235, 252–53, 481,
486–36
    general vs. specific prohibitions,
    502, 505n38, 513, 515, 519–20,
    534–35
prominence (discourse), 92, 166–68,
171–72, 179–81, 205n55, 215, 215n86,
225n17, 234n39, 259, 276–78,
280–90, 282n9, 305, 319, 319n56,
321, 321n65, 324, 330–33, 341, 453n55,
475, 482–83, 592n72, 596. *See also*
salience
    evaluative vs. thematic, 330–32,
    339–43, 340n29, 346, 349–50
prominence (grammatical), 122–59,
423
    aspect prominent, 122–24, 127–28,
    132–36, 144–59, 387, 407n98, 424,
    459, 627, 629
    tense prominent, 123–25, 127–28,
    130–32, 136–37, 154–59
    mood prominent, 124, 126–28, 132
Proto-Greek (PG), 133n14, 354, 419
Proto-Indo-European (PIE), 82n3,
83, 84n4, 87n12, 102–05, 103n53,
148, 185n3, 354–56, 418, 551–52, 578,
365–68, 370, 551n28, 578
prototype categories, 95n32, 96, 102,
124, 225, 265, 268, 379, 390, 390n44,

390n45, 395, 404-07, 406n94,
407n96, 410, 426, 481, 498, 547,
569-74, 569n20, 580, 585, 588-94.
*See also* transitive prototype
punctual, 27, 32, 39, 56n205, 58,
58n209, 58n210, 59n211, 59n212, 63,
63n219, 65, 69, 189, 390, 499-500,
500n30, 552, 630

**R**

realis-irrealis, 85, 95-96, 127, 148, 235,
268, 424, 439n28, 459, 529n60
reciprocal, 460, 572, 576, 585, 594,
602, 605-06, 619
reduplication, 87n12, 97n39, 107,
107n71, 135, 147, 147n26, 149-51, 154,
157, 193, 360-62, 368-71, 416, 418-19,
419n5, 420-22
reflexive, 572, 575-78, 585, 594,
602-06, 603n77, 614, 616, 619-20
relative clause, 237, 256, 258, 468-69,
554n33
    appositional vs. continuative,
    176-78, 180
Relevance Theory, 273-74, 274n1, 279,
289
remoteness, 46n169, 384n26, 424,
424n13
result state, resultative, 55-56,
55n203, 56n204, 58n207, 67, 72n242,
102-06, 102n50, 103n53, 104n64,
105n66, 106n68, 108n78, 109, 111-13,
170, 185n6, 236, 317, 318n51, 320,
321n65, 324, 388n39, 389, 421, 431,
433, 433n31, 447-50, 448n44, 449n47,
449n48, 454, 459-60, 466, 471, 484,
548, 550-52, 553n30, 554n33, 633
    target state vs. result state, 443n31,
    447-50, 449n48, 450n49
Rijksbaron, Albert, 81n1, 90n21,
91n23, 94n31, 95, 95n32, 95n33,
96n34, 99n44, 107n72, 107n73,
109, 185n4, 193n25, 210-11, 210n66,
210n70, 213, 305n22, 307, 307n2,
307n3, 384n26, 386, 576n28

Runge, Steven E., xxii (n10), 1-3, 13n1,
122n1, 125n5, 180n63, 184n1, 206,
209, 210n65, 211n73, 212n77, 212n80,
213, 213n82, 215n86, 215n87, 216,
221, 225n14, 225n15, 231n35, 233n37,
235n39, 236n45, 240n51, 245n55,
245n56, 250n62, 260n76, 261n77,
262n79, 288n13, 296n17, 332-33,
332n13, 346, 346n33, 385n27, 453n55,
458, 475n21, 539n1

**S**

salience, 92, 180n63, 223, 229, 233,
235, 238, 253, 256-61, 265, 269,
277n6, 283n9, 284, 286, 289-90,
463-64, 482. *See also* prominence
salience of participants, 572, 574,
592-93, 592n72, 595-601, 608-19
scope, 92, 94, 337, 339-40, 343, 349-51,
466, 494-97, 494n18, 490-91, 497,
497n20, 501, 513, 519-35, 565, 571-72,
575, 578, 586, 594, 603, 616, 627. *See
also* negation scope
scope of attention, 575, 577n36,
591-92, 595-96, 599, 601, 604,
610-14, 617
semantic, 2-3, 8-9, 11, 17, 17n17, 20, 26,
29-30, 32-34, 40-41, 47-50, 52, 63,
63n218, 67n225, 69, 73n243, 82-84,
82n3, 84n6, 88n15, 93-96, 99-103,
101n49, 102n51, 107-09, 110n86,
112n93, 113-14, 123, 132, 136, 143, 156,
174, 174n49, 234, 262n78, 263-65,
265n82, 273, 277, 277n6, 280-81,
281n9, 284, 287, 290, 291n15, 296,
296n17, 300, 304, 306, 317, 329-32,
335-39, 347, 359, 368-69, 372-74,
380, 384, 384n26, 385-87, 390n45,
391, 392n53, 393, 393n54, 397-98,
400n77, 402, 403n83, 404-05,
404n86, 406n94, 407, 410, 416, 419-
28, 430, 433-35, 433n10, 438, 442,
448-49, 448n44, 449n47, 450n51,
451, 453-55, 453n54, 453n55, 458,
482, 482n23, 484, 487, 489, 491-92,
492n13, 493-97, 493n17, 511n44, 513,

516, 519, 522, 526, 528, 534–35, 546,
    563, 564–65, 568–69, 571–75, 579–86,
    593–94, 597, 602, 609–20, 613n86,
    627–28, 635
  semantic vs. pragmatic, 99,
    108–09, 277, 287, 296n17, 332,
    335, 373–74, 385, 390n45, 391,
    393, 393n54, 397–98, 399n73,
    399n74, 401n77, 402, 403n83, 404,
    406n94, 410, 416, 627–28, 635. *See
    also* pragmatic
situation structure:
  situation time (TSit), 435, 438,
    440–44, 442n30, 449, 452–55
  post situation time (TPostSit), 443,
    443n31, 453, 455
  topic time (TTop), 438–40, 442–46,
    445n33, 446n36, 447n37, 451–55
  utterance time (TUtt), 438, 440–45,
    452–54
speech in discourse, 84–86, 88–90,
    88n16, 90n20, 164, 164n6, 176,
    180–81, 204, 206–09, 211–14, 216–17,
    225n15, 227, 229n32, 233, 266–67,
    285, 303, 303n21, 316, 331, 337–38,
    342–50, 358, 360, 472–76, 480–82,
    631, 634
  embedded, 89–90, 165, 229n32,
    266–67, 472–76
  reported, 164, 180–81, 267, 473, 634
  direct-indirect speech, 88n16, 209,
    212, 214, 217, 303, 303n21, 331, 338,
    634
spontaneous event/process, 571–72,
    576, 579, 579n46, 580–81, 585–86,
    594–601, 608, 612–16, 618–20
state of affairs, 49, 83, 85, 87–88,
    88n16, 91, 93–95, 96n34, 98–100, 114,
    147–48, 210, 212, 275, 314, 402n80,
    460–63, 465, 467–69, 471–72, 476,
    478–79, 481–82, 499, 502, 525, 531,
    596, 631
stative, 18n19, 32, 49, 51–53, 57, 68–69,
    71–72, 102–05, 106n69, 107, 109, 113,
    132, 142–43, 170, 172–73, 179, 206,

305n22, 311–13, 311n29, 312n30, 316–
    20, 323–24, 396–97, 397n65, 406n94,
    419, 419n2, 421, 423, 425–26, 459,
    484, 551n28, 553–55, 577–80, 578n40,
    629, 631, 633. For state predicates,
    *see* predicate class
stress, 309–10, 309n13, 375, 483
subject affectedness, 496, 572, 573–74,
    580, 590, 615, 618
subjectification, 108, 110, 110n86,
    112n93
subjective-objective, xxi, 15–16, 15n8,
    24, 26, 29, 32–33, 40–45, 48–9, 51,
    67, 110, 110n86, 254, 282n9, 390n45,
    423, 461, 507n40, 510n43, 545–48,
    558, 560, 629–30
subjunctive, 88n16, 93, 96, 96n34,
    99, 127, 129, 135, 139, 141–42, 148n31,
    185n5, 186, 188n10, 192n21, 200n41,
    201n44, 234–36, 235n42, 238, 268,
    286n12, 315, 336, 357, 365, 386, 490,
    513, 516, 520–21, 529, 535, 541–42, 554
subordination, subordinate clause,
    95, 96n34, 99, 165, 172–76, 180,
    180n63, 204, 212, 235, 253–54,
    356–57, 261, 261n77, 265, 269, 281,
    286–87, 306, 402n80, 465, 467–71,
    479, 482
  dependent vs. independent clause,
    235, 235n42, 254–59, 261–62, 265,
    268–69
  postnuclear subordinate clause,
    172, 174–75, 175n52, 180, 180n63,
    261n77, 266n83
  prenuclear subordinate clause,
    173–74, 176, 180, 180n63, 261n77
synchronic, 2–3, 95–96, 104n64,
    107, 368, 388, 425, 539, 564–65, 571,
    575–77, 617
synthetic, 40, 311, 549
  synthetic perfect, 541, 551, 553

**T**

tail-head linkage, 165, 172, 176, 176n53,
    176n54, 180, 261n77
telic-transformative, 579–80, 579n43

telicity, 48n183, 49, 55, 69, 72n239,
  436, 452, 484, 526n52, 544, 580, 629
  telic, 33, 49, 53, 60–63, 72, 93n28,
    103, 190, 305n22, 454, 484,
    498–500, 500n30, 544, 551–52, 579,
    579n43, 580, 598, 629
  atelic, 32, 49, 51, 53, 62–63, 72,
    93n28, 305n22, 446n34, 447–48,
    450–51, 451n52, 452, 454, 462,
    498–500, 504, 544, 551, 629
temporal structure/constituency,
  2, 15–16, 19, 25–31, 40, 42, 44–48,
  64, 98, 125, 408n101, 495, 507, 523,
  525–27, 530, 544–45. *See also* aspect
temporal, temporal reference, 3, 9,
  13n2, 15–20, 16n13, 23–31, 34–37,
  34n107, 36n117, 40–49, 45n165,
  45n166, 48n178, 64–71, 85, 87n12,
  88–89, 89n18, 92–98, 97n37, 112n93,
  124–25, 142–43, 148, 158, 176, 178,
  180, 185, 189, 206n59, 207, 223–24,
  247n57, 260, 264, 268, 277, 330–31,
  333, 350, 355, 358–59, 362, 369,
  372–74, 380–87, 384n26, 388n39,
  389, 391, 391n48, 393–96, 398–400,
  401n77, 402, 403n83, 404, 406,
  407–10, 406n94, 407n101, 409n102,
  424, 424n13, 441, 451, 459, 462, 493,
  513, 630, 632–34. *See also* tense
tense, xx, xxii, 1–4, 8, 13, 13n2, 14n3,
  15–18, 17n15, 18n19, 27–28, 28n65,
  35–36, 38, 40, 42n146, 44–45, 46n169,
  47, 48n169, 51, 52n196, 61, 63, 72–73,
  73n244, 81–82, 82n3, 84–87, 85n8,
  86n12, 87n14, 89, 89n17, 91, 95–99,
  95n33, 97n37, 103, 112–14, 123–38,
  124n3, 135n17, 140–59, 148n27,
  148n31, 158n35, 165–72, 185–86,
  203–04, 212, 217, 223, 225, 268,
  274–75, 275n4, 290, 291n15, 295–96,
  301n20, 304–05, 311, 314n38, 315,
  318–20, 322n68, 322n69, 324,
  329–32, 334–36, 335n18, 350, 353,
  355–57, 359, 362, 364–65, 368–74,
  370n54, 372n59, 380–81, 380n3,

380n4, 382n13, 384n26, 382–90,
  390n45, 392, 392n53, 394, 399n74,
  400n77, 401–03, 402n80, 403n83,
  403n84, 405–07, 404n85, 404n86,
  406n94, 407n101, 408, 409n101, 410,
  416, 419n5, 422–23, 424n13, 427, 431,
  432n7, 435, 435n16, 437–40, 439n38,
  446n34, 454, 459, 487, 488n5,
  494–95, 539–40, 543, 548–50, 552–53,
  554n34, 558–60, 626–28, 631–33, 635
  absolute-relative tense, 28n65,
    81n1, 124, 158, 390n45, 549–50,
    632
  tense reduction/neutralization,
    330–32
  tense vs. aspect, 13–20, 27–28,
    35–36, 40–47, 42n146, 52n196,
    72–73, 124–28, 159, 185–86, 374,
    380–82, 385–87, 392, 407–09,
    407n101, 409n102, 437–40, 543,
    545, 548–50, 558–59, 627–28, 631
  tense form, xxi, xxiv, 2–3, 7, 13n2,
    113, 153n34, 155–56, 166–68,
    166n10, 179, 190, 229, 268, 335n18,
    336–37, 381, 382n13, 397–400,
    401n77, 408, 410, 458, 461–62, 466,
    468–69, 472–73, 478, 478n23, 483,
    635
thematic/nonthematic, 163–64, 179,
  215n87, 224, 245n55, 253, 260, 277,
  330, 332, 340–41, 340n29, 343, 346,
  349–50. *See also* foreground/back-
  ground; theme-line/support
thematic/athematic verbs, 97n39,
  104n64, 146, 149, 190–91, 193,
  202n48, 335–36, 364–65, 367–68, 421
theme-line/support, 3, 163–64, 164n4,
  170, 179–81, 221–53, 221n1, 225n15,
  259, 261, 261n77, 266–68, 266n83,
  330, 339–41, 240n29, 350, 464, 470,
  472–79, 482–84, 482n23. *See also*
  foreground/background
-θη- aorist passive. *See* voice: middle
  (medio)-passive

thetic construction, 310, 310n18, 310n19, 322, 322n69, 206

time:
location in, 13–16, 28, 89, 124–25, 630. *See also* tense
time-relational view of aspect, 18, 20, 26n49, 34–37, 47–48
speech time (S), 35–36, 72, 89, 89n18, 112n93, 123, 155, 403n83, 444, 508
event time (E), 35–38, 52n196, 60, 72, 158
reference time (R), 35–38, 52n199, 60–62, 64, 66–68, 70, 108, 150, 155–56, 424, 431–33, 432n8, 440n29, 445, 446n36, 461–62, 473

token, 90n20, 98, 263n77, 314–15, 480, 482

topic, 243, 248, 309–10, 337
topic frame, 255–58
topic-comment, 206, 309, 309n14, 310, 322–23, 323n71

transitivity, 69, 124n3, 374, 420, 574, 579, 611–12, 615, 620
intransitive, 101n49, 106n69, 276n5, 336, 419–21, 419n2, 425, 427, 484, 498, 574, 578–79, 595, 599, 604, 607, 614, 618
transitive, 101n49, 108–09, 108n78, 336, 425–26, 508, 528n57, 572–74, 579, 579n46, 583, 588–94, 596, 611, 620
transitive prototype, 426, 573–74, 588–94, 596–97, 600–20

**V**

valence, 484

Vendler, Zeno, 49–50, 49n186, 53n200, 435n17, 436n19, 437n22, 497–98, 544, 544n8

verb:
phrase, 305n22, 307–08, 320, 444, 497
type. *See* predicate type
stem, 39, 82, 93–94, 186, 188n10, 189–91, 190n14, 193, 202n48,

211n74, 274–76, 295, 315, 335, 337, 355, 358, 363, 366, 380, 380n4, 383, 416–18, 422, 424, 439, 543, 545, 548, 550–52, 554, 558, 579–81, 614, 620, 627, 629–31, 633–35
constellation, 48–71, 53n198, 58n209

verbal aspect. *See* aspect

vivid, vividness, 204n52, 210–12, 331–33, 383, 453n55

vocative, 274

voice, 3, 96n35, 124n3, 134, 136, 139–40, 142, 144, 152–54, 186n6, 359, 374, 417–19, 458, 484, 541–42, 543n2, 563–20
active, 136, 139–40, 142, 144, 146, 149, 151–52, 274–75, 276n5, 319, 362, 364–65, 416–22, 424–25, 427, 433n10, 540–41, 542n2, 563–64, 566–69, 567n15, 568n18, 572–74, 578, 579n46, 580–84, 588–89, 591, 592n72, 593–02, 604–08, 610–11, 614–20
middle (medio)-passive, 3, 96n35, 123, 152–53, 153n34, 186n7, 191n17, 274 ex 1, 276n5, 315, 317, 356, 362, 364–65, 541–42, 542n2, 417–19, 421–27, 484, 563–20

**W**

Wallace, Daniel B., 22n32, 29, 29n71, 235n43, 258, 258n73, 307n1, 318n51, 382n18, 383, 383n21, 383n24, 459, 560n5, 486, 487n2, 396n19

# Index of Ancient Sources

## New Testament

### Matthew

| | |
|---|---|
| 1:19 | 608 |
| 1:20 | 566 |
| 1:22 | 170 |
| 1:24 | 439 |
| 2:13 | 338–39, 350 |
| 2:19 | 338–39, 350 |
| 2:20 | 122–23, 158 |
| 3:1 | 338–39 |
| 3:6 | 283 |
| 3:14 | 67 |
| 3:15 | 214n85, 323, 340, 346n32 |
| 4:4 | 346n32 |
| 4:5–7 | 347 |
| 4:6–7 | 347–48, 347n35 |
| 4:11 | 338, 340 |
| 4:18 | 283–84 |
| 4:23 | 284–85 |
| 4:24 | 285 |
| 5:18 | 249 |
| 6:17 | 604 |
| 7:6 | 608 |
| 8:7–8 | 347n35 |
| 8:8 | 346n32 |
| 8:25 | 427 |
| 8:30 | 310n19 |
| 9:38 | 610 |
| 10:5 | 175n52 |
| 10:28 | 524n51 |
| 10:30 | 319n56 |
| 11:4 | 346n32 |
| 11:19 | 285 |
| 11:25 | 346n32 |
| 12:4 | 323 |

| | |
|---|---|
| 12:39 | 346n32 |
| 12:46 | 315n44 |
| 12:48 | 346n32 |
| 13:2 | 170, 315n44 |
| 13:11 | 346n32 |
| 13:24 | 379, 382, 396 |
| 13:27–29 | 348–49 |
| 13:28a | 347 |
| 13:28–29 | 347n35, 348 |
| 13:37 | 346n32 |
| 13:46 | 453n55, 454 |
| 13:47 | 453n55 |
| 14:3 | 225n16 |
| 14:5 | 225n16 |
| 14:8 | 347 |
| 14:28 | 346n32 |
| 15:3 | 346n32 |
| 15:13 | 346n32 |
| 15:15 | 346n32 |
| 15:23 | 346n32 |
| 15:24 | 346n32 |
| 15:26 | 346n32 |
| 15:28 | 346n32 |
| 16:2 | 346n32 |
| 16:16 | 346n32 |
| 16:17 | 346n32 |
| 17:4 | 346n32 |
| 17:5 | 439, 440 |
| 17:11 | 346n32 |
| 17:17 | 346n32 |
| 17:22–23 | 347n35 |
| 17:23 | 601 |
| 17:25–26 | 347n35 |
| 18:3 | 609 |
| 18:20 | 319 |

| | |
|---|---|
| 18:25 | 593 |
| 19:4 | 346n32 |
| 19:6 | 599 |
| 19:7–8 | 342–43 |
| 19:16–22 | 343–46 |
| 19:18 | 346, 350 |
| 19:20 | 347 |
| 19:20–21 | 347n35, 350 |
| 19:27 | 346n32 |
| 19:28 | 192n21 |
| 20:13 | 346n32 |
| 20:22 | 346n32 |
| 21:4 | 170 |
| 21:11 | 225n15 |
| 21:21 | 346n32 |
| 21:24 | 346n32 |
| 21:27 | 346n32, 347 |
| 21:29 | 346n32 |
| 21:30 | 346n32 |
| 21:35 | 573 |
| 22:29 | 346n32 |
| 22:37 | 347 |
| 23:20 | 275 |
| 24:2 | 346n32 |
| 24:4 | 346n32 |
| 25:6 | 619 |
| 25:7 | 566 |
| 25:9 | 346n32 |
| 25:12 | 346n32 |
| 25:19–21 | 347n35 |
| 25:23 | 347n35 |
| 25:24 | 276 |
| 25:26 | 346n32 |
| 25:37 | 346n32 |
| 25:40 | 346n32 |

25:44.................346n32
25:45.................346n32
26:5 .................. 225n15
26:23.................346n32
26:25.................346n32
26:31–34.............347n35
26:33.................346n32
26:43 ................309n12
26:55.....................192
26:60....................347
26:61....................347
26:66.................346n32
26:75....................608
27:4 ....................... 466
27:11...................347
27:18 ................ 225n16
27:21 .................346n32
27:22–23 ...........347n35
27:25.................346n32
27:56 ................ 310n19
27:61 ................ 310n19
27:65....................347
28:2 ................. 225n16
28:5 .................346n32
28:19–20 ...........174n49,
                    280–81

**Mark**

1:6 ....................309n12
1:11.................... 72, 373
1:13 ................... 313n36
1:14–15 ....................174
1:21–22 .................... 171
1:31 ....................175n52
1:33 ................309n12
1:40 ............... 300, 303,
                    303n21, 304
2:3 .........................301
2:4 ................... 296, 301
2:5 ........................... 296
2:8 ........................... 296
2:12............. 175, 180n63
2:15 ...................... 294
2:17 ...................... 297
2:18............. 291, 309n12
3:1..................... 310n19

3:5 ...................297, 301
3:10 ................. 225n16
3:11 ................. 192n21
3:13 .........................291
3:20 .........................291
3:21 ................. 225n16
3:33..................... 297
4:35..........297, 303, 304
4:36 ...................... 297
4:38 .........................291
5:7 ...................... 297
5:11 .................. 310n19
5:15 ...................291, 452
5:19 ............. 319n58, 431,
                    446n34
5:21 .........................600
5:22 ............... 292, 297
5:23..................303n21
5:25–27 .............173–74
5:27b–c .............173n46
5:35......301, 302, 303n21
5:36 ...................... 297
5:38 ...................... 292
5:39 ...................... 297
5:40 ............... 292, 297
5:41 ...................... 298
6:1 ...................... 292
6:13................... 225n15
6:17................... 225n16
6:48 ......... 298, 303, 304
6:52 ...... 309n12, 225n16
6:56 ................ 317n50
7:1........... 298, 303, 304
7:32 ...................... 292
7:37............319, 446n34
8:1 ...........298, 301, 302
8:12...................... 298
8:17...................... 298
8:22 ...................... 292
9:2 ...................... 293
9:5 ...................... 298
9:6 ................. 225n16
9:19 ...................... 298
9:34 ............225n16, 566,
                    606, 619
10:1.................293, 299

10:17 .................170n28
10:19 .................516, 517
10:23 ...................... 299
10:24...................... 299
10:27 ...................... 299
10:32 ......................309
10:35 .................303n21
10:42 ...................... 299
10:49 .................303n21
10:52 ...................... 168
11:1........................ 294
11:2 ....................... 294
11:7 ....................... 293
11:17 ...... 319n58, 446n34
11:21...................... 299
11:22 ...................... 299
11:27................. 293, 302
11:33...................... 299
12:14 ...................... 299
12:41 ....................... 65
13:1 ........................ 302
14:4...................309n12
14:13................. 295, 303
14:17 ...................... 299
14:31 ................ 225n15
14:32 ...................... 293
14:37 ...................... 293
14:40...................309n12
14:41 ...................... 293
14:43 ...................... 302
14:44....................170
14:45 ...................... 299
14:63 ......................300
14:66 ......................302
14:67 ......................300
15:2 ......................300
15:14a....................169
15:16–17...........293, 304
15:17....................304
15:20–22 ................ 294
15:24 ............... 295, 304
15:26 .................309n12
15:27 ...................... 295
15:41..................... 55, 63
15:44 .................208n62
16:2................. 300, 304

16:4............300, 300n19
16:20 ............... 173n42

**Luke**

1:7..................... 321n65
1:10 ................... 314n38
1:12 ....................175n52
1:21 ...... 308–09, 309n13,
            313n36
1:22....... 314n38, 314n40,
            470n17, 371
1:25....... 319n58, 446n34
1:26....................176–77
1:62...........................371
2:8.................... 314n38
2:16...........................175
2:22 ....................... 598
2:23 ........... 314n38, 318,
            470n17, 467
2:29 ................. 206n59
2:33....... 309n12, 314n38
2:41....................169
2:51................... 314n38
3:2–3..................... 467
3:4 ........................ 467
3:22 .......... 379, 382, 396
3:23 ...................309n12
4:4 ......................... 473
4:6 ....................470n17
4:8 ......................... 474
4:10....................470n17
4:12 ........................ 474
4:17 ..........................318
4:18............. 468, 470n17
4:20 .......314n38, 314n40
4:31 .........................170
4:31–32.....................313
4:33–35.....................165
4:33–37.....................313
4:38 ................... 314n38
4:44 .................... 312–13
5:1.......... 315n45, 316n47
5:9 ..................... 225n16
5:16.............309, 314n38
5:17 ........ 309n13, 310–11,
     312n30, 314, 314n38

5:20 ....................... 474
5:23....................... 474
5:29 .................. 314n38
5:32...........432, 441, 476
6:12.................... 314n38
6:35.................. 282, 283
6:43 ................... 310n19
7:28 ....................... 474
7:31–32.................... 464
7:33–34 ................... 464
7:39 ........................ 475
7:47–50 ............. 475–76
7:50 ....................... 480
8:10 .................. 464n13
8:20 ..................464n13
8:29 ................. 225n16
8:32 ........... 310, 310n19,
            314n38
8:40...... 309n12, 314n38
8:42 ..........................66
8:48 ....................... 476
8:49 .............464n13, 67
8:52 ....................... 505
8:53 ....................59, 66
9..............................312
9:18 ...........309n12, 312,
            314n38
9:29 .........................312
9:36 ....................470n17
9:53....................314n38
10:7 ....................... 282
10:8–10 .................. 282
10:9 ....................... 476
10:11....................470n17
10:30 ............... 206n58
11:1........ 309n12, 314n38
11:13 ...................470n17
11:14.........................314
11:38 ......................603
11:40 ................. 576n31
11:44 ....................470n17
12:6................... 319n55
12:6–7....................319
12:7........321n65, 470n17
12:11 ........................514
12:29–30 ................ 470

12:31...................... 470
12:35 .................309n12
12:52 ................. 310n19
13:1 ................... 314n38
13:4 ...........................56
13:10 ......................314
13:12.................... 476
13:19 ...........................56
13:25–27 ................. 474
14:1 ................... 314n38
14:2.................... 205
14:6...........................609
14:16 .................. 206n58
14:17–20 ................. 463
14:22 ................. 463
14:23 .................... 463
15:1 ............308, 310n16
15:1–2 ................. 313n36
15:11 .................. 206n58
15:17 .................. 427
15:24 ................. 323n71
16:1 ...........206, 206n58
16:19 .........206, 206n58
17:2...................470n17
17:10 ..........319n58, 442,
            446n34, 476
17:14................. 178, 480
17:15–19 ....................179
17:19 .....................480
17:35 ................. 310n19
18:2.......................206
18:34 .................309n12
18:41 .....................480
18:42 .....................480
19:12 ................. 206n58
19:40 ......................275
19:46..................464n13
19:47.................. 314n38
19:48.................. 225n16
20:6.................... 323n71
20:9................. 206n58
20:19 ................. 225n16
21:5 ....................470n17
21:20.................470n17
21:21 .......................510
21:37 .................. 314n38

22:30 ...........192, 192n21
22:49 ...................... 38
22:57...................... 476
22:60 ................... 476
22:69 .................309n12
23:8 ................. 314n38
23:10.............. 315n44
23:15 ...........319, 319n55
23:34.................470n17
23:35 ............. 315n44
23:46 ................176
23:49 ............... 315n44
23:53 ............... 310n19
24:8 ...................... 566
24:13 ...........314, 558n37
24:29 .............470n17
24:32.................314n38,
          314n40, 322
24:38 ................ 321n65
24:46 ................. 476
24:53.................314n38

**John**
1:35 ................... 315n44
1:39 ............. 214, 214n83
1:46........................214
2:15........................ 595
2:16....................... 512
2:17................... 321n65
3:21................... 319n57
4:6 ..............191, 193n24
4:30 ................ 203n50
4:42 ................. 445n33
4:46 ...................... 205
5:5 ............ 205, 205n57
5:18.......................371
5:28 ................503, 504
5:37...................445n33
5:45..................432, 440
5:48 .................. 432n8
6:3 ................... 192–93
6:17................... 203n50
6:64 ........................38
6:69 ..........................68
7:37................... 315n44
8:2 ................... 203n50

8:8........................ 317
8:17......................318
8:31................209n63
8:31–32 ...................169
9:17....................... 362
9:35........432n8, 440n29
10:31 ......................206
10:32–33.................206
11:1–47 ......184, 194–200
11:1........................206
11:1–2 ................205, 217
11:3 .....206, 207, 207n61,
          214, 217
11:4 ............ 207, 214, 217
11:5 ..........................217
11:6 ............189, 557, 217
11:7 ................207, 214
11:7–16 ..................213
11:8 .............184n2, 206,
      206n59, 207, 214
11:9 ...................207, 214
11:11 ....207, 208, 213, 214
11:11–13.................. 207
11:12 ................ 214, 217
11:13 ......... 207, 208, 217
11:14.....187, 207, 214, 217
11:15 .............184n2, 214
11:16.....187, 205n55, 207,
          214, 217
11:17 ................. 189, 217
11:18.......................217
11:19.........208, 216, 217
11:20 ........... 191–92, 217
11:21............187, 205n56,
          207, 215–17
11:21–28 ..................213
11:22 ................. 215–16
11:23.................207, 215
11:24 ..............207, 215
11:25......207, 215, 315n45
11:25–26 ...... 201n43, 215
11:26 ..................184n2
11:27............ 184n2, 201,
          207, 215
11:28 .... 206, 207, 207n61
11:29 .........203, 212, 217

11:30 ............... 208, 217
11:31 ................. 194n26,
        200n42, 217
11:31–33 ....................216
11:32............187, 205n56,
        207n61, 217
11:33.....194n26, 202, 217
11:34.... 207, 214, 217, 426
11:34–43 ..................213
11:35 ............... 214, 217
11:36 ....207, 208, 216, 217
11:36–37 .......... 209, 216
11:37.................. 216, 217
11:38 .............184n2, 211,
        212n77, 216–17
11:39 .......... 207, 216, 217
11:39–41 .............205n55
11:40 ......184n2, 207, 216
11:41............ 207, 216, 217
11:42 ........... 184n2, 207
11:43.....207, 207n61, 216
11:44 .... 205n55, 207, 216
11:45...... 184n2, 202, 216
11:45–47 ...................216
11:46 ......... 207, 209, 217
11:47........ 207, 208, 217
11:48 ......................209
11:49–50 .................209
11:49–53 ................. 205
11:51–52 ...................209
11:53.......................209
11:54.......................557
12:14 .........................318
12:18 ................ 446n34
12:31................. 206n59
12:37 ................ 446n34
12:44 ......432n8, 440n29
13:4 ................... 203n49
13:12...... 319n58, 446n34
13:14.........................604
14:1 ........432n8, 440n29
14:5 ...................205n55
15:18 ............... 444, 445
16:5 ................... 206n59
16:9 .......432n8, 440n29
16:30................... 53, 57

17:1–2, 4, 7–8 .......553–54
17:7–8 ...................... 112
18:5................... 315n44
18:15–16 ................... 315
18:16 ................... 315n44
18:18 ...... 315n44, 315n45,
              316, 446n34
18:21 ...................445n33
18:25 .......................316
19:2......................557–58
19:3................... 203n50
19:21 ...................... 508
19:22 ...................... 317
19:25 ................... 315n44
19:32 ...................... 598
19:35 ......................170
20:1 ...................205n55
20:3 ................. 203n50
20:7......................205n55
20:11 ................... 315n44
20:14...................... 598
20:24–28...........205n55
20:26 ...................... 526
20:27 .............. 526, 503
20:30–31 .......... 205n55,
              317–19
20:31...............170, 201
21:2....................205n55
21:10 ................ 206n59
21:22 ......................189
21:24......................170

**Acts**
1:10 ....... 314n38, 314n40,
         315n44, 323n71
1:10–11 .....................177
1:12–14 ............... 314n38
1:13 ................... 314n38
1:14 ................... 314n38
1:17 ................... 323n71
1:18 ........................ 595
2:2 ................... 314n38
2:5 .........310n16, 314n38
2:6 ........................ 601
2:10 ...................175n52
2:13........................321

2:42 ................... 314n38
3:12 ................. 446n34
3:26 ........................275
4:9 ........................ 317
5:1................... 206n59
5:25................... 315n45,
              316, 319n55
6:11 ............ 445, 445n33
6:14....................445n33
7:27 .......................175
7:35.......................175
7:52 ................ 206n59
7:60 .............. 566, 619
8:1 ........314n38, 314n40
8:7–8 ............... 225n16
8:9................... 206n59
8:13 ................... 314n38
8:16 .............321–22n65
8:24 ...................191n16
8:27 ..................... 276
8:28 ...................314n40
8:32 ........................604
9:7 ................... 315n44
9:9................... 314n38
9:10 ....................... 205
9:28 ................. 314n38
9:36 ............ 177–78, 205
9:37 ........................178
10 ............................510
10:1................... 206n59
10:15 ...................... 511
10:24................. 314n38
10:30 ................. 314n38
11:5 ................... 314n38
11:9 ....................511n44
11:29–30...............177–78
12:5........................312
12:6....... 309n12, 314n38,
              314n40
12:12b ................. 314n38
12:20................. 314n38
13:12........................ 57
14:7............. 314n38, 322
14:8................. 206n59
15:39 .......................600
16:1 ........................ 205

16:9 ............ 315n45, 316
16:12 ................. 314n38
16:20 .............. 266n83
17:13...................191n16
18:7.........................313
18:18 .......................604
19:14 ...... 310n19, 314n38
19:32 .................309n12
19:36 ..................... 322
20:13.......... 321n65, 599
21:3 ................. 314n38
21:27 .......................600
21:29 ................. 225n16
21:33 .............319, 319n55,
              446n34
22:19................. 314n38
22:20 ................. 314n38
24:10...........175, 175n52,
              180n63
25:10 ............. 321n65
25:14 ......... 319n55, 320
26:26 ........... 309n12,
              319n55, 320
28:16.......................189
28:25...........172, 175n52,
              180n63, 266n83
28:30–31 ..................189

**Romans**
1:16–20 ....................241
2:24 ................... 467n15
3:4 ......... 467, 467n15
3:10 .................. 467n15
3:21....................... 476
3:21–27............. 288–89
3:31 ..................... 465
4 .............................241
4:13–16 ................... 246
4:17 .................. 467n15
5:1–2 ............. 237, 469
5:2 ........... 237, 452, 469
6:2 ........................ 287
6:4 ................... 243–45
6:4–14 ...............244–45
6:5–10 ............. 243–45
6:7 ................... 287

6:8 .......................... 287
6:11 ..................... 243–45
6:12 ......................... 243
6:16 ..........................481
7:1 ........................... 472
7:2 ........................471–72
7:3 .........................471
8:3 ......................... 258
8:36 ..................... 467n15
9:13 ..................... 467n15
9:33 ..................... 467n15
10:10 ................... 440n29
10:15 ................. 467n15
11:2–4 ...................... 477
11:5 ................... 475–77
11:8 ................... 467n15
11:20 ....................... 464
11:26 ................. 467n15
12:1 ......................... 234
12:3 ......................... 234
12:19 ................. 467n15
13:2 ......................... 476
13:13 ....................... 234
14:11 ................. 467n15
14:14 .........................481
14:19 ....................... 234
14:20–23 ............ 481–82
15:3 ................... 467n15
15:9 ................... 467n15
15:21 .......467n15, 445n33
15:22 .......................241

## 1 Corinthians

1:21 ..........................373
4:14 ............. 173n43, 317
7:20–21 ................... 250
7:29 ..................... 321n65
10:28 ........................ 508
11:13 ...................323n72
12:12 ....................... 259
15:2 ........................ 317
15:32 ....................... 234
15:52 ................. 190n13

## 2 Corinthians

2:13 ........452n53, 453n55

4:3 ........ 319n55, 320n62
11:25 ...........319n58, 446,
446n34

## Galatians

1:13 ......................... 61
1:20 .........................155
1:23 ................... 322n68
2:11 ..................... 321n65
2:16 ..................... 72n241
5:25 ......................... 234
6:12 ...................72n239

## Ephesians

2:1–5 ................. 255–56
2:5 ......................318n51
2:8 ........318, 319n55, 320
4:15 ....................... 234
4:18 ................... 321n65
4:26 ....................... 504
4:30 ........................600
6:4 ....................511, 522

## Philippians

1:20 ................. 206n59
2:2–4 ...................... 263
2:19–24 ............. 230–31
2:25–28 ................... 242
2:26 .......... 243, 322n68
3:17 ....................247–48
3:18–21 ................... 248
4:1 ......................247–48

## 1 Thessalonians

3:1 ........................... 397
4:1 .......................234n39
5:14 ....................234n39

## 1 Timothy

5:23 ..........................527

## 2 Timothy

1:18 ......................... 62
4:7 ........................ 434

## Hebrews

1:2–12 ..................... 478
1:13 ......................... 478
2:14 ....................465–66

2:17 ......................... 466
2:18 ......................... 465
3:2–3 ................. 470–71
4:2 ............. 319n55, 320
4:3 ............. 467, 467n15
4:7 ....................... 467n15
4:16 ....................... 236
5:5 ......................... 479
5:7–10 ..................... 467
5:11 .........................468
5:12–14 ................... 467
7:4–6 ..................... 479
7:9 ......................... 479
7:11 ...................465–66
7:20 ........... 319n55, 320
7:20–22 ............266–67
7:21 ......................... 607
7:22 ......................... 479
8:4 ............. 237–38, 477
8:5 ................... 467n15
8:6 ............. 237, 477, 479
8:13 ......................... 479
9:18 ......................... 479
9:26 ......................... 479
11:7 .......................... 55
11:17–19 ................. 479
11:28 .....319n58, 446n34,
446n35, 479
12:5 ......................... 479
13:5 ................... 467n15

## James

1:17 ................. 233, 251
1:13–17 ..................... 251
2:1 ...................233, 253
2:1–4 ........................ 232
2:1–13 ......................253
2:2–11 ......................252
2:11 ........................252
2:12 ........................252
2:13 ......................... 239
2:14 ........................ 240
2:19 ........432n8, 440n29
5:1–2 ...................... 250
5:15 .......446n34, 446n35

**1 Peter**
1:6 ........................... 322
1:13 ................... 604–05
1:24................. 566, 619
2:21......................191n17
5:12..........................156

**2 Peter**
3:7 ..................... 321n65

**1 John**
1:1.......................445n33

**Genesis**
8:6.......................... 362
12:3........................... 479
27:27........................ 611
38:9 ................... 192n21
41:48 ....................... 599

**Exodus**
2:1 ......................205n57

**Numbers**
17:27 ....................... 427
32:5........................ 530

**Deuteronomy**
8:3 .......................... 473

**Judges**
13:4.......................... 515

**1 Samuel**
1:1 ......................205n57

**1 Kings/3 Kingdoms**
18:37 ....................... 598

1:3.....................445n33
1:5......................445n33
4:3 .....................445n33
4:12 ...................321n65
5:10..................446n34

**2 John**
1:12 ................... 321n65

**Revelation**
3:12...........................156
5:7 ....................453n55

**Septuagint**

19:18 ...................... 477
22:31 ..................... 506

**2 Chronicles**
32:15 ....................... 504

**Tobit**
4:12 .......................... 517
4:5 .......................... 515

**Esther**
8:8................... 318n53

**2 Maccabees**
9:25 .......................... 157

**3 Maccabees**
6:18......................... 362

**Psalms**
9:19 ....................... 506
9:20...................... 506
105:17..................... 580

**Job**
1:1 ......................205n57

6:14......................... 596
7:11 ................... 315n44
8:4–5 ................ 453–54
8:5 .................... 453n55
9:18 .........................574
10:9 ..................... 595
10:10 ..................... 595
20:12.........................579

**Proverbs**
4:10–19................... 531
4:14................... 518, 532
4:15 ................... 517, 531
4:18...........................518

**Sirach**
1:28................... 517, 518
5:9 ..........................504

**Isaiah**
30:15 ................. 192n21

**Jeremiah**
10:2 ....................... 507
42:7..........................514
43:18 ....................... 155

**Baruch (Bar)**
3 Bar. 16.1................ 505
3 Bar. 13.3–5 ............ 505
4 Bar. 8.2 .................532
4 Bar. 8.3.................518

**Daniel**
1:12 .................... 528n57

**Apostolic Fathers**

**Ignatius of Antioch**
Ign. Trall. 8.2 .......... 512

**Epistle to Diognetus**
Diogn. 10.4 .............. 514

**Shepherd of Hermas**
Herm. Sim. 8.1.5..... 503

**2 Clement**
5.4 ........................... 524

## Other Ancient Sources

### Acts of Pilate
15:5 .......................... 518

### Ammonius (Ammon.)
Diff. 70 ................... 208

### Andocides
1.44 .......................... 192

### Appian
Pun. 11 ............... 528n57

### Demosthenes (Dem.)
Aristocr. 113 ............ 100
Con. 54.4 ............. 355n8
Con. 54.7 .......... 204n52
Cor. 198 ................... 551

### Herodotus (Hdt.)
Hist. 1.71.3 ......... 528n57

### Homer (Hom.)
h. Ap. 127 .......... 104n58
Il. 1.262 ............... 89n19
Il. 2.272–74 .......... 107
Il. 13.730–34 ............. 91
Il. 15.90 .................. 102
Il. 17.32 ..................... 90
Il. 18.546 ................... 94
Il. 21.106 .............. 187n8
Il. xxiii. 692–93 ....... 552
Od. 21.94 ................. 105
Od. 12.81–82 ..... 106n68

### Josephus (Jos.)
Life 271 .................... 157
A.J. 12.330 .............. 432
A.J. 12.338 ......... 447n37
A.J. 4.219 ................ 502
A.J. 4.244 ................ 510
B.J. 1.620 ................ 509

### Lucian
Bis acc. 16 .......... 528n57
Macr. 5 .............. 528n57

### Lysias (Lys.)
1:12 ..................... 185n5
1:10 ..................... 185n5
1.11–14 ............... 204n52
1.43 .......................... 111
frag. XVII.2 ...... 204n52

### Menander (Men.)
Mon. 205 ............... 100

### Petrie Papyri
P. Petr. 2.37,
    246/5 BC ............ 362

### PG Migne
28 ...................... 192n21
87.2 .................... 192n21

### Phrynichus Ecloga
313 ....................... 187n9
347 ...................... 187n9

### Plato (Pl.)
Critias 108c ............ 100
Parm. 141e .......... 552–53
Phaedo 64a ......... 186n7
Resp. 387d .............. 99
Resp. 561c ......... 528n57

### Plutarch (Plut.)
Adol. poet. aud. 4 .... 611
Def. Orac. 419E ....... 427
Para. 19 ............. 528n57

### Polybius (Plb.)
1.67.5 .................... 432
2.11.16 .............. 448n45

### Rigveda (RV)
10,68,7 .............. 104n59
10,28,1 ............... 104n61

### Sibylline Oracles (Sib. Or.)
5.440–1 .................. 502

### Sophocles (S.)
Ant. 441–43 ......... 185n5

Ant. 442–43 ............ 109

### Testament of Dan
T. Dan 4.3 ............... 522

### Testament of Gad
T. Gad 7.4 ............... 516

### Testament of Levi
2.9 ..................... 503n36

### Thucydides (Th.)
1.5.3 ....................... 111
3.3 .......................... 555
3.22.3 ................. 555–56
5.26.1 ..................... 109
7.77.4 ................ 192n21

### Xenophon (Xen.)
Cyr. 4.5.41 ......... 192n21
Cyr. 6.2.26–27 .... 528n57
Hell. 5.3.7 ................ 94
Hell. 2.1.21 ............... 98